Pro Spring

ROB HARROP AND JAN MACHACEK

Apress®

Pro Spring

Copyright © 2005 by Rob Harrop and Jan Machacek

ISBN-13 (pbk): 978-1-59059-461-2
ISBN-10 (pbk): 1-59059-461-4

Printed and bound in the United States of America 9 8 7 6

Lead Editor: Steve Anglin
Technical Reviewer: Dmitriy Kopylenko
Editorial Board: Steve Anglin, Dan Appleman, Ewan Buckingham, Gary Cornell, Tony Davis, Jason Gilmore, Jonathan Hassell, Chris Mills, Dominic Shakeshaft, Jim Sumser
Project Manager: Kylie Johnston
Copy Edit Manager: Nicole LeClerc
Copy Editor: Rebecca Rider
Production Manager: Kari Brooks-Copony
Production Editor: Janet Vail
Compositor: Susan Glinert Stevens
Proofreader: April Eddy
Indexer: John Collin
Artist: April Milne
Cover Designer: Kurt Krames
Manufacturing Manager: Tom Debolski

Distributed to the book trade in the United States by Springer-Verlag New York, Inc., 233 Spring Street, 6th Floor, New York, NY 10013, and outside the United States by Springer-Verlag GmbH & Co. KG, Tiergartenstr. 17, 69112 Heidelberg, Germany.

In the United States: phone 1-800-SPRINGER, fax 201-348-4505, e-mail orders@springer-ny.com, or visit http://www.springer-ny.com. Outside the United States: fax +49 6221 345229, e-mail orders@springer.de, or visit http://www.springer.de.

For information on translations, please contact Apress directly at 2560 Ninth Street, Suite 219, Berkeley, CA 94710. Phone 510-549-5930, fax 510-549-5939, e-mail info@apress.com, or visit http://www.apress.com.

The source code for this book is available to readers at http://www.apress.com in the Source Code section.

*This book is dedicated to all my friends and family who supported me
during the long hours of writing, especially my girlfriend, Sally, who somehow
manages to put up with having a computer geek for a boyfriend.*
—*Rob Harrop*

*To my parents for always being supportive and loving,
and to my sister, Marie, for being a great sister.*
—*Jan Machacek*

Contents at a Glance

PART 1 ■■■ Getting Started with Spring

PART 2 ■■■ Spring Basics

PART 3 ■■■ Aspect Oriented Programming with Spring

PART 4 ■■■ Data Access with Spring

PART 5 ■■■ Spring in the Middle Tier

PART 6 ■■■ Web Applications with Spring

PART 7 ■■■ Appendixes

Contents

PART 1 ▪▪▪ Getting Started with Spring

PART 2 ■■■ Spring Basics

PART 3 ■■■ Aspect Oriented Programming with Spring

PART 4 ■■■ Data Access with Spring

PART 5 ■■■ Spring in the Middle Tier

PART 6 ■■■ Web Applications with Spring

PART 7 ■■■ **Appendixes**

Foreword

Back in 2001, when I wrote the first lines of code that came to be the Spring Framework, I could not have envisaged the size of the community that would grow around the core ideas. The vision of a simpler, more productive J2EE—simplifying the programming model without sacrificing the power of the platform—resonated with many developers. In turn, as the community grew, their collective experience fed back into making the project stronger.

I welcome this book as another step in the growth of the Spring community. I'm excited to see the number of quality publications on Spring grow. While Spring's online documentation has always been excellent and a focus of major effort for us in the Spring team, a wide-ranging and sophisticated framework such as Spring needs to be approached from a number of angles. Reference documentation can tell you *what* a framework does, but it's even more important to know *why* and *when*. Books like this are far more than simply a reference on the framework; they place it in the context of real-world software development. Spring is perhaps unique among J2EE frameworks in that the architectural vision behind it was articulated in book form from its inception, in *Expert One-on-One J2EE Design and Development. Expert One-on-One J2EE Development without EJB* took this one step further, describing how Spring and other lightweight containers can be used as the basis of the next generation of J2EE architectures. Nevertheless, as the scope of Spring continues to expand at a rapid rate and the Spring core grows ever more sophisticated, it is increasingly important for developers to have books like *Pro Spring*, which cover both the big picture and the myriad of specific details that can help you be more productive.

I recently had the pleasure of meeting Rob Harrop for the first time, at JavaPolis 2004. We've worked together on various Spring features since Rob became a Spring developer, but it was good finally to meet face to face. Rob's enthusiasm for Spring—and technology in general—is infectious. He has a wide range of industry experience and a refreshingly practical, common-sense approach to applying it.

All those qualities come out in this book. It's evident on nearly every page that it reflects in-depth experience with Spring and J2EE as a whole. Rob is not only an author and open source developer—he is an *application developer*, like his readers. I firmly believe that the best writing on software development comes out of experience in the trenches, so this is my kind of book.

If you're new to Spring, this book will help you understand its core concepts and the background in areas such as transaction management and O/R mapping that underpins them. If you're already using Spring, you will learn about features you haven't yet seen and hopefully, gain a deeper understanding of those features you're already using.

Rod Johnson
Founder of the Spring Framework
London
December, 2004

About the Authors

 **ROB HARROP** is a software consultant specializing in delivering high-performance, highly-scalable enterprise applications. He is an experienced architect with a particular flair for understanding and solving complex design issues. With a thorough knowledge of both Java and .NET, Rob has successfully deployed projects across both platforms. He has extensive experience across a variety of sectors—in particular, retail and government.

Rob is the author of five books, including *Pro Spring*, a widely acclaimed, comprehensive resource on the Spring framework.

Rob has been a core developer of the Spring framework since June 2004 and currently leads the JMX and AOP efforts. He cofounded UK-based software company Cake Solutions in May 2001, having spent the previous two years working as lead developer for a successful dot com startup. Rob is a member of the JCP and is involved in the JSR-255 Expert Group for JMX 2.0.

 **JAN MACHACEK** is lead developer of UK-based software company Cake Solutions Limited, where he has helped design and implement enterprise-level applications for a variety of UK- and US-based clients. In his spare time, he enjoys exploring software architectures, nonprocedural and AI programming, and playing with computer hardware.

Jan is the coauthor of *Oracle Application Server 10g: J2EE Deployment and Administration* (Apress, 2004) and *Pro Visual Studio .NET* (Apress, 2004).

A proper computer geek, Jan loves the *Star Wars* and *The Lord of the Rings* series. Jan lives in Manchester, UK.

Jan authored Chapters 8 through 10, 12, 17 through 19, and Appendixes A and B.

About the Technical Reviewer

**DMITRIY KOPYLENKO** fell in love with computers when he was 15. When he got his first 80286 IBM PC/AT back in his hometown of Kharkov, Ukraine, he began to play with QBasic, Pascal, and later, X86 Assembler. Currently, Dmitriy works for the Enterprise Systems and Services division of Rutgers University, the state university of New Jersey, as a lead Java architect. Dmitriy designs and develops enterprise business systems with J2EE and the Spring framework. Dmitriy is also an active Spring framework developer. Dmitriy's current interests are Aspect Oriented Programming, exploring the possibilities of building real-time systems using RTSJ (JSR-1), and commercial aviation. He can be reached at dkopylen@rutgers.edu.

Acknowledgments

When writing a book, a substantial amount of work goes on behind the scenes, and authors are backed by an excellent team of editors, proofreaders, and technical reviewers. This book was no exception and I would like to thank everyone who worked on the book. Thanks in particular to the team at Apress, especially Steve Anglin and Kylie Johnston, for keeping the book on track and taking care of all the details that go into getting a book printed and on the shelves. I want to thank the rest of the Spring team, especially Dmitriy Kopylenko for his excellent input in his role as technical reviewer, Keith Donald for taking the time to check over the Spring Rich chapter and correct any mistakes, and last but not least, Rod Johnson for kindly agreeing to write the foreword.

Rob Harrop

Introduction

Recently, the Java world has witnessed a dramatic shift away from so-called "heavyweight" architectures such as Enterprise JavaBeans (EJB) toward lighter weight frameworks such as Spring. Complex and container-dependent services, such as ORM, and transaction management systems have been replaced with simpler alternatives such as Hibernate and Aspect Oriented Programming (AOP). At the core, Spring provides a comprehensive, lightweight container based on the principle of Inversion of Control (IoC), upon which you can build your own applications. On top of this container, Spring provides a myriad of useful services, bringing together a large range of highly competent open source projects into a single cohesive framework.

The quality of the Spring framework has seen it replacing traditional J2EE architectures in many cases; as a result, more and more developers see the need for comprehensive Spring skills. Despite Spring having quite an extensive suite of documentation and examples, we feel that many developers are still struggling to understand how to use Spring and, more importantly, how to use it effectively. Because of this and the fact that we are closely involved in Spring, we decided to write this book.

During the course of this book, you will learn how to use Spring to build better web and stand-alone applications and how to sift through the many choices available to you through the framework. Our aim is to provide you with all the knowledge you need to use Spring *effectively* in your own applications and to give you insight into what is happening behind the scenes in Spring.

For example, you will

- Learn the fundamentals of IoC in the context of AOP.

- Become aware of the seamlessness and power of Spring by referencing the easy-to-understand sample application we provide.

- Learn how to replace common EJB features with Spring alternatives, including Spring's comprehensive AOP-based transaction management framework.

- Learn to integrate and use these other open source projects with Spring: Apache Struts, Jakarta Velocity, Jakarta POI, and many more.

- Effectively manage your Spring components and applications using Spring's built-in JMX engine.

- Learn how to add scheduling to your Spring application with Quartz.

- Learn how to simplify mail sending with Spring and how to integrate JMS messaging into your application using Spring and ActiveMQ.

For more information on the content of this book, check out the Contents.

After reading this book, you will be equipped with all the knowledge you need to build applications effectively using Spring and its related open source projects.

Who This Book Is For

This book is aimed at experienced Java developers who have a solid understanding of the core Java platform. In addition, many of the chapters discuss J2EE technologies such as servlets, EJBs, and JMS; we assume that the reader is familiar with these concepts and spend little time introducing them. That said, this book does not assume that the reader has any prior experience with Spring or other IoC containers, and the first few chapters are aimed at helping Spring novices understand the basics of the framework.

Downloading the Code

Code will be available in ZIP file format in the Downloads section of the Apress website (www.apress.com).

Contacting the Authors

Contact Rob Harrop at robh@cakesolutions.net and Jan Machacek at jan@cakesolutions.net.

PART 1

■■■

Getting Started with Spring

CHAPTER 1

■ ■ ■

Introducing Spring

When we think of the community of Java developers, we are reminded of the hordes of gold rush prospectors of the late 1840s, frantically panning the rivers of North America looking for fragments of gold. As Java developers, our rivers run rife with open source projects, but, like the prospectors, finding a useful project can be time-consuming and arduous.

A common gripe with many open source Java projects is that they are conceived merely out of the need to fill the gap in the implementation of the latest buzzword-heavy technology or pattern. Having said that, many high quality, usable projects meet and address a real need for real applications and, during the course of this book, you will meet a subset of these projects. You will get to know one in particular rather well—Spring.

Throughout this book, you will see many applications of different open source technologies, all of which are unified under the Spring framework. When working with Spring, an application developer can use a large variety of open source tools, without needing to write reams of code and without coupling his application too closely to any particular tool.

In this chapter, as its title implies, we introduce you to the Spring framework, rather than looking at any solid examples or explanations. If you are already familiar with the Spring project, then you might want to skip this chapter and proceed straight to Chapter 2.

What Is Spring?

Perhaps one the hardest parts of actually explaining Spring as a technology is classifying exactly what it is. Typically, Spring is described as a lightweight framework for building Java applications, but that statement brings up two interesting points. First, you can use Spring to build any application in Java and, unlike many other frameworks such as Apache Struts, it is not just limited to web applications. Second, the lightweight part of the description doesn't really refer to the number of classes or the size of the distribution, but rather, it defines the principle of the Spring philosophy as a whole—that is, **minimal impact**. Spring is lightweight in the sense that you have to make few, if any, changes to your application code to gain the benefits of the Spring core, and should you choose to discontinue using Spring at any point, you will find doing so quite simple. Notice that we qualified that last statement to refer to the Spring core only—many of the extra Spring components, such as data access, require a much closer coupling to the Spring framework. However, the benefits of this coupling are quite clear, and throughout the book we present techniques for minimizing the impact this has on your application.

Inverting Control or Injecting Dependencies?

The core of the Spring framework is based on the principle of **Inversion of Control** (IoC). IoC is a technique that externalizes the creation and management of component dependencies. Consider an example where class Foo depends on an instance of class Bar to perform some kind of processing. Traditionally, Foo creates an instance of Bar using the new operator or obtains one from some kind of factory class. Using the IoC approach, an instance of Bar (or a subclass) is provided to Foo at runtime by some external process. This behavior, the injection of dependencies at runtime, leads to IoC being renamed the much more descriptive **Dependency Injection** (DI). The precise nature of the dependencies managed by DI is discussed in Chapter 4.

■**Note** As you will see in Chapter 4, using the term Dependency Injection when referring to Inversion of Control is always correct. In the context of Spring, you can use the terms interchangeably, without any loss of meaning.

Spring's DI implementation is based around two core Java concepts: JavaBeans and interfaces. When you use DI, you allow dependency configuration to be externalized from your code. JavaBeans provide a standard mechanism for creating Java resources that are configurable in a standard way. In Chapter 4, you will see how Spring uses the JavaBean specification to form the core of its DI configuration model; in fact, any Spring-managed resource is referred to as a **bean**. If you are unfamiliar with JavaBeans, then refer to the quick primer we present at the beginning of Chapter 4.

Interfaces and DI are technologies that are mutually beneficial. We are sure that no one reading this book will argue that designing and coding an application to interfaces makes for a flexible application, but the complexity of wiring together an application that is designed using interfaces is quite high and places an additional coding burden on developers. By using DI, you reduce the amount of code you need to utilize an interface-based design in your application to almost zero. Likewise, by using interfaces, you can get the most out of DI because your beans can utilize any interface implementation to satisfy their dependency.

In the context of DI, Spring acts more like a container than a framework—providing instances of your application classes with all the dependencies they need—but it does so in a much less intrusive way than, say, the EJB container that allows you to create persistent entity beans. Using Spring for DI relies on nothing more than following the JavaBeans naming conventions (a requirement that, as you will see in Chapter 5, you can bypass using Spring's method injection support) within your classes—there are no special classes from which to inherit or proprietary naming schemes to follow. If anything, the only change you make in an application that uses DI is to expose more properties on your JavaBeans, thus allowing more dependencies to be injected at runtime.

Although we leave the full discussion of DI until Chapter 4, it is worth taking a look at the benefits of using DI rather than a more traditional approach:

Reduce glue code: One of the biggest plus points of DI is its ability to reduce dramatically the amount of code you have to write to glue the different components of your application together. Often this code is trivial—where creating a dependency involves simply creating a new instance of an object. However, the glue code can get quite complex when you need to look up dependencies in a JNDI repository or when the dependencies cannot be invoked directly, as is the case with remote resources. In these cases, DI can really simplify the glue code by providing automatic JNDI lookup and automatic proxying of remote resources.

Externalize dependencies: You can externalize the configuration of dependencies, which allows you to reconfigure easily without needing to recompile your application. This gives you two interesting benefits. First, as you will see in Chapter 4, DI in Spring gives you the ideal mechanism for externalizing all the configuration options of your application for free. Second, this externalization of dependencies makes it much simpler to swap one implementation of a dependency for another. Consider the case where you have a DAO component that performs data operations against a PostgreSQL database and you want to upgrade to Oracle. Using DI, you can simply reconfigure the appropriate dependency on your business objects to use the Oracle implementation rather than the PostgreSQL one.

Manage dependencies in a single place: Using a traditional approach to dependency management, you create instances of your dependencies where they are needed—within the dependent class. In all but the most trivial of applications, you will have dependencies spread across the classes in your application, and changing them can prove problematic. When you use DI, all the information about dependencies is contained in a single repository, making the management of dependencies much simpler and less error prone.

Improve testability: When you design your classes for DI, you make it possible to replace dependencies easily. This comes in especially handy when you are testing your application. Consider a business object that performs some complex processing; for part of this, it uses a DAO object to access data stored in a relational database. For your test, you are not interested in testing the DAO; you simply want to test the business object with various sets of data. In a traditional approach, where the business object is responsible for obtaining an instance of the DAO itself, you have a hard time testing this, because you are unable to replace the DAO implementation easily with a mock implementation that returns your test data sets. Instead, you need to make sure that your test database contains the correct data and uses the full DAO implementation for your tests. Using DI, you can create a mock implementation of the DAO object that returns the test data sets and then you can pass this to your business object for testing. This mechanism can be extended for testing any tier of your application and is especially useful for testing web components where you can create mock implementations of `HttpServletRequest` and `HttpServletResponse`.

Foster good application design: Designing for DI means, in general, designing against interfaces. A typical injection-oriented application is designed so that all major components are defined as interfaces, and then concrete implementations of these interfaces are created and hooked together using the DI container. This kind of design was possible in Java before the advent of DI and DI-based containers such as Spring, but by using Spring, you get a whole host of DI features for free, and you are able to concentrate on building your application logic, not a framework to support it.

As you can see from this list, DI provides a lot of benefits for your application, but it is not without its drawbacks. In particular, DI can make it difficult for someone not intimately familiar with the code to see just what implementation of a particular dependency is being hooked into which objects. Typically, this is only a problem when developers are inexperienced with DI; after becoming more experienced, developers find that the centralized view of an application given by Spring DI enables them to see the whole picture. For the most part, the massive benefits far outweigh this small drawback but you should consider this when planning your application.

Beyond Dependency Injection

The Spring core alone, with its advanced DI capabilities, is a worthy tool, but where Spring really excels is in its myriad of additional features, all elegantly designed and built using the principles of DI. Spring provides features for all layers of an application, from helper application programming interfaces (APIs) for data access right through to advanced Model View Controller (MVC) capabilities. What is great about these features in Spring is that, although Spring often provides its own approach, you can easily integrate them with other tools in Spring, making these tools first-class members of the Spring family.

Aspect Oriented Programming with Spring

Aspect Oriented Programming (AOP) is one of the "technologies of the moment" in the Java space. AOP provides the ability to implement crosscutting logic—that is, logic that applies to many parts of your application—in a single place and to have that logic applied across your application automatically. AOP is enjoying an immense amount of time in the limelight at the moment; however, behind all the hype is a truly useful technology that has a place in any Java developer's toolbox.

There are two main kinds of AOP implementation. Static AOP, such as AspectJ (www.aspectj.org), provides a compile-time solution for building AOP-based logic and adding it to an application. Dynamic AOP, such as that in Spring, allows crosscutting logic to be applied arbitrarily to any other code at runtime. Both kinds of AOP have their place, and indeed, Spring provides features to integrate with AspectJ. This is covered in more detail in Chapter 7.

There are many applications for AOP. The typical one given in many of the traditional AOP examples involves performing some kind of logging, but AOP has found uses well beyond the trivial logging applications. Indeed, within the Spring framework itself, AOP is used for many purposes, particularly in transaction management. Spring AOP is covered in full detail in Chapters 7–9, where we show you typical uses of AOP within the Spring framework and your own application, as well as AOP performance and areas where traditional technologies are better suited than AOP.

Accessing Data in Spring

Data access and persistence seems to be **the** most discussed topic in the Java world. It seems that you cannot visit a community site such as www.theserverside.com without being bombarded with articles and blog entries for the latest, greatest data access tool. Spring provides excellent integration with a choice selection of these data access tools. In addition to this, Spring makes plain vanilla JDBC a viable option for many projects with its simplified wrapper APIs around the standard API.

As of Spring version 1.1, you have support for JDBC, Hibernate, iBATIS, and Java Data Objects (JDO), along with newly introduced support for Apache Jakarta's ObJect Relational Bridge (OJB).

The JDBC support in Spring makes building an application on top of JDBC realistic, even for more complex applications. The support for Hibernate, iBATIS, and JDO makes already simple APIs even simpler, thus easing the burden on developers. When using the Spring APIs to access data via any tool, you are able to take advantage of Spring's excellent transaction support. A full discussion of this is outside the scope of this chapter but is covered in full detail in Chapter 12.

One of the nicest features we find with Spring is the ability to mix and match data access technologies easily within an application. For instance, you may be running an application with Oracle, using Hibernate for much of your data access logic. However, if you want to take advantage of some Oracle-specific features, then it is simple to implement that part of your data access tier using Spring's JDBC APIs.

Managing Transactions

Spring provides an excellent abstraction layer for transaction management, allowing for programmatic and declarative transaction control. By using the Spring abstraction layer for transactions, you can make changing the underlying transaction protocol and resource managers simple. You can start with simple, local, resource-specific transactions and move to global, multi-resource transactions without having to change your code.

Transactions are covered in full detail in Chapter 12.

Simplifying and Integrating with J2EE

There has been a lot of discussion recently about the complexity of various J2EE APIs, especially those of EJB. It is evident from the proposed EJB 3.0 specification that this discussion has been taken on board by the expert group, hopefully with the result of a much more simplified EJB API.

In the meantime, however, you can use Spring to provide simplified support for many J2EE technologies. For EJB, there is a selection of classes for both building and accessing EJB resources. These classes reduce a lot of the grunt work from both tasks and provide a more DI-oriented API for EJBs.

For any resources stored in a JNDI-accessible location, Spring allows you to do away with the complex lookup code and have JNDI-managed resources injected as dependencies into other objects at runtime. As a side effect of this, your application becomes decoupled from JNDI, allowing you more scope for code reuse in the future.

As of version 1.0.2, Spring does not support JMS access. However, the CVS repository already contains a large array of classes that are to be introduced in 1.1. Using these classes simplifies all interaction with JMS destinations and should reduce a lot of the boilerplate code you need to write in order to use JMS from your Spring applications.

Chapter 13 covers all J2EE integration APIs, including the forthcoming JMS APIs.

MVC in the Web Tier

Although Spring can be used in almost any setting from desktop to Web, it provides a rich array of classes to support the creation of web-based applications. Using Spring, you have maximum flexibility when you are choosing how to implement your web front end.

For a web application of any complexity, it makes sense to use a framework that uses the MVC paradigm, a pattern that is proven to simplify application maintenance and increase code reuse. Perhaps the most well-known MVC framework for the Web is Apache Struts (http://struts.apache.org). Spring integrates fully with Struts, allowing you to apply Spring DI principles within your Struts classes.

In addition to Struts support, Spring provides its own excellent MVC implementation that you can use with a large array of different view technologies, from JSP and Apache's Jakarta Velocity to Microsoft's Excel and Adobe's PDF. The Spring MVC implementation is quite comprehensive and provides support classes that address 99 percent of all your requirements. For the remaining 1 percent, you can easily extend the MVC framework to add in your own functionality.

View support in Spring MVC is extensive and is constantly improving. In addition to standard support for JSP, which is greatly bolstered by the Spring tag libraries, you can take advantage of fully integrated support for Jakarta Velocity, FreeMarker, Jakarta Tiles (separate from Struts), and XSLT. In addition to this, you will find a set of base view classes that make it simple to add Excel and PDF output to your applications.

We cover the Spring MVC implementation in Chapters 17 and 18, with coverage for Apache Struts in Chapter 19.

Remoting Support

Accessing or exposing remote components in Java has never been the simplest of jobs. Using Spring, you can take advantage of extensive support for a wide range of remoting techniques to quickly expose and access remote services.

Spring provides support for a variety of remote access mechanisms, including Java RMI, JAXRPC, Caucho Hessian, and Caucho Burlap. In addition to these remoting protocols, Spring 1.1 has its own HTTP-based protocol that is based on standard Java serialization. By applying Spring's dynamic proxying capabilities, you can have a proxy to a remote resource injected as a dependency into one of your classes, thus removing the need to couple your application to a specific remoting implementation and also reducing the amount of code you need to write for your application.

In addition to making accessing remote components easy, Spring provides excellent support for exposing a Spring-managed resource as a remote service. Using this mechanism, you can export your service using any of the remoting mechanisms mentioned earlier without needing to have implementation-specific code in your application.

Mail Support

Sending e-mail is a typical requirement for many different kinds of application and is given first-class treatment within the Spring framework. Spring provides a simplified API for sending e-mail messages that fits nicely with the Spring DI capabilities. Spring supports pluggable implementations of the mail API and comes complete with two implementations: one uses JavaMail and the other uses Jason Hunter's `MailMessage` class from the `com.oreilly.servlet` package available from http://servlets.com/cos.

Spring provides the ability to create a prototype message in the DI container and use this as the base for all messages sent from your application. This allows for easy customization of mail parameters such as the subject and sender address. However, there is no support for customizing the message body outside of the code. In Chapter 15, we look at the mail support in detail and at a solution that combines Velocity and Spring, which allows the mail content to be externalized from the Java code.

Job Scheduling Support

Most nontrivial applications require some kind of scheduling capability. Whether this is for sending updates to customers or performing housekeeping tasks, the ability to schedule code to run at a predefined point in time is an invaluable tool for developers.

Spring provides support for two scheduling mechanisms: one uses the `Timer` class, which has been available since Java 1.3; and the other uses the Quartz scheduling engine. Scheduling based on the Timer class is quite primitive and is limited to fixed periods defined in milliseconds. When you are using Quartz, you can build complex schedules using the Unix cron format to define when tasks should be run.

The scheduling support in Spring is covered in full in Chapter 14.

Simplified Exception Handling

One area where Spring really helps to reduce the amount of repetitive, boilerplate code you need to write is in exception handling. The core of the Spring philosophy in this respect is that checked exceptions are overused in Java, and that a framework should not force you to catch any exception from which you are unlikely to be able to recover—a point of view that the authors agree with wholeheartedly.

In reality, many frameworks are designed to reduce the impact of having to write code to handle checked exceptions. However, many of these frameworks take the approach of sticking with checked exceptions but artificially reducing the granularity of the exception class hierarchy. One thing you will notice with Spring is that because of the convenience afforded to the developer from using unchecked exceptions, the exception hierarchy is remarkably granular.

Throughout the book you will see examples of where the Spring exception handling mechanisms can reduce the amount of code you have to write and, at the same time, improve your ability to identify, classify, and diagnose errors within your application.

Source Level Metadata

Source level metadata, often referred to as attributes, is getting quite a bit of coverage in the Java world at the moment, mainly due to the announcement that JSR-175, a standardized specification for attributes, will make it into Java 5.0. In addition to JSR-175, a wide range of open source projects for attributes, such as Jakarta Commons Attributes, provide the same functionality for current JVMs. Given that many applications continue to run on a 1.3 or 1.4 virtual machine and will for some time, this ability to support attributes in those applications is desired.

Spring provides a pluggable metadata solution so that you can plug any implementation into your application at any future point. Currently the only implementation available out of the box is Commons Attributes, but Spring will definitely have support for JSR-175 Attributes before Java 5.0 is released.

Spring's support for attributes is discussed at various points throughout the book, but it is first introduced during the discussions of AOP in Chapter 7.

The Spring Project

One of the most endearing things about the Spring project is the level of activity currently present in the community and the amount of cross-pollination between other projects such as CGLIB, Apache Geronimo, and AspectJ. One of the most touted benefits of open source is that if the project folded tomorrow, you would be left with the code; but let's face it—you do not want to be left with a codebase the size of Spring to support and improve upon. For this reason, it is comforting to know how well established and active the Spring community is.

Origins of Spring

The origins of Spring can be traced back to the book *Expert One-to-One J2EE Design and Development* by Rod Johnson (Wrox, 2002). In this book, Rod presented his interface 21 framework, a framework he developed to use in his own applications. Released into the open source world, this framework formed the foundation of the Spring framework as we know it today.

Spring proceeded quickly through the early beta and release candidate stages, and the first official 1.0 release was made available March 24, 2004. Since then, Spring has undergone two point releases and is currently in its 1.1 release (as of the time of writing).

The Spring Community

The Spring community is one of the best in any open source project we have encountered. The mailing lists and forums are always active, and progress on new features is usually rapid. The development team is truly dedicated to making Spring the most successful of all the Java application frameworks, and this shows in the quality of the code that is reproduced. Much of the ongoing development in Spring is in reworking existing code to be faster, smaller, neater, or all three.

As we mentioned already, Spring also benefits from excellent relationships with other open source projects, a fact that is extremely beneficial when you consider the large amount of dependency the full Spring distribution has.

From a user's perspective, perhaps one of the best features of Spring is the excellent documentation and test suite that accompany the distribution. Documentation is provided for almost all the features of Spring, making picking up the framework simple for new users. The test suite Spring provides is impressively comprehensive—the development team writes tests for everything. If they discover a bug, they fix that bug by first writing a test that highlights the bug and then getting the test to pass.

What does all this mean to you? Well, put simply, it means that you can be confident in the quality of the Spring framework and confident that, for the foreseeable future, the Spring development team will continue to improve upon what is already an excellent framework.

Spring for Microsoft .NET

The main Spring framework project is 100 percent Java based. However, due to the success of the Java version, developers in the .NET world started to feel a little bit left out; thus Mark Pollack and Rod Johnson have started the Spring .NET project. Aside from Rod, both projects have completely different development teams, so the .NET project should have minimal impact on the Spring Java. In fact, the authors believe that this is excellent news. Contrary to popular belief in the Java world, .NET is not a load of garbage produced by the Beast, a fact that the authors can attest to, having delivered several successful .NET applications to our clients. This project opens up whole new avenues for cross-pollination, especially since .NET already has the lead in some areas, such as source level metadata, and should lead to a better product on both fronts. Another side effect of this project is that it makes the move between platforms much easier for developers, because you can use Spring on both sides. This is given even more weight by the fact that other projects such as Hibernate and iBATIS now have .NET equivalents. You can find more information on Spring .NET at `www.springframework.net`.

The Spring Rich Client Platform

One of the offshoot projects of the main Spring project is the Spring Rich Client Platform (RCP), led by Keith Donald. Spring RCP provides a base library for building rich clients using familiar Spring concepts. Spring RCP is still in the early stages of development, but there is enough completed so that you can start putting together some interesting client applications. Spring RCP is covered in more detail in Appendix B.

The Spring IDE

The Spring IDE project is another offshoot of the main Spring project, and it functions as a plugin for the Eclipse platform. Using Spring IDE, you can get full source highlighting and code insight functionality for your Spring configuration files. You can also reduce the number of errors that can creep into your configuration files, thus speeding up the development cycle. Spring IDE is covered in more detail in Appendix C.

The Acegi Security System for Spring

Acegi is a security system project built on top of Spring. Acegi provides the full spectrum of security services required for Spring-based applications including multiple authentication backends, single sign-on support, and caching. We do not cover Acegi in any detail in this book, but you can find more details at `http://acegisecurity.sourceforge.net/`. Support for Acegi is provided through the Spring forums at `http://forum.springframework.org`.

The Future of Spring

At the time of writing, many new pieces of functionality are already planned for the 1.2 release. The main cruxes of this new block of functionality are modifications to the AOP implementation to allow for better integration with AspectJ; JMX integration that allows Spring beans to be published as JMX-managed resources; and Spring itself to be configured using JMX, portlet support, and a documentation tool for Spring configuration files.

Alternatives to Spring

Going back to our previous comments on the number of open source projects, you should not be surprised to learn that Spring is not the only framework offering Dependency Injection features or full end-to-end solutions for building applications. In fact, there are almost too many projects to mention. In the spirit of being open, we include a brief discussion of several of these frameworks here, but it is our belief that none of these platforms offers quite as comprehensive a solution as that available in Spring.

PicoContainer

PicoContainer (`www.picocontainer.org`) is an exceptionally small (50k) DI container that allows you to use DI for your application without introducing any other dependencies other than PicoContainer itself. Because PicoContainer is nothing more than a DI container, you may find that as your application grows, you need to introduce another framework, such as Spring, in which case you would have been better off using Spring from the start. However, if all you need is a tiny DI container, then PicoContainer is a good choice, but since Spring packages the DI container separate from the rest of the framework, you can just as easily use that and keep the flexibility for the future.

NanoContainer

NanoContainer (`www.nanocontainer.org`) is an extension to PicoContainer for managing trees of individual PicoContainers. Because Spring provides all the same functionality in the standard DI container, NanoContainer is not really a major improvement over Spring. Where NanoContainer becomes interesting is in its support for scripting languages that interact with the container. However, expect to see this functionality in Spring in the near future.

Keel Framework

The Keel Framework (`www.keelframework.org`) is more of a meta-framework in that most of its capabilities come from other frameworks that are all brought together under a single roof. For instance, DI functionality comes from the Apache Avalon container and web functionality comes from Struts or a similar framework. Keel has many implementations of the same components and links them all together into a cohesive structure, allowing you to swap out implementations with minimal impact on your application. Despite its wide feature set, Keel does not seem to have enjoyed the same level of acceptance as Spring. Although we have investigated Keel only briefly, we feel that this is partially to do with the level of accessibility. Spring is immediately accessible to developers of all levels, whereas Keel seems to be more complex. Having said that, the feature set is impressive, and this is certainly a direct competitor to Spring.

The Rest of the Book

Now that you have had a whirlwind tour of Spring, you are no doubt aching to get started with all the different components available. In the next chapter, we discuss all the information you need to know to get up and running with a basic Spring application. We show you how to obtain the Spring framework and discuss the packaging options, the test suite, and the documentation. Also, Chapter 2 introduces some basic Spring code, including the time-honored "Hello World!" example in all its DI-based glory.

Our main aims with this book are to provide as comprehensive a reference to the Spring framework as we can and, at the same time, give plenty of practical, application-focused advice without it seeming like a clone of the documentation. To help with this, we build a full application using Spring throughout the book to illustrate how to use Spring technologies. Chapter 3 discusses the sample application in full detail.

Summary

In this chapter, we presented you with a high-level view of the Spring framework complete with discussions of all the major features, and we guided you to the relevant sections of the book where these features are discussed in detail. After reading this chapter, you should have some kind of idea about what Spring can do for you; all that remains is to see how it can do it. On that note, it is time to proceed.

CHAPTER 2

■■■

Getting Started

Often the hardest part of coming to grips with any new development tool is knowing where to begin. Typically, this problem is worse when the tool offers as many choices as Spring. Fortunately, getting started with Spring isn't actually that hard if you know where to look first. In this chapter, we present you with all the basic knowledge you need to get off to a flying start. Specifically, we will look at the following:

Obtaining Spring: The first logical step is to obtain or build the Spring JAR files. If you want to get up and running quickly with the standard Spring distribution, simply download the latest Spring distribution from the Spring website at `www.springframework.org`. However, if you want to be on the cutting edge of Spring developments, check out the latest version of the source code from Spring's CVS repository.

Spring packaging options: Spring packaging is modular; it allows you to pick and choose which components you want to use in your application and to include only those components when you are distributing your application.

Spring dependencies: The full distribution of Spring includes a voluminous set of dependencies, but in many cases, you only need a subset of these dependencies. In this section, we look at which Spring features require which dependencies; this information helps you reduce the size of your application to the absolute minimum.

Spring samples: Spring comes with a large selection of sample applications that make ideal reference points for building your own applications. In this section, we will take a look inside the sample applications to give you a feel for the amount of sample code that is available. If you couple this with the sample application you build during the course of this book, you should have more than enough of a codebase from which to start building your own applications.

Test suite and documentation: One of the things members of the Spring community are most proud of is their comprehensive test suite and documentation set. Testing is a big part of what the team does. By using Clover (`www.cenqua.com/clover/index.html`), the team actively monitors the percentage test coverage and is constantly striving to push this percentage higher. The documentation set provided with the standard distribution is excellent—we were even lucky enough to have a professional proofreader donate her time to check our atrocious grammar and spelling! This means that the developers can focus on getting down the information that matters, and someone is there to alert them when what they produce doesn't make sense.

Putting a Spring into Hello World: All bad punning aside, we feel that the best way to get started with any new programming tool is to dive right in and write some code. In this section, we are going to look at some simple examples, including a full DI-based implementation of everyone's favorite, Hello World! Don't be alarmed if you don't understand all the code examples right away; full discussions follow later in the book.

If you are already familiar with the basics of the Spring framework, feel free to proceed straight to Chapter 3 for a discussion of the sample application that you will be building during the course of this book. However, even if you are familiar with the basics of Spring, you may find some of the discussions in this chapter interesting, especially those on packaging and dependencies.

Obtaining the Spring Framework

Before you can get started with any Spring coding, you need to obtain the Spring code. You have two options for retrieving the code: you can download a packaged distribution from the Spring website, or you can check out the code from the Spring CVS repository.

Downloading a Standard Distribution

Spring hosts its development on SourceForge at `www.sourceforge.net/projects/springframework`. Visit this page to download the latest release of Spring (version 1.1 at the time of writing). If you want to download an older release, click the Files link at the top of the page to view a list of all previous releases.

You will find that each release since 1.0 M4 is available in two flavors: one with all the dependencies included and one without. If you are only going to use a subset of Spring's components, then you might want to download the version without dependencies and then handpick the dependencies that you need using the information in the "Analyzing Spring Dependencies" section later in this chapter. However, bear in mind that you typically use Spring for many projects, and for the sake of an extra few minutes' download time, you can easily have all of the dependencies at hand. Also worth bearing in mind is that the dependencies packaged with Spring were used to compile the distribution, so you can be certain that they are the correct version.

Unless otherwise stated, when we are discussing the sample application, we assume that you have downloaded the full 1.1 distribution including all its dependencies.

Checking Spring Out of CVS

Spring is under constant development with many new features, such as JMX integration, already in the pipeline for version 1.2. If you want to get a grip on new features before they make their way into a release, then obtaining the latest codebase from CVS is the best way of going about it.

To check out the latest version of the Spring code, first install CVS, which you can download from www.cvshome.org, and then run the following command:

```
cvs -d:pserver:anonymous@cvs.sourceforge.net:/cvsroot/springframework login
```

When prompted for your password, simply press Enter to send a blank password. Next, enter the following command to check out the HEAD of the CVS repository, which contains the latest changes that have been committed:

```
cvs -d:pserver:anonymous@cvs.sourceforge.net:/cvsroot/springframework co spring
```

This command gives you the absolute latest version of the code, including two separate source trees: one contains the main source for Spring including any new features considered stable enough to be in the main tree; and the other, the sandbox, contains code still classified as work in progress. New code in the main tree is likely to make it into the next release, but code in the sandbox might not. Be aware that any new code is subject to change without notice; for this reason, avoid basing any of your new applications around unreleased code.

Older versions of Spring are stored in CVS tagged by their version number, so you can download any version of Spring directly from CVS. If you are unsure of the tags to use, you can find them by browsing the CVS repository online at http://cvs.sourceforge.net/viewcvs.py/springframework/.

Understanding Spring Packaging

When you obtain a distribution of Spring, you may be surprised to find that rather than distributing a single JAR file with all the code in it, the Spring team opted to create a single JAR that contains a full distribution and eight separate JARs that contain individual Spring components. In future releases, it is likely that the number of component JARs will increase, thus enabling you to be more selective of the features you include in your code.

The Full Distribution

The spring.jar file available in every release contains **almost** the full distribution of the Spring framework classes. We say almost because it doesn't actually contain any of the mock classes that are distributed with Spring as testing aids. This is a good decision by the Spring team, because you almost never have to distribute mock classes in a release of your application; instead, you use them in the development environment to aid your testing process. Aside from this one omission, the spring.jar file contains every class in the main Spring source tree.

The Component Distributions

In addition to the spring.jar file, Spring comes with another eight JAR files as mentioned earlier; one contains the mock classes and the other seven contain individual components of the Spring framework. Table 2-1 lists these JAR files along with a description of their corresponding components.

Table 2-1. *Spring Component Distributions*

JAR File	Description
spring-aop.jar	This JAR contains all the classes you need to use Spring's AOP features within your application. You also need to include this JAR in your application if you plan to use other features in Spring that use AOP, such as declarative transaction management.
spring-context.jar	This package contains classes that provide many extensions to the Spring core. You will find that all classes need to use Spring's ApplicationContext feature (covered in Chapter 5), along with classes for EJB, JNDI, and mail integration. Also contained in this package are the Spring remoting classes, classes for integration with templating engines such as Velocity and FreeMarker and the base validation classes. It is worth bearing in mind that many of the classes contained in this package are really out of place, and features such as remoting and EJB support would be better packaged into additional JAR files.
spring-core.jar	This is one JAR file that you need for every application. In this JAR file, you will find all the classes for accessing configuration files, creating and managing beans, and performing DI. If all you want for your application is basic DI support, then all you need is this JAR file. Also, in this JAR, you will find a selection of extremely useful utility classes that are used throughout the Spring codebase and that you can also use in your own application.
spring-dao.jar	This JAR contains all the base classes for Spring DAO support, including all classes for accessing data using JDBC and Spring's transaction abstraction layer. In order to use the declarative transaction support, you need to include spring-aop.jar in your application as well.
spring-mock.jar	As we mentioned earlier, Spring provides a set of mock classes to aid in testing your applications. Many of these mock classes are used within the Spring test suite, so they are well tested and make testing your applications much simpler. Certainly we have found great use for the mock HttpServletRequest and HttpServletResponse classes in unit tests for our web applications.
spring-orm.jar	This JAR extends Spring's standard DAO feature set with support for Hibernate, iBATIS and JDO. Many of the classes in this JAR depend on classes contained in spring-dao.jar, so you definitely need to include that in your application as well. In the future, individual ORM tools may be packaged separately, because you do not need to include classes for Hibernate and JDO when your application is using iBATIS.
spring-web.jar	This JAR file contains the core classes for using Spring in your web applications, including classes for loading an ApplicationContext feature automatically, Struts integration classes, file upload support classes, and a bunch of useful classes for performing repetitive tasks such as parsing int values from the query string.
spring-webmvc.jar	This JAR contains all the classes for Spring's own MVC framework. If you are using a separate MVC framework for your application, then you won't need any of the classes from this JAR file. Spring MVC is covered in more detail in Chapters 17 and 18.

Choosing a Distribution Option

Choosing which of these distribution options to use is actually quite simple. If you are building a web application and you will be using Spring throughout it, then you may as well use the spring.jar file and save yourself the hassle of having to maintain the different files. Likewise, if all you want is a simple DI container for your application, then you should be okay with just spring-core.jar. If the size of your release is critical, then you will almost certainly want to pick the JAR files containing just the features that you need.

Bear in mind that the component distributions are not really that granular; you will almost certainly end up including whole sets of classes in your application that you do not need. You may be able to make your application slightly smaller, but the big space savings come from knowing exactly which of Spring's dependencies you need to include in your application and discarding the rest.

Analyzing Spring Dependencies

Spring has over 60 separate dependencies, all of which are available as part of the full Spring download. If you are building Spring from source, then you are going to need all of these dependencies. However, at runtime, most likely you will require only a subset of the dependencies and you can really minimize the size of your distribution by including only the necessary dependencies.

Due to the large number of dependencies, Spring groups them together to make working with them easier. These groups are represented as subdirectories of the main lib directory in the root of the distribution. Table 2-2 describes these groups along with a list of the JAR files in each group and a discussion of what the dependencies are used for.

Table 2-2. *Spring Dependencies*

Dependency Group	JAR Files	Description
ant	ant.jar, ant-junit.jar, ant-launcher.jar	Spring uses Apache Ant as its build tool and also for many other tasks such as documentation generation and test running. Ant is not used at all at runtime so you do not need to include this JAR file in your distribution.
aopalliance	aopalliance.jar	The AOP Alliance (http://aopalliance.sourceforge.net/) is a combined, open source collaboration between many projects to provide a standard set of interfaces for AOP in Java. Spring's AOP implementation is based on the standard AOP Alliance APIs. You only need this JAR file if you plan to use any of Spring's AOP or AOP-based features.
axis	axis.jar, saaj.jar, wsdl4j.jar	Spring uses the Apache Axis project to support the JAXRPC capabilities in Spring remoting. You only need these files if you are using JAXRPC Remoting.
caucho	burlap-2.1.12.jar, hessian-2.1.12.jar	Spring remoting provides support for a wide variety of different protocols, including Caucho's Burlap and Hessian. You only need the JARs in this group if you are using the corresponding protocols in your application.
cglib	cglib-full-2.0.2.jar	CGLIB is used to generate dynamic proxy classes for use in both the core DI and AOP implementations. You almost always need to include CGLIB with your application, because it is used to implement a wide range of Spring's functionality.

Table 2-2. *Spring Dependencies (Continued)*

Dependency Group	JAR Files	Description
cos	cos.jar	COS stands for com.oreilly.servlet, which is a collection of useful classes for working with Servlets and web-based applications. Spring uses COS in two areas: for handling file uploads and for sending e-mail. In both cases, COS is just an implementation choice, so you only need to include cos.jar if you choose to use COS over one of the other implementations.
dom4j	dom4j.jar	You must have dom4j when you are using Hibernate, so you need to include this JAR file if you plan to use Hibernate for ORM in your application.
easymock	easymock.jar, easymockclassextension.jar	EasyMock is used in the Spring test suite, so you only need to use this JAR for building and running the test suite; you do not need to distribute this with your application.
freemarker	freemaker.jar	Spring provides wrapper classes around the FreeMarker templating engine and also provides support for using FreeMarker templates as views for your web applications. This is required whenever you are using FreeMarker.
hibernate	ehcache.jar, hibernate2.jar, odmg.jar	These JAR files are required when you are using Spring's Hibernate integration and support classes. If you are using a different ORM tool, such as iBATIS, you can leave these JARs out of your application. When you are using Hibernate, you must also include the CGLIB JAR file in your application.
hsqldb	hsqldb.jar	The hsqldb.jar file is used by the Spring sample applications.
ibatis	ibatis-common.jar , ibatis-sqlmap.jar, ibatis-sqlmap-2.jar	These files are required when you are using Spring's iBATIS integration classes, but you can leave them out of your application if you are using JDBC or another ORM tool such as Hibernate or JDO.
itext	itext-1.02b.jar	Spring uses iText to provide PDF support in the web tier. Only include this JAR if your web applications need to generate PDF output.
j2ee	activation.jar, connector-api.jar, ejb.jar, jaxrpc.jar, jdbc2_0-stdext.jar, jms.jar, jstl.jar, jta.jar, mail.jar, servlet.jar, xml-apis.jar	As you can see, there is a large array of different J2EE-related JAR files. You need the activation.jar and mail.jar files if you want to use the JavaMail implementation of Spring's mail support. You need connector-api.jar to use the JCA Connector for Hibernate, ejb.jar to use Spring's EJB support, and jms.jar for Spring's JMS support. For web applications, you need servlet.jar and jstl.jar if you want to use Spring's JSTL support. The jaxrpc.jar file is required for JAXRPC support in Spring remoting and jta.jar is used for JTA transaction support. The remaining two jars, jdbc2_0-stdext.jar and xml-apis.jar, are needed for JDBC and XML configuration support respectively—but only when you are using a 1.3 JVM.

Table 2-2. *Spring Dependencies (Continued)*

Dependency Group	JAR Files	Description
jakarta	jakarta-commons commons-attributes-api.jar, commons-attributes-compiler.jar, commons-beanutils.jar, commons-collections.jar, commons-dbcp.jar, commons-digester.jar, commons-discovery.jar, commons-fileupload.jar, commons-lang.jar, commons-logging.jar, commons-pool.jar, commons-validator.jar	Many of the components from the Jakarta Commons project are used by Spring. You need the commons-attribute-api.jar if you want to use source level metadata in your application, plus you need the compiler JAR file to compile the attributes into your application. The BeanUtils, Collections, Digester, Discovery, and Validator JAR files are used by Struts, and Hibernate uses Collections as well. DBCP is used by Spring's JDBC support when you are using DBCP connection pools, and Pooling is required by some of the sample applications. FileUpload is required if you want to use the corresponding Spring wrapper to handle file uploads in your web applications. Finally, Logging is used throughout Spring, so you need to include it in every Spring-based application.
jakarta-taglibs	standard.jar	This is the Jakarta JSTL implementation and it is used by some of the Spring sample applications.
jboss	jboss-common-jdbc-wrapper.jar	This is required when you are using Spring's JDBC classes in an application running on the JBoss application server.
jdo	jdo.jar	This is required for Spring's JDO support.
jdom	jdom.jar	JDOM is required when you are using iBATIS 1.3 with Spring. The version of iBATIS covered in this chapter is 2.0.
jotm	jotm.jar, xapool.jar	The jotm.jar file is required is you plan to use JOTM in conjunction with Spring's transaction abstraction layer. You only need xapool.jar if you plan to use XAPool for connection pooling in your application.
junit	junit.jar	JUnit is not required at all at runtime; it is only used for building and running the test suite.
log4j	log4j-1.2.8.jar	This is required when you want to use Spring to configure log4j logging.
poi	poi-2.5.jar	This adds support for Microsoft Excel output to Spring's MVC framework.
quartz	quartz.jar	This is used for Spring Quartz-based scheduling support.
regexp	Jakarta-oro-2.0.7.jar	This is required when you are using regular expressions to specify pointcuts in AOP. You can find more details on this in Chapter 6.
struts	struts-1.1.jar	The Struts JAR is required whenever you want to use Struts in conjunction with Spring to build a web application.

Table 2-2. *Spring Dependencies (Continued)*

Dependency Group	JAR Files	Description
velocity	velocity-1.4.jar, velocity-tools-generic-1.1.jar	Spring provides wrapper classes around Velocity to DI-enable it and also to reduce the amount of code you need to write to use Velocity in your application. In addition to this, Spring provides classes to support the use of Velocity as the view provider in the web tier. If you are using any of these features, you need to include the Velocity JAR files in your distribution.
xdoclet	xjavadoc-1.0.jar	Commons Attributes uses this to parse your source code files and extract the attribute information. Include this JAR file if you are using Spring's Commons Attributes support.

As you can see, Spring's dependencies are quite varied, and for most applications, you only need a fraction of the full dependency set. It is worthwhile spending the time to pick out exactly what dependencies you need and only adding those to your application. In this way, you can keep the size of your application down; this is a particular benefit to those of you who frequently need to deploy to remote locations. Keeping the size of your application as small as possible is especially important if you plan to distribute your application over the Web to people who may be downloading over a slow link.

The Sample Applications

An area where many open source, and indeed commercial, products fail is in providing enough well-documented sample code to make it easy for people to get started. Thankfully, Spring comes with a complete set of nifty sample applications that demonstrate a wide selection of the features in Spring. A point to note is that the sample applications are treated as first-class citizens of the framework by the development team, and they are constantly being improved and worked on by the team. For this reason, you generally find that, after you get what you can from the test suite, the samples are a great place to get started when you are looking at new features.

The Petclinic Application

Petclinic is an interesting sample application that was built to showcase Spring's data access support. In it, you find a web-based application for querying and updating the database of a fictional veterinary office. The interesting thing about this application is that it comes with a selection of interchangeable DAO implementations that highlight how easy it is to decouple your application from the data access logic when you are using Spring.

The Hibernate DAO implementation really shows off Spring's Hibernate support by implementing each of the eight DAO methods with a single line. The JDBC implementation is equally as interesting. First, much of the JDBC logic is contained in an abstract base class.

This class provides hook methods for subclasses when you need to use provider-specific SQL features—in the Petclinic case, this happens with the auto generation of primary keys. Second, when you are looking at the base class, it is interesting to see how much of the repetitive error handling code that is prevalent when you are using JDBC is removed. Third, it is very interesting to see how data access is handled in a much more object-oriented way.

This project also contains a very solid example of how to build a web application using Spring's MVC support, so if you are planning to use Spring MVC for one of your own applications, make sure you take a look at this sample first.

We cover JDBC support in Chapter 8, Hibernate in Chapter 9, and Spring MVC in Chapters 17 and 18.

The jPetStore Application

The jPetStore is based on the jPetStore sample created by Clinton Begin for iBATIS. As far as sample applications go, this one is huge. It contains a full DAO layer, created using Spring and iBATIS, with implementations for Oracle, Microsoft SQL Server, MySQL, and PostgreSQL. The business tier is fully Spring managed and, coupled with the DAO layer, it presents a good example of Spring-managed transactions.

Also included with this application is a solid example of how to use both Spring MVC and Struts. This application also highlights how to use Spring remoting using JAXRPC.

Spring MVC is covered in Chapters 17 and 18, Struts integration is covered in Chapter 19, iBATIS is covered in Chapter 10, and Spring remoting is covered in Chapter 16.

The Tiles-Example Application

Tiles is one of our favorite open source tools because it reduces a lot of the drudge work when you are building user interfaces for the Web, and it really helps separate individual UI elements into reusable fragments. Because of this, the Tiles support in Spring is especially welcome, and this sample application makes getting started with Tiles in your own sample application easy.

We cover Tiles in detail in Chapter 18.

The ImageDB Application

This is one of our favorite sample applications because it shows off loads of useful Spring features. Specifically, you see how to load and store LOBs in a database, how to handle file uploads, and how to schedule jobs using the Quartz job scheduler. As if that weren't enough, you also see how to use Velocity as the view technology in the web tier.

We cover LOBs in Chapter 8, file uploads in Chapter 17, job scheduling in Chapter 14, and Velocity support in Chapter 18.

The Countries Application

This is an intriguing example that demonstrates some of the more advanced features of Spring MVC. It looks at using HandlerInterceptors to provide common preprocessing for your Controllers as well as utilizing Excel and PDF output for the view technology. This example is quite small and is certainly worth a look if you are planning to use Excel or PDF within your application. We cover HandlerInterceptors in Chapter 17 and Excel and PDF integration in Chapter 18.

Spring Documentation

One of the aspects of Spring that makes it such a useful framework for real developers who are building real applications is its wealth of well-written, accurate documentation. One of the key goals for the 1.1 release was to ensure that all the documentation was finished off and polished by the development team. This means that every feature of Spring is not only fully documented in the JavaDoc, but is also covered in the Spring reference manual included in every distribution.

If you haven't yet familiarized yourself with the Spring JavaDoc and the reference manual, do so now. This book does not aim to be a replacement for either of these resources; rather, it aims to be a complementary reference, demonstrating how to build a Spring-based application from the ground up.

Verifying Your Spring Distribution

With every distribution, you get the full source code for the test suite along with the Ant script you need to run the tests and produce the test report. If you think your distribution has a bug, first run the test suite to see if the bug is highlighted in one of the tests. Although many open source projects claim that most bugs are in user code and not in their code, Spring can back this up with a test suite that consists of some 1500+ tests.

Putting a Spring into Hello World

Hopefully by this point in the book you appreciate that Spring is a solid, well-supported project that has all the makings of a great tool for application development. However, one thing is missing—we haven't shown you any code yet. We are sure that you are dying to see Spring in action, and because we can not go any longer without getting into the code, let us do just that. Do not worry if you do not fully understand all the code in this section; we go into much more detail on all the topics as we proceed through the book.

Now, we are sure you are all familiar with the traditional Hello World example, but just in case you have been living on the Moon for the last 30 years, Listing 2-1 shows the Java version in all its glory.

Listing 2-1. *Typical Hello World Example*

```
package com.apress.prospring.ch2;
public class HelloWorld {

    public static void main(String[] args) {
        System.out.println("Hello World!");
    }
}
```

As far as examples go, this one is pretty simple—it does the job but it is not very extensible. What if we want to change the message? What if we want to output the message differently, maybe to stderr instead of stdout, or enclosed in HTML tags rather than as plain text?

We are going to redefine the requirements for the sample application and say that it must support a simple, flexible mechanism for changing the message, and it must be simple to change the rendering behavior. In the basic Hello World example, you can make both of these changes quickly and easily by just changing the code as appropriate. However, in a bigger application, recompiling takes time and it requires the application to be fully tested again. No, a better solution is to externalize the message content and read it in at runtime, perhaps from the command line arguments shown in Listing 2-2.

Listing 2-2. *Using Command Line Arguments with Hello World*

```
package com.apress.prospring.ch2;

public class HelloWorldWithCommandLine {

    public static void main(String[] args) {
        if(args.length > 0) {
            System.out.println(args[0]);
        } else {
            System.out.println("Hello World!");
        }
    }
}
```

This example accomplishes what we wanted—we can now change the message without changing the code. However, there is still a problem with this application: the component responsible for rendering the message is also responsible for obtaining the message. Changing how the message is obtained means changing the code in the renderer. Add to this the fact that we still cannot change the renderer easily; doing so means changing the class that launches the application.

If we take this application a step further, away from the basics of Hello World, a better solution is to refactor the rendering and message retrieval logic into separate components. Plus, if we really want to make our application flexible, we should have these components implement interfaces and define the interdependencies between the components and the launcher using these interfaces.

By refactoring the message retrieval logic, we can define a simple MessageProvider interface with a single method, getMessage(), as shown in Listing 2-3.

Listing 2-3. *The MessageProvider Interface*

```
package com.apress.prospring.ch2;

public interface MessageProvider {

public String getMessage();
}
```

As you can see in Listing 2-4, the MessageRenderer interface is implemented by all components that can render messages.

Listing 2-4. *The MessageRenderer Interface*

```
package com.apress.prospring.ch2;

public interface MessageRenderer {

    public void render();

    public void setMessageProvider(MessageProvider provider);
    public MessageProvider getMessageProvider();
}
```

As you can see, the MessageRenderer interface has a single method, render(), and also a single JavaBean-style property, MessageProvider. Any MessageRenderer implementations are decoupled from message retrieval and delegate it instead to the MessageProvider with which they are supplied. Here MessageProvider is a dependency of MessageRenderer. Creating simple implementations of these interfaces is easy (see Listing 2-5).

Listing 2-5. *The HelloWorldMessageProvider Class*

```
    package com.apress.prospring.ch2;

public class HelloWorldMessageProvider implements MessageProvider {

    public String getMessage() {

        return "Hello World!";
    }

}
```

In Listing 2-5, you can see that we have created a simple MessageProvider that always returns "Hello World!" as the message. The StandardOutMessageRenderer class (shown in Listing 2-6) is just as simple.

Listing 2-6. *The StandardOutMessageRenderer Class*

```
package com.apress.prospring.ch2;

public class StandardOutMessageRenderer implements MessageRenderer {

    private MessageProvider messageProvider = null;

    public void render() {
        if (messageProvider == null) {
            throw new RuntimeException(
                    "You must set the property messageProvider of class:"
                            + StandardOutMessageRenderer.class.getName());
        }
```

```
            System.out.println(messageProvider.getMessage());
        }

        public void setMessageProvider(MessageProvider provider) {
            this.messageProvider = provider;
        }

        public MessageProvider getMessageProvider() {
            return this.messageProvider;
        }
    }
```

Now all that remains is to rewrite the main() of our entry class as shown in Listing 2-7.

Listing 2-7. *Refactored Hello World*

```
    package com.apress.prospring.ch2;

public class HelloWorldDecoupled {

    public static void main(String[] args) {
        MessageRenderer mr = new StandardOutMessageRenderer();
        MessageProvider mp = new HelloWorldMessageProvider();
        mr.setMessageProvider(mp);
        mr.render();
    }
}
```

The code here is fairly simple: we instantiate instances of HelloWorldMessageProvider and StandardOutMessageRenderer, although the declared types are MessageProvider and MessageRenderer, respectively. Then we pass the MessageProvider to the MessageRenderer and invoke MessageRenderer.render(). Here is the output from this example, as expected:

```
Hello World!
```

Now this example is more like what we are looking for, but there is one small problem. Changing the implementation of either the MessageRenderer or MessageProvider interfaces means a change to the code. To get around this, we can create a simple factory class that reads the implementation class names from a properties file and instantiates them on behalf of the application (see Listing 2-8).

Listing 2-8. *The MessageSupportFactory Class*

```
package com.apress.prospring.ch2;

import java.io.FileInputStream;
import java.util.Properties;
```

```java
public class MessageSupportFactory {

    private static MessageSupportFactory instance = null;

    private Properties props = null;

    private MessageRenderer renderer = null;

    private MessageProvider provider = null;

    private MessageSupportFactory() {
        props = new Properties();

        try {
            props.load(new FileInputStream("ch2/src/conf/msf.properties"));

            // get the implementation classes
            String rendererClass = props.getProperty("renderer.class");
            String providerClass = props.getProperty("provider.class");

            renderer = (MessageRenderer)
                                Class.forName(rendererClass).newInstance();
            provider = (MessageProvider)
                                Class.forName(providerClass).newInstance();
        } catch (Exception ex) {
            ex.printStackTrace();
        }
    }

    static {
        instance = new MessageSupportFactory();
    }

    public static MessageSupportFactory getInstance() {
        return instance;
    }

    public MessageRenderer getMessageRenderer() {
        return renderer;
    }

    public MessageProvider getMessageProvider() {
        return provider;
    }
}
```

The implementation here is trivial and naïve, the error handling is simplistic, and the name of the configuration file is hard coded, but we already have a substantial amount of code.

A fuller implementation, one suitable for a production system, would have much more code, but for the purposes of this chapter, the example code is adequate. The configuration file for this class is quite simple:

```
renderer.class=com.apress.prospring.ch2.StandardOutMessageRenderer
provider.class=com.apress.prospring.ch2.HelloWorldMessageProvider
```

A simple modification to the `main()` method (as shown in Listing 2-9) and we are in business.

Listing 2-9. *Using MessageSupportFactory*

```
package com.apress.prospring.ch2;

public class HelloWorldDecoupledWithFactory {

    public static void main(String[] args) {
        MessageRenderer mr =
                    MessageSupportFactory.getInstance().getMessageRenderer();
        MessageProvider mp =
                    MessageSupportFactory.getInstance().getMessageProvider();
        mr.setMessageProvider(mp);
        mr.render();
    }
}
```

Before we move on to see how we can introduce Spring into this application, let's quickly recap what we have done. Starting with the simple Hello World application, we defined two additional requirements that the application must fulfill. The first was that changing the message should be simple, and the second was that changing the rendering mechanism should also be simple. To meet these requirements, we introduced two interfaces: `MessageProvider` and `MessageRenderer`. The `MessageRenderer` interface depends on an implementation of the `MessageProvider` interface to be able to retrieve a message to render. Finally, we added a simple factory class to retrieve the names of the implementation classes and instantiate them as applicable.

Refactoring with Spring

The final example from the previous section met the goals we laid out for our sample application, but there are still problems with it. The first problem is that we had to write a lot of glue code to piece the application together, while at the same time keeping the components loosely coupled. The second problem was that we still had to provide the implementation of `MessageRenderer` with an instance of `MessageProvider` manually. We can solve both of these problems using Spring.

To solve the problem of too much glue code, we can completely remove the `MessageSupportFactory` class from the application and replace it with a Spring class, `DefaultListableBeanFactory`. Don't worry too much about this class; for now it is enough to know that this class acts as a more generic version of our `MessageSupportFactory` with a few extra tricks up its sleeve (see Listing 2-10).

Listing 2-10. *Using DefaultListableBeanFactory*

```
package com.apress.prospring.ch2;

import java.io.FileInputStream;
import java.util.Properties;

import org.springframework.beans.factory.BeanFactory;
import org.springframework.beans.factory.support.DefaultListableBeanFactory;
import org.springframework.beans.factory.support.PropertiesBeanDefinitionReader;

public class HelloWorldSpring {

    public static void main(String[] args) throws Exception {

        // get the bean factory
        BeanFactory factory = getBeanFactory();

        MessageRenderer mr = (MessageRenderer) factory.getBean("renderer");
        MessageProvider mp = (MessageProvider) factory.getBean("provider");

        mr.setMessageProvider(mp);
        mr.render();
    }

    private static BeanFactory getBeanFactory() throws Exception {
        // get the bean factory
        DefaultListableBeanFactory factory = new DefaultListableBeanFactory();

        // create a definition reader
        PropertiesBeanDefinitionReader rdr = new PropertiesBeanDefinitionReader(
                factory);

        // load the configuration options
        Properties props = new Properties();
        props.load(new FileInputStream("./ch2/src/conf/beans.properties"));

        rdr.registerBeanDefinitions(props);

        return factory;
    }
}
```

In Listing 2-10, you can see that the main() method obtains an instance of DefaultListableBeanFactory, typed as BeanFactory, and from this, it obtains the MessageRenderer and MessageProvider instances using the BeanFactory.getBean() method.

Don't worry too much about the getBeanFactory() method for now; just know that this method reads the BeanFactory configuration from a properties file and then returns the configured instance. This properties file is identical to the one we used for MessageSupportFactory:

```
renderer.class=com.apress.prospring.ch2.StandardOutMessageRenderer
provider.class=com.apress.prospring.ch2.HelloWorldMessageProvider
```

The BeanFactory interface and its implementing classes form the core of Spring's DI container. As mentioned in Chapter 1, Spring makes extensive use of JavaBeans conventions for its DI container, and for this reason, Spring refers to any managed component as a **bean**, hence the getBean() method.

Now although we have written more code in the startup class, we have removed the need to create any factory code at all, and at the same time, we have gained a much more robust factory implementation with better error handling and a fully decoupled configuration mechanism. However, there is still a small problem with this code. The startup class must have knowledge of the MessageRenderer's dependencies and must obtain these dependencies and pass them to the MessageRenderer. In Listing 2-10, Spring acts as no more than a sophisticated factory class, creating and supplying instances of classes as needed. By finally employing Spring's DI capabilities, we can glue the application together externally using the BeanFactory configuration. This requires a minor modification to the configuration file:

```
# The MessageRenderer
renderer.class=com.apress.prospring.ch2.StandardOutMessageRenderer
renderer.messageProvider(ref)=provider

# The MessageProvider
provider.class=com.apress.prospring.ch2.HelloWorldMessageProvider
```

Notice that, aside from the comments, all we have added is the line that assigns the provider bean to the MessageProvider property of the renderer bean. The (ref) keyword means that the value of the property is to be treated as a reference to another bean and not as a literal value. With this configuration, we can remove any references to the MessageProvider interface in the startup class, as shown in Listing 2-11.

Listing 2-11. *Using Dependency Injection*

```
package com.apress.prospring.ch2;

import java.io.FileInputStream;
import java.util.Properties;

import org.springframework.beans.factory.BeanFactory;
import org.springframework.beans.factory.support.DefaultListableBeanFactory;
import org.springframework.beans.factory.support.PropertiesBeanDefinitionReader;

public class HelloWorldSpringWithDI {

    public static void main(String[] args) throws Exception {
```

```
        // get the bean factory
        BeanFactory factory = getBeanFactory();

        MessageRenderer mr = (MessageRenderer) factory.getBean("renderer");
        mr.render();
    }

    private static BeanFactory getBeanFactory() throws Exception {
        // get the bean factory
        DefaultListableBeanFactory factory = new DefaultListableBeanFactory();

        // create a definition reader
        PropertiesBeanDefinitionReader rdr = new PropertiesBeanDefinitionReader(
                factory);

        // load the configuration options
        Properties props = new Properties();
        props.load(new FileInputStream("./ch2/src/conf/beans.properties"));

        rdr.registerBeanDefinitions(props);

        return factory;
    }
}
```

As you can see, the main() method now just obtains the MessageRenderer bean and calls render(); Spring has created the MesssageProvider implementation and injected it into the MessageRenderer implementation. Notice that we didn't have to make any changes to the classes that are being wired together using Spring. In fact, these classes have no reference to Spring whatsoever and are completely oblivious to its existence. However, this isn't always the case. Your classes can implement Spring-specified interfaces to interact in a variety of ways with the DI container. For instance, it is possible to remove the check in MessageRenderer.render() to see if the MessageProvider implementation has been set and make this check just once. However, this relies on a Spring-specific interface, and we will leave that discussion for Chapter 5.

Summary

In this chapter, we have presented you with all the background information you need to get up and running with Spring. We showed you how to obtain both the Spring release distribution and the current development version directly from CVS. We described how Spring is packaged and the dependencies you need for each of Spring's features. Using this information, you can make informed decisions about which of the Spring JAR files your application needs and which dependencies you need to distribute with your application. Spring's documentation, sample applications, and test suite provide Spring users with an ideal base from which to start their Spring development, so we took some time to investigate what is available in the Spring distribution. Finally, we presented an example of how, using Spring DI, it is possible to make the traditional Hello World a loosely coupled, extendable message rendering application.

The important thing to realize is that we only scratched the surface of Spring DI in this chapter, and we barely made a dent in Spring as a whole. In the next chapter, we take an in-depth look at the sample application that we will be building, paying particular attention to how we can use Spring to solve common design issues and how we have made our application simpler and more manageable using Spring.

CHAPTER 3

■■■

The Sample Application

The examples in each chapter of this book are tailored to the current discussion and are suitably simple to prevent the example itself from clouding the issue at hand. For the most part, these examples provide a sufficient explanation for the topic they are demonstrating. That said, the examples are taken in isolation and are not based on a real-world scenario, which can make understanding how the different Spring features work together difficult. To overcome this, we built a basic blog application, SpringBlog, that highlights most of the topics discussed in this book and shows how the different Spring features work together.

You should note that this application is purposely very simple, and indeed, many of its features were conceived so we could highlight a particular piece of Spring functionality. Despite its simplicity, the SpringBlog application does demonstrate how a Spring-based application is constructed and how the components are glued together.

In this chapter, you get to take a peek at the finished SpringBlog application. We then discuss the Spring features used to implement different parts of the application. This chapter also highlights some of the decisions we made when designing the SpringBlog application and why we made them. More than anything, this chapter serves as a road map to the rest of the book, allowing you to highlight an area that is important to your own application and immediately identify where that area is covered in the book.

Specifically, this chapter covers two main topics:

Requirements of the SpringBlog application: In this section, we discuss the requirements of the SpringBlog application and sneak a peek at the finished product of these requirements. We also discuss why we chose to include certain requirements and why we ignored others when we built the sample application.

Implementing the SpringBlog application: In this section, we take a high-level look at how the requirements discussed in the previous section are implemented using Spring. This section does not go into any detail on the individual Spring features; instead, it discusses the features generally and points you to other chapters that contain more complete descriptions.

If you are already comfortable with the design of Spring applications or you already know which chapters are most important to your application, feel free to skip this chapter. If you are completely new to Spring, reading this chapter will give you a good idea of where the different Spring components fit into your applications.

Requirements of the SpringBlog Application

When defining the requirements for the SpringBlog application, our main goal was to highlight certain Spring features in the context of a full application. For this reason, we included a few features, such as auditing and obscenity filtering, that you would not expect to see in a traditional blog application but that are useful features nonetheless and provide a way to highlight certain features of the Spring framework. On the flip side of this, certain features that you would expect to see, such as authentication and authorization, are not covered fully in the requirements because their implementation has little to do with Spring.

This section provides a full rundown of the features included in the SpringBlog application.

Security and Authentication

Most blog applications provide some kind of security that prevents unauthorized users from creating, editing, and removing blog entries. Because Spring does not provide anything in the way of security support, we have not defined security as a requirement of the SpringBlog system.

As you can see in Figure 3-1, the SpringBlog application does provide some support for user identity.

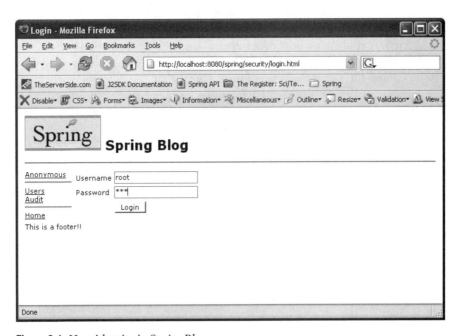

Figure 3-1. *User identity in SpringBlog*

In SpringBlog, you are assigned the Anonymous identity automatically. Using the Login function, you can validate your details against the user list in the database and assign yourself a different identity. Internally, SpringBlog uses this identity as part of the audit process, but it has no functionality for restricting user access based on this identity.

Although we have not discussed application security in any detail in this book, it is still a very important topic. Traditionally, a J2EE application utilizes the security features provided by the container to secure an application at both the servlet and EJB levels. For web applications built using Spring, servlet container security is still a viable option, with which many of you are more than familiar. Although Spring itself does not offer a security framework, many open source projects are available that do. A project of particular note is Acegi Security (http://acegisecurity.sourceforge.net/), which is specifically designed to be used with Spring applications.

Viewing Blog Entries

An obvious requirement for any blog system is that it can display blog entries to users. As Figure 3-2 shows, the SpringBlog application displays the latest postings to the blog on the home page.

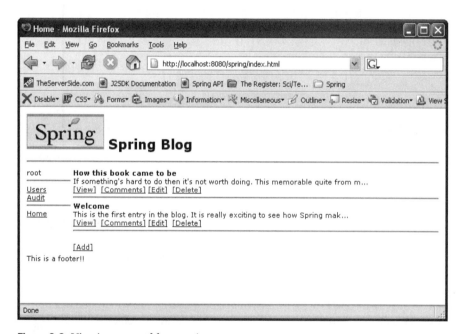

Figure 3-2. *Viewing recent blog entries*

You can configure the number of entries to be displayed using standard Spring configuration mechanisms. Clicking the View link for a particular blog entry displays just that entry, along with the list of comments posted for that entry and the files that have been attached to it, as shown in Figure 3-3.

Figure 3-3. *Viewing a blog entry*

Posting Blog Entries

Without the ability to post blog entries, there would be nothing to display. You can post a new blog entry using the entry form shown in Figure 3-4, which you can access using the Add link on the home page.

Once you have created a blog entry, you can edit it by clicking the Edit link in the entry's listing. Behind the scenes, SpringBlog uses the same HTML form both for creating and editing a blog entry, but it uses different Spring `Controllers` to handle each action.

In addition to the Create and Edit functions, SpringBlog also allows you to delete a blog entry by clicking the Delete link in the listing for the entry you want to delete. As Figure 3-5 shows, SpringBlog prompts you for confirmation before it allows a deletion to proceed.

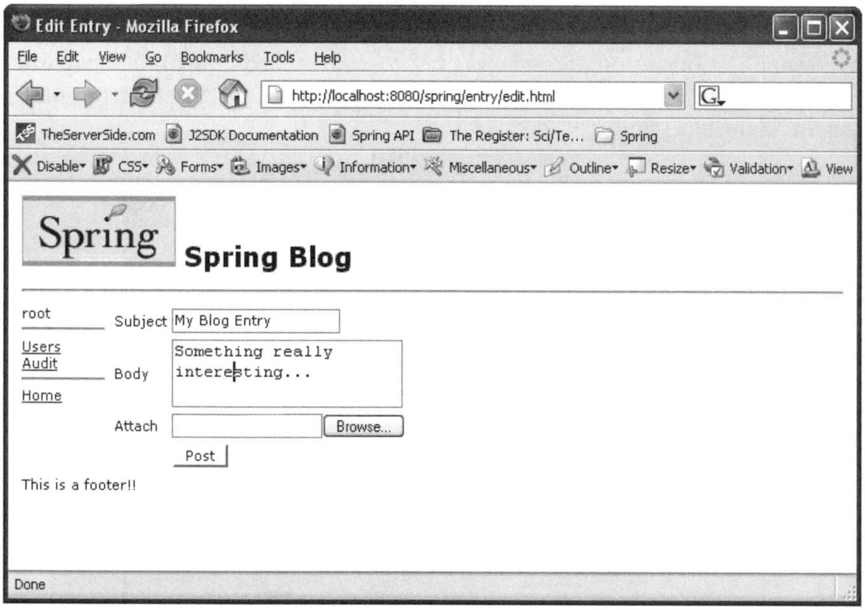

Figure 3-4. *Posting a blog entry*

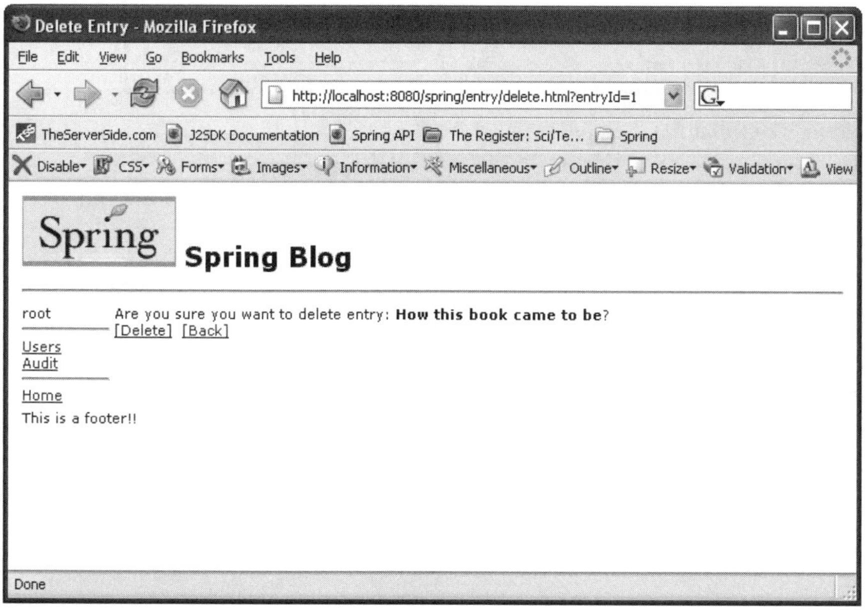

Figure 3-5. *Confirming entry deletion*

Commenting on a Blog Entry

As with most blog applications, SpringBlog allows users to express their opinions about particular entries by posting comments. Users can post comments using the Add link from an entry's comments page, as shown in Figure 3-6.

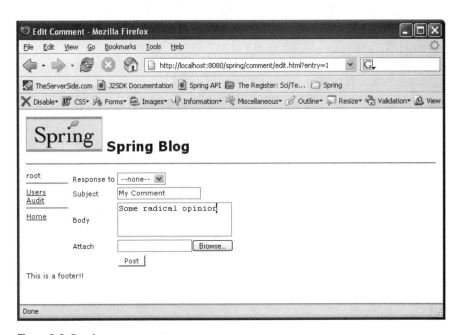

Figure 3-6. *Posting a comment*

As is the case with the entry posting functionality, this functionality also allows you to edit and delete comments.

Filtering Out Obscenities

One of the features of Spring we really wanted to highlight in SpringBlog was AOP, but we did not want to go down the traditional route of using logging as an example, and AOP-based transaction management is already built into Spring. Although most blogs do not use any kind of obscenity filter, we decided that ours would. During design, it seemed that using AOP was the best way to apply this feature across the application.

With this functionality in place, when you try to post an entry such as that shown in Figure 3-7, you actually get a posting like the one in Figure 3-8.

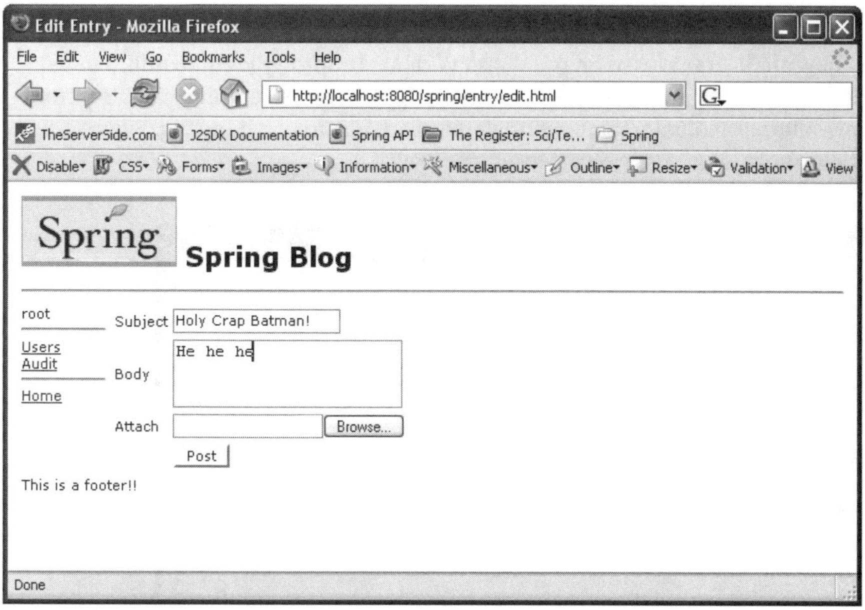

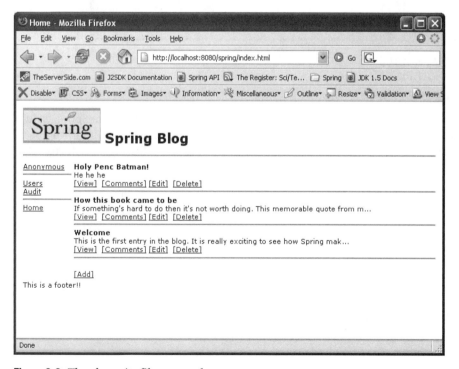

Figure 3-7. *Attempting to post an obscenity*

Figure 3-8. *The obscenity filter at work*

Attaching Files to a Blog Entry or Comment

Unlike many blog applications used on the World Wide Web, SpringBlog allows files to be uploaded with blog entries and comments. In reality, this feature poses quite a large security risk, but it does allow us to demonstrate Spring's excellent file upload handling. Figure 3-9 shows a file being uploaded alongside a new entry.

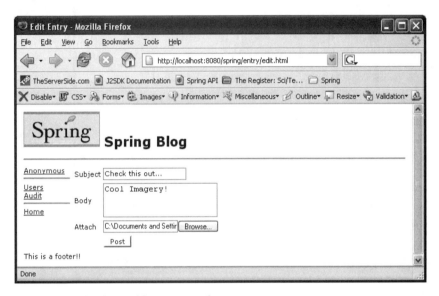

Figure 3-9. *Uploading a file to SpringBlog*

Auditing Blog Actions

One feature that we included purely to support the demonstration of a particular Spring feature is auditing. By introducing the need for all blog operations to be logged for auditing purposes, we made each blog operation require multiple database operations; this requires the use of a database transaction which, obviously, we manage using Spring's transaction management features.

You can view the currently stored audit data by clicking the Audit link in the left-hand navigation bar, as shown in Figure 3-10.

From the View Audit Records screen, you can also remove audit records over a certain age using the purge functionality.

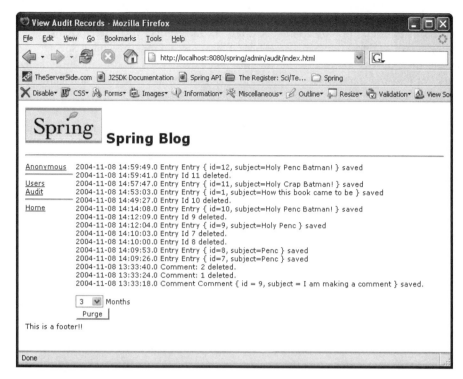

Figure 3-10. *Viewing audit data*

Implementing SpringBlog

One of the best reasons for using Spring is that it makes designing and building an application using traditional OOP practices much simpler than when you are using standard J2EE features. With Spring, you are free to design your applications as you see fit and have Spring worry about wiring the different components together. Spring removes the need for false patterns, such as Factory and Singleton, that hinder testing and do not solve the problems for which they are designed half as well as they would like.

In this section, we present a high-level overview of the design and implementation decisions of the SpringBlog application with pointers to where each topic is discussed in detail.

Application Design

The design of SpringBlog is very simple, with each tier defined in terms of interfaces rather than concrete classes. In each tier, the interfaces that correspond to that tier define only the methods exposed by that tier to other tiers classified as client tiers; no methods or properties are used to configure parameters. Instead, the configuration methods are declared on the classes that implement the interfaces in each tier and configuration data is injected using Spring's IoC-based configuration mechanisms. Chapter 11 presents a full discussion of the different interfaces that make up SpringBlog, how they are wired together using Spring, and factors affecting interface granularity. In particular, when we discuss decoupling the auditing functionality from the main blog functionality, you will see an example of how increasing the interface granularity improves application testability.

The SpringBlog application also contains a basic Domain Object Model (DOM) that encapsulates both data and behavior. In Chapter 11, we take the time to look at the different flavors of the DOM you may have seen in projects that you have worked on, and we discuss the factors you must consider when deciding whether to encapsulate behavior in the DOM or in separate service objects.

Implementing the Data Access Tier

Data access is a topic close to many developers' hearts and it is often the subject of many heated discussions on developer forums across the Internet. In recent times, the focus in the Java world has been on Object-Relational Mapping (ORM) tools as a replacement for JDBC, which many see as an overcomplicated mess. A big part of Spring's feature set lies in its support for data access technologies. All in all, Spring supports five different data access mechanisms: plain JDBC, Hibernate, iBATIS, Java Data Objects (JDO), and Apache ObJect Relational Bridge (OJB).

With the SpringBlog application, we wanted to show how easy it is to switch between data access implementations, so we built three different implementations of the Data Access Tier: one using JDBC, one using Hibernate, and a third using iBATIS.

Spring's support for JDBC is fantastic, removing the need for much of the spaghetti code that was required when using JDBC directly to catch and handle `Exceptions` correctly. In Chapter 8, you will see how to use Spring to simplify your JDBC code; in that chapter, we also present some patterns for maximizing JDBC reuse across multiple database systems.

Hibernate is perhaps the most well-known ORM tool in the Java world, and it has enjoyed considerable success due to the ease with which it can be used to develop high-performance data access code. Although Hibernate has quite a simple API, the error-handling code you need to use Hibernate is quite verbose; Spring simplifies this greatly, reducing most Hibernate operations to just a single line of code. Chapter 9 discusses Spring's support for Hibernate and how we use Spring and Hibernate to build the second implementation of our Data Access Tier.

Strictly speaking, iBATIS is not an ORM tool in that it does not remove all responsibility from the developer for creating the SQL statements needed to map Java objects to data in the RDMBS. Instead, iBATIS introduces the concept of a SQL map, allowing you to specify a variety of SQL queries and how these queries map to both input and output parameters. iBATIS is incredibly powerful and is the personal favorite of both authors. Chapter 10 discusses iBATIS in detail and shows how we built our third data access implementation.

In all cases, we use Spring's infrastructure classes for each data access tool. These classes integrate with Spring's transaction architecture, which allows transactions to be managed in a platform- and resource-provider-independent way in the Business Tier of the SpringBlog application.

Implementing Business Logic

The SpringBlog application is fairly simple, and aside from the basic storage and retrieval of blog data, there are very few business rules in the system. However, there are two particular business functions in the SpringBlog application that exploit two of the most interesting Spring features: the AOP-based obscenity filter and the audit log.

Using AOP for Obscenity Filtering

AOP is a hot topic in the Java world at the moment and as a result, Java developers are fortunate to have a wide range of different AOP implementations available to them. Spring AOP support comes in two forms: the Spring native AOP framework and integration with the AspectJ AOP framework. Chapters 6 and 7 discuss both Spring AOP and AspectJ integration in detail.

For the SpringBlog application, we wanted to provide a practical example of AOP usage rather than the traditional (and boring) logging example. One of the features that we were working on for the sample application was an obscenity filter, and during design, it became apparent that AOP was the ideal mechanism for implementing this filter. In Chapter 7, you will see how we built the obscenity filter and how we used AOP to apply the filter selectively to methods on the core business interface, `BlogManager`.

Using Spring Transaction Support

As developers, one of the features of Spring that we found most impressive was the transaction support. Spring's transaction support provides a simple mechanism to control transactions across one or more resource providers, either programmatically or declaratively. Chapter 12 discusses the transaction framework in detail, focusing specifically on database transactions using both local and distributed transactions. In Chapter 13, you can see how you can use the same transaction architecture to manage JMS transactions.

For the SpringBlog application, we defined a requirement that all operations in the blog be audited and logged to the database. To ensure that an operation is rolled back if the audit process fails, we used the Spring transaction framework to encapsulate each operation and its audit process in a single transaction. We discuss this in Chapter 12; Appendix A demonstrates the technique we used to test to make sure the transaction rollback was functioning correctly.

Implementing the Web Tier

As with support for data access technologies, Spring is well known for its support for a wide range of different web application frameworks and tools. Chapters 17–19 provide a detailed discussion of the Spring MVC framework, the different view technologies used by Spring, and Spring/Struts integration.

Spring MVC and Struts

In keeping with the multiple implementations available for the Data Access Tier, we built two implementations for the Web Tier, one using Spring MVC and the other using Struts. In Chapter 17, we discuss the creation of the Spring MVC-based Web Tier, and in Chapter 19, we look at the Struts-based alternative.

Using Tiles

With most web applications, only a portion of the screen changes each time a new request is processed, and common elements such as the header and navigation bar remain the same. Using Tiles, you can assemble your pages from individual parts called **tiles**, enabling common elements to be defined once and reused across the application. Chapter 18 looks at using Tiles with a Spring application and shows how we used Tiles to build the sample application.

Using Non-JSP Views

Nowadays it is uncommon for web applications to be restricted to purely HTML content; other content types such as PDF and Microsoft Excel are becoming more prevalent. Also, it is not uncommon to see other frameworks such as FreeMarker and Velocity used to produce text-based content. In Chapter 18, you will see how to use a variety of different view technologies with Spring and how we used these technologies in the SpringBlog application.

Summary

In this chapter, you looked at the SpringBlog application that we discuss throughout the book and you were introduced to various discussions of the different features in SpringBlog, how they are implemented, and where in the book they are discussed.

In the next chapter, we discuss the core of the Spring framework—its IoC container. Chapter 4 extends the examples we covered in Chapter 2 and discusses the different kinds of IoC and how they are supported in Spring.

PART 2

■■■

Spring Basics

CHAPTER 4

■■■

Introducing Inversion
of Control

In Chapter 1, during the first discussion of Inversion of Control (IoC), you might recall that we mentioned that it had been renamed, by Martin Fowler, the more descriptive Dependency Injection (DI). However, this is not strictly true; in reality, DI is a specialized form of IoC, although you will often find that the two terms are used interchangeably. In this chapter, we take a much more detailed look at IoC and DI, formalizing the relationship between the two concepts and looking in great detail at how Spring fits into the picture.

After defining both and looking at Spring's relationship with them, we will explore the concepts that are essential to Spring's implementation of DI. This chapter only covers the basics of Spring's DI implementation; we discuss more advanced DI features in Chapter 5 and look at DI in the context of application design in both Chapters 5 and 11. More specifically this chapter will cover the following topics:

Inversion of Control concepts: In this section, we discuss the various kinds of IoC including Dependency Injection and Dependency Lookup. This section looks at the differences between the various IoC approaches and presents the pros and cons of each.

Inversion of Control in Spring: This section looks at IoC capabilities available in Spring and how these capabilities are implemented. In particular, this section looks at Dependency Injection and the setter-based and constructor-based approaches Spring offers. This section also provides the first full discussion of the `BeanFactory` interface, which is central to the whole Spring framework.

XML configuration for Spring `BeanFactories`: The final part of this chapter focuses on using the XML-based configuration approach for the `BeanFactory` configuration. This section starts out with a discussion of DI configuration and moves on to look at additional services provided by the `BeanFactory` such as bean inheritance, lifecycle management, and autowiring.

Inversion of Control and Dependency Injection

At its core, IoC, and therefore DI also, aims to offer a simpler mechanism for provisioning component dependencies (often referred to as an object's **collaborators**) and managing these dependencies throughout their lifecycles. A component that requires certain dependencies is often referred to as the **dependent object** or, in the case of IoC, the target. This is a rather grand way of saying that IoC provides services through which a component can access its dependencies and services for interacting with the dependencies throughout their life. In general, IoC can be decomposed into two subtypes: Dependency Injection and Dependency Lookup. These subtypes are further decomposed into concrete implementations of the IoC services. From this definition, you can clearly see that when we are talking about DI we are always talking about IoC, but when we are talking about IoC we are not always talking about DI.

Types of Inversion of Control

You may be wondering why there are two different types of IoC and why these types are split further into different implementations. There seems to be no clear answer to this question; certainly the different types provide a level of flexibility, but to us, it seems that IoC is more of a mixture of old and new ideas; the two different types of IoC represent this.

Dependency Lookup is a much more traditional approach and at first glance, it seems more familiar to Java programmers. Dependency Injection is a newer, less well-established approach that, although it appears counterintuitive at first, is actually much more flexible and usable than Dependency Lookup.

With Dependency Lookup–style IoC, a component must acquire a reference to a dependency, whereas with Dependency Injection, the dependencies are literally injected into the component by the IoC container. Dependency Lookup comes in two types: Dependency Pull and Contextualized Dependency Lookup (CDL). Dependency Injection also has two common flavors: Constructor Dependency Injection and Setter Dependency Injection.

■**Note** For the discussions in this section, we are not concerned with how the fictional IoC container comes to know about all the different dependencies, just that at some point, it performs the actions described for each mechanism.

Dependency Pull

To a Java developer, Dependency Pull is the most familiar type of IoC. In Dependency Pull, dependencies are pulled from a registry as required. Anyone who has ever written code to access an EJB has used Dependency Pull. Spring also offers Dependency Pull as a mechanism for retrieving components the framework manages; you saw this in action in Chapter 2. Listing 4-1 shows a typical Dependency Pull lookup in a Spring-based application.

Listing 4-1. *Dependency Pull in Spring*

```
public static void main(String[] args) throws Exception {

    // get the bean factory
    BeanFactory factory = getBeanFactory();

    MessageRenderer mr = (MessageRenderer) factory.getBean("renderer");
    mr.render();
}
```

This kind of IoC is not only prevalent in J2EE-based applications, which make extensive use of JNDI lookups to obtain dependencies from a registry, but it is also pivotal to working with Spring in many environments.

Contextualized Dependency Lookup

Contextualized Dependency Lookup (CDL) is similar, in some respects, to Dependency Pull, but in CDL, lookup is performed against the container that is managing the resource, not from some central registry, and it is usually performed at some set point. CDL works by having the component implement an interface similar to that in Listing 4-2.

Listing 4-2. *Component Interface for CDL*

```
package com.apress.prospring.ch4;

public interface ManagedComponent {

    public void performLookup(Container container);
}
```

By implementing this interface, a component is signaling to the container that it wishes to obtain a dependency. When the container is ready to pass dependencies to a component, it calls performLookup() on each component in turn. The component can then look up its dependencies using the Container interface, as shown in Listing 4-3.

Listing 4-3. *Obtaining Dependencies in CDL*

```
package com.apress.prospring.ch4;

public class ContextualizedDependencyLookup implements ManagedComponent {

    private Dependency dep;

    public void performLookup(Container container) {
        this.dep = (Dependency) container.getDependency("myDependency");
    }

}
```

Constructor Dependency Injection

Constructor Dependency Injection is Dependency Injection where a component's dependencies are provided to it in its constructor(s). The component declares a constructor or a set of constructors taking as arguments its dependencies, and the IoC container passes the dependencies to the component when it instantiates it, as shown in Listing 4-4.

Listing 4-4. *Constructor Dependency Injection*

```
package com.apress.prospring.ch4;

public class ConstructorInjection {

    private Dependency dep;

    public ConstructorInjection(Dependency dep) {
        this.dep = dep;
    }
}
```

Setter Dependency Injection

In Setter Dependency Injection, the IoC container injects a component's dependencies into the component via JavaBean-style setter methods. A component's setters expose the set of the dependencies the IoC container can manage. Listing 4-5 shows a typical Setter Dependency Injection–based component.

Listing 4-5. *Setter Dependency Injection*

```
package com.apress.prospring.ch4;

public class SetterInjection {

    private Dependency dep;

    public void setMyDependency(Dependency dep) {
        this.dep = dep;
    }
}
```

Within the container, the dependency requirement exposed by the setMyDependency() method is referred to by the JavaBeans-style name, myDependency. In practice, setter injection is the most widely used injection mechanism, and it is one of the simplest IoC mechanisms to implement.

Injection vs. Lookup

Choosing which style of IoC to use—Injection or Lookup—is not usually a difficult decision. In many cases, the type of IoC you use is mandated by the container you are using. For instance, if you are using EJB 2.0, then you must use Lookup-style IoC to obtain the EJB from the J2EE container. In Spring, aside from initial bean lookups, your components and their dependencies are always wired together using Injection-style IoC.

▨**Note** When you are using Spring, you can access EJB resources without needing to perform an explicit lookup. Spring can act as an adapter between Lookup- and Injection-style IoC systems, thus allowing you to manage all resources using Injection.

The real question is this: Given the choice, which method should you use, Injection or Lookup? The answer to this is most definitely Injection. If you look at the code in Listings 4-4 and 4-5, you can clearly see that using Injection has zero impact on your components' code. The Dependency Pull code, on the other hand, must actively obtain a reference to the registry and interact with it to obtain the dependencies, and using CDL requires your classes to implement a specific interface and look up all dependencies manually. When you are using Injection, the most your classes have to do is allow dependencies to be injected using either constructors or setters.

Using Injection, you are free to use your classes completely decoupled from the IoC container supplying dependent objects with their collaborators manually, whereas with Lookup, your classes are always dependent on classes and interfaces defined by the container. Another drawback with Lookup is that it becomes very difficult to test your classes in isolation from the container. Using Injection, testing your components is trivial, because you can simply provide the dependencies yourself using the appropriate constructor or setter.

▨**Note** For a more complete discussion of testing using Dependency Injection and Spring, refer to Appendix A.

Lookup-based solutions are, by necessity, more complex than Injection-based ones. Although complexity is nothing to be afraid of, we question the validity of adding unneeded complexity to a process as core to your application as dependency management.

All of these reasons aside, the biggest reason to choose Injection over Lookup is that it makes your life easier. You write substantially less code when you are using Injection, and the code that you do write is simple and can, in general, be automated by a good IDE. You will notice that all of the code in the Injection samples is passive, in that it doesn't actively try to accomplish a task; the most exciting thing you see in Injection code is objects getting stored in a field—not much can go wrong there! Passive code is much simpler to maintain than active code, because there is very little that can go wrong. Consider the following code taken from Listing 4-3:

```
public void performLookup(Container container) {
    this.dep = (Dependency) container.getDependency("myDependency");
}
```

In this code, plenty could go wrong: the dependency key could change, the container instance could be null, or the returned dependency might be the incorrect type. We refer to this code as having a lot of moving parts because plenty of things can break. Using Lookup might decouple the components of your application, but it adds complexity in the additional code required to couple these components back together in order to perform any useful tasks.

Setter Injection vs. Constructor Injection

Now that we have established which method of IoC is preferable, we still need to choose whether to use setter injection or constructor injection. Constructor injection is particularly useful when you absolutely must have an instance of the dependency class before your component is used. Many containers, Spring included, provide a mechanism for ensuring that all dependencies are defined when you use setter injection, but by using constructor injection you assert the requirement for the dependency in a container-agnostic manner.

Setter injection is useful in a variety of different cases. If the component is exposing its dependencies to the container but is happy to provide its own defaults, then setter injection is usually the best way to accomplish this. Another benefit of setter injection is that it allows dependencies to be declared on an interface, although this is not as useful as you might first think. Consider a typical business interface with one business method, defineMeaningOfLife(). If, in addition to this method, you define a setter for injection such as setEncylopedia(), then you are mandating that all implementations must use or at least be aware of the encyclopedia dependency. You do not need to define this setter at all—any decent IoC container, Spring included, can work with the component in terms of the business interface but still provide the dependencies of the implementing class. An example of this may clarify this matter slightly. Consider the business interface in Listing 4-6.

Listing 4-6. *The Oracle Interface*

```
package com.apress.prospring.ch4;

public interface Oracle {

    public String defineMeaningOfLife();
}
```

Notice that the business interface does not define any setters for dependency injection. This interface could be implemented as shown in Listing 4-7.

Listing 4-7. *Implementing the Oracle Interface*

```
package com.apress.prospring.ch4;

public class BookwormOracle implements Oracle {

    private Encyclopedia enc;
```

```
public void setEncyclopedia(Encyclopedia enc) {
    this.enc = enc;
}

public String defineMeaningOfLife() {
    return "Encyclopedias are a waste of money - use the Internet";
}

}
```

As you can see, the BookwormOracle class not only implements the Oracle interface but also defines the setter for Dependency Injection. Spring is more than comfortable dealing with a structure like this—there is absolutely no need to define the dependencies on the business interface. The ability to use interfaces to define dependencies is an often-touted benefit of setter injection, but in actuality, you should strive to keep setters used solely for injection out of your business interfaces. Unless you are absolutely sure that all implementations of a particular business interface require a particular dependency, let each implementation class define its own dependencies and keep the business interface for business methods.

Although you shouldn't always place setters for dependencies in a business interface, placing setters and getters for configuration parameters in the business interface is a good idea and makes setter injection a valuable tool. We consider configuration parameters to be a special case for dependencies. Certainly your components depend on the configuration data, but configuration data is significantly different from the types of dependency you have seen so far. We will discuss the differences shortly, but for now, consider the business interface shown in Listing 4-8.

Listing 4-8. *The NewsletterSender Interface*

```
package com.apress.prospring.ch4;

public interface NewsletterSender {

    public void setSmtpServer(String smtpServer);
    public String getSmtpServer();

    public void setFromAddress(String fromAddress);
    public String getFromAddress();

    public void send();
}
```

The NewsletterSender interface is implemented by classes that send a set of newsletters via e-mail. The send() method is the only business method, but notice that we have defined two JavaBean properties on the interface. Why are we doing this, when we just said that you shouldn't define dependencies in the business interface? The reason is that these values, the SMTP server address and the address the e-mails are sent from, are not dependencies in the practical sense; rather, they are configuration details that affect how all implementations of the NewsletterSender interface function. Spring's Dependency Injection capabilities form the ideal solution to the external configuration of application components, not for dependency provision but as a mechanism for externalizing component configuration settings. The question here then is: What is the difference between a configuration parameter and any other kind of dependency? In most cases, you can clearly see whether a dependency should be classed as a configuration parameter, but if you are not sure, look for the following three characteristics that point to a configuration parameter:

1. **Configuration parameters are passive.** In the `NewsletterSender` example shown in Listing 4-8, the SMTP server parameter is an example of a passive dependency. Passive dependencies are not used directly to perform an action; instead, they are used internally or by another dependency to perform their actions. In the `MessageRenderer` example from Chapter 2, the `MessageProvider` dependency was not passive—it performed a function that was necessary for the `MessageRenderer` to complete its task.

2. **Configuration parameters are usually information, not other components.** By this we mean that a configuration parameter is usually some piece of information that a component needs to complete its work. Clearly the SMTP server is a piece of information required by the `NewsletterSender`, but the `MessageProvider` is really another component that the `MessageRenderer` needs to function correctly.

3. **Configuration parameters are usually simple values or collections of simple values.** This is really a by-product of points 1 and 2, but configuration parameters are usually simple values. In Java this means they are a primitive (or the corresponding wrapper class) or a `String` or collections of these values. Simple values are generally passive. This means you can't do much with a `String` other than manipulate the data it represents; and you almost always use these values for information purposes—for example, an `int` value that represents the port number that a network socket should listen on, or a `String` that represents the SMTP server through which an e-mail program should send messages.

When considering whether to define configuration options in the business interface, also consider whether the configuration parameter is applicable to all implementations of the business interface or just one. For instance, in the case of implementations of `NewsletterSender`, it is obvious that all implementations need to know which SMTP server to use when sending e-mails. However, we would probably choose to leave the configuration option that flags whether to send secure e-mail off the business interface, because not all e-mail APIs are capable of this and it is correct to assume that many implementations will not take security into consideration at all.

■**Note** Recall that in Chapter 2, we chose to define the dependencies in the business purposes. This was for illustration purposes and should not be treated in any way as best practice.

Setter injection also allows you to swap dependencies for a different implementation on the fly without creating a new instance of the parent component. Currently Spring doesn't support this feature, but as soon as Spring is JMX aware, this feature will present itself. Perhaps the biggest benefit of setter injection is that it is the least intrusive of the Injection mechanisms.

If you are defining constructors for injection on a class that would otherwise just have the default constructor, then you are affecting all code that uses that class in a non-IoC environment. Extra setters that are defined on a class for IoC purposes do not affect the ability of other classes to interact with it.

In general, setter-based injection is the best choice, because it has the least effect on your code's usability in non-IoC settings. Constructor injection is a good choice when you want to ensure that dependencies are being passed to a component, but bear in mind that many containers provide their own mechanism for doing this with setter injection. Most of the code in the sample application uses setter injection, although there are a few examples of constructor injection.

Inversion of Control in Spring

As we mentioned earlier, Inversion of Control is a big part of what Spring does, and the core of Spring's implementation is based on Dependency Injection, although Dependency Lookup features are provided as well. When Spring provides collaborators to a dependent object automatically, it does so using Dependency Injection. In a Spring-based application, it is always preferable to use Dependency Injection to pass collaborators to dependent objects rather than have the dependent objects obtain the collaborators via Lookup. Although Dependency Injection is the preferred mechanism for wiring together collaborators and dependent objects, you need Dependency Lookup to access the dependent objects. In many environments, Spring cannot automatically wire up **all** of your application components using Dependency Injection and you must use Dependency Lookup to access the initial set of components. When you are building web applications using Spring's MVC support, Spring can avoid this by gluing your entire application together automatically. Wherever it is possible to use Dependency Injection with Spring, you should do so; otherwise you can fall back on the Dependency Lookup capabilities. You will see examples of both in action during the course of this chapter, and we are sure to point them out when they first arise.

An interesting feature of Spring's IoC container is that it has the ability to act as an adaptor between its own Dependency Injection container and external Dependency Lookup containers. We look at this in more detail in Chapter 5.

Spring supports both constructor and setter injection and bolsters the standard IoC feature set with a whole host of useful additions to make your life easier.

The rest of this chapter introduces the basics of Spring's DI container complete with plenty of examples.

Dependency Injection with Spring

Spring's support for Dependency Injection is comprehensive and, as you will see in Chapter 5, goes beyond the standard IoC feature set we have discussed so far. The rest of this chapter addresses the basics of Spring's Dependency Injection container, looking at both setter and constructor injection, along with a detailed look at how Dependency Injection is configured in Spring.

Beans and BeanFactories

The core of Spring's Dependency Injection container is the BeanFactory. A BeanFactory is responsible for managing components and their dependencies. In Spring, the term **bean** is used to refer to any component managed by the container. Typically your beans adhere, at some level, to the JavaBeans specification, but this is not required, especially if you plan to use Constructor Injection to wire your beans together.

Your application interacts with the Spring DI container via the BeanFactory interface. At some point, your application must create an instance of a class that implements the BeanFactory interface and configure it with bean and dependency information. After this is complete, your application can access the beans via the BeanFactory and get on with its processing. In some cases, all of this setup is handled automatically, but in many cases, you need to code the setup yourself. All of the examples in this chapter require manual setup of the BeanFactory implementation.

Although a BeanFactory can be configured programmatically, it is more common to see it configured externally using some kind of configuration file. Internally, bean configuration is represented by instances of classes that implement the BeanDefinition interface. The bean configuration stores not only information about a bean itself, but also about the beans that it depends on. For any BeanFactory class that also implements the BeanDefinitionRegistry interface, you can read the BeanDefinition data from a configuration file, using either PropertiesBeanDefinitionReader or XmlBeanDefinitionReader. The two main BeanFactory implementations that come with Spring implement BeanDefinitionRegistry.

So you can identify your beans within the BeanFactory, each bean is assigned a name. Each bean has at least one name but can have any number. Any names after the first are considered aliases for the same bean. You use bean names to retrieve a bean from the BeanFactory and also to establish dependency relationships—that is, bean X depends on bean Y.

BeanFactory Implementations

The description of the BeanFactory might make using it seem overly complex, but in practice, this is not the case. In fact, we discussed all of the concepts in the previous section and in the simple example in Chapter 2. Listing 4-9 shows the code from Chapter 2.

Listing 4-9. *Using the BeanFactory*

```
package com.apress.prospring.ch2;

import java.io.FileInputStream;
import java.util.Properties;

import org.springframework.beans.factory.BeanFactory;
import org.springframework.beans.factory.support.DefaultListableBeanFactory;
import org.springframework.beans.factory.support.PropertiesBeanDefinitionReader;
```

```java
public class HelloWorldSpringWithDI {

    public static void main(String[] args) throws Exception {

        // get the bean factory
        BeanFactory factory = getBeanFactory();

        MessageRenderer mr = (MessageRenderer) factory.getBean("renderer");
        mr.render();
    }

    private static BeanFactory getBeanFactory() throws Exception {
        // get the bean factory
        DefaultListableBeanFactory factory = new DefaultListableBeanFactory();

        // create a definition reader
        PropertiesBeanDefinitionReader rdr = new PropertiesBeanDefinitionReader(
                factory);

        // load the configuration options
        Properties props = new Properties();
        props.load(new FileInputStream("./ch2/src/conf/beans.properties"));

        rdr.registerBeanDefinitions(props);

        return factory;
    }
}
```

In this example, you can see that we are using the DefaultListableBeanFactory—one of the two main BeanFactory implementations supplied with Spring—and that we are reading in the BeanDefinition information from a properties file using the PropertiesBeanDefinitionReader. Once the BeanFactory implementations is created and configured, we retrieve the MessageRenderer bean using its name, renderer, which is configured in the properties file.

In addition to the PropertiesBeanDefinitionReader, Spring also provides XmlBeanDefinitionReader, which allows you to manage your bean configuration using XML rather than properties. Although properties are ideal for small, simple applications, they can quickly become cumbersome when you are dealing with a large number of beans. For this reason, it is preferable to use the XML configuration format for all but the most trivial of applications. This leads nicely to a discussion of the second of the two main BeanFactory implementations: XmlBeanFactory.

The XmlBeanFactory is derived from DefaultListableBeanFactory and simply extends it to perform automatic configuration using the XmlBeanDefinitionReader. So rather than create some code like this:

```
package com.apress.prospring.ch4;

import org.springframework.beans.factory.support.DefaultListableBeanFactory;
import org.springframework.beans.factory.xml.XmlBeanDefinitionReader;
import org.springframework.core.io.FileSystemResource;

public class XmlConfig {

    public static void main(String[] args) {
        DefaultListableBeanFactory factory = new DefaultListableBeanFactory();
        XmlBeanDefinitionReader rdr = new XmlBeanDefinitionReader(factory);
        rdr.loadBeanDefinitions(new FileSystemResource("ch4/src/conf/beans.xml"));
        Oracle oracle = (Oracle)factory.getBean("oracle");
    }
}
```

you can do this instead:

```
package com.apress.prospring.ch4;

import org.springframework.beans.factory.xml.XmlBeanFactory;
import org.springframework.core.io.FileSystemResource;

public class XmlConfigWithBeanFactory {

    public static void main(String[] args) {
        XmlBeanFactory factory = new XmlBeanFactory(new FileSystemResource(
                "ch4/src/conf/beans.xml"));
        Oracle oracle = (Oracle)factory.getBean("oracle");
    }
}
```

For the rest of this book, including the sample application, we will be using the XML configuration format exclusively. You are free to investigate the properties format yourself—you will find plenty of examples throughout the Spring codebase.

Of course, you are free to define your own BeanFactory implementations, although be aware that doing so is quite involved; you need to implement a lot more interfaces than just BeanFactory to get the same level of functionality you have with the supplied BeanFactory implementations. If all you want to do is define a new configuration mechanism, then create your definition reader and wrap this in a simple BeanFactory implementation derived from DefaultListableBeanFactory. This is the approach the XmlBeanFactory class takes; check the Spring code for more details.

Configuring the BeanFactory

The key to getting set up with any Spring-based application is creating the BeanFactory configuration file for your application. A basic configuration without any bean definitions looks like this:

```
<!DOCTYPE beans PUBLIC "-//SPRING//DTD BEAN//EN"
 "http://www.springframework.org/dtd/spring-beans.dtd">
<beans>
</beans>
```

Each bean is then defined using a <bean> tag under the root of the <beans> tag. The <bean> tag has two required attributes: id and class. The id attribute is used to give the bean its default name and the class attribute specifies the type of the bean. Listing 4-10 returns to the Hello World example from Chapter 2 to show how the two beans, renderer and provider, are defined within the configuration file.

Listing 4-10. *Configuring the Hello World Example with XML*

```
<!DOCTYPE beans PUBLIC "-//SPRING//DTD BEAN//EN"

"http://www.springframework.org/dtd/spring-beans.dtd">
<beans>
    <bean id="renderer"
          class="com.apress.prospring.ch2.StandardOutMessageRenderer"/>
    <bean id="provider"
          class="com.apress.prospring.ch2.HelloWorldMessageProvider"/>
</beans>
```

We can modify the code from Chapter 2 to read this configuration using the XmlBeanFactory. Listing 4-11 shows how.

Listing 4-11. *Reading the Hello World Configuration from XML*

```
package com.apress.prospring.ch4;

import org.springframework.beans.factory.BeanFactory;
import org.springframework.beans.factory.xml.XmlBeanFactory;
import org.springframework.core.io.FileSystemResource;

import com.apress.prospring.ch2.MessageProvider;
import com.apress.prospring.ch2.MessageRenderer;

public class HelloWorldXml {

    public static void main(String[] args) throws Exception {

        // get the bean factory
        BeanFactory factory = getBeanFactory();

        MessageRenderer mr = (MessageRenderer) factory.getBean("renderer");
        MessageProvider mp = (MessageProvider) factory.getBean("provider");
```

```
        mr.setMessageProvider(mp);
        mr.render();
    }

    private static BeanFactory getBeanFactory() throws Exception {
        // get the bean factory
        XmlBeanFactory factory = new XmlBeanFactory(new FileSystemResource(
                "ch4/src/conf/beans.xml"));

        return factory;
    }
}
```

Notice that there is no difference between the main() in Listing 4-11 and the main() method in Listing 2-10 in Chapter 2, but here there is substantially less code in the getBeanFactory() method. The interesting point to note here is that the code in the main() method didn't change. This is because it was working with the BeanFactory interface, not some subinterface or class. Although you may need to work with the specific BeanFactory type during configuration, you do not need to during the rest of your application when all you are doing is locating beans using getBean(). This is a good pattern to follow and you should avoid coupling your application too closely to any particular BeanFactory implementation.

Note that there is a problem with the code in Listing 4-11, a problem we encountered and fixed in Chapter 2—the application still has to pass the provider bean to the reference bean to satisfy its dependency. In Chapter 2, we modified the configuration; Spring did this for us using setter injection. We can, of course, also do this using the XML configuration provider.

Using Setter Injection

To configure setter injection using the XML provider, you need to specify <property> tags under the <bean> tag for each <property> into which you wish to inject a dependency. For example, to assign the provider bean to the messageProvider property of the renderer bean, we simply change the <bean> tag for the renderer bean as follows:

```
<bean id="renderer"
      class="com.apress.prospring.ch2.StandardOutMessageRenderer">
    <property name="messageProvider">
        <ref local="provider"/>
    </property>
</bean>
```

From this code, you can see that we are assigning the provider bean to the messageProvider property. We use the <ref> tag to assign a bean reference to a property (discussed in more detail shortly). Now we can remove the unnecessary property assignments from the Hello World example, as shown in Listing 4-12.

Listing 4-12. *Configuring Dependency Injection with XML*

```
package com.apress.prospring.ch4;

import org.springframework.beans.factory.BeanFactory;
import org.springframework.beans.factory.xml.XmlBeanFactory;
import org.springframework.core.io.FileSystemResource;

import com.apress.prospring.ch2.MessageRenderer;

public class HelloWorldXmlWithDI {

    public static void main(String[] args) throws Exception {

        // get the bean factory
        BeanFactory factory = getBeanFactory();
        MessageRenderer mr = (MessageRenderer) factory.getBean("renderer");
        mr.render();
    }

    private static BeanFactory getBeanFactory() throws Exception {
        // get the bean factory
        XmlBeanFactory factory = new XmlBeanFactory(new FileSystemResource(
                "ch4/src/conf/beans.xml"));

        return factory;
    }
}
```

This example makes full use of Spring's Dependency Injection capabilities and is fully configured using the XML format.

Using Constructor Injection

In the previous example, the MessageProvider implementation, HelloWorldMessageProvider, returned the same hard-coded message for each call of the getMessage() method. In the Spring configuration file, you can easily create a configurable MessageProvider that allows the message to be defined externally, as shown in Listing 4-13.

Listing 4-13. *The ConfigurableMessageProvider Class*

```
package com.apress.prospring.ch4;

import com.apress.prospring.ch2.MessageProvider;

public class ConfigurableMessageProvider implements MessageProvider {
```

```
    private String message;

    public ConfigurableMessageProvider(String message) {
        this.message = message;
    }

    public String getMessage() {
        return message;
    }

}
```

As you can see, it is impossible to create an instance of ConfigurableMessageProvider without providing a value for the message (unless you supply null). This is exactly what we want, and this class is ideally suited for use with Constructor Injection. Listing 4-14 shows how you can redefine the provider bean definition to create an instance of ConfigurableMessageProvider, injecting the message using Constructor Injection.

Listing 4-14. *Using Constructor Injection*

```
<bean id="provider" class="com.apress.prospring.ch4.ConfigurableMessageProvider">
    <constructor-arg>
        <value>This is a configurable message</value>
    </constructor-arg>
</bean>
```

In this code, instead of using a <property> tag, we used a <constructor-arg> tag. Because we are not passing in another bean this time, just a String literal, we use the <value> tag instead of the <ref> to specify the value for the constructor argument.

When you have more than one constructor argument or your class has more than one constructor, you need to give each <constructor-arg> tag an index attribute to specify the index of the argument, starting at 0, in the constructor signature. It is always best to use the index attribute whenever you are dealing with constructors that have multiple arguments to avoid confusion between the parameters and ensure that Spring picks the correct constructor.

Avoiding Constructor Confusion

In some cases, Spring finds it impossible to tell which constructor you want it to use for constructor injection. This usually arises when you have two constructors with the same number of arguments and the types used in the arguments are represented in exactly the same way. Consider the code in Listing 4-15.

Listing 4-15. *Constructor Confusion*

```
package com.apress.prospring.ch4;

import org.springframework.beans.factory.BeanFactory;
import org.springframework.beans.factory.xml.XmlBeanFactory;
import org.springframework.core.io.FileSystemResource;

public class ConstructorConfusion {

    private String someValue;

    public ConstructorConfusion(String someValue) {
        System.out.println("ConstructorConfusion(String) called");
        this.someValue = someValue;
    }

    public ConstructorConfusion(int someValue) {
        System.out.println("ConstructorConfusion(int) called");
        this.someValue = "Number: " + Integer.toString(someValue);
    }

    public static void main(String[] args) {
        BeanFactory factory = new XmlBeanFactory(new FileSystemResource(
                "./ch4/src/conf/beans.xml"));

        ConstructorConfusion cc = (ConstructorConfusion)
                                        factory.getBean("constructorConfusion");
        System.out.println(cc);
    }

    public String toString() {
        return someValue;
    }
}
```

Here, you can clearly see what this code does—it simply retrieves a bean of type
ConstructorConfusion from the BeanFactory and writes the value to stdout. Now look at
the configuration code in Listing 4-16.

Listing 4-16. *Confused Constructors*

```
<bean id="constructorConfusion"
      class="com.apress.prospring.ch4.ConstructorConfusion">
    <constructor-arg>
        <value>90</value>
    </constructor-arg>
</bean>
```

Which of the constructors is called in this case? Running the example yields the following output:

```
ConstructorConfusion(String) called
90
```

This shows that the constructor with the String argument was called. This is not the desired effect, since we want to prefix any integer values passed in using constructor injection with Number:, as shown in the int constructor. To get around this, we need to make a small modification to the configuration, shown in Listing 4-17.

Listing 4-17. *Overcoming Constructor Confusion*

```
<bean id="constructorConfusion"
      class="com.apress.prospring.ch4.ConstructorConfusion">
    <constructor-arg type="int">
        <value>90</value>
    </constructor-arg>
</bean>
```

Notice now that the <constructor-arg> tag has an additional attribute, type, that specifies the type of argument that Spring should look for. Running the example again with the corrected configuration yields the correct output:

```
ConstructorConfusion(int) called
Number: 90
```

Injection Parameters

In the two previous examples, you saw how to inject other components and values into a bean using both setter injection and constructor injection. Spring supports a myriad of options for injection parameters, allowing you to inject not only other components and simple values, but also Java Collections, externally defined properties, and even beans in another factory. You can use all of these injection parameter types for both setter injection and constructor injection by using the corresponding tag under the <property> and <constructor-args> tags, respectively.

Injecting Simple Values

Injecting simple values into your beans is easy. To do so, simply specify the value in the configuration tag, wrapped inside a <value> tag. By default, the <value> tag can not only read String values, but it can also convert these values to any primitive or primitive wrapper class. Listing 4-18 shows a simple bean that has a variety of properties exposed for injection.

Listing 4-18. *Injecting Simple Values*

```
package com.apress.prospring.ch4;

import org.springframework.beans.factory.xml.XmlBeanFactory;
import org.springframework.core.io.FileSystemResource;

public class InjectSimple {

    private String name;

    private int age;

    private float height;

    private boolean isProgrammer;

    private Long ageInSeconds;

    public static void main(String[] args) {
        XmlBeanFactory factory = new XmlBeanFactory(new FileSystemResource(
                "./ch4/src/conf/beans.xml"));
        InjectSimple simple = (InjectSimple)factory.getBean("injectSimple");
        System.out.println(simple);
    }

    public void setAgeInSeconds(Long ageInSeconds) {
        this.ageInSeconds = ageInSeconds;
    }

    public void setIsProgrammer(boolean isProgrammer) {
        this.isProgrammer = isProgrammer;
    }
```

```
public void setAge(int age) {
    this.age = age;
}

public void setHeight(float height) {
    this.height = height;
}

public void setName(String name) {
    this.name = name;
}

public String toString() {
    return    "Name :" + name + "\n"
            + "Age:" + age + "\n"
            + "Age in Seconds: " + ageInSeconds + "\n"
            + "Height: " + height + "\n"
            + "Is Programmer?: " + isProgrammer;
    }
}
```

In addition to the properties, the InjectSimple class also defines the main() method that creates an XmlBeanFactory and then retrieves an InjectSimple bean from Spring. The property values of this bean are then written to stdout. The configuration for this bean is shown in Listing 4-19.

Listing 4-19. *Configuring Simple Value Injection*

```
<bean id="injectSimple" class="com.apress.prospring.ch4.InjectSimple">
        <property name="name">
            <value>John Smith</value>
        </property>
        <property name="age">
            <value>35</value>
        </property>
        <property name="height">
            <value>1.78</value>
        </property>
        <property name="isProgrammer">
            <value>true</value>
        </property>
        <property name="ageInSeconds">
                <value>1103760000</value>
        </property>
    </bean>
```

You can see from Listings 4-18 and 4-19 that is it is possible to define properties on your bean that accept String values, primitive values, or primitive wrapper values and then inject values for these properties using the `<value>` tag. Here is the output created by running this example as expected:

```
Name: John Smith
Age: 35
Age in Seconds: 1103760000
Height: 1.78
Is Programmer?: true
```

In Chapter 5, you will see how to expand the range of types that can be injected using the `<value>` tag.

Injecting Beans in the Same Factory

As you have already seen, it is possible to inject one bean into another using the `<ref>` tag. Listing 4-20 shows a class that exposes a setter to allow a bean to be injected.

Listing 4-20. *Injecting Beans*

```
package com.apress.prospring.ch4;

public class InjectRef {

    private Oracle oracle;

    public void setOracle(Oracle oracle) {
        this.oracle = oracle;
    }
}
```

To configure Spring to inject one bean into another, you first need to configure two beans: one to be injected and one to be the target of the injection. Once this is done, you simply configure the injection using the `<ref>` tag on the target bean. Remember that `<ref>` must come under either `<property>` or `<constructor-arg>` depending on whether you are using setter or constructor injection. Listing 4-21 shows an example of this configuration.

Listing 4-21. *Configuring Bean Injection*

```
<bean id="injectRef" class="com.apress.prospring.ch4.InjectRef">
    <property name="oracle">
        <ref local="oracle"/>
    </property>
</bean>
<bean id="oracle" class="com.apress.prospring.ch4.BookwormOracle"/>
```

An important point to note is that the type being injected does not have to be the exact type defined on the target; the types just need to be compatible. Compatible means that if the declared type on the target is an interface, then the injected type must implement this interface. If the declared type is a class, then the injected type must either be the same type or a subtype. In this example, the InjectRef class defines the setOracle() method to receive an instance of Oracle, which is an interface, and the injected type is BookwormOracle, a class that implements Oracle. This is a point that causes confusion for some developers, but it is really quite simple. Injection is subject to the same typing rules as any Java code, so as long as you are familiar with how Java typing works, then understanding typing in injection is easy.

In the previous example, the id of the bean to inject was specified using the local attribute of the <ref> tag. As you will see later, in the section titled "Understanding Bean Naming," you can give a bean more than one name so that you can refer to it using a variety of aliases. When you use the local attribute, it means that the <ref> tag only ever looks at the bean's id and never at any of its aliases. To inject a bean by any name, use the bean attribute of the <ref> tag instead of the local attribute. Listing 4-22 shows an alternative configuration for the previous example using an alternative name for the injected bean.

Listing 4-22. *Injecting Using Bean Aliases*

```
<bean id="injectRef" class="com.apress.prospring.ch4.InjectRef">
    <property name="oracle">
        <ref bean="wiseworm"/>
    </property>
</bean>
<bean id="oracle"
      name="wiseworm"
      class="com.apress.prospring.ch4.BookwormOracle"/>
```

In this example, the oracle bean is given an alias using the name attribute, and then it is injected into the injectRef bean by using this alias in conjunction with the bean attribute of the <ref> tag. Don't worry too much about the naming semantics at this point—we discuss this in much more detail later in the chapter.

Injection and BeanFactory Nesting

So far the beans we have been injecting have been located in the same bean factory as the beans they are injected into. However, Spring supports a hierarchical structure for BeanFactories so that one factory is considered the parent of another. By allowing BeanFactories to be nested, Spring allows you to split your configuration into different files—a godsend on larger projects with lots of beans.

When nesting BeanFactories, Spring allows beans in what is considered the child factory to reference beans in the parent factory. The only drawback is that this can only be done in configuration. It is impossible to call getBean() on the child BeanFactory to access a bean in the parent BeanFactory.

BeanFactory nesting using the XmlBeanFactory is very simple to get a grip on. To nest one XmlBeanFactory inside another, simply pass the parent XmlBeanFactory as a constructor argument to the child XmlBeanFactory. This is shown in Listing 4-23.

Listing 4-23. *Nesting XmlBeanFactories*

```
BeanFactory parent = new XmlBeanFactory(new FileSystemResource(
              "./ch4/src/conf/parent.xml"));
      BeanFactory child = new XmlBeanFactory(new FileSystemResource(
              "./ch4/src/conf/beans.xml"), parent);
```

Inside the configuration file for the child BeanFactory, referencing a bean in the parent
BeanFactory works exactly like referencing a bean in the child BeanFactory, unless you have a
bean in the child BeanFactory that shares the same name. In that case, you simply replace the
bean attribute of the <ref> tag with parent and you are on your way. Listing 4-24 shows a
sample configuration file for the parent BeanFactory.

Listing 4-24. *Parent BeanFactory Configuration*

```
<bean id="injectBean" class="java.lang.String">
      <constructor-arg>
          <value>Bean In Parent</value>
      </constructor-arg>
</bean>
<bean id="injectBeanParent" class="java.lang.String">
      <constructor-arg>
          <value>Bean In Parent</value>
      </constructor-arg>
</bean>
```

As you can see, this configuration simply defines two beans: injectBean and
injectBeanParent. Both are String objects with the value Bean In Parent. Listing 4-25
shows a sample configuration for the child BeanFactory.

Listing 4-25. *Child BeanFactory Configuration*

```
<bean id="target1" class="com.apress.prospring.ch4.SimpleTarget">
      <property name="val">
          <ref bean="injectBeanParent"/>
      </property>
</bean>

<bean id="target2" class="com.apress.prospring.ch4.SimpleTarget">
      <property name="val">
          <ref bean="injectBean"/>
      </property>
</bean>

<bean id="target3" class="com.apress.prospring.ch4.SimpleTarget">
      <property name="val">
          <ref parent="injectBean"/>
      </property>
</bean>
```

```
<bean id="injectBean" class="java.lang.String">
    <constructor-arg>
        <value>Bean In Child</value>
    </constructor-arg>
</bean>
```

Notice that we have defined four beans here. The injectBean in this listing is similar to the injectBean in the parent except that the String it represents has a different value, indicating that it is located in the child BeanFactory.

The target1 bean is using the bean attribute of the <ref> tag to reference the bean named injectBeanParent. Because this bean only exists in the parent BeanFactory, target1 receives a reference to that bean. There are two points of interest here. First, you can use the bean attribute to reference beans in both the child and parent BeanFactories. This makes it easy to reference the beans transparently, allowing you to move beans between configuration files as your application grows. The second point of interest is that you can't use the local attribute to refer to beans in the parent BeanFactory. The XML parser checks to see that the value of the local attribute exists as a valid element in the same file, preventing it from being used to reference beans in the parent factory.

The target2 bean is using the bean attribute of the <ref> tag to reference the injectBean. Because that bean is defined in both BeanFactories, the target2 bean receives a reference to the injectBean in its own BeanFactory.

The target3 bean is using the parent attribute of the <ref> tag to reference the injectBean directly in the parent BeanFactory. Because target3 is using the parent attribute of the <ref> tag, the injectBean declared in the child BeanFactory is ignored completely.

The code in Listing 4-26 demonstrates the semantics discussed here by retrieving each of the three targetX beans from the child BeanFactory and outputting the value of the val property in each case.

Listing 4-26. *The HierarchicalBeanFactoryUsage Class*

```java
package com.apress.prospring.ch4;

import org.springframework.beans.factory.BeanFactory;
import org.springframework.beans.factory.xml.XmlBeanFactory;
import org.springframework.core.io.FileSystemResource;

public class HierarchicalBeanFactoryUsage {

    public static void main(String[] args) {
        BeanFactory parent = new XmlBeanFactory(new FileSystemResource(
                "./ch4/src/conf/parent.xml"));
        BeanFactory child = new XmlBeanFactory(new FileSystemResource(
                "./ch4/src/conf/beans.xml"), parent);

        SimpleTarget target1 = (SimpleTarget) child.getBean("target1");
        SimpleTarget target2 = (SimpleTarget) child.getBean("target2");
        SimpleTarget target3 = (SimpleTarget) child.getBean("target3");
```

```
            System.out.println(target1.getVal());
            System.out.println(target2.getVal());
            System.out.println(target3.getVal());
        }
}
```

Here is the output from running this example:

```
Bean In Parent
Bean In Child
Bean In Parent
```

As expected, the target1 and target3 beans both get a reference to beans in the parent BeanFactory, whereas the target2 bean gets a reference to a bean in the child BeanFactory.

Using Collections for Injection

Often your beans need access to collections of objects rather than just individual beans or values. Therefore, it should come as no surprise that Spring allows you to inject a collection of objects into one of your beans. Using the collection is simple: you choose either <list>, <map>, <set>, or <props> to represent a List, Map, Set, or Properties instance, and then you pass in the individual items just as you would with any other injection. The <props> tag only allows for Strings to be passed in as the value because the Properties class only allows for property values to be Strings. When using <list>, <map>, or <set>, you can use any tag you use when injecting into a property, even another collection tag. This allows you to pass in a List of Maps, a Map of Sets, or even a List of Maps of Sets of Lists! Listing 4-27 shows a class that can have all four collection types injected into it.

Listing 4-27. *Collection Injection*

```
package com.apress.prospring.ch4;

import java.util.Iterator;
import java.util.List;
import java.util.Map;
import java.util.Properties;
import java.util.Set;

import org.springframework.beans.factory.BeanFactory;
import org.springframework.beans.factory.xml.XmlBeanFactory;
import org.springframework.core.io.FileSystemResource;

public class CollectionInjection {

    private Map map;

    private Properties props;

    private Set set;
```

```java
    private List list;

    public static void main(String[] args) {
        BeanFactory factory = new XmlBeanFactory(
                            new FileSystemResource("./ch4/src/conf/beans.xml"));

        CollectionInjection instance = (CollectionInjection)

        factory.getBean("injectCollection");
        instance.displayInfo();
    }

    public void setList(List list) {
        this.list = list;
    }

    public void setSet(Set set) {
        this.set = set;
    }

    public void setMap(Map map) {
        this.map = map;
    }

    public void setProps(Properties props) {
        this.props = props;
    }

    public void displayInfo() {

        // display the Map
        Iterator i = map.keySet().iterator();

        System.out.println("Map contents:\n");
        while (i.hasNext()) {
            Object key = i.next();
            System.out.println("Key: " + key + " - Value: " + map.get(key));
        }

        // display the properties
        i = props.keySet().iterator();
        System.out.println("\nProperties contents:\n");
        while (i.hasNext()) {
            String key = i.next().toString();
            System.out.println("Key: " + key + " - Value: "
                    + props.getProperty(key));
        }
```

```
        // display the set
        i = set.iterator();
        System.out.println("\nSet contents:\n");
        while (i.hasNext()) {
            System.out.println("Value: " + i.next());
        }

        // display the list
        i = list.iterator();
        System.out.println("\nList contents:\n");
        while (i.hasNext()) {
            System.out.println("Value: " + i.next());
        }
    }
}
```

That is quite a lot of code, but it actually does very little. The main() method retrieves a CollectionInjection bean from Spring and then calls the displayInfo() method. This method just outputs the contents of the List, Map, Properties, and Set instances that will be injected from Spring. In Listing 4-28, you can see the configuration required to inject values for each of the properties on the CollectionInjection class.

Listing 4-28. *Configuring Collection Injection*

```xml
<bean id="injectCollection" class="com.apress.prospring.ch4.CollectionInjection">
        <property name="map">
            <map>
                <entry key="someValue">
                    <value>Hello World!</value>
                </entry>
                <entry key="someBean">
                    <ref local="oracle"/>
                </entry>
            </map>
        </property>
        <property name="props">
            <props>
                <prop key="firstName">
                    Rob
                </prop>
                <prop key="secondName">
                    Harrop
                </prop>
            </props>
        </property>
```

```
        <property name="set">
            <set>
                <value>Hello World!</value>
                <ref local="oracle"/>
            </set>
        </property>
        <property name="list">
            <list>
                <value>Hello World!</value>
                <ref local="oracle"/>
            </list>
        </property>
    </bean>
```

In this code, you can see that we have injected value into all four setters exposed on the ConstructorInjection class. For the map property, we have injected a Map instance using the <map> tag. Notice that each entry is specified using an <entry> tag and each has a String key and then an entry value. This entry value can be any value you can inject into a property separately; this example shows the use of the <value> and <ref> tags to add a String value and a bean reference to the Map. For the props property, we use the <props> tag to create an instance of java.util.Properties and populate it using <prop> tags. Notice that although the <prop> tag is keyed in a similar manner to the <entry> tag, you can only specify a String value for each property that goes in the Properties instance.

Both the <list> and <set> tags work in exactly the same way: you specify each element using any of the individual value tags such as <value> and <ref> that are used to inject a single value into a property. In Listing 4-28, you can see that we have added a String value and a bean reference to both the List and the Set.

Here is the output generated by Listing 4-28. As expected, it simply lists the elements added to the collections in the configuration file.

```
Map contents:

Key: someValue - Value: Hello World!
Key: someBean - Value: com.apress.prospring.ch4.BookwormOracle@1ccce3c

Properties contents:

Key: secondName - Value: Harrop
Key: firstName - Value: Rob

Set contents:

Value: com.apress.prospring.ch4.BookwormOracle@1ccce3c
Value: Hello World!

List contents:

Value: Hello World!
Value: com.apress.prospring.ch4.BookwormOracle@1ccce3c
```

Remember, with the <list>, <map>, and <set> elements, you can employ any of the tags used to set the value of noncollection properties to specify the value of one of the entries in the collection. This is quite a powerful concept because you are not limited just to injecting collections of primitive values, you can also inject collections of beans or other collections.

Using this functionality, it is much easier to modularize your application and provide different, user-selectable implementations of key pieces of application logic. Consider a system that allows corporate staff to create, proofread, and order their personalized business stationery online. In this system, the finished artwork for each order is sent to the appropriate printer when it is ready for production. The only complication is that some printers want to receive the artwork via e-mail, some via FTP, and still more using Secure Copy Protocol (SCP). Using Spring's collection injection, you can create a standard interface for this functionality, as shown in Listing 4-29.

Listing 4-29. *The ArtworkSender Interface*

```
package com.apress.prospring.ch4;

public interface ArtworkSender {

    public void sendArtwork(String artworkPath, Recipient recipient);

    public String getFriendlyName();

    public String getShortName();
}
```

From this interface, you can create multiple implementations, each of which is capable of describing itself to a human, such as the ones shown in Listing 4-30.

Listing 4-30. *The FtpArtworkSender Class*

```
package com.apress.prospring.ch4;

public class FtpArtworkSender implements ArtworkSender {

    public void sendArtwork(String artworkPath, Recipient recipient) {
        // ftp logic here...
    }

    public String getFriendlyName() {
        return "File Transfer Protocol";
    }

    public String getShortName() {
        return "ftp";
    }
}
```

With the implementations in place, you simply pass a `List` to your `ArtworkManager` class and you are on your way. Using the `getFriendlyName()` method, you can display a list of delivery options for the system administrator to choose from when you are configuring each stationery template. In addition, your application can remain fully decoupled from the individual implementations if you just code to the `ArtworkSender` interface.

Understanding Bean Naming

Spring supports quite a complex bean naming structure that allows you the flexibility to handle many different situations. Every bean must have at least one name that is unique within the containing `BeanFactory`. Spring follows a simple resolution process to determine what name is used for the bean. If you give the `<bean>` tag an `id` attribute, then the value of that attribute is used as the name. If no `id` attribute is specified, Spring looks for a `name` attribute and, if one is defined, it uses the first name defined in the `name` attribute. (We say the first name because it is possible to define multiple names within the `name` attribute; this is covered in more detail shortly.) If neither the `id` nor the `name` attribute is specified, Spring uses the bean's class name as the name, provided, of course, that no other bean is using the same name. Listing 4-31 shows a sample configuration that uses all three naming schemes.

Listing 4-31. *Bean Naming*

```
<bean id="string1" class="java.lang.String"/>
<bean name="string2" class="java.lang.String"/>
<bean class="java.lang.String"/>
```

Each of these approaches is equally valid from a technical point of view, but which is the best choice for your application? To start with, avoid using the automatic name by class behavior. This doesn't allow you much flexibility to define multiple beans of the same type, and it is much better to define your own names. That way, if Spring changes the default behavior in the future, your application continues to work. When choosing whether to use `id` or `name`, always use `id` to specify the bean's default name. The `id` attribute in the XML is declared as an XML identity in the DTD for the Spring configuration file. This means that not only can the XML parser perform validation on your file, but any good XML editor should be able to do the same, thus reducing the number of errors as a result of mistyped bean names. Essentially, this allows your XML editor to validate that the bean you are referencing in the `local` attribute of a `<ref>` tag actually exists.

The only drawback of using the `id` attribute is that you are limited to characters that are allowed within XML element IDs. If you find that you cannot use a character you want in your name, then you can specify that name using the `name` attribute, which does not have to adhere to the XML naming rules. That said, you should still consider giving your bean a name using `id`, and then you can define the desirable name using name aliasing as discussed in the next section.

Bean Name Aliasing

Spring allows a bean to have more than one name. You can achieve this by specifying a comma- or semicolon-separated list of names in the `name` attribute of the bean's `<bean>` tag. You can do this in place of, or in conjunction with, using the `id` attribute. Listing 4-32 shows a simple `<bean>` configuration that defines multiple names for a single bean.

Listing 4-32. *Configuring Multiple Bean Names*

```
<bean  id="name1" name="name2,name3,name4" class="java.lang.String"/>
```

As you can see, we have defined four names: one using the id attribute, and the other three as a comma-separated list in the name attribute. Listing 4-33 shows a sample Java routine that grabs the same bean from the BeanFactory four times using the different names and verifies that they are the same bean.

Listing 4-33. *Accessing Beans Using Aliases*

```
package com.apress.prospring.ch4;

import org.springframework.beans.factory.BeanFactory;
import org.springframework.beans.factory.xml.XmlBeanFactory;
import org.springframework.core.io.FileSystemResource;

public class BeanNameAliasing {

    public static void main(String[] args) {
        BeanFactory factory = new XmlBeanFactory(
                           new FileSystemResource("./ch4/src/conf/beans.xml"));

        String s1 = (String)factory.getBean("name1");
        String s2 = (String)factory.getBean("name2");
        String s3 = (String)factory.getBean("name3");
        String s4 = (String)factory.getBean("name4");

        System.out.println((s1 == s2));
        System.out.println((s2 == s3));
        System.out.println((s3 == s4));
    }
}
```

This code prints true three times to stdout for the configuration contained in Listing 4-32 verifying that the beans accessed using different names are in fact the same bean.

You can retrieve a list of the bean's aliases by calling BeanFactory.getAliases(String) and passing in any one of the bean's names. The number of names returned in the list is always one less than the total number of names assigned to the bean, because Spring considers one of the names to be the default. Which name is the default depends on how you configured the bean. If you specified a name using the id attribute, then that is always the default. If you did not use the id attribute, then the first name in the list passed to the name attribute may be used.

Bean name aliasing is a strange beast because it is not something you tend to use when you are building a new application. If you are going to have many other beans inject another bean, then they may as well use the same name to access that bean. However, as your application goes into production and maintenance work gets carried out, modifications made, and so on, bean name aliasing becomes more useful.

Consider the following scenario: you have an application in which 50 different beans, configured using Spring, all require an implementation of the Foo interface. Twenty-five of the beans use the StandardFoo implementation with the bean name standardFoo and the other 25 use the SuperFoo implementation with the superFoo bean name. Six months after you put the application into production, you decide to move the first 25 beans to the SuperFoo implementation. To do this you have three options.

The first is to change the implementation class of the standardFoo bean to SuperFoo. The drawback of this approach is that you have two instances of the SuperFoo class lying around when you really only need one. In addition, you now have two beans to make changes to when the configuration changes.

The second option is to update the injection configuration for the 25 beans that are changing, which changes the beans' names from standardFoo to superFoo. This approach is not the most elegant way to proceed—you could perform a find and replace, but then rolling back your changes when management isn't happy means retrieving an old version of your configuration from your version control system.

The third, and most ideal, approach is to remove (or comment out) the definition for the standardFoo bean and make standardFoo an alias to the superFoo. This change requires minimal effort and restoring the system to its previous configuration is just as simple.

Bean Instantiation Modes

By default, all beans in Spring are singletons. This means that Spring maintains a single instance of the bean, all dependent objects use the same instance, and all calls to BeanFactory.getBean() return the same instance. We demonstrated this in the previous example shown in Listing 4-33, where we were able to use identity comparison (==) rather than the equals() comparison to check if the beans were the same.

The term **singleton** is used interchangeably in Java to refer to two distinct concepts: an object that has a single instance within the application, and the Singleton design pattern. We refer to the first concept as singleton and to the Singleton pattern as Singleton. The Singleton design pattern was popularized in the seminal *Design Patterns: Elements of Reusable Object Oriented Software* by Erich Gamma, et al. (Addison-Wesley, 1995). The problem arises when people confuse the need for singleton instances with the need to apply the Singleton pattern. Listing 4-34 shows a typical implementation of the Singleton pattern in Java.

Listing 4-34. *The Singleton Design Pattern*

```
package com.apress.prospring.ch4;

public class Singleton {

    private static Singleton instance;

    static {
        instance = new Singleton();
    }

    public static Singleton getInstance() {
        return instance;
    }
}
```

This pattern achieves its goal of allowing you to maintain and access a single instance of a class throughout your application, but it does so at the expense of increased coupling. Your application code must always have explicit knowledge of the `Singleton` class in order to obtain the instance—completely removing the ability to code to interfaces. In reality, the Singleton pattern is actually two patterns in one. The first, and desired, pattern involves maintenance of a single instance of an object. The second, and less desirable, is a pattern for object lookup that completely removes the possibility of using interfaces. Using the Singleton pattern also makes it very difficult to swap out implementations arbitrarily, because most objects that require the `Singleton` instance access the Singleton object directly. This can cause all kinds of headaches when you are trying to unit test your application because you are unable to replace the Singleton with a mock for testing purposes.

Fortunately, with Spring you can take advantage of the singleton instantiation model without having to work around the Singleton design pattern. All beans in Spring are, by default, created as `Singleton` instances, and Spring uses the same instances to fulfill all requests for that bean. Of course, Spring is not just limited to use of the singleton instance; it can still create a new instance of the bean to satisfy every dependency and every call to `getBean()`. It does all of this without any impact on your application code, and for this reason, we like to refer to Spring as being **instantiation mode agnostic**. This is a very powerful concept. If you start off with an object that is a singleton, but then discover that it is not really suited to multithread access, you can change it to a non-singleton without affecting any of your application code.

■**Note** Although changing the instantiation mode of your bean won't affect your application code, it does cause some problems if you rely on Spring's lifecycle interfaces. We cover this in more detail in Chapter 5.

Changing the instantiation mode from singleton to non-singleton is simple (see Listing 4-35).

Listing 4-35. *Non-Singleton Bean Configuration*

```
<bean id="nonSingleton" class="java.lang.String" singleton="false">
      <constructor-arg>
          <value>Rob Harrop</value>
      </constructor-arg>
</bean>
```

As you can see, the only difference between this bean declaration and any of the declarations you have seen so far is that we set the singleton attribute to `false`. Listing 4-36 shows the effect this setting has on your application.

Listing 4-36. *Non-Singleton Beans in Action*

```
package com.apress.prospring.ch4;

import org.springframework.beans.factory.BeanFactory;
import org.springframework.beans.factory.xml.XmlBeanFactory;
import org.springframework.core.io.FileSystemResource;

public class NonSingleton {

    public static void main(String[] args) {

        BeanFactory factory = new XmlBeanFactory(new FileSystemResource(
            "./ch4/src/conf/beans.xml"));

        String s1 = (String)factory.getBean("nonSingleton");
        String s2 = (String)factory.getBean("nonSingleton");

        System.out.println("Identity Equal?: " + (s1 ==s2));
        System.out.println("Value Equal:? " + s1.equals(s2));
        System.out.println(s1);
        System.out.println(s2);
    }
}
```

Running this example gives you the following output:

```
Identity Equal?: false
Value Equal:? true
Rob Harrop
Rob Harrop
```

You can see from this that although the values of the two String objects are clearly equal, the identities are not, despite the fact that both instances were retrieved using the same bean name.

Choosing an Instantiation Mode

In most scenarios, it is quite easy to see which instantiation mode is suitable. Typically we find that singleton is the default mode for our beans. In general, singletons should be used in the following scenarios:

- **Shared objects with no state:** When you have an object that maintains no state and has many dependent objects. Because you do not need synchronization if there is no state, you do not really need to create a new instance of the bean each time a dependent object needs to use it for some processing.

- **Shared object with read-only state:** This is similar to the previous point, but you have some read-only state. In this case, you still do not need synchronization, so creating an instance to satisfy each request for the bean is just adding additional overhead.

- **Shared object with shared state:** If you have a bean that has state that must be shared, then singleton is the ideal choice. In this case, ensure that your synchronization for state writes is as granular as possible.

- **High throughput objects with writable state:** If you have a bean that is used a great deal in your application, then you may find that keeping a singleton and synchronizing all write access to the bean state allows for better performance than constantly creating hundreds of instances of the bean. When using this approach, try to keep the synchronization as granular as possible without sacrificing consistency. You will find that this approach is particularly useful when your application creates a large number of instances over a long period of time, when your shared object has only a small amount of writable state, or when the instantiation of a new instance is expensive.

You should consider using non-singletons in the following scenarios:

- **Objects with writable state:** If you have a bean that has a lot of writable state, then you may find that the cost of synchronization is greater than the cost of creating a new instance to handle each request from a dependent object.

- **Objects with private state:** In some cases, your dependent objects need a bean that has private state so that they can conduct their processing separately from other objects that depend on that bean. In this case, singleton is clearly not suitable and you should use non-singleton.

The main benefit you gain from Spring's instantiation management is that your applications can immediately benefit from the lower memory usage associated with singletons, and with very little effort on your part. Then, if you find that singleton does not meet the needs of your application, it is a trivial task to modify your configuration to use non-singleton mode.

Resolving Dependencies

During normal operation, Spring is able to resolve dependencies by simply looking at your configuration file. In this way, Spring can ensure that each bean is configured in the correct order so that each bean has its dependencies correctly configured. If Spring did not perform this and just created the beans and configured them in any order, a bean could be created and configured before its dependencies. This is obviously not what you want and would cause all sorts of problems within your application.

Unfortunately, Spring is not aware of any dependencies that exist between beans in your code. For instance, take one bean, bean A, which obtains an instance of another bean, bean B, in the constructor via a call to getBean(). In this case, Spring is unaware that bean A depends on bean B and, as a result, it may instantiate bean A before bean B. You can provide Spring with additional information about your bean dependencies using the depends-on attribute of the <bean> tag. Listing 4-37 shows how the scenario for bean A and bean B would be configured.

Listing 4-37. *Manually Defining Dependencies*

```
<bean id="A" class="com.apress.prospring.ch4.BeanA" depends-on="b"/>
<bean id="B" class="com.apress.prospring.ch4.BeanB"/>
```

In this configuration, we are asserting that bean A depends on bean B. Spring takes this into consideration when instantiating the beans and ensures that bean B is created before bean A.

When developing your applications, avoid designing your applications to use this feature; instead, define your dependencies by means of setter and constructor injection contracts. However, if you are integrating Spring with legacy code, then you may find that the dependencies defined in the code require you to provide extra information to the Spring framework.

Auto-Wiring Your Beans

In all the examples so far, we have had to define explicitly, via the configuration file, how the individual beans are wired together. If you don't like having to wire all your components together, then you can have Spring attempt to do so automatically. By default, auto-wiring is disabled. To enable it, you specify which method of auto-wiring you wish to use using the autowire attribute of the bean you wish to auto-wire.

Spring supports four modes for auto-wiring: byName, byType, constructor, and autodetect. When using byName auto-wiring, Spring attempts to wire each property to a bean of the same name. So, if the target bean has a property named foo and a foo bean is defined in the BeanFactory, the foo bean is assigned to the foo property of the target.

When using byType auto-wiring, Spring attempts to wire each of the properties on the target bean automatically using a bean of the same type in the BeanFactory. So if you have a property of type String on the target bean and a bean of type String in the BeanFactory, then Spring wires the String bean to the target bean's String property. If you have more than one bean of the same type, in this case String, in the same BeanFactory, then Spring is unable to decide which one to use for the auto-wiring and throws an exception.

The constructor auto-wiring mode functions just like byType wiring, except that it uses constructors rather than setters to perform the injection. Spring attempts to match the greatest numbers of arguments it can in the constructor. So, if your bean has two constructors, one that accepts a String and one that accepts a String and an Integer, and you have both a String and an Integer bean in your BeanFactory, Spring uses the two-argument constructor.

The final mode, autodetect, instructs Spring to choose between constructor and byType modes automatically. If your bean has a default (no arguments) constructor, then Spring uses byType; otherwise, it uses constructor.

Listing 4-38 shows a simple configuration that auto-wires four beans of the same type using each of the different modes.

Listing 4-38. *Configuring Auto-Wiring*

```
<!DOCTYPE beans PUBLIC "-//SPRING//DTD BEAN//EN"

"http://www.springframework.org/dtd/spring-beans.dtd">

<beans>
    <bean id="foo" class="com.apress.prospring.ch4.autowiring.Foo"/>
    <bean id="bar" class="com.apress.prospring.ch4.autowiring.Bar"/>

    <bean id="targetByName" autowire="byName"
            class="com.apress.prospring.ch4.autowiring.Target"/>
    <bean id="targetByType" autowire="byType"
            class="com.apress.prospring.ch4.autowiring.Target"/>
    <bean id="targetConstructor" autowire="constructor"
            class="com.apress.prospring.ch4.autowiring.Target"/>
    <bean id="targetAutodetect" autowire="autodetect"
            class="com.apress.prospring.ch4.autowiring.Target"/>
</beans>
```

This configuration should look very familiar to you now. Notice that each of the Target beans has a different value for the autowire attribute. Listing 4-39 shows a simple Java application that retrieves each of the Target beans from the BeanFactory.

Listing 4-39. *Auto-Wiring Collaborators*

```
package com.apress.prospring.ch4.autowiring;

import org.springframework.beans.factory.BeanFactory;
import org.springframework.beans.factory.xml.XmlBeanFactory;
import org.springframework.core.io.FileSystemResource;

public class Target {

    private Foo foo;
    private Foo foo2;

    private Bar bar;

    public Target() {

    }

    public Target(Foo foo) {
        System.out.println("Target(Foo) called");
    }
```

```java
    public Target(Foo foo, Bar bar) {
        System.out.println("Target(Foo, Bar) called");
    }

    public void setFoo(Foo foo) {
        this.foo = foo;
        System.out.println("Property foo set");
    }

    public void setFoo2(Foo foo) {
        this.foo2 = foo;
        System.out.println("Property foo2 set");
    }

    public void setMyBarProperty(Bar bar) {
        this.bar = bar;
        System.out.println("Property myBarProperty set");
    }

    public static void main(String[] args) {
        BeanFactory factory = new XmlBeanFactory(new FileSystemResource(
                "./ch4/src/conf/autowiring.xml"));

        Target t = null;

        System.out.println("Using byName:\n");
        t = (Target) factory.getBean("targetByName");

        System.out.println("\nUsing byType:\n");
        t = (Target) factory.getBean("targetByType");

        System.out.println("\nUsing constructor:\n");
        t = (Target) factory.getBean("targetConstructor");

        System.out.println("\nUsing autodetect:\n");
        t = (Target) factory.getBean("targetAutodetect");

    }
}
```

In this code, you can see that the Target class has three constructors: a no argument constructor, a constructor that accepts a Foo instance, and a constructor that accepts a Foo and a Bar instance. In addition to these constructors, the Target bean has three properties: two of type Foo and one of type Bar. Each of these properties and constructors writes a message to stdout when it is called. The main method simply retrieves each of the Target beans declared in the BeanFactory, triggering the auto-wire process. Here is the output from running this example:

```
Using byName:
    Property foo set

Using byType:
Property foo set
Property foo2 set
Property myBarProperty set

Using constructor:
Target(Foo, Bar) called

Using autodetect:
Property foo set
Property foo2 set
Property myBarProperty set
```

From the output, you can see that when Spring uses byName, the only property that is set is the foo property, because this is the only property with a corresponding bean entry in the configuration file. When using byType, Spring sets the value of all three properties. The foo and foo2 properties are set by the foo bean and the myBarProperty is set by the bar bean. When using constructor, Spring uses the two-argument constructor, because Spring can provide beans for both arguments and does not need to fall back to another constructor. In this case, autodetect functions just like byType because we defined a default constructor. If we had not done this, autodetect would have functioned just like constructor.

When to Use Auto-Wiring

In most cases, the answer to the question of whether you should use auto-wiring is definitely "No!" Auto-wiring can save you time in small applications, but in many cases, it leads to bad practices and is inflexible in large applications. Using byName seems like a good idea, but it may lead you to give your classes artificial property names so that you can take advantage of the auto-wiring functionality. The whole idea behind Spring is that you can create your classes how you like and have Spring work for you, not the other way around. You may be tempted to use byType until you realize that you can only have one bean for each type in your BeanFactory— a restriction that is problematic when you need to maintain beans with different configurations of the same type. The same argument applies to the use of constructor auto-wiring. This mode follows the same semantics as byType and to autodetect, which is simply byType and constructor bundled together.

In some cases, auto-wiring can save you time, but it does not really take that much extra effort to define your wiring explicitly, and you benefit from explicit semantics and full flexibility on property naming and on how many instances of the same type you manage. For any non-trivial application, steer clear of auto-wiring at all costs.

Checking Dependencies

When creating bean instances and wiring together dependencies, Spring does not, by default, check to see that every property on a bean has a value. In many cases, you do not need Spring to perform this check, but if you have a bean that absolutely must have a value for all of its properties, then you can ask Spring to check this for you.

As pointed out in the documentation, this is not always effective, because you may provide a default value for some properties and you may just want to assert that only one particular property must also have a value; the dependency checking capabilities of Spring do not take these features into consideration. That said, it can be quite useful in certain circumstances to have Spring perform this check for you. In many cases, it allows you to remove checks from your code and have Spring perform them just once at startup.

Besides the default of no checking, Spring has three modes for dependency checking: simple, objects, and all. The simple mode checks to see whether all properties that are either Collections or a built-in type have a value. In this mode, Spring does not check to see whether or not properties of any other types are set. This mode can be quite useful for checking whether all the configuration parameters for a bean are set because they are typically either built-in values or Collections of built-in values.

The objects mode checks any property not covered by the simple mode, but it does not check properties that are covered by simple. So if you have a bean that has two properties, one of type int and the other of type Foo, then objects checks whether a value is specified for the Foo property but does not check for the int property.

The all mode checks all properties, essentially performing the checks of both the simple and objects mode. Listing 4-40 shows a simple class that has two properties: one int property and one property of the same type as the class itself.

Listing 4-40. *The SimpleBean Class*

```
package com.apress.prospring.ch4.depcheck;

import org.springframework.beans.factory.BeanFactory;
import org.springframework.beans.factory.xml.XmlBeanFactory;
import org.springframework.core.io.FileSystemResource;

public class SimpleBean {

    private int someInt;

    private SimpleBean nestedSimpleBean;

    public void setSomeInt(int someInt) {
        this.someInt = someInt;
    }

    public void setNestedSimpleBean(SimpleBean nestedSimpleBean) {
        this.nestedSimpleBean = nestedSimpleBean;
    }
```

```
public static void main(String[] args) {
    BeanFactory factory = new XmlBeanFactory(new FileSystemResource(
            "./ch4/src/conf/depcheck.xml"));

    SimpleBean simpleBean1 = (SimpleBean)factory.getBean("simpleBean1");
    SimpleBean simpleBean2 = (SimpleBean)factory.getBean("simpleBean2");
    SimpleBean simpleBean3 = (SimpleBean)factory.getBean("simpleBean3");
    }
}
```

The main() method in this code retrieves three beans, all of type SimpleBean, from the
BeanFactory. Listing 4-41 shows the configuration for this BeanFactory.

Listing 4-41. *Configuring Dependency Checks*

```
<!DOCTYPE beans PUBLIC "-//SPRING//DTD BEAN//EN"

"http://www.springframework.org/dtd/spring-beans.dtd">
<beans>
    <bean id="simpleBean1" class="com.apress.prospring.ch4.depcheck.SimpleBean"
        dependency-check="simple">
        <property name="someInt">
            <value>16</value>
        </property>
    </bean>

    <bean id="simpleBean2" class="com.apress.prospring.ch4.depcheck.SimpleBean"
        dependency-check="objects">
        <property name="nestedSimpleBean">
            <ref local="nestedSimpleBean"/>
        </property>
    </bean>

    <bean id="simpleBean3" class="com.apress.prospring.ch4.depcheck.SimpleBean"
        dependency-check="all">
        <property name="someInt">
            <value>16</value>
        </property>
        <property name="nestedSimpleBean">
            <ref local="nestedSimpleBean"/>
        </property>
    </bean>

    <bean id="nestedSimpleBean"
        class="com.apress.prospring.ch4.depcheck.SimpleBean"/>
</beans>
```

As you can see from this configuration, each of the beans being retrieved from the BeanFactory in the Java app in Listing 4-40 has a different setting for the dependency-check attribute. The configuration currently ensures that all properties that need to be populated as per the dependency-check attribute have values, and as a result, the Java application runs without error. Try commenting out some of the <property> tags and see what happens then— Spring throws an org.springframework.beans.factory.UnsatisfiedDependencyException, indicating which property should have a value and does not have one.

Bean Inheritance

In some cases, you many need multiple definitions of beans that are the same type or implement a shared interface. This can become problematic if you want these beans to share some configuration settings but differ in others. The process of keeping the shared configuration settings in sync is quite error-prone, and on large projects, doing so can be quite time-consuming. To get around this, Spring allows you to define a <bean> definition that inherits its property settings from another bean in the same BeanFactory. You can override the values of any properties on the child bean as required, which allows you to have full control, but the parent bean can provide each of your beans with a base configuration. Listing 4-42 shows a simple configuration with two beans, one of which is the child of the other.

Listing 4-42. *Configuring Bean Inheritance*

```
<bean id="inheritParent" class="com.apress.prospring.ch4.inheritance.SimpleBean">
    <property name="name">
        <value>Rob Harrop</value>
    </property>
    <property name="age">
        <value>22</value>
    </property>
</bean>

<bean id="inheritChild" class="com.apress.prospring.ch4.inheritance.SimpleBean"
        parent="inheritParent">
    <property name="age">
        <value>35</value>
    </property>
</bean>
```

In this code, you can see that the <bean> tag for the inheritChild bean has an extra attribute, parent, which indicates that Spring should consider the inheritParent bean the parent of the bean. Because the inheritChild bean has its own value for the age property, Spring passes this value to the bean. However, inheritChild has no value for the name property, so Spring uses the value given to the inheritParent bean. Listing 4-43 shows the code for the SimpleBean class used in a previous configuration.

Listing 4-43. *The SimpleBean Class*

```
package com.apress.prospring.ch4.inheritance;

import org.springframework.beans.factory.BeanFactory;
import org.springframework.beans.factory.xml.XmlBeanFactory;
import org.springframework.core.io.FileSystemResource;

public class SimpleBean {

    public String name;

    public int age;

    public static void main(String[] args) {
        BeanFactory factory = new XmlBeanFactory(new FileSystemResource(
                "./ch4/src/conf/beans.xml"));

        SimpleBean parent = (SimpleBean)factory.getBean("inheritParent");
        SimpleBean child = (SimpleBean)factory.getBean("inheritChild");

        System.out.println("Parent:\n" + parent);
        System.out.println("Child:\n" + child);
    }

    public void setName(String name) {
        this.name = name;
    }

    public void setAge(int age) {
        this.age = age;
    }

    public String toString() {
        return    "Name: " + name + "\n"
                + "Age:" + age;
    }
}
```

As you can see, the main() method of the SimpleBean class grabs both the inheritChild and inheritParent beans from the BeanFactory and writes the contents of their properties to stdout. Here is the output from this example:

```
Parent:
Name: Rob Harrop
Age: 22
Child:
Name: Rob Harrop
Age: 35
```

As expected, the `inheritChild` bean inherited the value for its `name` property from the `inheritParent` bean, but was able to provide its own value for the `age` property.

Considerations for Using Bean Inheritance

Child beans inherit both constructor arguments and property values from the parent beans, so you can use both styles of injection with bean inheritance. This level of flexibility makes bean inheritance a powerful tool for building applications with more than a handful of bean definitions. If you are declaring a lot of beans of the same value with shared property values, then avoid the temptation to use copy and paste to share the values; instead, set up an inheritance hierarchy in your configuration.

When you are using inheritance, remember that bean inheritance does not have to match a Java inheritance hierarchy. It is perfectly acceptable to use bean inheritance on five beans of the same type. Think of bean inheritance as more like a templating feature than an inheritance feature. Be aware, however, that if you are changing the type of the child bean, then that type must be compatible with the type of the parent bean.

Summary

In this chapter, we covered a lot of ground with both the Spring core and IoC in general. We showed you examples of the different types of IoC and presented a discussion of the pros and cons of using each mechanism in your applications. We looked at which IoC mechanisms Spring provides and when and when not to use each within your applications. While exploring IoC, we introduced the Spring `BeanFactory`, which is the core component for Spring's IoC capabilities, and more specifically, we focused on the `XmlBeanFactory` that allows external configuration of Spring using XML.

This chapter also introduced you to the basics of Spring's IoC feature set including setter injection, constructor injection, auto-wiring, and bean inheritance. In the discussion of configuration, we demonstrated how you can configure your bean properties with a wide variety of different values, including other beans, using the `XmlBeanFactory`.

This chapter only scratches the surface of Spring and Spring's IoC container. In the next chapter, we look at some IoC-related features specific to Spring, and we take a more detailed look at other functionality available in the Spring core.

CHAPTER 5

■■■

Beyond the Basics

In the previous chapter, we took a detailed look at the concept of Inversion of Control (IoC) and how it fits into the Spring framework. However, as we said at the end of the last chapter, we have only really scratched the surface of what the Spring core can do.

Spring provides a wide array of services that supplement and extend the basic IoC capabilities provided by the BeanFactory and associated implementations. A number of projects provide IoC containers, but none so far provides the same comprehensive feature set Spring provides. In this chapter, we are going to look in detail at some additional IoC-related features offered in Spring along with other functionality offered by the Spring core. Specifically, we will be looking at the following:

- **Managing the bean lifecycle:** So far all the beans you have seen have been fairly simple and completely decoupled from the Spring container. In this section, we look at some strategies you can employ to enable your beans so they receive notifications from the Spring container at various points throughout their lifecycle. You can do this either by implementing specific interfaces laid out by Spring or by specifying methods that Spring can call via reflection.

- **Making your beans "Spring aware":** In some cases, you want a bean to be able to interact with the BeanFactory that configured it. For this reason, Spring offers two interfaces, BeanNameAware and BeanFactoryAware, that allow your bean to obtain its own name and a reference to its BeanFactory, respectively. This section of the chapter looks at implementing these interfaces and some practical considerations for using them in your application.

- **Using method injection:** As of release 1.1, Spring provides a new mechanism for managing dependencies when working with beans of different lifecycles (singletons and non-singletons). In addition to this, Spring provides functionality to allow you to replace any method of any bean with a new implementation, without touching the original code.

- **Using FactoryBeans:** As its name implies, the FactoryBean interface is intended to be implemented by any bean that acts as a factory for other beans. The FactoryBean interface provides a mechanism by which you can easily integrate your own factories with the Spring BeanFactory.

- **Working with JavaBeans `PropertyEditors`:** The `PropertyEditor` interface is a standard interface provided in the `java.beans` package. `PropertyEditors` are used to convert property values to and from `String` representations. Spring uses `PropertyEditors` extensively, mainly to read values specified in the `BeanFactory` configuration and convert them into the correct types. In this section of the chapter, we discuss the set of `PropertyEditors` supplied with Spring and how you can use them within your application. We also take a look at implementing custom `PropertyEditors`.

- **Learning about the Spring `ApplicationContext`:** The `ApplicationContext` is an extension of the `BeanFactory` intended for use in full applications. The `ApplicationContext` interface provides a useful set of additional functionality, including internationalized message provision, resource loading, and event publishing. `ApplicationContext` also enables a much simpler configuration and, in many cases, such as when you are building web applications, you can create and configure an `ApplicationContext` automatically. In this chapter, we take a detailed look at the `ApplicationContext` and the features it offers. We also jump ahead of ourselves a little and look at how the `ApplicationContext` simplifies the use of Spring when you are building web applications.

Spring's Impacts on Application Portability

All of the features discussed in this chapter are specific to Spring, and in many cases, are not available in other IoC containers. Although many IoC containers offer lifecycle management functionality, they probably do so through a different set of interfaces than Spring. If the portability of your application between different IoC containers is truly important, then you might want to avoid using some of the features that couple your application to Spring.

Remember, however, that by setting a **constraint**—that your application is portable between IoC containers—you are losing out on the wealth of functionality Spring offers. Because you are likely to be making a strategic choice to use Spring, it makes sense that you use it to the best of its ability.

Be careful not to create a requirement for portability out of thin air. In many cases, the end users of your application do not care if the application can run on three different IoC containers, they just want it to run. In our experience, it is often a mistake to try to build an application on the lowest common denominator of features available in your chosen technology. Doing so often sets your application at a disadvantage right from the get-go. However, if your application *requires* IoC container portability, then do not see this as a drawback—it is a true requirement, and therefore, one your application should fulfill. In *Expert One-on-One: J2EE Development without EJB* (Wrox, 2004), Rod Johnson and Jürgen Höller describe these types of requirement as **phantom requirements** and provide a much more detailed discussion of phantom requirements and how they can affect your project.

Although using these features may couple your application to the Spring framework, in reality, you are increasing the portability of your application in the wider scope. Consider that you are using a freely available, open source framework that has no particular vendor affiliation. An application built using Spring's IoC container runs anywhere Java runs. For J2EE applications, Spring opens up new possibilities for portability. Spring provides many of the same capabilities as J2EE and also provides classes to abstract and simplify many other aspects of J2EE. In many cases, it is possible to build a web application using Spring that runs in a simple servlet container, but with the same level of sophistication as an application targeted at a full-blown J2EE application server. By coupling to Spring, you can increase your application's portability by replacing many features that are either vendor-specific or rely on vendor-specific configuration with equivalent features in Spring.

Bean Lifecycle Management

An important part of any IoC container, Spring included, is that beans can be constructed in such a way that they receive notifications at certain points in their lifecycle. This enables your beans to perform relevant processing at certain points throughout their life. The number of possible notifications is huge, but in general, two lifecycle events are particularly relevant to a bean: post-initialization and pre-destruction.

In the context of Spring, the post-initialization event is raised as soon as Spring finishes setting all the property values on the bean and finishes any dependency checks that you configured it to perform. The pre-destruction event is fired just before Spring destroys the bean instance. Both of these lifecycle events are only fired for beans that are singletons. Spring doesn't manage the lifecycle of beans that are configured as non-singletons.

Spring provides two mechanisms a bean can use to hook into each of these events and perform some additional processing: interface-based or method-based. Using the interface-based mechanism, your bean implements an interface specific to the type of notification it wishes to receive, and Spring notifies the bean via a callback method defined in the interface. For the method-based mechanism, Spring allows you to specify, in your BeanFactory configuration, the name of a method to call when the bean is initialized and the name of a method to call when the bean is destroyed.

In the case of both events, the mechanisms achieve exactly the same goal. The interface mechanism is used extensively throughout Spring so that you don't have to remember to specify the initialization or destruction each time you use one of Spring's components. However, in your own beans, you may be better served using the method-based mechanism because your beans do not need to implement any Spring-specific interfaces. Although we stated that portability often isn't as important a requirement as many texts lead you to believe, this does not mean you should sacrifice portability when a perfectly good alternative exists. That said, if you are coupling your application to Spring in other ways, using the interface method allows you to specify the callback once and then forget about it. If you are defining a lot of beans of the same type that need to take advantage of the lifecycle notifications, then using the interface mechanism is the perfect way to avoid needing to repeat yourself—an extra coding burden that can lead to hard-to-diagnose errors and an application that is problematic to maintain.

Overall, the choice of which mechanism you use for receiving lifecycle notifications depends on your application requirements. If you are concerned about portability or you are just defining one or two beans of a particular type that need the callbacks, then use the method-based mechanism. If you are not too concerned about portability or you are defining many beans of the same type that need the lifecycle notifications, then using the interface-based mechanism is the best way to ensure that your beans always receive the notifications they are expecting. If you plan to use a bean across many different Spring projects, then you almost certainly want the functionality of that bean to be as self-contained as possible, so you should definitely use the interface-based mechanism.

Hooking into Bean Creation

By being aware of when it is initialized, a bean can check to see whether all its required dependencies are satisfied. Although Spring can check dependencies for you, it is pretty much an all-or-nothing approach, and it doesn't offer any opportunities for applying additional logic to the dependency resolution procedure. Consider a bean that has four dependencies declared as setters, two of which are required and one of which has a suitable default in the event that no dependency is provided. Using an initialization callback, your bean can check for the dependencies it requires, throwing an exception or providing a default as needed.

A bean cannot perform these checks in its constructor because at this point, Spring has not had an opportunity to provide values for the dependencies it can satisfy. The initialization callback in Spring is called *after* Spring finishes providing the dependencies that it can and performs any dependency checks that you ask it to.

You are not limited to using the initialization callback just to check dependencies; you can do anything you want in the callback, but it is most useful for the purpose we have described. In many cases, the initialization callback is also the place to trigger any actions that your bean must take automatically in response to its configuration. For instance, if you build a bean to run scheduled tasks, the initialization callback provides the ideal place to start the scheduler—after all, the configuration data is set on the bean.

■**Note** You will not have to write a bean to run scheduled tasks because this is something Spring can do automatically through its integration with the Quartz scheduler. We cover this in more detail in Chapter 14.

Specifying an Initialization Method

As we mentioned previously, one way to receive the initialization callback is to designate a method on your bean as an initialization method and tell Spring to use this method as an initialization method. As discussed, this callback mechanism is useful when you only have a few beans of the same type or when you want to keep your application decoupled from Spring. Another reason for using this mechanism is to enable your Spring application to work with beans that were built previously or were provided by third-party vendors.

Specifying a callback method is simply a case of specifying the name in the init-method attribute of a bean's <bean> tag. Listing 5-1 shows a basic bean with two dependencies.

Listing 5-1. *The SimpleBean Class*

```
package com.apress.prospring.ch5.lifecycle;

import org.springframework.beans.factory.BeanCreationException;
import org.springframework.beans.factory.BeanFactory;
import org.springframework.beans.factory.xml.XmlBeanFactory;
import org.springframework.core.io.FileSystemResource;
```

```java
public class SimpleBean {

    private static final String DEFAULT_NAME = "Luke Skywalker";

    private String name = null;

    private int age = Integer.MIN_VALUE;

    public void setName(String name) {
        this.name = name;
    }

    public void setAge(int age) {
        this.age = age;
    }

    public void init() {
        System.out.println("Initializing bean");

        if (name == null) {
            System.out.println("Using default name");
            name = DEFAULT_NAME;
        }

        if (age == Integer.MIN_VALUE) {
            throw new IllegalArgumentException(
                    "You must set the age property of any beans of type "
                                    + SimpleBean.class);
        }
    }

    public String toString() {
        return "Name: " + name + "\nAge: " + age;
    }

    public static void main(String[] args) {
        BeanFactory factory = new XmlBeanFactory(new FileSystemResource(
                "./ch5/src/conf/lifecycle/initMethod.xml"));

        SimpleBean simpleBean1 = getBean("simpleBean1", factory);
        SimpleBean simpleBean2 = getBean("simpleBean2", factory);
        SimpleBean simpleBean3 = getBean("simpleBean3", factory);
    }
```

```
    private static SimpleBean getBean(String beanName, BeanFactory factory) {
        try {
            SimpleBean bean =(SimpleBean) factory.getBean(beanName);
            System.out.println(bean);
            return bean;
        } catch (BeanCreationException ex) {
            System.out.println("An error occured in bean configuration: "
                    + ex.getMessage());
            return null;
        }
    }

}
```

Notice that we have defined a method, init(), to act as the initialization callback. The init() method checks to see if the name property has been set, and if it has not, it uses the default value stored in the DEFAULT_VALUE constant. The init() method also checks to see if the age property is set and throws an IllegalArgumentException if it is not.

The main() method of the SimpleBean class attempts to obtain three beans from the BeanFactory, all of type SimpleBean, using its own getBean() method. Notice that in the getBean() method, if the bean is obtained successfully, then its details are written to stdout. If an exception is thrown in the init() method, as will occur in this case if the age property is not set, then Spring wraps that exception in a BeanCreationException. The getBean() method catches these exceptions and writes a message to stdout informing us of the error.

Listing 5-2 shows a BeanFactory configuration that defines the beans used in Listing 5-1.

Listing 5-2. *Configuring the SimpleBeans*

```
<!DOCTYPE beans PUBLIC "-//SPRING//DTD BEAN//EN"
"http://www.springframework.org/dtd/spring-beans.dtd">
<beans>
    <bean id="simpleBean1"
            class="com.apress.prospring.ch5.lifecycle.SimpleBean"
            init-method="init">
        <property name="name">
            <value>Rob Harrop</value>
        </property>
        <property name="age">
            <value>100</value>
        </property>
    </bean>
    <bean id="simpleBean2"
            class="com.apress.prospring.ch5.lifecycle.SimpleBean"
            init-method="init">
        <property name="age">
            <value>100</value>
        </property>
    </bean>
```

```
    <bean id="simpleBean3"
          class="com.apress.prospring.ch5.lifecycle.SimpleBean"
          init-method="init">
        <property name="name">
            <value>Rob Harrop</value>
        </property>
    </bean>
</beans>
```

As you can see, the <bean> tag for each of the three beans has an init-method attribute that tells Spring that it should invoke the init() method as soon as it finishes configuring the bean. The simpleBean1 bean has values for both the name and age properties, so it passes through the init() method with absolutely no changes. The simpleBean2 bean has no value for the name property, meaning that in the init() method, the name property is given the default value. Finally, the simpleBean3 bean has no value for the age property. The logic defined in the init() method treats this as an error so an IllegalArgumentException is thrown. Running this example yields the following output:

```
Initializing bean
Name: Rob Harrop
Age: 100
Initializing bean
Using default name
Name: Luke Skywalker
Age: 100
Initializing bean
An error occured in bean configuration: ➡
Error creating bean with name 'simpleBean3' defined in file ➡
[D:\projects\pro-spring\.\ch5\src\conf\lifecycle.xml]: ➡
Initialization method 'init' threw exception; ➡
nested exception is java.lang.IllegalArgumentException: ➡
You must set the age property of any beans of type class ➡
com.apress.prospring.ch5.lifecycle.SimpleBean
```

From this output you can see that simpleBean1 was configured correctly with the values that we specified in the configuration file. For simpleBean2, the default value for the name property was used because no value was specified in the configuration. Finally, for simpleBean3, no bean instance was created because the init() method raised an error due to the lack of a value for the age property.

As you can see, using the initialization method is an ideal way to ensure that your beans are configured correctly. By using this mechanism, you can take full advantage of the benefits of IoC without losing any of the control you get from manually defining dependencies. The only constraint on your initialization method is that it cannot accept any arguments. You can define any return type, although it is ignored by Spring, and you can even use a static method, but the method must accept no arguments.

The benefits of this mechanism are negated when using a static initialization method, because you cannot access any of the bean's state to validate it. If your bean is using static state as a mechanism for saving memory and you are using a static initialization method to validate this state, then you should consider moving the static state to instance state and using a non-static initialization method. If you use Spring's singleton management capabilities, the end effect is the same, but you have a bean that is much simpler to test and you also have the increased effect of being able to create multiple instances of the bean with their own state when necessary. Of course, there are instances in which you need to use static state shared across multiple instances of a bean, in which case, you can always use a static initialization method.

Implementing the InitializingBean Interface

The InitializingBean interface defined in Spring allows you to define inside your bean code that you want the bean to receive notification that Spring has finished configuring it. In the same way as when you are using an initialization method, this gives you the opportunity to check the bean configuration to ensure that it is valid, providing any default values along the way.

The InitializingBean interface defines a single method, afterPropertiesSet(), that serves the same purpose as the init() method in Listing 5-1. Listing 5-3 shows a reimplementation of the previous example using the InitializingBean interface in place of the initialization method.

Listing 5-3. *Using the InitializingBean Interface*

```
package com.apress.prospring.ch5.lifecycle;

import org.springframework.beans.factory.BeanCreationException;
import org.springframework.beans.factory.BeanFactory;
import org.springframework.beans.factory.InitializingBean;
import org.springframework.beans.factory.xml.XmlBeanFactory;
import org.springframework.core.io.FileSystemResource;

public class SimpleBeanWithInterface implements InitializingBean {

    private static final String DEFAULT_NAME = "Luke Skywalker";

    private String name = null;

    private int age = Integer.MIN_VALUE;

    public void setName(String name) {
        this.name = name;
    }

    public void setAge(int age) {
        this.age = age;
    }

    public void afterPropertiesSet() throws Exception {
        System.out.println("Initializing bean");
```

```
        if (name == null) {
            System.out.println("Using default name");
            name = DEFAULT_NAME;
        }

        if (age == Integer.MIN_VALUE) {
            throw new IllegalArgumentException(
                    "You must set the age property of any beans of type " +
                    SimpleBean.class);
        }
    }

    public String toString() {
        return "Name: " + name + "\nAge: " + age;
    }

    public static void main(String[] args) {
        BeanFactory factory = new XmlBeanFactory(new FileSystemResource(
                "./ch5/src/conf/lifecycle/initInterface.xml"));

        SimpleBeanWithInterface simpleBean1 = getBean("simpleBean1", factory);
        SimpleBeanWithInterface simpleBean2 = getBean("simpleBean2", factory);
        SimpleBeanWithInterface simpleBean3 = getBean("simpleBean3", factory);
    }

    private static SimpleBeanWithInterface getBean(String beanName,
            BeanFactory factory) {
        try {
            SimpleBeanWithInterface bean =
                            (SimpleBeanWithInterface) factory.getBean(beanName);
            System.out.println(bean);
            return bean;
        } catch (BeanCreationException ex) {
            System.out.println("An error occured in bean configuration: "
                    + ex.getMessage());
            return null;
        }
    }
}
```

As you can see, not much in this example has changed. Aside from the obvious class name change, the only difference is that this class implements `InitializingBean` and the initialization logic has moved into the `InitializingBean.afterPropertiesSet()` method.

In Listing 5-4, you can see the configuration for this example.

Listing 5-4. *Configuration Using InitializingBean*

```
<!DOCTYPE beans PUBLIC "-//SPRING//DTD BEAN//EN"
"http://www.springframework.org/dtd/spring-beans.dtd">
<beans>
    <bean id="simpleBean1"
          class="com.apress.prospring.ch5.lifecycle.SimpleBeanWithInterface">
        <property name="name">
            <value>Rob Harrop</value>
        </property>
        <property name="age">
            <value>100</value>
        </property>
    </bean>
    <bean id="simpleBean2"
          class="com.apress.prospring.ch5.lifecycle.SimpleBeanWithInterface">
        <property name="age">
            <value>100</value>
        </property>
    </bean>
    <bean id="simpleBean3"
          class="com.apress.prospring.ch5.lifecycle.SimpleBeanWithInterface">
        <property name="name">
            <value>Rob Harrop</value>
        </property>
    </bean>
</beans>
```

Again, not much of a difference between the configuration code in Listing 5-4 and the configuration code from Listing 5-2. The noticeable difference is the omission of the init-method attribute. Because the SimpleBeanWithInterface class implements the InitializingBean interface, Spring knows which method to call as the initialization callback, thus removing the need for any additional configuration. The output from this example is shown here:

```
Initializing bean
Name: Rob Harrop
Age: 100
Initializing bean
Using default name
Name: Luke Skywalker
Age: 100
Initializing bean
An error occured in bean configuration: ➥
Error creating bean with name 'simpleBean3' defined in file ➥
[D:\projects\pro-spring\.\ch5\src\conf\lifecycle\initInterface.xml]: ➥
Initialization of bean failed; ➥
nested exception is java.lang.IllegalArgumentException: ➥
You must set the age property of any beans of type class ➥
com.apress.prospring.ch5.lifecycle.SimpleBean
```

As you can see, there is no difference in the output of the two examples; both work in exactly the same way. As we discussed earlier, both approaches have their benefits and drawbacks. Using an initialization method, you have the benefit of keeping your application decoupled from Spring, but you have to remember to configure the initialization method for every bean that needs it. Using `InitializingBean`, you have the benefit of being able to specify the initialization callback once for all instances of your bean class, but you have to couple your application to do so. In the end, you should let the requirements of your application drive the decision about which approach to use. If portability is an issue, then use the initialization method, otherwise use the `InitializingBean` interface to reduce the amount of configuration your application needs and the chance of errors creeping into your application due to misconfiguration.

Order of Resolution

You can use both an initialization method and the `InitializingBean` on the same bean instance. In this case, Spring invokes `InitializingBean.afterPropertiesSet()` first, followed by your initialization method. This can be useful if you have an existing bean that performs some initialization in a specific method, but you need to add some more initialization code when you use Spring. However, a better approach is to call your bean's initialization method from `afterPropertiesSet()`. This way, if Spring changes the initialization order in a future release, your code continues to work as it should.

Hooking into Bean Destruction

When using a `BeanFactory` implementation that implements the `ConfigurableListableBeanFactory` interface (such as `XmlBeanFactory`), you can signal the `BeanFactory` that you want to destroy all singleton instances with a call to `destroySingletons()`. Typically, you do this when your application shuts down, and it allows you to clean up any resources that your beans might be holding open, thus allowing your application to shut down gracefully. This callback also provides the perfect place to flush any data you are storing in memory to persistent storage and to allow your beans to end any long-running processes they may have started.

To allow your beans to receive notification that `destroySingletons()` has been called, you have two options, both similar to the mechanisms available for receiving an initialization callback. The destruction callback is often used in conjunction with the initialization callback. In many cases, you create and configure a resource in the initialization callback and then release the resource in the destruction callback.

Executing a Method When a Bean Is Destroyed

To designate a method to be called when a bean is destroyed, you simply specify the name of the method in the `destroy-method` attribute of the bean's `<bean>` tag. Spring calls it just before it destroys the singleton instance of the bean. Listing 5-5 shows a simple class that implements `InitializingBean`, and in the `afterPropertiesSet()` method, it creates an instance of `FileInputStream` and stores this in a private field.

Listing 5-5. *Using a destroy-method Callback*

```java
package com.apress.prospring.ch5.lifecycle;

import java.io.FileInputStream;
import java.io.IOException;
import java.io.InputStream;

import org.springframework.beans.factory.InitializingBean;
import org.springframework.beans.factory.config.ConfigurableListableBeanFactory;
import org.springframework.beans.factory.xml.XmlBeanFactory;
import org.springframework.core.io.FileSystemResource;

public class DestructiveBean implements InitializingBean {

    private InputStream is = null;

    public String filePath = null;

    public void afterPropertiesSet() throws Exception {

        System.out.println("Initializing Bean");

        if (filePath == null) {
            throw new IllegalArgumentException(
                    "You must specify the filePath property of " +
                            DestructiveBean.class);
        }

        is = new FileInputStream(filePath);
    }

    public void destroy() {

        System.out.println("Destroying Bean");

        if (is != null) {
            try {
                is.close();
                is = null;
            } catch (IOException ex) {
                System.err.println("WARN: An IOException occured"
                        + " trying to close the InputStream");
            }
        }
    }
}
```

```
    public void setFilePath(String filePath) {
        this.filePath = filePath;
    }

    public static void main(String[] args) throws Exception {
        ConfigurableListableBeanFactory factory = new XmlBeanFactory(
                new FileSystemResource(
                        "./ch5/src/conf/lifecycle/disposeMethod.xml"));


        DestructiveBean bean = (DestructiveBean)
                                        factory.getBean("destructiveBean");

        System.out.println("Calling destroySingletons()");
        factory.destroySingletons();
        System.out.println("Called destroySingletons()");
    }
}
```

This code also defines a destroy() method, in which the FileInputStream is closed and set to null, releasing the resource and allowing it to be garbage collected. The main() method retrieves a bean of type DestructiveBean from the XmlBeanFactory and then invokes ConfigurableListableBeanFactory.destroySingletons(), instructing Spring to destroy all the singletons it is managing. Both the initialization and destruction callbacks write a message to stdout informing us that they have been called. In Listing 5-6, you can see the configuration for the destructiveBean bean.

Listing 5-6. *Configuring a destroy-method Callback*

```
<!DOCTYPE beans PUBLIC "-//SPRING//DTD BEAN//EN"
"http://www.springframework.org/dtd/spring-beans.dtd">
<beans>
    <bean id="destructiveBean"
          class="com.apress.prospring.ch5.lifecycle.DestructiveBean"
          destroy-method="destroy">
        <property name="filePath">
            <value>d:/tmp/test.txt</value>
        </property>
    </bean>
</beans>
```

Notice that we have specified the destroy() method as the destruction callback using the destroy-method attribute. Running this example yields the following output:

```
Initializing Bean
Calling destroySingletons()
Destroying Bean
Called destroySingletons()
```

As you can see, Spring first invokes the initialization callback, and the DestructiveBean
instance creates the FileInputStream instance and stores it. Next, during the call to
destroySingletons(), Spring iterates over the set of singletons it is managing, in this
case just one, and invokes any destruction callbacks that are specified. This is where the
DestructiveBean instance closes the FileInputStream and sets the reference to null.

Implementing the DisposableBean Interface

As with initialization callbacks, Spring provides an interface, in this case DisposableBean, that
can be implemented by your beans as a mechanism for receiving destruction callbacks. The
DisposableBean interface defines a single method, destroy(), which is called just before the
bean is destroyed. Using this mechanism is orthogonal to using the InitializingBean interface
to receive initialization callbacks. Listing 5-7 shows a modified implementation of the
DestructiveBean class that implements the DisposableBean interface.

Listing 5-7. *Implementing DisposableBean*

```
package com.apress.prospring.ch5.lifecycle;

import java.io.FileInputStream;
import java.io.IOException;
import java.io.InputStream;

import org.springframework.beans.factory.DisposableBean;
import org.springframework.beans.factory.InitializingBean;
import org.springframework.beans.factory.config.ConfigurableListableBeanFactory;
import org.springframework.beans.factory.xml.XmlBeanFactory;
import org.springframework.core.io.FileSystemResource;

public class DestructiveBeanWithInterface implements InitializingBean,
        DisposableBean {

    private InputStream is = null;

    public String filePath = null;

    public void afterPropertiesSet() throws Exception {

        System.out.println("Initializing Bean");

        if (filePath == null) {
            throw new IllegalArgumentException(
                    "You must specify the filePath property of " +
                            DestructiveBean.class);
        }
```

```java
        is = new FileInputStream(filePath);
    }

    public void destroy() {

        System.out.println("Destroying Bean");

        if (is != null) {
            try {
                is.close();
                is = null;
            } catch (IOException ex) {
                System.err.println("WARN: An IOException occured"
                        + " trying to close the InputStream");
            }
        }
    }

    public void setFilePath(String filePath) {
        this.filePath = filePath;
    }

    public static void main(String[] args) throws Exception {
        final ConfigurableListableBeanFactory factory = new XmlBeanFactory(
                new FileSystemResource(
                        "./ch5/src/conf/lifecycle/disposeInterface.xml"));

        DestructiveBeanWithInterface bean =
            (DestructiveBeanWithInterface)factory.getBean("destructiveBean");

        System.out.println("Calling destroySingletons()");
        factory.destroySingletons();
        System.out.println("Called destroySingletons()");

    }

}
```

Again, there is not much difference between the code that uses the callback method mechanism and the code that uses the callback interface mechanism. In this case, we even used the same method names. Listing 5-8 shows an amended configuration for this example.

Listing 5-8. *Configuration Using the DisposableBean Interface*

```
<!DOCTYPE beans PUBLIC "-//SPRING//DTD BEAN//EN"
"http://www.springframework.org/dtd/spring-beans.dtd">
<beans>
    <bean id="destructiveBean"
        class="com.apress.prospring.ch5.lifecycle.DestructiveBeanWithInterface">
        <property name="filePath">
            <value>d:/tmp/test.txt</value>
        </property>
    </bean>
</beans>
```

As you can see, aside from the different class name, the only difference is the omission of the destroy-method attribute.

Running this example yields the following output:

```
Initializing Bean
Calling destroySingletons()
Destroying Bean
Called destroySingletons()
```

Again, the output from the two different mechanisms is exactly the same. The destruction callback is an ideal mechanism for ensuring that your applications shut down gracefully and do not leave resources open or in an inconsistent state. However, you still have to decide whether to use the destruction method callback or the DisposableBean interface. Again, let the requirements of your application drive your decision in this respect; use the method callback where portability is an issue, otherwise use the DisposableBean interface to reduce the amount of configuration required.

Using a Shutdown Hook

The only drawback of the destruction callbacks in Spring is that they are not fired automatically; you need to remember to call destroySingletons() before your application is closed. When your application runs as a servlet, you can simply call destroySingletons() in the servlet's destroy() method. However, in a stand-alone application, things are not quite so simple, especially if you have multiple exit points out of your application. Fortunately, there is a solution. Java allows you to create a **shutdown hook**, a thread that is executed just before the application shuts down. This is the perfect way to invoke the destroySingletons() method of your BeanFactory. The easiest way to take advantage of this mechanism is to create a class that implements the Runnable interface and have the run() method call destroySingletons(). This is shown in Listing 5-9.

Listing 5-9. *Implementing a Shutdown Hook*

```
package com.apress.prospring.ch5.lifecycle;

import org.springframework.beans.factory.config.ConfigurableListableBeanFactory;

public class ShutdownHook implements Runnable {

    private ConfigurableListableBeanFactory factory;

    public ShutdownHook(ConfigurableListableBeanFactory factory) {
        this.factory = factory;
    }

    public void run() {
        System.out.println("Destroying Singletons");
        factory.destroySingletons();
        System.out.println("Singletons Destroyed");
    }

}
```

Using this class, you can then create an instance of Thread and register this Thread as a shutdown hook using Runtime.addShutdownHook(). This is shown in Listing 5-10.

Listing 5-10. *Registering a Shutdown Hook*

```
package com.apress.prospring.ch5.lifecycle;

import org.springframework.beans.factory.config.ConfigurableListableBeanFactory;
import org.springframework.beans.factory.xml.XmlBeanFactory;
import org.springframework.core.io.FileSystemResource;

public class ShutdownHookExample {

    public static void main(String[] args) {
        ConfigurableListableBeanFactory factory = new XmlBeanFactory(
                new FileSystemResource(
                        "./ch5/src/conf/lifecycle/disposeInterface.xml"));

        Runtime.getRuntime().addShutdownHook(
                new Thread(new ShutdownHook(factory)));
        DestructiveBeanWithInterface bean =
            (DestructiveBeanWithInterface)factory.getBean("destructiveBean");
    }
}
```

Notice that we obtain a reference to the current `Runtime` using `Runtime.getRuntime()` and then call `addShutdownHook()` on this reference. Running this example results in the following output:

```
Initializing Bean
Destroying Singletons
Destroying Bean
Singletons Destroyed
```

As you can see, the `destroySingletons()` method is invoked, even though we didn't write any code to invoke it explicitly as the application was shutting down.

Making Your Beans "Spring Aware"

One of the biggest selling points of Dependency Injection over Dependency Lookup as a mechanism for achieving Inversion of Control is that your beans do not need to be aware of the implementation of the container that is managing them. To a bean that uses constructor injection, the Spring container is the same as the container provided by PicoContainer. However, in certain circumstances, you may need a bean that is using Dependency Injection to obtain its dependencies so it can interact with the container for some other reason. An example of this may be a bean that automatically configures a shutdown hook for you, and thus it needs access to the `BeanFactory`. In other cases, a bean may wish to know what its name is so it can perform some additional processing based on this name.

That said, this feature is really intended for internal Spring use. Giving the name some kind of business meaning is generally a bad idea and can lead to configuration problems where bean names have to be artificially manipulated to support their business meaning. However, we have found that being able to have a bean find out its name at runtime is really useful for logging. Consider a situation where you have many beans of the same type running under different configurations. The bean name can be included in log messages to help you differentiate between which one is generating errors and which ones are working fine when something goes wrong.

Using the BeanNameAware Interface

The `BeanNameAware` interface, which can be implemented by a bean that wants to obtain its own name, has a single method: `setBeanName(String)`. Spring calls the `setBeanName()` method after it has finished configuring your bean but before any lifecycle callbacks (initialization or destroy) are called. In most cases, the implementation of the `setBeanName()` interface is just a single line that stores the value passed in by the container in a field for use later on. Listing 5-11 shows a simple bean that obtains its name using `BeanNameAware` and then later uses this bean name when writing log messages.

Listing 5-11. *Implementing BeanNameAware*

```
package com.apress.prospring.ch5.interaction;

import org.apache.commons.logging.Log;
import org.apache.commons.logging.LogFactory;
import org.springframework.beans.factory.BeanNameAware;

public class LoggingBean implements BeanNameAware {

    private static final Log log = LogFactory.getLog(LoggingBean.class);

    private String beanName = null;

    public void setBeanName(String beanName) {
        this.beanName = beanName;
    }

    public void someOperation() {
        if(log.isInfoEnabled()) {
            log.info("Bean [" + beanName + "] - someOperation()");
        }
    }
}
```

This implementation is fairly trivial. Remember that BeanNameAware.setBeanName() is called before the first instance of the bean is returned to your application via a call to BeanFactory.getBean(), so there is no need to check to see if the bean name is available in the someOperation() method. Listing 5-12 shows a simple configuration for this example.

Listing 5-12. *Configuring the LoggingBean Example*

```
<!DOCTYPE beans PUBLIC "-//SPRING//DTD BEAN//EN"
"http://www.springframework.org/dtd/spring-beans.dtd">
<beans>
    <bean id="loggingBean"
          class="com.apress.prospring.ch5.interaction.LoggingBean"/>
</beans>
```

As you can see, no special configuration is required to take advantage of the BeanNameAware interface. In Listing 5-13 you can see a simple example application that retrieves the Logging-Bean instance from the BeanFactory and then calls the someOperation() method.

Listing 5-13. *The LoggingBeanExample Class*

```
package com.apress.prospring.ch5.interaction;

import org.springframework.beans.factory.BeanFactory;
import org.springframework.beans.factory.xml.XmlBeanFactory;
import org.springframework.core.io.FileSystemResource;

public class LoggingBeanExample {

    public static void main(String[] args) {
        BeanFactory factory = new XmlBeanFactory(new FileSystemResource(
                "./ch5/src/conf/interaction/logging.xml"));

        LoggingBean bean = (LoggingBean)factory.getBean("loggingBean");
        bean.someOperation();
    }
}
```

This example generates the following log output—notice the inclusion of the bean name in the log message for the call to someOperation():

```
Aug 4, 2004 4:10:35 PM ➥
org.springframework.beans.factory.xml.XmlBeanDefinitionReader loadBeanDefinitions
INFO: Loading XML bean definitions from file ➥
[D:\projects\pro-spring\.\ch5\src\conf\interaction\logging.xml]
Aug 4, 2004 4:10:35 PM ➥
org.springframework.beans.factory.support.AbstractBeanFactory getBean
INFO: Creating shared instance of singleton bean 'loggingBean'
Aug 4, 2004 4:10:35 PM ➥
com.apress.prospring.ch5.interaction.LoggingBean someOperation
INFO: Bean [loggingBean] - someOperation()
```

Using the BeanNameAware interface is really quite simple, and it is put to good use when you are improving the quality of your log messages. Avoid being tempted to give your bean names business meaning just because you can access them; by doing so, you are coupling your classes to Spring for a feature that brings negligible benefit. If your beans need some kind of name internally, then have them implement an interface such as Nameable with a method setName() and then give each bean a name using Dependency Injection. This way you can keep the names you use for configuration concise and you won't need to manipulate your configuration unnecessarily to give your beans names with business meaning.

Using the BeanFactoryAware Interface

Using the BeanFactoryAware method, it is possible for your beans to get a reference to the BeanFactory that configured them. The main reason this interface was created was to allow a bean to access other beans programmatically, using getBean(). You should, however, avoid this practice and use Dependency Injection to provide your beans with their collaborators. If you use the lookup-based getBean() approach to obtain dependencies when you can use

Dependency Injection, you are adding unnecessary complexity to your beans and coupling them to the Spring framework without good reason.

Of course, the BeanFactory isn't just used to look up beans; it performs a great many other tasks. As you saw previously, one of these tasks is to destroy all singletons, notifying each of them in turn before doing so. In the previous section, you saw how to create a shutdown hook to ensure that the BeanFactory is instructed to destroy all singletons before the application shuts down. By using the BeanFactoryAware interface, you can build a bean that can be configured in a BeanFactory to create and configure a shutdown hook bean automatically. Listing 5-14 shows the code for this bean.

Listing 5-14. *The ShutdownHookBean Class*

```
package com.apress.prospring.ch5.interaction;

import org.springframework.beans.BeansException;
import org.springframework.beans.factory.BeanFactory;
import org.springframework.beans.factory.BeanFactoryAware;
import org.springframework.beans.factory.config.ConfigurableListableBeanFactory;

public class ShutdownHookBean implements BeanFactoryAware,
        Runnable {

    private ConfigurableListableBeanFactory factory;

    public void setBeanFactory(BeanFactory factory) throws BeansException {

        if (factory instanceof ConfigurableListableBeanFactory) {
            this.factory = (ConfigurableListableBeanFactory) factory;
            Runtime.getRuntime().addShutdownHook(new Thread(this));
        }
    }

    public void run() {
        if (factory != null) {
            System.out.println("Destroying Singletons");
            factory.destroySingletons();
            System.out.println("Singletons Destroyed");
        }
    }
}
```

Most of this code should seem familiar to you by now. The BeanFactoryAware interface defines a single method, setBeanFactory(BeanFactory), which Spring calls to pass your bean a reference to its BeanFactory. In Listing 5-14, the ShutdownHookBean class checks to see if the BeanFactory is of type ConfigurableListableBeanFactory, meaning it has a destroySingletons() method; if it does, it saves the reference to a field. You can also see that if the BeanFactory is a ConfigurableListableBeanFactory, the bean registers itself as a shutdown hook with the current Runtime instance. Listing 5-15 shows how to configure this bean to work with the DestructiveBeanWithInterface bean used in the previous section.

Listing 5-15. *Configuring the ShutdownHookBean*

```
<!DOCTYPE beans PUBLIC "-//SPRING//DTD BEAN//EN"
"http://www.springframework.org/dtd/spring-beans.dtd">
<beans>
    <bean id="destructiveBean"
          class="com.apress.prospring.ch5.lifecycle.DestructiveBeanWithInterface">
        <property name="filePath">
            <value>d:/tmp/test.txt</value>
        </property>
    </bean>
    <bean id="shutdownHook"
          class="com.apress.prospring.ch5.interaction.ShutdownHookBean"/>
</beans>
```

Notice that no special configuration is required. Listing 5-16 shows a simple example application that uses the ShutdownHookBean to manage the destruction of singleton beans.

Listing 5-16. *Using ShutdownHookBean*

```
package com.apress.prospring.ch5.interaction;

import org.springframework.beans.factory.config.ConfigurableListableBeanFactory;
import org.springframework.beans.factory.xml.XmlBeanFactory;
import org.springframework.core.io.FileSystemResource;

import com.apress.prospring.ch5.lifecycle.DestructiveBeanWithInterface;
public class ShutdownHookBeanExample {

    public static void main(String[] args) {
        ConfigurableListableBeanFactory factory = new XmlBeanFactory(
                new FileSystemResource(
                        "./ch5/src/conf/interaction/shutdownHook.xml"));

        // make sure the shutdown hook is created
        factory.preInstantiateSingletons();

        DestructiveBeanWithInterface bean =
        (DestructiveBeanWithInterface)factory.getBean("destructiveBean");
    }
}
```

This code should seem quite familiar to you, but note that we have included a call to `ConfigurableListableBeanFactory.preInstantiateSingletons()`. By default, Spring lazily instantiates singleton beans as they are needed. This is a problem for the `ShutdownHookBean`, because it needs to be instantiated to register itself as a shutdown hook. Invoking `preInstantiateSingletons()` causes Spring to run through all its singleton bean definitions and create the instances, invoking any callback methods as appropriate. Running this example yields the following output, as expected:

```
Initializing Bean
Destroying Singletons
Destroying Bean
Singletons Destroyed
```

As you can see, even though no calls to `destroySingletons()` are in the main application, the `ShutdownHookBean` is registered as a shutdown hook and called `destroySingletons()` just before the application shut down.

Using Method Injection

A new IoC-oriented feature introduced with Spring 1.1 is **Method Injection**, which allows greater flexibility for interactions between collaborators. Spring's Method Injection capabilities come in two loosely related forms, **Lookup Method Injection** and **Method Replacement**. Lookup Method Injection provides a new mechanism by which a bean can obtain one of its dependencies, and Method Replacement allows you to replace the implementation of any method on a bean arbitrarily, without having to change the original source code.

In order to provide these two features, Spring uses the dynamic bytecode enhancement capabilities of CGLIB. If you want to use Lookup Method Injection or Method Replacement in your application, make sure you have the CGLIB JAR file on your classpath. Since version 1.1, Spring has included a fully packaged CGLIB JAR file, which includes the ASM bytecode manipulation library as well.

Lookup Method Injection

Lookup Method Injection was added to Spring to overcome the problems encountered when a bean depends on another bean with a different lifecycle—specifically, when a singleton depends on a non-singleton. In this situation, both setter and constructor injection result in the singleton maintaining a single instance of what should be a non-singleton bean. In some cases, you will want to have the singleton bean obtain a new instance of the non-singleton every time it requires the bean in question.

Typically, you can achieve this by having the singleton bean implement `BeanFactoryAware`. Then, using the `BeanFactory` instance, the singleton bean can look up a new instance of the non-singleton dependency every time it needs it. Lookup Method Injection allows the singleton bean to declare that it requires a non-singleton dependency and receive a new instance of the non-singleton bean each time it needs to interact with it, without needing to implement any Spring-specific interfaces.

Lookup Method Injection works by having your singleton declare a method, the lookup method, which returns an instance of the non-singleton bean. When you obtain a reference to the singleton in your application, you are actually receiving a reference to a dynamically created subclass on which Spring has implemented the lookup method. A typical implementation involves defining the lookup method, and thus the bean class, as abstract. This prevents any strange errors from creeping in when you forget to configure the Method Injection and you are working directly against the bean class with the empty method implementation instead of the Spring-enhanced subclass. This topic is quite complex and is best shown by example.

In this example, we create one non-singleton bean and two singleton beans that both implement the same interface. One of the singletons obtains an instance of the non-singleton bean using "traditional" setter injection; the other uses Method Injection. Listing 5-17 shows the MyHelper bean, which in our example is the non-singleton bean.

Listing 5-17. *The MyHelper Bean*

```
package com.apress.prospring.ch5.mi;

public class MyHelper {

    public void doSomethingHelpful() {
        // do something!
    }
}
```

This bean is decidedly unexciting, but it serves the purposes of this example perfectly. In Listing 5-18, you can see the DemoBean interface, which is implemented by both of the singleton beans.

Listing 5-18. *The DemoBean Interface*

```
package com.apress.prospring.ch5.mi;

public interface DemoBean {

    public MyHelper getMyHelper();
    public void someOperation();
}
```

This bean has two methods: getMyHelper() and someOperation(). The sample application uses the getMyHelper() method to get a reference to the MyHelper instance and, in the case of the method lookup bean, to perform the actual method lookup. The someOperation() method is a simple method that depends on the MyHelper class to do its processing.

Listing 5-19 shows the StandardLookupDemoBean class, which uses setter injection to obtain an instance of the MyHelper class.

Listing 5-19. *The StandardLookupDemoBean Class*

```
package com.apress.prospring.ch5.mi;

public class StandardLookupDemoBean implements DemoBean {

    private MyHelper helper;

    public void setMyHelper(MyHelper helper) {
        this.helper = helper;
    }

    public MyHelper getMyHelper() {
        return this.helper;
    }

    public void someOperation() {
        helper.doSomethingHelpful();
    }
}
```

This code should all look familiar, but notice that the someOperation() method uses
the stored instance of MyHelper to complete its processing. In Listing 5-20, you can see the
AbstractLookupDemoBean class, which uses Method Injection to obtain an instance of the
MyHelper class.

Listing 5-20. *The AbstractLookupDemoBean Class*

```
package com.apress.prospring.ch5.mi;

public abstract class AbstractLookupDemoBean implements DemoBean {

    public abstract MyHelper getMyHelper();

    public void someOperation() {
        getMyHelper().doSomethingHelpful();
    }
}
```

Notice that the getMyHelper() method is declared as abstract, and that this method is
called by the someOperation() method to obtain a MyHelper instance. In Listing 5-21, you can
see the configuration code required for this example.

Listing 5-21. *Configuring Method Lookup Injection*

```
<!DOCTYPE beans PUBLIC "-//SPRING//DTD BEAN//EN"
"http://www.springframework.org/dtd/spring-beans.dtd">
<beans>
    <bean id="helper" class="com.apress.prospring.ch5.mi.MyHelper"
        singleton="false"/>
    <bean id="abstractLookupBean"
        class="com.apress.prospring.ch5.mi.AbstractLookupDemoBean">
        <lookup-method name="getMyHelper" bean="helper"/>
    </bean>
    <bean id="standardLookupBean"
        class="com.apress.prospring.ch5.mi.StandardLookupDemoBean">
        <property name="myHelper">
            <ref local="helper"/>
        </property>
    </bean>
</beans>
```

The configuration for the helper and standardLookupBean beans should look familiar to
you by now. For the abstractLookupBean, you need to configure the lookup method using the
<lookup-method> tag. The name attribute of the <lookup-method> tag tells Spring the name of the
method on the bean that it should override. This method must not accept any arguments and
the return type should be that of the bean you want to return from the method. The bean attribute
tells Spring which bean the lookup method should return.

The final piece of code for this example is shown in Listing 5-22.

Listing 5-22. *The LookupDemo Class*

```
package com.apress.prospring.ch5.mi;

import org.springframework.beans.factory.BeanFactory;
import org.springframework.beans.factory.xml.XmlBeanFactory;
import org.springframework.core.io.FileSystemResource;
import org.springframework.util.StopWatch;

public class LookupDemo {

    public static void main(String[] args) {
        BeanFactory factory = new XmlBeanFactory(new FileSystemResource(
                "./ch5/src/conf/mi/lookup.xml"));

        DemoBean abstractBean = (DemoBean) factory.getBean("abstractLookupBean");
        DemoBean standardBean = (DemoBean) factory.getBean("standardLookupBean");
```

```
        displayInfo(standardBean);
        displayInfo(abstractBean);

    }

    public static void displayInfo(DemoBean bean) {
        MyHelper helper1 = bean.getMyHelper();
        MyHelper helper2 = bean.getMyHelper();

        System.out.println("Helper Instances the Same?: "
                + (helper1 == helper2));

        StopWatch stopWatch = new StopWatch();
        stopWatch.start("lookupDemo");

        for (int x = 0; x < 100000; x++) {
            MyHelper helper = bean.getMyHelper();
            helper.doSomethingHelpful();
        }

        stopWatch.stop();

        System.out.println("100000 gets took " + stopWatch.getTotalTimeMillis()
                + " ms");

    }
}
```

In this code, you can see that we retrieve the abstractLookupBean and the standardLookupBean from the BeanFactory and pass each reference to the displayInfo() method. The first part of the displayInfo() method creates two local variables of MyHelper and assigns them each a value by calling getMyHelper() on the bean passed to it. Using these two variables, it writes a message to stdout indicating whether or not the two references point to the same object. For the abstractLookupBean class, a new instance of MyHelper should be retrieved for each call to getMyHelper(), so the references should not be the same. For standardLookupBean, a single instance of MyHelper is passed to the bean by setter injection, and this instance is stored and returned for every call to getMyHelper(), so the two references should be the same.

Note The StopWatch class used in the previous example is a utility class available with Spring. You'll find StopWatch very useful when you need to perform simple performance tests and when you are testing your applications.

The final part of the displayInfo() method runs a simple performance test to see which of the beans is faster. Clearly the standardLookupBean should be faster because it returns the same instance each time, but it is interesting to see the difference. Here is the output we received from this example:

```
Helper Instances the Same?: true
100000 gets took 16 ms
Helper Instances the Same?: false
100000 gets took 2063 ms
```

As you can see, the helper instances are, as expected, the same when we use standardLookupBean and different when we use abstractLookupBean. There is a noticeable performance difference when we use the standardLookupBean, but that is to be expected.

Considerations for Method Lookup Injection

Method Lookup Injection is intended for use when you want to work with two beans of different lifecycles. Avoid the temptation to use Method Lookup Injection when the beans share the same lifecycle, especially if they are singletons. Listing 5-22 shows a noticeable difference in performance between using Method Injection to obtain new instances of a dependency and using standard DI to obtain a single instance of a dependency. Also, make sure you don't use Method Lookup Injection needlessly, even when you have beans of different lifecycles.

Consider a situation in which you have three singletons that share a dependency in common. You want each singleton to have its own instance of the dependency, so you create the dependency as a non-singleton, but you are happy with each singleton using the same instance of the collaborator throughout its life. In this case, setter injection is the ideal solution; Method Lookup Injection just adds unnecessary overhead.

As we mentioned before, Method Lookup Injection was created so you could avoid having lots of beans that implemented BeanFactoryAware and performed lookups manually using getBean(). So how does performing manual lookups with BeanFactoryAware compare to Method Lookup Injection from a performance perspective? Listing 5-23 shows another implementation of the DemoBean interface that also implements BeanFactoryAware and uses the getBean() method to look up its non-singleton dependency manually.

Listing 5-23. *The BeanFactoryAwareLookupDemoBean Class*

```
package com.apress.prospring.ch5.mi;

import org.springframework.beans.BeansException;
import org.springframework.beans.factory.BeanFactory;
import org.springframework.beans.factory.BeanFactoryAware;

public class BeanFactoryAwareLookupDemoBean implements BeanFactoryAware,
        DemoBean {

    private BeanFactory factory = null;
```

```
    public void setBeanFactory(BeanFactory factory) throws BeansException {
        this.factory = factory;
    }

    public MyHelper getMyHelper() {
        return (MyHelper) factory.getBean("helper");
    }

    public void someOperation() {
        getMyHelper().doSomethingHelpful();
    }
}
```

As you can see, the getMyHelper() performs a lookup each time it is called, returning a new instance of the helper bean each time. In Listing 5-24 you can see a simple performance test that compares this class with the AbstractLookupDemoBean class that uses Method Lookup Injection.

Listing 5-24. *Comparing Performance*

```
package com.apress.prospring.ch5.mi;

import org.springframework.beans.factory.BeanFactory;
import org.springframework.beans.factory.xml.XmlBeanFactory;
import org.springframework.core.io.FileSystemResource;
import org.springframework.util.StopWatch;

public class LookupPerformance {

    public static void main(String[] args) {

        BeanFactory factory = new XmlBeanFactory(new FileSystemResource(
                "./ch5/src/conf/mi/lookup.xml"));

        DemoBean abstractBean = (DemoBean) factory.getBean("abstractLookupBean");
        DemoBean factoryBean = (DemoBean) factory.getBean("factoryLookupBean");

        testPerf(abstractBean);
        testPerf(factoryBean);
    }

    public static void testPerf(DemoBean bean) {
        StopWatch stopWatch = new StopWatch();
        stopWatch.start("perfTest");
```

```
        for (int x = 0; x < 1000000; x++) {
            MyHelper helper = bean.getMyHelper();
            helper.doSomethingHelpful();
        }

        stopWatch.stop();

        System.out.println("1000000 gets took "
                + stopWatch.getTotalTimeSeconds() + " seconds");
    }
}
```

When we ran this example on our machine, we received the following output:

```
1000000 gets took 17.563 seconds
1000000 gets took 17.375 seconds
```

As you can see, there is barely any difference in the performance of the two different mechanisms; the manual lookup approach is marginally faster. Given that the difference in performance is negligible, we recommend that you use Method Lookup Injection when you are working with beans of different lifecycles rather than implementing BeanFactoryAware and performing the lookup manually. Using Method Lookup Injection, you can keep your beans decoupled from Spring without any noticeable performance loss.

When you are using Method Lookup Injection, there are a few design guidelines that you should bear in mind when building your classes. In the earlier examples, we declared the lookup method in an interface. The only reason we did this was we did not have to duplicate the displayInfo() method twice for two different bean types. As we mentioned earlier, generally you do not need to pollute a business interface with unnecessary definitions that are used solely for IoC purposes. Another point to bear in mind is that although you don't have to make your lookup method abstract, doing so prevents you from forgetting to configure the lookup method and then using a blank implementation by accident.

Method Replacement

Although the Spring documentation classifies method replacement as a form of injection, it is very different from what you have seen so far. So far, we have used injection purely to supply beans with their collaborators. Using method replacement, you can replace the implementation of any method on any beans arbitrarily without having to change the source of the bean you are modifying.

Internally you achieve this by creating a subclass of the bean class dynamically. You use CGLIB and redirect calls to the method you want to replace to another bean that implements the MethodReplacer interface.

In Listing 5-25 you can see a simple bean that declares two overloads of a formatMessage() method.

Listing 5-25. *The ReplacementTarget Class*

```
package com.apress.prospring.ch5.mi;

public class ReplacementTarget {

    public String formatMessage(String msg) {
        return "<h1>" + msg + "</h1>";
    }

    public String formatMessage(Object msg) {
        return "<h1>" + msg + "</h1>";
    }
}
```

You can replace any of the methods on the ReplacementTarget class using Spring's method replacement functionality. In this example, we show you how to replace the formatMessage(String method) and we also compare the performance of the replaced method with that of the original.

To replace a method, you first need to create an implementation of the MethodReplacer class; this is shown in Listing 5-26.

Listing 5-26. *Implementing MethodReplacer*

```
package com.apress.prospring.ch5.mi;

import java.lang.reflect.Method;

import org.springframework.beans.factory.support.MethodReplacer;

public class FormatMessageReplacer implements MethodReplacer {

    public Object reimplement(Object target, Method method, Object[] args)
            throws Throwable {

        if (isFormatMessageMethod(method)) {

            String msg = (String) args[0];

            return "<h2>" + msg + "</h2>";
        } else {
            throw new IllegalArgumentException("Unable to reimplement method "
                    + method.getName());
        }
    }
}
```

```
private boolean isFormatMessageMethod(Method method) {

    // check correct number of params
    if (method.getParameterTypes().length != 1) {
        return false;
    }

    // check method name
    if (!("formatMessage".equals(method.getName()))) {
        return false;
    }

    // check return type
    if (method.getReturnType() != String.class) {
        return false;
    }

    // check parameter type is correct
    if (method.getParameterTypes()[0] != String.class) {
        return false;
    }

    return true;
}

}
```

The MethodReplacer interface has a single method, reimplement(), that you must implement. Three arguments are passed to reimplement(): the bean on which the original method was invoked, a Method instance that represents the method that is being overridden, and the array of arguments passed to the method. The reimplement() method should return the result of your reimplemented logic and, obviously, the type of the return value should be compatible with the return type of the method you are replacing. In Listing 5-27, the FormatMessageReplacer first checks to see if the method that is being overridden is the formatMessage(String) method; if so, it executes the replacement logic—in this case, surrounding the message with <h2> and </h2>—and returns the formatted message to the caller. It is not necessary to check to see if the message is correct, but this can be useful if you are using a few MethodReplacers with similar arguments. Using a check helps prevent a situation where a different MethodReplacer with compatible arguments and return types is used accidentally.

Listing 5-27 shows a BeanFactory that defines two beans of type ReplacementTarget—one has the formatMessage(String) method replaced and the other does not.

Listing 5-27. *Configuring Method Replacement*

```
<!DOCTYPE beans PUBLIC "-//SPRING//DTD BEAN//EN"
"http://www.springframework.org/dtd/spring-beans.dtd">
<beans>
    <bean id="methodReplacer"
          class="com.apress.prospring.ch5.mi.FormatMessageReplacer"/>
    <bean id="replacementTarget"
          class="com.apress.prospring.ch5.mi.ReplacementTarget">
        <replaced-method name="formatMessage" replacer="methodReplacer">
            <arg-type>String</arg-type>
        </replaced-method>
    </bean>
    <bean id="standardTarget"
          class="com.apress.prospring.ch5.mi.ReplacementTarget"/>
</beans>
```

As you can see from Listing 5-27, the MethodReplacer implementation is declared as a bean in the BeanFactory. We then used the <replaced-method> tag to replace the formatMessage(String) method on the replacementTargetBean. The name attribute of the <replaced-method> tag specifies the name of the method to replace and the replacer attribute is used to specify the name of the MethodReplacer bean that we want to replace the method implementation. In cases where there are overloaded methods such as in the ReplacementTarget class, you can use the <arg-type> tag to specify the method signature to match. The <arg-type> supports pattern matching, so String is matched to java.lang.String and also to java.lang.StringBuffer.

Listing 5-28 shows a simple demo application that retrieves both the standardTarget and replacementTarget beans from the BeanFactory, executes their formatMessage(String) methods, and then runs a simple performance test to see which is faster.

Listing 5-28. *Method Replacement in Action*

```
package com.apress.prospring.ch5.mi;

import org.springframework.beans.factory.BeanFactory;
import org.springframework.beans.factory.xml.XmlBeanFactory;
import org.springframework.core.io.FileSystemResource;
import org.springframework.util.StopWatch;

public class MethodReplacementExample {

    public static void main(String[] args) {
        BeanFactory factory = new XmlBeanFactory(new FileSystemResource(
                "./ch5/src/conf/mi/replacement.xml"));
```

```
        ReplacementTarget replacementTarget =
                        (ReplacementTarget) factory.getBean("replacementTarget");
        ReplacementTarget standardTarget =
                        (ReplacementTarget) factory.getBean("standardTarget");

        displayInfo(replacementTarget);
        displayInfo(standardTarget);
    }

    private static void displayInfo(ReplacementTarget target) {
        System.out.println(target.formatMessage("Hello World!"));

        StopWatch stopWatch = new StopWatch();
        stopWatch.start("perfTest");

        for (int x = 0; x < 1000000; x++) {
            String out = target.formatMessage("foo");
        }

        stopWatch.stop();

        System.out.println("1000000 invocations took: "
                + stopWatch.getTotalTimeMillis() + " ms");
    }
}
```

You should be very familiar with this code by now, so we won't go into any detail on it. On our machine, running this example yields the following output:

```
<h2>Hello World!</h2>
1000000 invocations took: 3609 ms
<h1>Hello World!</h1>
1000000 invocations took: 844 ms
```

As expected, the output from the replacementTarget bean reflects the overridden implementation the MethodReplacer provides. Interestingly, though, the dynamically replaced method is over four times slower than the statically defined method. Removing the check for a valid method in the MethodReplacer made a negligible difference (between 20 and 150 milliseconds) across a number of executions, so we can conclude that most of the overhead is in the CGLIB subclass.

When to Use Method Replacement

We will resist the temptation to say "Never." and instead say that method replacement can prove quite useful in a variety of circumstances, especially when you only want to override a particular method for a single bean rather than all beans of the same type. That said, we still prefer to use standard Java mechanisms for overriding methods rather than depending on runtime bytecode enhancement.

If you are going to use method replacement as part of your application, we recommend that you use one `MethodReplacer` per method or group of overloaded methods. Avoid the temptation to use a single `MethodReplacer` for lots of unrelated methods; this results in lots of unnecessary `String` comparisons while your code works out which method it is supposed to reimplement. We have found that performing simple checks to ensure that the `MethodReplacer` is working with the correct method is useful and doesn't add too much overhead to your code. If you are really concerned about performance, you can simply add a `boolean` property to your `MethodReplacer`, which allows you to turn the check on and off using Dependency Injection.

Using FactoryBeans

One of the problems that you will face when using Spring is how to create and then inject dependencies that cannot be created simply by using the new operator. To overcome this problem, Spring provides the `FactoryBean` interface that acts as an adaptor for objects that cannot be created and managed using the standard Spring semantics. Typically, you use `FactoryBeans` to create beans you cannot use the new operator to create such as those you access through static factory methods, although this is not always the case. Simply put, a `FactoryBean` is a bean that acts as a factory for other beans. `FactoryBeans` are configured within your `BeanFactory` like any normal bean, but when Spring uses the `FactoryBean` to satisfy a dependency or lookup request, it does not return the `FactoryBean`; instead, it invokes the `FactoryBean.getObject()` method and returns the result of that invocation.

`FactoryBeans` are used to great effect in Spring; the most noticeable uses are the creation of transactional proxies, which we cover in Chapter 12, and the automatic retrieval of resources from a JNDI context, which we cover in Chapter 13. However, `FactoryBeans` are not just useful for building the internals of Spring; you'll find them really useful when you build your own applications, because they allow you to manage many more resources using IoC than would otherwise be available.

The MessageDigestFactoryBean

Often the projects that we work on require some kind of cryptographic processing; typically, this involves generating a **message digest** or **hash** of a user's password to be stored in a database. In Java, the `MessageDigest` class provides functionality for creating a digest of any arbitrary data. `MessageDigest` itself is abstract, and you obtain concrete implementations by calling `MessageDigest.getInstance()` and passing in the name of the digest algorithm you want to use. For instance, if we want to use the MD5 algorithm to create a digest, we use the following code to create the `MessageDigest` instance:

```
MessageDigest md5 = MessageDigest.getInstance("MD5");
```

If we want to use Spring to manage the creation of the `MessageDigest` object, the best we can do without a `FactoryBean` is have a property, `algorithmName`, on our bean and then use an initialization callback to call `MessageDigest.getInstance()`. Using a `FactoryBean`, we can encapsulate this logic inside a bean. Then any beans that require a `MessageDigest` instance can simply declare a property, `messageDigest`, and use the `FactoryBean` to obtain the instance. Listing 5-29 shows an implementation of `FactoryBean` that does just this.

Listing 5-29. *The MessageDigestFactoryBean Class*

```java
package com.apress.prospring.ch5.factory;

import java.security.MessageDigest;

import org.springframework.beans.factory.FactoryBean;
import org.springframework.beans.factory.InitializingBean;

public class MessageDigestFactoryBean implements FactoryBean, InitializingBean {

    private String algorithmName = "MD5";

    private MessageDigest messageDigest = null;

    public Object getObject() throws Exception {
        return messageDigest.clone();
    }


    public Class getObjectType() {
        return MessageDigest.class;
    }


    public boolean isSingleton() {
        return true;
    }

    public void afterPropertiesSet() throws Exception {
        messageDigest = MessageDigest.getInstance(algorithmName);
    }

    public void setAlgorithmName(String algorithmName) {
        this.algorithmName = algorithmName;
    }
}
```

The FactoryBean interface declares three methods: getObject(), getObjectType(), and isSingleton(). Spring calls the getObject() method to retrieve the Object created by the FactoryBean. This is the actual Object that is passed to other beans that use the FactoryBean as a collaborator. In Listing 5-29, you can see that the MessageDigestFactoryBean passes a clone of the stored MessageDigest instance that is created in the InitializingBean.afterPropertiesSet() callback.

The getObjectType() method allows you to tell Spring what type of Object your FactoryBean will return. This can be null if you know in advance, but if you specify a type, Spring can use it for auto-wiring purposes. We return MessageDigest as our type, because we do not know what concrete type will be returned, not that it matters because all beans will define their dependencies using MessageDigest anyway

The isSingleton() property allows you to inform Spring whether the FactoryBean is managing a singleton instance or not. Remember that by setting the singleton attribute of the FactoryBean's <bean> tag, you tell Spring about the singleton status of the FactoryBean itself, not the Objects it is returning.

Now let's see how the FactoryBean is employed in an application. In Listing 5-30, you can see a simple bean that maintains two MessageDigest instances and then displays the digests of a message passed to its digest() method.

Listing 5-30. *The MessageDigester Class*

```java
package com.apress.prospring.ch5.factory;

import java.security.MessageDigest;

import sun.misc.BASE64Encoder;

public class MessageDigester {

    private MessageDigest digest1 = null;
    private MessageDigest digest2 = null;

    public void setDigest1(MessageDigest digest1) {
        this.digest1 = digest1;
    }

    public void setDigest2(MessageDigest digest2) {
        this.digest2 = digest2;
    }

    public void digest(String msg) {
        System.out.println("Using digest1");
        digest(msg, digest1);

        System.out.println("Using digest2");
        digest(msg, digest2);
    }

    private void digest(String msg, MessageDigest digest) {
        System.out.println("Using algorithm: " + digest.getAlgorithm());
        digest.reset();
        byte[] bytes = msg.getBytes();
        byte[] out = digest.digest(bytes);
        BASE64Encoder enc = new BASE64Encoder();
        System.out.println(enc.encode(out));
    }
}
```

Our apologies for using the Sun-specific BASE64Encoder class. We wanted to be able to display the digest data, but we didn't want to overcomplicate the example with the necessary code for Base64. If you're not running a Sun JVM, then you can remove the BASE64Encoder and output the bytes directly to the screen, or you can replace it with a class that performs a similar operation.

Listing 5-31 shows a simple BeanFactory configuration that configures two MessageDigestFactoryBeans, one for the SHA1 algorithm and the other using the default (MD5) algorithm.

Listing 5-31. *Configuring FactoryBeans*

```
<!DOCTYPE beans PUBLIC "-//SPRING//DTD BEAN//EN"
"http://www.springframework.org/dtd/spring-beans.dtd">
<beans>
    <bean id="shaDigest"
        class="com.apress.prospring.ch5.factory.MessageDigestFactoryBean">
        <property name="algorithmName">
            <value>SHA1</value>
        </property>
    </bean>
    <bean id="defaultDigest"
        class="com.apress.prospring.ch5.factory.MessageDigestFactoryBean"/>
    <bean id="digester"
        class="com.apress.prospring.ch5.factory.MessageDigester">
        <property name="digest1">
            <ref local="shaDigest"/>
        </property>
        <property name="digest2">
            <ref local="defaultDigest"/>
        </property>
    </bean>
</beans>
```

As you can see, not only have we configured the two MessageDigestFactoryBeans, but we have also configured a MessageDigester, using the two MessageDigestFactoryBeans, to provide values for the digest1 and digest2 properties. In Listing 5-32, you see a basic example class that retrieves the MessageDigester bean from the BeanFactory and creates the digest of a simple message.

Listing 5-32. *Using MessageDigester*

```
package com.apress.prospring.ch5.factory;

import org.springframework.beans.factory.BeanFactory;
import org.springframework.beans.factory.xml.XmlBeanFactory;
import org.springframework.core.io.FileSystemResource;

public class MessageDigestExample {
```

```
    public static void main(String[] args) {
        BeanFactory factory = new XmlBeanFactory(new FileSystemResource(
                "./ch5/src/conf/factory/factory.xml"));

        MessageDigester digester = (MessageDigester) factory
                .getBean("digester");
        digester.digest("Hello World!");

    }
}
```

Running this example gives the following output:

```
Using digest1
Using algorithm: SHA1
Lve95gjOVATpfV8EL5X4nxwjKHE=
Using digest2
Using algorithm: MD5
7Qdih1MuhjZehB6Sv8UNjA==
```

As you can see, the MessageDigest bean is provided with two MessageDigest implementations, SHA1 and MD5, despite the fact that no MessageDigests are configured in the BeanFactory. This is the FactoryBean at work.

FactoryBeans are the perfect solution when you are working with classes that cannot be created using the new operator. If you work with objects that are created using a factory method and you want to use these classes in a Spring application, then create a FactoryBean to act as an adaptor, allowing your classes to take full advantage of Spring's IoC capabilities.

Accessing a FactoryBean Directly

Given that Spring automatically satisfies any references to a FactoryBean by the objects produced by that FactoryBean, you may be wondering if you can actually access the FactoryBean directly. The answer is "Yes."

Accessing the FactoryBean is actually very simple: you simply prefix the bean name with an ampersand in the call to getBean(), as shown in Listing 5-33.

Listing 5-33. *Accessing FactoryBeans Directly*

```
package com.apress.prospring.ch5.factory;

import java.security.MessageDigest;

import org.springframework.beans.factory.BeanFactory;
import org.springframework.beans.factory.xml.XmlBeanFactory;
import org.springframework.core.io.FileSystemResource;
```

```
public class AccessingFactoryBeans {

    public static void main(String[] args) {
        BeanFactory factory = new XmlBeanFactory(new FileSystemResource(
                "./ch5/src/conf/factory/factory.xml"));

        MessageDigest digest =
                                (MessageDigest) factory.getBean("shaDigest");

        MessageDigestFactoryBean factoryBean =
                        (MessageDigestFactoryBean) factory.getBean("&shaDigest");
    }
}
```

This feature is used in a few places in the Spring code, but your application should really have no reason to use it. The FactoryBean interface is intended to be used as a piece of supporting infrastructure to allow you to use more of your application's classes in an IoC setting. Avoid accessing the FactoryBean directly and invoking getObject() manually; if you do not, you are making extra work for yourself and are unnecessarily coupling your application to a specific implementation detail that could quite easily change in the future.

JavaBeans PropertyEditors

For those of you not entirely familiar with JavaBeans concepts, a PropertyEditor is a class that converts a property's value to and from its native type representation into a String. Originally, this was conceived as a way to allow property values to be entered, as String values, into an editor and have them transformed into the correct type. However, because PropertyEditors are inherently lightweight classes, they have found uses in many different settings, including Spring.

Because a good portion of property values in a Spring-based application start life in the BeanFactory configuration file, they are essentially Strings. However, the property that these values are set on may not be String-typed. So, to save you from having to create a load of String-typed properties artificially, Spring allows you to define PropertyEditors to manage the conversion of String-based property values into the correct types.

The Built-in PropertyEditors

Spring comes with seven built-in PropertyEditor implementations that are preregistered with the BeanFactory. Listing 5-34 shows a simple bean that declares seven properties, one for each of the types supported by the built-in PropertyEditors.

Listing 5-34. *Using the Built-in PropertyEditors*

```java
package com.apress.prospring.ch5.pe;

import java.io.File;
import java.net.URL;
import java.util.Locale;
import java.util.Properties;

import org.springframework.beans.factory.BeanFactory;
import org.springframework.beans.factory.xml.XmlBeanFactory;
import org.springframework.core.io.FileSystemResource;

public class PropertyEditorBean {

    private Class cls;

    private File file;

    private URL url;

    private Locale locale;

    private Properties properties;

    private String[] strings;

    private byte[] bytes;

    public void setClass(Class cls) {
        System.out.println("Setting class: " + cls.getName());
        this.cls = cls;
    }

    public void setFile(File file) {
        System.out.println("Setting file: " + file.getName());
        this.file = file;
    }

    public void setLocale(Locale locale) {
        System.out.println("Setting locale: " + locale.getDisplayName());
        this.locale = locale;
    }
```

```
    public void setProperties(Properties properties) {
        System.out.println("Loaded " + properties.size() + " properties");
        this.properties = properties;
    }

    public void setStrings(String[] strings) {
        System.out.println("Loaded " + strings.length + " Strings");
        this.strings = strings;
    }

    public void setUrl(URL url) {
        System.out.println("Setting URL: " + url.toExternalForm());
        this.url = url;
    }

    public void setBytes(byte[] bytes) {
        System.out.println("Adding " + bytes.length + " bytes");
        this.bytes = bytes;
    }

    public static void main(String[] args) {
        BeanFactory factory = new XmlBeanFactory(new FileSystemResource(
                "./ch5/src/conf/pe/builtin.xml"));
        PropertyEditorBean bean = (PropertyEditorBean) factory
                .getBean("builtInSample");
    }
}
```

In Listing 5-34, you can see that PropertyEditorBean has seven properties, each corresponding to one of the built-in PropertyEditors. In Listing 5-35, you can see a simple BeanFactory configuration specifying values for all of these properties.

Listing 5-35. *Configuration Using PropertyEditors*

```
<!DOCTYPE beans PUBLIC "-//SPRING//DTD BEAN//EN"
"http://www.springframework.org/dtd/spring-beans.dtd">
<beans>
    <bean id="builtInSample"
          class="com.apress.prospring.ch5.pe.PropertyEditorBean">
        <property name="class">
            <value>java.lang.String</value>
        </property>
        <property name="file">
            <value>d:/tmp/test.txt</value>
        </property>
        <property name="locale">
            <value> en-GB </value>
        </property>
```

```
            <property name="url">
                <value>http://www.springframework.org</value>
            </property>
            <property name="properties">
                <value>
                    name=foo
                    age=19
                </value>
            </property>
            <property name="strings">
                <value>rob,jan,rod,jurgen,alef</value>
            </property>
            <property name="bytes">
                <value>Hello World</value>
            </property>
        </bean>
</beans>
```

As you can see, although all the properties on the PropertyEditorBean are not Strings, the values for the properties are specified as simple Strings. Running this example yields the following output:

```
Setting class: java.lang.String
Setting file: test.txt
Setting locale:  en-gb
Setting URL: http://www.springframework.org
Loaded 2 properties
Loaded 5 Strings
Adding 11 bytes
```

As you can see, Spring has, using the built-in PropertyEditors, converted the String representations of the various properties to the correct types. Table 5-1 summarizes the built-in PropertyEditors available in Spring.

Table 5-1. *Spring PropertyEditors*

PropertyEditor	Description
ByteArrayPropertyEditor	This PropertyEditor converts a String value into an array of bytes.
ClassEditor	The ClassEditor converts from a fully qualified class name into a Class instance. When using this PropertyEditor, be careful not to include any extraneous spaces on either side of the class name when using XmlBeanFactory, because this results in a ClassNotFoundException.
FileEditor	The FileEditor converts a String file path into a File instance. Spring does not check to see if the file exists.
LocaleEditor	The LocaleEditor converts the String representation of a locale, such as en-GB, into a java.util.Locale instance.

Table 5-1. *Spring PropertyEditors (Continued)*

PropertyEditor	Description
PropertiesEditor	PropertiesEditor converts a String in the format key1=value1\n key2=value2\n key*n*=value*n* into an instance of java.util.Properties with the corresponding properties configured.
StringArrayPropertyEditor	The StringArrayPropertyEditor class converts a comma-separated list of Strings into a String array.
URLEditor	The URLEditor converts a String representation of a URL into an instance of java.net.URL.

This set of PropertyEditors provides a good base for working with Spring and makes configuring your application with common components such as Files and URLs much simpler.

Creating a Custom PropertyEditor

Although the built-in PropertyEditors cover some of the standard cases of property type conversion, there may come a time when you need to create your own PropertyEditor to support a class or a set of classes you are using in your application.

Spring has full support for registering custom PropertyEditors; the only downside is that the java.beans.PropertyEditor interface has a lot of methods, many of which are irrelevant to the task at hand—converting property types. Thankfully, Spring provides the PropertyEditorSupport class, which your own PropertyEditors can extend, leaving you to implement only a single method: setAsText().

Many of the applications that we build use regular expressions. In a recent application we built using Spring, we wanted to externalize the regular expressions we used in the application. At first glance, we thought the way to do this was to expose the regular expressions as String-typed properties and then, in an initialization callback, compile the String patterns in java.util.regex.Pattern objects. However, by employing a custom PropertyEditor, we discovered that we could expose Pattern type properties and have the PropertyEditor perform the compilation as the property values are set.

Listing 5-36 shows the code for the PatternPropertyEditor class.

Listing 5-36. *The PatternPropertyEditor Class*

```
package com.apress.prospring.ch5.pe;

import java.beans.PropertyEditorSupport;
import java.util.regex.Pattern;

public class PatternPropertyEditor extends PropertyEditorSupport {

    public void setAsText(String text) throws IllegalArgumentException {
        Pattern pattern = Pattern.compile(text);
        setValue(pattern);
    }
}
```

As you can see, very little code is involved in the custom PropertyEditor; we simply use the supplied text as the source of the Pattern.compile() method. Calling the setValue() method sets the value of the underlying property.

In Listing 5-37, you can see a simple bean that searches a String using a Pattern instance and displays the result.

Listing 5-37. *The CustomEditorExample Bean*

```java
package com.apress.prospring.ch5.pe;

import java.util.regex.Matcher;
import java.util.regex.Pattern;

import org.springframework.beans.factory.config.ConfigurableListableBeanFactory;
import org.springframework.beans.factory.config.CustomEditorConfigurer;
import org.springframework.beans.factory.xml.XmlBeanFactory;
import org.springframework.core.io.FileSystemResource;

public class CustomEditorExample {

    private Pattern searchPattern;

    private String textToSearch;

    public static void main(String[] args) {
        ConfigurableListableBeanFactory factory = new XmlBeanFactory(
                new FileSystemResource("./ch5/src/conf/pe/custom.xml"));

        CustomEditorConfigurer config =
                    (CustomEditorConfigurer) factory.getBean("customEditorConfigurer");

        config.postProcessBeanFactory(factory);

        CustomEditorExample bean =
                            (CustomEditorExample) factory.getBean("exampleBean");

        System.out.println(bean.getMatchCount());
    }

    public void setSearchPattern(Pattern searchPattern) {
        this.searchPattern = searchPattern;
    }

    public void setTextToSearch(String textToSearch) {
        this.textToSearch = textToSearch;
    }
```

```
    public int getMatchCount() {
        Matcher m = searchPattern.matcher(textToSearch);

        int count = 0;
        while (m.find()) {
            count++;
        }

        return count;
    }
}
```

The most complex part of using a custom `PropertyEditor` is the registration process. You can register your `PropertyEditor` with Spring in one of two ways. The first is by calling `ConfigurableBeanFactory.registerCustomEditor()` and passing the type for which the editor should be used and an instance of the editor itself. The second, and preferred, mechanism is to define a bean of type `CustomEditorConfigurer` in your `BeanFactory` configuration, specifying the editors in a `Map`-typed property of that bean.

The `CustomEditorConfigurer` is an example of a `BeanFactoryPostProcessor`, a class that can make changes to a `BeanFactory`'s configuration before the application uses it. Other common `BeanFactoryPostProcessor`s are `PropertyPlaceholderConfigurer` and `PropertyOverrideConfigurer`. You can find more information about these classes in the Spring documentation. The only drawback of using a `BeanFactoryPostProcessor` with a `BeanFactory` is that they are not applied automatically. However, as you will see shortly, this is not a problem you encounter when using the `ApplicationContext`, which is one of the reasons `ApplicationContext` is preferred over `BeanFactory` for most applications.

Listing 5-38 shows a `BeanFactory` configuration that configures a `CustomEditorConfigurer` and the `PatternPropertyEditor`.

Listing 5-38. *Using CustomEditorConfigurer*

```
<!DOCTYPE beans PUBLIC "-//SPRING//DTD BEAN//EN"
"http://www.springframework.org/dtd/spring-beans.dtd">
<beans>
    <bean name="customEditorConfigurer"
        class="org.springframework.beans.factory.config.CustomEditorConfigurer">
        <property name="customEditors">
            <map>
                <entry key="java.util.regex.Pattern">
                    <bean
                        class="com.apress.prospring.ch5.pe.PatternPropertyEditor"/>
                </entry>
            </map>
        </property>
    </bean>
```

```
    <bean id="exampleBean"
        class="com.apress.prospring.ch5.pe.CustomEditorExample">
        <property name="searchPattern">
            <value>(dog|fox)</value>
        </property>
        <property name="textToSearch">
            <value>The quick brown fox jumped over the lazy dog.</value>
        </property>
    </bean>
</beans>
```

You should notice three points in this configuration. The first is that the custom PropertyEditors are injected into the CustomEditorConfigurer class using the Map-typed customEditors property. The second point is that each entry in the Map represents a single PropertyEditor with the key of the entry being the name of the class for which the PropertyEditor is used. As you can see, the key for the PatternPropertyEditor is java.util.regex.Pattern, which signifies that this is the class for which the editor should be used. The final point of interest here is that we used an anonymous bean declaration as the value of the single Map entry. No other bean needs to access this bean, so it needs no name and as a result, you can declare it inside of the <entry> tag.

Listing 5-39 shows the code for CustomEditorExample class that is registered as a bean in Listing 5-38.

Listing 5-39. *The CustomEditorExample Class*

```
package com.apress.prospring.ch5.pe;

import java.util.regex.Matcher;
import java.util.regex.Pattern;

import org.springframework.beans.factory.config.ConfigurableListableBeanFactory;
import org.springframework.beans.factory.config.CustomEditorConfigurer;
import org.springframework.beans.factory.xml.XmlBeanFactory;
import org.springframework.core.io.FileSystemResource;

public class CustomEditorExample {

    private Pattern searchPattern;

    private String textToSearch;

    public static void main(String[] args) {
        ConfigurableListableBeanFactory factory = new XmlBeanFactory(
                new FileSystemResource("./ch5/src/conf/pe/custom.xml"));

        CustomEditorConfigurer config = (CustomEditorConfigurer) factory
                .getBean("customEditorConfigurer");
```

```
        config.postProcessBeanFactory(factory);

        CustomEditorExample bean = (CustomEditorExample) factory
                .getBean("exampleBean");

        System.out.println(bean.getMatchCount());
    }

    public void setSearchPattern(Pattern searchPattern) {
        this.searchPattern = searchPattern;
    }

    public void setTextToSearch(String textToSearch) {
        this.textToSearch = textToSearch;
    }

    public int getMatchCount() {
        Matcher m = searchPattern.matcher(textToSearch);

        int count = 0;
        while (m.find()) {
            count++;
        }

        return count;
    }
}
```

Most of this code is fairly intuitive; the only point of interest is the call to `CustomEditorConfigurer.postProcessBeanFactory()`, which passes in the `BeanFactory` instance. This is where the custom editors are registered in Spring; you should call this before you attempt to access any beans that need to use the custom `PropertyEditors`.

Choosing a Registration Process

We did not show the programmatic registration process because we believe that in all cases, the declarative process is better suited to the needs of most, if not all, applications. When you are using the programmatic process, adding a new `PropertyEditor` means changing the application code, whereas with the declarative mechanism, you can simply update the configuration. Using the declarative mechanism also encourages you to define your editors as beans, which makes it so that you can configure them using Dependency Injection.

When using a `BeanFactory`, you require roughly the same amount of Java code for each mechanism as when you are registering a single `PropertyEditor`. When using an `ApplicationContext`, you require no Java code whatsoever to use the declarative mechanism, which strengthens the argument against using the programmatic mechanism.

PropertyEditors Summary

By using custom `PropertyEditors`, you can avoid exposing a lot of unnecessary `String`-typed properties on your beans. However, they are not always the ideal solution. We chose the regular expression editor to demonstrate this. Although we started off with a regular expression `PropertyEditor`, we eventually moved to a `FactoryBean` instead. The reason we chose a `FactoryBean` is because you can only have one `PropertyEditor` per type, and if you need different configurations, you are stuck. We reached a point where we needed one `Pattern` object configured to be in multiline mode and another to be configured in single-line mode. Because we could only have a single `PropertyEditor` registered for the `Pattern` type, we could only chose one of these options, thus we needed to move to a `FactoryBean`.

In general, you can use a `PropertyEditor` when the entire identity and configuration of the `Object` can be represented as a `String`, or where the configuration can be changed or derived from the identity. `Pattern` instances are immutable, so you cannot change the configuration, and it is impossible to tell whether a pattern should be in multiline or single-line mode. In all other cases, you may be better off with a `FactoryBean`.

The Spring ApplicationContext

So far, all interaction with Spring has been via the `BeanFactory` interface and its subinterfaces. Although using the `BeanFactory` interface is a good way of interacting with Spring for simple applications, it can prove unwieldy when used in larger applications. Recall that in some of the previous examples we had to call control methods on the `BeanFactory`, such as `preInstantiateSingletons()`, or we had to invoke a `BeanFactoryPostProcessor` manually, as in the case of the `CustomEditorConfigurer`. This is where the `ApplicationContext` comes in.

`ApplicationContext` is an extension of `BeanFactory`, providing all the same functionality, but it also reduces the amount of code you need to interact with it and adds new features into the pot for good measure. When using an `ApplicationContext`, you can control bean instantiation declaratively on a bean-by-bean basis, and any `BeanFactoryPostProcessors` registered in the `ApplicationContext` are executed for you automatically.

The main function of the `ApplicationContext` is to provide a much richer framework on which to build your applications. An `ApplicationContext` is much more aware of the beans that you configure within it, and in the case of many of the Spring infrastructure classes and interfaces, such as `BeanFactoryPostProcessor`, it interacts with them on your behalf, reducing the amount of code you need to write in order to use Spring.

The biggest benefit of using `ApplicationContext` is that it allows you to configure and manage Spring and Spring-managed resources in a completely declarative way. This means that wherever possible, Spring provides support classes to load an `ApplicationContext` into your application automatically, thus removing the need for you to write any code to access the `ApplicationContext`. In practice, this feature is currently only available when you are building web applications with Spring, so Spring also provides implementations of `ApplicationContext` you can create yourself.

In addition to providing a model that is focused more on declarative configuration, the ApplicationContext supports the following features not present in a BeanFactory:

- Internationalization

- Event publication

- Resource management and access

- Additional lifecycle interfaces

- Improved automatic configuration of infrastructure components

So should you use ApplicationContext or BeanFactory? Unless you are looking for a really lightweight IoC solution for your application, you should almost certainly use ApplicationContext. The additional support functionality provided by ApplicationContext really makes your life easier, reducing the amount of code you need to write and providing some useful additional features. When you are building a web application with Spring, having an ApplicationContext provided for you automatically makes choosing ApplicationContext over BeanFactory a real no-brainer.

Implementations of ApplicationContext

Like BeanFactory, ApplicationContext is an interface, and you are free to provide your own implementations. Of course, creating an ApplicationContext is no trivial feat, so Spring provides three implementations intended for use in production application. All three implementations use the same configuration format as the XmlBeanFactory. In fact, as you will see, they offer more complete support for the format than XmlBeanFactory.

For stand-alone applications where the ApplicationContext cannot be loaded automatically, you can choose from either FileSystemXmlApplicationContext or ClasspathXmlApplicationContext. These names are pretty self-explanatory, and functionally, these classes are quite similar. With FileSystemXmlApplicationContext, you can load the configuration from anywhere in the file system provided your application has permissions. Using ClasspathXmlApplicationContext, you can load from anywhere on the classpath; this is useful if you want to package the configuration with a bunch of classes inside a JAR file.

The XmlWebApplicationContext is intended solely for use in a web application environment, and as you will see in Chapter 17, by using either ContextLoaderListener or ContextLoaderServlet, you can load the ApplicationContext configuration automatically for your web application.

For the rest of the chapter, we will be using the FileSystemXmlApplicationContext to run the examples.

Using ApplicationContextAware

Earlier in the chapter you saw how a bean can obtain a reference to its BeanFactory by implementing the BeanFactoryAware interface. In the same way, a bean can obtain a reference to its ApplicationContext by implementing ApplicationContextAware. Listing 5-40 shows a bean that implements this interface.

Listing 5-40. *Implementing ApplicationContextAware*

```
package com.apress.prospring.ch5.context;

import org.springframework.beans.BeansException;
import org.springframework.context.ApplicationContext;
import org.springframework.context.ApplicationContextAware;
import org.springframework.context.support.FileSystemXmlApplicationContext;

public class ContextAwareDemo implements ApplicationContextAware {

    private ApplicationContext ctx;

    public void setApplicationContext(ApplicationContext applicationContext)
            throws BeansException {
        ctx = applicationContext;
    }

    public static void main(String[] args) {
        ApplicationContext ctx = new FileSystemXmlApplicationContext(
                "./ch5/src/conf/appContext/aware.xml");

        ContextAwareDemo demo = (ContextAwareDemo) ctx.getBean("contextAware");
        demo.displayAppContext();
    }

    public void displayAppContext() {
        System.out.println(ctx);
    }
}
```

As you can see, the `ApplicationContextAware` interface declares a single method, `setApplicationContext()`, and implementing the interface is very much like implementing `BeanFactoryAware`. In the `main()` method, we create an instance of `FileSystemXmlApplicationContext`, and from this, we obtain an instance of the `ContextAwareDemo` bean. Listing 5-41 shows the configuration for this example.

Listing 5-41. *Configuration for ContextAwareDemo Class*

```
<!DOCTYPE beans PUBLIC "-//SPRING//DTD BEAN//EN"
"http://www.springframework.org/dtd/spring-beans.dtd">
<beans>
    <bean id="contextAware"
            class="com.apress.prospring.ch5.context.ContextAwareDemo"/>
</beans>
```

Notice that although we are using `ApplicationContext` and not `BeanFactory`, the configuration format is exactly the same, meaning that using `ApplicationContext` is no more difficult than using `BeanFactory`. Running this example gives the following output:

```
org.springframework.context.support.FileSystemXmlApplicationContext: ➡
displayName=[org.springframework.context.support.FileSystemXmlApplicationContext;➡
hashCode=26281671]; ➡
startup date=[Fri Aug 06 16:02:33 BST 2004]; ➡
root of ApplicationContext hierarchy
```

As you can see, the ContextAwareDemo is able to obtain a reference to its ApplicationContext and display its details. The same comments about the use of the BeanFactoryAware interface also apply to this interface.

Controlling Bean Initialization

Recall that in an earlier example, we built a ShutdownHookBean class that automatically registered a shutdown hook Thread with the JVM to dispose of all singletons in the BeanFactory. You might also remember that in order to ensure that the ShutdownHookBean was instantiated, we had to call the preInstantiateSingletons() method of the BeanFactory. This is slightly annoying because it means that an application has to have prior knowledge of the configuration; it also means that all singletons, not just the one we want, are instantiated in advance.

When using ApplicationContext, there is a solution to this problem: the lazy-init attribute. By setting the lazy-init attribute on a bean's <bean> tag to false, you are telling the ApplicationContext that you want to create the bean in advance and it should not wait until it is first requested. Listing 5-42 shows a revised configuration for the shutdown hook bean example.

Listing 5-42. *Using lazy-init*

```
<!DOCTYPE beans PUBLIC "-//SPRING//DTD BEAN//EN"
"http://www.springframework.org/dtd/spring-beans.dtd">
<beans>
    <bean id="destructiveBean"
          class="com.apress.prospring.ch5.lifecycle.DestructiveBeanWithInterface">
        <property name="filePath">
            <value>d:/tmp/test.txt</value>
        </property>3
    </bean>
    <bean id="shutdownHook"
          class="com.apress.prospring.ch5.interaction.ShutdownHookBean"
          lazy-init="false"/>
</beans>
```

Notice that for the shutdownHook bean, we set the lazy-init attribute to false. Although lazy-init is false by default in many of the Spring implementations of ApplicationContext, there is no harm in making it explicit—this way the ApplicationContext implementation won't affect your bean. In Listing 5-43, you can see a revised driver application for this example, which omits the call to preInstantiateSingletons().

Listing 5-43. *The LazyInitDemo Class*

```
package com.apress.prospring.ch5.context;

import org.springframework.context.ApplicationContext;
import org.springframework.context.support.FileSystemXmlApplicationContext;

import com.apress.prospring.ch5.lifecycle.DestructiveBeanWithInterface;

public class LazyInitDemo {

    public static void main(String[] args) {
        ApplicationContext ctx = new FileSystemXmlApplicationContext(
                "./ch5/src/conf/appContext/lazy.xml");

        DestructiveBeanWithInterface bean =
                    (DestructiveBeanWithInterface) ctx.getBean("destructiveBean");
    }
}
```

Running this example results in the same output as before, but without the need to call preInstantiateSingletons():

```
Initializing Bean
Destroying Singletons
Destroying Bean
Singletons Destroyed
```

This is clearly beneficial because it lets you have fine-grained control over when each bean in your application is created without having to modify any of the application code.

Internationalization with MessageSource

One area in which Spring really excels is in support for internationalization (i18n). Using the MessageSource interface, your application can access String resources, called messages, stored in a variety of different languages. For each language you want to support in your application, you maintain a list of messages that are keyed to correspond to messages in other languages. For instance, if I wanted to display "The quick brown fox jumped over the lazy dog" in English and in Czech, I would create two messages, both keyed as msg; the one for English would say, "The quick brown fox jumped over the lazy dog," and the one for Czech would say, "Príšerne žlutoucký kun úpel dábelské ódy."

Although you don't need to use ApplicationContext to use MessageSource, the ApplicationContext interface actually extends MessageSource and provides special support for loading messages and for making them available in your environment. The automatic loading of messages is available in any environment, but automatic access is only provided in certain Spring-managed scenarios, such as when you are using Spring's MVC framework to build a web application. Although any class can implement ApplicationContextAware and thus access the automatically loaded messages, we suggest a better solution later in this chapter in the section entitled "Using MessageSource in Stand-Alone Applications."

Before we continue, if you are unfamiliar with i18n support in Java, we suggest that you at least check out the JavaDocs for the `Locale` and `ResourceBundle` classes.

Using ApplicationContext and MessageSource

Aside from `ApplicationContext`, Spring provides three `MessageSource` implementations: `ResourceBundleMessageSource`, `ReloadableResourceMessageSource`, and `StaticMessageSource`. The `StaticMessageSource` is not really meant to be used in a production application because you can't configure it externally, and this is generally one of the main requirements when you are adding i18n capabilities to your application. The `ResourceBundleMessageSource` loads messages using a Java `ResourceBundle`. `ReloadableResourceMessageSource` is essentially the same, except it supports scheduled reloading of the underlying source files.

All of the implementations, `ApplicationContext` included, implement another interface `HierarchicalMessageSource`, which allows for many `MessageSource` instances to be nested. This is key to the way `ApplicationContext` works with `MessageSources`.

To take advantage of `ApplicationContext`'s support for `MessageSource`, you must define a bean in your configuration of type `MessageSource` and with the name `messageSource`. `ApplicationContext` takes this `MessageSource` and nests it within itself, allowing you to access the messages using the `ApplicationContext`. This can be hard to visualize, so take a look at the following example.

Listing 5-44 shows a simple application that accesses a set of messages for both the English and Czech locales.

Listing 5-44. *Exploring MessageSource Usage*

```
package com.apress.prospring.ch5.context;

import java.util.Locale;

import org.springframework.context.ApplicationContext;
import org.springframework.context.support.FileSystemXmlApplicationContext;
public class MessageSourceDemo {

    public static void main(String[] args) {
        ApplicationContext ctx = new FileSystemXmlApplicationContext(
                "./ch5/src/conf/appContext/messageSource.xml");

        Locale english = Locale.ENGLISH;
        Locale czech = new Locale("cs", "CZ");

        System.out.println(ctx.getMessage("msg", null, english));
        System.out.println(ctx.getMessage("msg", null, czech));

        System.out.println(ctx.getMessage("nameMsg", new Object[] { "Rob",
                "Harrop" }, english));
    }
}
```

Don't worry about the calls to getMessage() just yet; we return to those shortly. For now, just know that they retrieve a keyed message for the locale specified. In Listing 5-45 you can see the configuration used by this application.

Listing 5-45. *Configuring a MessageSource Bean*

```
<!DOCTYPE beans PUBLIC "-//SPRING//DTD BEAN//EN"
"http://www.springframework.org/dtd/spring-beans.dtd">
<beans>
    <bean id="messageSource"
class="org.springframework.context.support.ResourceBundleMessageSource">
            <property name="basenames">
                <list>
                    <value>buttons</value>
                    <value>labels</value>
                </list>
            </property>
    </bean>
</beans>
```

Here we are defining a ResourceBundleMessageSource bean with the name messageSource as required and configuring it with a set of names to form the base of its file set. A Java ResourceBundle, which is used by ResourceBundle, works on a set of properties files that are identified by base names. When looking for a message for a particular Locale, the ResourceBundle looks for a file that is named as a combination of the base name and the Locale name. For instance, if the base name is foo and we are looking for a message in the en-GB (British English) Locale, then the ResourceBundle looks for a file called foo_en_GB.properties.

Running this application (with the appropriate ResourceBundle files created and present in the classpath) yields the following output:

```
The quick brown fox jumped over the lazy dog
Príšerne žlutoucký kun úpel dábelské ódy
My name is Rob Harrop
```

The translation of the Czech is "Terribly yellow horse was groaning devilish odes." Now this example just raises even more questions. What did those calls to getMessage() mean? Why did we use ApplicationContext.getMessage() rather than access the ResourceBundleMessageSource bean directly? We'll answer each of these questions in turn.

The getMessage() Method

The MessageSource interface defines three overloads for the getMessage() method. These are described in Table 5-2.

Table 5-2. *Overloads for MessageSource.getMessage()*

Method Signature	Description
getMessage(String, Object[], Locale)	This is the standard getMessage() method. The String argument is the key of the message corresponding to the key in the properties file. In Listing 5-44, the first call to getMessage() used msg as the key, and this corresponded to the following entry in the properties file for the en locale: msg=The quick brown fox jumped over the lazy dog. The Object[] array argument is used for replacements in the message. In the third call to getMessage() in Listing 5-44, we passed in an array of two Strings. The message that was keyed as nameMsg was My name is {0} {1}. The numbers surrounded in braces are placeholders, and each one is replaced with the corresponding entry in the argument array. The final argument, Locale, tells ResourceBundleMessageSource which properties file to look in. Even though the first and second calls to getMessage() in the example used the same key, they returned different messages that correspond to the Locale that was passed in to getMessage().
getMessage(String, Object[], String, Locale)	This overload works in the same way as getMessage(String, Object[], Locale), other than the second String argument, which allows you to pass in a default value in case a message for the supplied key is not available for the supplied Locale.
getMessage(MessageSourceResolvable, Locale)	This overload is a special case. We discuss it in further detail in the section entitled "The MessageSourceResolvable Interface."

Why Use ApplicationContext as a MessageSource?

To answer this question, we need to jump a little ahead of ourselves and look at the web application support in Spring. The answer, in general, to this question is that you shouldn't use the ApplicationContext as a MessageSource when doing so couples your bean to the ApplicationContext unnecessarily (this is discussed in more detail in the next section). You should use the ApplicationContext when you are building a web application using Spring's MVC framework.

The core interface in Spring MVC is Controller. Unlike frameworks like Struts that require that you implement your controllers by inheriting from a concrete class, Spring simply requires that you implement the Controller interface. Having said that, Spring provides a collection of useful base classes that you will, more often than not, use to implement your own controllers. All of these base classes are themselves subclasses (directly or indirectly) of the ApplicationObjectSupport class.

Remember that in a web application setting, the ApplicationContext is loaded automatically. ApplicationObjectSupport accesses this ApplicationContext, wraps it in a MessageSourceAccessor object, and makes that available to your controller via the protected getMessageSourceAccessor() method. MessageSourceAccessor provides a wide array of convenience methods for working with MessageSources. This form of "auto injection" is quite beneficial; it removes the need for all of your controllers to expose a messageSource property.

However, this is not the best reason for using `ApplicationContext` as a `MessageSource` in your web application. The main reason to use `ApplicationContext` rather than a manually defined `MessageSource` bean is that Spring does, where possible, expose `ApplicationContext`, as a `MessageSource`, to the view tier. This means that when you are using Spring's JSP tag library, the `<spring:message>` tag automatically reads messages from the `ApplicationContext`, and when you are using JSTL, the `<fmt:message>` tag does the same.

All of these benefits mean that it is better to use the `MessageSource` support in `ApplicationContext` when you are building a web application, rather than manage an instance of `MessageSource` separately. This is especially true when you consider that all you need to do to take advantage of this feature is configure a `MessageSource` bean with the name `messageSource`.

Using MessageSource in Stand-Alone Applications

When you are using `MessageSources` in stand-alone applications where Spring offers no additional support other than to nest the `messageSource` bean automatically in the `ApplicationContext`, it is best to make the `MessageSources` available using Dependency Injection. You can opt to make your bean `ApplicationContextAware`, but doing so precludes their use in a `BeanFactory` context. Add to this the fact that you complicate testing without any discernible benefit, and it is clear that you should stick to using Dependency Injection to access `MessageSource` objects in a stand-alone setting.

The MessageSourceResolvable Interface

You can use an `Object` that implements `MessageSourceResolvable` in place of a key and a set of arguments when you are looking up a message from a `MessageSource`. This interface is most widely used in the Spring validation libraries to link `Error` objects to their internationalized error messages. You will see an example of how to use `MessageSourceResolvable` in Chapter 17 when we look at error handling in the Spring MVC library.

Using Application Events

Another feature of the `ApplicationContext` not present in the `BeanFactory` is the ability to publish and receive events using the `ApplicationContext` as a broker. An event is class-derived from `ApplicationEvent`, which itself derives from the `java.util.EventObject`. Any bean can listen for events by implementing the `ApplicationListener` interface; the `ApplicationContext` automatically registers any bean that implements this interface as a listener when it is configured. Events are published using the `ApplicationContext.publishEvent()` method, so the publishing class must have knowledge of the `ApplicationContext`. In a web application, this is simple because many of your classes are derived from Spring framework classes that allow access to the `ApplicationContext` through a protected method. In a stand-alone application, you can have your publishing bean implement `ApplicationContextAware` to enable it to publish events.

Listing 5-46 shows an example of a basic event class.

Listing 5-46. *Creating an Event Class*

```
package com.apress.prospring.ch5.event;

import org.springframework.context.ApplicationEvent;

public class MessageEvent extends ApplicationEvent {

    private String msg;
    public MessageEvent(Object source, String msg) {
        super(source);
        this.msg = msg;
    }

    public String getMessage() {
        return msg;
    }
}
```

This code is quite basic; the only point of note is that the ApplicationEvent has a single constructor that accepts a reference to the source of the event. This is reflected in the constructor for MessageEvent. In Listing 5-47 you can see the code for the listener.

Listing 5-47. *The MessageEventListener Class*

```
package com.apress.prospring.ch5.event;

import org.springframework.context.ApplicationEvent;
import org.springframework.context.ApplicationListener;

public class MessageEventListener implements ApplicationListener {


    public void onApplicationEvent(ApplicationEvent event) {
        if(event instanceof MessageEvent) {
            MessageEvent msgEvt = (MessageEvent)event;
            System.out.println("Received: " + msgEvt.getMessage());
        }
    }
}
```

The ApplicationListener interface defines a single method, onApplicationEvent, that is called by Spring when an event is raised. The MessageEventListener is only interested in events of type MessageEvent, so it checks to see whether the event raised is of that type and, if so, it writes the message to stdout. Publishing events is simple; it is just a matter of creating an instance of the event class and passing it to the ApplicationContext.publishEvent() method, as shown in Listing 5-48.

Listing 5-48. *Publishing an Event*

```java
package com.apress.prospring.ch5.event;

import org.springframework.beans.BeansException;
import org.springframework.context.ApplicationContext;
import org.springframework.context.ApplicationContextAware;
import org.springframework.context.support.FileSystemXmlApplicationContext;

public class Publisher implements ApplicationContextAware {

    private ApplicationContext ctx;

    public static void main(String[] args) {
        ApplicationContext ctx = new FileSystemXmlApplicationContext(
                "./ch5/src/conf/events/events.xml");

        Publisher pub = (Publisher) ctx.getBean("publisher");
        pub.publish("Hello World!");
        pub.publish("The quick brown fox jumped over the lazy dog");
    }

    public void setApplicationContext(ApplicationContext applicationContext)
            throws BeansException {
        this.ctx = applicationContext;

    }

    public void publish(String message) {
        ctx.publishEvent(new MessageEvent(this, message));
    }
}
```

Here you can see that the Publisher class retrieves an instance of itself from the ApplicationContext and then, using the publish() method, publishes two MessageEvents to the ApplicationContext. The Publisher bean instance accesses the ApplicationContext by implementing ApplicationContextAware. Listing 5-49 shows the configuration for this example.

Listing 5-49. *Configuring ApplicationListener Beans*

```xml
<!DOCTYPE beans PUBLIC "-//SPRING//DTD BEAN//EN"
"http://www.springframework.org/dtd/spring-beans.dtd">
<beans>
    <bean id="publisher"
          class="com.apress.prospring.ch5.event.Publisher"/>
    <bean id="messageEventListener"
          class="com.apress.prospring.ch5.event.MessageEventListener"/>
</beans>
```

Notice that you do not need a special configuration to register the `MessageEventListener` with the `ApplicationContext`; it is picked up automatically by Spring. Running this example results in the following output:

```
Received: Hello World!
Received: The quick brown fox jumped over the lazy dog
```

Considerations for Event Usage

There are many cases in an application where certain components need to be notified of certain events. Often you do this by writing code to notify each component explicitly or by using a messaging technology such as JMS. The drawback of writing code to notify each component in turn is that you are coupling those components to the publisher, in many cases unnecessarily.

Consider a situation where you cache product details in your application to avoid trips to the database. Another component allows product details to be modified and persisted to the database. To avoid making the cache invalid, the update component explicitly notifies the cache that the user details have changed. In this example, the update component is coupled to a component that, really, has nothing to do with its business responsibility. A better solution would be to have the update component publish an event every time a product's details are modified, and then have interested components, such as the cache, listen for that event. This has the benefit of keeping the components decoupled, which makes it simple to remove the cache if you need to, or to add another listener that is interested in knowing when a product's details change.

Using JMS in this case would be overkill, because the process of invalidating the product's entry in the cache is quick and is not business critical. The use of the Spring event infrastructure adds very little overhead to your application.

Typically, we use events for reactionary logic that executes quickly and is not part of the main application logic. In the previous example, the invalidation of a product in cache happens in reaction to the updating of product details, it executes quickly (or it should), and it is not part of the main function of the application. For processes that are long running and form part of the main business logic, we prefer to use JMS or similar messaging systems such as MSMQ in the Microsoft world. In a recent project we built an e-commerce system with some complex order fulfillment logic. For this, we chose to use JMS because it is more suited to long-running processes and as the system grows, we can, if necessary, factor the JMS-driven order processing onto a separate machine.

Accessing Resources

Often an application needs to access a variety of resources in different forms. You might need to access some configuration data stored in a file in the file system, some image data stored in a JAR file on the classpath, or maybe some data on a server elsewhere. Spring provides a unified mechanism for accessing resources in a protocol-independent way. This means that your application can access a file resource in the same way, whether it is stored in the file system, the classpath, or on a remote server.

At the core of Spring's resource support is the `Resource` interface. The Resource interface defines seven self-explanatory methods: `exists()`, `getDescription()`, `getFile()`, `getFileName()`, `getInputStream()`, `getURL()`, and `isOpen()`. In addition to these seven methods, there is one that is not quite so self-explanatory: `createRelative()`. The `createRelative()`

method creates a new Resource instance using a path that is relative to the instance on which it is invoked. You can provide your own Resource implementations, although that is outside the scope of this chapter, but in most cases, you use one of the built-in implementations for accessing file, classpath, or URL resources.

Internally, Spring uses another interface, ResourceLoader, and the default implementation, DefaultResourceLoader, to locate and create Resource instances. However, you generally won't interact with DefaultResourceLoader, instead using another ResourceLoader implementation—ApplicationContext.

Listing 5-50 shows a sample application that accesses three resources using ApplicationContext.

Listing 5-50. *Accessing Resources*

```
package com.apress.prospring.ch5.resource;

import org.springframework.context.ApplicationContext;
import org.springframework.context.support.FileSystemXmlApplicationContext;
import org.springframework.core.io.Resource;

public class ResourceDemo {

    public static void main(String[] args) throws Exception{
        ApplicationContext ctx = new FileSystemXmlApplicationContext(
        "./ch5/src/conf/events/events.xml");

        Resource res1 = ctx.getResource("file:///d:/tmp/test.txt");
        displayInfo(res1);
        Resource res2 = ctx.getResource("classpath:lib/commons-logging.jar");
        displayInfo(res2);
        Resource res3 = ctx.getResource("http://www.google.co.uk");
        displayInfo(res3);
    }

    private static void displayInfo(Resource res) throws Exception{
        System.out.println(res.getClass());
        System.out.println(res.getURL().getContent());
        System.out.println("");
    }
}
```

You should note that the configuration file used in this example is unimportant. Notice that in each call to getResource() we pass in a URI for each resource. You will recognize the common file: and http: protocols that we pass in for res1 and res3. The classpath: protocol we use for res2 is Spring-specific and indicates that the ResourceLoader should look in the classpath for the resource. Running this example results in the following output:

```
class org.springframework.core.io.UrlResource
sun.net.www.content.text.PlainTextInputStream@4cee32

class org.springframework.core.io.ClassPathResource
java.io.BufferedInputStream@12b7eea

class org.springframework.core.io.UrlResource
sun.net.www.protocol.http.HttpURLConnection$HttpInputStream@cd5f8b
```

Notice that for both the `file:` and `http:` protocols, Spring returns a `UrlResource` instance. Spring does include a `FileSystemResource` class, but the `DefaultResourceLoader` does not use this class at all. Once a `Resource` instance is obtained, you are free to access the contents as you see fit, using `getFile()`, `getInputStream()`, or `getURL()`. In some cases, such as when you are using the `http:` protocol, the call to `getFile()` results in a `FileNotFoundException`. For this reason, we recommend that you use `getInputStream()` to access resource contents because it is likely to function for all possible resource types.

Summary

In this chapter, you have seen a wide range of Spring-specific features that complement the core IoC capabilities. You saw how to hook into the lifecycle of a bean and to make it aware of the Spring environment. We demonstrated how to use Method Injection to overcome the problem of dealing with beans with incompatible lifecycles, and we introduced `FactoryBeans` as a solution for IoC-enabling a wider set of classes. We also looked at how you can use `PropertyEditors` to simplify application configuration and to remove the need for artificial `String-typed` properties. Finally, we finished with an in-depth look at the additional features offered by the `ApplicationContext` including i18n, event publication, and resource access.

In the next chapter, we will look at the impact IoC, and in particular Dependency Injection, has on the design of the sample application. We will pay particular attention to the amount of up-front design that is required, the compatibility of Spring with test-driven development (TDD) processes, and the realization that Spring allows us to design and build applications the way that we want.

PART 3

■■■

Aspect Oriented Programming with Spring

Introducing Spring AOP

Over the last 18 months, Aspect Oriented Programming (AOP) has become a hot topic in the Java world. Many articles, discussions, and implementations of AOP have become available for Java programmers who want to get into this world. AOP is often referred to as a tool for implementing crosscutting concerns. When you cut through the unfamiliar terminology, this means that you use AOP for modularizing individual pieces of logic, known as **concerns,** and you apply these concerns to many parts of an application. Logging and security are typical examples of crosscutting concerns that are present in many applications. Consider an application that logs the start and end of every method for debugging purposes. You will probably refactor the logging code into a special class, but you still have to call methods on that class twice per method in your application in order to perform the logging. Using AOP, you can simply specify that you want the methods on your logging class to be invoked before and after each method call in your application.

It is important that you understand that AOP complements OOP, rather than competes with it. OOP is very good at solving a wide variety of problems that we, as programmers, encounter. However, if you take the logging example again, it is quite plain to see that OOP is lacking when it comes to implementing crosscutting logic on a large scale. Using AOP on its own to develop an entire application is practically impossible, given that AOP functions on top of OOP. Likewise, although it is certainly possible to develop entire applications using OOP, you can work smarter by employing AOP to solve certain problems that involve crosscutting logic.

We are going to cover AOP in this chapter and the next. In particular, this chapter covers the following topics:

- **AOP basics:** Before we begin discussing Spring's AOP implementation, we cover the basics of AOP as a technology. Most of the concepts covered in this section are not specific to Spring and can be found in any AOP implementation. If you are already familiar with another AOP implementation, then feel free to skip over this section.

- **Types of AOP:** There are two distinct types of AOP, static and dynamic. In static AOP, like that provided by AspectJ (http://eclipse.org/aspectj/), the crosscutting logic is applied to your code at compile time, and you cannot change it without modifying the code and recompiling. With dynamic AOP, like Spring AOP, crosscutting logic is applied dynamically, at runtime. This allows you to make changes in the distribution of crosscutting without recompiling the application. These types of AOP are complementary and, when used together, they form a powerful combination that you can use in your applications.

■Note Static and dynamic AOP are distinct from the static and dynamic crosscutting concepts. The differentiation between static and dynamic crosscutting is largely academic and is of no relevance to Spring AOP. For more information on this topic and on AOP as a whole, we recommend that you read *AspectJ in Action: Practical Aspect-Oriented Programming* by Ramnivas Laddad (Manning, 2003).

- **Spring AOP architecture:** In this section, we get down to the nitty-gritty of Spring's AOP implementation. Spring AOP is only a subset of the full AOP feature-set found in other implementations like AspectJ. In this section, we take a high-level look at which features are present in Spring, how they are implemented, and why some features are excluded from the Spring implementation.

- **Proxies in Spring AOP:** Proxies are a huge part of how Spring AOP works, and you must understand them to get the most out of Spring AOP. In this section, we look at the two different kinds of proxy: JDK dynamic proxy and CGLIB proxy. In particular, we look at the different scenarios in which Spring uses each proxy, the performance of the two proxy types, and some simple guidelines to follow in your application to get the most from Spring AOP.

- **Using Spring AOP:** In this section, we look at some practical examples of AOP usage. We start off with a simple Hello World example to ease you into Spring's AOP code, then we continue with a detailed description of the different AOP features that are available in Spring, complete with examples.

In this chapter, we cover Spring AOP in isolation from much of the rest of the framework. In Chapter 7, we take a much more framework-oriented view of Spring AOP, including how to configure AOP using an `ApplicationContext`.

AOP Concepts

As with most technologies, AOP comes with its own specific set of concepts and terms. It is important that you understand what these terms mean before we explain how to use AOP in an application. The following list explains the core concepts of AOP:

- **Joinpoints:** A **joinpoint** is a well-defined point during the execution of your application. Typical examples of joinpoints include a call to a method, the method invocation itself, class initialization, and object instantiation. Joinpoints are a core concept of AOP and define the points in your application at which you can insert additional logic using AOP.

- **Advice:** The code that is executed at a particular joinpoint is called the **advice**. There are many different types of advice, including **before**, which executes before the joinpoint, and **after**, which executes after it.

- **Pointcuts:** A **pointcut** is a collection of joinpoints that you use to define when advice should be executed. By creating pointcuts, you gain fine-grained control over how you apply advice to the components in your application. As mentioned previously, a typical joinpoint is a method invocation. A typical pointcut is the collection of all method invocations in a particular class. Often you can compose pointcuts in complex relationships to further constrain when advice is executed. We discuss pointcut composition in more detail in the next chapter.

- **Aspects:** An **aspect** is the combination of advice and pointcuts. This combination results in a definition of the logic that should be included in the application and where it should execute.

- **Weaving:** This is the process of actually inserting aspects into the application code at the appropriate point. For compile-time AOP solutions, this is, unsurprisingly, done at compile time, usually as an extra step in the build process. Likewise, for runtime AOP solutions, the weaving process is executed dynamically at runtime.

- **Target:** An object whose execution flow is modified by some AOP process is referred to as the **target object.** Often you see the target object referred to as the **advised object.**

- **Introduction:** This is the process by which you can modify the structure of an object by introducing additional methods or fields to it. You can use introduction to make any object implement a specific interface without needing the object's class to implement that interface explicitly.

Don't worry if you find these concepts confusing; this will all become clear when you see some examples. Also be aware that you are shielded from many of these concepts in Spring AOP and some are not relevant due to Spring's choice of implementation. We will discuss each of these features in the context of Spring as we progress through the chapter.

Types of AOP

As we mentioned earlier, there are two distinct types of AOP: static and dynamic. The difference between them is really the point at which the weaving process occurs and how this process is achieved.

Static AOP

Many of the first AOP implementations were static. In static AOP, the weaving process forms another step in the build process for an application. In Java terms, you achieve the weaving process in a static AOP implementation by modifying the actual bytecode of your application, changing and extending the application code as necessary. Clearly, this is a well-performing way of achieving the weaving process because the end result is just Java bytecode, and you do not perform any special tricks at runtime to determine when advice should be executed.

The drawback of this mechanism is that any modifications you make to the aspects, even if you simply want to add another joinpoint, require you to recompile the entire application. AspectJ is an excellent example of a static AOP implementation.

Dynamic AOP

Dynamic AOP implementations, like Spring AOP, differ from static AOP implementations in that the weaving process is performed dynamically at runtime. How this is achieved is implementation-dependent, but as you will see, Spring's adopted approach is to create proxies for all advised objects, allowing for advice to be invoked as required. The slight drawback of dynamic AOP is that, typically, it does not perform as well as static AOP, but the performance is steadily increasing. The major benefit of dynamic AOP implementations is the ease with which you can modify the entire aspect set of an application without needing to recompile the main application code.

Choosing an AOP Type

Choosing whether to use static or dynamic AOP is actually quite a hard decision. There is no reason for you to choose a single implementation exclusively, because both have their benefits. Indeed, Spring 1.1 introduced features that allow Spring to integrate with AspectJ, allowing you to use both types of AOP with ease. We cover this feature in more detail in Chapter 7. In general, the static AOP implementations have been around longer, and they tend to have more feature-rich implementations, with a greater number of available joinpoints. Indeed, Spring supports only a subset of the features available with AspectJ. Typically, if performance is absolutely critical or you need an AOP feature that is not implemented in Spring, then you will want to use AspectJ. In most other cases, Spring AOP is ideal for what you are trying to achieve. Make sure you are aware that many AOP-based features are already available in Spring, such as declarative transaction management. Reimplementing these using AspectJ is a waste of time and effort, especially since Spring has tried-and-tested implementations ready for you to use.

Most importantly, let the requirements of your application drive your choice of AOP implementation, and don't restrict yourself to a single implementation if a combination of implementations would better suit your application. In general, we have found that Spring AOP is less complex than AspectJ, so it tends to be our first choice. If we find that Spring AOP won't do what we want it to do, or we discover during application tuning that performance is poor, then we move to AspectJ instead.

AOP in Spring

You can think of Spring's AOP implementation as coming in two logical parts. The first part is the AOP core, which provides fully decoupled, purely programmatic AOP functionality. The second part of the AOP implementation is the set of framework services that make AOP easier to use in your applications. On top of this, other components of Spring, such as the transaction manager and EJB helper classes, provide AOP-based services to simplify the development of your application. In this chapter, we focus solely on the basics of the AOP core. The framework services and the advanced functionality of the core are covered in Chapter 7.

Spring AOP is really a subset of the full AOP feature set, implementing only a handful of the constructs available in implementations like AspectJ. Don't be fooled into thinking Spring AOP is not useful, however. Indeed, one of the most powerful aspects of Spring AOP is that it is so simple to use because it is unencumbered with extraneous features that you often do not need. The implementation of only a subset of the AOP feature set is a specific design goal of Spring, allowing Spring to focus on simple access to the most common features of AOP. To make sure that you are not left without the AOP features that you need, in the 1.1 release, Spring's designers designed Spring to fully integrate with AspectJ.

The AOP Alliance

The AOP Alliance (http://aopalliance.sourceforge.net/) is a joint effort between representatives of many open source AOP projects, including Rod Johnson of Spring, to define a standard set of interfaces for AOP implementations. The AOP Alliance is being very conservative, resisting the temptation to over-constrain AOP while it is still growing, and as a result they have only defined interfaces for a subset of AOP features. Wherever applicable, Spring uses the AOP Alliance interfaces rather than defining its own. This allows you to reuse certain advice across multiple AOP implementations that support the AOP Alliance interfaces.

Hello World in AOP

Before we dive into discussing the Spring AOP implementation in detail, we want to present a simple example to provide some context for these discussions. In this example, we take a simple class that outputs the message "World", and then using AOP, we transform an instance of this class at runtime to output "Hello World!" instead. Listing 6-1 shows the basic MessageWriter class.

Listing 6-1. *The MessageWriter Class*

```
package com.apress.prospring.ch6;

public class MessageWriter {

    public void writeMessage() {
        System.out.print("World");
    }
}
```

The MessageWriter class is nothing special; it has just one method that writes the message "World" to stdout. We want to advise—that is, add some advice to—this class so that the writeMessage() method actually writes "Hello World!" instead.

To do this, we need to execute some code before the method body executes to write "Hello", and some code after the method body executes to write "!". In AOP terms, what we need is an **around advice**—that is, advice that executes around a joinpoint. In this case, the joinpoint is the invocation of the writeMessage() method. Listing 6-2 shows the implementation of the around advice, the MessageDecorator class.

Listing 6-2. *Implementing Around Advice*

```
package com.apress.prospring.ch6;

import org.aopalliance.intercept.MethodInterceptor;
import org.aopalliance.intercept.MethodInvocation;

public class MessageDecorator implements MethodInterceptor {

    public Object invoke(MethodInvocation invocation) throws Throwable {
        System.out.print("Hello ");
        Object retVal = invocation.proceed();
        System.out.println("!");
        return retVal;
    }
}
```

The MethodInterceptor interface is the AOP Alliance standard interface for implementing around advice for method invocation joinpoints. The MethodInvocation object represents the method invocation that is being advised, and using this object, we control when the method invocation is actually allowed to proceed. Because this is around advice, we are essentially capable of performing some actions before the method is invoked and some actions after it is invoked but before it returns. In Listing 6-2, we simply write Hello to stdout, invoke the method with a call to MethodInvocation.proceed(), and then write ! to stdout.

The final step in this sample is to weave the MessageDecorator advice into the code. To do this, we create an instance of MessageWriter, the target, and then create a proxy of this instance, instructing the proxy factory to weave in the MessageDecorator advice. This is shown in Listing 6-3.

Listing 6-3. *Weaving the MessageDecorator Advice*

```
package com.apress.prospring.ch6;

import org.springframework.aop.framework.ProxyFactory;

public class HelloWorldAOPExample {

    public static void main(String[] args) {
        MessageWriter target = new MessageWriter();

        // create the proxy
        ProxyFactory pf = new ProxyFactory();

        pf.addAdvice(new MessageDecorator());
        pf.setTarget(target);

        MessageWriter proxy = (MessageWriter) pf.getProxy();
```

```
        // write the messages
        target.writeMessage();
        System.out.println("");
        proxy.writeMessage();
    }
}
```

The important part here is that we use the `ProxyFactory` class to create the proxy of the target object, weaving in the advice at the same time. We pass the `MessageDecorator` advice to the `ProxyFactory` with a call to `addAdvice()` and specify the target for weaving with a call to `setTarget()`. Once the target is set and some advice is added to the `ProxyFactory`, we generate the proxy with a call to `getProxy()`. Finally, we call `writeMessage()` on both the original target object and the proxy object. Here are the results of running this example:

```
World
Hello World!
```

As you can see, calling `writeMessage()` on the untouched target object resulted in a standard method invocation, and no extra content is written to `stdout`. However, the invocation of the proxy caused the code in the `MessageDecorator` to execute, creating the desired output of `Hello World!` From this example, you can see that the advised class had no dependencies on Spring or the AOP Alliance interfaces; the beauty of Spring AOP, and indeed AOP in general, is that you can advise almost any class, even if that class was created without AOP in mind. The only restriction, in Spring AOP at least, is that you can't advise final classes, because they cannot be overridden and therefore cannot be proxied.

Spring AOP Architecture

The core architecture of Spring AOP is based around proxies. When you want to create an advised instance of a class, you must use the `ProxyFactory` class to create a proxy of an instance of that class, first providing the `ProxyFactory` with all the aspects that you want to be woven into the proxy. Using `ProxyFactory` is a purely programmatic approach to creating AOP proxies. For the most part, you don't need to use this in your application; instead you can rely on the `ProxyFactoryBean` class to provide declarative proxy creation. However, it is important to understand how proxy creation works. For the rest of this chapter, we will use the programmatic approach to proxy creation. In the next chapter, we discuss using `ProxyFactoryBean` when creating proxies.

Internally, Spring has two proxy implementations: JDK dynamic proxy and CGLIB proxy. In previous releases of Spring, there was not much difference between the two proxy types, and CGLIB proxies were only used when you wanted to proxy classes rather than interfaces, or when you explicitly specified them. As of the 1.1 release of Spring, the CGLIB proxy is noticeably faster than JDK dynamic proxies in most cases. This is especially true when you are running on a 1.3 VM, which suffers from poor reflection performance. Understanding proxies and how they are used internally is key to getting the best performance out of your application. We discuss proxies in great detail later in the chapter, in the section titled "All About Proxies."

Joinpoints in Spring

One of the more noticeable simplifications in Spring AOP is that it only supports one joinpoint type: method invocation. At first glance, this might seem like a severe limitation if you are familiar with other AOP implementations like AspectJ, which supports many more joinpoints, but in fact this actually makes Spring more accessible.

The method invocation joinpoint is by far the most useful joinpoint available, and using it, you can achieve many of the tasks that make AOP useful in day-to-day programming. Remember that if you need to advise some code at a joinpoint other than a method invocation, you can always use Spring and AspectJ together.

Aspects in Spring

In Spring AOP, an aspect is represented by an instance of a class that implements the `Advisor` interface. Spring provides a selection of convenience `Advisor` implementations that you can use in your applications, thus removing the need for you to create lots of different `Advisor` implementations for your example. There are two subinterfaces of `Advisor`: `IntroductionAdvisor` and `PointcutAdvisor`. The `PointcutAdvisor` interface is implemented by all Advisors that use pointcuts to control the applicability of advice to joinpoints.

In Spring, introductions are treated as special kinds of advice. Using the `IntroductionAdvisor` interface, you can control those classes to which an introduction applies. We cover this in more detail in the next chapter.

We discuss the different `PointcutAdvisor` implementations in detail later in this chapter in the section titled "Advisors and Pointcuts in Spring."

About the ProxyFactory Class

The `ProxyFactory` class controls the weaving and proxy creation process in Spring AOP. Before you can actually create a proxy, you must specify the advised or target object. You can do this, as you saw earlier, using the `setTarget()` method. Internally, `ProxyFactory` delegates the proxy creation process to an instance of `DefaultAopProxyFactory`, which in turn delegates to either `Cglib2AopProxy` or `JdkDynamicAopProxy`, depending on the settings of your application. We discuss proxy creation in more detail later in this chapter.

Using the `ProxyFactory` class, you control which aspects you want to weave into the proxy. As mentioned earlier, you can weave only an aspect—that is, advice combined with a pointcut— into advised code. However, in some cases you want an advice to apply to the invocation of all methods in a class, not just a selection. For this reason, the `ProxyFactory` class provides the `addAdvice()` method that you saw in Listing 6-3. Internally, `addAdvice()` wraps the advice you pass it in an instance of `DefaultPointcutAdvisor`, which is the standard implementation of `PointcutAdvisor`, and configures it with a pointcut that includes all methods by default. When you want more control over the `Advisor` that is created, or when you want to add an introduction to the proxy, create the `Advisor` yourself and use the `addAdvisor()` method of the `ProxyFactory()`.

You can use the same `ProxyFactory` instance to create many different proxies, each with different aspects. To help with this, `ProxyFactory` has `removeAdvice()` and `removeAdvisor()` methods, which allow you to remove any advice or `Advisors` from the `ProxyFactory` that you previously passed to it. To check whether or not a `ProxyFactory` has a particular advice attached to it, call `adviceIncluded()`, passing in the advice object for which you want to check.

Be aware that `ProxyFactory` defines quite a few methods that have deprecated in favor of other methods such as `addAdvice()`. You can find full details of these methods in the JavaDoc. Avoid using the deprecated methods, because they will likely be removed in future versions of Spring, and there is an alternative to each of them. If you stick with the methods used in this book, you will be okay.

Creating Advice in Spring

Spring supports five different flavors of advice, described in Table 6-1.

Table 6-1. *Advice Types in Spring*

Advice Name	Interface	Description
Before	`org.springframework.aop` `.MethodBeforeAdvice`	Using before advice, you can perform custom processing before a joinpoint executes. Because a joinpoint in Spring is always a method invocation, this essentially allows you to perform preprocessing before the method executes. A before advice has full access to the target of the method invocation as well as the arguments passed to the method, but it has no control over the execution of the method itself.
After returning	`org.springframework.aop` `.AfterReturningAdvice`	After returning advice is executed after the method invocation at the joinpoint has finished executing and has returned a value. The after returning advice has access to the target of the method invocation, the arguments passed to the method, and the return value as well. Because the method has already executed when the after returning advice is invoked, it has no control over the method invocation at all.
Around	`org.aopalliance.intercept` `.MethodInterceptor`	In Spring, around advice is modeled using the AOP Alliance standard of a method interceptor. Your advice is allowed to execute before and after the method invocation, and you can control the point at which the method invocation is allowed to proceed. You can choose to bypass the method altogether if you want, providing your own implementation of the logic.
Throws	`org.springframework.aop` `.ThrowsAdvice`	Throws advice is executed after a method invocation returns, but only if that invocation threw an exception. It is possible for a throws advice to catch only specific exceptions, and if you choose to do so, you can access the method that threw the exception, the arguments passed into the invocation, and the target of the invocation.
Introduction	`org.springframework.aop` `.IntroductionInterceptor`	Spring models introductions as special types of interceptors. Using an introduction interceptor, you can specify the implementation for methods that are being introduced by the advice. Introductions are covered in more detail in the next chapter.

We have found that these advice types, coupled with the method invocation joinpoint, allow us to perform about 90 percent of the tasks we want to perform with AOP. For the other 10 percent, which we use only rarely, we fall back on AspectJ.

Interfaces for Advice

From our previous discussion of the ProxyFactory class, recall that advice is added to a proxy either directly, using the addAdvice() method, or using an Advisor, with the addAdvisor() method. In previous releases of Spring, we had an addXXX() method for each type of advice; indeed, these methods are still present, albeit deprecated. Originally, each advice interface was separate from the others, but more recently, a well-defined hierarchy has been created for advice interfaces. This hierarchy is based on the AOP Alliance interfaces and is shown in detail in Figure 6-1.

This kind of hierarchy has the benefit of not only being sound OO design, but it also means that you can deal with advice types generically, as in using a single addAdvice() method on the ProxyFactory, and you can add new advice types easily without having to modify the ProxyFactory class.

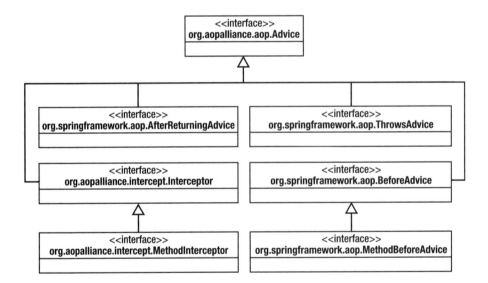

Figure 6-1. *Interfaces for Spring advice types*

Creating Before Advice

Before advice is one of the most useful advice types available in Spring. A before advice can modify the arguments passed to a method and can prevent the method from executing by raising an exception. In the next chapter, you will see before advice used frequently when we look at how AOP is used in the SpringBlog application. In this section, we show you two examples of using before advice: a simple example that writes a message to stdout containing the name of the method before the method executes, and a simple security advice that you can use to restrict access to methods on an object.

In Listing 6-4, you can see the code for the SimpleBeforeAdvice class.

Listing 6-4. *The SimpleBeforeAdvice Class*

```
package com.apress.prospring.ch6;

import java.lang.reflect.Method;

import org.springframework.aop.MethodBeforeAdvice;
import org.springframework.aop.framework.ProxyFactory;

public class SimpleBeforeAdvice implements MethodBeforeAdvice {

    public static void main(String[] args) {
        MessageWriter target = new MessageWriter();

        // create the proxy
        ProxyFactory pf = new ProxyFactory();

        pf.addAdvice(new SimpleBeforeAdvice());
        pf.setTarget(target);

        MessageWriter proxy = (MessageWriter) pf.getProxy();

        // write the messages
        proxy.writeMessage();
    }

    public void before(Method method, Object[] args, Object target)
            throws Throwable {
        System.out.println("Before method: " + method.getName());
    }

}
```

In this code, you can see that we have advised an instance of the MessageWriter class that we created earlier with an instance of the SimpleBeforeAdvice class. The MethodBeforeAdvice interface, which is implemented by SimpleBeforeAdvice, defines a single method, before(), which the AOP framework calls before the method at the joinpoint is invoked. Remember that, for now, we are using the default pointcut provided by the addAdvice() method, which matches all methods in a class. The before() method is passed three arguments: the method that is to be invoked, the arguments that will be passed to that method, and the Object that is the target of the invocation. The SimpleBeforeAdvice class uses the Method argument of the before() method to write a message to stdout containing the name of the method to be invoked. Running this example gives us the following output:

```
Before method: writeMessage
World
```

As you can see, the output from the call to writeMessage() is shown, but just before it, you can see the output generated by the SimpleBeforeAdvice.

Securing Method Access Using Before Advice

The last example was fairly trivial and didn't really show the power of AOP. In this section, we are going to build a before advice that checks user credentials before allowing the method invocation to proceed. If the user credentials are invalid, an exception is thrown by the advice, thus preventing the method from executing. The example in this section is simplistic. It allows users to authenticate with any password, and it also allows only a single, hard-coded user access to the secured methods. However, it does illustrate how easy it is to use AOP to implement a crosscutting concern such as security.

Listing 6-5 shows the SecureBean class. This is the class that we will be securing using AOP.

Listing 6-5. *The SecureBean Class*

```
package com.apress.prospring.ch6.security;

public class SecureBean {

    public void writeSecureMessage() {
        System.out.println("Every time I learn something new, "
                + "it pushes some old stuff out of my brain");
    }
}
```

The SecureBean class imparts a small pearl of wisdom from Homer Simpson, wisdom that we don't want everyone to see. Because this example requires users to authenticate, we are somehow going to need to store their details. Listing 6-6 shows the UserInfo class we use to store a user's credentials.

Listing 6-6. *The UserInfo Class*

```
package com.apress.prospring.ch6.security;

public class UserInfo {
    private String userName;

    private String password;

    public UserInfo(String userName, String password) {
        this.userName = userName;
        this.password = password;
    }

    public String getPassword() {
        return password;
    }
    public String getUserName() {
        return userName;
    }
}
```

There is nothing really of interest in this class; it simply holds data about the user so that we can do something useful with it. Listing 6-7 shows the SecurityManager class, which is responsible for authenticating users and storing their credentials for later retrieval.

Listing 6-7. *The SecurityManager Class*

```
package com.apress.prospring.ch6.security;

public class SecurityManager {

    private static ThreadLocal threadLocal = new ThreadLocal();

    public void login(String userName, String password) {
        // assumes that all credentials
        // are valid for a login
        threadLocal.set(new UserInfo(userName, password));
    }

    public void logout() {
        threadLocal.set(null);
    }

    public UserInfo getLoggedOnUser() {
        return (UserInfo) threadLocal.get();
    }
}
```

The application uses the SecurityManager class to authenticate a user and, later, to retrieve the details of the currently authenticated user. The application authenticates a user using the login() method. In a real application, the login() method would probably check the supplied application against a database or LDAP directory, but here we assume all users are allowed to authenticate. The login() method creates a UserInfo object for the user and stores it on the current thread using a ThreadLocal. The logout() method sets any value that might be stored in the ThreadLocal to null. Finally, the getLoggedOnUser() method returns the UserInfo object for the currently authenticated user. This method returns null if no user is authenticated.

In order to check whether or not a user is authenticated and if so, whether or not the user is permitted to access the methods on SecureBean, we need to create an advice that executes before the method and checks the UserInfo object returned by SecurityManager.getLoggedOnUser() against the set of credentials for allowed users. The code for this advice, SecurityAdvice, is shown in Listing 6-8.

Listing 6-8. *The SecurityAdvice Class*

```
package com.apress.prospring.ch6.security;

import java.lang.reflect.Method;

import org.springframework.aop.MethodBeforeAdvice;

public class SecurityAdvice implements MethodBeforeAdvice {

    private SecurityManager securityManager;

    public SecurityAdvice() {
        this.securityManager = new SecurityManager();
    }

    public void before(Method method, Object[] args, Object target)
            throws Throwable {
        UserInfo user = securityManager.getLoggedOnUser();

        if (user == null) {
            System.out.println("No user authenticated");
            throw new SecurityException(
                    "You must login before attempting to invoke the method: "
                            + method.getName());
        } else if ("robh".equals(user.getUserName())) {
            System.out.println("Logged in user is robh - OKAY!");
        } else {
            System.out.println("Logged in user is " + user.getUserName()
                    + " NOT GOOD :(");
            throw new SecurityException("User " + user.getUserName()
                    + " is not allowed access to method " + method.getName());
        }

    }

}
```

The SecurityAdvice class creates an instance of SecurityManager in its constructor and then stores this instance in a field. You should note that the application and the SecurityAd-vice don't need to share the same SecurityManager instance, because all data is stored with the current thread using ThreadLocal. In the before() method, we perform a simple check to see if the user name of the authenticated user is robh. If so, we allow the user access; otherwise, an exception is raised. Also notice that we check for a null UserInfo object, which indicates that the current user is not authenticated.

In Listing 6-9, you can see a sample application that uses the SecurityAdvice class to secure the SecureBean class.

Listing 6-9. *The SecurityExample Class*

```java
package com.apress.prospring.ch6.security;

import org.springframework.aop.framework.ProxyFactory;

public class SecurityExample {

    public static void main(String[] args) {
        // get the security manager
        SecurityManager mgr = new SecurityManager();

        // get the bean
        SecureBean bean = getSecureBean();

        // try as robh
        mgr.login("robh", "pwd");
        bean.writeSecureMessage();
        mgr.logout();

        // try as janm
        try {
            mgr.login("janm", "pwd");
            bean.writeSecureMessage();
        } catch(SecurityException ex) {
            System.out.println("Exception Caught: " + ex.getMessage());
        } finally {
            mgr.logout();
        }

        // try with no credentials
        try {
            bean.writeSecureMessage();
        } catch(SecurityException ex) {
            System.out.println("Exception Caught: " + ex.getMessage());
        }

    }

    private static SecureBean getSecureBean() {
        // create the target
        SecureBean target = new SecureBean();

        // create the advice
        SecurityAdvice advice = new SecurityAdvice();
```

```
            // get the proxy
            ProxyFactory factory = new ProxyFactory();
            factory.setTarget(target);
            factory.addAdvice(advice);
            SecureBean proxy = (SecureBean)factory.getProxy();

            return proxy;

        }
    }
```

In the getSecureBean() method, we create a proxy of the SecureBean class that is advised using an instance of SecurityAdvice. This proxy is returned to the caller. When the caller invokes any method on this proxy, the call is first routed to the instance of SecurityAdvice for a security check. In the main() method, we test three different scenarios, invoking the SecureBean.writeSecureMessage() method with two different sets of user credentials and then no user credentials at all. Because the SecurityAdvice only allows method calls to proceed if the currently authenticated user is robh, we expect that the only successful scenario in Listing 6-9 is the first of these scenarios. Running this example gives the following output:

```
Logged in user is robh - OKAY!
Every time I learn something new, it pushes some old stuff out of my brain
Logged in user is janm NOT GOOD :(
Exception Caught: User janm is not allowed access to method writeSecureMessage
No user authenticated
Exception Caught: You must login before attempting to invoke the method:➥
writeSecureMessage
```

As you can see, only the first invocation of SecureBean.writeSecureMessage() was allowed to proceed. The remaining invocations were prevented by the SecurityException thrown by the SecurityAdvice.

This example is simple, but it does highlight the usefulness of the before advice. Security is a typical example of before advice, but we also find it useful when a scenario demands the modification of arguments going into the method. In Chapter 7, we show you how to use before advice to create an obscenity filter for the SpringBlog application.

Creating After Returning Advice

As its name implies, after returning advice is executed after the method invocation at the join-point returns. Given that the method has already executed, you can't change the arguments that are passed to it. Although you can read these, you can't change the execution path, nor can you prevent the method from executing. These restrictions are expected; what is not expected, however, is the fact that you cannot modify the return value in the after returning advice; you are simply restricted to performing some additional processing. Although after returning advice cannot modify the return value of a method invocation, it can throw an exception that can be sent up the stack instead of the return value.

In this section, we look at two examples of using after returning advice in an application. The first example simply writes a message to stdout after the method has been invoked. The second example shows how you can use after returning advice to add additional error checking to a method. Consider a class, KeyGenerator, that generates keys for cryptographic purposes. Many cryptographic algorithms suffer from the problem that a small number of keys in the keyspace are considered weak. A weak key is any key whose characteristics make it significantly easier to derive the original message without knowing the key. For the DES algorithm, there are a total of 2^{56} possible keys. From this keyspace, 4 keys are considered weak and another 12 are considered semi-weak. Although the chance of one of these keys being generated randomly is ridiculously small (1 in 2^{52}), testing for the keys is so simple that it seems almost lax to ignore the test. In the second example of this section, we build an after returning advice that checks for weak keys generated by the KeyGenerator and raises an exception if one is found.

■**Note** For more information on weak keys and cryptography at large, we recommend that you read *Applied Cryptography* by Bruce Schneier (Wiley, 1995).

In Listing 6-10, you can see the SimpleAfterReturningAdvice class, which demonstrates the use of after returning advice by writing a message to stdout after a method has returned.

Listing 6-10. *The SimpleAfterReturningAdvice Class*

```
package com.apress.prospring.ch6;

import java.lang.reflect.Method;

import org.springframework.aop.AfterReturningAdvice;
import org.springframework.aop.framework.ProxyFactory;

public class SimpleAfterReturningAdvice implements AfterReturningAdvice {

    public static void main(String[] args) {
        MessageWriter target = new MessageWriter();

        // create the proxy
        ProxyFactory pf = new ProxyFactory();

        pf.addAdvice(new SimpleAfterReturningAdvice());
        pf.setTarget(target);

        MessageWriter proxy = (MessageWriter) pf.getProxy();

        // write the messages
        proxy.writeMessage();
    }
```

```
    public void afterReturning(Object returnValue, Method method, Object[] args,
            Object target) throws Throwable {
        System.out.println("");
        System.out.println("After method: " + method.getName());
    }
}
```

This example is really not that different from the SimpleBeforeAdvice class that you saw earlier. Notice that the AfterReturningAdvice interface declares a single method, afterReturning(), which is passed the return value of method invocation, a reference to the method that was invoked, the arguments that were passed to the method, and the target of the invocation. Running this example results in the following output:

```
World
After method: writeMessage
```

The output is very similar to that of the before advice example except that, as expected, the message written by the advice appears after the message written by the writeMessage() method.

A good use of after returning advice is to perform some additional error checking when it is possible for a method to return an invalid value. In the scenario we described earlier, it is possible for a cryptographic key generator to generate a key that is considered weak for a particular algorithm. Ideally, the key generator would check for these weak keys, but since the chance of these keys arising is often very small, many generators do not check. By using an after returning advice, we can advise the method that generates the key and performs this additional check. Listing 6-11 shows an extremely primitive key generator.

Listing 6-11. *The KeyGenerator Class*

```
package com.apress.prospring.ch6.crypto;

import java.util.Random;

public class KeyGenerator {

    public static final long WEAK_KEY = 0xFFFFFFFF0000000L;
    public static final long STRONG_KEY = 0xACDF03F590AE56L;

    private Random rand = new Random();

    public long getKey() {
        int x = rand.nextInt(3);

        if(x == 1) {
            return WEAK_KEY;
        } else {
            return STRONG_KEY;
        }
    }
}
```

It is plain to see that this key generator is ridiculously insecure, but we didn't want you to have to wait around for years while a real key generator produced a weak key, so we created this generator, which has a 1-in-3 chance of producing a weak key. In Listing 6-12, you can see the WeakKeyCheckAdvice that checks to see if the result of the getKey() method is a weak key.

Listing 6-12. *Checking for Weak Keys*

```
package com.apress.prospring.ch6.crypto;

import java.lang.reflect.Method;

import org.springframework.aop.AfterReturningAdvice;

public class WeakKeyCheckAdvice implements AfterReturningAdvice {

    public void afterReturning(Object returnValue, Method method,
            Object[] args, Object target) throws Throwable {

        if ((target instanceof KeyGenerator)
                && ("getKey".equals(method.getName()))) {
            long key = ((Long) returnValue).longValue();

            if (key == KeyGenerator.WEAK_KEY) {
                throw new SecurityException(
                        "Key Generator generated a weak key. Try again");
            }
        }
    }
}
```

In the afterReturning() method, we check first to see if the method that was executed at the joinpoint was the getKey() method. If so, we then check the result value to see if it was the weak key. If we find that the result of the getKey() method was a weak key, then we throw a SecurityException to inform the calling code of this. Listing 6-13 shows a simple application that demonstrates the use of this advice.

Listing 6-13. *Testing the WeakKeyCheckAdvice Class*

```
package com.apress.prospring.ch6.crypto;

import org.springframework.aop.framework.ProxyFactory;

public class AfterAdviceExample {
```

```
    public static void main(String[] args) {
        KeyGenerator keyGen = getKeyGenerator();

        for(int x = 0; x < 10; x++) {
            try {
                long key = keyGen.getKey();
                System.out.println("Key: " + key);
            } catch(SecurityException ex) {
                System.out.println("Weak Key Generated!");
            }
        }

    }

    private static KeyGenerator getKeyGenerator() {

        KeyGenerator target = new KeyGenerator();

        ProxyFactory factory = new ProxyFactory();
        factory.setTarget(target);
        factory.addAdvice(new WeakKeyCheckAdvice());

        return (KeyGenerator)factory.getProxy();
    }
}
```

After creating an advised proxy of a KeyGenerator target, the AfterAdviceExample class attempts to generate ten keys. If a SecurityException is thrown during a single generation, then a message is written to stdout informing the user that a weak key was generated, otherwise the generated key is displayed. A single run of this on our machine generated the following output:

```
Weak Key Generated!
Key: 48658904092028502
Key: 48658904092028502
Key: 48658904092028502
Key: 48658904092028502
Key: 48658904092028502
Weak Key Generated!
Weak Key Generated!
Key: 48658904092028502
Weak Key Generated!
```

As you can see, the KeyGenerator class sometimes generates weak keys, as expected, and the WeakKeyCheckAdvice ensures that a SecurityException is raised whenever a weak key is encountered.

Creating Around Advice

Around advice functions like a combination of before and after advice, with one big difference—you can modify the return value. Not only that, you can also prevent the method from actually executing. This means that using around advice, you can essentially replace the entire implementation of a method with new code. Around advice in Spring is modeled as an interceptor using the MethodInterceptor interface. There are many uses for around advice, and you will find that many features of Spring are created using method interceptors, such as the remote proxy support and the transaction management features. Method interception is also a good mechanism for profiling the execution of your application, and it forms the basis of the example in this section.

We are not going to build a simple example for method interception; instead, we refer back to the first example in Listing 6-2, which shows how to use a basic method interceptor to write out a message on either side of a method invocation. Notice from this earlier example that the invoke() method of the MethodInterceptor class does not provide the same set of arguments as the MethodBeforeAdvice and AfterReturningAdvice—that is, the method is not passed the target of the invocation, the method that was invoked, or the arguments used. However, you can get access to this data using the MethodInvocation object that is passed to invoke(). You will see a demonstration of this in the following example.

For this example, we want to achieve some way to advise a class so that we get basic information about the runtime performance of its methods. Specifically, we want to know how long the method took to execute. To achieve this, we can use the StopWatch class included in Spring, and we clearly need a MethodInterceptor, because we need to start the StopWatch before the method invocation and stop it right afterward.

Listing 6-14 shows the WorkerBean class that we are going to profile using the StopWatch class and an around advice.

Listing 6-14. *The WorkerBean Class*

```
package com.apress.prospring.ch6.profiling;

public class WorkerBean {

    public void doSomeWork(int noOfTimes) {
        for(int x = 0; x < noOfTimes; x++) {
            work();
        }
    }

    private void work() {
        System.out.print("");
    }
}
```

This is a very simple class. The doSomeWork() method accepts a single argument, noOfTimes, and calls the work() method exactly the number of times specified by this method. The work() method simply has a dummy call to System.out.print(), which passes in an empty String. This prevents the compiler from optimizing out the work() method, and thus the call to work().

In Listing 6-15, you can see the ProfilingInterceptor class that uses the StopWatch class to profile method invocation times. We use this interceptor to profile the WorkerBean class shown in Listing 6-14.

Listing 6-15. *The ProfilingInterceptor Class*

```
package com.apress.prospring.ch6.profiling;

import java.lang.reflect.Method;

import org.aopalliance.intercept.MethodInterceptor;
import org.aopalliance.intercept.MethodInvocation;
import org.springframework.util.StopWatch;

public class ProfilingInterceptor implements MethodInterceptor {

    public Object invoke(MethodInvocation invocation) throws Throwable {
        // start the stop watch
        StopWatch sw = new StopWatch();
        sw.start(invocation.getMethod().getName());

        Object returnValue = invocation.proceed();

        sw.stop();
        dumpInfo(invocation, sw.getTotalTimeMillis());
        return returnValue;
    }

    private void dumpInfo(MethodInvocation invocation, long ms) {
        Method m = invocation.getMethod();
        Object target = invocation.getThis();
        Object[] args = invocation.getArguments();

        System.out.println("Executed method: " + m.getName());
        System.out.println("On object of type: " + target.getClass().getName());

        System.out.println("With arguments:");
        for (int x = 0; x < args.length; x++) {
            System.out.print("    > " + args[x]);
        }
        System.out.print("\n");

        System.out.println("Took: " + ms + " ms");
    }
}
```

In the invoke() method, which is the only method in the MethodInterceptor interface, we create an instance of StopWatch and then start it running immediately, allowing the method

invocation to proceed with a call to MethodInvocation.proceed(). As soon as the method invocation has ended and the return value has been captured, we stop the StopWatch and pass the
total number of milliseconds taken, along with the MethodInvocation object, to the dumpInfo()
method. Finally, we return the Object returned by MethodInvocation.proceed() so that the
caller obtains the correct return value. In this case, we did not want to disrupt the call stack in
any way; we were simply acting as an eavesdropper on the method invocation. If we had
wanted to, we could have changed the call stack completely, redirecting the method call to
another object or a remote service, or we could simply have reimplemented the method logic
inside the interceptor and returned a different return value.

The dumpInfo() method simply writes some information about the method call to stdout,
along with the time taken for the method to execute. In the first three lines of dumpInfo(), you
can see how you can use the MethodInvocation object to determine the method that was invoked,
the original target of the invocation, and the arguments used.

Listing 6-16 shows the ProfilingExample class that first advises an instance of WorkerBean
with a ProfilingInterceptor and then profiles the doSomeWork() method.

Listing 6-16. *The ProfilingExample Class*

```java
package com.apress.prospring.ch6.profiling;

import org.springframework.aop.framework.ProxyFactory;

public class ProfilingExample {

    public static void main(String[] args) {
        WorkerBean bean = getWorkerBean();
        bean.doSomeWork(10000000);
    }

    private static WorkerBean getWorkerBean() {
        WorkerBean target = new WorkerBean();

        ProxyFactory factory = new ProxyFactory();
        factory.setTarget(target);
        factory.addAdvice(new ProfilingInterceptor());

        return (WorkerBean)factory.getProxy();
    }
}
```

You should be more than familiar with this code by now. Running this example on our
machine produces the following output:

```
Executed method: doSomeWork
On object of type: com.apress.prospring.ch6.profiling.WorkerBean
With arguments:
    > 10000000
Took: 4141 ms
```

From this output, you can see which method was executed, what the class of the target was, what arguments were passed in, and how long the invocation took.

Creating Throws Advice

Throws advice is similar to after returning advice in that it executes after the joinpoint, which is always a method invocation, but throws advice only executes if the method threw an exception. Throws advice is also similar to after returning advice in that it has little control over program execution. If you are using a throws advice, you can't choose to ignore the exception that was raised and return a value for the method instead. The only modification you can make to the program flow is to change the type of exception that is thrown. This is actually quite a powerful idea and can make application development much simpler. Consider a situation where you have an API that throws an array of poorly defined exceptions. Using a throws advice, you can advise all classes in that API and reclassify the exception hierarchy into something more manageable and descriptive. Of course, you can also use throws advice to provide centralized error logging across your application, thus reducing the amount of error logging code that is spread across your application.

As you saw from the diagram in Figure 6-1, throws advice is implemented by the ThrowsAdvice interface. Unlike the interfaces you have seen so far, ThrowsAdvice does not define any methods; instead, it is simply a marker interface used by Spring. The reason for this is that Spring allows typed throws advice, which allows you to define exactly which Exception types your throws advice should catch. Spring achieves this by detecting methods with certain signatures using reflection. Spring looks for two distinct method signatures. This is best demonstrated with a simple example. Listing 6-17 shows a simple bean with two methods that both simply throw exceptions of different types.

Listing 6-17. *The ErrorBean Class*

```
package com.apress.prospring.ch6;

public class ErrorBean {

    public void errorProneMethod() throws Exception {
        throw new Exception("Foo");
    }

    public void otherErrorProneMethod() throws IllegalArgumentException {
        throw new IllegalArgumentException("Bar");
    }
}
```

In Listing 6-18, you can see the SimpleThrowsAdvice class that demonstrates both of the method signatures that Spring looks for on a throws advice.

Listing 6-18. *The SimpleThrowsAdvice Class*

```java
package com.apress.prospring.ch6;

import java.lang.reflect.Method;

import org.springframework.aop.ThrowsAdvice;
import org.springframework.aop.framework.ProxyFactory;

public class SimpleThrowsAdvice implements ThrowsAdvice {

    public static void main(String[] args) throws Exception {
        ErrorBean errorBean = new ErrorBean();

        ProxyFactory pf = new ProxyFactory();
        pf.setTarget(errorBean);
        pf.addAdvice(new SimpleThrowsAdvice());

        ErrorBean proxy = (ErrorBean) pf.getProxy();

        try {
            proxy.errorProneMethod();
        } catch (Exception ignored) {

        }

        try {
            proxy.otherErrorProneMethod();
        } catch (Exception ignored) {

        }

    }

    public void afterThrowing(Exception ex) throws Throwable {
        System.out.println("***");
        System.out.println("Generic Exception Capture");
        System.out.println("Caught: " + ex.getClass().getName());
        System.out.println("***\n");
    }

    public void afterThrowing(Method method, Object[] args, Object target,
            IllegalArgumentException ex) throws Throwable {
        System.out.println("***");
        System.out.println("IllegalArgumentException Capture");
        System.out.println("Caught: " + ex.getClass().getName());
        System.out.println("Method: " + method.getName());
        System.out.println("***\n");
    }
}
```

We are sure that you understand the code in the main() method, so now we will just focus on the two afterThrowing() methods. The first thing Spring looks for in a throws advice is one or more public methods called afterThrowing(). The return type of the methods is unimportant, although we find it best to stick with void because this method can't return any meaningful value. The first afterThrowing() method in the SimpleThrowsAdvice class has a single argument of type Exception. You can specify any type of Exception as the argument, and this method is ideal when you are not concerned about the method that threw the exception or the arguments that were passed to it. Note that this method catches Exception and any subtypes of Exception unless the type in question has its own afterThrowing() method.

In the second afterThrowing() method, we declared four arguments to catch the Method that threw the exception, the arguments that were passed to the method, and the target of the method invocation. The order of the arguments in this method is important, and you must specify all four. Notice that the second afterThrowing() method catches exceptions of type IllegalArgumentException (or its subtype). Running this example produces the following output:

```
***
Generic Exception Capture
Caught: java.lang.Exception
***

***
IllegalArgumentException Capture
Caught: java.lang.IllegalArgumentException
Method: otherErrorProneMethod
***
```

As you can see, when a plain old Exception is thrown, the first afterThrowing() method is invoked, but when an IllegalArgumentException is thrown, the second afterThrowing() method is invoked. Spring only invokes a single afterThrowing() method for each Exception and, as you saw from the example in Listing 6-18, Spring uses the method whose signature contains the best match for the Exception type. In the situation where your after throwing advice has two afterThrowing() methods, both declared with the same Exception type but one with a single argument and the other with four arguments, Spring invokes the four-argument afterThrowing() method.

As we mentioned earlier, after throwing advice is useful in a variety of situations; it allows you to reclassify entire Exception hierarchies as well as build centralized Exception logging for your application. We have found that after throwing advice is particularly useful when we are debugging a live application, because it allows us to add extra logging code without needing to modify the application's code.

Choosing an Advice Type

In general, the choice of which advice type you want to use is driven by the requirements of your application, but you should choose the most specific advice type for your need. That is to say, don't use an around advice when a before advice will do. In most cases, an around advice can accomplish everything that the other three advice types can, but it may be overkill for what you are trying to achieve. By using the most specific type of advice, you are making the intention of your code clearer and you are also reducing the possibility of errors. Consider an advice that counts method calls. When you are using before advice, all you need to code is the counter, but with an around advice, you need to remember to invoke the method and return the value to the caller. These small things can allow spurious errors to creep into your application. By keeping the advice type as focused as possible, you reduce the scope for errors.

Advisors and Pointcuts in Spring

Thus far, all the examples you have seen have used the `ProxyFactory.addAdvice()` method to configure advice for a proxy. As we mentioned earlier, this method delegates to `addAdvisor()` behind the scenes, creating an instance of `DefaultPointcutAdvisor` and configuring it with a pointcut that points to all methods. In this way, the advice is deemed to apply to all methods on the target. In some cases, such as when you are using AOP for logging purposes, this may be desirable, but in other cases you may want to limit the methods to which an advice applies.

Of course, you could simply check in advice itself that the method that is being advised is the correct one, but this approach has several drawbacks. First, hard coding the list of acceptable methods into the advice reduces the advice's reusability. By using pointcuts, you can configure the methods to which an advice applies, without needing to put this code inside the advice; this clearly increases the reuse value of the advice. The second and third drawbacks with hard coding the list of methods into the advice are performance related. To check the method being advised in the advice, you need to perform the check each time any method on the target is invoked. This clearly reduces the performance of your application. When you use pointcuts, the check is performed once for each method and the results are cached for later use. The other performance-related drawback of not using pointcuts to restrict the list-advised methods is that Spring can make optimizations for non-advised methods when creating a proxy, which results in faster invocations on non-advised methods. These optimizations are covered in greater detail when we discuss proxies later in the chapter.

We would strongly recommend that you avoid the temptation to hard code method checks into your advice and instead use pointcuts wherever possible to govern the applicability of advice to methods on the target. That said, in some cases it is necessary to hard code the checks into your advice. Consider the earlier example of the after returning advice designed to catch weak keys generated by the `KeyGenerator` class. This kind of advice is closely coupled to the class it is advising and it is wise to check inside the advice to ensure that it is applied to the incorrect type. We refer to this coupling between advice and target as **target affinity**. In general, you should use pointcuts when your advice has little or no target affinity—that is, it can apply to any type or a wide range of types. When your advice has strong target affinity, try to check that the advice is being used correctly in the advice itself; this helps reduce head-scratching errors when an advice is misused. We also recommend that you avoid advising methods needlessly. As you will see, this results in a noticeable drop in invocation speed that can have a large impact on the overall performance of your application.

The Pointcut Interface

Pointcuts in Spring are created by implementing the `Pointcut` interface, as shown in Listing 6-19.

Listing 6-19. *The Pointcut Interface*

```
public interface Pointcut {

    ClassFilter getClassFilter ();

    MethodMatcher getMethodMatcher();
}
```

As you can see from this code, the Pointcut interface defines two methods, getClassFilter() and getMethodMatcher(), which return instances of ClassFilter and MethodMatcher, respectively. When creating your own pointcuts from scratch, you must implement both the ClassFilter and MethodMatcher interfaces as well. Thankfully, as you will see in the next section, this is usually unnecessary because Spring provides a selection of Pointcut implementations that cover almost if not all of your use cases.

When determining whether a Pointcut applies to a particular method, Spring first checks to see if the Pointcut applies to the method's class using the ClassFilter instance returned by Pointcut.getClassFilter(). Listing 6-20 shows the ClassFilter interface.

Listing 6-20. *The ClassFilter Interface*

```
public interface ClassFilter {

    boolean matches(Class clazz);
}
```

As you can see, the ClassFilter interface defines a single method, matches(), that is passed an instance of Class that represents the class to be checked. As you have no doubt determined, the matches() method returns true if the pointcut applies to the class and false otherwise.

The MethodMatcher interface is more complex than the ClassFilter interface, as is shown in Listing 6-21.

Listing 6-21. *The MethodMatcher Interface*

```
public interface MethodMatcher {

    boolean matches(Method m, Class targetClass);

    boolean isRuntime();

    boolean matches(Method m, Class targetClass, Object[] args);

}
```

Spring supports two different types of `MethodMatcher`, static and dynamic, determined by the return value of `isRuntime()`. Before using a `MethodMatcher`, Spring calls `isRuntime()` to determine whether the `MethodMatcher` is static, indicated by a return value of `false`, or dynamic, indicated by a return value of `true`.

For a static pointcut, Spring calls the `matches(Method, Class)` method of the `MethodMatcher` once for every method on the target, caching the return value for subsequent invocations of those methods. In this way, the check for method applicability is performed only once for each method and subsequent invocations of a method do not result in an invocation of `matches()`.

With dynamic pointcuts, Spring still performs a static check using `matches(Method, Class)` the first time a method is invoked to determine the overall applicability of a method. However, in addition to this and provided that the static check returned `true`, Spring performs a further check for each invocation of a method using the `matches(Method, Class, Object[])` method. In this way, a dynamic `MethodMatcher` can determine whether a pointcut should apply based on a particular invocation of a method, not just on the method itself.

Clearly, static pointcuts—that is, pointcuts whose `MethodMatcher` is static—perform much better than dynamic pointcuts because they avoid the need for an additional check per invocation. That said, dynamic pointcuts provide a greater level of flexibility for deciding whether to apply an advice. In general, we recommend that you use static pointcuts wherever you can. However, in cases where your advice adds substantial overhead, it may be wise to avoid any unnecessary invocations of your advice by using a dynamic pointcut.

In general, you rarely create your own `Pointcut` implementations from scratch because Spring provides abstract base classes for both static and dynamic pointcuts. We look at these base classes, along with other `Pointcut` implementations, over the next few sections.

Available Pointcut Implementations

Spring provides seven implementations of the `Pointcut` interface: two abstract classes intended as convenience classes for creating static and dynamic pointcuts; and five concrete classes, one for composing multiple pointcuts together, one for handling control flow pointcuts, one for performing simple name-based matching, and two for defining pointcuts using regular expressions. These implementations are summarized in Table 6-2.

Table 6-2. *Summary of Spring Pointcut Implementations*

Implementation Class	Description
`org.springframework.aop` `.support.ComposablePointcut`	The `ComposablePointcut` class is used to compose two or more pointcuts together with operations such as `union()` and `intersection()`. This class is covered in more detail in the next chapter.
`org.springframework.aop` `.support.ControlFlowPointcut`	The `ControlFlowPointcut` is a special case pointcut that matches all methods within the **control flow** of another method—that is, any method that is invoked either directly or indirectly as the result of another method being invoked. We cover `ControlFlowPointcut` in more detail in the next chapter.
`org.springframework.aop.support` `.DynamicMethodMatcherPointcut`	The `DynamicMethodMatcherPointcut` is intended as a base class for building dynamic pointcuts.

Table 6-2. *Summary of Spring Pointcut Implementations (Continued)*

Implementation Class	Description
org.springframework.aop.support .JdkRegexpMethodPointcut	The JdkRexepMethodPointcut allows you to define pointcuts using JDK 1.4 regular expression support. This class requires JDK 1.4 or higher.
org.springframework.aop.support .NameMatchMethodPointcut	Using the NameMatchMethodPointcut, you can create a pointcut that performs simple matching against a list of method names.
org.springframework.aop.support .Perl5RegexpMethodPointcut	The Perl5RegexpMethodPointcut allows you to define pointcuts using Perl 5 regular expression syntax. This class depends on the Jakarta ORO project and can be used on JDKs older than 1.4.
org.springframework.aop .StaticMethodMatcherPointcut	The StaticMethodMatcherPointcut class is intended as a base for building static pointcuts.

We cover the five basic implementations in detail in the following sections. We leave discussions of the more advanced ComposablePointcut and ControlFlowPointcut classes until the next chapter.

Using DefaultPointcutAdvisor

Before you can use any Pointcut implementation, you must first create an Advisor, or more specifically a PointcutAdvisor. Remember from our earlier discussions that an Advisor is Spring's representation of an aspect, a coupling of advice and pointcuts that governs which methods should be advised and how they should be advised. Spring provides four implementations of PointcutAdvisor, but for now we concern ourselves we just one— DefaultPointcutAdvisor. DefaultPointcutAdvisor is a simple PointcutAdvisor for associating a single Pointcut with a single Advice.

Creating a Static Pointcut Using StaticMethodMatcherPointcut

In this section, we we will create a simple static pointcut using the StaticMethodMatcherPointcut class as a base. StaticMethodMatcherPointcut requires you to implement only a single method, matches(Method, Class); the rest of the Pointcut implementation is handled automatically. Although this is the only method you are required to implement, you may also want to override the getClassFilter() method as we do in this example to ensure that only methods of the correct type get advised.

For this example, we have two classes, BeanOne and BeanTwo, with identical methods defined in both. Listing 6-22 shows the BeanOne class.

Listing 6-22. *The BeanOne Class*

```
package com.apress.prospring.ch6.staticpc;

public class BeanOne {

    public void foo() {
        System.out.println("foo");
    }

    public void bar() {
        System.out.println("bar");
    }
}
```

The BeanTwo class has identical methods to BeanOne. With this example, we want to be able to create a proxy of both classes using the same DefaultPointcutAdvisor, but have the advice apply to only the foo() method of the BeanOne class. To do this, we created the SimpleStaticPointcut class, as shown in Listing 6-23.

Listing 6-23. *The SimpleStaticPointcut Class*

```
package com.apress.prospring.ch6.staticpc;

import java.lang.reflect.Method;

import org.springframework.aop.ClassFilter;
import org.springframework.aop.support.StaticMethodMatcherPointcut;

public class SimpleStaticPointcut extends StaticMethodMatcherPointcut {

    public boolean matches(Method method, Class cls) {
        return ("foo".equals(method.getName()));
    }

    public ClassFilter getClassFilter() {
        return new ClassFilter() {
            public boolean matches(Class cls) {
                return (cls == BeanOne.class);
            }
        };

    }
}
```

Here you can see that we implemented the matches(Method, Class) method as required by the StaticMethodMatcher base class. The implementation simply returns true if the name of the method is foo, otherwise it returns false. Notice that we have also overridden the getClassFilter() method to return a ClassFilter instance whose matches() method only returns true for the BeanOne class. With this static pointcut, we are saying that only methods of the BeanOne class will be matched, and furthermore, only the foo() method of that class will be matched.

Listing 6-24 shows the SimpleAdvice class that simply writes out a message on either side of the method invocation.

Listing 6-24. *The SimpleAdvice Class*

```
package com.apress.prospring.ch6.staticpc;

import org.aopalliance.intercept.MethodInterceptor;
import org.aopalliance.intercept.MethodInvocation;

public class SimpleAdvice implements MethodInterceptor {

    public Object invoke(MethodInvocation invocation) throws Throwable {
        System.out.println(">> Invoking " + invocation.getMethod().getName());
        Object retVal = invocation.proceed();
        System.out.println(">> Done");
        return retVal;
    }
}
```

In Listing 6-25, you can see a simple driver application for this example that creates an instance of DefaultPointcutAdvisor using the SimpleAdvice and SimpleStaticPointcut classes.

Listing 6-25. *The StaticPointcutExample Class*

```
package com.apress.prospring.ch6.staticpc;

import org.aopalliance.aop.Advice;
import org.springframework.aop.Advisor;
import org.springframework.aop.Pointcut;
import org.springframework.aop.framework.ProxyFactory;
import org.springframework.aop.support.DefaultPointcutAdvisor;

public class StaticPointcutExample {

    public static void main(String[] args) {
        BeanOne one = new BeanOne();
        BeanTwo two = new BeanTwo();

        BeanOne proxyOne;
        BeanTwo proxyTwo;
```

```
        // create pointcut, advice and advisor
        Pointcut pc = new SimpleStaticPointcut();
        Advice advice = new SimpleAdvice();
        Advisor advisor = new DefaultPointcutAdvisor(pc, advice);

        // create BeanOne proxy
        ProxyFactory pf = new ProxyFactory();
        pf.addAdvisor(advisor);
        pf.setTarget(one);
        proxyOne = (BeanOne)pf.getProxy();

        // create BeanTwo proxy
        pf = new ProxyFactory();
        pf.addAdvisor(advisor);
        pf.setTarget(two);
        proxyTwo = (BeanTwo)pf.getProxy();

        proxyOne.foo();
        proxyTwo.foo();

        proxyOne.bar();
        proxyTwo.bar();

    }
}
```

Notice that the DefaultPointcutAdvisor instance is then used to create two proxies: one for an instance of BeanOne and one for an instance of BeanTwo. Finally, both the foo() and bar() methods are invoked on the two proxies.

Running this example results in the following output:

```
>> Invoking foo
foo
>> Done
foo
bar
```

As you can see, the only method for which the SimpleAdvice was actually invoked was the foo() method for the BeanOne class, exactly as expected. Restricting the methods that an advice applies is quite simple and, as you will see when we discuss the different proxy options, is key to getting the best performance out of your application.

Creating a Dynamic Pointcut Using DyanmicMethodMatcherPointcut

As we will demonstrate in this section, creating a dynamic pointcut is not much different from creating a static one. For this example, we create a dynamic pointcut for the class shown in Listing 6-26.

Listing 6-26. *The SampleBean Class*

```
package com.apress.prospring.ch6.dynamicpc;1

public class SampleBean {

    public void foo(int x) {
        System.out.println("Invoked foo() with: "  +x);
    }

    public void bar() {
        System.out.println("Invoked bar()");
    }
}
```

For this example, we want to advise only the foo() method, but unlike the previous example, we want to advise this method only if the int argument passed to it is greater or less than 100.

As with static pointcuts, Spring provides a convenience base class for creating dynamic pointcuts—DynamicMethodMatcherPointcut. The DynamicMethodMatcherPointcut class has a single abstract method, matches(Method, Class, Object[]), that you must implement, but as you will see, it is also prudent to implement the matches(Method, Class) method to control the behavior of the static checks. Listing 6-27 shows the SimpleDynamicPointcut class.

Listing 6-27. *The SimpleDynamicPointcut Class*

```
package com.apress.prospring.ch6.dynamicpc;

import java.lang.reflect.Method;

import org.springframework.aop.ClassFilter;
import org.springframework.aop.support.DynamicMethodMatcherPointcut;

public class SimpleDynamicPointcut extends DynamicMethodMatcherPointcut {

    public boolean matches(Method method, Class cls) {
        System.out.println("Static check for " + method.getName());
        return ("foo".equals(method.getName()));
    }

    public boolean matches(Method method, Class cls, Object[] args) {
        System.out.println("Dynamic check for " + method.getName());

        int x = ((Integer) args[0]).intValue();

        return (x != 100);
    }
```

```
    public ClassFilter getClassFilter() {
        return new ClassFilter() {

            public boolean matches(Class cls) {
                return (cls == SampleBean.class);
            }
        };
    }
}
```

As you can see from the code in Listing 6-27, we override the getClassFilter() method in a similar manner to the previous example shown in Listing 6-23. This removes the need to check the class in the method matching methods—something that is especially important for the dynamic check. Although we are only required to implement the dynamic check, we implement the static check as well. The reason for this is that we know the bar() method will never be advised. By indicating this using the static check, Spring makes it so it never has to perform a dynamic check for this method. If we neglect the static check, Spring performs a dynamic check each time the bar() method is invoked even though it always returns false. In the matches(Method, Class, Object[]) method, you can see that we return false if the value of the int argument passed to the foo() method is false, otherwise we return true. Note that in the dynamic check, we know that we are dealing with the foo() method, because no other method makes it past the static check.

In Listing 6-28, you can see an example of this pointcut in action.

Listing 6-28. *The DynamicPointcutExample Class*

```
package com.apress.prospring.ch6.dynamicpc;

import org.springframework.aop.Advisor;
import org.springframework.aop.framework.ProxyFactory;
import org.springframework.aop.support.DefaultPointcutAdvisor;

import com.apress.prospring.ch6.staticpc.SimpleAdvice;

public class DynamicPointcutExample {

    public static void main(String[] args) {
        SampleBean target = new SampleBean();

        // create advisor
        Advisor advisor = new DefaultPointcutAdvisor(
                new SimpleDynamicPointcut(), new SimpleAdvice());

        // create proxy
        ProxyFactory pf = new ProxyFactory();
        pf.setTarget(target);
        pf.addAdvisor(advisor);
        SampleBean proxy = (SampleBean)pf.getProxy();
```

```
        proxy.foo(1);
        proxy.foo(10);
        proxy.foo(100);

        proxy.bar();
        proxy.bar();
        proxy.bar();
    }
}
```

Notice that we have used the same advice class as in the static pointcut example. However, in this example, only the first two calls to foo() should be advised. The dynamic check prevents the third call to foo() from being advised and the static check prevents the bar() method from being advised. Running this example yields the following output:

```
Static check for foo
Static check for bar
Static check for hashCode
Static check for clone
Static check for toString
Static check for foo
Dynamic check for foo
>> Invoking foo
Invoked foo() with: 1
>> Done
Dynamic check for foo
>> Invoking foo
Invoked foo() with: 10
>> Done
Dynamic check for foo
Invoked foo() with: 100
Invoked bar()
Invoked bar()
Invoked bar()
```

As we expected, only the first two invocations of the foo() method were advised. Notice that none of the bar() invocations is subject to a dynamic check, thanks to the static check on bar(). An interesting point to note here is that the foo() method is actually subject to **two** static checks: one during the initial phase when all methods are checked and another when it is first invoked.

As you can see, dynamic pointcuts offer a greater degree of flexibility than static pointcuts, but due to the additional runtime overhead they require, you should only use a dynamic pointcut when absolutely necessary.

Using Simple Name Matching

Often when creating a pointcut, you want to match based on just the name of the method, ignoring method signature and return type. In this case, you can avoid needing to create a subclass of StaticMethodMatcherPointcut and use the NameMatchMethodPointcut to match against a list of method names instead. When you are using NameMatchMethodPointcut, no consideration is given to the signature of the method, so if you have methods foo() and foo(int), they are both matched for the name foo.

Now for a demonstration. Listing 6-29 shows a simple class with four methods.

Listing 6-29. *The NameBean Class*

```
package com.apress.prospring.ch6.namepc;

public class NameBean {

    public void foo() {
        System.out.println("foo");
    }

    public void foo(int x) {
        System.out.println("foo " + x);
    }

    public void bar() {
        System.out.println("bar");
    }

    public void yup() {
        System.out.println("yup");
    }
}
```

For this example, we want to match the foo(), foo(int), and bar() methods using the NameMatchMethodPointcut; this translates to matching the names foo and bar. This is shown in Listing 6-30.

Listing 6-30. *Using the NameMatchMethodPointcut*

```
package com.apress.prospring.ch6.namepc;

import org.springframework.aop.Advisor;
import org.springframework.aop.framework.ProxyFactory;
import org.springframework.aop.support.DefaultPointcutAdvisor;
import org.springframework.aop.support.NameMatchMethodPointcut;

import com.apress.prospring.ch6.staticpc.SimpleAdvice;

public class NamePointcutExample {

    public static void main(String[] args) {
        NameBean target = new NameBean();
```

```
// create advisor
NameMatchMethodPointcut pc = new NameMatchMethodPointcut();
pc.addMethodName("foo");
pc.addMethodName("bar");
Advisor advisor = new DefaultPointcutAdvisor(pc, new SimpleAdvice());

// create the proxy
ProxyFactory pf = new ProxyFactory();
pf.setTarget(target);
pf.addAdvisor(advisor);
NameBean proxy = (NameBean)pf.getProxy();

proxy.foo();
proxy.foo(999);
proxy.bar();
proxy.yup();
    }
}
```

There is no need to create a class for the pointcut; you can simply create an instance of NameMatchMethodPointcut and you are on your way. Notice that we have added two names to the pointcut, foo and bar, using the addMethodName() method. Running this example results in the following output:

```
>> Invoking foo
foo
>> Done
>> Invoking foo
foo 999
>> Done
>> Invoking bar
bar
>> Done
yup
```

As expected, the foo(), foo(int), and bar() methods are advised, thanks to the pointcut, but the yup() method is left unadvised.

Creating Pointcuts with Regular Expressions

In the previous section, we discussed how to perform simple matching against a predefined list of methods. But what if you don't know all of the methods' names in advance, and instead you know the pattern that the names follow? For instance, what if you want to match all methods whose names starts with get? In this case, you can use one of the regular expression pointcuts, either JdkRegexpMethodPointcut or Perl5RegexpMethodPointcut, to match a method name based on a regular expression.

The code in Listing 6-31 shows a simple class with three methods.

Listing 6-31. *The RegexpBean Class*

```
package com.apress.prospring.ch6.regexppc;

public class RegexpBean {

    public void foo1() {
        System.out.println("foo1");
    }

    public void foo2() {
        System.out.println("foo2");
    }

    public void bar() {
        System.out.println("bar");
    }
}
```

Using a regular expression-based pointcut, we can match all methods in this class whose name starts with foo. This is shown in Listing 6-32.

Listing 6-32. *Using Regular Expressions for Pointcuts*

```
package com.apress.prospring.ch6.regexppc;

import org.springframework.aop.Advisor;
import org.springframework.aop.framework.ProxyFactory;
import org.springframework.aop.support.DefaultPointcutAdvisor;
import org.springframework.aop.support.JdkRegexpMethodPointcut;

import com.apress.prospring.ch6.staticpc.SimpleAdvice;

public class RegexpPointcutExample {

    public static void main(String[] args) {
        RegexpBean target = new RegexpBean();

        // create the advisor
        JdkRegexpMethodPointcut pc = new JdkRegexpMethodPointcut();
        pc.setPattern(".*foo.*");
        Advisor advisor = new DefaultPointcutAdvisor(pc, new SimpleAdvice());
```

```
        // create the proxy
        ProxyFactory pf = new ProxyFactory();
        pf.setTarget(target);
        pf.addAdvisor(advisor);
        RegexpBean proxy = (RegexpBean)pf.getProxy();

        proxy.foo1();
        proxy.foo2();
        proxy.bar();
    }
}
```

Notice we do not need to create a class for the pointcut; instead, we just create an instance of JdkRegexpMethodPointcut (which could just as easily be Perl5RegexpMethodPointcut), specify the pattern to match, and we are done. The interesting thing to note is the pattern. When matching method names, Spring matches the fully qualified name of the method, so for foo1(), Spring is matching against com.apress.prospring.ch6.regexppc.RegexpBean.foo1, hence the leading .* in the pattern. This is a powerful concept because it allows you to match all methods within a given package, without needing to know exactly which classes are in that package and what the names of the methods are. Running this example yields the following output:

```
>> Invoking foo1
foo1
>> Done
>> Invoking foo2
foo2
>> Done
bar
```

As you would expect, only the foo1() and foo2() methods have been advised, because the bar() method does not match the regular expression pattern.

Convenience Advisor Implementations

For many of the Pointcut implementations, Spring also provides a convenience Advisor implementation that acts as the Pointcut as well. For instance, instead of using the NameMatchMethodPointcut coupled with a DefaultPointcutAdvisor in the previous example, we could simply have used a NameMatchMethodPointcutAdvisor, as shown in Listing 6-33.

Listing 6-33. *Using NameMatchMethodPointcutAdvisor*

```
package com.apress.prospring.ch6.namepc;

import org.springframework.aop.framework.ProxyFactory;
import org.springframework.aop.support.NameMatchMethodPointcutAdvisor;

import com.apress.prospring.ch6.staticpc.SimpleAdvice;
```

```
public class NamePointcutUsingAdvisor {

    public static void main(String[] args) {
        NameBean target = new NameBean();

        // create advisor
        NameMatchMethodPointcutAdvisor advisor = new
            NameMatchMethodPointcutAdvisor(new SimpleAdvice());
        advisor.addMethodName("foo");
        advisor.addMethodName("bar");

        // create the proxy
        ProxyFactory pf = new ProxyFactory();
        pf.setTarget(target);
        pf.addAdvisor(advisor);
        NameBean proxy = (NameBean) pf.getProxy();

        proxy.foo();
        proxy.foo(999);
        proxy.bar();
        proxy.yup();
    }
}
```

Notice in Listing 6-33 that rather than create an instance of NameMatchMethodPointcut, we configure the pointcut details on the instance of NameMatchMethodPointcutAdvisor itself. In this way, the NameMatchMethodPointcutAdvisor is acting as both the Advisor and the Pointcut.

You can find full details of the different convenience Advisor implementations by exploring the JavaDoc for the org.springframework.aop.support package. There is no noticeable performance difference between the two approaches, and aside from there being slightly less code in the second approach, there is very little difference in the actual coding approach. We prefer to stick with the first approach because we feel that the intent is slightly clearer in the code. At the end of the day, the style you choose comes down to personal preference.

All About Proxies

So far, we have taken only a cursory look at the proxies generated by ProxyFactory. We mentioned that there are two types of proxy available in Spring: JDK proxies created using the JDK Proxy class and CGLIB-based proxies created using the CGLIB Enhancer class. Understanding the differences between these proxies is key to making the AOP code in your application perform as well as it can. In this section, we take a detailed look at the differences between the proxies and how these differences affect the performance of your application.

You may be wondering exactly what the difference between the two proxies is and why Spring needs two different types of proxy. Prior to version 1.1 of Spring, the two types of proxy shared much in common in the way they were implemented, and the performance of both types of proxy was very similar. The reason that there are two types of proxy is because of the poor performance of `Proxy` under JDK 1.3. Spring overcame this by providing CGLIB proxies, which performed comparably to the JDK 1.4 proxies when running on a 1.3 JVM.

The initial intention of the CGLIB proxy was to overcome the performance issues of the `Proxy` class on JDK 1.3, and the implementation was as similar to that of the JDK proxy as possible. The only drawback with this was that Spring was not taking full advantage of the feature-set available with CGLIB. In version 1.1, things have changed dramatically. The CGLIB proxy is now heavily optimized and outperforms the JDK proxy quite dramatically in many cases. Before we take a look at the differences in proxy implementations, we first must make sure you understand exactly what the generated proxies have to do.

▓**Caution** Before version 1.1 of Spring, a bug in the CGLIB proxy code resulted in an inordinate amount of dynamically generated classes being created unnecessarily. In the long run, this resulted in excess memory being used and eventually `OutOfMemoryErrors` occurring. This bug is fixed in Spring 1.1, so if you are having problems with earlier versions of Spring related to memory usage, you might want to upgrade.

Understanding Proxies

The core goal of a proxy is to intercept method invocations, and where necessary, execute chains of advice that apply to a particular method. The management and invocation of advice is largely proxy independent and is managed by the Spring AOP framework. However, the proxy is responsible for intercepting calls to all methods and passing them as necessary to the AOP framework for the advice to be applied.

In addition to this core functionality, the proxy must also support a set of additional features. It is possible to configure the proxy to expose itself via the `AopContext` class so that you can retrieve the proxy and invoke advised methods on the proxy from the target object. The proxy is responsible for ensuring that when this option is enabled via `ProxyFactory.setExposeProxy()`, the proxy class is appropriately exposed. In addition to this, all proxy classes implement the `Advised` interface by default, which allows for, among other things, the advice chain to be changed after the proxy has been created. A proxy must also ensure that any methods that return `this`—that is, return the proxied target—do in fact return the proxy and not the target.

As you can see, a typical proxy has quite a lot of work to perform, and all of this logic is implemented in both the JDK and CGLIB proxies. As of version 1.1 of Spring, the way in which this logic is implemented differs quite drastically depending on which of the proxy types you are using.

Using JDK Dynamic Proxies

JDK proxies are the most basic type of proxy available in Spring. Unlike the CGLIB proxy, the JDK proxy can only generate proxies of interfaces, not classes. In this way, any object you wish to proxy must implement at least one interface. In general, it is good design to use interfaces for your classes, but it is not always possible, especially when you are working with third-party or legacy code. In this case, you **must** use the CGLIB proxy.

When you are using the JDK proxy, all method calls are intercepted by the JVM and routed to the invoke() method of the proxy. This method then determines whether or not the method in question is advised, and if so, it invokes the advice chain and then the method itself using reflection. In addition to this, the invoke() method performs all the logic discussed in the previous section.

The JDK proxy makes no determination between methods that are advised and unadvised until it is in the invoke() method. This means that for unadvised methods on the proxy, the invoke() method is still called, all the checks are still performed, and the method is still invoked using reflection. Obviously this incurs a runtime overhead each time the method is invoked, even though the proxy often performs no additional processing other than to invoke the unadvised method via reflection.

You can instruct the ProxyFactory to use a JDK proxy by specifying the list of interfaces to proxy using setProxyInterfaces().

Using CGLIB Proxies

With the JDK proxy, all decisions about how to handle a particular method invocation are handled at runtime each time the method is invoked. When you use CGLIB, you avoid this approach in favor of one that performs much better. A full discussion of the inner workings of CGLIB is well beyond the scope of this chapter, but essentially CGLIB dynamically generates the bytecode for a new class on the fly for each proxy, reusing already generated classes wherever possible. This approach allows you to make extensive optimizations.

When a CGLIB proxy is first created, CGLIB asks Spring how it wants to handle each method. This means that many of the decisions that are performed in each call to invoke() on the JDK proxy are performed just once for the CGLIB proxy. Because CGLIB generates actual bytecode, there is also a lot more flexibility in the way you can handle methods. For instance, the CGLIB proxy generates the appropriate bytecode to invoke any unadvised methods directly, dramatically reducing the overhead introduced by the proxy. In addition to this, the CGLIB proxy determines whether it is possible for a method to return this; if not, it allows the method call to be invoked directly, again reducing the overhead substantially.

The CGLIB proxy also handles fixed advice chains differently than the JDK proxy. A fixed advice chain is one that you guarantee will not change after the proxy has been generated. By default, you are able to change the advisors and advice on a proxy even after it is created, although this is rarely a requirement. The CGLIB proxy handles fixed advice chains in a particular way, reducing the runtime overhead for executing an advice chain.

In addition to all these optimizations, the CGLIB proxy utilizes the bytecode generation capabilities to gain a slight increase in performance when invoking advised methods; this results in advised methods that perform slightly better than those on JDK proxies.

Comparing Proxy Performance

So far, all we have done is discuss in loose terms the differences in implementation between the different proxy types. In this section, we are going to run a simple performance test to compare the performance of the CGLIB proxy with the JDK proxy.

Listing 6-34 shows the code for the performance test.

Listing 6-34. *Testing Proxy Performance*

```java
package com.apress.prospring.ch6.proxies;

import org.springframework.aop.Advisor;
import org.springframework.aop.framework.Advised;
import org.springframework.aop.framework.ProxyFactory;
import org.springframework.aop.support.DefaultPointcutAdvisor;

public class ProxyPerfTest {

    public static void main(String[] args) {
        ISimpleBean target = new SimpleBean();

        Advisor advisor = new DefaultPointcutAdvisor(new TestPointcut(),
                new NoOpBeforeAdvice());

        runCglibTests(advisor, target);
        runCglibFrozenTests(advisor, target);
        runJdkTests(advisor, target);
    }

    private static void runCglibTests(Advisor advisor, ISimpleBean target) {
        ProxyFactory pf = new ProxyFactory();
        pf.setTarget(target);
        pf.addAdvisor(advisor);

        ISimpleBean proxy = (ISimpleBean)pf.getProxy();
        System.out.println("Running CGLIB (Standard) Tests");
        test(proxy);
    }

    private static void runCglibFrozenTests(Advisor advisor, ISimpleBean target) {
        ProxyFactory pf = new ProxyFactory();
        pf.setTarget(target);
        pf.addAdvisor(advisor);
        pf.setFrozen(true);

        ISimpleBean proxy = (ISimpleBean)pf.getProxy();
        System.out.println("Running CGLIB (Frozen) Tests");
        test(proxy);
    }

    private static void runJdkTests(Advisor advisor, ISimpleBean target) {
        ProxyFactory pf = new ProxyFactory();
        pf.setTarget(target);
        pf.addAdvisor(advisor);
        pf.setInterfaces(new Class[]{ISimpleBean.class});
```

```
    ISimpleBean proxy = (ISimpleBean)pf.getProxy();
    System.out.println("Running JDK Tests");
    test(proxy);
}

private static void test(ISimpleBean bean) {
    long before = 0;
    long after = 0;

    // test advised method
    System.out.println("Testing Advised Method");
    before = System.currentTimeMillis();
    for(int x = 0; x < 500000; x++) {
        bean.advised();
    }
    after = System.currentTimeMillis();;

    System.out.println("Took " + (after - before) + " ms");

    // testing unadvised method
    System.out.println("Testing Unadvised Method");
    before = System.currentTimeMillis();
    for(int x = 0; x < 500000; x++) {
        bean.unadvised();
    }
    after = System.currentTimeMillis();;

    System.out.println("Took " + (after - before) + " ms");

    // testing equals() method
    System.out.println("Testing equals() Method");
    before = System.currentTimeMillis();
    for(int x = 0; x < 500000; x++) {
        bean.equals(bean);
    }
    after = System.currentTimeMillis();;

    System.out.println("Took " + (after - before) + " ms");

    // testing hashCode() method
    System.out.println("Testing hashCode() Method");
    before = System.currentTimeMillis();
    for(int x = 0; x < 500000; x++) {
        bean.hashCode();
    }
    after = System.currentTimeMillis();;
```

```
        System.out.println("Took " + (after - before) + " ms");

        // testing method on Advised
        Advised advised = (Advised)bean;

        System.out.println("Testing Advised.getProxyTargetClass() Method");
        before = System.currentTimeMillis();
        for(int x = 0; x < 500000; x++) {
            advised.getProxyTargetClass();
        }
        after = System.currentTimeMillis();;

        System.out.println("Took " + (after - before) + " ms");

        System.out.println(">>>\n");
    }
}
```

In this code you can see that we are testing three kinds of proxy: a standard CGLIB proxy, a CGLIB proxy with a frozen advice chain, and a JDK proxy. For each proxy type, we run the following five test cases:

- **Advised method:** A method that is advised. The advice type used in the test is a before advice that performs no processing so it reduces the effects of the advice itself on the performance tests.

- **Unadvised method:** A method on the proxy that is unadvised. Often your proxy has many methods that are not advised. This test looks at how well unadvised methods perform for the different proxies.

- **The equals() method:** This test looks at the overhead of invoking the equals() method. This is especially important when you use proxies as keys in a HashMap or similar collection.

- **The hashCode() method:** As with the equals() method, the hashCode() method is important when you are using HashMaps or similar collections.

- **Executing methods on the Advised interface:** As we mentioned earlier, a proxy implements the Advised interface by default, allowing you to modify the proxy after creation and to query information about the proxy. This test looks at how quick methods on the Advised interface can be accessed using the different proxy types.

We ran the test on a Pentium 4 3.0GHz machine with 2GB of RAM. When running the test, we set the initial heap size of the JVM to 1024MB to reduce the effects of heap resizing on test results. The results are shown in Table 6-3.

Table 6-3. *Proxy Performance Test Results (ms)*

	CGLIB (Standard)	CGLIB (Frozen)	JDK
Advised Method	343	172	516
Unadvised Method	47	47	391
equals()	47	31	343
hashCode()	16	16	391
Advised.getProxyTargetClass()	0	16	266

From the results in this table, it is clear to see that the CGLIB proxy performs much better than the JDK proxies. A standard CGLIB proxy only performs marginally better than the JDK proxy when executing an advised method, but there is a noticeable difference when you are using a proxy with a frozen advice chain. For unadvised methods, the CGLIB proxy is over eight times faster than the JDK proxy. Similar figures apply to the equals() and hashCode() methods, which are noticeably faster when you are using the CGLIB proxy. Notice that hashCode() is faster than equals(). The reason for this is that equals() is handled in a specific way to ensure that the equals() contract is preserved for the proxies. For methods on the Advised interface, you will notice that they are also faster on the CGLIB proxy, although not to the same degree. The reason for this is that Advised methods are handled early on in the intercept() method and they avoid much of the logic that is required for other methods.

From the test results, notice that for the standard CGLIB proxy, the invocation on Advised.getProxyTargetClass() took 0 milliseconds. This indicates that this call was optimized out by the JIT compiler. On subsequent runs of the test, we noticed that sometimes calls to hashCode() were also optimized out when either CGLIB proxy was used. Interestingly, none of the method calls was ever optimized out for the JDK proxy.

Which Proxy to Use?

Deciding which proxy to use is typically an easy decision. The CGLIB proxy can proxy both classes and interfaces, whereas the JDK proxy can only proxy interfaces. Add to this the fact that the CGLIB proxy clearly performs better than the JDK proxy and it becomes apparent that the CGLIB proxy is the correct choice. The only thing to be aware of when using the CGLIB proxy is that a new class is generated for each distinct proxy, although with version 1.1, the reuse of proxy classes is now functioning correctly, reducing the runtime overhead of frequent class generation and reducing the amount of memory used by the CGLIB proxy classes. When proxying a class, the CGLIB proxy is the default choice because it is the only proxy capable of generating a proxy of a class. In order to use the CGLIB proxy when proxying an interface, you must set the value of the optimize flag in the ProxyFactory to true using the setOptimize() method.

Summary

In this chapter, we introduced the core concepts of AOP and then looked at how these concepts translate into the Spring AOP implementation. We discussed the features that are and are not implemented in Spring AOP and we pointed to AspectJ as an AOP solution for those features Spring does not implement. We spent some time explaining the details of the advice types available in Spring, and you have seen examples of the four types in action. We also looked at how you limit the methods to which an advice applies using pointcuts. In particular, we looked at the five basic pointcut implementations available with Spring. Finally, we covered the details of how the AOP proxies are constructed, the different options, and what makes them different. We concluded the discussion of proxies with a comparison of the performance between three different proxy types and we concluded that the CGLIB proxy performs the best and is suitable for most, if not all, the proxies you will use.

In Chapter 7, we will complete our discussion of the pointcuts available in Spring by looking at `ComposablePointcut` and `ControlFlowPointcut` in detail. We will spend some time looking at how you utilize Spring's AspectJ integration to extend the AOP feature-set available to your application. We will also look at how AOP is supported by Spring framework services, which means you can define and configure advice declaratively rather than programmatically. Chapter 7 finishes with a look at how we used AOP in the sample application to solve a real problem encountered during its development.

CHAPTER 7

■ ■ ■

More on Spring AOP

In this chapter, we go into more detail about the AOP features available in Spring. In particular, we look at the topic in a much more real-world light: we explore the framework services in Spring that allow for transparent application of AOP, we cover real-world usage of AOP in the context of the sample application, and we also discuss overcoming the limitations of Spring AOP using Spring/AspectJ integration. More specifically, this chapter covers the following:

- **Advanced use of pointcuts:** This chapter finishes discussing pointcutting by looking at both `ComposablePointcut` and `ControlFlowPointcut`. This section also summarizes the whole pointcut discussion and looks at the appropriate techniques you should employ when you are using pointcuts in your application.

- **Introductions:** Mentioned briefly in the previous chapter, introductions allow you to add interface implementations dynamically to any object on the fly using the familiar interceptor concept.

- **AOP framework services:** We skipped over this topic completely in the previous chapter and focused solely on assembling AOP proxies and advice chains manually. However, in true Spring fashion, the framework fully supports configuring AOP transparently and declaratively. In this section, we look at how you can use the `ProxyFactoryBean` to inject declaratively defined AOP proxies into your application objects as collaborators, thus making your application completely unaware that it is working with advised objects. This section also looks at the autoproxying facilities Spring provides to ease the burden of configuring many different proxies.

- **Integrating AspectJ:** AspectJ is a fully featured, statically compiled AOP implementation. The feature set of AspectJ is much greater than that of Spring AOP, but it is much more complicated to use than Spring. As mentioned in the previous chapter, AspectJ is a good solution when you find that Spring AOP lacks a feature you need. As of version 1.1 of Spring, you can take full advantage of Spring features when configuring your AspectJ aspects.

- **AOP in the sample application:** In this section, we discuss how we solved some problems in the sample application using AOP. Specifically, we look at how we used Spring AOP to create an obscenity filter for the SpringBlog application that can be applied across as many methods as possible.

In order to run some of the examples in this chapter, you need to obtain AspectJ. You can download it from `http://eclipse.org/aspectj`. We used version 1.2 of AspectJ for the examples in this chapter.

Advanced Use of Pointcuts

In the last chapter, we looked at five basic `Pointcut` implementations Spring provides; for the most part, we found that these meet the needs of our applications. However, sometimes you need more flexibility when defining pointcuts. Spring provides two additional `Pointcut` implementations, `ComposablePointcut` and `ControlFlowPointcut`, that provide exactly the flexibility you need.

Using Control Flow Pointcuts

Spring control flow pointcuts, implemented by the `ControlFlowPointcut` class, are similar to the `cflow` construct available in many other AOP implementations, although they are not quite as powerful. Essentially, a control flow pointcut in Spring pointcuts all method calls below a given method or below all methods in a class. This is quite hard to visualize and is better explained using an example.

Listing 7-1 shows a `SimpleBeforeAdvice` that writes a message out describing the method it is advising.

Listing 7-1. *The SimpleBeforeAdvice Class*

```
package com.apress.prospring.ch7.cflow;

import java.lang.reflect.Method;

import org.springframework.aop.MethodBeforeAdvice;

public class SimpleBeforeAdvice implements MethodBeforeAdvice {


    public void before(Method method, Object[] args, Object target)
            throws Throwable {
        System.out.println("Before method: " + method);
    }

}
```

This advice class allows us to see which methods are being pointcut by the `ControlFlowPointcut`. In Listing 7-2, you can see a `simple` class with one method—the method that we want to advise.

Listing 7-2. *The TestBean Class*

```
package com.apress.prospring.ch7.cflow;

public class TestBean {

    public void foo() {
        System.out.println("foo()");
    }
}
```

In Listing 7-2, you can see the simple foo() method that we want to advise. We have, however, a special requirement—we only want to advise this method when it is called from another, specific method. Listing 7-3 shows a simple driver program for this example.

Listing 7-3. *Using the ControlFlowPointcut Class*

```
package com.apress.prospring.ch7.cflow;

import org.springframework.aop.Advisor;
import org.springframework.aop.Pointcut;
import org.springframework.aop.framework.ProxyFactory;
import org.springframework.aop.support.ControlFlowPointcut;
import org.springframework.aop.support.DefaultPointcutAdvisor;

public class ControlFlowExample {

    public static void main(String[] args) {
        ControlFlowExample ex = new ControlFlowExample();
        ex.run();
    }

    public void run() {
        TestBean target = new TestBean();

        // create advisor
        Pointcut pc = new ControlFlowPointcut(ControlFlowExample.class, "test");
        Advisor advisor = new DefaultPointcutAdvisor(pc,
                new SimpleBeforeAdvice());

        // create proxy
        ProxyFactory pf = new ProxyFactory();
        pf.setTarget(target);
        pf.addAdvisor(advisor);

        TestBean proxy = (TestBean) pf.getProxy();

        System.out.println("Trying normal invoke");
        proxy.foo();
        System.out.println("Trying under ControlFlowExample.test()");
        test(proxy);
    }

    private void test(TestBean bean) {
        bean.foo();
    }
}
```

In Listing 7-3, the advised proxy is assembled with `ControlFlowPointcut` and then the `foo()` method is invoked twice: once directly from the `run()` method and once from the `test()` method. Here is the line of particular interest:

```
Pointcut pc = new ControlFlowPointcut(ControlFlowExample.class, "test");
```

In this line, we are creating a `ControlFlowPointcut` instance for the `test()` method of the `ControlFlowExample` class. Essentially, this says, "pointcut all methods that are called from the `ControlFlowExample.test()` method." Note that although we said "pointcut all methods," in fact, this really means "pointcut all methods on the proxy object that is advised using the `Advisor` corresponding to this instance of `ControlFlowPointcut`." Running this example yields the following output:

```
Trying normal invoke
foo()
Trying under ControlFlowExample.test()
Before method: public void com.apress.prospring.ch7.cflow.TestBean.foo()
foo()
```

As you can see, when the `foo()` method is first invoked outside of the control flow of the `test()` method, it is unadvised. When it executes for a second time, this time inside the control flow of the `test()` method, the `ControlFlowPointcut` indicates that its associated advice applies to the method, and thus the method is advised. Note that if we had called another method from within the `test()` method, one that was not on the advised proxy, it would not have been advised.

Control flow pointcuts can be extremely useful, allowing you to advise an object selectively only when it is executed in the context of another. However, be aware that you take a substantial performance hit for using control flow pointcut over other pointcuts. Figures from the Spring documentation indicate that a control flow pointcut is typically five times slower than other pointcuts on a 1.4 JVM and ten times slower on a 1.3 JVM.

Using ComposablePointcut

In previous pointcutting examples, we used just a single pointcut for each `Advisor`. In most cases, this is usually enough, but in some cases, you may need to compose two or more pointcuts together to achieve the desired goal. Consider the situation where you want to pointcut all getter and setter methods on a bean. You have a pointcut for getters and a pointcut for setters, but you don't have one for both. Of course, you could just create another pointcut with the new logic, but a better approach is to combine the two pointcuts into a single pointcut using `ComposablePointcut`.

The `ComposablePointcut` supports two methods: `union()` and `intersection()`. By default, `ComposablePointcut` is created with a `ClassFilter` that matches all classes and a `MethodMatcher` that matches all methods, although you can supply your own initial `ClassFilter` and `MethodMatcher` during construction. The `union()` and `intersection()` methods are both overloaded to accept `ClassFilter` and `MethodMatcher` arguments.

Invoking the `union()` method for a `MethodMatcher` replaces the `MethodMatcher` of the `ComposablePointcut` with an instance of `UnionMethodMatcher` using the current `MethodMatcher` of the `ComposablePointcut` and the `MethodMatcher` passed to the `union()` method as arguments. The `UnionMethodMatcher` then returns `true` for a match if either of its wrapped `MethodMatchers` return `true`. You can invoke the `union()` method as many times as you want, with each call creating a new `UnionMethodMatcher` that wraps the current `MethodMatcher` of the `ComposablePointcut` with the MethodMatcher passed to union(). A similar structure is followed when you are using ClassFilter with the union() method.

Internally, the intersection() method works in a similar way to the union(). However, the IntersectionMethodMatcher class only returns true for a match if both of the embedded MethodMatchers return true for a match. Essentially, you can think of the union() method as an **any** match, in that it returns true if any of the matchers it is wrapping return true; and you can think of the intersection() method as an **all** match, in that it only returns true if all its wrapped matchers return true.

As with control flow pointcuts, this is quite difficult to visualize, and it is much easier to understand with an example. Listing 7-4 shows a simple bean with three methods.

Listing 7-4. *The SampleBean Class*

```
package com.apress.prospring.ch7.composable;

public class SampleBean {

    public String getName() {
        return "Rob Harrop";
    }

    public void setName(String name) {

    }

    public int getAge() {
        return 100;
    }
}
```

With this example, we are going to generate three different proxies using the same ComposablePointcut instance, but each time, we are going to modify the ComposablePointcut using either the union() or intersection() method. Following this, we will invoke all three methods on the SampleBean proxy and look at which ones have been advised. Listing 7-5 shows the code for this.

Listing 7-5. *Investigating ComposablePointcut*

```
package com.apress.prospring.ch7.composable;

import java.lang.reflect.Method;

import org.springframework.aop.Advisor;
import org.springframework.aop.ClassFilter;
import org.springframework.aop.framework.ProxyFactory;
import org.springframework.aop.support.ComposablePointcut;
import org.springframework.aop.support.DefaultPointcutAdvisor;
import org.springframework.aop.support.StaticMethodMatcher;
```

```java
import com.apress.prospring.ch7.cflow.SimpleBeforeAdvice;

public class ComposablePointcutExample {

    public static void main(String[] args) {
        // create target
        SampleBean target = new SampleBean();


        ComposablePointcut pc = new ComposablePointcut(ClassFilter.TRUE,
                new GetterMethodMatcher());

        System.out.println("Test 1");
        SampleBean proxy = getProxy(pc, target);
        testInvoke(proxy);

        System.out.println("Test 2");
        pc.union(new SetterMethodMatcher());
        proxy = getProxy(pc, target);
        testInvoke(proxy);

        System.out.println("Test 3");
        pc.intersection(new GetAgeMethodMatcher());
        proxy = getProxy(pc, target);
        testInvoke(proxy);

    }

    private static SampleBean getProxy(ComposablePointcut pc, SampleBean target) {
        // create the advisor

        Advisor advisor = new DefaultPointcutAdvisor(pc,
                new SimpleBeforeAdvice());

        // create the proxy
        ProxyFactory pf = new ProxyFactory();
        pf.setTarget(target);
        pf.addAdvisor(advisor);

        return (SampleBean) pf.getProxy();
    }
```

```java
private static void testInvoke(SampleBean proxy) {
    proxy.getAge();
    proxy.getName();
    proxy.setName("Rob Harrop");
}

private static class GetterMethodMatcher extends StaticMethodMatcher {

    public boolean matches(Method method, Class cls) {
        return (method.getName().startsWith("get"));
    }

}

private static class GetAgeMethodMatcher extends StaticMethodMatcher {
    public boolean matches(Method method, Class cls) {
        return "getAge".equals(method.getName());
    }
}

private static class SetterMethodMatcher extends StaticMethodMatcher {

    public boolean matches(Method method, Class cls) {
        return (method.getName().startsWith("set"));
    }

}
}
```

The first thing to notice in this example is the set of three private MethodMatcher implementations. The GetterMethodMatcher matches all methods that start with get. This is the default MethodMatcher that we use to assemble the ComposablePointcut. Because of this, we expect that the first round of invocations on the SampleBean methods will result in only the getAge() and getName() methods being advised.

The SetterMethodMatcher matches all methods that start with set, and it is combined with the ComposablePointcut using union() for the second round of invocations. At this point, we have a union of two MethodMatchers: one that matches all methods starting with get and one that matches all methods starting with set. To this end, we expect that all invocations during the second round will be advised.

The GetAgeMethodMatcher is very specific and only matches the getAge() method. This MethodMatcher is combined with the ComposablePointcut using intersection() for the third round for invocations. Because the GetAgeMethodMatcher is being composed using intersection(), the only method that we expect to be advised in the third round of invocations is getAge(), because this is the only method that matches all the composed MethodMatchers.

Running this example results in the following output:

```
Test 1
Before method: public int com.apress.prospring.ch7.composable.SampleBean.getAge()
Before method: public java.lang.String ➥
com.apress.prospring.ch7.composable.SampleBean.getName()
Test 2
Before method: public int com.apress.prospring.ch7.composable.SampleBean.getAge()
Before method: public java.lang.String ➥
com.apress.prospring.ch7.composable.SampleBean.getName()
Before method: public void
com.apress.prospring.ch7.composable.SampleBean.setName(java.lang.String)
Test 3
Before method: public int com.apress.prospring.ch7.composable.SampleBean.getAge()
```

As expected, the first round of invocations on the proxy saw only the getAge() and getName() methods being advised. For the second round, when the SetterMethodMatcher had been composed with the union() method, all methods were advised. In the final round, as a result of the intersection of the GetAgeMethodMatcher, only the getAge() method was advised.

Although this example only demonstrated the use of MethodMatchers in the composition process, it is just as simple to use ClassFilter when you are building the pointcut. Indeed, you can use a combination of MethodMatchers and ClassFilters when building your composite pointcut.

Composition and the Pointcut Interface

In the last section, you saw how to create a composite pointcut using multiple MethodMatchers and ClassFilters. You can also create composite pointcuts using other objects that implement the Pointcut interface. You can perform an intersection of Pointcuts using the ComposablePointcut.intersection() method, but for a union, you need to use the org.springframework.aop.support.Pointcuts class that has both intersection() and union() methods.

Composition of Pointcuts works in the same way as it does for MethodMatchers, so we do not go into any detail here. You can find more information about composition by reading the JavaDoc for the Pointcuts class.

Pointcutting Summary

From the discussions in this chapter and in the previous chapter, you can see that Spring offers a powerful set of Pointcut implementations that should meet most, if not all, of your application's requirements. Remember that if you can't find a pointcut to suit your needs, you can create your own implementation from scratch by implementing Pointcut, MethodMatcher, and ClassFilter.

There are two patterns you use to combine pointcuts and advisors together. The first pattern, the one that we have used so far, involves having the pointcut implementation decoupled from the advisor. In the code we have seen up to this point, we have created instances of Pointcut implementations and then used the DefaultPointcutAdvisor to add advice along with the Pointcut to the proxy.

The second option, one that is adopted by many of the examples in the Spring documentation, is to encapsulate the Pointcut inside your own Advisor implementation. This way, you have a class that implements both Pointcut and PointcutAdvisor, with the PointcutAdvisor.getPointcut() method simply returning this. This is an approach many classes, such as StaticMethodMatcherPointcutAdvisor, use in Spring.

We find that the first approach is the most flexible, allowing you to use different Pointcut implementations with different Advisor implementations. However, the second approach is useful in situations where you are going to be using the same combination of Pointcut and Advisor in different parts of your application, or indeed, across many different applications. The second approach is useful when each Advisor must have a separate instance of a Pointcut; by making the Advisor responsible for creating the Pointcut, you can ensure that this is the case.

If you recall the discussion on proxy performance from the previous chapter, you will remember that unadvised methods perform much better than methods that are advised. For this reason, you should ensure that, by using Pointcuts, you only advise the methods that are absolutely necessary. This way you reduce the amount of unnecessary overhead added to your application by using AOP.

Getting Started with Introductions

Introductions are an important part of the AOP feature set available in Spring. By using introductions, you can introduce new functionality to an existing object dynamically. In Spring, you can introduce an implementation of any interface to an existing object. You may well be wondering exactly why this is useful—why would you want to add functionality dynamically at runtime when you can simply add that functionality at development time? The answer to this question is easy. You add functionality dynamically when the functionality is crosscutting and is not easily implemented using traditional advice.

The Spring documentation gives two atypical examples of introduction use: object locking and modification detection. In the case of object locking, which is implemented in the Spring documentation, we have an interface, Lockable, that defines the method for locking and unlocking an object. The intended application for this interface involves enabling the application to lock an object so that its internal state cannot be modified. Now you could simply implement this interface manually for every class you wish to make lockable. However, this would result in a lot of duplicated code across many classes. Sure, you can refactor the implementation into an abstract base class, but then you lose your one shot at concrete inheritance, and you still have to check the lock status in every method that modifies the state of the object. Clearly this is not an ideal situation and has the potential to lead to many bugs, and no doubt some maintenance nightmares.

By using introductions, you can overcome all of these issues. Using an introduction, you can centralize the implementation of the Lockable interface into a single class, and then, at runtime, have any object you wish adopt this implementation of Lockable. Not only does the object adopt the implementation of Lockable but it also becomes an instance of Lockable, in that it passes the instanceof test for the Lockable interface, even though its class does not implement this interface.

Clearly this overcomes the problem of centralizing the implementation logic without affecting the concrete inheritance hierarchy of your classes, but what about all the code you need to write to check the lock status? Well, an introduction is simply an extension of a method interceptor, and as such, it can intercept any method on the object on which the introduction was made. Using this feature, you could check the lock status before any calls are made to setter methods and throw an `Exception` if the object is locked. All of this code is encapsulated in a single place, and none of the `Lockable` objects needs to be aware of this.

Introductions are key to providing declarative services in applications. For instance, if you build an application that is fully aware of the `Lockable` interface, by using introductions, you declaratively define exactly which objects should be made `Lockable`.

We won't be spending any more time looking at the `Lockable` interface and how to implement it using introductions because it is fully discussed in the Spring documentation. Instead we focus on the other, unimplemented, example from the documentation—object modification detection. However, before we start we will take a look at the basics behind building an introduction.

Introduction Basics

Spring treats introductions as a special type of advice, more specifically, as a special type of around advice. Because introductions apply solely at the class level, you cannot use pointcuts with introductions; semantically, the two don't match. An introduction adds new interface implementations to a class and a pointcut defines which methods an advice applies. You create an introduction by implementing the `IntroductionInterceptor` class, which extends the `MethodInterceptor` interface. Figure 7-1 shows this structure along with the methods of both interfaces.

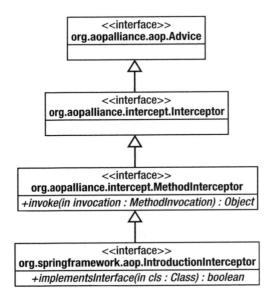

Figure 7-1. *Interface structure for introductions*

As you can see, the `MethodInterceptor` interface defines an `invoke()` method. Using this method, you provide the implementation for the interfaces that you are introducing and perform interception for any additional methods as required. Implementing all methods for an interface inside a single method can prove troublesome, and it is likely to result in an awful lot of code that you will have to wade through just to decide which method to invoke. Thankfully, Spring provides a default implementation of IntroductionInterceptor, DelegatingIntroductionInterceptor, which makes creating introductions much simpler. To build an introduction using DelegatingIntroductionInterceptor, you create a class that both inherits from DelegatingIntroductionInterceptor and implements the interfaces you want to introduce. The DelegatingIntroductionInterceptor then simply delegates all calls to introduced methods to the corresponding method on itself. Don't worry if this seems a little unclear; you will see an example of it in the next section.

Just as you need to use a PointcutAdvisor when you are working with pointcut advice, you need to use an IntroductionAdvisor to add introductions to a proxy. The default implementation of IntroductionAdvisor is DefaultIntroductionAdvisor, which should suffice for most, if not all, of your introduction needs. You should be aware that adding an introduction using ProxyFactory.addAdvice() is not permitted and results in an AopConfigException being thrown.

When using standard advice—that is, not introductions—it is possible for the same advice instance to be used for many different objects. The Spring documentation refers to this as the **per-class lifecycle,** although you can use a single advice instance for many different classes. For introductions, the introduction advice forms a part of the state of the advised object, and as a result, you must have a distinct advice instance for every advised object. This is called the **per-instance lifecycle**. Because you must ensure that each advised object has a distinct instance of the introduction, it is often preferable to create a subclass of DefaultIntroductionAdvisor that is responsible for creating the introduction advice. This way, you only need to ensure that a new instance of your advisor class is created for each object, because it will automatically create a new instance of the introduction.

That covers the basics of introduction creation. We will now move on to discuss how you can use introductions to solve the problem of object modification detection.

Object Modification Detection with Introductions

Object modification detection is a useful technique for many reasons. Typically you apply modification detection to prevent unnecessary database access when you are persisting object data. If an object is passed to a method for modification but it comes back unmodified, there is little point in issuing an update statement to the database. Using a modification check in this way can really increase application throughput, especially when the database is already under a substantial load or is located on some remote network making communication an expensive operation.

Unfortunately, this kind of functionality is difficult to implement by hand because it requires you to add to every method that can modify object state to check if the object state is actually being modified. When you consider all the null checks that have to be made and the checks to see if the value is actually changing, you are looking at around eight lines of code per method. You could refactor this into a single method, but you still have to call this method every time you need to perform the check. Spread this across a typical application with many different classes that require modification checks and you have a disaster waiting to happen.

This is clearly a place where introductions will help. We do not want to have to make it so each class that requires modification checks inherits from some base implementation, losing its only chance for inheritance as a result, nor do we really want to be adding checking code to each and every state-changing method. Using introductions, we can provide a flexible solution to the modification detection problem without having to write a bunch of repetitive, error-prone code.

In this example, we are going to build a full modification check framework using introductions. The modification check logic is encapsulated by the IsModified interface, an implementation of which will be introduced into the appropriate objects, along with interception logic to perform modification checks automatically. For the purposes of this example, we use JavaBeans conventions, in that we consider a modification to be any call to a setter method. Of course, we don't just treat all calls to a setter method as a modification—we check to see if the value being passed to the setter is different from the one currently stored in the object. The only flaw with this solution is that setting an object back to its original state will still reflect a modification if any one of the values on the object changed. However, the implementation here is nontrivial and suffices for most requirements. Implementing the more complete solution would result in an overly complex example.

The IsModified Interface

Central to the modification check solution is the IsModified interface, which our fictional application uses to make intelligent decisions about object persistence. We do not look at how the application would use IsModified; instead we focus on the implementation of the introduction.

Listing 7-6 shows the IsModified interface.

Listing 7-6. *The IsModified Interface*

```
package com.apress.prospring.ch7.introductions;

public interface IsModified {

    public boolean isModified();
}
```

Nothing special here—just a single method, isModified(), indicating whether or not an object has been modified.

Creating a Mixin

The next step is to create the code that implements IsModified and that is introduced to the objects; this is referred to as a **mixin.** As we mentioned earlier, it is much simpler to create mixins by subclassing DelegatingIntroductionInterceptor rather than to create one directly using IntroductionInterceptor. Our mixin class, IsModifiedMixin, subclasses DelegatingIntroductionInterceptor and also implements the IsModified interface. This is shown in Listing 7-7.

Listing 7-7. *The IsModifiedMixin Class*

```
package com.apress.prospring.ch7.introductions;

import java.lang.reflect.Method;
import java.util.HashMap;
import java.util.Map;
```

```java
import org.aopalliance.intercept.MethodInvocation;
import org.springframework.aop.support.DelegatingIntroductionInterceptor;

public class IsModifiedMixin extends DelegatingIntroductionInterceptor
        implements IsModified {

    private boolean isModified = false;

    private Map methodCache = new HashMap();

    public boolean isModified() {
        return isModified;
    }

    public Object invoke(MethodInvocation invocation) throws Throwable {

        if (!isModified) {
            if ((invocation.getMethod().getName().startsWith("set"))
                    && (invocation.getArguments().length == 1)) {

                // invoke the corresponding get method to see
                // if the value has actually changed
                Method getter = getGetter(invocation.getMethod());

                if (getter != null) {
                    // modification check is unimportant
                    // for write only methods
                    Object newVal = invocation.getArguments()[0];
                    Object oldVal = getter.invoke(invocation.getThis(), null);

                    if((newVal == null) && (oldVal == null)) {
                        isModified = false;
                    } else if((newVal == null) && (oldVal != null)) {
                        isModified = true;
                    } else if((newVal != null) && (oldVal == null)) {
                        isModified = true;
                    } else {
                        isModified = (!newVal.equals(oldVal));
                    }
                }

            }
        }

        return super.invoke(invocation);
    }
```

```
        private Method getGetter(Method setter) {
            Method getter = null;

            // attempt cache retrieval.
            getter = (Method) methodCache.get(setter);

            if (getter != null) {
                return getter;
            }

            String getterName = setter.getName().replaceFirst("set", "get");
            try {
                getter = setter.getDeclaringClass().getMethod(getterName, null);

                // cache getter
                synchronized (methodCache) {
                    methodCache.put(setter, getter);
                }

                return getter;
            } catch (NoSuchMethodException ex) {
                // must be write only
                return null;
            }
        }
    }
}
```

The first thing to notice here is the implementation of IsModified, which is made up of the private modified field and the isModified() method. This example highlights why you must have one mixin instance per advised object—the mixin introduces not only methods to the object but also state. If you share a single instance of this mixin across many different objects, then you are also sharing the state, which means all objects show as modified the first time a single object becomes modified.

You do not actually have to implement the invoke() method for a mixin, but in this case, doing so allows us to detect automatically when a modification occurs. The implementation for the modification check is fairly trivial. We start by only performing the check if the object is still unmodified; we do not need to check for modifications once we know that the object has been modified. Next, we check to see if the method is a setter, and if it is, we retrieve the corresponding getter method. Note that we cache the getter/setter pairs for quicker future retrieval. Finally, we compare the value returned by the getter with that passed to the setter to determine whether or not a modification has occurred. Notice that we check for the different possible combinations of null and set the modifications appropriately. It is important to remember that when you are using DelegatingIntroductionInterceptor, you must call super.invoke() when overriding invoke() because it is the DelegatingIntroductionInterceptor that actually dispatches the invocation to the correct location, either the advised object or the mixin itself.

You can implement as many interfaces as you like in your mixin, each of which is automatically introduced into the advised object. If you need to implement an interface on the mixin and you do not want to introduce that interface, you can simply call suppressInterface() from the mixin constructor after invoking super(), to prevent that interface from being exposed.

Creating an Advisor

The next step is to create an Advisor to wrap the creation of the mixin class. This step is optional, but it does help ensure that a new instance of the mixin is being used for each advised object. Listing 7-8 shows the IsModifiedAdvisor() class.

Listing 7-8. *Creating an Advisor for Your Mixin*

```
package com.apress.prospring.ch7.introductions;

import org.springframework.aop.support.DefaultIntroductionAdvisor;

public class IsModifiedAdvisor extends DefaultIntroductionAdvisor {

    public IsModifiedAdvisor() {
        super(new IsModifiedMixin());
    }
}
```

Notice that we have extended the DefaultIntroductionAdvisor to create our IsModifiedAdvisor. The implementation of this advisor is trivial and self-explanatory.

Putting It All Together

Now that we have a mixin class and an Advisor class, we can test out the modification check framework. Listing 7-9 shows a simple class that we use to test out the IsModifiedMixin.

Listing 7-9. *The TargetBean Class*

```
package com.apress.prospring.ch7.introductions;

public class TargetBean {

    private String name;

    public void setName(String name) {
        this.name = name;
    }

    public String getName() {
        return name;
    }
}
```

This bean has a single property, name, that we use when we are testing the modification check mixin. Listing 7-10 shows how to assemble the advised proxy and then tests the modification check code.

Listing 7-10. *Using the IsModifiedMixin*

```
package com.apress.prospring.ch7.introductions;

import org.springframework.aop.IntroductionAdvisor;
import org.springframework.aop.framework.ProxyFactory;

public class IntroductionExample {

    public static void main(String[] args) {
        // create the target
        TargetBean target = new TargetBean();
        target.setName("Rob Harrop");

        // create the advisor
        IntroductionAdvisor advisor = new IsModifiedAdvisor();

        // create the proxy
        ProxyFactory pf = new ProxyFactory();
        pf.setTarget(target);
        pf.addAdvisor(advisor);
        pf.setOptimize(true);

        TargetBean proxy = (TargetBean)pf.getProxy();
        IsModified proxyInterface = (IsModified)proxy;

        // test interfaces
        System.out.println("Is TargetBean?: " + (proxy instanceof TargetBean));
        System.out.println("Is IsModified?: " + (proxy instanceof IsModified));

        // test is modified implementation
        System.out.println("Has been modified?: " + proxyInterface.isModified());
        proxy.setName("Rob Harrop");
        System.out.println("Has been modified?: " + proxyInterface.isModified());
        proxy.setName("Joe Schmoe");
        System.out.println("Has been modified?: " + proxyInterface.isModified());

    }
}
```

Notice that when we are creating the proxy, we set the optimize flag to true to force the use of the CGLIB proxy. The reason for this is that when you are using the JDK proxy to introduce a mixin, the resulting proxy will not be an instance of the object class (in this case TargetBean);

the proxy only implements the mixin interfaces, not the original class. With the CGLIB proxy, the original class is implemented by the proxy along with the mixin interfaces.

Notice in the code that we test first to see if the proxy is an instance of TargetBean and then to see if it is an instance of IsModified. Both tests return true when you are using the CGLIB proxy, but only the IsModified test returns true for the JDK proxy. Finally, we test the modification check code by first setting the name property to its current value and then to a new value, checking the value of the isModified flag each time. Running this example results in the following output:

```
Is TargetBean?: true
Is IsModified?: true
Has been modified?: false
Has been modified?: false
Has been modified?: true
```

As expected, both instanceof tests return true. Notice that the first call to isModified(), before any modification occurred, returns false. The next call, after we set the value of name to the same value, also returns false. For the final call, however, after we set the value of name to a new value, the isModified() method returns true, indicating that the object has in fact been modified.

Introductions Summary

Introductions are one of the most powerful features of Spring AOP; they allow you not only to extend the functionality of existing methods, but also to extend the set of interfaces and object implements dynamically. Using introductions is the perfect way to implement crosscutting logic that your application interacts with through well-defined interfaces. In general, this is the kind of logic that you want to apply declaratively rather than programmatically. By using the IsModifiedMixin defined in this example and the framework services discussed in the next section, we can declaratively define which objects are capable of modification checks, without needing to modify the implementations of those objects.

Obviously, because introductions work via proxies, they add a certain amount of overhead, and all methods on the proxy are considered to be advised, because you cannot use pointcuts in conjunction with introductions. However, in the case of many of the services you can implement using introductions such as the object modification check, this performance overhead is a small price to pay for the reduction in code required to implement the service, as well the increase in stability and maintainability that comes from fully centralizing the service logic.

Framework Services for AOP

Up to now, we have had to write a lot of code to advise objects and generate the proxies for them. Although this in itself is not a huge problem, it does mean that all advice configuration is hardcoded into your application, removing some of the benefits of being able to advise a method implementation transparently. Thankfully, Spring provides additional framework services that allow you to create an advised proxy in your application configuration and then inject this proxy into a target bean just like any other dependency.

Using the declarative approach to AOP configuration is preferable to the manual, programmatic mechanism. When you use the declarative mechanism, you not only externalize the configuration of advice, but you also reduce the chance of coding errors. You can also take advantage of DI and AOP combined to enable AOP so it can be used in a completely transparent environment.

Configuring AOP Declaratively

Declarative configuration of AOP does not require any special configuration wizardry. AOP configuration is just like standard bean configuration; the only difference is that instead of exposing your bean directly, you use the ProxyFactoryBean class, which implements FactoryBean, to create a proxy automatically.

Introducing ProxyFactoryBean

The ProxyFactoryBean class is the central class for declarative AOP configuration. It is an implementation of FactoryBean that allows you to specify a bean to target and it provides a set of advice and advisors for that bean that are eventually merged into an AOP proxy. Because you can use both advisor and advice with the ProxyFactoryBean, you can configure not only the advice declaratively, but the pointcuts as well.

ProxyFactoryBean shares a common interface with ProxyFactory and ProxyConfig, and as a result, it exposes many of the same flags such as frozen, optimize, and exposeProxy. The values for these flags are passed directly to the underlying ProxyFactory, which allows you to configure the factory declaratively as well.

ProxyFactoryBean in Action

Using ProxyFactoryBean is actually very simple. You define a bean that will be the target bean and then using ProxyFactoryBean, you define the bean that your application will actually access, using the target bean as the proxy target. Where possible, define the target bean as an anonymous bean inside the proxy bean declaration. This prevents your application from accidentally accessing the unadvised bean. However, in some cases, such as the sample we are about to show you, you may want to create more than one proxy for the same bean, so you should use a normal top-level bean for this case.

Listings 7-11 and 7-12 show two classes, one of which has a dependency on the other.

Listing 7-11. *The MyDependency Class*

```
package com.apress.prospring.ch7.pfb;

public class MyDependency {

    public void foo() {
        System.out.println("foo()");
    }

    public void bar() {
        System.out.println("bar()");
    }
}
```

Listing 7-12. *The MyBean Class*

```
package com.apress.prospring.ch7.pfb;

public class MyBean {

    private MyDependency dep;

    public void execute() {
        dep.foo();
        dep.bar();
    }

    public void setDep(MyDependency dep) {
        this.dep = dep;
    }
}
```

For this example, we are going to create two proxies for a single MyDependency instance, both with the same basic advice shown in Listing 7-13.

Listing 7-13. *The MyAdvice Class*

```
package com.apress.prospring.ch7.pfb;

import java.lang.reflect.Method;

import org.springframework.aop.MethodBeforeAdvice;

public class MyAdvice implements MethodBeforeAdvice {

    public void before(Method method, Object[] args, Object target)
            throws Throwable {
        System.out.println("Executing: " + method);
    }

}
```

The first proxy will just advise the target using the advice directly, thus all methods will be advised. For the second proxy, we will configure a JdkRegexpMethodPointcut and a DefaultPointcutAdvisor so that only the foo() method of the MyDependency class is advised. To test the advice, we will create two bean definitions of type MyBean, each of which will be injected with a different proxy. Then we will invoke the execute() method on each of these beans and observe what happens when the advised methods on the dependency are invoked.

Listing 7-14 shows the configuration for this example.

Listing 7-14. *Declarative AOP Configuration*

```
<!DOCTYPE beans PUBLIC "-//SPRING//DTD BEAN//EN"
"http://www.springframework.org/dtd/spring-beans.dtd">
<beans>
    <bean id="myBean1" class="com.apress.prospring.ch7.pfb.MyBean">
        <property name="dep">
            <ref local="myDependency1"/>
        </property>
    </bean>

    <bean id="myBean2" class="com.apress.prospring.ch7.pfb.MyBean">
        <property name="dep">
            <ref local="myDependency2"/>
        </property>
    </bean>

    <bean id="myDependencyTarget"
          class="com.apress.prospring.ch7.pfb.MyDependency"/>

    <bean id="myDependency1"
          class="org.springframework.aop.framework.ProxyFactoryBean">
        <property name="target">
            <ref local="myDependencyTarget"/>
        </property>
        <property name="interceptorNames">
            <list>
                <value>advice</value>
            </list>
        </property>
    </bean>

    <bean id="myDependency2"
          class="org.springframework.aop.framework.ProxyFactoryBean">
        <property name="target">
            <ref local="myDependencyTarget"/>
        </property>
        <property name="interceptorNames">
            <list>
                <value>advisor</value>
            </list>
        </property>
    </bean>

    <bean id="advice" class="com.apress.prospring.ch7.pfb.MyAdvice"/>
```

```xml
<bean id="advisor"
        class="org.springframework.aop.support.DefaultPointcutAdvisor">
    <property name="advice">
        <ref local="advice"/>
    </property>
    <property name="pointcut">
        <bean class="org.springframework.aop.support.JdkRegexpMethodPointcut">
            <property name="pattern">
                <value>.*foo.*</value>
            </property>
        </bean>
    </property>
</bean>
</beans>
```

This code should be familiar to you. Notice that we are not really doing anything special; we are simply setting the properties that we set in code using Spring's DI capabilities. The only points of interest are that we use an anonymous bean for the pointcut and we use the ProxyFactoryBean class. We prefer to use anonymous beans for pointcuts when they are not being shared because it keeps the set of beans that are directly accessible as small and as application-relevant as possible. The important point to realize when you are using ProxyFactoryBean is that the ProxyFactoryBean declaration is the one to expose to your application and the one to use when you are fulfilling dependencies. The underlying target bean declaration is not advised, so you should only use this bean when you want to bypass the AOP framework, although in general, your application should not be aware of the AOP framework and thus should not want to bypass it. For this reason, you should use anonymous beans wherever possible to avoid accidental access from the application.

Listing 7-15 shows a simple class that grabs the two MyBean instances from the ApplicationContext and then runs the execute() method for each one.

Listing 7-15. *The ProxyFactoryBeanExample Class*

```java
package com.apress.prospring.ch7.pfb;

import org.springframework.context.ApplicationContext;
import org.springframework.context.support.FileSystemXmlApplicationContext;

public class ProxyFactoryBeanExample {

    public static void main(String[] args) {
        ApplicationContext ctx = new FileSystemXmlApplicationContext(
                "./ch7/src/conf/pfb.xml");

        MyBean bean1 = (MyBean)ctx.getBean("myBean1");
        MyBean bean2 = (MyBean)ctx.getBean("myBean2");

        System.out.println("Bean 1");
        bean1.execute();
```

```
                System.out.println("\nBean 2");
                bean2.execute();
        }
}
```

Running this example results in the following output:

```
Bean 1
Executing: public void com.apress.prospring.ch7.pfb.MyDependency.foo()
foo()
Executing: public void com.apress.prospring.ch7.pfb.MyDependency.bar()
bar()

Bean 2
Executing: public void com.apress.prospring.ch7.pfb.MyDependency.foo()
foo()
bar()
```

As expected, both the foo() and bar() methods in the first proxy are advised, because no pointcut was used in its configuration. For the second proxy, however, only the foo() method was advised due to the pointcut used in the configuration.

Using ProxyFactoryBean for Introductions

You can not only use the ProxyFactoryBean class for advising an object, but also for introducing mixins to your objects. Remember from our earlier discussion on introductions that you must use an IntroductionAdvisor to add an introduction; you cannot add an introduction directly. The same rule applies when you are using ProxyFactoryBean with introductions. When you are using ProxyFactoryBean, it becomes much easier to configure your proxies if you created a custom Advisor for your mixin as discussed earlier. Listing 7-16 shows a sample configuration for the IsModifiedMixin introduction we discussed earlier.

Listing 7-16. *Configuring Introductions with ProxyFactoryBean*

```
<!DOCTYPE beans PUBLIC "-//SPRING//DTD BEAN//EN"
"http://www.springframework.org/dtd/spring-beans.dtd">
<beans>
    <bean id="bean"
          class="org.springframework.aop.framework.ProxyFactoryBean">
        <property name="target">
            <bean id="beanTarget"
                  class="com.apress.prospring.ch7.introductions.TargetBean">
                <property name="name">
                    <value>Rob Harrop</value>
                </property>
            </bean>
        </property>
```

```
            <property name="interceptorNames">
                <list>
                    <value>advisor</value>
                </list>
            </property>
            <property name="proxyTargetClass">
                <value>true</value>
            </property>
        </bean>

        <bean id="advisor"
              class="com.apress.prospring.ch7.introductions.IsModifiedAdvisor"/>
</beans>
```

As you can see from the configuration, we use the IsModifiedAdvisor class as the advisor for the ProxyFactoryBean, and because we do not need to create another proxy of the same target object, we use an anonymous declaration for the target bean. Listing 7-17 shows a modification of the previous introduction example that obtains the proxy from the ApplicationContext.

Listing 7-17. *The IntroductionConfigExample Class*

```java
package com.apress.prospring.ch7.introductions;

import org.springframework.context.ApplicationContext;
import org.springframework.context.support.FileSystemXmlApplicationContext;

public class IntroductionConfigExample {

    public static void main(String[] args) {
        ApplicationContext ctx = new FileSystemXmlApplicationContext(
                "./ch7/src/conf/introductions.xml");

        TargetBean bean = (TargetBean) ctx.getBean("bean");
        IsModified mod = (IsModified) bean;

        // test interfaces
        System.out.println("Is TargetBean?: " + (bean instanceof TargetBean));
        System.out.println("Is IsModified?: " + (bean instanceof IsModified));

        // test is modified implementation
        System.out.println("Has been modified?: " + mod.isModified());
        bean.setName("Rob Harrop");
        System.out.println("Has been modified?: " + mod.isModified());
        bean.setName("Joe Schmoe");
        System.out.println("Has been modified?: " + mod.isModified());
    }
}
```

Running this example yields exactly the same output as the previous introduction example, but this time the proxy is obtained from the `ApplicationContext` and no configuration is present in the application code.

ProxyFactoryBean Summary

When you use `ProxyFactoryBean`, you can configure AOP proxies that provide all the flexibility of the programmatic method without needing to couple your application to the AOP configuration. Unless you need to perform decisions at runtime as to how your proxies should be created, it is best to use the declarative method of proxy configuration over the programmatic method.

Using Automatic Proxying

When you use `ProxyFactoryBean`, you gain an excellent way to create advised beans external to your application. However, the `ProxyFactoryBean` approach does require some level of configuration, and for applications that make extensive use of AOP, this configuration can be quite time-consuming to create. For this reason, Spring provides some convenience classes to create proxies of beans in your `ApplicationContext` automatically. Aside from the obvious benefit of reduced coding, this feature also prevents an application from retrieving the unadvised bean, because Spring actually swaps the bean for the proxy in the `ApplicationContext`.

Here are the three core options you have for autoproxying with Spring:

- **Using the `BeanNameAutoProxyCreator` class:** This class allows you to specify a list of bean names and the set of advice and advisors to apply to them. Spring automatically proxies all beans with the specified advice. In addition, you can use wildcards in the bean names, which enables you to match all beans following a similar naming scheme.

- **Using the `DefaultAdvisorAutoProxyCreator`:** This is an extremely powerful autoproxy class that automatically proxies all beans in your `ApplicationContext` with any advisor that is relevant. This class only works with advisors, not advice, because it relies on the pointcut of the advisor when determining whether or not the advisor should be applied to a particular bean.

- **Using source level metadata:** This is a special case of `DefaultAdvisorAutoProxyCreator` usage. When using source level metadata, the `Advisor` used by `DefaultAdvisorAutoProxyCreator` uses pointcuts that are driven by the source level metadata. For example, when configuring transactions in Spring, you can define the transaction behavior at method level using metadata, and then using `DefaultAdvisorAutoProxyCreator`, you can have the transactional proxy created automatically for you. We will not be looking at how you use this feature in your own applications, but we do look at using metadata-driven proxying in Chapter 12 when we discuss transaction management with Spring. If you want to use this feature in your own applications, then we suggest you start by looking at the source code for the classes described in Chapter 12.

Using BeanNameAutoProxyCreator

The BeanNameAutoProxyCreator is the ideal class when you want to apply the same set of advice to an arbitrary set of beans in your ApplicationContext automatically. BeanNameAutoProxyCreator requires that you specify the names of the beans that are the advice and the names of the beans to be advised, and that's it. When specifying the names of the beans to be advised, you can use wildcards, which allows you to autoproxy a set of beans that follow the same naming structure. In fact, this is one of the best features of BeanNameAutoProxyCreator—it allows you to apply a set of advice uniformly to a set of beans based on the way they are named. Provided that you have some kind of naming convention in place for beans that are related, it is simple to apply advice across whole sets of related beans.

Listing 7-18 shows a simple class, AutoBean, that we are going to autoproxy in this example.

Listing 7-18. *The AutoBean Class*

```
package com.apress.prospring.ch7.autoproxying;

public class AutoBean {

    public void foo() {
        System.out.println("foo()");
    }
}
```

For this example, we are going to define two beans of type AutoBean in our ApplicationContext and then autoproxy them using BeanNameAutoProxyCreator to add the SimpleBeforeAdvice class that we created earlier. The configuration for this is shown in Listing 7-19.

Listing 7-19. *Using BeanNameAutoProxyCreator*

```
<!DOCTYPE beans PUBLIC "-//SPRING//DTD BEAN//EN"
"http://www.springframework.org/dtd/spring-beans.dtd">
<beans>

    <bean id="proxyCreator"
      class="org.springframework.aop.framework.autoproxy.BeanNameAutoProxyCreator">
        <property name="beanNames">
            <list>
                <value>foo*</value>
                <value>barBean</value>
            </list>
            </property>
```

```
                <property name="interceptorNames">
                    <list>
                        <value>advice</value>
                    </list>
                </property>
            </bean>

        <bean id="fooBean" class="com.apress.prospring.ch7.autoproxying.AutoBean"/>
        <bean id="barBean" class="com.apress.prospring.ch7.autoproxying.AutoBean"/>

        <bean id="advice" class="com.apress.prospring.ch7.cflow.SimpleBeforeAdvice"/>
    </beans>
```

Here you can see that we have defined two beans, fooBean and barBean, both of type
AutoBean. These are the beans we are going to proxy. The advice bean will be the advice that is
applied to both beans. Notice that for the proxyCreator bean, we have defined the list of interceptor names as we would with the ProxyFactoryBean. Also supplied to proxyCreator is the list
of bean names. We have specified barBean and foo*. The foo* name will match any bean whose
name begins with foo.

In Listing 7-20, you can see an example of how the automatically generated proxies are
accessed.

Listing 7-20. *Accessing the Auto Generated Proxies*

```
package com.apress.prospring.ch7.autoproxying;

import org.springframework.context.ApplicationContext;
import org.springframework.context.support.FileSystemXmlApplicationContext;

public class BeanNameExample {

    public static void main(String[] args) {
        ApplicationContext ctx = new FileSystemXmlApplicationContext(
        "./ch7/src/conf/bnapc.xml");

        AutoBean fooBean = (AutoBean)ctx.getBean("fooBean");
        AutoBean barBean = (AutoBean)ctx.getBean("barBean");

        fooBean.foo();
        barBean.foo();
    }
}
```

Notice that when accessing the beans, we use the bean names as defined in the ApplicationContext configuration. The reason for this is that the BeanNameAutoProxyCreator actually replaces the original bean instance with the automatically generated proxy instance. Running this example results in the following output:

```
Before method: public void com.apress.prospring.ch7.autoproxying.AutoBean.foo()
foo()
Before method: public void com.apress.prospring.ch7.autoproxying.AutoBean.foo()
foo()
```

As you can see, both calls to AutoBean.foo() were advised, as we expected. This example only autogenerated two proxies, so you do not really get a full appreciation of the amount of configuration code saved. However, when you need to proxy three or more beans, you really start to notice the configuration savings. Whenever you need to advise a set of beans in an identical manner, the BeanNameAutoProxyCreator is an ideal solution, especially if all your beans share a similar naming structure.

Using DefaultAdvisorAutoProxyCreator

Using the DefaultAdvisorAutoProxyCreator enables you to advise any bean in your ApplicationContext automatically by simply providing the appropriate advisors. The DefaultAdvisorAutoProxyCreator uses the pointcut of each advisor in the ApplicationContext to decide whether it applies to a particular bean. It performs this check for each advisor present and for each bean in your ApplicationContext. If a bean has no applicable advisors in the ApplicationContext, meaning none of the defined pointcuts match any of the joinpoints on the bean, then no proxy is created for it.

For this example we are going to use the AutoBean class from the previous example, but also the OtherBean class as shown in Listing 7-21.

Listing 7-21. *The OtherBean Class*

```
package com.apress.prospring.ch7.autoproxying;

public class OtherBean {

    public void foo() {
        System.out.println("foo()");
    }
}
```

As you can see, this is just a duplicate of the AutoBean class, but it helps illustrate the part pointcuts play when you are using DefaultAdvisorAutoProxyCreator. The next piece of the puzzle is a pointcut that only matches the AutoBean class and matches all methods on that class. This code is shown in Listing 7-22.

Listing 7-22. *The MyPointcut Class*

```
package com.apress.prospring.ch7.autoproxying;

import org.springframework.aop.ClassFilter;
import org.springframework.aop.MethodMatcher;
import org.springframework.aop.Pointcut;

public class MyPointcut implements Pointcut {

    public ClassFilter getClassFilter() {
        return new ClassFilter() {

            public boolean matches(Class cls) {
                return (cls == AutoBean.class);
            }
        };
    }

    public MethodMatcher getMethodMatcher() {
        return MethodMatcher.TRUE;
    }
}
```

Here you can see a pointcut with a `ClassFilter` that only matches the `AutoBean` class and a `MethodMatcher` that matches all methods. Because of the `ClassFilter` in this pointcut, any `Advisor` that is associated with it is only applied to beans of type `AutoBean`. Listing 7-23 shows a configuration using the `DefaultAdvisorAutoProxyCreator`.

Listing 7-23. *Using DefaultAdvisorAutoProxyCreator*

```
<!DOCTYPE beans PUBLIC "-//SPRING//DTD BEAN//EN"
"http://www.springframework.org/dtd/spring-beans.dtd">
<beans>

    <bean id="proxyCreator"
class="org.springframework.aop.framework.autoproxy.DefaultAdvisorAutoProxyCreator"/>

    <bean id="autoBean" class="com.apress.prospring.ch7.autoproxying.AutoBean"/>
    <bean id="otherBean" class="com.apress.prospring.ch7.autoproxying.OtherBean"/>

    <bean id="advisor"
          class="org.springframework.aop.support.DefaultPointcutAdvisor">
          <property name="pointcut">
              <bean class="com.apress.prospring.ch7.autoproxying.MyPointcut"/>
          </property>
```

```
            <property name="advice">
                <bean class="com.apress.prospring.ch7.cflow.SimpleBeforeAdvice"/>
            </property>
        </bean>
</beans>
```

Here you can see that we have set up the advisor bean with an instance of MyPointcut as the pointcut and SimpleBeforeAdvice as the advice. The DefaultAdvisorAutoProxyCreator bean, which requires no configuration beyond its declaration, attempts to advise both autoBean and otherBean automatically with the advisor bean. However, the MyPointcut on the advisor bean prevents it from being applied to otherBean because the ClassFilter only matches the AutoBean class. Listing 7-24 shows an example of accessing both autoBean and otherBean in an application.

Listing 7-24. *The DefaultCreatorExample Class*

```
package com.apress.prospring.ch7.autoproxying;

import org.springframework.aop.support.AopUtils;
import org.springframework.context.ApplicationContext;
import org.springframework.context.support.FileSystemXmlApplicationContext;

public class DefaultCreatorExample {

    public static void main(String[] args) {
        ApplicationContext ctx = new FileSystemXmlApplicationContext(
        "./ch7/src/conf/dpac.xml");

        AutoBean autoBean = (AutoBean)ctx.getBean("autoBean");
        OtherBean otherBean = (OtherBean)ctx.getBean("otherBean");

        autoBean.foo();
        System.out.println(AopUtils.isAopProxy(autoBean));

        otherBean.foo();
        System.out.println(AopUtils.isAopProxy(otherBean));
    }
}
```

Here you can see that we grab both autoBean and otherBean from the ApplicationContext and then invoke the foo() method on both. Only the foo() method of autoBean is advised. Notice that we also use the AopUtils class supplied by Spring to test whether or not the two beans are actually AOP proxies. Because otherBean had no valid advisors in the ApplicationContext, it should not have been proxied; the output from this example shows this to be true:

```
Before method: public void com.apress.prospring.ch7.autoproxying.AutoBean.foo()
foo()
true
foo()
false
```

As you can see, the only advised method was the foo() method of autoBean, and otherBean was not a proxy. The DefaultAdvisorAutoProxyCreator class is a useful class when you have a set of advisors or pointcuts that are capable of filtering out non-target classes appropriately. However, in a large application, it can become difficult to see exactly where advice will be applied and you may find that you are adding unnecessary advice to your objects.

Autoproxying Summary

Using autoproxying can save you a lot of configuration coding, but it is not as explicit as using ProxyFactoryBean, and it can quickly become confusing as to which beans are being advised, especially when you are using DefaultAdvisorAutoProxyCreator. That said, the BeanNameAutoProxyCreator class is extremely useful for advising beans in large amounts, and it does not make your configuration too confusing. In general, we find that BeanNameAutoProxyCreator is very useful for applying uniform advice across a large selection of beans, but when we are dealing with just one or two beans, we prefer to stick to ProxyFactoryBean, because it makes the configuration much more explicit.

AspectJ Integration

AOP provides a powerful solution to many of the common problems that arise with OOP-based applications. When using Spring AOP, you can take advantage of a select subset of AOP functionality that, in most cases, allows you to solve problems you encounter in your application. However, in some cases, you may wish to use some AOP features that are outside the scope of Spring AOP. In this case, you need to look at an AOP implementation with a fuller feature set. Our preference, in this case, is to use AspectJ, and because you can now configure AspectJ aspects using Spring, AspectJ forms the perfect complement to Spring AOP.

About AspectJ

AspectJ is a fully featured AOP implementation that uses a compile-time weaving process to introduce aspects into your code. In AspectJ, aspects and pointcuts are built using a Java-like syntax, which reduces the learning curve for Java developers. We are not going to spend too much time looking at AspectJ and how it works because that is way beyond the scope of this book. Instead, we present some simple AspectJ examples and show you how to configure them using Spring. For more information on AspectJ, you should definitely read *AspectJ in Action* by Raminvas Laddad (Manning, 2003).

■Note We are not going to cover how to compile and weave AspectJ aspects into your application. Refer to the AspectJ documentation for details on how to achieve this. Alternatively, Eclipse users can download the AspectJ integration package and take advantage of full IDE integration and auto-compilation.

Using Singleton Aspects

By default, AspectJ aspects are singletons, in that you get a single instance per classloader. The problem Spring faces with any AspectJ aspect is that it cannot create the aspect instance because that is handled by AspectJ itself. However, each aspect exposes a method, aspectOf(), which can be used to access the aspect instance. Using the aspectOf() method and a special feature of Spring configuration, you can have Spring configure the aspect for you. The benefits of this cannot be understated. You can take full advantage of AspectJ's powerful AOP feature set without losing out on Spring's excellent DI and configuration abilities. This also means that you do not need two separate configuration methods for your application; you can use the same Spring ApplicationContext approach for all your Spring-managed beans and for your AspectJ aspects.

There is actually nothing particularly special or difficult about configuring AspectJ aspects using Spring, as the following example shows. In Listing 7-25, you can see a basic class, MessageWriter, that we will advise using AspectJ.

Listing 7-25. *The MessageWriter Class*

```
package com.apress.prospring.ch7.aspectj;

public class MessageWriter {

    public void writeMessage() {
        System.out.println("foobar!");
    }

    public void foo() {
        System.out.println("foo");
    }
}
```

For this example, we are going to use AspectJ to advise the writeMessage() method and write out a message before and after the method invocation. These messages will be configurable using Spring.

Listing 7-26 shows the MessageWrapper aspect.

Listing 7-26. *MessageWrapper Aspect*

```
package com.apress.prospring.ch7.aspectj;

public aspect MessageWrapper {

    private String prefix;
    private String suffix;

    public void setPrefix(String prefix) {
        this.prefix = prefix;
    }
```

```
    public void setSuffix(String suffix) {
        this.suffix = suffix;
    }

    pointcut doWriting() :
        execution(*
            com.apress.prospring.ch7.aspectj.MessageWriter.writeMessage());

    before() : doWriting() {
        System.out.println(prefix);
    }

    after() : doWriting() {
        System.out.println(suffix);
    }
}
```

Much of this code should look familiar. Essentially we create an aspect called MessageWrapper and, just like a normal Java class, we give the aspect two properties, suffix and prefix, which we will use when advising the writeMessage() method. Next, we define a named pointcut, doWriting(), for a single joinpoint, in this case, the execution of the writeMessage() method. (AspectJ has a huge number of joinpoints, but coverage of those is outside the scope of this example.) Finally, we define two lots of advice: one that executes before the doWriting() pointcut and one that executes after it. The before advice writes a line containing the prefix and the after advice writes a line containing the suffix. Listing 7-27 shows how this aspect is configured in Spring.

Listing 7-27. *Configuring an AspectJ Aspect*

```
<?xml version="1.0" encoding="UTF-8"?>
<!DOCTYPE beans PUBLIC "-//SPRING//DTD BEAN//EN"
"http://www.springframework.org/dtd/spring-beans.dtd">
<beans>
  <bean id="aspect"
        class="com.apress.prospring.ch7.aspectj.MessageWrapper"
            factory-method="aspectOf">
    <property name="prefix">
        <value>Ha Ha!</value>
    </property>
      <property name="suffix">
        <value>Ho Ho!</value>
    </property>
  </bean>
</beans>
```

As you can see, much of the configuration of the aspect bean is very similar to standard bean configuration. The only difference is the use of the factory-method attribute of the <bean> tag. The factory-method attribute is intended to allow classes that follow a traditional Factory pattern to be integrated seamlessly into Spring. For instance, if you have a class Foo with a private constructor and then a static factory method, getInstance(), using factory-method allows a bean of this class to be managed by Spring. The aspectOf() method exposed by every AspectJ aspect allows you to access the instance of the aspect and thus allows Spring to set the properties of the aspect. Listing 7-28 shows a simple driver application for this example.

Listing 7-28. *AspectJ Configuration in Action*

```
package com.apress.prospring.ch7.aspectj;

import org.springframework.context.ApplicationContext;
import org.springframework.context.support.FileSystemXmlApplicationContext;

public class AspectJExample {

    public static void main(String[] args) {
        ApplicationContext ctx = new FileSystemXmlApplicationContext(
                "./ch7/src/conf/aspectj.xml");
        MessageWriter writer = new MessageWriter();
        writer.writeMessage();
        writer.foo();
    }
}
```

Notice that first we load the ApplicationContext to allow Spring to configure the aspect. Next we create an instance of MessageWriter and then invoke the writeMessage() and foo() methods. The output from this example is as follows:

```
Ha Ha!
foobar!
Ho Ho!
foo
```

As you can see, the advice in the MessageWrapper aspect was applied to the writeMessage() method and the prefix and suffix values specified in the ApplicationContext configuration were used by the advice when writing out the before and after messages.

Features Coming Soon

Currently the only feature implemented in the Spring/AspectJ integration is the ability to configure singleton aspects. Because this is the most important feature required, it was the feature that was placed at the top of the list. For the 1.2 release, expect to see support for perthis, pertarget, and percflow aspects as well as the current support for singleton aspects. Also planned for 1.2 is an AspectJ-style pointcut expression language for Spring, which will allow a greater range of pointcuts to be defined in Spring.

AOP in the Sample Application

So far, you have seen lots of small examples of how to use the Spring AOP features, but as of yet, we have not looked at some practical uses of AOP in an application. Typical examples in this field are logging and security, and we have looked at these, albeit briefly, over the course of this chapter and the last. However, AOP is not just limited to use in logging and security, and it can be put to great use when you are implementing any application-specific logic that is crosscutting— that is, any logic in your application that needs to be called from a large number of separate components. In this section, we show you how we use Spring AOP in the sample SpringBlog application to solve a problem involving crosscutting logic.

Filtering Obscenities in SpringBlog

One of the problems we faced when building the SpringBlog application was how to filter obscenities uniformly out of postings on the blog. This includes top-level blog entries as well as any comments made about a particular entry. We needed to ensure that neither an entry nor a comment could be created containing obscenities, and that existing entries and comments could not be modified to contain obscenities. Specifically, we wanted the ability to obfuscate obscenities contained in postings automatically with non-offensive alternatives. Taking this further, we decided that in some cases, the blog owner might actually want to be able to add obscenities to their entries, acting as their own moderator, but want to restrict blog readers from posting comments containing obscenities.

The traditional approach to this problem would be to define an interface, ObscenityFilter, and then build an implementation of this interface and make it accessible through some factory class. Then in each method where an entry or comment is created or modified, you invoke the ObscenityFilter to remove obscenities from the posting. In the SpringBlog application, all business logic is exposed through the BlogManager interface. BlogManager exposes two methods, saveEntry() and saveComment(), both of which need to check for obscenities in their respective Entry and Comment objects.

There are two main problems with this. First, each implementation of BlogManager is going to have to remember to implement this check. You can reduce this burden slightly by creating a common base class for all BlogManager implementations, but nothing prevents a programmer from creating a BlogManager implementation directly and forgetting to check the ObscenityFilter. The second problem with this approach is that it relies on the same logic being present in two methods; this increases the maintenance burden and the chance of spurious errors creeping into the code.

Using Spring AOP, we can create a much more elegant solution to this problem by factoring the obscenity check into a before advice that we can apply to any method that accepts the Entry or Comment object as an argument. We could have opted to make this advice much more flexible, allowing it to explore any JavaBean for String-typed properties, but we had no use for this feature in the application; following the principles of YAGNI (You Aren't Gonna Need It), we decided to keep the implementation simple and to the point.

An interesting point about this implementation is that, for the most part, we just followed good OOP practice as suggested in the traditional approach. We defined an interface, ObscenityFilter, and then built an implementation. Thanks to Spring DI, we were able to avoid the need to create a factory class, but by following good practices, we were able to build an obscenity filter that can be used equally well in both AOP and non-AOP settings.

The BlogPosting Interface

Within the blog, there are two distinct types of postings: a main blog entry, represented by an Entry object, and a comment about an entry, represented by a Comment object. Although these two objects represent different kinds of posting, they do share similar characteristics, such as body, subject, attachments, and date of posting. For this reason, we created an interface, BlogPosting, that allows Comments and Entries to be manipulated at the same time. Because all the String-typed properties of Comment and Entry are exposed on the BlogPosting interface, we use the BlogPosting interface in our obscenity filter advice. Listing 7-29 shows the BlogPosting interface.

Listing 7-29. *The BlogPosting Interface*

```
package com.apress.prospring.domain;

import java.util.Date;
import java.util.List;

public interface BlogPosting {

    public List getAttachments();
    public void setAttachments(List attachments);

    public String getBody();
    public void setBody(String body);

    public Date getPostDate();
    public void setPostDate(Date postDate);

    public String getSubject();
    public void setSubject(String subject);
}
```

Implementing ObscenityFilter

For the SpringBlog application, we decided to create an implementation of ObscenityFilter that allows the list of obscenities to filter to be specified as a List and that replaces the obscenities using the ROT13 algorithm. Listing 7-30 shows the ObscenityFilter interface.

Listing 7-30. *The ObscenityFilter Interface*

```
package com.apress.prospring.business;

public interface ObscenityFilter {

    public boolean containsObscenities(String data);

    public String obfuscateObscenities(String data);
}
```

The basic usage of the ObscenityFilter interface involves a call to containsObscenities() to see if a particular String contains obscenities. If it does, then a call to obfuscateObscenities() takes the String containing obscenities and returns a String with them obfuscated. Our basic implementation of this interface is shown in Listing 7-31.

Listing 7-31. *The ListBasedObscenityFilter Class*

```java
package com.apress.prospring.business;

import java.util.List;
import java.util.regex.Matcher;
import java.util.regex.Pattern;

public class ListBasedObscenityFilter implements ObscenityFilter {

    private List obscenities = null;

    private Pattern obscenityPattern = null;

    public void setObscenities(List obscenities) {
        this.obscenities = obscenities;

        buildRegex();
    }

    private void buildRegex() {
        StringBuffer sb = new StringBuffer();

        int size = obscenities.size();

        for (int x = 0; x < size; x++) {
            if (x != 0) {
                sb.append("|");
            }
            sb.append("(");
            sb.append(obscenities.get(x));
            sb.append(")");
        }

        obscenityPattern =
                Pattern.compile(sb.toString(), Pattern.CASE_INSENSITIVE);
    }
```

```java
    public boolean containsObscenities(String data) {
        Matcher m = obscenityPattern.matcher(data);
        return m.find();
    }

    public String obfuscateObscenities(String data) {
        Matcher m = obscenityPattern.matcher(data);
        StringBuffer out = new StringBuffer(data.length());

        while (m.find()) {
            if (m.group(0) != null) {
                m.appendReplacement(out, rot13(m.group(0)));
            }
        }

        return out.toString();
    }

    private String rot13(String in) {
        char[] chars = in.toCharArray();

        for (int x = 0; x < chars.length; x++) {
            char c = chars[x];
            if (c >= 'a' && c <= 'm')
                c += 13;
            else if (c >= 'n' && c <= 'z')
                c -= 13;
            else if (c >= 'A' && c <= 'M')
                c += 13;
            else if (c >= 'A' && c <= 'Z') c -= 13;

            chars[x] = c;
        }

        return new String(chars);
    }
}
```

Here you can see that the ListBasedObscenityFilter class exposes the List-typed obscenities property, allowing the list of obscenities to filter to be specified externally. In particular, this allows the list of obscenities to be specified in the Spring configuration file. Once the list of obscenities is specified, we build a regular expression from the list, which allows the obscenity filter to match and replace obscenities easily.

The obfuscateObscenities() method uses the regular expression that we created previously to replace any obscenities in the supplied data with the ROT13 equivalent. The ROT13 algorithm is very basic, and essentially, it just rotates each letter in a String by 13 places. Listing 7-32 shows a basic JUnit test case for the ListBasedObscenityFilter that demonstrates typical usage.

Listing 7-32. *Testing the ListBasedObscenityFilter*

```
package com.apress.prospring.business;

import java.util.ArrayList;
import java.util.List;

import junit.framework.TestCase;

public class ObscenityFilterTest extends TestCase {

    public void testReplaceObscenity() {

        ListBasedObscenityFilter filter = new ListBasedObscenityFilter();
        List list = new ArrayList();
        list.add("crap");
        list.add("damn");
        list.add("arse");
        list.add("bugger");

        filter.setObscenities(list);

        String testData = "Crap! Kiss my arse, you damn bugger!";

        assertTrue("Test data should contain obscenities", filter
                .containsObscenities(testData));

        String val = filter.obfuscateObscenities(testData);

        System.out.println(val);

        assertTrue(val.indexOf("arse") == -1);
        assertTrue(val.indexOf("Crap") == -1);
        assertTrue(val.indexOf("damn") == -1);
        assertTrue(val.indexOf("bugger") == -1);
        assertTrue(val.indexOf("Kiss") > -1);
    }
}
```

As you can see, we specify a list of obscenities and then, using some test data containing these obscenities, we check to make sure the ObscenityFilter correctly identifies the obscenities and replaces them, without touching other words in the String. Running this test results in a pass and the following obfuscated message being written to stdout:

```
Penc! Kiss my nefr, you qnza ohttre
```

As you can see, the basic sentence structure is preserved, but the obscene words are replaced with nonsense.

Creating the ObscenityFilterAdvice

With the `ListBasedObscenityFilter` implementation finished, all that remains is creating an advice that allows obscenity filter capabilities to be applied declaratively to any method that accepts `Entry` or `Comment` arguments. The basis of the `ObscenityFilterAdvice` is to modify the arguments passed to the method so that any `String` properties of the `Entry` or `Comment` objects are replaced with their obfuscated alternatives. Because we only need to look at the arguments passed to a method and perhaps modify them, a before advice is ideal for this. Listing 7-33 shows the implementation of `ObscenityFilterAdvice`.

Listing 7-33. *The ObscenityFilterAdvice Class*

```
package com.apress.prospring.business.aop;

import java.lang.reflect.Method;

import org.springframework.aop.MethodBeforeAdvice;

import com.apress.prospring.business.ObscenityFilter;
import com.apress.prospring.domain.BlogPosting;

public class ObscenityFilterAdvice implements MethodBeforeAdvice {

    private ObscenityFilter filter;

    public void setObscenityFilter(ObscenityFilter filter) {
        this.filter = filter;
    }

    public void before(Method method, Object[] args, Object target)
            throws Throwable {
        for (int x = 0; x < args.length; x++) {
            if (args[x] instanceof BlogPosting) {
                BlogPosting arg = (BlogPosting) args[x];
                if (filter.containsObscenities(arg.getBody())) {
                    arg.setBody(filter.obfuscateObscenities(arg.getBody()));
                }
                if (filter.containsObscenities(arg.getSubject())) {
                    arg.setSubject(filter
                            .obfuscateObscenities(arg.getSubject()));
                }
            }
        }
    }
}
```

Here you can see a basic before advice. We defined a single property, `obscenityFilter`, allowing the `ObscenityFilter` implementation to be defined externally. In the `before()` method, we check each argument to see if it is an instance of BlogPosting. If so, we test the body and subject properties, replacing them with obfuscated values as appropriate. Configuring this advice in the ApplicationContext is simple and is shown in Listing 7-34.

Listing 7-34. *Configuring the ObscenityFilterAdvice*

```
<bean id="obscenityFilterAdvisor"
      class="com.apress.prospring.business.aop.ObscenityFilterAdvice">
    <property name="obscenityFilter">
        <bean class="com.apress.prospring.business.ListBasedObscenityFilter">
            <property name="obscenities">
                <list>
                    <value>crap</value>
                </list>
            </property>
        </bean>
    </property>
</bean>
```

As you can see, we define the obscenityFilterAdvisor bean with an anonymous inner bean for the ObscenityFilter. Notice that we are able to set the list of obscenities in the configuration. Using ProxyFactoryBean, we can advise any object in the ApplicationContext with this advice, but we do not show this here because we have special requirements for the BlogManager bean related to transaction processing. The configuration of the BlogManager proxy is discussed in more detail in Chapter 12.

Obscenity Filter Summary

As you can see from the example in this section, AOP has plenty of practical uses in a real application. We found that by using AOP for the obscenity filter, we were able to keep the code for the BlogManager implementations much cleaner and were also able to reduce the amount of code duplication within the application. When you build your own applications with Spring, it is worth it to take the time to identify crosscutting logic. Once you have done this, define the interfaces to interact with it, build the implementations, and then instead of using a factory and embedding calls against your interfaces throughout your code, use Spring AOP to weave the logic into your application transparently.

Summary

In this chapter, we concluded our discussion on AOP. We looked at the advanced options for pointcutting, as well as how to extend the set of interfaces implemented by an object using introductions. A large part of this chapter focused on using Spring framework services to configure AOP declaratively, thus avoiding the need to hardcode AOP proxy construction logic into your code. We spent some time looking at how Spring and AspectJ are integrated to allow you to use the added power of AspectJ without losing any of the flexibility of Spring. Finally, we looked at how we can use AOP to solve an application-specific problem in the sample application.

In the next chapter, we move on to a completely different topic—how we can use Spring's JDBC support to radically simplify the creation of JDBC-based data access code.

PART 4

■■■

Data Access with Spring

CHAPTER 8

■■■

Spring JDBC Support

In the previous chapters, you saw how easy it is to build a fully Spring-managed application. You now have a solid understanding of bean configuration and Aspect Oriented Programming (AOP)—in other words, you know how to wire up the entire application using Spring. However, one of the parts of the puzzle is missing: How do you get the data that drives the application?

Apart from simple throwaway command line utilities, almost every application needs to persist data to some kind of data store. The most usual and convenient data store is a relational database.

The most notable open source databases are perhaps MySQL (www.mysql.com) and PostgreSQL (www.postgresql.org). MySQL is very fast, but it lacks support for more advanced features such as stored procedures and an internal scripting language. On the other hand, it runs on almost any operating system and platform. PostgreSQL is a bit pickier when it comes to the host platform, but it supports lots of advanced features. It is also worth noting that PL/pgSQL is very close to Oracle's PL/SQL.

Even if you choose the fastest and most reliable database, you cannot afford to loose the offered speed and flexibility by using a poorly designed and implemented data access layer. Applications tend to use the data access layer very frequently; thus any unnecessary bottlenecks in the data access code impact the entire application, no matter how well designed it is.

In this chapter, we show you how you can use Spring to simplify the implementation of data access code using JDBC. We start off by looking at the horrendous amount of code you would normally need to write without Spring and then compare it to a data access class implemented using Spring's data access classes. The result is truly amazing—Spring allows you to use the full power of human-tuned SQL queries while minimizing the amount of support code you need to implement. Specifically, we will discuss the following:

- **Comparing traditional JDBC code and Spring JDBC support:** We explore how Spring simplifies the old-style JDBC code while keeping the same functionality. You will also see how Spring accesses the low-level JDBC API and how this low-level API is mapped into convenience classes such as `JdbcTemplate`.

- **Connecting to the database:** Even though we do not go into every little detail of database connection management, we do show you the fundamental differences between a simple Connection and a DataSource. Naturally, we discuss how Spring manages the DataSources and which DataSources you can use in your applications.

- **Mapping the data to Java objects:** We show you how to effectively and easily map the selected data to Java objects. You also learn that Spring JDBC is a viable alternative to Object-Relational Mapping (ORM) tools.

- **Inserting, updating, and deleting data:** Finally, we discuss how you can implement the insert, update, and delete operations so that any changes to the database you are using do not have a devastating impact on the code you have written.

WHAT IS A DATABASE?

Developers sometimes struggle to describe what a database is. In one case, a database represents the actual data, and in other cases, it may represent a piece of software that manages the data, an instance of a process of this software, or even the physical machine that runs the manager process.

Formally, a database is a collection of data; the database software (such as Oracle, PostgreSQL, MySQL, etc.) is called database management software, or, more specifically, a relational database management system (RDBMS); the instance of RDBMS is called a database engine; and finally, the machine that runs the database engine is called the database server.

However, most developers immediately understand the meaning of the term database from the context in which it is used. This is why we use this term to represent all four meanings just described.

Exploring the JDBC Infrastructure

JDBC provides a standard way for Java applications to access data stored in a database. The core of the JDBC infrastructure is a driver that is specific to each database; it is this driver that allows Java code to access the database.

Once a driver is loaded, it registers itself with a `java.sql.DriverManager` class. This class manages a list of drivers and provides static methods for establishing connections to the database. The `DriverManager`'s `getConnection()` method returns a driver-implemented `java.sql.Connection` interface. This interface allows you to run SQL statements against the database.

The JDBC framework is quite complex and well tested; however, with this complexity comes difficulty in development. The first level of complexity lies in making sure your code manages the connections to the database. A connection is a scarce resource and is very expensive to establish. Generally, the database creates a thread or spawns a child process for each connection. Also, the number of concurrent connections is usually limited, and an excessive number of open connections slows the database down.

We will show you how Spring helps manage this complexity, but before we can proceed any further, we need to show you how to select, delete, and update data in pure JDBC.

In Listing 8-1, we create a simple DAO interface with methods for selecting all entries, creating a new entry, and deleting an entry from the database. Keeping in mind what we already know about database connections, we take the cautious and expensive approach of creating a connection for each statement. This greatly degrades the performance of Java and adds extra stress to the database because a connection has to be established for each query. However, if we kept a connection open, we could bring the database server to a halt. In Listing 8-1, the `TestDao` interface is empty for the moment; we will add appropriate methods to it later.

Listing 8-1. *Creating a JDBC Connection*

```java
public class PlainTestDao implements TestDao {

    static {
        try {
            Class.forName("org.gjt.mm.mysql.Driver");
        } catch (ClassNotFoundException ex) {
            // noop
        }
    }

    private Connection getConnection() throws SQLException {
        return DriverManager.
            getConnection("jdbc:mysql://localhost:3306/psch10", "janm", "");
    }

    private void closeConnection(Connection connection) {
        if (connection == null) return;

        try {
            connection.close();
        } catch (SQLException ex) {
            // noop
        }
    }
}
```

This code is far from complete, but it gives you an idea of the steps you need to perform to just open a connection. This code does not even deal with **connection pooling**, a common technique for managing connections to the database more effectively. We do not discuss connection pooling at this point (connection pooling is discussed in the "Database Connections and DataSources" section later in this chapter); instead, in Listing 8-2, we show a full implementation of our DAO class using plain JDBC.

Listing 8-2. *Plain JDBC DAO Implementation*

```java
package com.apress.prospring.ch10.plain;

// imports omitted for clarity
public class PlainTestDao implements TestDao {

    static {
        try {
            Class.forName("org.gjt.mm.mysql.Driver");
        } catch (ClassNotFoundException ex) {
            // noop
        }
    }
```

```java
    private Connection getConnection() throws SQLException {
        return DriverManager.getConnection("jdbc:mysql://localhost:3306/psch10",
            "janm", "");
    }

    private void closeConnection(Connection connection) {
        if (connection == null) return;

        try {
            connection.close();
        } catch (SQLException ex) {
            // noop
        }
    }

    public List getAll() {
        List result = new ArrayList();

        Connection connection = null;
        try {
            connection = getConnection();
            PreparedStatement statement = connection.prepareStatement(
                "select * from Test");
            ResultSet resultSet = statement.executeQuery();
            while (resultSet.next()) {
                Test test = new Test();
                test.setName(resultSet.getString("Name"));
                test.setTestId(resultSet.getInt("TestId"));
                result.add(test);
            }
        } catch (SQLException ex) {
            ex.printStackTrace();
        } finally {
            closeConnection(connection);
        }

        return result;
    }

    public void insert(Test test) {
        Connection connection = null;
        try {
            connection = getConnection();
            PreparedStatement statement = connection.prepareStatement(
                "insert into Test (Name) values (?)");
            statement.setString(1, test.getName());
            statement.execute();
```

```
            ResultSet generatedKeys = statement.getGeneratedKeys();
            if (generatedKeys.next()) {
                test.setTestId(generatedKeys.getInt("TestId"));
            }
        } catch (SQLException ex) {
            ex.printStackTrace();
        } finally {
            closeConnection(connection);
        }
    }

    public void delete(int testId) {
        Connection connection = null;
        try {
            connection = getConnection();
            PreparedStatement statement = connection.prepareStatement(
                "delete from Test where TestId=?");
            statement.setInt(1, testId);
            statement.execute();
        } catch (SQLException ex) {
            ex.printStackTrace();
        } finally {
            closeConnection(connection);
        }
    }
}
```

As you can see from this listing, a lot of code needs to be moved to a helper class or—even worse—duplicated in each DAO class. This is the main disadvantage of JDBC from the application programmer's point of view—you just do not have time to code dull and repeated code in every DAO class. Instead, you want to concentrate on writing code that actually does what you need the DAO class to do: select, update, and delete the data. The more helper code you need to write, the more checked exceptions you need to handle, and the more bugs you may introduce in your code.

This is where a DAO framework and Spring come in. The framework eliminates the code that does not actually perform any custom logic and allows you to forget about all the housekeeping that needs to be performed and Spring's extensive JDBC support makes your life a lot easier.

Spring JDBC Infrastructure

The code we have discussed in the first part of the chapter is not very complex, but it is annoying to write, and because there is so much of it to write, the likelihood of coding errors is quite high. It is time to take a look at how Spring makes things easier and more elegant.

Overview and Used Packages

JDBC support in Spring is divided into the four packages detailed in Table 8-1; each handles different aspects of JDBC access.

Table 8-1. *Spring JDBC Packages*

Package	Description
org.springframework.jdbc.core	This package contains the foundations of JDBC classes in Spring; namely SQLExceptionTranslator, which is responsible for processing exceptions from JDBC calls to Spring JDBC runtime exceptions, and a core JDBC class, the JdbcTemplate.
org.springframework.jdbc.datasource	Contains helper classes and DataSource implementations that you can use to run JDBC code outside of a J2EE container.
org.springframework.jdbc.object	Contains classes that help convert the data returned from the database into objects or lists of objects. These objects and lists are plain Java objects and therefore are disconnected from the database.
org.springframework.jdbc.support	The most important class in this package is SQLException translation support. This allows Spring to recognize error codes used by the database and map them to higher-level exceptions.

Let us start the discussion of Spring JDBC support by looking at the lowest-level functionality. The first thing you need to do before you can even think about running SQL queries is establish a connection to the database.

Database Connections and DataSources

First of all, you can use Spring to manage the database connection for you by providing a bean that implements javax.sql.DataSource. The difference between a DataSource and a Connection is that a DataSource provides and manages Connections.

DriverManagerDataSource is the simplest implementation of a DataSource. By looking at the class name, you can guess that it simply calls the DriverManager to obtain a connection. This makes DriverManagerDataSource unsuitable for anything other than testing. The configuration of DriverManagerDataSource is quite simple, as you can see in Listing 8-3; you just need to supply the driver class name, a connection URL, a user name, and a password.

Listing 8-3. *Spring-Managed DriverManagerDataSource dataSource Bean*

```
<?xml version="1.0" encoding="UTF-8"?>
<!DOCTYPE beans PUBLIC "-//SPRING//DTD BEAN//EN" ➡
"http://www.springframework.org/dtd/spring-beans.dtd">
<beans>
```

```
    <bean id="dataSource"
        class="org.springframework.jdbc.datasource.DriverManagerDataSource"
        destroy-method="close">
        <property name="driverClassName">
            <value>org.postgresql.Driver</value></property>
        <property name="url">
            <value>jdbc:postgresql://localhost/janm</value></property>
        <property name="username"><value>janm</value></property>
        <property name="password"><value></value></property>
    </bean>
</beans>
```

In real-world applications you can use Apache Jakarta Commons `BasicDataSource`
(`http://jakarta.apache.org/commons/dbcp/`) or a DataSource implemented by a J2EE application
server, which may further increase the performance of the application. You could use a DataSource
in the plain JDBC code and get the same pooling benefits; however, in most cases, you would
still miss a central place to configure the data source. Spring, on the other hand, allows you to
declare a `dataSource` bean and set the connection properties in the application context definition
files (see Listing 8-4).

Listing 8-4. *Spring-Managed dataSource Bean*

```
<?xml version="1.0" encoding="UTF-8"?>
<!DOCTYPE beans PUBLIC "-//SPRING//DTD BEAN//EN" ➟
"http://www.springframework.org/dtd/spring-beans.dtd">
<beans>

    <bean id="dataSource" class="org.apache.commons.dbcp.BasicDataSource"
        destroy-method="close">
        <property name="driverClassName">
            <value>org.postgresql.Driver</value></property>
        <property name="url">
            <value>jdbc:postgresql://localhost/janm</value></property>
        <property name="username"><value>janm</value></property>
        <property name="password"><value></value></property>
    </bean>
</beans>
```

Most likely you recognize the bold properties in the listing. They represent the values you
normally pass to JDBC to obtain a `Connection` interface. This particular Spring-managed
DataSource is implemented in `org.apache.commons.dbcp.BasicDataSource`. The most important
bit is that the `dataSource` bean implements `javax.sql.DataSource`, and you can immediately
start using it in your data access classes.

Another way to configure a `dataSource` bean is to use JNDI. If the application you are
developing is going to run in a J2EE container, you can take advantage of the container-managed
connection pooling. To use a JNDI-based data source, you need to change the `dataSource` bean
declaration, as shown in Listing 8-5.

Listing 8-5. *Spring-Managed JNDI dataSource Bean*

```xml
<?xml version="1.0" encoding="UTF-8"?>
<!DOCTYPE beans PUBLIC "-//SPRING//DTD BEAN//EN" ➥
"http://www.springframework.org/dtd/spring-beans.dtd">
<beans>
    <bean id="dataSource"
        class="org.springframework.jndi.JndiObjectFactoryBean">
        <property name="jndiName">
            <value>java:comp/env/jdbc/springch8</value>
        </property>
    </bean>
</beans>
```

If you take the JNDI approach, you must not forget to add a resource reference (resource-ref) in the application descriptor file (see Listing 8-6).

Listing 8-6. *A Resource Reference in Descriptor Files*

```xml
<root-node>
    <resource-ref>
        <res-ref-name>jdbc/springch8</res-ref-name>
        <res-type>javax.sql.DataSource</res-type>
        <res-auth>Container</res-auth>
    </resource-ref>
</root-node>
```

The <root-node> is a placeholder value; you need to change it depending on how your module is packaged. For example, it becomes web-app if the application is a web module. Most likely, you will need to configure the resource-ref in an application server–specific descriptor file as well. However, notice that the resource-ref element configures the jdbc/springch8 reference name and that the dataSource bean's jndiName is set to java:comp/env/**jdbc/springch8**.

As you can see, Spring allows you to configure the DataSource in almost any way you like, and it hides the actual implementation or location of the data source from the rest of the application's code. In other words, your DAO classes do not know and do not need to know where the DataSource points to.

The connection management is also delegated to the dataSource bean, which in turn performs the management itself or uses the J2EE container to do all the work.

Using DataSources in DAO Classes

We start with a simple implementation of a UserDao interface. We will add more features as we go along, and explain the Spring JDBC classes as we do so. Let us begin with an empty UserDao interface and a JdbcUserDao implementation (see Listing 8-7).

Listing 8-7. *UserDao Interface and Implementation*

```
public interface TestDao {
}

public class JdbcTestDao implements TestDao {
}
```

First we will add a dataSource property to the implementation. The reason we want to add the dataSource property to the **implementation** class rather than the **interface** should be quite obvious: the interface does not need to know how the data is going to be retrieved and updated. By adding get/setDataSource methods to the interface, we—in the best-case scenario—force the implementations to declare the getter and setter stubs. Clearly this is not a very good design practice. Take a look at the modified JdbcUserDao class in Listing 8-8.

Listing 8-8. *JdbcUserDao with dataSource Property*

```
public class JdbcTestDao implements TestDao {
    private DataSource dataSource;
    public void setDataSource(DataSource dataSource) {
        this.dataSource = dataSource;
    }
}
```

We can now instruct Spring to configure our userDao bean using the JdbcUserDao implementation and set the dataSource property (see Listing 8-9).

Listing 8-9. *Spring Application Context File with dataSource and userDao Beans*

```
<?xml version="1.0" encoding="UTF-8"?>
<!DOCTYPE beans PUBLIC "-//SPRING//DTD BEAN//EN" ➥
"http://www.springframework.org/dtd/spring-beans.dtd">
<beans>

    <bean id="dataSource" class="org.apache.commons.dbcp.BasicDataSource"
        destroy-method="close">
        <!-- omitted for clarity -->
    </bean>

    <bean id="testDao " class="com.apress.prospring.data.jdbc.JdbcTestDao">
        <property name="dataSource"><ref local="dataSource"/></property>
    </bean>

</beans>
```

Spring now creates the testDao bean by instantiating the JdbcTestDao class with the dataSource property set to the dataSource bean.

It is good practice to make sure that all required properties on a bean have been set. The easiest way to do this is to implement the `InitializingBean` interface and provide an implementation for the `afterPropertiesSet()` method (see Listing 8-10). This way you make sure that all required properties have been set on your `JdbcTestDao`. For further discussion of bean initialization, refer to Chapter 5.

Listing 8-10. *JdbcTestDao Implementation with InitializingBean*

```
public class JdbcTestDao implements TestDao, InitializingBean {
    private DataSource dataSource;

    public void afterPropertiesSet() throws Exception {
        if (dataSource == null) {
            throw new BeanCreationException("Must set dataSource on UserDao");
        }
        // more initialization code
    }

    public void setDataSource(DataSource dataSource) {
        this.dataSource = dataSource;
    }
}
```

The code we have looked at so far uses Spring to manage the data source and introduces the TestDao interface and its JDBC implementation. We also set the `dataSource` property on the JdbcTestDao class in the Spring application context file. Now we expand the code by adding the actual DAO operations to the interface and implementation.

Exception Handling

Because Spring advocates using runtime exceptions rather than checked exceptions, you need a mechanism to translate the checked `SQLException` into a runtime Spring JDBC exception. Because Spring's SQL exceptions are runtime exceptions, they can be much more granular than checked exceptions.[1]

Spring provides a default implementation of the `SQLExceptionTranslator` interface, which takes care of translating the generic SQL error codes into Spring JDBC exceptions. In most cases, this implementation is sufficient enough, but we can extend Spring's default implementation and set our new `SQLExceptionTranslator` implementation to be used in `JdbcTemplate`, as shown in Listing 8-11.

---

1. By definition, this is not a feature of runtime exceptions, but it is very inconvenient to have to declare a long list of checked exceptions in the throws clause, hence checked exceptions tend to be much more coarse-grained than their runtime equivalents.

Listing 8-11. *Custom SQLExceptionTranslator*

```
public class MySQLErrorCodesTransalator
    extends SQLErrorCodeSQLExceptionTranslator {
    protected DataAccessException customTranslate(String task,
        String sql, SQLException sqlex) {
        if (sqlex.getErrorCode() == -12345)
            return new DeadlockLoserDataAccessException(task, sqlex);
        return null;
    }
}

// another class file, another method:

JdbcTemplate jt = new JdbcTemplate();
jt.setDataSource(dataSource);
// create a custom translator and set the datasource ➥
// for the default translation lookup
MySQLErrorCodesTransalator tr = new MySQLErrorCodesTransalator();
tr.setDataSource(dataSource);
jt.setExceptionTranslator(tr);
// use the JdbcTemplate for this SqlUpdate
SqlUpdate su = new SqlUpdate();
su.setJdbcTemplate(jt);
su.setSql("update orders set shipping_charge = shipping_charge * 1.05");
su.compile();
su.update();
```

Obviously, nothing can stop you from creating the SQLExceptionTranslator as a Spring-managed bean and using the JdbcTemplate bean in your DAO classes. Don't worry if you don't remember reading about the JdbcTemplate class, we are going now going to discuss it in more detail.

The JdbcTemplate Class

This class represents the core of Spring's JDBC support. It can execute all types of SQL statements. In the most simplistic view, you can classify the data definition and data manipulation statements. Data definition statements cover creating various database objects (tables, views, stored procedures, etc). Data manipulation statements manipulate the data and can be classified as select and update statements. A select statement generally returns a set of rows; each row has the same set of columns. An update statement modifies the data in the database but does not return any results.

The `JdbcTemplate` class allows you to issue any type of SQL statement to the database and return any type of result.

Let's start with a simple query that returns a single value. A good example is a query that returns the last generated primary key value—for instance, `select last_insert_id()` in MySQL. This statement returns an `int` value. We can use `JdbcTemplate` to retrieve the value, as shown in Listing 8-12.

Listing 8-12. *Using JdbcTemplate to Retreive an int Value*

```
package com.apress.prospring.ch10.spring;

public abstract class JdbcAbstractTestDao
    extends JdbcDaoSupport implements TestDao {

    protected void retrieveIdentity(final Test test) {
        JdbcTemplate jt = new JdbcTemplate(getDataSource());
        test.setTestId(jt.queryForInt("select last_insert_id()"));
    }
}i
```

The other methods of `JdbcTemplate` return `Long`, `Object`, and `int` values and are very self-explanatory.

In Listing 8-13, we demonstrate how to return a list of two domain objects as a result of an inner join operation using the execute method of `JdbcTemplate`.

Listing 8-13. *JdbcTemplate Example*

```
package com.apress.prospring.ch10.spring;

public abstract class JdbcAbstractTestDao
    extends JdbcDaoSupport implements TestDao {

    public List getAll() {
        JdbcTemplate jt = new JdbcTemplate(getDataSource());
        return (List)jt.execute(
            new PreparedStatementCreator() {

                public PreparedStatement createPreparedStatement(
                    Connection connection)
                    throws SQLException {
                    return connection.prepareStatement(
                        "select t.*, td.* from Tests t " +
                        "inner join TestDetails td on t.TestId = td.Test");
                }

            },
            new PreparedStatementCallback() {
```

```
            private int testId = -1;

            public Object doInPreparedStatement(PreparedStatement ps)
                throws SQLException, DataAccessException {
                int testId;
                List result = new ArrayList();
                int lastTestId = -1;
                Test test = null;
                ResultSet rs = ps.executeQuery();
                while (rs.next()) {
                    testId = rs.getInt("TestId");
                    if (testId != lastTestId) {
                        test = new Test();
                        test.setTestId(testId);
                        test.setName(rs.getString("Name"));
                        test.setDetails(new ArrayList());
                    }
                    TestDetail td = new TestDetail();
                    td.setData(rs.getString("Data"));
                    td.setTest(rs.getInt("Test"));
                    td.setTestDetailId(rs.getInt("TestDetailId"));
                    test.getDetails().add(td);
                }
                return result;
            }

        });
    }
}
```

This code demonstrates how to use this fundamental class. As you can see in Listing 8-13, you have full control over how you create and use the PreparedStatement. Here, we created a JdbcTemplate instance with implementations of PreparedStatementCreator and PreparedStatementCallback. In the creator, we created a PreparedStatement that selects rows from two inner joined tables. The result is a subset of a Cartesian product of the Test and TestDetail tables. Here, we iterate through the result and create appropriate instances of Test and TestDetail objects.

This code adequately demonstrates how to use JdbcTemplate. The bottom line is that anything you can do in JDBC you can do in Spring, but you do not need to manage the JDBC checked exceptions, which makes your code less cluttered and easier to read.

It is worth noting that other Spring JDBC support classes (such as MappingSqlQuery and SqlUpdate) use JdbcTemplate internally to perform the requested database operations. We cover these high-level classes in the next section of the chapter.

Selecting the Data as Java Objects

You have learned how to use JdbcTemplate to perform raw data operations, but there is too much code to write, and in most cases, writing code for various select statements results in massive code duplication. Also, the queryForList() method returns a List of Map instance because it is not aware of the columns being selected. Unfortunately you still need to write lots of code to retrieve the data using ResultSets and create appropriate domain objects.

In Listing 8-14, we show the use of Spring JDBC support classes. We are going to start the discussion with the use of the MappingSqlQuery class that will process the result set and create appropriate domain objects. Subclasses of MappingSqlQuery must implement its mapRow method. This method gets the values from the underlying ResultSet and returns the appropriate domain object.

Listing 8-14. *MappingSqlQuery Usage*

```
package com.apress.prospring.ch10.spring;

import java.sql.ResultSet;
import java.sql.SQLException;
import java.sql.Types;
import java.util.List;

import javax.sql.DataSource;

import org.springframework.jdbc.core.SqlParameter;
import org.springframework.jdbc.core.support.JdbcDaoSupport;
import org.springframework.jdbc.object.MappingSqlQuery;

import com.apress.prospring.ch10.TestDao;
import com.apress.prospring.ch10.domain.Test;

public class JdbcTestDao implements TestDao, InitializingBean {
    private DataSource dataSource;

    private static final String SELECT_BY_NAME_SQL =
        "select * from Test where Name=?";

    abstract class AbstractSelect extends MappingSqlQuery {

        public AbstractSelect(DataSource dataSource, String sql) {
            super(dataSource, sql);
        }
```

```
        protected Object mapRow(ResultSet rs, int rowNum) throws SQLException {
            Test test = new Test();

            test.setName(rs.getString("Name"));
            test.setTestId(rs.getInt("TestId"));

            return test;
        }
    }

    class SelectByName extends AbstractSelect {
        public SelectByName (DataSource dataSource) {
            super(dataSource, SELECT_BY_NAME_SQL);
            declareParameter(new SqlParameter(Types.VARCHAR));
        }
    }

    public void afterPropertiesSet() throws Exception {
        if (dataSource == null) {
            throw new BeanCreationException("Must set dataSource on UserDao");
        }
        // more initialization code
    }

    public void setDataSource(DataSource dataSource) {
        this.dataSource = dataSource;
    }
}
```

The code in Listing 8-14 looks like it can actually do some database work! Let's review what we have implemented.

First, we have the AbstractSelect class that extends MappingSqlQuery. This class maps the ResultSet columns and returns the appropriate Test domain object. All query classes that select users inevitably return User objects, so we can use the AbstractSelect class as a super-class of all select classes. The SelectByName class exemplifies this approach. The constructor takes only a single DataSource parameter, because this class performs one specific SQL query. This particular query requires two VARCHAR parameters, username and password. We declare the parameters using a call to declareParameter().

AbstractSelect is a superclass for all concrete Select implementations that no longer have to implement the mapRow() method to create an instance of the domain object. This implies that all select statements need to return the same set of columns in order for AbstractSelect.mapRow() to be able to create the domain object.

You may be wondering why AbstractSelect is still marked as abstract; after all, it already implements the mapRow() abstract method. There is a simple explanation for this: we should not use the AbstractSelect class to perform any SQL query, because different queries may use different parameters, and by marking this class abstract, we are forcing ourselves to subclass AbstractSelect for every SQL query.

A more important benefit, however, is that by implementing each individual query in its own class, we can take advantage of the fact that most databases precompile the queries and cache the compiled query plan. This may not be very critical in simple `select * from Table` queries similar to those that result in a full table scan, but it becomes more important as the queries get more complex.

■**NOTE**   Some databases do not use the precompiled plans. The rationale behind this is that the statistics used to create the query plan may become out of date very quickly as records are inserted into the database. If a table has 100 rows, for example, it is not worth the effort to use index operations, but if a table has 1,000,000 rows, then the additional work of an Index Scan operation is well justified. It is not impossible to imagine that a query plan was created for a table of 100 rows and, in the meantime, the number of rows increased to a million. If this was the case, the database would be using a very inefficient query plan, and the query time saved by using the precompiled query plan would be insignificant.

Listing 8-15 shows how to use the concept of the `AbstractSelect` class in a `TestDao` implementation.

Listing 8-15. *TestDao Interface*

```
package com.apress.prospring.ch10;

import java.util.List;

public interface TestDao {

    public List getByName(String name);

}
```

To implement the method declared in the `TestDao` interface, we are going to use the `SelectByName` inner class (see Listing 8-16). To use this class, we need to instantiate, and we will do so in the `afterPropertiesSet()` method declared in `InitializingBean`.

Listing 8-16. *Implementation of getByName*

```
package com.apress.prospring.data.jdbc;

public class JdbcTestDao implements TestDao, InitializingBean {

    private DataSource dataSource;

    private static final String SELECT_BY_NAME_SQL =
        "select * from Test where Name=?";

    abstract class AbstractSelect extends MappingSqlQuery {
```

```
        public AbstractSelect(DataSource dataSource, String sql) {
            super(dataSource, sql);
        }

        protected Object mapRow(ResultSet rs, int rowNum) throws SQLException {
            Test test = new Test();

            test.setName(rs.getString("Name"));
            test.setTestId(rs.getInt("TestId"));

            return test;
        }
    }

    class SelectByName extends AbstractSelect {

        public SelectByName(DataSource dataSource) {
            super(dataSource, SELECT_BY_NAME_SQL);
            declareParameter(new SqlParameter(Types.VARCHAR));
        }
    }

    private SelectByName selectByName;

    public void afterPropertiesSet() throws Exception {
        if (dataSource == null) {
            throw new BeanCreationException("Must set dataSource on testDao");
        }

        selectByName = new SelectByName(dataSource);
    }

    public List getByName(String name) {
        return selectByName.execute(new Object[] { name });
    }

}
```

This code links all pieces of the puzzle together. We created an abstract subclass of Spring's MappingSqlQuery named AbstractSelect, which takes care of mapping the results retrieved from the database into a Test object. We then subclassed AbstractSelect in SelectByName to execute the SQL query that selects rows from the Test table to return a test whose name matches the parameters passed to the method. In the SelectByName constructor, we have declared that name is the only parameter and is stored as VARCHAR in the database table. To select the Test objects by name, we need to pass the parameter value to the execute() method in an Object[] array containing a single value. The execute() method returns a List of objects returned by the mapRow() method. Because SelectByName is a subclass of AbstractSelect, and because the AbstractSelect.mapRow() method returns an instance of the Test class, we can safely cast the Objects in the List to Tests.

Keep in mind that the order in which the parameters are passed is critical to the execute() method: if we accidentally change the order of the parameters, we do not get the correct results.

Let us step back and look at the code we have written. If this is the only DAO implementation class in the application, it is just fine the way it is. However, most applications have more than one DAO class. If this is the case, we need to create a DAO class that has a dataSource property and implements InitializingBean and the appropriate DAO interface. This has a nasty code smell and as a result, we need to refactor the code. Spring supports this situation by providing a JdbcDaoSupport class.

The refactored JdbcTestDao class is shown in Listing 8-17.

Listing 8-17. *Refactored JdbcTestDao*

```
public class JdbcTestDao
    extends JdbcDaoSupport implements TestDao, InitializingBean {

    private DataSource dataSource;

    private static final String SELECT_BY_NAME_SQL =
        "select * from Test where Name=?";

    abstract class AbstractSelect extends MappingSqlQuery {
        /* omitted for clarity */
    }

    class SelectByName extends AbstractSelect { /* omitted for clarity */ }

    private SelectByName selectByName;

    protected void initDao() throws Exception {
        super.initDao();
        selectByName = new SelectByName(getDataSource());
    }

    public void afterPropertiesSet() throws Exception {
        if (dataSource == null)
            throw new BeanCreationException("Must set dataSource on testDao");

        selectByName = new SelectByName(dataSource);
    }

    public void setDataSource(DataSource dataSource) {
        this.dataSource = dataSource;
    }

    public List getByName(String name) {
        return selectByName.execute(name);
    }
}
```

This code is much cleaner after we remove the stricken-out lines and add the lines in bold. We had to remove some of the code because JdbcDaoSupport implements InitializingBean's afterPropertiesSet as final, and it also has the dataSource property. Because we still need to instantiate the query inner classes, JdbcDaoSupport allows us to override the initDao() method, which is called after all properties have been set on JdbcDaoSupport. We can access the dataSource property by calling the getDataSource() method.

The code we now have looks like it does not need any more refactoring, and indeed, that would be true if we were only selecting and updating data. Before we take a look at the inevitable catch with inserts, we will discuss data updates.

Updating Data

Fast and efficient selects are important; however, applications must also be able to update existing data. Updates are surprisingly less complicated than selects. Because update operations do not return any data, you do not need to create abstract selection classes that map the results to objects. To perform an update, we need to create a simple subclass of SqlUpdate, specify the SQL statement that performs the update, and declare parameters the SQL statement expects (see Listing 8-18).

Listing 8-18. *Implementation of an Update*

```
public class JdbcTestDao

    extends JdbcDaoSupport implements TestDao {

    private static final String UPDATE_SQL =
        "update Test set Name=? where TestId=?";

    abstract class AbstractSelect extends MappingSqlQuery {
        /* omitted for clarity */
    }

    class SelectByName extends AbstractSelect { /* omitted for clarity */ }

    class Update extends SqlUpdate {
        public Update(DataSource dataSource) {
            super(dataSource, UPDATE_SQL);
            declareParameter(new SqlParameter(Types.VARCHAR));    // Name
            declareParameter(new SqlParameter(Types.INTEGER));    // TestId
        }
    }

    private SelectByName selectByName;
    private Update update;
```

```
    protected void initDao() throws Exception {
        super.initDao();
        selectByName = new SelectByName(getDataSource());
        update = new Update(getDataSource());
    }

    public void update(Test test) {
        update.update(new Object[] { test.getName(),
            new Integer(test.getTestId()) });
    }

}
```

The code is very simple; the only thing you need to be mindful of is the order of the values in the values array.

A special case of an update is a delete. To our code, a delete operation is the same as an update operation. It takes a number of parameters and does not return any data. Hence the Delete class is also a subclass of SqlUpdate.

Listing 8-19. *Delete Class Declaration and Implementation*

```
public class JdbcTestDao

    extends JdbcDaoSupport implements TestDao {

    private static final String UPDATE_SQL =
        "update Test set Name=? where TestId=?";
    private static final String DELETE_SQL =
        "delete from Test where TestId=?";

    abstract class AbstractSelect extends MappingSqlQuery {
        /* omitted for clarity */
    }

    class SelectByName extends AbstractSelect { /* omitted for clarity */ }

    class Update extends SqlUpdate { /* omitted for clarity */ }

    class Delete extends SqlUpdate {
        public Delete(DataSource dataSource) {
            super(dataSource, DELETE_SQL);
            declareParameter(new SqlParameter(Types.INTEGER));    // TestId
        }
    }

    private SelectByName selectByName;
    private Update update;
    private Delete delete;
```

```
protected void initDao() throws Exception {
    super.initDao();
    selectByName = new SelectByName(getDataSource());
    update = new Update(getDataSource());
    delete = new Delete(getDataSource());
}

public void delete(int testId) {
    delete.update(testId);
}
```

}

The Delete class calls the constructor of the superclass with the dataSource parameter and a specific SQL delete query. Just as we did for the update and select classes, we create an individual delete class for each delete operation.

Again, this code is very simple and because we are passing only a single int parameter, we can take advantage of one of the overloaded execute() methods that takes one int parameter. We do not need to create an array of Objects containing a single Integer.

Inserting Data

Generally speaking, inserts are actually updates to the data. However, there is one major difference: in most cases, inserts have to deal with primary keys. Depending on your database, you may have to set the primary key before you issue the insert statement. Your database may support implicit serial, auto_increment, or identity types; in this case, you need to select the generated key after performing the insert operation.

As you can see, an originally trivial update operation gets more complicated. You need to perform a select and update or an update and select, depending on your database. When you are developing a large system, you usually decide for one database and stick with this choice. Writing only ANSI SQL code is nice, but if you have invested in a sophisticated database, you will want to use its non-ANSI features. Even so, you should always design your data layer code so that if you ever need to change the database, the impact on your code is minimal. This is why we are going to further refactor our DAO classes. Instead of the JdbcTestDao class, we will employ an abstract JdbcAbstractTestDao that performs the majority of the DAO operations and delegate the retrieval of the primary keys to the subclasses.

Unfortunately, even this approach is not ideal because we need to decide whether we are going to select the primary key *before* or *after* the insert operation. Of course you could refactor the DAO classes further. You could create JdbcAbstractPKBeforeInsertTestDao as a subclass of JdbcAbstractTestDao whose implementation of the insert() method would get the primary key value before the insert operation, and JdbcAbstractPKAfterInsertTestDao whose insert() method would get the primary key value after the insert operation. We would not recommend that you do this, because full database portability may be a phantom requirement. If the system you are developing is using the Oracle database and the client has already invested in the database, chances are slim that they will change their mind and tell you to program the DAO against MySQL. However, for the sake of argument, in the next section, we implement a JdbcAbstractTestDao whose insert() method gets the generated primary key *after* the insert operation. Even though this is not an exhaustive example, we believe it is enough to demonstrate the point.

Getting the Primary Key Value

Each database has its own ways to select the generated key, whether it is select last_insert_id() in MySQL, select last_value from Sequence in PostgreSQL, or select @@IDENTITY in Microsoft SQL Server. However, all these identity selections have one thing in common: the database *generates* the identity as part of the insert command. Several databases require you to first obtain a new identity and then insert it. Oracle is such database; if we use Oracle, we have to modify our code to first select the new identity and then perform the insert, with the value of the primary key specified in the insert statement. The abstract class that contains most of the common SQL code has to be rewritten to satisfy the requirements of generating the identity before an insert. Obtaining an identity before an insert operation is a preferred method, and if your database supports it, you should explicitly select a new primary key from a sequence and then perform an insert. Consider what would happen if the Table table were defined as shown in Listing 8-20.

Listing 8-20. *Table Definition*

```
create table Table (
    TableId serial not null,
    Column varchar(50) not null,
    constraint PK_TableId primary key (TableId)
)
```

The serial data type is specific to PostgreSQL; the TableId column would have to be defined as TableId int identity not null in Microsoft SQL Server or TableId int not null auto_increment in MySQL. Let us then consider two transactions, A and B, and a sequence named sequence table_tableid_seq, all of which are running concurrently in PostgreSQL as demonstrated in Table 8-2.

Table 8-2. *Potential Risk in Selecting Generated Key After an Insert*

Time	Transaction/Process A	Transaction/Process B
0	insert into Table (Column) values ('value 1);	
1		insert into Table (Column) values ('value 2);
3		select last_value from table_tableid_seq
4	select last_value from table_tableid_seq	

A quick look at the sequence of operations performed by the two transactions or processes reveals that in Time 4, Process A retrieves a value generated by the insert operation performed by Process B. Process B, on the other hand, gets the correct value in Time 3. You may argue that this is not a problem when all your code does is just insert and then not use the generated primary key. However, if you change the code to rely on the generated value, you must make sure you are getting the correct value.

A better approach is to select the next primary key value and then attempt an insert (see Table 8-3). If another transaction commits an insert operation with the same primary key before your transaction is committed, the database reports a primary key constraint violation; you must design your code to cope with this and retry the insert operation. This way you can guarantee that the primary key value is correct.

Table 8-3. *Selecting a Primary Key Value Before an Insert Operation*

Time	Transaction/Process A	Transaction/Process B
0	select next_value from table_tableid_seq	
1	insert into Table (TableId, Column) values (tableId, 'value 1');	select next_value from table_tableid_seq
2	commit	insert into Table (TableId, Column) values (tableId, 'value 2');
3		commit

Table 8-3 illustrates a scenario where both transactions select the next value from the sequence, store it, and attempt an insert with this value. Transaction A succeeds, but Transaction B fails because Transaction A already inserted a record with the same primary key. Process B can retry the insert and, with a bit of luck and less concurrent inserts, it will get the next value and commit the insert before another transaction manages to complete the same procedure.

Unfortunately, MySQL does not support sequences. If you are using it, you must take a chance that no other transaction will commit and thus change the last generated key before you select it. This does not stop you from refactoring your JDBC data access code to work with all databases that only allow you to select the last generated primary key *after* the insert operation.

Now we are going to refactor the DAO classes: first we create a JdbcAbstractUserDao class that extends JdbcDaoSupport and implements UserDao interfaces. We will keep as much generic JDBC code as possible in the abstract class. The only thing that is most likely to be database-specific is identity selection.

Listing 8-21 shows the code we have after refactoring.

Listing 8-21. *JdbcAbstractTestDao Class*

```
public abstract class JdbcAbstractTestDao
    extends JdbcDaoSupport implements TestDao {

    private static final String INSERT_SQL = "insert into Test (Name) values (?)";

    abstract class AbstractSelect extends MappingSqlQuery {
        /* ommited for clarity */
    }
    class SelectByName extends AbstractSelect {
        /* ommited for clarity */
    }
```

```
    class Update extends SqlUpdate { /* ommited for clarity */ }
    class Delete extends SqlUpdate { /* ommited for clarity */ }

    class Insert extends SqlUpdate {
        public Insert(DataSource dataSource) {
            super(dataSource, INSERT_SQL);
            declareParameter(new SqlParameter(Types.VARCHAR));    // Name
        }
    }

    protected abstract String getIdentitySql();

    protected void retrieveIdentity(final Test test) {
        test.setTestId(getJdbcTemplate().queryForInt(getIdentitySql()));
    }

    private SelectByName selectByName;
    private Update update;
    private Delete delete;
    private Insert insert;

    protected void initDao() throws Exception {
        super.initDao();
        selectByName = new SelectByName(getDataSource());
        update = new Update(getDataSource());
        delete = new Delete(getDataSource());
        insert = new Insert(getDataSource());
    }

    public void insert(Test test) {
        insert.update(new Object[] { test.getName() });
        retrieveIdentity(test);
    }

    // other TestDao methods omitted for clarity

}
```

As you can see, we created an abstract class that takes care of all the operations declared in the TestDao interface. It also takes care of selecting the last generated identity from the database using a call to the retrieveIdentity() method. This method uses the utility method, getJdbcTemplate(), provided by the JdbcDaoSupport class. Because the new abstract class is a subclass of JdbcDaoSupport and because JdbcDaoSupport already contains final getters and setters for the DataSource, the final step is to provide an implementation for our abstract class for the MySQL database (see Listing 8-22).

Listing 8-22. *MySQL Implementation for JdbcAbstractTestDao*

```
package com.apress.prospring.data.jdbc;

public class MySqlTestDao extends JdbcAbstractTestDao {

    protected String getIdentitySql() {
        return "select last_insert_id()";
    }

}
```

This class implements the getIdentitySql() method to return a SQL statement that returns an int of the last generated identity. Let's assume that we had to change the database to PostgreSQL and that the UserId column in the Users table is declared as UserId serial not null primary key. PostgreSQL creates an implicit sequence named users_userid_seq. You can implement the JdbcPostgreSqlUserDao class, as shown in Listing 8-23.

Listing 8-23. *PostgreSQL Implementation for JdbcAbstractTestDao*

```
package com.apress.prospring.data.jdbc;

public class PostgreSqlTestDao extends JdbcAbstractTestDao {

    protected String getIdentitySql() {
        return "select last_value from test_testid_seq";
    }

}
```

And lo! We have support for both MySQL and PostgreSQL all with just a few lines of code.

Transactions

Transactions are a very important part of database design. In most cases, they are used to enforce data integrity. There are a few important design decisions you should consider when you are implementing transactions. First of all, DAO classes and methods should be very granular, and therefore should result in just one insert or update statement. It then follows that transactions should be managed by the Business Tier.

Consider this scenario: you need to create a record for a test record and test detail. Each test must have at least one detail, making it a 1:N relationship. Let the Test bean represent the test domain object and TestDetail represent the test detail domain object. The Test object has a List property that holds a collection of TestDetail objects. You want to insert the test and its details into the database, and to ensure the data integrity, you want to use transactions. However, you should not extend the scope of the TestDao interface so that you can insert the test details.

Instead, create a separate DAO for `TestDetail` and implement the `insert(TestDetail)` method. Then create a `TestManager` object that has properties for `TestDao` and `TestDetailDao` and uses Spring to automatically manage transactions.

For further discussion of transaction management, refer to Chapter 12.

Why JDBC?

The final thing you may ask is why you should go through all the trouble with JDBC code when multiple Object-Relational Mapping (ORM) tools greatly simplify the job. The answer is that JDBC allows you to fully harvest the power of the database you are using. Several excellent ORM tools (iBATIS and Hibernate) are covered in this book, but none give you the power to fully control the data selection and object creation. This may not be a major issue for simple applications, but if you're implementing a more complex application, you may want to implement various caching models. True, both iBATIS and Hibernate support caching, but the caching engine in your application may be far too complex for ORM tools.

To be more specific, iBATIS allows you to forget all about JDBC inner classes and manually code the SQL statements, which makes all nonstandard features of your database easily accessible. However, there are several drawbacks, such as your inability to implement custom enumerations.

Consider a situation where you have a relatively small and fixed number of user roles in your system. Let's consider just three roles: administrator, user, and guest. You want to represent these roles as `UserRole` domain objects. However, you do not want to create an instance of `UserRole` for each user because each individual `UserRole` should only exist once on the heap. There is no reason to be creating 1,000 identical `UserRole` objects for 1,000 users! In JDBC, you can easily use canonicalization to do this, assigning an appropriate single instance of `UserRole` in the `mapRow()` method.

Hibernate has support for custom enumerations, which can be used to model this scenario, but it has limited support for custom SQL queries. Furthermore, it may create very complex object graphs, especially when dealing with tree structures. If you need to model something similar to a directory structure, you would probably define the table to store the directory name and parent ID as a foreign key, and the domain object to store the name and another directory domain object as a parent. To make sure all references are solved, Hibernate needs to build the entire tree, which results in a lot of heap space being used and a lot of unnecessary database work.

Using JDBC Data Access in the Sample Application

All the concepts introduced here are used in the sample application. The beans that implement the data access interfaces are defined in applicationContext-jdbc.xml. To make sure SpringBlog uses this implementation, edit the web.xml file and make sure the contextConfigLocation includes the applicationContext-jdbc.xml, as shown in Listing 8-24.

Listing 8-24. *web.xml for JDBC Data Access Layer Implementation*

```
<?xml version="1.0" encoding="ISO-8859-1"?>
<!DOCTYPE web-app PUBLIC
    "-//Sun Microsystems, Inc.//DTD Web Application 2.3//EN"
    "http://java.sun.com/dtd/web-app_2_3.dtd">
<web-app>
    <context-param>
        <param-name>contextConfigLocation</param-name>
        <param-value>
            /WEB-INF/applicationContext.xml
            /WEB-INF/applicationContext-db.xml
            /WEB-INF/applicationContext-jdbc.xml
        </param-value>
    </context-param>

    <!-- the rest of the file omitted -->

</web-app>
```

The implementation classes are all located in the com.apress.prospring.data.jdbc package. We have tried to make the implementation of the JDBC classes as database-independent as possible by using an abstract class that is common for all databases and then providing an implementation of the abstract class for MySQL, as explained in the "Inserting Data" section earlier in this chapter. The UML diagram in Figure 8-1 shows the EntryDao interface, the JdbcAbstractEntryDao that performs the database-independent functions, and the JdbcMysqlEntryDao that provides MySQL-specific functionality to the JdbcAbstractEntryDao.

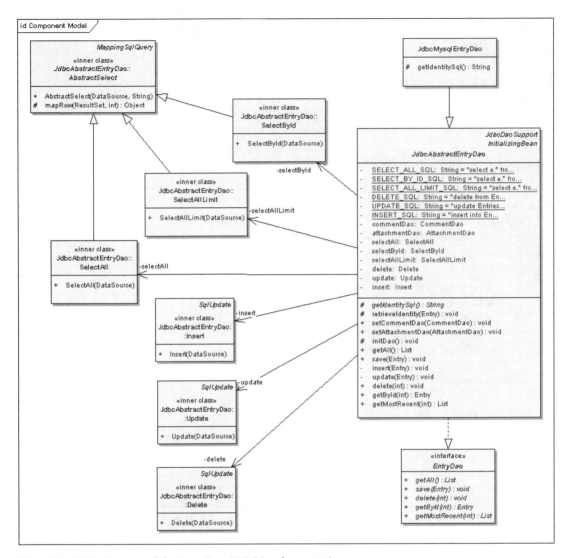

Figure 8-1. *UML diagram of the EntryDao JDBC implementation*

The diagram in Figure 8-1 also shows the inner classes used in the JdbcAbstractEntryDao implementation. All classes that return data are subclasses of AbstractSelect, which takes care of mapping the rows retrieved from the database to the Entry domain objects. The concrete implementations of AbstractSelect provide the SQL select statement that will be executed. The Insert, Update, and Delete inner classes all extend the SqlUpdate class, provide the SQL statement for the actual update operation, and define the required parameters.

We have chosen to merge the insert and update operations into the save() method. The motivation is that the data access implementation knows how to tell a domain object that needs to be inserted from a domain object that needs to be updated. In the case of relational databases using an integer primary key, the unsaved object has its primary key value set to 0, whereas the object that references an existing row has the primary key value set greater than 0.

Listing 8-25 shows the implementation of the save() method calling the insert() or update() method appropriately.

Listing 8-25. *Implementaion of the save(), insert(), and update() Methods*

```
public abstract class JdbcAbstractEntryDao extends JdbcDaoSupport implements
        EntryDao, InitializingBean {

    // rest of the code omitted

    protected abstract String getIdentitySql();

    protected void retrieveIdentity(final Entry entry) {
        entry.setEntryId(getJdbcTemplate().queryForInt(getIdentitySql()));
    }

    public void save(Entry entry) {
        if (entry.getEntryId() == 0)
            insert(entry);
        else
            update(entry);
    }

    private void insert(Entry entry) {
        Object[] values = new Object[] { entry.getSubject(), entry.getBody(),
                entry.getPostDate() };
        insert.update(values);
        retrieveIdentity(entry);

    }

    private void update(Entry entry) {
        Object[] values = new Object[] { entry.getSubject(), entry.getBody(),
                entry.getPostDate(), new Integer(entry.getEntryId()) };
        update.update(values);
    }
}
```

The code from Listing 8-25 also explains why the JdbcAbstractEntryDao is an abstract class: when a row is inserted into the Entries table, we need to retrieve the value generated for the primary key. To do this, the insert() method calls the retrieveIdentity() method, which gets the integer value by executing a SQL statement returned by the getIdentitySql() method.

The getIdentitySql() method is the only method that must be implemented to support each individual database. We implement this method for MySQL in JdbcMysqlEntryDao, as shown in Listing 8-26.

Listing 8-26. *JdbcMysqlEntryDao Implementation*

```
package com.apress.prospring.data.jdbc;

public class JdbcMysqlEntryDao extends JdbcAbstractEntryDao {

    protected String getIdentitySql() {
        return "select LAST_INSERT_ID()";
    }
}
```

The update and delete operations in Listing 8-25 are implemented almost exactly as the same operations were implemented in the "Updating Data" and "Inserting Data" sections earlier in this chapter.

Selecting the data from the database tables is a trivial task of extending the AbstractSelect query to make sure the correct SQL statements are passed to the database; all this has already been covered in the "Selecting the Data as Java Objects" section earlier in this chapter.

The last thing we have to deal with is selecting data from more than one table. This is best explained by the getById() method, which returns an Entry domain object identified by its primary key, but it also loads all Attachment and Comment objects associated with the Entry. The JdbcAbstractEntryDao class uses CommentDao and AttachmentDao to load and set the attachments and comments properties of the Entry domain object. This means that the getById() method issues three select statements to the database: one to load the Entry object, one to load the List of Attachments, and another one to load the List of Comments. Fortunately, this is not a major problem, because the getById() method is not called very frequently and more importantly, it only loads a single Entry domain object. This is known as *N+1* complexity, which we discuss in more detail in Chapters 9 and 10.

Summary

This chapter showed you how to use Spring to simplify JDBC programming. You learned how to connect to a database and perform selects, updates, deletes, and inserts. We also discussed primary key considerations and transaction support and hinted that there is another way to implement the data access layer of your application, through Object-Relational Mapping tools. We take a look at these tools in the next chapters.

■■■

CHAPTER 9

Using Hibernate in Spring Applications

In the previous chapter you saw how to use JDBC in Spring applications. However, even though Spring goes a long way toward simplifying JDBC development, you still have a lot of code to write.

In this chapter, we are going to take a look at one of the object-relational mapping (ORM) frameworks that has wide support in Spring—Hibernate.

Hibernate started off as an independent project, but it became part of JBoss. This proves that Hibernate is indeed a robust and fast framework that can bring a rapid application development (RAD) approach to DAO implementations.

Just like any other RAD tool, with Hibernate, there is a tradeoff between ease of use and speed and low-level features you can access. As you will see, Hibernate performs adequately and offers enough features to manipulate the data, even from its high-level APIs.

In particular, we are going to discuss the following topics:

Configuration: We are going to discuss the various configuration files you need to successfully use Hibernate in your data access layer.

Creating mapping files: You need to create these mapping files to tell Hibernate how to map the tables in your database to the domain objects. We are going to discuss mappings that represent the various table relationships.

CRUD operations: You will learn how to effectively select data from the database using outer joins wherever possible and how to insert data to the database and make sure Hibernate sets the correct value of the primary key to the inserted domain object. Finally, you will learn how to effectively implement optimistic concurrency in data updates.

What Is Hibernate?

There are two basic kinds of ORM frameworks. The first allows you to fully control the SQL statements, and you have to make sure that you are selecting the correct columns. Hibernate represents the second kind of ORM tools, the kind where the framework generates the SQL statements for you. This speeds up development incredibly because you only have to write the mapping files and the framework takes care of the database operations and correctly processes the results.

Hibernate also allows you to specify the SQL dialect it should use for the queries. As a result, Hibernate generates almost ideal queries that are tailored to the specific database you are using. The dialect controls the syntax for joins, limit/top clauses, and many other database-specific SQL features.

One of the most useful aspects of Hibernate is that it allows you to define your own persisted enum types—regular Java classes that implement a specific interface. This helps you implement object canonicalization, which may give your application quite a performance boost.

Hibernate Versions

The current production version of Hibernate is 2.1.6, and therefore we focus on the version 2 line in this chapter. However, by the time this book is published, version 3.0 may have reached the production stage. In fact, the Spring community is already making all the necessary preparations for adding support to Hibernate 3 when it is finally released.

Configuring Hibernate in a Spring Application

If you want to use Hibernate in your application, you must start by configuring a dataSource (as shown in Listing 9-1), which defines the connection to a database.

Listing 9-1. *dataSource Bean Definition*

```
<?xml version="1.0" encoding="UTF-8"?>
<!DOCTYPE beans PUBLIC "-//SPRING//DTD BEAN//EN" ➡
"http://www.springframework.org/dtd/spring-beans.dtd">

<beans>

    <!-- Data source bean -->
    <bean id="dataSource" class="org.apache.commons.dbcp.BasicDataSource"
        destroy-method="close">
        <property name="driverClassName">
            <value>org.postgresql.Driver</value></property>
        <property name="url">
            <value>jdbc:postgresql://localhost/prospring</value></property>
        <property name="username"><value>janm</value></property>
        <property name="password"><value>GenOme64</value></property>
    </bean>
</beans>
```

The dataSource bean defines a connection to the prospering PostgreSQL database that is running on the local machine using the specified user name and password. You also need to create a sessionFactory bean (see Listing 9-2) that all the Hibernate DAO implementations are going to use.

Listing 9-2. *sessionFactory Bean Definition*

```xml
<?xml version="1.0" encoding="UTF-8"?>
<!DOCTYPE beans PUBLIC "-//SPRING//DTD BEAN//EN" ➥
"http://www.springframework.org/dtd/spring-beans.dtd">

<beans>
    <bean id="dataSource" …/>

    <bean id="sessionFactory"
        class="org.springframework.orm.hibernate.LocalSessionFactoryBean">
        <property name="dataSource"><ref local="dataSource"/></property>
        <property name="mappingResources">
            <value>sample.hbm.xml</value></property>
        <property name="hibernateProperties">
            <props>
                <prop key="hibernate.dialect">
                    net.sf.hibernate.dialect.PostgresSQLDialect</prop>
            </props>
        </property>
    </bean>
</beans>
```

As you can see in Listing 9-2, there are several notable settings in the sessionFactory bean. First of all, you must set a reference to the dataSource bean. You then need to set the mappingResources, which is a Spring Resource reference, to at least one Hibernate mapping file. The location of these files is specific to the application type you are developing. It is important to realize that the configuration files are **resources,** and as such, they are handled by ResourceLoaders, usually the default ResourceLoader. (More information on resources is covered in Chapter 4.)

Finally, you need to set the hibernate.dialect property on the session factory, which allows Hibernate to generate the SQL queries effectively. Each dialect also specifies additional features the database supports. For example, MySQLDialect supports identity key generation, whereas PostgreSQLDialect supports sequence key generation, not identity. You have no way of finding out what the next primary key value is going to be in MySQL, because MySQL only generates the primary key value on insert. For this reason as well as others, it is vital that you set this property according to the database you are using.

In a larger-scale application, you do not usually use a single Hibernate mapping file. Instead, you usually split the mapping files for each class. If this is the case, you have to modify the mappingResources property of the sessionFactory bean as we have done in Listing 9-3.

Listing 9-3. *sessionFactory Bean Definition with mappingResources Specified*

```
<?xml version="1.0" encoding="UTF-8"?>
<!DOCTYPE beans PUBLIC "-//SPRING//DTD BEAN//EN" ➥
"http://www.springframework.org/dtd/spring-beans.dtd">

<beans>
    <bean id="dataSource" …/>

    <bean id="sessionFactory"
        class="org.springframework.orm.hibernate.LocalSessionFactoryBean">
        <property name="dataSource"><ref local="dataSource"/></property>
        <property name="mappingResources">
          <list>
                <value>sample.hbm.xml</value>
          </list>
        </property>
        <property name="hibernateProperties">
            <props>
                <prop key="hibernate.dialect">
                    net.sf.hibernate.dialect.PostgresSQLDialect</prop>
            </props>
        </property>
    </bean>
</beans>
```

Because Hibernate needs a lot of configuration files to function properly, it is important to place the mapping files in appropriate source folders and then use the build script to place them correctly in the distribution archive. The location of these files is shown in Table 9-1.

Table 9-1. *Locations of the Configuration Files*

File	Source Location	Build/Run Location
sample.hbm.xml	src/hibernate	build
applicationContext	src/conf	build

The build script, build.xml, takes care of building the application and makes sure that the configuration files are copied from their source location to the appropriate destination to run the application. But before you can move ahead to complete the configuration files and make the application work, we need to take a closer look at the Hibernate mapping files.

Mapping Files

Put simply, the mapping files define classes, properties of these classes, and how these classes and their properties map to the database tables and columns so that Hibernate can persist the classes to the database. These mapping files can get quite complex (especially when you are using many-to-many inverse mappings), but in most cases, they are very straightforward.

Simple Mappings

Let us begin with the script for a simple table that has just three columns and a matching domain object (see Listing 9-4).

Listing 9-4. *SQL Script for the Test Table*

```
create table Test (
    TestId serial not null,
    Name varchar(50) not null,
    RunDate timestamp not null,

    constraint PK_TestId primary key (TestId)
);

insert into Test (Name, RunDate) values ('foobar', '2004-01-01');
```

The domain object (shown in Listing 9-5) is going to have properties for all three columns and is going to override the toString() method to return a human-readable representation of the object's data.

Listing 9-5. *Test Domain Object*

```
package com.apress.prospring.ch9.domain;

import java.util.Date;

public class Test {

    private int testId;
    private String name;
    private Date runDate;

    public String toString() {
        // implementation
    }
    // Getters and Setters
}
```

Now let's take a look at our sample mapping file (see Listing 9-6). It maps the Test domain object's properties to columns in the Test table.

Listing 9-6. *Hibernate Mapping File for the Test Object and Table*

```
<?xml version="1.0" encoding="UTF-8"?>
<!DOCTYPE hibernate-mapping PUBLIC
        "-//Hibernate/Hibernate Mapping DTD//EN"
        "http://hibernate.sourceforge.net/hibernate-mapping-2.0.dtd">

<hibernate-mapping auto-import="true">

    <class name="com.apress.prospring.ch9.domain.Test" table="Test">
        <id name="testId" column="TestId" type="int" unsaved-value="0">
            <generator class="sequence">
                <param name="sequence">Test_TestId_Seq</param>
            </generator>
        </id>
        <property name="name" column="Name"/>
        <property name="runDate" column="RunDate"/>
    </class>

</hibernate-mapping>
```

The code in bold instructs Hibernate to create an instance of the Test domain object for the rows selected from the Test table. It also sets the value of property testId to the value in column TestId, name to the value of the Name column, and runDate to the value of the RunDate column.

This code also specifies that on insert, Hibernate uses a sequence to set the primary key value. This is the only database-specific setting because not all databases support sequences or identities. For instance, if you want to design the application to support different databases, you have to create separate mapping files for each database that you want to use. Alternatively, you can use a database-independent generator for the primary key value, such as hilo. This approach works well if the primary key is a numeric type; however, if the primary key is GUID, the hilo generator is not going to work and you have to rely on the database to provide the correct primary key value.

One-to-Many Mappings

Hibernate allows you to map a one-to-many relationship very easily. To demonstrate this, we create a fairly typical Customer to Customer Address relationship. The SQL demonstrates this 1:*N* relationship in an obvious way, as shown in Listing 9-7.

Listing 9-7. *SQL Script for 1:N Example*

```
create table Customers (
    CustomerId serial not null,
    FirstName varchar(50) not null,
    LastName varchar(50) not null,
```

```
        constraint PK_CustomerId primary key (CustomerId)
);

create table CustomerAddresses (
        CustomerAddressId serial not null,
        Customer int not null,
        Line1 varchar(50) not null,
        Line2 varchar(50) not null,
        City varchar(50) not null,
        PostCode varchar(50) not null,

        constraint PK_CustomerAddressId primary key (CustomerAddressId),
        constraint FK_Customer foreign key (Customer)
            references Customers (CustomerId)
            on delete cascade
);
```

The domain objects (shown in Listing 9-8) are going to reflect the structure shown in Listing 9-7. However, the Customer object is going to have a Set of CustomerAddresses.

Listing 9-8. *Customer and CustomerAddress Domain Objects*

```
package com.apress.prospring.ch9.domain;

// in Customer.java
import java.util.Set;

public class Customer {

    private int customerId;
    private String firstName;
    private String lastName;
    private Set addresses;
    public String toString() {
        // implementation
    }
    // Getters and setters
}

// in CustomerAddress.java
public class CustomerAddress {

    private int customerAddressId;
    private int customer;
    private String line1;
    private String line2;
    private String city;
    private String postCode;
```

```
    public String toString() {
        // implementation
    }
    // Getters and setters
}
```

These domain classes are a box-standard representation of the data, except that the Customer object has a Set of addresses. Traditionally, we would not include the addresses property in the Customer domain object. In Listing 9-9, we tell Hibernate that the addresses property should be populated by data selected from the CustomerAddresses table where Customer = CustomerId.

Listing 9-9. *The customer.hbm.xml Mapping File*

```xml
<?xml version="1.0" encoding="UTF-8"?>
<!DOCTYPE hibernate-mapping PUBLIC
        "-//Hibernate/Hibernate Mapping DTD//EN"
        "http://hibernate.sourceforge.net/hibernate-mapping-2.0.dtd">

<hibernate-mapping auto-import="true">

    <class name="com.apress.prospring.ch9.domain.Customer" table="Customers">
        <id name="customerId" column="CustomerId" type="int" unsaved-value="0">
            <generator class="sequence">
                <param name="sequence">Customers_CustomerId_Seq</param>
            </generator>
        </id>
        <property name="firstName" column="FirstName"/>
        <property name="lastName" column="LastName"/>
        <set name="addresses">
            <key column="Customer"/>
            <one-to-many
                class="com.apress.prospring.ch9.domain.CustomerAddress"/>
        </set>
    </class>

    <class name="com.apress.prospring.ch9.domain.CustomerAddress"
        table="CustomerAddresses">
        <id name="customerAddressId" column="CustomerAddressId"
            type="int" unsaved-value="0">
            <generator class="sequence">
                <param name="sequence">CustomerAddresses_CustomerId_Seq</param>
            </generator>
        </id>
```

```
        <property name="customer" column="Customer"/>
        <property name="line1" column="Line1"/>
        <property name="line2" column="Line2"/>
        <property name="city" column="City"/>
        <property name="postCode" column="PostCode"/>
    </class>

</hibernate-mapping>
```

The mapping states that the `Customer` object has a `Set` property named `addresses`. The elements in this set should be `CustomerAddress` objects selected from the CustomerAddresses table where the ID of the `Customer` object is equal to the value in the `Customer` column.

Hibernate suffers from a $1+N$ complexity. For example, assume that we have two rows in the Customers table; if this is the case, Hibernate performs two queries to the CustomerAddresses table to get the addresses for each `Customer` object returned from the first query. Hence the number of queries is 1 (to get the `Customer` objects) + N (to select N CustomerAddresses objects for the N Customers selected in the first query).

The log from the sample application shown in Listing 9-10, which we are going to finish later in this chapter, demonstrates this.

Listing 9-10. *Log Messages Showing 1 + N Complexity in Select*

```
(1) select customer0_.CustomerId as CustomerId, customer0_.FirstName as
    FirstName, customer0_.LastName as LastName from Customers customer0_
(2) select addresses0_.Customer as Customer__,
    addresses0_.CustomerAddressId as Customer1___,
    addresses0_.CustomerAddressId as Customer1_0_,
    addresses0_.Customer as Customer0_,
    addresses0_.Line1 as Line10_,
    addresses0_.Line2 as Line20_, addresses0_.City as City0_,
    addresses0_.PostCode as PostCode0_ from
    CustomerAddresses addresses0_ where addresses0_.Customer=?
(3) select addresses0_.Customer as Customer__,
    addresses0_.CustomerAddressId as Customer1___,
    addresses0_.CustomerAddressId as Customer1_0_,
    addresses0_.Customer as Customer0_,
    addresses0_.Line1 as Line10_,
    addresses0_.Line2 as Line20_, addresses0_.City as City0_,
    addresses0_.PostCode as PostCode0_ from
    CustomerAddresses addresses0_ where addresses0_.Customer=?
```

Many-to-Many Mappings

The most complex mapping type (and also the type that requires the most work in updates and inserts) is *M:N*. This relationship is modeled by a join table, which creates two 1:*N* relationships.

In Listing 9-11, we add two more tables to the schema from Listing 9-7.

Listing 9-11. *Many-to-Many SQL Schema*

```sql
create table Permissions (
    PermissionId int not null,
    Name varchar(50) not null,

    constraint PK_PermissionId primary key (PermissionId)
);

create table CustomerPermissions (
    CustomerPermissionId serial not null,
    Permission int not null,
    Customer int not null,

    constraint PK_CustomerPermissionId primary key (CustomerPermissionId),
    constraint PK_Permission foreign key (Permission)
        references Permissions(PermissionId) on delete cascade,
    constraint PK_Customer foreign key (Customer) references Customers(CustomerId)
        on delete cascade
);
```

The domain object for Permission is simply going to map the columns from the table to its properties. As well as the mapping for the Permission domain object, Listing 9-12 shows mapping for the roles property to the Customer domain object. Most importantly, the listing also shows the many-to-many relationship between the Customer and Permission domain objects.

Listing 9-12. *The customer.hbm.xml Mapping File*

```xml
<?xml version="1.0" encoding="UTF-8"?>
<!DOCTYPE hibernate-mapping PUBLIC
        "-//Hibernate/Hibernate Mapping DTD//EN"
        "http://hibernate.sourceforge.net/hibernate-mapping-2.0.dtd">

<hibernate-mapping auto-import="true">

    <class name="com.apress.prospring.ch9.domain.Customer" table="Customers">
        <id name="customerId" column="CustomerId" type="int" unsaved-value="0">
            <generator class="sequence">
                <param name="sequence">Customers_CustomerId_Seq</param>
            </generator>
        </id>
        <property name="firstName" column="FirstName"/>
        <property name="lastName" column="LastName"/>
        <set name="addresses" outer-join="true">
            <key column="Customer"/>
            <one-to-many class="com.apress.prospring.ch9.domain.CustomerAddress"/>
        </set>
```

```
        <set name="permissions" outer-join="true" inverse="true"
            table="CustomerPermissions">
            <key column="Customer"/>
            <many-to-many class="com.apress.prospring.ch9.domain.Permission"
                    column="Permission"/>
        </set>
    </class>

    <class name="com.apress.prospring.ch9.domain.CustomerAddress"
        table="CustomerAddresses">
        <id name="customerAddressId" column="CustomerAddressId"
            type="int" unsaved-value="0">
            <generator class="sequence">
                <param name="sequence">CustomerAddresses_CustomerAddressId_Seq
                </param>
            </generator>
        </id>
        <property name="customer" column="Customer"/>
        <property name="line1" column="Line1"/>
        <property name="line2" column="Line2"/>
        <property name="city" column="City"/>
        <property name="postCode" column="PostCode"/>
    </class>

    <class name="com.apress.prospring.ch9.domain.Permission" table="Permissions">
        <id name="permissionId" column="PermissionId" type="int">
            <generator class="sequence"/>
        </id>
        <property name="name" column="Name"/>
    </class>

</hibernate-mapping>
```

The many-to-many mapping is represented here by the Set of Permission objects. In this code, we instruct Hibernate to select all rows from the Permissions that have a record in CustomerPermissions where Customer = CustomerId. In SQL, Hibernate runs the query shown in Listing 9-13.

Listing 9-13. *Generated SQL Statement for Many-to-Many Mapping*

```
select permission0_.Customer as Customer__,
    permission0_.Permission as Permission__,
    permission1_.PermissionId as Permissi1_0_,
    permission1_.Name as Name0_
from CustomerPermissions permission0_ inner join Permissions permission1_ on
    permission0_.Permission=permission1_.PermissionId
where permission0_.Customer=?
```

As you can see, *M:N* selects also suffer from the $1 + N$ performance problem, which is magnified by the inner join operation.

You can reduce the complexity of the select operation[1] by setting the `hibernate.max_fetch_depth` property in the `hibernateProperties` of the `sessionFactory` (see Listing 9-14). This tells Hibernate to attempt to perform a single outer join select rather than multiple separate select statements.

Listing 9-14. *max_fetch_depth Setting*

```
<?xml version="1.0" encoding="UTF-8"?>
<!DOCTYPE beans PUBLIC "-//SPRING//DTD BEAN//EN"➡
 "http://www.springframework.org/dtd/spring-beans.dtd">

<beans>

    <!-- Data source bean -->
    <bean id="dataSource" …/>


    <bean id="sessionFactory"
        class="org.springframework.orm.hibernate.LocalSessionFactoryBean">
        <!-- etc -->
        <property name="hibernateProperties">
            <props>
                <prop
                    key="hibernate.dialect">
                        net.sf.hibernate.dialect.PostgreSQLDialect
                </prop>
                <prop key="hibernate.max_fetch_depth">3</prop>
            </props>
        </property>
    </bean>

</beans>
```

The `hibernate.max_fetch_depth` property sets the maximum number of tables to be joined for single-ended associations (one-to-one, many-to-one). Generally, you should set this to values between 1 and 3 because 0 disables outer joins completely and outer joining more than three tables may result in SQL statements that are too complex and too much work for the database.

Without setting the `hibernate.max_fetch_depth` property, if you select all customers from the sample database, you get eight select statements. When we added this property to the `sessionFactory`, the number of select statements dropped to 5.

---

1. You are not actually reducing the complexity of the operation; you are merely delegating some work to the database. After all, databases are designed and optimized particularly for joins.

The Hibernate Query Language

Hibernate does not use SQL for its statements. It uses its own query language called Hibernate Query Language (HQL), which is very similar to SQL. Because HQL is so similar to SQL, it takes almost no time to learn and makes the internals of the framework a bit easier to work with.

HQL is fully covered in Hibernate documentation; but we are going to discuss just a few major points here. First of all, HQL is case-sensitive. Unlike in SQL, the column names (bean properties) as well as table names (object names) are case sensitive. This is because HQL uses object names rather than table names to select the data. When you are writing an HQL statement, you do not actually have to worry about which tables are going to be used to build the result—it is up to Hibernate to find which tables map to which classes and issue the select statement to the database.

HQL is also an object-oriented language because it must include support for polymorphism. You will see from the examples in the rest of the chapter that other parts of the language, such as where, order by, group by, having, and many other clauses, are almost exactly the same as their SQL counterparts.

Possibly the most difficult part of the language that you have to get used to is that you select data from classes that are mapped in the mapping files. Rather than writing `select *` `from Test` to select all the rows from table Test, you have to write `select t from Test as t`. In this case, however, Test is a reference to the Test domain object, not the Test table.

Selecting Data

Now that we have configured Hibernate in a Spring application and mentioned that we are not going to be using SQL but HQL, we can dive in and implement the DAO that actually returns some meaningful data.

Simple Mappings

First let's go back to our Test table and Test domain objects, create a simple TestDao interface, and implement it in HibernateTestDao (see Listing 9-15).

Listing 9-15. *TestDao Interface*

```
package com.apress.prospring.ch9.data;

import java.util.List;

import com.apress.prospring.ch9.domain.Test;

public interface TestDao {

    public List getAll();

    public Test getById(int testId);
```

```
    public void save(Test test);

    public void delete(int testId);
}
```

In Listing 9-16, we implement only the getAll() and getById(int) methods; we leave the others as stubs.

Listing 9-16. *TestDao Hibernate Implementation*

```
package com.apress.prospring.ch9.data;

import java.util.List;

import org.springframework.orm.hibernate.support.HibernateDaoSupport;

import com.apress.prospring.ch9.domain.Test;


public class HibernateTestDao extends HibernateDaoSupport implements TestDao {

    public List getAll() {
        return getHibernateTemplate().find("from Test");
    }

    public Test getById(int testId) {
        return (Test)getHibernateTemplate().load(Test.class,
            new Integer(testId));
    }

    public void save(Test test) {
    }

    public void delete(int testId) {
    }

}
```

HibernateDaoSupport is a convenience superclass that allows us to use the getHibernate-Template() method, which returns HibernateTemplate, which, in turn, delegates calls to Hibernate methods.

Let's take a look at what's going on in the TestDao methods implemented in the HibernateTestDao class. The getAll() method calls the find(String) method on HibernateTemplate. This method automatically prefixes the select statement with select <alias>, therefore all you need to specify as a parameter to the find call is from Test. The getById(int) method calls the load () method on HibernateTemplate. This method takes two parameters: the class that will be returned, and a primary key, in our case, testId. The latter parameter returns an object, but you can safely cast it to Test and return the selected value.

To make sure that all the code we've written so far actually runs, we create a simple Main class, which builds Spring application context from an XML file on a classpath. Before we can do this, we have to make one last modification to the applicationContext.xml file—add the testDao bean (see Listing 9-17).

Listing 9-17. *Modified applicationContext.xml File*

```xml
<?xml version="1.0" encoding="UTF-8"?>
<!DOCTYPE beans PUBLIC "-//SPRING//DTD BEAN//EN" ➥
"http://www.springframework.org/dtd/spring-beans.dtd">

<beans>

    <bean id="dataSource" … />
    <bean id="sessionFactory" … />

    <bean id="testDao" class="com.apress.prospring.ch9.data.HibernateTestDao">
        <property name="sessionFactory"><ref local="sessionFactory"/></property>
    </bean>
</beans>
```

And this is it. We have the database ready, we have configured the Hibernate sessionFactory, and we have configured the testDao bean that implements the TestDao interface. Spring sets its sessionFactory property to an instance of the sessionFactory bean. We can give the code we have written so far a good test in Listing 9-18.

Listing 9-18. *Main Class Implementation*

```java
package com.apress.prospring.ch9;

import java.util.Iterator;
import java.util.List;

import org.springframework.context.ApplicationContext;
import org.springframework.context.support.ClassPathXmlApplicationContext;

import com.apress.prospring.ch9.data.TestDao;
import com.apress.prospring.ch9.domain.Test;

public class Main {

    private ApplicationContext context;

    private void test() {
        TestDao testDao = (TestDao)context.getBean("testDao");
        List tests = testDao.getAll();
```

```
        for (Iterator i = tests.iterator(); i.hasNext();) {
            Test test = (Test)i.next();
            System.out.println(test);
        }
    }

    private void run() {
        System.out.println("Initializing application");
        context = new ClassPathXmlApplicationContext("applicationContext.xml");

        test();

        System.out.println("Done");
    }

    public static void main(String[] args) {
        new Main().run();
    }

}
```

Here, you can see that the context is built in the run() method, and the test() method gets the TestDao implementation and calls getAll() to return a List of Test domain objects. Finally, we iterate over the contents of the list and print the individual items.

The result of running Ant using the build.xml script produces the following output:

```
Buildfile: d:\projects\pro-spring\ch9\build.xml
init:
compile:
run:
    [java] Initializing application
    ...
    [java] INFO: Creating shared instance of singleton bean 'sessionFactory'
    [java] Sep 2, 2004 11:30:16 AM net.sf.hibernate.cfg.Environment <clinit>
    [java] INFO: Hibernate 2.1.6
    [java] Sep 2, 2004 11:30:16 AM net.sf.hibernate.cfg.Environment <clinit>
    [java] INFO: hibernate.properties not found
    [java] Sep 2, 2004 11:30:16 AM net.sf.hibernate.cfg.Environment <clinit>
    [java] INFO: using CGLIB reflection optimizer
    [java] Sep 2, 2004 11:30:16 AM net.sf.hibernate.cfg.Binder bindRootClass
    [java] INFO: Mapping class: com.apress.prospring.ch9.domain.Test -> Test
    [java] Sep 2, 2004 11:30:16 AM ➥
org.springframework.orm.hibernate.LocalSessionFactoryBean afterPropertiesSet
    [java] INFO: Building new Hibernate SessionFactory
    [java] Sep 2, 2004 11:30:16 AM net.sf.hibernate.cfg.➥
Configuration secondPassCompile
    [java] INFO: processing one-to-many association mappings
    [java] Sep 2, 2004 11:30:16 AM net.sf.hibernate.cfg.➥
```

```
Configuration secondPassCompile
     [java] INFO: processing one-to-one association property references
     [java] Sep 2, 2004 11:30:16 AM net.sf.hibernate.cfg.➥
Configuration secondPassCompile
     [java] INFO: processing foreign key constraints
     [java] Sep 2, 2004 11:30:16 AM net.sf.hibernate.dialect.Dialect <init>
     [java] INFO: Using dialect: net.sf.hibernate.dialect.PostgreSQLDialect
     [java] Sep 2, 2004 11:30:16 AM net.sf.hibernate.cfg.➥
SettingsFactory buildSettings
     [java] INFO: Use outer join fetching: true
     [java] Sep 2, 2004 11:30:16 AM ➥
   net.sf.hibernate.connection.ConnectionProviderFactory newConnectionProvider
     [java] INFO: Initializing connection provider: org.springframework.orm.➥
hibernate.LocalDataSourceConnectionProvider
     [java] Sep 2, 2004 11:30:16 AM ➥
   net.sf.hibernate.transaction.TransactionManagerLookupFactory ➥
   getTransactionManagerLookup
     [java] Sep 2, 2004 11:30:17 AM net.sf.hibernate.cfg.➥
SettingsFactory buildSettings
     [java] INFO: Use scrollable result sets: true
     [java] Sep 2, 2004 11:30:17 AM net.sf.hibernate.cfg.➥
SettingsFactory buildSettings
     [java] INFO: Use JDBC3 getGeneratedKeys(): false
     [java] Sep 2, 2004 11:30:17 AM net.sf.hibernate.cfg.➥
SettingsFactory buildSettings
     [java] INFO: Optimize cache for minimal puts: false
     [java] Sep 2, 2004 11:30:17 AM net.sf.hibernate.cfg.➥
SettingsFactory buildSettings
     [java] INFO: Query language substitutions: {}
     [java] Sep 2, 2004 11:30:17 AM net.sf.hibernate.cfg.➥
SettingsFactory buildSettings
     [java] INFO: cache provider: net.sf.hibernate.cache.EhCacheProvider
     [java] Sep 2, 2004 11:30:17 AM net.sf.hibernate.cfg.➥
Configuration configureCaches
     [java] INFO: instantiating and configuring caches
     [java] Sep 2, 2004 11:30:17 AM net.sf.hibernate.impl.SessionFactoryImpl <init>
     [java] Sep 2, 2004 11:30:17 AM net.sf.hibernate.impl.➥
SessionFactoryObjectFactory addInstance
     [java] INFO: Not binding factory to JNDI, no JNDI name configured
     [java] Sep 2, 2004 11:30:17 AM ➥
   org.springframework.orm.hibernate.HibernateTransactionManager ➥
   afterPropertiesSet
     ...
     [java] Test { testId=1, name=foobar, runDate=2004-01-01 00:00:00.0}
     [java] Done
BUILD SUCCESSFUL
Total time: 2 seconds
```

As you can see, the application selects all rows from the Test table and prints out every one. However, before it can do this, it needs to configure the Hibernate framework. The output lists messages Hibernate produces on startup.

One-to-Many and Many-to-Many Selects

The code you need to write for these mappings is exactly the same as for simple mappings. First, in Listing 9-19, we create the CustomerDao interface and its implementation, HibernateCustomerDao.

Listing 9-19. *CustomerDao Interface and Its Implementation*

```
package com.apress.prospring.ch9.data;

import java.util.List;

import com.apress.prospring.ch9.domain.Customer;

// in CustomerDao.java:
public interface CustomerDao {
    public List getAll();
    public void save(Customer customer);
}

// in HibernateCustomerDao
public class HibernateCustomerDao
    extends HibernateDaoSupport
    implements CustomerDao {

    public List getAll() {
        return getHibernateTemplate().find("from Customer");
    }
    // other methods omitted for clarity
}
```

The CustomerDao interface defines only two methods: getAll() and save(). Both methods are fairly self-explanatory and the implementation on the Java side is very simple—we let Hibernate and Spring do all the hard work. In Listing 9-20, we modify the applicationContext.xml file and the Main class to test the code we have.

Listing 9-20. *Modified ApplicationContext.xml File*

```
<?xml version="1.0" encoding="UTF-8"?>
<!DOCTYPE beans PUBLIC "-//SPRING//DTD BEAN//EN" ➥
"http://www.springframework.org/dtd/spring-beans.dtd">

<beans>

    <bean id="dataSource" … />
    <bean id="sessionFactory" … />

    <bean id="customerDao"
        class="com.apress.prospring.ch9.data.HibernateCustomerDao">
        <property name="sessionFactory"><ref local="sessionFactory"/></property>
    </bean>
</beans>
```

Finally, in Listing 9-21, we add the customer() method to the Main class and call it from the run() method.

Listing 9-21. *Main Class Modification to Test the CustomerDao and Mappings*

```
package com.apress.prospring.ch9;

public class Main {
    public void customer() {
        CustomerDao customerDao =
            (CustomerDao)context.getBean("customerDao");
        List customers = customerDao.getAll();
        for (Iterator i = customers.iterator(); i.hasNext(); j++) {
            Customer customer = (Customer)i.next();
            System.out.println(customer);
        }
    }
    // the rest of the code omitted for clarity
}
```

The output produced by running the application is exactly what we expected: two Customer objects, with all their properties set.

```
Customer { customerId=1, firstName=Jan, lastName=Machacek,
addresses=[
    CustomerAddress { customerAddressId=2, line1=Line 1, line2=Line 2,
        city=Hradec Kralove, postCode=500 04 },
    CustomerAddress { customerAddressId=1, line1=Line 1, line2=Line 2,
        city=Manchester, postCode=M1 4HH }],
```

```
permissions=[
    Permission { permissionId=2, name=Edit Customer },
    Permission { permissionId=3, name=Delete Customer },
    Permission { permissionId=1, name=View Customer }] }
Customer { customerId=2, firstName=Rob, lastName=Harrop,
addresses=[
    CustomerAddress { customerAddressId=3, line1=Line 1, line2=Line 2,
        city=Denton, postCode=SK1 2AB }],
permissions=[Permission { permissionId=1, name=View Customer }] }
```

Advanced Selects

If you need to perform more advanced selects, you can take advantage of the features of HQL. We are not going to go into a detailed description here; but as an example, in Listing 9-22, we show a query that selects all the puny customers with just one permission.

Listing 9-22. *More Complex Selects*

```
package com.apress.prospring.ch9.data;

public class HibernateCustomerDao
    extends HibernateDaoSupport
    implements CustomerDao {

    // other methods omitted for clarity

    public List getAllWithOnlyOnePermission() {
        return getHibernateTemplate().find(
                "from Customer as c having c.permissions.size = ?",
                new Object[] { new Integer(1) });
    }

}
```

This code fragment clearly shows that you can use HQL to perform almost anything you can do with SQL; it also shows how to pass parameters to an HQL query. Just as you do with JDBC, you pass the parameters in as an array of Objects.

Updating and Inserting Data

Update and insert operations are very simple to program; actually we have very little code to write. All we need to do is to make sure our mappings are correct; we can then leave Hibernate to do all the hard work. Let's start with the TestDao.save(Test) implementation (see Listing 9-23).

Listing 9-23. *TestDao.save(Test) Implementation*

```
package com.apress.prospring.ch9.data;

import java.util.List;

import org.springframework.orm.hibernate.support.HibernateDaoSupport;

import com.apress.prospring.ch9.domain.Test;


public class HibernateTestDao extends HibernateDaoSupport implements TestDao {

    public void save(Test test) {
        getHibernateTemplate().saveOrUpdate(test);
    }
    // other methods omitted for clarity
}
```

This code is very simple. Hibernate decides whether to perform an insert or an update based on the value of the property defined in the ID element.

In Listing 9-24, we look at the mapping of the Test domain object's identity property. Hibernate uses the value of the identity property to determine whether it needs to perform an insert or an update.

Listing 9-24. *Hibernate Mapping File for the Test Object*

```
<?xml version="1.0" encoding="UTF-8"?>
<!DOCTYPE hibernate-mapping PUBLIC
        "-//Hibernate/Hibernate Mapping DTD//EN"
        "http://hibernate.sourceforge.net/hibernate-mapping-2.0.dtd">

<hibernate-mapping auto-import="true">

    <class name="com.apress.prospring.ch9.domain.Test" table="Test">
        <id name="testId" column="TestId" type="int" unsaved-value="0">
            <generator class="sequence">
                <param name="sequence">Test_TestId_Seq</param>
            </generator>
        </id>
        <!-- etc -->
    </class>

</hibernate-mapping>
```

The mapping defines that the primary key is stored in a property named testId, with an unsaved value of 0. The saveOrUpdate() method checks the primary key property, and if the value is equal to the value specified in the unsaved-value attribute, Hibernate performs an insert operation; otherwise, it performs an update. To demonstrate this, in Listing 9-25, we add a few lines to the Main class.

Listing 9-25. *Main Class Implementation Showing the TestDao Method Usage*

```
package com.apress.prospring.ch9;

public class Main {

    private ApplicationContext context;

    private void test() {
        TestDao testDao = (TestDao)context.getBean("testDao");
        Test test = new Test();
        test.setName("name");
        test.setRunDate(new Date());
        testDao.save(test);
    }

    // the rest of the code omitted for clarity

}
```

When we instantiate the Test object, testId is initialized to the default value for the int primitive, which is 0. The value 0 is also defined in the unsaved-value attribute in the mapping file, which means that a subsequent call to testDao.save(test) performs the SQL operations shown in Listing 9-26.

Listing 9-26. *SQL Statements Generated by the insert Operation*

```
select nextval ('Test_TestId_Seq')
insert into Test (Name, RunDate, TestId) values (?, ?, ?)
```

Hibernate correctly identifies that the Test domain object is not saved in the database yet, and it selects the next value for the primary key from the sequence and performs the insert operation.

If we set the testId property to a value other than 0, Hibernate tries to perform an update. Hibernate does not check for concurrent updates, but it does check the number of rows updated, which must be 1. Any other value indicates that you tried to update a row that does not exist. The code fragment in Listing 9-27 simulates an update of a nonexistent row.

Listing 9-27. *Code Fragment from Main.test() Method*

```
Test test = new Test();
test.setTestId(-1);
test.setName("name");
test.setRunDate(new Date());
testDao.save(test);
```

If we run the code fragment in Listing 9-27, Hibernate throws a `HibernateException` to indicate that the number of update rows is incorrect.

Concurrency

Hibernate supports versioned data for optimistic locking. The concept of optimistic locking means that the database allows many users to read a row, but it allows only the first user to perform an update. All other users need to reread the data in order to save it. This allows for much higher performance, but it may inconvenience users. However, in most cases, versioned concurrency offers the best performance while keeping the implementation simple and requires only one additional column in each versioned table.

Hibernate offers two ways of versioning the data: by version number or by timestamp. The concept of version numbers is quite simple; each row in the table has an additional column that specifies the version of the row. An update operation is allowed only if the version in the domain object matches the version in the table. An update operation also increases the version number.

Timestamping works in a similar way. Each row has a column that specifies the last time the row was saved. An update operation fails if the timestamp value in the table is newer than the timestamp in the domain object.

Because both methods require an additional column in each row, we recommend that you use versioning because it is a more reliable way of ensuring the data integrity.

The code in Listing 9-28 adds versioning support to our Test table and Test domain object.

Listing 9-28. *Alter Script for the Test Table*

```
alter table Test add column Version int not null default 0;
```

Now we need to modify the Test object, add an `int version` property, and modify the mapping file by adding the version element (see Listing 9-29).

Listing 9-29. *Version Element in the Mapping File*

```
<?xml version="1.0" encoding="UTF-8"?>
<!DOCTYPE hibernate-mapping PUBLIC
        "-//Hibernate/Hibernate Mapping DTD//EN"
        "http://hibernate.sourceforge.net/hibernate-mapping-2.0.dtd">

<hibernate-mapping auto-import="true">
```

```xml
    <class name="com.apress.prospring.ch9.domain.Test" table="Test">
        <id name="testId" column="TestId" type="int" unsaved-value="0">
            <generator class="sequence">
                <param name="sequence">Test_TestId_Seq</param>
            </generator>
        </id>
        <version name="version" column="Version" unsaved-value="negative"/>
        <property name="name" column="Name"/>
        <property name="runDate" column="RunDate"/>
    </class>

</hibernate-mapping>
```

Provided that we have added the version property to the Test domain object and have run the alter SQL script, we can now check that versioning works (see Listing 9-30).

Listing 9-30. *test() Method in Main*

```java
package com.apress.prospring.ch9;

public class Main {

    private void test() {
        TestDao testDao = (TestDao)context.getBean("testDao");
        Test test1, test2;
        test1 = testDao.getById(1);
        test2 = testDao.getById(1);
        test1.setName("new Name");
        test2.setName("other name");
        testDao.save(test1);
        testDao.save(test2);
    }

    // other methods omitted for clarity
}
```

The code in Listing 9-30 simulates concurrent updates. If test1 is loaded by Alice and test2 by Bob, then Alice is allowed to update the record, but Bob's update is rejected. However, if Bob saved the record first, Alice's changes are rejected. The output of running the build script shown here clearly demonstrates that the version is checked and that testDao.save(test2) throws an exception:

```
select test0_.TestId as TestId0_, test0_.Version as Version0_,
    test0_.Name as Name0_, test0_.RunDate as RunDate0_ from Test test0_
where test0_.TestId=?
select test0_.TestId as TestId0_, test0_.Version as Version0_,
    test0_.Name as Name0_, test0_.RunDate as RunDate0_ from Test test0_
```

```
where test0_.TestId=?
update Test set Version=?, Name=?, RunDate=? where TestId=? and Version=?
update Test set Version=?, Name=?, RunDate=? where TestId=? and Version=?
StaleObjectStateException:27 - An operation failed due to stale data
net.sf.hibernate.StaleObjectStateException: ➥
Row was updated or deleted by another transaction ➥
(or unsaved-value mapping was incorrect) for ➥
com.apress.prospring.ch9.domain.Test instance with identifier: 1
```

As you can see, implementing optimistic locking is very simple, but you must add another column to each table that contains versioned data.

There is another way to implement optimistic locking that may (in very few cases) further improve user experience, but it requires much more memory; in this case, in addition to "working" values, you also need to keep original values. Also, when you are performing an update, you need to check that the original values match in the where clause. Because you are comparing the values of the columns in the database and the original values stored in the domain object, you do not need to add an additional column, but the domain objects require double the memory to store the original and new property values.

Why Hibernate?

You have seen how Hibernate can speed up the development cycle. It is quite amazing how quickly you can implement changes in the data structure. Hibernate also supports persisted enum types, which is very useful for object canonicalization.

Of course, all this flexibility comes at a price. First of all, you are somewhat limited by the fact that you cannot manually optimize the SQL statements. You may also find that some of the features of the framework influence your decisions about the design of the application, sometimes even resulting in implementing the application in a certain way, not because it is the best way to do it, but because you know that Hibernate works well with that design.

Perhaps the worst part of Hibernate is that you cannot easily control the data you are selecting, and this can lead to some very inefficient queries. This is especially true for 1:N and M:N selects, which can get too complex. However, this is not a fault of Hibernate; it is a feature of the technology. If you do not want to start writing messy JDBC code, but you want to get more control over the object creation and SQL code, read Chapter 10, which deals with iBATIS.

Using Hibernate in the Sample Application

The SpringBlog application comes with an applicationContext-hibernate.xml file that allows you to use Hibernate as an implementation for the data access interfaces. If you want to use Hibernate, you need to modify the web.xml file to make sure you are using the applicationContext-hibernate.xml file in the contextConfigLocation element (see Listing 9-31).

Listing 9-31. *web.xml for Hibernate Data Access Layer Implementaion*

```xml
<?xml version="1.0" encoding="ISO-8859-1"?>
<!DOCTYPE web-app PUBLIC
    "-//Sun Microsystems, Inc.//DTD Web Application 2.3//EN"
    "http://java.sun.com/dtd/web-app_2_3.dtd">
<web-app>
    <context-param>
        <param-name>contextConfigLocation</param-name>
        <param-value>
            /WEB-INF/applicationContext.xml
            /WEB-INF/applicationContext-db.xml
            /WEB-INF/applicationContext-hibernate.xml
        </param-value>
    </context-param>

    <!-- the rest of the file omitted -->

</web-app>
```

The implementation classes are located in the com.apress.prospring.data.hibernate package. All Hibernate DAO implementation classes extend the HibernateDaoSupport class to get access to the utility methods, namely getHibernateTemplate(). We need to configure LocalSessionFactoryBean to get access to the SessionFactory class, which maintains the Session instances Hibernate uses to perform the database operations. The declaration of the sessionFactory bean is shown in Listing 9-32.

Listing 9-32. *sessionFactory Bean Definition*

```xml
<?xml version="1.0" encoding="UTF-8"?>
<!DOCTYPE beans PUBLIC "-//SPRING//DTD BEAN//EN"
    "http://www.springframework.org/dtd/spring-beans.dtd">
<beans>
    <bean id="sessionFactory"
        class="org.springframework.orm.hibernate.LocalSessionFactoryBean">
        <property name="dataSource"><ref bean="dataSource"/></property>
        <property name="mappingResources">
            <list>
                <value>Entry.hbm.xml</value>
                <value>Comment.hbm.xml</value>
                <value>User.hbm.xml</value>
                <value>Attachment.hbm.xml</value>
            </list>
        </property>
```

```
        <property name="hibernateProperties">
            <props>
                <prop key="hibernate.dialect">
                    net.sf.hibernate.dialect.MySQLDialect</prop>
                <prop key="hibernate.max_fetch_depth">3</prop>
            </props>
        </property>
    </bean>
</beans>
```

The sessionFactory bean sets the mappingResources that contain the Hibernate mappings for the domain objects. Even though you can keep all the mappings in one large file, we decided to split them into several files to keep the code clear.

Next, we set the hibernate.dialect property in hibernateProperties to MySQLDialect, indicating that the database server is MySQL. Finally, we set the hibernate.max_fetch_depth property; this specifies that Hibernate will construct the SQL statements to select the data with no more than three outer joins.

The mapping files are not particularly complex; the most complicated one is the Entry.hbm.xml for the Entry domain object. In Listing 9-33, you can see that it references mapping from the Comments.hbm.xml and Attachment.hbm.xml files, whereas Comment.hbm.xml references mapping from the User.hbm.xml mapping file.

Listing 9-33. *Entry Domain Object Mappings*

```
// Entry.hbm.xml
<?xml version="1.0"?>
<!DOCTYPE hibernate-mapping PUBLIC "-//Hibernate/Hibernate Mapping DTD//EN"
    "http://hibernate.sourceforge.net/hibernate-mapping-2.0.dtd">
<hibernate-mapping>

    <class name="com.apress.prospring.domain.Entry" table="Entries">
        <id name="entryId" type="int" unsaved-value="0" >
            <generator class="identity"/>
        </id>

        <property name="subject" type="string" not-null="true"/>
        <property name="body" type="string" not-null="true"/>
        <property name="postDate" type="timestamp" not-null="true"/>
        <set name="comments">
            <key column="Entry"/>
            <one-to-many class="com.apress.prospring.domain.Comment"/>
        </set>
```

```xml
            <set name="attachments" table="EntryAttachments">
                <key column="Entry"/>
                <many-to-many
                    class="com.apress.prospring.domain.Attachment"
                    column="Attachment" foreign-key="Attachment"/>
            </set>
        </class>

</hibernate-mapping>
```

// **Comment.hbm.xml**

```xml
<?xml version="1.0"?>
<!DOCTYPE hibernate-mapping PUBLIC "-//Hibernate/Hibernate Mapping DTD//EN"
    "http://hibernate.sourceforge.net/hibernate-mapping-2.0.dtd">
<hibernate-mapping>

    <class name="com.apress.prospring.domain.Comment" table="Comments">
        <id name="commentId" type="int" unsaved-value="0" >
            <generator class="identity"/>
        </id>

        <property name="subject" type="string" not-null="true"/>
        <property name="body" type="string" not-null="true"/>
        <property name="postDate" type="timestamp" not-null="true"/>
        <property name="entry" type="int" not-null="true"/>
        <property name="replyTo" type="int" not-null="false"/>
        <many-to-one name="postedBy"
            class="com.apress.prospring.domain.User" column="PostedBy">
            <column name="UserId"/>
        </many-to-one>
        <set name="attachments" table="CommentAttachments">
            <key column="Comment"/>
            <many-to-many class="com.apress.prospring.domain.Attachment"
                column="Attachment" foreign-key="Attachment"/>
        </set>
    </class>

</hibernate-mapping>
```

// **User.hbm.xml**

```xml
<?xml version="1.0"?>
<!DOCTYPE hibernate-mapping PUBLIC "-//Hibernate/Hibernate Mapping DTD//EN"
    "http://hibernate.sourceforge.net/hibernate-mapping-2.0.dtd">
```

```
<hibernate-mapping>

    <class name="com.apress.prospring.domain.User" table="Users">
        <id name="userId" type="int" unsaved-value="0" >
            <generator class="identity"/>
        </id>

        <property name="username" type="string" not-null="true"/>
        <property name="password" type="string" not-null="true"/>
        <property name="email" type="string" not-null="true"/>
        <property name="type" type="int" not-null="true"/>
    </class>

</hibernate-mapping>
```

Let's take a look at the mapping in more detail. First of all, the Entry domain object has the Set comments property and inherits the Set attachments property. The mapping specifies that the data for the attachments property should be the Attachment objects for rows selected from the Attachments table joined with the EntryAttachments table where EntryAttachments.Entry = Entry.EntryId and Attachment.AttachmentId = EntryAttachments.Attachment. This is effectively a many-to-many relationship.

Next, the mapping specifies that the data for the comments property should be the Comment domain objects. Hibernate knows that the Comment objects are stored in the Comments table, so the only thing we need to specify is the foreign key, Entry. The mapping for the Comment object specifies the attachments property as an Attachment object that is created from rows selected from the Attachments table joined with the CommentAttachments table where CommentAttachment.Comment = Comments.CommentId and Attachment.AttachmentId = CommentAttachments.Attachment.

Finally, the Comment objects contain a reference to the User who created the comment. This is represented by the many-to-one mapping to the User object selected from the Users table where Users.UserId = Comment.PostedBy.

Very little remains to be written about the DAO implementations, because all the work associated with selecting, updating, and deleting data is done by Hibernate. This means that the implementation files contain a lot less code than their JDBC versions. Take a look at Listing 9-34, which shows a **complete** implementation of the UserDao interface.

Listing 9-34. *HibernateUserDao Implementation*

```
package com.apress.prospring.data.hibernate;

import java.util.List;

import org.springframework.orm.hibernate.support.HibernateDaoSupport;

import com.apress.prospring.data.UserDao;
import com.apress.prospring.domain.User;
```

```
public class HibernateUserDao extends HibernateDaoSupport implements UserDao {

    public User getByUsernameAndPassword(String username, String password) {
        List users = getHibernateTemplate().findByNamedParam(
            "select u from User as u where u.username=:username and " +
            "u.password=:password", new String[] { "username", "password" },
                new Object[] { username, password });
        if (users.size() == 1) {
            return (User)users.get(0);
        }
        return null;
    }

    public void save(User user) {
        getHibernateTemplate().saveOrUpdate(user);
    }

    public void delete(int userId) {
        User user = new User();
        user.setUserId(userId);
        getHibernateTemplate().delete(user);
    }

    public List getAll() {
        return getHibernateTemplate().find("select u from User as u");
    }

}
```

The only slightly complex method in this code is getByUsernameAndPassword() because it needs to pass two named parameters (username and password) to Hibernate. Hibernate executes the query and returns a List of matching User objects. We need to check that the number of objects in the List is 1 and return the first object from the List. If there are zero or more than one result, we return null. Because the HibernateTemplate.delete() method requires an Object parameter representing the domain object to be deleted, we need to construct an instance of the User object and set its userId property before passing it as a parameter to the HibernateTemplate.delete() method.

There is one more interesting point to mention in the implementation of the Hibernate data access layer: in HibernateEntryDao.save(), we need to make sure the class of the entry parameter passed to the saveOrUpdate() method is Entry.class. The reason why is because in the web layer, we use an object that extends the Entry domain object and passes it to the Blog-Manager.saveEntry() method, which, in turn, calls the EntryDao.save() method implemented in HibernateEntryDao.save(). Unfortunately, Hibernate does not know how to persist the subclass of the Entry object and throws an exception. Listing 9-35 shows how we deal with the situation.

Listing 9-35. *HibernateEntryDao.save() Implementation*

```
package com.apress.prospring.data.hibernate;

import java.util.List;

import org.springframework.orm.hibernate.support.HibernateDaoSupport;

import com.apress.prospring.data.EntryDao;
import com.apress.prospring.domain.Entry;

public class HibernateEntryDao extends HibernateDaoSupport implements EntryDao {

    public void save(Entry entry) {
        Entry ex = new Entry();
        ex.setEntryId(entry.getEntryId());
        ex.setBody(entry.getBody());
        ex.setEntryId(entry.getEntryId());
        ex.setPostDate(entry.getPostDate());
        ex.setSubject(entry.getSubject());
        getHibernateTemplate().saveOrUpdate(ex);
    }

    // other methods omitted
}
```

Here, we actually create an instance of the Entry object and set its properties from the entry parameter; we then use the local Entry instance in the call to the saveOrUpdate() method.

The last problem we have to solve in the HibernateEntryDao implementation is how to limit the number of Entry objects returned. We do not want to get all the rows from the Entries table and then create another List and copy the first count objects. Instead, we want to tell Hibernate not to return more than count objects. Listing 9-36 shows how we finally solve this problem using the HibernateTemplate.execute() method and implementing the HibernateCallback interface.

Listing 9-36. *Limiting the Maximum Number of Objects Returned*

```
package com.apress.prospring.data.hibernate;

import java.sql.SQLException;
import java.util.List;

import net.sf.hibernate.HibernateException;
import net.sf.hibernate.Query;
import net.sf.hibernate.Session;

import org.springframework.orm.hibernate.HibernateCallback;
import org.springframework.orm.hibernate.support.HibernateDaoSupport;
```

```
import com.apress.prospring.data.EntryDao;
import com.apress.prospring.domain.Entry;

public class HibernateEntryDao
    extends HibernateDaoSupport implements EntryDao {

    // other methods omitted

    public List getMostRecent(final int count) {
        return (List) getHibernateTemplate().execute(new HibernateCallback() {
            public Object doInHibernate(Session session)
                throws HibernateException, SQLException {
                Query query = session.createQuery("from Entry");
                query.setMaxResults(count);
                return query.list();
            }

        });
    }
}
```

Even though the implementation of the data access layer using Hibernate is very simple, the complexity of the queries the database needs to process for a complex object structure, such as the Entry object, is very large. Because of this, the overall performance of the application suffers, mainly because the web layer does not know that once it retrieves a List of Entry domain objects, all dependant objects are also loaded. We can change the Web Tier to reflect the fact that the entire object tree is loaded, but doing so introduces dependency on a particular DAO implementation, and we do not want to do that.

Summary

In this chapter, you learned how to use Hibernate in your Spring applications. Using Hibernate is just like using any other RAD tool. In simple applications, you get very good performance for very little programming; however, if you want or need to take full control over the data access layer of your application, you may find that Hibernate is simply too slow. It is not a fault of the framework itself; it is just that sometimes the queries to build the objects defined in the mapping files are simply too complex. The good news is that Spring allows you to start off with Hibernate and then move toward other DAO implementations if you find that Hibernate's performance does not meet your expectations.

In the next chapter, we will take a look at iBATIS, which represents the second type of ORM framework. You will see that even though there is a bit more code involved, iBATIS is a viable alternative to Hibernate.

CHAPTER 10

■ ■ ■

iBATIS Integration

In the previous chapter, you saw how to use JDBC in Spring applications. Even though Spring goes a long way toward simplifying JDBC development, you will find that you still have a lot of code to write with JDBC.

One elegant solution to avoiding all this code is to use an object-relational mapping (ORM) tool, which maps the data rows and creates appropriate Java objects. In order for such mapping tools to access Java objects in a standardized fashion, they have to follow Java bean naming conventions. For example, the mapping tools can also set referenced objects that result from a join operation.

There are two basic types of ORM frameworks: those in which you can rely on the framework to generate the SQL statements entirely, or those in which you can take a slightly more manual approach and write the SQL statements yourself. The first case speeds up development, but sometimes the SQL code is not efficient enough. With the second approach, you write the SQL code yourself, making sure to select the correct columns that the ORM framework uses to create instances of the Java beans.

In this chapter, we are going to focus on implementing the data access layer of a Spring application using iBATIS. Specifically, we will cover the following:

Configuration: We discuss the various configuration files you need to successfully use iBATIS in the data layer of your application.

Mapping files: In this section, you learn how to create the mapping files and how iBATIS uses these files to perform the mapping of the selected rows to the properties of the domain objects.

CRUD operations: You learn how to implement the select, delete, and update operations using iBATIS. You learn how to implement select operations that represent all types of data relationships. Finally, we discuss how you can make sure that the insert operations are using the correct primary key values.

What Is iBATIS?

iBATIS represents the second of the two types of ORM tools mentioned in this chapter's introduction; it allows the developer to write the custom SQL code they need to populate the bean properties. iBATIS uses the same approach for data inserts and updates, which is very good news indeed. Sometimes you do not want to update the entire row (especially when the row is quite large); in a lot of cases, you just have one value to update. It also allows you to fully use your database's extensions to the standard SQL syntax. You may object to the fact that portability is an important feature of a J2EE application, but remember that in most cases, full database portability is often a phantom requirement (for further discussion of application design in Spring, check out Chapter 5). Besides, because iBATIS uses XML mapping files, you can easily have different mapping files for different databases. This is similar to the level of abstraction you gain from using stored procedures.[1]

iBATIS Versions

iBATIS has two distinct versions that have similar high-level functions, but the syntax of the configuration files is very different. Spring supports both versions of iBATIS, but iBATIS authors recommend that you develop new projects using the newer version. This is why we do not discuss iBATIS support for the older version.

Infrastructure and Configuration

Let's take a look at iBATIS configuration and mapping files. One central XML file contains references to mapping files that define the Java beans and all database operations. You can specify the location of this reference configuration file when you create an instance of the iBATIS beans in Spring.

The mapping files usually represent a single domain object and appropriate SQL code for persisting that object's data to the database. It is important that you realize that all mapping files are loaded at startup, and the mappings specified are validated against the actual objects. If a property is not present in the domain object, the bean creation fails.

Unlike stand-alone iBATIS applications, the only things you need to configure in a Spring iBATIS application are the reference file and the mapping files. The Spring iBATIS factory bean (org.springframework.orm.ibatis.SqlMapClientFactoryBean) takes care of loading the configuration files. Just like with JDBC, you should not create and manage database transactions manually in the iBATIS mapping files; always delegate the transaction management to Spring.

Figure 10-1 gives you a basic overview of the structure of the configuration files. We take a more detailed look at the recommended file locations and the exact content of the files in the next section.

---

1. Some databases do not even support stored procedures

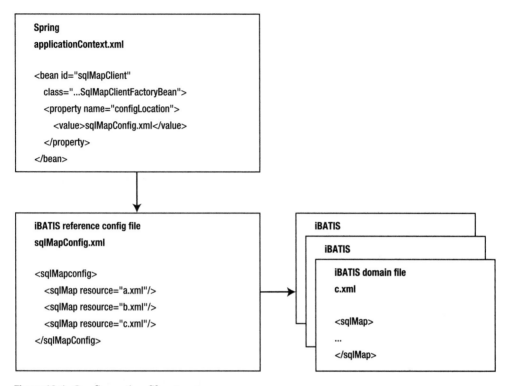

Figure 10-1. *Configuration files structure*

Mapping Files

Let's begin with a description of the reference configuration file. Unlike stand-alone iBATIS applications, you normally only include references to the concrete sqlMap files.

Listing 10-1 shows a sample reference configuration file.

Listing 10-1. *SqlMapConfig.XML Reference Configuration File*

```
<?xml version="1.0" encoding="UTF-8" ?>
<!DOCTYPE sqlMapConfig
    PUBLIC "-//iBATIS.com//DTD SQL Map Config 2.0//EN"
    "http://www.ibatis.com/dtd/sql-map-config-2.dtd">

<sqlMapConfig>
    <sqlMap resource="Test.xml" />
</sqlMapConfig>
```

As you can see in Listing 10-2, the configuration file references a single sqlMap file, Test.xml, which in turn declares the domain object type.

Listing 10-2. *sqlMap File for Test Class*

```
<?xml version="1.0" encoding="UTF-8" standalone="no"?>
<!DOCTYPE sqlMap PUBLIC "-//iBATIS.com//DTD SQL Map 2.0//EN" ➥
"http://www.ibatis.com/dtd/sql-map-2.dtd">

<sqlMap>

</sqlMap>
```

At this point, we have the basic infrastructure of the application ready. The missing piece of the puzzle is the Spring context file that links all the configuration files together (see Listing 10-3).

Listing 10-3. *Spring applicationContext.xml File*

```
<?xml version="1.0" encoding="UTF-8"?>
<!DOCTYPE beans PUBLIC "-//SPRING//DTD BEAN//EN" ➥
"http://www.springframework.org/dtd/spring-beans.dtd">

<beans>

    <!-- SqlMap setup for iBATIS Database Layer -->
    <bean id="sqlMapClient"
        class="org.springframework.orm.ibatis.SqlMapClientFactoryBean">
        <property name="configLocation">
            <value>sqlMapConfig.xml</value>
        </property>
    </bean>

</beans>
```

Listing 10-3 shows you how to instruct Spring to create an instance of the sqlMapClient bean, which loads the sqlMapConfig.xml file. We now have a configured sqlMapClient bean that can be used in the DAO implementations. All we need to do is define the DAO interfaces, create the implementation, and create the dataSource bean; but before we can do that, we must take a more detailed look at the map files.

In Table 10-1, we review the files we have and how we are going to structure them.

Table 10-1. *Locations of the Configuration Files*

File	Source Location	Build/Run Location
sqlMapClient.xml	src/ibatis	build
Test.xml	src/ibatis	build
applicationContext	src/conf	build

The build script, build.xml, takes care of building the application and makes sure that the configuration files are copied from their source location to the appropriate destination to run the application. Before we can move ahead and complete the configuration files and make the application work, we need to take a closer look at the sqlMap files.

The location of the files is specific to the application type you are developing. It is important to realize that the configuration files are **resources** and as such, they are handled by ResourceLoaders; usually the default ResourceLoader. Refer to Chapter 5 for more information on resources.

SqlMap Files

sqlMap defines types, result maps, and database statements. Even though you can use a single file, it is a good idea to create a separate sqlMap file for each domain object. If you follow this simple rule, you will keep the sqlMap files easy to read, and as the number of domain objects grows, the project will remain easy to manage.

In Listing 10-4, we create a simple database with a single table to demonstrate the iBATIS functionality.

Listing 10-4. *SQL Create Script*

```
create table Test (
    TestId serial not null,
    Name varchar(50) not null,
    RunDate timestamp not null,

    constraint PK_TestId primary key (TestId)
);

insert into Test (Name, RunDate) values ('foo', '2004-01-01');
```

Next, we create a domain object to map in the sqlMap file. The domain object (see Listing 10-5) has the same class name as the sqlMap file, Test, and it is going to have the same properties as the Test table columns.

Listing 10-5. *Test Domain Object*

```
package com.apress.prospring.ch12.domain;

import java.util.Date;

public class Test {

    private int testId;
    private String name;
    private Date runDate;

    // Operations
```

```java
    public String toString() {
        StringBuffer result = new StringBuffer(50);
        result.append("Test { testId: ");
        result.append(testId);
        result.append(", name: ");
        result.append(name);
        result.append(", runDate: ");
        result.append(runDate);
        result.append(" }");
        return result.toString();
    }

    // Getters and setters

    public String getName() {
        return name;
    }

    public void setName(String name) {
        this.name = name;
    }

    public Date getRunDate() {
        return runDate;
    }

    public void setRunDate(Date runDate) {
        this.runDate = runDate;
    }

    public int getTestId() {
        return testId;
    }

    public void setTestId(int testId) {
        this.testId = testId;
    }
}
```

The domain object has three properties, testId, name, and runDate. We need to tell iBATIS how to interpret the data that will be selected from the database. To do this, we create a resultMap element that tells iBATIS what object to instantiate and what properties to set (see Listing 10-6).

Listing 10-6. *sqlMap File for the Test Domain Object*

```xml
<?xml version="1.0" encoding="UTF-8" standalone="no"?>
<!DOCTYPE sqlMap PUBLIC "-//iBATIS.com//DTD SQL Map 2.0//EN" ➥
"http://www.ibatis.com/dtd/sql-map-2.dtd">

<sqlMap>

    <typeAlias type="com.apress.prospring.ch12.domain.Test" alias="test"/>

    <resultMap class="test" id="result">
        <result property="testId" column="TestId"/>
        <result property="name" column="Name"/>
        <result property="runDate" column="RunDate"/>
    </resultMap>

</sqlMap>
```

Listing 10-6 actually shows how to create a typeAlias that tells iBATIS that Test actually means com.apress.prospring.ch12.domain.Test; this is a merely a convenience feature to save you typing. Table 10-2 lists all predefined aliases and their corresponding Java types.

Table 10-2. *Predefined iBATIS Type Aliases*

Alias	Java Type	Details
boolean	java.lang.Boolean	Use #value# to access the object's primitive boolean property.
byte	java.lang.Byte	Use #value# to access the object's primitive byte property.
short	java.lang.Short	Use #value# to access the object's primitive short property.
int	java.lang.Integer	Use #value# to access the object's primitive int property.
long	java.lang.Long	Use #value# to access the object's primitive long property.
float	java.lang.Float	Use #value# to access the object's primitive float property.
double	java.lang.Double	Use #value# to access the object's primitive double property.
string	java.lang.String	Use #value# to access the object's value.
date	java.util.Date	Use #value# to access the object's value.
decimal	java.math.BigDecimal	Use #value# to access the object's value.
map	java.util.Map	Use #key# to get or set the item in the Map.

Next, we define a resultMap with an ID of result. When a resultMap with the name result is used, iBATIS instantiates the Test object and sets its properties with the values in the appropriate columns (see Listing 10-7).

Listing 10-7. *sqlMap File for the Select Statement of the Test Domain Object*

```xml
<?xml version="1.0" encoding="UTF-8" standalone="no"?>
<!DOCTYPE sqlMap PUBLIC "-//iBATIS.com//DTD SQL Map 2.0//EN" ➥
"http://www.ibatis.com/dtd/sql-map-2.dtd">

<sqlMap>

    <typeAlias type="com.apress.prospring.ch12.domain.Test" alias="test"/>

    <resultMap class="test" id="result">
        <result property="testId" column="TestId"/>
        <result property="name" column="Name"/>
        <result property="runDate" column="RunDate"/>
    </resultMap>

    <select id="getAllTests" resultMap="result">
        select * from Test
    </select>
</sqlMap>
```

Don't worry if you don't understand what a select node does or what to use it for, we will discuss this further in the "Selecting Data" section later in this chapter.

Configuring iBATIS and Spring

Finally, we can define the TestDao interface and its iBATIS implementation and then add the familiar dataSource bean.

■**NOTE** If you cannot remember how to configure dataSource beans, go back to Chapter 8 where we discussed different DataSources you can use in a Spring application.

In Listing 10-8, we begin with TestDao, a DAO interface, and the SqlMapClientTestDao implementation.

Listing 10-8. *TestDao Interface*

```
package com.apress.prospring.ch12.data;

import java.util.List;

import com.apress.prospring.ch12.domain.Test;

public interface TestDao {
    public List getAll();
    public List getByNameAndRunDate(String name, Date runDate);
    public void save(Test test);
    public void delete(int testId);
    public Test getById(int testId);
    public List getByNameAndRunDate(String name, Date runDate);
    public void updateName(int testId, String name);
}
```

We now proceed to implement this interface (see Listing 10-9). We use a convenience Spring superclass, SqlMapClientDaoSupport. Just like JdbcDaoSupport, this class already has a property for a dataSource and provides getSqlMapClientTemplate(), which allow us to call iBATIS methods.

Listing 10-9. *TestDao iBATIS Implementation*

```
package com.apress.prospring.ch12.data;

import java.util.List;

import org.springframework.orm.ibatis.support.SqlMapClientDaoSupport;

import com.apress.prospring.ch12.domain.Test;

public class SqlMapClientTestDao
    extends SqlMapClientDaoSupport
    implements TestDao {

    // TestDao methods are implemented as stubs
}
```

In Listing 10-10, we finish the applicationContext.xml file to link the beans together.

Listing 10-10. *Spring applicationContext.xml File*

```xml
<?xml version="1.0" encoding="UTF-8"?>
<!DOCTYPE beans PUBLIC "-//SPRING//DTD BEAN//EN" ➥
"http://www.springframework.org/dtd/spring-beans.dtd">

<beans>
    <!-- Data source bean -->
    <bean id="dataSource" class="org.apache.commons.dbcp.BasicDataSource"
        destroy-method="close">
        <property name="driverClassName">
            <value>org.postgresql.Driver</value>
        </property>
        <property name="url">
            <value>jdbc:postgresql://localhost/prospring</value></property>
        <property name="username"><value>janm</value></property>
        <property name="password"><value>****</value></property>
    </bean>

    <!-- SqlMap setup for iBATIS Database Layer -->
    <bean id="sqlMapClient"
        class="org.springframework.orm.ibatis.SqlMapClientFactoryBean">
        <property name="configLocation">
            <value>sqlMapConfig.xml</value>
        </property>
    </bean>

    <bean id="testDao"
        class="com.apress.prospring.ch12.data.SqlMapClientTestDao">
        <property name="dataSource"><ref local="dataSource"/></property>
        <property name="sqlMapClient"><ref local="sqlMapClient"/></property>
    </bean>

</beans>
```

We're almost there, now. We have a full Spring application context file with the dataSource, sqlMapClient, and testDao beans. We can now create a Main class (see Listing 10-11) that creates the application context from the context file on the classpath and selects and prints the data.

Listing 10-11. *The Sample Application's Main Class*

```java
package com.apress.prospring.ch12;

import java.util.Iterator;
import java.util.List;
```

```
import org.springframework.context.ApplicationContext;
import org.springframework.context.support.ClassPathXmlApplicationContext;

import com.apress.prospring.ch12.data.TestDao;
import com.apress.prospring.ch12.domain.Test;


public class Main {

    private ApplicationContext context;

    private void run() {
        System.out.println("Initializing application");
        context = new ClassPathXmlApplicationContext("applicationContext.xml");

        System.out.println("Getting testDao");
        TestDao testDao = (TestDao)context.getBean("testDao");

        System.out.println("Done");
    }

    public static void main(String[] args) {
        new Main().run();
    }

}
```

The framework for the application is now ready. Once executed, the Spring application context is loaded and all beans are successfully configured. However, we cannot see any data just yet, so let's move on to the next section.

Selecting Data

In this section, we discuss how to select rows from the database together with how to pass parameters from DAO implementations to the select statements. We start by discussing select operations from a single table that uses a single domain object, then we move on to discuss selecting data from 1:1, 1:N, and finally M:N database relationships.

Simple Selects

We start with a select all statement that does not need any parameters and selects the data from only one table into one domain object (see Listing 10-12); the only addition to the Test.xml sqlMap file is the select node.

Listing 10-12. *sqlMap File for the Test Domain Object*

```xml
<?xml version="1.0" encoding="UTF-8" standalone="no"?>
<!DOCTYPE sqlMap PUBLIC "-//iBATIS.com//DTD SQL Map 2.0//EN" ➥
"http://www.ibatis.com/dtd/sql-map-2.dtd">

<sqlMap>

    <typeAlias type="com.apress.prospring.ch12.domain.Test" alias="test"/>

    <resultMap class="test" id="result">
        <result property="testId" column="TestId"/>
        <result property="name" column="Name"/>
        <result property="runDate" column="RunDate"/>
    </resultMap>

    <select id="getAllTests" resultMap="result">
        select * from Test
    </select>
</sqlMap>
```

This simple `<select>` node actually tells iBATIS that there is a SQL statement named getAllTests and that this statement is a select statement. The SQL code for the statement is select * from Test and the resultMap is result, which in turn represents test, aka the Test domain object. In Listing 10-13, we implement the TestDao's getAll() method to actually see all this in action.

Listing 10-13. *TestDao getAll() iBATIS Implementation*

```java
package com.apress.prospring.ch12.data;

import java.util.List;

import org.springframework.orm.ibatis.support.SqlMapClientDaoSupport;

import com.apress.prospring.ch12.domain.Test;

public class SqlMapClientTestDao
    extends SqlMapClientDaoSupport
    implements TestDao {

    public List getAll() {
        return getSqlMapClientTemplate().queryForList("getAllTests", null);
    }

    // other TestDao methods are implemented as stubs
}
```

This is really **all** the code you need to write! The getAll() method delegates the database call, domain object instantiation to iBATIS. All we need to provide is the name of the statement, which must be defined in one of the sqlMap files referenced from the SqlMapConfig file. iBATIS locates the statement, checks that it is a select statement, performs the database operation, processes the resultSet, and then for each row, instantiates the domain object, sets its properties, and adds it to the resulting List.

In Listing 10-14, we make a final change to the Main class to utilize the new implementation.

Listing 10-14. *Modified Main Class*

```
package com.apress.prospring.ch12;

public class Main {

    private ApplicationContext context;

    private void run() {
        System.out.println("Initializing application");
        context = new ClassPathXmlApplicationContext("applicationContext.xml");

        System.out.println("Getting testDao");
        TestDao testDao = (TestDao)context.getBean("testDao");
        List tests = testDao.getAll();
        for (Iterator i = tests.iterator(); i.hasNext();) {
            Test test = (Test)i.next();
            System.out.println(test);
        }
        System.out.println("Done");
    }
    // the rest of the code ommited for brevity
}
```

When we run the application, it creates the Spring ApplicationContext, which is used to get a TestDao bean and finally, we call its getAll() method to get a List of Test domain objects. The output is exactly what we expect, as shown in Listing 10-15.

Listing 10-15. *Running the Sample Application*

```
Buildfile: d:\projects\pro-spring\ch12\build.xml
init:
compile:
    [javac] Compiling 1 source file to D:\projects\pro-spring\ch12\build
run:
    [java] Initializing application
    [java] Debug messages ommited
    [java] Getting testDao
    [java] Test { testId: 1, name: foo, runDate: Thu Jan 01 00:00:00 GMT 2004 }
```

```
    [java] Done
BUILD SUCCESSFUL
Total time: 3 seconds
```

Eureka! The application runs, connects to the database, selects the data, and returns a List of our domain objects. In most cases, however, you do need to filter out the rows that are selected. In other words, you need to pass parameters to the select statements. In Listing 10-16, we begin with a select by primary key operation, implemented in the getById(int) method.

Listing 10-16. *sqlMap File for the Test Domain Object*

```xml
<?xml version="1.0" encoding="UTF-8" standalone="no"?>
<!DOCTYPE sqlMap PUBLIC "-//iBATIS.com//DTD SQL Map 2.0//EN" ➥
"http://www.ibatis.com/dtd/sql-map-2.dtd">

<sqlMap>
    <!-- as previous -->
    <select id="getTestById" resultMap="result" parameterClass="int">
        select * from Test where TestId=#value#
    </select>
</sqlMap>
```

Here, we added the getTestById select statement with a parameter class of int, which is a type alias for java.lang.Integer. The implementation of the getById(int) method (shown in Listing 10-17) is quite simple as well. All we need to do is pass the primary key value to iBATIS.

Listing 10-17. *TestDao getById(int) iBATIS Implementation*

```java
package com.apress.prospring.ch12.data;

import java.util.List;

import org.springframework.orm.ibatis.support.SqlMapClientDaoSupport;

import com.apress.prospring.ch12.domain.Test;

public class SqlMapClientTestDao
    extends SqlMapClientDaoSupport
    implements TestDao {

    public Test getById(int testId) {
        return (Test)getSqlMapClientTemplate().queryForObject(
            "getTestById", new Integer(testId));
    }

    // other TestDao methods are implemented as stubs
}
```

The implementation calls the queryForObject() method that returns a single java.lang.Object or a null that results from executing the select statement. If more than one row is selected, a DataAccessException is thrown. Even though the result of queryForObject() is java.lang.Object, we can safely cast it to Test because the resultMap used states that the object type is Test. We are also passing an Integer object with its value set to the primary key value as a parameter instance to the iBATIS call. Again, the code is very straightforward and easy to follow.

There are some cases where you will want to pass more than one value to the database operation. You are free to use any type, but in most cases, you will find yourself using either the domain object or a java.util.Map. There is no difference between using a Map or a concrete domain object in sqlMap files; however, in the Java code, you gain type safety if you use the domain objects. The rule of thumb is that if you find yourself updating only a few fields in a table with a large number of columns, you are better off using a Map. If, on the other hand, you are updating all or most of the columns in a table, it is better to use the domain object. In Listing 10-18, we show you both implementations.

Listing 10-18. *sqlMap File for the Test Domain Object*

```xml
<?xml version="1.0" encoding="UTF-8" standalone="no"?>
<!DOCTYPE sqlMap PUBLIC "-//iBATIS.com//DTD SQL Map 2.0//EN" ➥
"http://www.ibatis.com/dtd/sql-map-2.dtd">

<sqlMap>
    <!-- as previous -->
    <select id="getTestsByNameAndRunDateMap"
        resultMap="result" parameterClass="map">
        select * from Test where Name like #name# and RunDate=#runDate#
    </select>

    <select id="getTestsByNameAndRunDateDO"
        resultMap="result" parameterClass="test">
        select * from Test where Name like #name# and RunDate=#runDate#
    </select>

</sqlMap>
```

Here, we added two select statements: one uses the parameterClass of the map, and the other one uses the Test domain object. Apart from this, the body of the select statements is exactly the same. In Listing 10-19, you can see that the Java implementation of TestDao is also very similar.

Listing 10-19. *TestDao getByNameAndRunDate*() iBATIS Implementation*

```
package com.apress.prospring.ch12.data;

import java.util.List;

import org.springframework.orm.ibatis.support.SqlMapClientDaoSupport;

import com.apress.prospring.ch12.domain.Test;

public class SqlMapClientTestDao
    extends SqlMapClientDaoSupport
    implements TestDao {

    public List getByNameAndRunDateMap(String name, Date runDate) {
        Map params = new HashMap();
        params.put("name", name);
        params.put("runDate", runDate);
        return getSqlMapClientTemplate().queryForList(
            "getTestsByNameAndRunDateMap", params);
    }

    public List getByNameAndRunDateDO(String name, Date runDate) {
        Test test = new Test();
        test.setName(name);
        test.setRunDate(runDate);
        return getSqlMapClientTemplate().queryForList(
            "getTestsByNameAndRunDateMap", test);
    }

    // other TestDao methods are implemented as stubs
}
```

The two methods demonstrate different ways in which we can pass data to the select statements. In the getByNameAndRunDateMap method, we create a Map instance and put the values required in the select statement, while the code in the getByNameAndRunDateDO method instantiates the Test domain object, sets the property values, and passes the instance of the domain object to the iBATIS call. You'll experience a slight performance hit when you use Map to update the same number of fields. We have tested 25,000 select calls using a Map and the domain object as parameters to the iBATIS calls. The Map implementation took 13,594 ms, whereas the domain object implementation took 12,328 ms.

One-to-One Selects

To demonstrate how to select data in 1:1 mapping, we add another table and another domain object. To demonstrate this, let's create a few tables and domain objects. In Listing 10-20, we create the Customers and CustomerDetails tables.

Listing 10-20. *One-to-One Relationship SQL Script*

```
create table CustomerDetails (
    CustomerDetailId serial not null,
    Data varchar(255) not null,

    constraint PK_CustomerDetailId primary key (CustomerDetailId)
);

create table Customers (
    CustomerId serial not null,
    FirstName varchar(50) not null,
    LastName varchar(50) not null,
    CustomerDetail int not null,
    CustomerGossip int null,

    constraint PK_CustomerId primary key (CustomerId),
    constraint FK_CustomerDetail foreign key (CustomerDetail)
        references CustomerDetails(CustomerDetailId) on delete cascade,
    constraint FK_CustomerGossip foreign key (CustomerGossip)
        references CustomerDetails(CustomerDetailId) on delete cascade
);

create index IX_Customers_CustomerDetail on Customers
    using btree (CustomerDetail);
create index IX_Customers_CustomerGossip on Customers
    using btree (CustomerGossip);

insert into CustomerDetails (Data) values ('Doeth!');
insert into CustomerDetails (Data) values ('The Force is strong with him');
insert into CustomerDetails (Data) values ('Will tell for a bottle of Tequilla');
insert into Customers (FirstName, LastName, CustomerDetail, CustomerGossip)
    values ('Jan', 'Machacek', 1, null);
insert into Customers (FirstName, LastName, CustomerDetail, CustomerGossip)
    values ('Rob', 'Harrop', 2, 3);
```

As you can see from the SQL script, a record in the Customers table must have one record in the CustomerDetails table referenced by CustomerDetail and may have one record in the CustomerDetails table referenced by CustomerGossip.

On the Java front, we create the two domain objects: CustomerDetail and Customer (as shown in Listing 10-21).

Listing 10-21. *Customer and CustomerDetail Domain Objects*

```java
// Customer.java:
package com.apress.prospring.ch12.domain;
public class Customer {

    private int customerId;
    private String firstName;
    private String lastName;
    private CustomerDetail customerDetail;
    private CustomerDetail customerGossip;
    // getters and setters as usual
}


// CustomerDetail.java:
package com.apress.prospring.ch12.domain;
public class CustomerDetail {

    private int customerDetailId;
    private String data;
}
```

The domain objects also override the toString() method to return a nice text representation of the instance data.

Next, in Listing 10-22, we create an sqlMap for the domain objects.

Listing 10-22. *Customer.xml sqlMap File*

```xml
<?xml version="1.0" encoding="UTF-8" standalone="no"?>
<!DOCTYPE sqlMap PUBLIC "-//iBATIS.com//DTD SQL Map 2.0//EN" ➥
"http://www.ibatis.com/dtd/sql-map-2.dtd">

<sqlMap>

    <typeAlias type="com.apress.prospring.ch12.domain.Customer" alias="customer"/>
    <typeAlias type="com.apress.prospring.ch12.domain.CustomerDetail"
        alias="customerDetail"/>

    <resultMap class="customer" id="result">
        <result property="customerId" column="CustomerId"/>
        <result property="firstName" column="FirstName"/>
        <result property="lastName" column="LastName"/>
    </resultMap>

    <resultMap class="customerDetail" id="gossipResult">
        <result property="customerDetailId" column="CustomerDetailId"/>
        <result property="data" column="Data"/>
    </resultMap>
```

```
<resultMap class="customer" id="resultDetail" extends="result">
    <result property="customerDetail.customerDetailId"
        column="CustomerDetailId"/>
    <result property="customerDetail.data" column="CustomerDetailData"/>
    <result property="customerGossip" select="getCustomerGossipById"
        column="CustomerGossip"/>
</resultMap>

<select id="getCustomerById" resultMap="resultDetail" parameterClass="int">
    select
        c.CustomerId as CustomerId,
        c.FirstName as FirstName,
        c.LastName as LastName,
        c.CustomerDetail as CustomerDetail,
        c.CustomerGossip as CustomerGossip,
        cd.CustomerDetailId as CustomerDetailId,
        cd.Data as CustomerDetailData
    from
        Customers c inner join CustomerDetails cd on
        c.CustomerDetail = cd.CustomerDetailId
    where
        c.CustomerId=#value#
</select>

<select id="getCustomerGossipById" resultMap="gossipResult"
    parameterClass="int">
    select * from CustomerDetails where CustomerDetailId=#value#
</select>

</sqlMap>
```

This sqlMap file has a lot of new features, so let's take a closer look at them. First of all, we are using resultMap inheritance. This is useful for situations where you want to create a resultMap that adds more fields to the super resultMap. Let's say you're implementing a search method that returns a list of customers based on their lastName. You are not interested in customerDetail or customerGossip properties, so you can leave them set to their default value, null. However, if you are getting a customer by customerId, you want to get all available information about the customer. This is why we created a simple result resultMap and then created the resultDetail resultMap that extends the result and adds definitions for customerDetail and customerGossip.

In Listing 10-23, you can take a closer look at the resultDetail, which also reveals that we are telling iBATIS that there will always be data for a customerDetail object, while there may not be data for customerGossip.

Listing 10-23. *Detail of the resultDetail resultMap*

```
<sqlMap>
    <resultMap class="customer" id="resultDetail" extends="result">
        <result property="customerDetail.customerDetailId"
            column="CustomerDetailId"/>
        <result property="customerDetail.data" column="CustomerDetailData"/>
        <result property="customerGossip" select="getCustomerGossipById"
            column="CustomerGossip"/>
    </resultMap>
</sqlMap>
```

The code in bold in Listing 10-23 states that the CustomerDetailId and CustomerDetailData columns will always be present in the resultSet, and that they should be set on the customerDetail object's customerDetailId and data properties. The customerGossip object, on the other hand, should be set to the result of the getCustomerGossipById select statement. This statement takes a single int parameter. The value of this parameter should be taken from the CustomerGossip column of the Customers table. In other words, the customerDetail property is never null, whereas customerGossip can be null. On the other hand, the CustomerDao interface and its implementation are very simple, as you can see in Listing 10-24.

Listing 10-24. *The CustomerDao Interface and Its Implementation*

```
// CustomerDao.java
package com.apress.prospring.ch12.data;

import com.apress.prospring.ch12.domain.Customer;

public interface CustomerDao {
    public Customer getById(int customerId);
}

// SqlMapClientCustomerDao.java
package com.apress.prospring.ch12.data;

import org.springframework.orm.ibatis.support.SqlMapClientDaoSupport;
import com.apress.prospring.ch12.domain.Customer;

public class SqlMapClientCustomerDao
    extends SqlMapClientDaoSupport implements CustomerDao {
    public Customer getById(int customerId) {
        return (Customer)getSqlMapClientTemplate().
            queryForObject("getCustomerById", new Integer(customerId));
    }
}
```

We must not forget to include the new Customer.xml sqlMap in the SqlMapConfig.xml file and to add the customerDao bean to the applicationContext.xml file. Once all the changes to the configuration files are complete, we can add the code in Listing 10-25 to the Main class.

Listing 10-25. *New Code to Test 1:1 Relationship*

```
CustomerDao customerDao = (CustomerDao)context.getBean("customerDao");

Customer janm = customerDao.getById(1);
Customer robh = customerDao.getById(2);

System.out.println(janm);
System.out.println(robh);
```

Running the Main class using the test data from the SQL script produces the following output:

```
Buildfile: d:\projects\pro-spring\ch12\build.xml
init:
compile:
run:
    [java] Initializing application
    [java] Customer { customerId: 1, firstName: Jan, lastName: Machacek, ➥
customerDetail: CustomerDetail { customerDetailId: 1, data: Doeth! }, ➥
customerGossip: null }
    [java] Customer { customerId: 2, firstName: Rob, lastName: Harrop, ➥
customerDetail: CustomerDetail { customerDetailId: 2, data: ➥
The Force is strong with him }, ➥
customerGossip: CustomerDetail { customerDetailId: 3, data: ➥
Will tell for a bottle of Tequilla } }
    [java] Done
BUILD SUCCESSFUL
Total time: 2 seconds
```

Performance

There is one performance issue you need to consider: using a select statement to set a property on a domain object results in *N+1* select operations being performed. Consider a situation where you load a single User object: an extra query is run to select the UserDetail row to set the userGossip property. This may become a major issue. Imagine a situation where we issue a select statement that returns 100 User domain objects. iBATIS now needs to run 100 separate selects to set the userGossip property, making the total number of queries 101.

We have seen a way around this, though—we can return the userDetail object as a part of the result set and then no more queries need to be executed. Unfortunately, we cannot use inner joins if the 1:1 relationship is optional.

The best way to solve this situation is to set the properties only if you really need them. Use a simplified resultMap that sets only the basic properties for selects that return a large number of rows, and use this basic resultMap as a super map for a detailed map that sets all properties.

One-to-one relationships are not very common; the most common relationship ever is one-to-many, which we are going to discuss next.

One-to-Many Selects

Let's move away from the nasty customerGossip objects we have used in the previous section and implement standard order tables. Each order can have zero or more lines. As you can see in Listing 10-26, adding to SQL script is simple enough.

Listing 10-26. *Adding to the Create SQL Script*

```
create table Orders (
    OrderId serial not null,
    Customer int not null,

    constraint PK_OrderId primary key (OrderId),
    constraint FK_Customer foreign key (Customer) references Customers(CustomerId)
);

create index IX_Orders_Customer on Orders using btree (Customer);

create table OrderLines (
    OrderLineId serial not null,
    "Order" int not null,
    Product varchar(200) not null,
    Price decimal(10, 2) not null,

    constraint PK_OrderLineId primary key (OrderLineId),
    constraint FK_Order foreign key ("Order") references Orders(OrderId)
);

create index IX_OrderLines_Order on OrderLines using btree ("Order");

insert into Orders (Customer) values (1);
insert into OrderLines ("Order", Product, Price)
    values (1, 'Punch people over the internet client application', 19.95);
insert into OrderLines ("Order", Product, Price)
    values (1, 'The Mangelfreuzer Switch', 12.95);
```

The Java domain objects are also going to be pretty standard. The Order object is going to contain all the properties for columns in the Orders table plus a List for holding instances of the OrderLine domain object, which, in turn, is going to have properties for all columns in the OrderLines table.

In Listing 10-27, we begin the implementation of the iBATIS mapping files by creating the sqlMap file, Order.xml.

Listing 10-27. *The Order.xml sqlMap File*

```xml
<?xml version="1.0" encoding="UTF-8" standalone="no"?>
<!DOCTYPE sqlMap PUBLIC "-//iBATIS.com//DTD SQL Map 2.0//EN" ➥
"http://www.ibatis.com/dtd/sql-map-2.dtd">

<sqlMap>

    <typeAlias type="com.apress.prospring.ch12.domain.Order" alias="order"/>
    <typeAlias type="com.apress.prospring.ch12.domain.OrderLine"
        alias="orderLine"/>

    <resultMap class="order" id="result">
        <result property="orderId" column="OrderId"/>
        <result property="customer" column="Customer"/>
        <result property="orderLines" select="getOrderLinesByOrder"
            column="OrderId"/>
    </resultMap>

    <resultMap class="orderLine" id="resultLine">
        <result property="orderLineId" column="OrderLineId"/>
        <result property="order" column="Order"/>
        <result property="product" column="Product"/>
        <result property="price" column="Price"/>
    </resultMap>

    <select id="getOrderById" resultMap="result" parameterClass="int">
        select * from Orders where OrderId=#value#
    </select>

    <select id="getOrderLinesByOrder" resultMap="resultLine" parameterClass="int">
        select * from OrderLines where "Order"=#value#
    </select>

</sqlMap>
```

The elements in the sqlMap file from Listing 10-28 should be no surprise. We have two types, `order` and `orderLine`. We have also declared that to set the `orderLines` property, iBATIS must execute the `getOrderLinesByOrder` select statement and add the results of that query to the `orderLines` `List` property of the `Order` object. The domain objects follow the properties we declared in the sqlMap file (as shown in Listing 10-28).

Listing 10-28. *Order and OrderLine Domain Objects*

```java
// Order.java
package com.apress.prospring.ch12.domain;

import java.util.List;

public class Order {

    private int orderId;
    private int customer;
    private List orderLines;

    // Getters and Setters
}

// OrderLine.java
package com.apress.prospring.ch12.domain;

import java.math.BigDecimal;

public class OrderLine {

    private int orderLineId;
    private int order;
    private String product;
    private BigDecimal price;

    // Getters and Setters
}
```

The OrderDao interface and its implementation are also very simple (see Listing 10-29); it merely passes the required parameters to the iBATIS calls.

Listing 10-29. *OrderDao Interface and Its Implementation*

```java
// OrderDao.java
package com.apress.prospring.ch12.data;

import com.apress.prospring.ch12.domain.Order;


public interface OrderDao {
    public Order getById(int orderId);
}
```

```
// SqlMapClientOrderDao.java
package com.apress.prospring.ch12.data;

import org.springframework.orm.ibatis.support.SqlMapClientDaoSupport;

import com.apress.prospring.ch12.domain.Order;

public class SqlMapClientOrderDao
    extends SqlMapClientDaoSupport implements OrderDao {

    public Order getById(int orderId) {
        return (Order)getSqlMapClientTemplate().queryForObject(
            "getOrderById", new Integer(orderId));
    }

}
```

If we add a reference to the new sqlMap file to SqlMapConfig.xml and add a bean definition for orderDao to the applicationContext.xml file, we can use the code in the Main class (see Listing 10-30) to test the application.

Listing 10-30. *Testing Code for the OderDao Implementation*

```
OrderDao orderDao = (OrderDao)context.getBean("orderDao");
Order order = orderDao.getById(1);
System.out.println(order);
```

The result of running this code is the following nice output that shows that Order with OrderId: 1 has two order lines:

```
Buildfile: d:\projects\pro-spring\ch12\build.xml
init:
compile:
    [javac] Compiling 5 source files to D:\projects\pro-spring\ch12\build
run:
    [java] Order { orderId: 1, customer: 1, orderLines:
        [OrderLine
            { orderLineId: 2, order: 1, product: The Mangelfreuzer Switch,
price12.95 },
        OrderLine
            { orderLineId: 1, order: 1, product: Punch people over the internet ➥
client application, price19.95 }] }
    [java] Done
BUILD SUCCESSFUL
Total time: 4 seconds
```

Performance

In one-to-many relationships, you have no way to avoid N+1 selects. However, you can still use the basic resultMap to set the basic properties, and then you can extend this simple resultMap in a detailed resultMap that sets all properties. This makes a lot of sense: if you are displaying a list of orders, you do not really need to know the orderLines. You only need this extra information when you want to display a detailed summary of the order. This usually means selecting an order domain object by its primary key, which results in another query being executed to return all order lines.

Excellent! We already have two relationships: one-to-one and one-to-many. The last one remaining is many-to-many.

Many-to-Many Selects

Finally, a many-to-many select is a simple question of creating two one-to-many selects. For example, consider the User and Role objects. A User can appear in more than one Role and one Role can be assigned to more than one User. We need a linking table UserRole, that creates a 1:N relationship between User and UserRole and a 1:M relationship between UserRole and Role; making the whole relationship M:N.

Updating Data

Now that you have learned how to select data from the database, you must be keen to learn how to update existing data. The updates are very similar to selects, we use parameter maps and domain objects extensively. Let's start with the simplest example: updating all columns in the Test table. In Listing 10-31, we modify the sqlMap file for the Test domain objects and add an update statement.

Listing 10-31. *sqlMap File for the Test Domain Object*

```
<?xml version="1.0" encoding="UTF-8" standalone="no"?>
<!DOCTYPE sqlMap PUBLIC "-//iBATIS.com//DTD SQL Map 2.0//EN" ➥
"http://www.ibatis.com/dtd/sql-map-2.dtd">

<sqlMap>
    <!-- as previous -->

    <update id="updateTest" parameterClass="test">
        update Tests set Name=#name#, RunDate=#runDate# where TestId=#testId#
    </update>

</sqlMap>
```

As expected, the update SQL statement is in the body of an update element in the sqlMap file, and it does exactly what is expected of it—it updates the Name and RunDate columns in a row identified by TestId and passed in through the int parameterClass. The int parameterClass is an alias for java.lang.Integer, and we can access its int property in #value#.

The implementation in the Java code is slightly more complex; because our TestDao interface contains only one method to update or insert the domain object, we need to decide whether the object is to be updated or inserted (see Listing 10-32).

Listing 10-32. *TestDao save() iBATIS Implementation*

```java
package com.apress.prospring.ch12.data;

import java.util.List;

import org.springframework.orm.ibatis.support.SqlMapClientDaoSupport;

import com.apress.prospring.ch12.domain.Test;

public class SqlMapClientTestDao
    extends SqlMapClientDaoSupport
    implements TestDao {
    private void insert(Test test) {

    }

    private void update(Test test) {
        getSqlMapClientTemplate().update("updateTest", test);
    }

    public void save(Test test) {
        if (test.getTestId() == 0) {
            insert(test);
        } else {
            update(test);
        }
    }

    // other TestDao methods are implemented as stubs
}
```

Having only a single method for insert and update saved coding, and because our DAO implementation knows how the domain object is stored, it can decide whether to perform an insert or update. Now we are going to ignore the insert(Test) method for the moment and focus on the update(Test) method.

Similar rules to type usage apply to the update statements: you are free to use any Java type or iBATIS alias. To demonstrate this, we create a method that updates the name of a Test record identified by its primary key. Again, we have two options: we can either use a Map instance or the domain object. Tests show that using a Map is slightly slower.[2] When using a Map, we are creating another instance of java.lang.Integer, whereas when we are using the Test domain

---

2. It is important to keep in mind that Map is slower in **this case.** If you find yourself updating only 2 fields out of 20, it is definitely more efficient to use a Map.

object, we can use the setTestId(int) method and pass the primitive rather than instance of java.lang.Integer. Listing 10-33 shows two update elements: the first one takes the Test domain object and the second one a Map.

Listing 10-33. *sqlMap File for the Test Domain Object*

```xml
<?xml version="1.0" encoding="UTF-8" standalone="no"?>
<!DOCTYPE sqlMap PUBLIC "-//iBATIS.com//DTD SQL Map 2.0//EN" ➥
"http://www.ibatis.com/dtd/sql-map-2.dtd">

<sqlMap>
    <!-- as previous -->

    <update id="updateTestNameDO" parameterClass="test">
        update Test set Name=#name# where TestId=#testId#
    </update>

    <update id="updateTestNameMap" parameterClass="map">
        update Test set Name=#name# where TestId=#testId#
    </update>
</sqlMap>
```

The implementation of the DAO interface is going to be very straightforward (see Listing 10-34). We are not going to discuss the Map implementation; we leave this to you in case you wish to do your own performance testing.

Listing 10-34. *TestDao updateName() iBATIS Implementation*

```java
package com.apress.prospring.ch12.data;

import java.util.List;

import org.springframework.orm.ibatis.support.SqlMapClientDaoSupport;

import com.apress.prospring.ch12.domain.Test;

public class SqlMapClientTestDao
    extends SqlMapClientDaoSupport
    implements TestDao {

    public void updateName(int testId, String name) {
        Test test = new Test();
        test.setTestId(testId);
        test.setName(name);
        getSqlMapClientTemplate().update("updateTestNameDO", test);
    }

    // other TestDao methods are implemented as stubs
}
```

The performance tests on my workstation reveal that the Map implementation took 19,063 ms to perform 5,000 updates, whereas the domain object implementation took 15,937 ms in a table of less than 1,000 rows. Do not be too concerned about using Maps; if your application is performing more complicated updates, the overhead of object creation and lookup is absolutely minimal compared to the actual database work.

There is one final point to make about data updates. Each DAO interface-implementation pair should be responsible for updating its own domain objects. Consider this situation: you have two domain objects: Order and OrderLine. Order has a List that contains instances of OrderLine objects. You may be tempted to code the SQL statement for the save() operation in the OrderDao implementation so that it saves all its OrderLines, but this is not a very good idea. If you do this, the OrderDao and OrderLineDao no longer have clear responsibilities. You have to document that once OrderDao.save(Order) is called, you do not need to call OrderLineDao.save(OrderLine) for each OrderLine in Order. Also, you probably included the entire operation in a transaction, which is not the best idea because you should try not to control the transactions manually in the code. Delegate transaction management to Spring; if you can't wait to read about transaction management, go to Chapter 12.

Deleting Data

Now that we have covered data selects and updates, we can take a look at deletes. A delete is very similar to an update; just like an update, it takes a number of parameters and does not return any results. Let's start by implementing a delete(int) method in TestDao that deletes a row in the Test table identified by the primary key. In Listing 10-35, we modify the sqlMap Test.xml file and TestDao implementation.

Listing 10-35. *sqlMap File for the Test Domain Object*

```
<?xml version="1.0" encoding="UTF-8" standalone="no"?>
<!DOCTYPE sqlMap PUBLIC "-//iBATIS.com//DTD SQL Map 2.0//EN" ➡
"http://www.ibatis.com/dtd/sql-map-2.dtd">

<sqlMap>
    <!-- as previous -->

    <delete id="deleteTest" parameterClass="int">
        delete from Test where TestId=#value#
    </delete>
</sqlMap>
```

The <delete> node declares a delete operation named deleteTest, which takes one parameter of type int that represents the primary key.

The addition to the DAO implementation class simply calls the delete method, passing it the name of the delete statement and the primary key value wrapped in a java.lang.Integer (as shown in Listing 10-36).

Listing 10-36. *TestDao delete(int) iBATIS Implementation*

```
import com.apress.prospring.ch12.domain.Test;

public class SqlMapClientTestDao
    extends SqlMapClientDaoSupport
    implements TestDao {

    public void delete(int testId) {
        getSqlMapClientTemplate().delete("deleteTest", new Integer(testId));
    }

    // other TestDao methods are implemented as stubs
}
```

The Java code is very simple and does exactly what we expect it to do: it removes a row from the table identified by its primary key.

The same considerations about concern slush[3] apply to the delete operations: a DAO implementation class should only delete rows that belong to its domain object. It is absolutely valid to use on delete cascade in your foreign key definitions, which effectively means that a delete of a master record propagates to the child rows, but do not delete the referenced records yourself.

Inserting Data

It is time to tackle the last data operation—insert. An insert is very similar to an update operation, with one exception: you need to generate the primary key value before you perform the insert, or you need to get the generated primary key value after the insert.[4]

For the insert example, we are going to use PostgreSQL, which allows us to demonstrate how to select a primary key value before, as well as after, an insert operation. If you are using automatically generated values and your database system offers no way to know what the next primary key value is going to be, it certainly offers a way to retrieve a value that was generated by the **last** insert operation. The catch is in the word "last." In a high-contention system, another insert operation may complete and change the last generated value before you can select it. The result is that even though the rows have been inserted with unique primary keys, your application has two different domain objects with the same value for their primary key. This problem is discussed more extensively in Chapter 8.

Let's take a look at the ideal scenario: we select the next value from a sequence and attempt an insert operation. It is impossible for two processes to get the same value from a sequence as each select nextval('<sequence>') increases the sequence counter. Our insert operation consists of two separate steps: selecting the next value from the sequence and performing the actual insert operation. We also want to modify the property of the domain object that stores

---

3. Technically, this is **just** a same-layer concern slush. The real and nasty concern slush happens when a web layer contains parts of business logic, for example.
4. Most databases let you create a table without a primary key, but you should **always** have a primary key in a table.

the primary key value. It sounds complicated, but with iBATIS, it is not at all difficult. Listing 10-37 shows how to select a value from the sequence and then perform the insert operation.

Listing 10-37. *SqlMap File Showing How to Select the Primary Key Values*

```xml
<?xml version="1.0" encoding="UTF-8" standalone="no"?>
<!DOCTYPE sqlMap PUBLIC "-//iBATIS.com//DTD SQL Map 2.0//EN" "http://www.ibatis.com/
dtd/sql-map-2.dtd">

<sqlMap>
    <!-- as previous -->

    <insert id="insertTest" parameterClass="test">
        <selectKey keyProperty="testId" resultClass="int">
            select nextval('Test_TestId_Seq')
        </selectKey>
        insert into Test (TestId, Name, RunDate) values (#testId#, #name#,
#runDate#)
    </insert>
</sqlMap>
```

If you look at the `<insert>` element, you can see that the first step is to select a key from the sequence and then simply use the selected key in the insert operation. The `<selectKey>` element also sets the domain object's `testId` property to the value of the selected value from the sequence. The Java implementation of the `insert(Test)` method is incredibly simple, as you can see in Listing 10-38.

Listing 10-38. *TestDao insert(This) iBATIS Implementation*

```java
import com.apress.prospring.ch12.domain.Test;

public class SqlMapClientTestDao
    extends SqlMapClientDaoSupport
    implements TestDao {

    private void insert(Test test) {
        getSqlMapClientTemplate().insert("insertTest", test);
    }

    // other TestDao methods are implemented as stubs
}
```

That is all the code you have to write, honest. In Listing 10-39, we modify the source code for the Main class to test that our new object does indeed get inserted.

Listing 10-39. *Main Class Calling the save(Test) Method*

```
package com.apress.prospring.ch12;

public class Main {

    private ApplicationContext context;

    private void run() {
        // get the context and testDao
        Date today = Calendar.getInstance().getTime();

        System.out.println("Inserting new Test record");
        Test test = new Test();
        test.setName("new one");
        test.setRunDate(today);
        testDao.save(test);

        System.out.println("Test inserted " + test);

    }

    public static void main(String[] args) {
        new Main().run();
    }

}
```

Running the build script, shown in the following output, proves that we are selecting the next value from the sequence, setting the testId property to the sequence value, and inserting a row with the selected testId primary key.

```
Buildfile: d:\projects\pro-spring\ch12\build.xml
init:
compile:
    [javac] Compiling 2 source files to D:\projects\pro-spring\ch12\build
run:
    [java] Getting testDao
    [java] Inserting new Test record
    [java] Test inserted Test { testId: 4, name: new one,
        runDate: Wed Aug 25 17:10:33 BST 2004 }
    [java] Test { testId: 1, name: foo, runDate: Thu Jan 01 00:00:00 GMT 2004 }
    [java] Test { testId: 2, name: bar, runDate: Fri Jan 02 00:00:00 GMT 2004 }
    [java] Test { testId: 4, name: new one, runDate: Wed Aug 25 17:10:33 BST 2004 }
    [java] Took 13203 ms
    [java] Took 27329 ms
    [java] Done
BUILD SUCCESSFUL
Total time: 43 seconds
```

Unfortunately, some databases do not support sequences or do not allow us to obtain the value that **is** generated for the primary key in an insert operation. The only thing we can do is to get the value generated by the last insert operation. One such database is MySQL. If we use MySQL, we have to modify the SQL script (as shown in Listing 10-40) as well as the <insert> element in the SqlMap file.

Listing 10-40. *MySQL Create Script*

```
create table Test (
    TestId int auto_increment not null,
    Name varchar(50) not null,
    RunDate timestamp not null,

    constraint PK_TestId primary key (TestId)
);
```

The only difference is the TestId column definition; instead of using sequence data type, we are using int with the auto_increment modifier. This tells MySQL that it should generate a unique value for the primary key if no value is supplied for the column in the insert statement.

The sqlMap also needs to be modified to select the generated key after the insert operation (see Listing 10-41).

Listing 10-41. *sqlMap File for the Test Domain Object for MySQL*

```
<?xml version="1.0" encoding="UTF-8" standalone="no"?>
<!DOCTYPE sqlMap PUBLIC "-//iBATIS.com//DTD SQL Map 2.0//EN" "http://www.ibatis.com/
dtd/sql-map-2.dtd">

<sqlMap>
    <!-- as previous -->

    <insert id="insertTest" parameterClass="test">
        insert into Test (TestId, Name, RunDate) values (#testId#, #name#,
#runDate#)
        <selectKey keyProperty="testId" resultClass="int">
            select select last_insert_id()
        </selectKey>
    </insert>
</sqlMap>
```

The implementation of TestDao remains the same. If we create a MySQL database, create the Test table in it, modify the dataSource bean connection properties, and run the application, we get the same output in almost all cases,[5] and we also get the correct value for the generated primary key.

---

5. The chances of selecting a primary key value generated by another insert operation are remote. An insert operation takes thousands of CPU instructions to finish; the chance that the scheduler of the operating system will switch threads so that this situation would arise are as likely as another Big Bang happening in your coffee mug–but remember, even the Big Bang has happened at least once!

What Is Missing?

Even though iBATIS offers a very good performance-to-code complexity ratio, several features are missing. Perhaps the most annoying absence is lack of support for persistent enumerations and object canonicalization.

Take a User domain object for example. Usually a limited number of Roles are used in the system. If a User object has a userRole property, a select statement that returned 1,000 User objects also creates 1,000 UserRole objects, even though most of the UserRole objects actually represent the same Role. This is very inefficient and results in a lot of memory being used up. This is a similar situation to java.lang.Boolean where you can create 1,000 Booleans that represent Boolean.TRUE. Even though these 1,000 objects represent the **same information**, you have 1,000 distinct objects. Another side effect is that you have to use the equals(Object) method to compare the values whereas if you had 1,000 references to the same object, you could use the == operator.

Finally, a persistent enumeration would be a nice addition to iBATIS. Hibernate allows you to use persistent enumeration. This is actually an object that has public static <T> fromInt() and public int toInt() methods, which return an int value that represents value in the enumeration. Hibernate, however, creates instance of the object.

The issues just discussed are the only problems in iBATIS we can think of, which makes it an exceptional DAO framework.

Overall Performance

The performance of iBATIS is very good. Because iBATIS allows you to write your own SQL statements in the sqlMap files, you are free to use additional features of the database server you are using. You also have full control over the data that is selected into the columns. For instance, there is no reason why you cannot perform the code in Listing 10-42.

Listing 10-42. *sqlMap File for the Test Domain Object*

```xml
<?xml version="1.0" encoding="UTF-8" standalone="no"?>
<!DOCTYPE sqlMap PUBLIC "-//iBATIS.com//DTD SQL Map 2.0//EN" ➥
"http://www.ibatis.com/dtd/sql-map-2.dtd">

<sqlMap>

    <typeAlias type="com.apress.prospring.ch12.domain.Test" alias="test"/>

    <resultMap class="test" id="result">
        <result property="testId" column="TestId"/>
        <result property="name" column="Name"/>
        <result property="runDate" column="RunDate"/>
    </resultMap>

    <select id="getAllTests" resultMap="result">
        select (1+1) as TestId, 'foo' as Name, '2004-01-01' as RunDate
    </select>
</sqlMap>
```

Even though this is not a typical select statement, it demonstrates your full control over the selected data and the way the data is selected.

You need to consider possible performance implications of $N+1$ selects when selecting object properties of domain objects. In most cases, however, you can absorb the performance hit by splitting the resultMaps into a basic one that is used for selects that return large number of rows and one that extends the basic resultMap to set more complex properties when you know that the number of rows is not going to be very large. As always, do not guess, measure the performance!

As we have already stated in the chapter introduction, the most important advantage of iBATIS is that it does not generate any code. Therefore, you have no data selection language to learn and you do not have to translate to the database's SQL code. This allows you to use nonstandard extensions to the SQL language provided by your database.

Bean configuration in separate XML files also help you to keep the code relatively easy to manage.

The actual data operations are incredibly simple; the built-in types allow you to pass almost any parameters to the database operations without having to create specific Java beans for them.

We have highlighted several limitations in the code. The one that bothers us the most is that there is no support for persistent enumerations and object canonicalization. This is an unfortunate side effect of almost every ORM framework we have worked with so far. You have to sacrifice a bit of the ideal design to accommodate the features or the lack of features of the framework you are using. However, iBATIS is the least obtrusive framework we have seen so far. However, we do encourage you to read about Hibernate—it is a truly data-RAD tool and the SQL code it generates is actually very good.

Using iBATIS in the Sample Application

The SpringBlog application comes with an applicationContext-ibatis.xml file that allows you to use iBATIS as implementation for the data access interfaces. If you want to use iBATIS, you need to modify the web.xml file to make sure you are using the applicationContext-ibatis.xml in the contextConfigLocation element (see Listing 10-43).

Listing 10-43. *web.xml for iBATIS Data Access Layer Implementaion*

```
<?xml version="1.0" encoding="ISO-8859-1"?>
<!DOCTYPE web-app PUBLIC
    "-//Sun Microsystems, Inc.//DTD Web Application 2.3//EN"
    "http://java.sun.com/dtd/web-app_2_3.dtd">
<web-app>
    <context-param>
        <param-name>contextConfigLocation</param-name>
        <param-value>
            /WEB-INF/applicationContext.xml
            /WEB-INF/applicationContext-db.xml
            /WEB-INF/applicationContext-ibatis.xml
        </param-value>
    </context-param>
</context-param>
```

```
    <!-- the rest of the file omitted -->

</web-app>
```

The applicationContext-ibatis.xml file contains a definition for the `SqlMapClientFactoryBean` bean, which is used in the subsequent iBATIS DAO implementations. The only configuration setting we used in Listing 10-43 is the `configLocation` property, which specifies the location of the master mapping file. The bean definition is shown in Listing 10-44.

Listing 10-44. *sqlMapClient Bean Definition*

```
<?xml version="1.0" encoding="UTF-8"?>
<!DOCTYPE beans PUBLIC "-//SPRING//DTD BEAN//EN"
"http://www.springframework.org/dtd/spring-beans.dtd">
<beans>
    <!-- SqlMap setup for iBATIS Database Layer -->
    <bean id="sqlMapClient"
        class="org.springframework.orm.ibatis.SqlMapClientFactoryBean">
        <property name="configLocation">
            <value>WEB-INF/sql-map-config.xml</value>
        </property>
    </bean>
</beans>
```

The sql-map-config.xml file is located in /data/src/ibatis and it references the Attachment.xml, Audit.xml, Comment.xml, Entry.xml, and User.xml files that contain mapping definitions for the respective domain objects. The build.xml Ant script packages the sql-map-config.xml file to the WEB-INF directory. Because iBATIS loads the mapping file names specified in the sql-map-config.xml file (shown in Listing 10-45) using the current classpath, the Attachment.xml, Audit.xml, Comment.xml, Entry.xml, and User.xml files are packaged to the WEB-INF/classes directory.

Listing 10-45. *sql-map-config.xml File*

```
<?xml version="1.0" encoding="UTF-8" ?>
<!DOCTYPE sqlMapConfig
    PUBLIC "-//iBATIS.com//DTD SQL Map Config 2.0//EN"
    "http://www.ibatis.com/dtd/sql-map-config-2.dtd">

<sqlMapConfig>
    <sqlMap resource="Comment.xml" />
    <sqlMap resource="User.xml" />
    <sqlMap resource="Entry.xml" />
    <sqlMap resource="Audit.xml" />
    <sqlMap resource="Attachment.xml" />
</sqlMapConfig>
```

The implementation classes are located in the `com.apress.prospring.data.ibatis` package. All iBATIS DAO implementation classes extend the `SqlMapClientDaoSupport` class to get access to the utility methods, namely the `getSqlMapClientTemplate()`. This is why we need to set a reference to the `sqlMapClient` bean, as shown in Listing 10-46.

Listing 10-46. *iBATIS DAO Bean Definitions*

```xml
<?xml version="1.0" encoding="UTF-8"?>
<!DOCTYPE beans PUBLIC "-//SPRING//DTD BEAN//EN"
"http://www.springframework.org/dtd/spring-beans.dtd">
<beans>
    <!-- SqlMap setup for iBATIS Database Layer -->
    <bean id="sqlMapClient"
        class="org.springframework.orm.ibatis.SqlMapClientFactoryBean">
        <property name="configLocation">
            <value>WEB-INF/sql-map-config.xml</value>
        </property>
    </bean>

    <bean id="userDao"
        class="com.apress.prospring.data.ibatis.SqlMapClientDaoSupport ">
        <property name="dataSource"><ref bean="dataSource"/></property>
        <property name="sqlMapClient"><ref local="sqlMapClient"/></property>
    </bean>

    <!-- other beans similar -->

</beans>
```

Unlike the JDBC implementation, the `SqlMapClientEntryDao` class does not require references to the `AttachmentDao` and `CommentDao` implementations. Instead, the mapping file for the Entry domain object specifies how to select the data needed to create domain objects that will be added to the `attachments` and `comments` properties. Listing 10-47 shows the mapping for the Entry domain object.

Listing 10-47. *Mapping File for the Entry Domain Object*

```xml
<?xml version="1.0" encoding="UTF-8" standalone="no"?>
<!DOCTYPE sqlMap PUBLIC "-//iBATIS.com//DTD SQL Map 2.0//EN" ➥
"http://www.ibatis.com/dtd/sql-map-2.dtd">

<sqlMap>
    <typeAlias type="com.apress.prospring.domain.Entry" alias="entry"/>
    <resultMap class="entry" id="result">
        <result property="entryId" column="EntryId"/>
        <result property="subject" column="Subject"/>
        <result property="body" column="Body"/>
        <result property="postDate" column="PostDate" javaType="java.util.Date"/>
```

```
        <result property="attachments" column="entryId"
            select="getAttachmentByEntry"/>
        <result property="comments" column="entryId"
            select="getCommentByEntry"/>
    </resultMap>
</sqlMap>
```

The getAttachmentByEntry and getCommentByEntry select elements are declared in the Attachment.xml and Comment.xml mapping files. As expected, they return a List of Attachment and Comment objects. Therefore, selecting a single Entry object results in three select statements issued to the database, demonstrating the *N*+1 problem, as discussed in the "Selecting Data" section.

Another piece of code that deserves special attention includes the insert elements of the mapping files. Each insert element in the iBATIS mapping files can include a selectKey element, which specifies code required to select or generate the primary key value. An example of how to use the selectKey element is shown in Listing 10-48.

Listing 10-48. *Using the selectKey Element*

```
<?xml version="1.0" encoding="UTF-8" standalone="no"?>
<!DOCTYPE sqlMap PUBLIC "-//iBATIS.com//DTD SQL Map 2.0//EN" ➥
"http://www.ibatis.com/dtd/sql-map-2.dtd">

<sqlMap>
    <typeAlias type="com.apress.prospring.domain.Entry" alias="entry"/>
    <insert id="insertEntry" parameterClass="entry">
        insert into Entries (Subject, Body, PostDate)
            values (#subject#, #body#, #postDate#)
        <selectKey keyProperty="entryId" resultClass="int">
            select LAST_INSERT_ID() as value
        </selectKey>
    </insert>
</sqlMap>
```

In Listing 10-48, we use the approach we explained in the "Inserting Data" section of the chapter to implement the mapping files in the SpringBlog application. Because we used select LAST_INSERT_ID() as value in the selectKey element, our mapping files are specific to the MySQL database. If you want to use a different database, most likely you will need to modify this code.

If the database you are using supports sequences, it is much better to move the selectKey element before the insert code to make sure the primary key is set correctly. Listing 10-49 shows how to do this in PostgreSQL.

Listing 10-49. *Using Sequences in the selectKey Element*

```xml
<?xml version="1.0" encoding="UTF-8" standalone="no"?>
<!DOCTYPE sqlMap PUBLIC "-//iBATIS.com//DTD SQL Map 2.0//EN" ➥
"http://www.ibatis.com/dtd/sql-map-2.dtd">

<sqlMap>
    <typeAlias type="com.apress.prospring.domain.Entry" alias="entry"/>
    <insert id="insertEntry" parameterClass="entry">
        <selectKey keyProperty="entryId" resultClass="int">
            select nextval('entries_entryid_seq')
        </selectKey>
        insert into Entries (EntryId, Subject, Body, PostDate)
            values (#entryId#, #subject#, #body#, #postDate#)
    </insert>
</sqlMap>
```

This mapping clearly shows that we first retrieve the primary key value from the entries_entryid_seq sequence and then insert a new row with the primary key already set. Further discussion of this topic is in Chapter 8.

For the remaining iBATIS data access layer implementation details, refer to the source code because it uses only features discussed in this chapter.

Summary

In this chapter, you have learned how to use iBATIS in your Spring applications. We believe that iBATIS offers the best trade-off between ease of development and code control. In fact, iBATIS does not generate the SQL code, which means that all your code is not interpreted in any way by the ORM framework. Caching is there to speed up data access in time-critical applications, and if you are aware of the few limitations of the framework, we believe you will be able to write very efficient, elegant, and high-performing applications.

For more information about iBATIS, its latest source code, binaries, and documentation, go to www.ibatis.com.

PART 5

■■■

Spring in the Middle Tier

■ ■ ■

CHAPTER 11

Designing and Implementing Spring-Based Applications

Application design is perhaps one of the most widely covered topics in application development, particularly in the Java world, which seems both to benefit and suffer from an overabundance of books on architecture issues and design patterns. In this chapter, we are not going to rehash all of the information contained in these books, nor are we attempting to provide an exhaustive guide to application design. Although we hate to admit it, you won't find any frighteningly clever and original solutions in this chapter. What you will find, however, is a discussion of tried and tested OOP practices that result in applications which have clearly defined component responsibilities and which are also easy to test and maintain. This chapter looks at the impact Spring has on application design, paying particular attention to patterns and practices that you will find easy to apply when you are building your application with Spring. Much of this chapter focuses on the design decisions we made when building the SpringBlog application, and we use that application as the basis for our examples and discussions.

This chapter is not just about application design. We also focus on how we used many of the Spring technologies covered so far to implement the data access and business logic tiers of the SpringBlog application.

Specifically, in this chapter we look at the following:

- **Interface-driven design:** Interface-driven design is a traditional OOP best practice. When you use interface-driven design, the main components of your application are defined in terms of interfaces rather than concrete classes. Java offers first-class support for this kind of design with its notion of interfaces separate from classes. In this section of the chapter, we discuss interface-driven design in general terms and why you should use it in your applications.

- **Building a Domain Object Model:** In this section of the chapter, we look at the notion of a **Domain Object Model (DOM)**, a collection of objects that provides an abstract model of the data in an application's problem domain. By creating a DOM for your application, you are creating a set of objects for modeling application data and behavior that matches some abstract idea of your problem domain. Using a DOM provides a great number of benefits for your application, not the least of which is reducing the level of impedance between an application's code and the real-world problems it is attempting to solve.

- **The Data Access Tier:** Most applications nowadays need to access some kind of persistent data store, typically a relational database. Chapters 8 through 10 discussed Spring's support for a variety of different data access methods. In this section of the chapter, we look at the design issues related to building a Data Access Tier to service the rest of your application.

- **Building the Business Tier:** An application's Business Tier is where all of the business logic that makes up the application is encapsulated. In this section, we look at how the Business Tier interacts with the Domain Object Model and Data Access Tier to provide a unified interface to access application functionality. We also look at the business requirements of the SpringBlog application and how this translates into an interface design and an implementation of that interface. This section also touches briefly on the topic of transactions, looking at how the design of your Business Tier can affect the choices available when you are specifying transaction settings.

- **Data validation in Spring:** An important part of any application's logic is data validation. You should definitely consider data validation part of an application's business logic, although the rendering of validation errors is outside the scope of the Business Tier. Spring provides a validation framework that accurately reflects this. In this section, we also cover how the data validation rules for SpringBlog are defined using the Spring validation framework. Chapter 17 looks at how this validation logic is employed by the Spring web framework.

You should note that this chapter does not cover design or implementation of the application's Web Tier; that is covered in greater detail in Chapters 17 through 19. In particular, we do not cover how the SpringBlog Business Tier is utilized by the web front end, nor do we explore how Spring uses the validation logic to support data validation and error reporting in the front end. Both of these topics are covered in Chapters 17 through 19.

Designing to Interfaces

As a best practice, designing to interfaces is relatively ancient when compared to the seemingly unending stream of new best practices that emerge on a weekly basis; it is also one of the most enduring. One of the main design goals of Spring is to ease the development of applications that are designed and implemented around a set of well-defined interfaces. Before we can look at designing a Spring-based application in any detail, we should explore exactly why designing to interfaces is such a big thing and how Spring goes about making it easier.

Why Design to Interfaces?

There are many reasons you should design and code your applications to interfaces rather than to a concrete class hierarchy, but perhaps the biggest reason is to reduce coupling. If components in your application talk to each other in terms of interfaces rather than concrete types, it becomes very easy to swap out a component if it becomes problematic. This capability allows you to swap out one implementation for another, without having to touch the rest of the application code; indeed, it is possible for your application to be working with many different implementations of the same interface without even being aware that it is doing so.

Remember also that, in Java, a class only has one shot at concrete inheritance but can implement as many interfaces as necessary. By defining application components in terms of interfaces rather than classes, you are not going to constrain an implementing class to a particular base class unnecessarily.

One of the most important benefits gained by this loose coupling is the increase in testability. As the heads of a busy development team, we are constantly seeking new ways to improve the test coverage in the applications we produce as a direct way of improving the quality of the product we send to the customer. By designing to interfaces, we can swap out an implementation of an interface for a mock implementation, which allows us more flexibility when testing. For example, a requirement of the SpringBlog application is that each operation that results in a new posting or a post being modified should result in an audit message being written. This process should work under a transaction so that if the writing of the audit message fails, then blog modification is rolled back. Originally we had the audit log encapsulated as a private method of our implementation of BlogManager (the main business interface). The problem with this was that it made testing a rollback very difficult. To get around this, we refactored the auditing logic behind a new interface, AuditService, and then we created a MockAuditService implementation that threw an exception. This allows us to test that the transactional behavior was correct. This actual scenario is discussed in more detail in Chapter 12.

What we find when we design to interfaces is that we do not need to do huge amounts of up-front design. Typically, to start with, we lay out the main component interfaces as we see them, and then as the application progresses, we refactor certain pieces of functionality, introducing new interfaces as we find the code becoming unwieldy or hard to test.

The Factory Pattern

One of the key problems you will encounter when implementing an application where all the components are defined in terms of interfaces is how your application goes about locating instances of classes that implement the interfaces. A traditional solution to this is to use the Factory pattern. The Factory pattern defines a class whose responsibility is to provide application components with implementations of other application components; in this case, the available components are defined in terms of interfaces, not concrete implementations. Consider a system that has a business interface OrderService. Other components in the system want to obtain implementations of this interface without knowing ahead of time which implementation they need. To implement such a system, we can build a Factory class like the one shown in Listing 11-1.

Listing 11-1. *A Basic Factory Implementation*

```
package com.apress.prospring.ch11.factory;

public class BasicFactory {

    private static final BasicFactory instance;

    private OrderService orderService;
```

```
    static {
        instance = new BasicFactory();
    }

    public static BasicFactory getInstance() {
        return instance;
    }

    public BasicFactory() {
        this.orderService = new DefaultOrderService();
    }

    public OrderService getOrderService() {
        return this.orderService;
    }
}
```

This is a simplistic Factory implementation, but it does illustrate the basic Factory approach. Now any application that wishes to get access to an implementation of OrderService simply uses the getOrderService() method of the BasicFactory class.

Drawbacks of the Basic Factory Pattern

In its basic form, the Factory pattern has three main drawbacks:

- There is no way to change an implementing class without a recompile.

- There is no way to make multiple implementations available transparently to different components. This is part of a larger problem in that the Factory class requires each component to have some knowledge of the Factory and which method on the Factory to invoke.

- There is no way simply to switch instantiation models. In Listing 11.1, we maintained a singleton instance of DefaultOrderService, but if we wanted to return many instances, we would have to recompile the Factory class.

These drawbacks are discussed in detail in the next three sections.

Externally Configurable Factories

From the example in Listing 11-1, you can see that changing the implementation class means changing the BasicFactory class and recompiling. One of the benefits of interface-based design is that you can swap out implementations for new ones very easily. However, having to recompile the Factory removes some of the ease with which this can be done. In many projects in the past, before Spring was available, we created factories which allowed the implementation class for interfaces to be specified in an external configuration file. This solved the initial problem, but it added more development burden to our project and it did not really help out with the two remaining problems.

Supporting Multiple Implementations Transparently

Supporting multiple implementations transparently is perhaps the biggest drawback of the traditional Factory pattern. The basic method on the BasicFactory class, getOrderService(), can only return one particular implementation (or a random choice), but it cannot choose which implementation to return based on the caller. This leads, naturally, to an implementation such as that shown in Listing 11-2.

Listing 11-2. *Basic Support for Multiple Implementations*

```
package com.apress.prospring.ch11.factory;

public class MultiFactory {

    private static final BasicFactory instance;

    private OrderService orderService;
    private OrderService superOrderService;

    static {
        instance = new BasicFactory();
    }

    public static BasicFactory getInstance() {
        return instance;
    }

    public MultiFactory() {
        this.orderService = new DefaultOrderService();
        this.superOrderService = new SuperOrderService();
    }

    public OrderService getOrderService() {
        return this.orderService;
    }

    public OrderService getSuperOrderService() {
        return this.superOrderService;
    }
}
```

With this implementation, components that need to access the SuperOrderService implementation can call the getSuperOrderService() method. However, this approach just negates the benefit of a Factory. Although the components are not coupled by class to a particular implementation, they are coupled by the method they call on the Factory. Another drawback to this approach is that each new implementation requires a change to the Factory code and a change to the component that needs the new implementation. Having to add a new method for each new implementation makes this approach very difficult to configure externally.

Another implementation that tries to solve the problem of transparent support for multiple implementations requires components that invoke the getOrderService() method to pass in their class to the getOrderService() method so that the Factory can decide, based on the class of the caller, which implementation to return. This implementation suffers from numerous problems, not least of which is that it only works with classes, meaning two instances of the same class cannot have different implementations of the OrderService. You will also find that the implementation of the getOrderService() method quickly becomes messy when you have many components that need an OrderService implementation.

Yet another approach to this problem is to use a lookup-style approach by having each component look up the implementation with a key. So instead of calling getOrderService(), a component calls getOrderService("someKey"). The problem with this approach is that in order to maintain full flexibility, each component must use a separate key so that its implementation can be changed separately from the others. This in turn means that without some complex configuration logic, it is going to be difficult to share an instance of the same implementation class across components with different keys.

The root of this problem lies in the fact that a component actively has to ask for an implementation class, and to gain full flexibility, it must ask in a way that is different from all other instances of all other components. This is a problem that is not solved using the traditional Factory pattern.

Supporting Multiple Instantiation Modes

Another problem is supporting multiple instantiation modes of an implementation class for different components. This problem suffers from many of the issues discussed in the preceding section, and again, the core of this problem is that a component actively has to ask for an implementation class. This problem is also not solved using the traditional Factory pattern.

Thankfully, Spring solves all of these problems; we discuss how in the next section.

Impact of Spring on Interface-Based Design

Spring has a huge impact on applications that are designed using interfaces. Because Spring takes care of wiring all the components together, you no longer have to worry about creating Factory classes that consider every possible situation.

On the surface, when you are building interface-based applications, the biggest benefit from Spring is the reduction in glue code that you have to write. This benefit is further enhanced by the excellent, out-of-the-box support for external configuration of component dependencies. However, the biggest benefit comes from Spring's use of Dependency Injection. Because Spring removes the responsibility for dependency location from components themselves and simply asks that components allow it to provide them with the dependencies, Spring is able to solve the last two of the three problems discussed previously.

Dependency Injection means that Spring can provide any instance of any implementation class to any instance of any application component without requiring any special coding in the application component whatsoever. This is coupled with the fact that Spring can freely manage the lifecycle of any instance of any dependency that it is managing for an application component.

Basically this means that Spring has all the features that we need to design interface-based applications, and we do not have to worry about how we are going to glue the components together come implementation time.

Building a Domain Object Model

A Domain Object Model (DOM) is a set of classes that models concepts from your problem domain. We really cannot do justice to the concept of a DOM in just a small portion of this chapter, so we recommend that you read *Patterns of Enterprise Application Architecture* by Martin Fowler (Addison-Wesley, 2002) or *Domain Driven Design: Tackling Complexity in the Heart of Software* by Eric Evans (Addison-Wesley, 2003) for a more complete description of the DOM pattern. Although we do not go into great detail on this pattern, we do show you why we chose to create a DOM for the SpringBlog application and how we built our DOM.

Spring and the Domain Object Model

Given that this is a book on Spring, you might find it strange that we dedicate considerable page space to a topic that is not directly related to Spring in any way. Of the applications that we have built using Spring, the only objects that are consistently not managed by Spring are Domain Objects. The reason for this is that, really, Spring does not need to be involved with Domain Objects. Generally, you create many instances of your Domain Objects using the new() operator, and although you can have Spring create new instances for you as you need them, it seems like overkill to have to call BeanFactory.getBean() every time you need a new Domain Object instance. This is especially true when you consider that, typically, Domain Objects do not take advantage of Dependency Injection, because they generally have few dependencies outside of the DOM itself, and they don't require much configuration.

You might well be wondering, then, why so much attention to the DOM? The answer is simple. The DOM affects so many other parts of the application, parts that are managed by Spring, that getting it right is very important to getting your whole application right.

DOM != Value Object

The important thing to understand about the DOM pattern is that it is not the same as the Value Object (often called Data Transfer Object) pattern. The Value Object pattern was created to overcome a shortcoming in the original EJB specification that meant that all calls to an EJB were remote. Configuring the state of an EJB typically means many calls, all of which are remote. Using a Value Object, object state is transferred in bulk using a single remote call, thus reducing the performance hit of making many remote calls.

NOTE   Officially the Value Object pattern is not the same as the Data Transfer Object pattern. Martin Fowler defines a Value Object as "A small simple object, like money or date range, whose equality isn't based on identity." The confusion arises, however, from the Core J2EE Patterns catalog that uses the term Value Object for many of the examples of the Data Transfer Object pattern. In this section, we use Value Object and Data Transfer Object interchangeably, but we are talking about the Data Transfer Object pattern.

A DOM is an object-based representation of the application problem domain, intended to allow the programmer to code in terms of objects that exist in the problem domain, not objects that exist inside the computer. Where a Value Object purely encompasses state, it is perfectly acceptable for a Domain Object to encompass both state and behavior (although you may choose not to encapsulate behavior inside Domain Objects).

Another key difference between Domain Objects and Value Objects is that a Value Object's structure is driven by the need to transfer data remotely, whereas a Domain Object is modeled to represent a real-world concept and is not driven by some need of the application infrastructure. As we discuss later, we believe there are no hard-and-fast rules for modeling Domain Objects; you have to choose a level of granularity that matches your application and the functions it will perform.

It is possible for an application to have both Domain Objects and Value Objects. In this approach, Value Objects are used by the Business Tier to communicate with the Data Access Tier. These Value Objects are then converted as appropriate into Domain Objects and passed into the Presentation Tier for rendering. In our opinion, this approach is really not worth the hassle. With Spring, the data access framework is so powerful that it is simple to map data directly to Domain Objects. However, this approach is sometimes problematic when you have a DOM that is quite far removed from the model in the underlying data store. This issue is discussed in greater detail in the later section entitled "Modeling Domain Objects."

Why Create a Domain Object Model?

Creating a DOM requires some up-front effort in order to identify Domain Objects and then create an in-code representation of these Objects. However, in all but the most trivial of applications, this up-front effort is far outweighed by the time you will save and the bugs you will avoid when it comes to implementing business logic to do something with your Domain Objects. We find that using a good DOM makes creating the code to solve business problems much easier, since you are able to code in terms of the problem rather than in terms of the machine. A good DOM makes it easier for developers to transform application requirements into application features.

Modeling Domain Objects

There are a great many different methodologies and approaches to Domain Object modeling. Some practices advocate letting the underlying data store drive your object model, whereas some practices say, "Let the business domain drive the object model." In practice, we have found that a happy medium between these two approaches results in a DOM that is both easy to work with and well performing.

For small applications with only five or six database tables, it is often easier just to create one Domain Object that corresponds to each database table. Although these objects are not strictly Domain Objects—in that their creation is not driven by the problem domain, but rather the data structure—they are close enough for the purposes of such a simple application. Indeed, in many small applications, the result of an extensive domain modeling process is an object model that matches the database structure entirely.

For larger applications, a little more thought has to be put into the real-world problem domain and the underlying data store. When we are building a DOM for an application, we usually focus on three main points:

- How the problem domain is structured

- How the Domain Objects will be used

- How the underlying data store is constructed

What we are looking for is a DOM that is as close to the ideal model as possible without affecting the performance of the data store too much and without having too great an impact on code that has to use the Domain Objects.

Typically, a DOM is quite granular, and you might end up with more than one class for a single logical concept. For instance, consider the concept of an order in a purchasing system. Typically an order is modeled as a single Order object with one or more OrderLine objects that represent each line item of the order. Trying to model an order using a single object leads to an object model that is unnecessarily coarse and unwieldy, not to mention difficult to implement. You should always look for opportunities to increase the granularity of your Domain Objects when it makes working with the DOM easier.

You will also find that your DOM contains objects that do not exist in your data store. For instance, a typical purchasing system has some notion of a shopping cart, perhaps represented by Cart and CartItem objects. Unless you are required to persist contents across user sessions, chances are these Domain Objects do not have corresponding tables for data storage. Remember, you are not simply building an object-oriented representation of your database, you are modeling the business domain. This point cannot be stressed enough. We have seen plenty of projects that created a pseudo-DOM derived directly from the data store, and inevitably these projects suffered from the lack of abstraction that can be gained from a well-defined DOM.

We have found that a solid DOM comes from taking the time to look at your problem domain, identifying the objects in the domain, and then looking at how the natural granularity of these objects fits into the requirements of your application. Although we take both the utilization of the Domain Objects and the underlying data store into consideration, we don't like to let these have undue influence on our DOM.

It is important to remember that the goal of building a DOM is to create a set of classes that help you and other developers build the application at a level of abstraction that is closer to the application's problem domain. In general, we consider all other concerns secondary when building a DOM. If you find that performance is suffering due to the design of your DOM, feel free to tweak away, but we don't recommend that you do this on a hunch. Make absolutely sure that your DOM is to blame. You don't want to reduce the benefits of your DOM out of the mistaken belief that it is performing badly.

Database Modeling and Domain Object Modeling

Although database modeling and Domain Object modeling are quite similar, the results you get from each are rarely the same, and indeed, you rarely want them to be. When modeling a database, you are looking for the structure that allows you to store and retrieve data in the most efficient and consistent manner. When you are building a DOM, performance is obviously important, but so is building an API that is easy to work with and makes assembling your business logic simple. In general, we have found that it is best to model the database in the way that is best for the database, and model the DOM, initially at least, in the way that is best for the DOM. You can make any changes later on, if and when you identify performance bottlenecks.

Modeling Domain Object Relationships

The most common mistake we see in a DOM, especially when the DOM is driven by the design of the database, is that Domain Objects are created to represent relationships between other Domain Objects. This comes from the fact that a many-to-many relationship between two tables in a database must have a third table to construct the relationship. Relationships in a DOM should be modeled in a much more OOP-style way, with Domain Objects maintaining references to other Domain Objects or lists of Domain Objects.

A common mistake when populating Domain Object data from a database, such as what would be done in the Data Access Tier of an application, is to assume that all related Domain Objects must be loaded from the database as well—this is not so. See the later section entitled "Domain Object Relationships" for a more detailed discussion of this problem.

To Encapsulate Behavior or Not?

You are not forced to have your Domain Objects encapsulate any behavior at all; indeed, you can choose to have your Domain Objects represent just the state of your problem domain. In most cases, we have found that it is better to factor out much of the business logic into a set of service objects that work with Domain Objects rather than encapsulate this logic inside the Domain Objects. Typically, we place all logic that interacts with components outside of the DOM into the service objects. In this way, we are reducing the coupling between the DOM and components involved in application logic. This allows the DOM to be used in a wider variety of scenarios, and often, you will find that the DOM can be reused in other applications that solve problems in the same domain.

Where we like to encapsulate behavior in the DOM is in situations where the logic is implemented purely in interactions between Domain Objects. The jPetStore sample application included with Spring provides a great example of this that can be mapped to our purchasing system example. In this scenario, a user has a shopping cart, represented by a `Cart` object, and a list of `CartItem` objects. When the user is ready to purchase the items in her cart and create an order, the application has to create an `Order` object along with a list of `OrderLine` objects that corresponds to the data modeled by the `Cart` and `CartItem` objects. This is a perfect example of when behavior should be encapsulated inside the DOM. The conversion from `Cart` to `Order` is coded purely in terms of Domain Objects with no dependencies on other components in your application. In jPetStore, the `Order` class has an `initOrder()` method that accepts two arguments, `Account` and `Cart`. All the logic required to create an `Order` based on the `Cart` object for the user represented by the `Account` object is represented in this method.

As with most things related to modeling, there are no hard-and-fast rules about when to put logic inside a Domain Object and when to factor it out into a service object. You should avoid placing logic inside your Domain Objects when it causes your Domain Objects to depend on other application components outside of the DOM. In this way, you are ensuring that your DOM is as reusable as possible. On the flipside of this, logic that involves only Domain Objects is ideally placed in the DOM, which allows it to be used wherever the DOM is used.

The SpringBlog Domain Object Model

Because the SpringBlog application is actually quite simple, the DOM is also quite simple. Figure 11-1 shows the SpringBlog DOM.

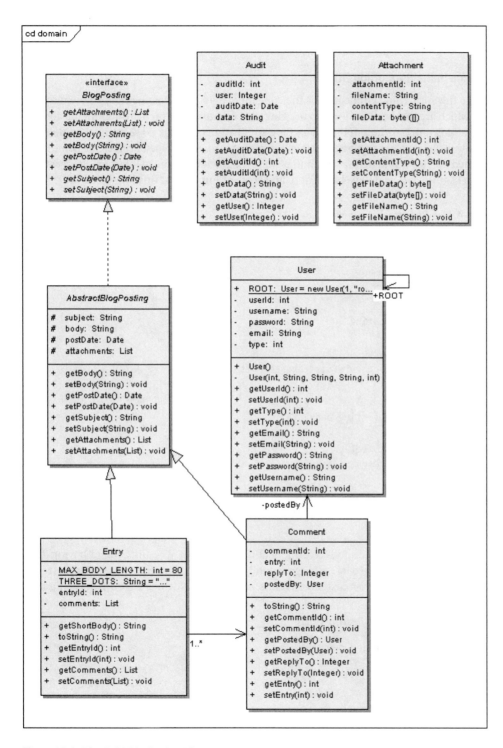

Figure 11-1. *The DOM in SpringBlog*

Although this is quite a simple DOM, it does highlight some of the points we have been talking about. These are discussed in the next three sections.

Inheritance in the SpringBlog DOM

Central to the SpringBlog application is the concept of a posting. Postings come in two types: entries, which are top-level postings to the blog; and comments, which are comments about a particular blog entry. Although the SpringBlog application contains no security, the intention is that only the blog owner can create entries whereas any anonymous user can create comments. We decided that we would define common postings characteristics in an interface, BlogPosting, shown in Listing 11-4, and have both Entry and Comment implement this interface.

Listing 11-4. *The BlogPosting Interface*

```
package com.apress.prospring.domain;

import java.util.Date;
import java.util.List;

public interface BlogPosting {

    public List getAttachments();
    public void setAttachments(List attachments);

    public String getBody();
    public void setBody(String body);

    public Date getPostDate();
    public void setPostDate(Date postDate);

    public String getSubject();
    public void setSubject(String subject);
}
```

However, this results in undue code duplication, with both Entry and Comment having their own implementations of BlogPosting. To get around this, we introduce the AbstractBlogPosting class and have Entry and Comment extend this class. AbstractBlogPosting is shown in Listing 11-5.

Listing 11-5. *The AbstractBlogPosting Class*

```
package com.apress.prospring.domain;

import java.util.Date;
import java.util.List;
```

```java
public abstract class AbstractBlogPosting implements BlogPosting {

    protected String subject;

    protected String body;

    protected Date postDate;

    protected List attachments;

    public String getBody() {
        return body;
    }

    public void setBody(String body) {
        this.body = body;
    }

    public Date getPostDate() {
        return postDate;
    }

    public void setPostDate(Date postDate) {
        this.postDate = postDate;
    }

    public String getSubject() {
        return subject;
    }

    public void setSubject(String subject) {
        this.subject = subject;
    }

    public List getAttachments() {
        return attachments;
    }

    public void setAttachments(List attachments) {
        this.attachments = attachments;
    }

}
```

By extending this base class, we move all the BlogPosting implementation details out of Entry and Comment, reducing code duplication. As an example of this, Listing 11-6 shows the code for the Entry class.

Listing 11-6. *The Entry Class*

```
package com.apress.prospring.domain;

public class Entry extends AbstractBlogPosting {

    private static final int MAX_BODY_LENGTH = 80;

    private static final String THREE_DOTS = "...";

    private int entryId;

    public String getShortBody() {
        if (body.length() <= MAX_BODY_LENGTH)
            return body;
        StringBuffer result = new StringBuffer(MAX_BODY_LENGTH + 3);
        result.append(body.substring(0, MAX_BODY_LENGTH));
        result.append(THREE_DOTS);

        return result.toString();
    }

    public String toString() {
        StringBuffer result = new StringBuffer(50);
        result.append("Entry { id=");
        result.append(entryId);
        result.append(", subject=");
        result.append(subject);
        result.append(" }");

        return result.toString();
    }

    public int getEntryId() {
        return entryId;
    }

    public void setEntryId(int entryId) {
        this.entryId = entryId;
    }
}
```

This is a pattern that is used extensively in Spring and throughout the SpringBlog application. Common functionality is defined in interfaces rather than abstract classes, but we provide a default implementation of the interface as an abstract class. The reason for this is that, where possible, we can take advantage of the abstract base class as with Entry and Comment, thus removing the need for each class to implement the BlogPosting interface directly. However, should a requirement arise for the Entry class to extend the Foo class, then we can simply implement the BlogPosting interface directly in Entry. The main point to remember here is that you do not define common functionality in terms of abstract classes because doing so restricts you to a set inheritance hierarchy. Instead, define common functionality in terms of interfaces, along with default implementations of these interfaces as abstract base classes. This way you can take advantage of the inherited implementation wherever possible, but you are not artificially constraining your inheritance hierarchy.

A point of note here is that we did not reflect this inheritance tree in the database. That is to say, we didn't create a BlogPosting table to store the shared data, and then two tables, Entry and Comment, to store the entity-specific data. The main reason for this is that we didn't think that an application of the size of SpringBlog warranted the complexity of that structure, plus this example highlights our point about having a DOM that is different in structure than the database. The main reason for defining this inheritance hierarchy, besides that it is a good design, is to allow the SpringBlog application to work with the common data in the Entry and Comment objects, without having to differentiate between the two. A good example of this is the obscenity filter that we covered in Chapter 7.

Domain Behavior in SpringBlog

Although the SpringBlog domain model is simplistic, we still need to encapsulate some logic in the domain model. Because the body of a blog posting could potentially be very long, we wanted a mechanism to get a snippet of the body to use when it displays a list of blog postings. For this reason, we create the Entry.getShortBody() method shown in Listing 11-7.

Listing 11-7. *Behavior in the Entry Class*

```
package com.apress.prospring.domain;

public class Entry extends AbstractBlogPosting {

    private static final int MAX_BODY_LENGTH = 80;

    private static final String THREE_DOTS = "...";

    public String getShortBody() {
        if (body.length() <= MAX_BODY_LENGTH)
            return body;
        StringBuffer result = new StringBuffer(MAX_BODY_LENGTH + 3);
        result.append(body.substring(0, MAX_BODY_LENGTH));
        result.append(THREE_DOTS);

        return result.toString();
    }
    /* omitted for clarity */
}
```

Here you can see that to build the short body, we take the first 80 characters of the body and simply append three dots to the end. This is a simplistic implementation, but it does highlight a typical scenario for encapsulating logic in the DOM.

Domain Object Relationships

In the DOM in Figure 11-1, notice that we defined an association between Entry and Attachment, and Comment and Attachment. As part of the SpringBlog requirements, we want to be able to upload and store files with both types of posting. In the database, we have a table to store the attachments called, strangely enough, attachments. Then to associate attachments with an entry or a comment, we have two other tables: entryattachments and commentattachments. A common mistake we see is that people create Domain Objects to model these relationships, rather than using standard Java features to relate the objects together. When you have a one-to-one relationship in your database, you can model this in the DOM by having one object maintain a reference to the other. For one-to-many or many-to-many relationships, using Java Collections makes it simple to represent these complex relationships in a familiar manner that is simple to work with in code. Listing 11-8, a snippet from the AbstractBlogPosting class, shows how we use a List to store the Attachment objects for each posting.

Listing 11-8. *Using List for Domain Object Relationships*

```
package com.apress.prospring.domain;

import java.util.List;

public abstract class AbstractBlogPosting implements BlogPosting {

    protected List attachments;

    public List getAttachments() {
        return attachments;
    }

    public void setAttachments(List attachments) {
        this.attachments = attachments;
    }
}
```

Rather than using additional objects to model relationships, we use a simple List to model the one-to-many relationship. Aside from reducing the amount of code we need to type, this method prevents the DOM from becoming polluted with needless classes, and allows familiar Java concepts such as Iterators to be used when navigating relationships.

Canonicalization and Memory Considerations for a DOM

A consideration when modeling objects in your domain is the amount of memory taken up by these objects. Typically you have many instances of the same class in your application at the same time. Often you have the same logical entity represented by many different instances of a Domain Object at the same time. In many cases, you can't avoid this, but for some scenarios, you can avoid this by preventing multiple instances of a Domain Object from being created to represent the same logical entity—this technique is called canonicalization.

■**NOTE** This canonicalization pattern is often referred to as the Typesafe Enum pattern.

Before we look at this technique, we should first discuss scenarios where applying it is valid. Consider again the purchasing system. One of the Domain Objects for the purchasing system is Product. Now it is possible for more than one user to be looking at the same product at the same time. Typically, this results in multiple instances of Product being created to represent the same physical product. Our fictional purchasing system sells over 10,000 different product lines, and it is this number that makes canonicalization impractical, as you will see.

Another Domain Object in the purchasing system is ShippingCompany, which represents one of the companies that ships orders to the user. Our system only offers three choices of shipping company, yet there may be many more instances of shipping companies around in the JVM at any one time. This low number of fixed data sets makes the ShippingCompany ideal for canonicalization. Basic canonicalization works by making the constructor of the class private and then defining all possible instances of the class as public static final members. Listing 11-9 shows an example of this for the ShippingCompany class.

Listing 11-9. *Canonicalization for Domain Objects*

```
package com.apress.prospring.ch11.domain;

public class ShippingCompany {

    public static final ShippingCompany UPS = new ShippingCompany(1, "UPS");

    public static final ShippingCompany DHL = new ShippingCompany(2, "DHL");

    public static final ShippingCompany FEDEX = new ShippingCompany(3, "FEDEX");

    private final int id;

    private final String name;

    private ShippingCompany(int id, String name) {
        this.id = id;
        this.name = name;
    }

    public int getId() {
        return this.id;
    }

    public String getName() {
        return this.name;
    }
```

```
    public static ShippingCompany fromInt(int id) {
        if (id == UPS.id) {
            return UPS;
        } else if (id == DHL.id) {
            return DHL;
        } else if (id == FEDEX.id) {
            return FEDEX;
        } else {
            return null;
        }
    }
}
```

Here you can see that the three instances of the ShippingCompany class are created as public static final members. It is not possible for external classes to create more instances of ShippingCompany because the constructor is declared private. The fromInt() method isn't necessary and is in fact something that we inherited from Hibernate. The fromInt() method is useful when loading canonicalized objects from the data store. We discuss canonicalization from a data access point of view later in the chapter.

When you have a large number of objects to canonicalize—say you have an application that performs lots of processing on Country objects—you may find that caching is a better solution than canonicalization. We are not going to discuss caching in this chapter. For a more detailed discussion, read *Expert One-on-One J2EE Development without EJB* by Rod Johnson and Juergen Hoeller (Wrox, 2004).

Domain Object Model Summary

In this section, we looked at the DOM for the SpringBlog application and we spent some time discussing the basics of Domain Object modeling and implementation. There is no doubt that this topic is much greater than what we have covered here. Indeed, a whole range of books is available that discusses the topic in detail. We only scratched the surface here, and we focused on why you want to build a DOM, what the focus is when building one, and some general topics related to the SpringBlog application.

Although it is certainly possible to build applications without defining and building a DOM, it is our experience that taking the time to do so pays off in reduced complexity, lower maintenance costs, and fewer bugs.

Designing and Building the Data Access Tier

In the last 3 years, we don't think we can honestly say that we have built an application for a customer that did not access some kind of data store—in most cases a relational database. The fact remains that data is an important part of building applications, and being able to store, retrieve, and manipulate that data quickly and reliably is, perhaps, even more important.

In this section, we take a look at the ubiquitous Data Access Tier, paying particular attention to the design pattern known as the Data Access Object (DAO). As with the DOM, the DAO pattern has had a huge amount of text written about it—usually related to the implementation of individual DAOs themselves. Because we covered the implementation of the SpringBlog

DAOs in Chapters 8, 9, and 10, we won't spend too much time looking at that here. Instead, we look at some of the practical considerations that go into designing a good set of DAOs.

Why Have a Data Access Tier?

At our company, we take on quite a few developers on a trainee scheme. When we get these developers in and show them our applications, the first thing that many of them ask is "Why do you bother with a Data Access Tier?" For most Java developers, the answer to this question is plainly, and often painfully, obvious, borne out of many late nights spent debugging spaghetti JSPs with embedded data access code. Aside from it being good design practice to encapsulate all data access logic behind a well-defined set of interfaces, building a Data Access Tier makes applications, and hence developers' lives, simpler. A good DAO provides an isolated area, away from the business logic, where the developer can concentrate on mapping the quite often different DOM to the database schema. Putting all your data access logic in one place reduces the need to spread, and often duplicate, the code across your application, an approach that inevitably leads to debugging and maintenance nightmares—not to mention programmers going prematurely gray.

Typically, it doesn't take that much effort to design a good Data Access Tier, and in many cases, the implementation time is much shorter than when you are spreading code throughout your application, because you are avoiding unnecessary duplication.

Practical Design Considerations

The task of designing and building a Data Access Tier is fairly simple; indeed, the most complex part is actually creating the data access code itself. However, you should bear in mind a few practical considerations when creating your Data Access Tier that lead you to build DAOs that are simpler to use and easier to extend.

Domain Objects or Data Transfer Objects?

As we mentioned earlier, one school of thought says that when you invoke your Data Access Tier, generally from the service objects in your Business Tier, then you should create Data Transfer Objects from your Domain Objects. Honestly, we cannot think of a reason you would want to do this; in our eyes, it seems that this practice has sprung up out of confusion on how certain J2EE patterns should be used. We have never used this technique in any of our applications, because we have never had a problem passing Domain Objects straight to our DAOs. If any of you know of a scenario where this approach is useful, then let us know, and we'll include it in the second edition.

More Interfaces

At the risk of sounding like a broken record, use interfaces. Define your DAOs in terms of interfaces, not classes. When writing code in your service objects to work with your DAOs, code to the interfaces, not the implementation classes. Remember that when you are using Spring, it is a trivial job to pass an instance of the appropriate DAO implementation to your service tier, so using interfaces for your DAOs places very little additional coding burden on you.

Use the Base Interface Implementation Pattern

As we did with the BlogPosting interface earlier, it is often useful to define an abstract base class to the basis of the interface implementation. In this way different implementations of the same DAO can share common functionality, reducing the need for duplication. The difference between defining base classes for business interfaces and for DAO interfaces is that with DAO interfaces you often do not need to define them, because Spring has already taken care of this for you. For instance, consider the UML model in Figure 11-2, which shows a portion of the DAO structure in SpringBlog.

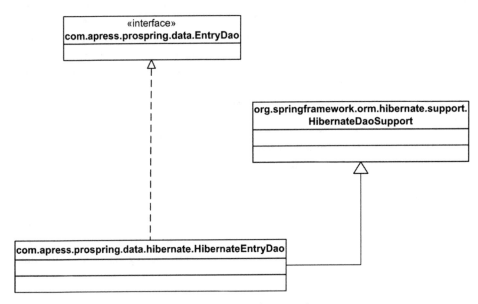

Figure 11-2. *Using Spring base class for DAO implementations*

Here you can see that we have defined the EntryDao interface, and for this, we have built an implementation using Hibernate—HibernateEntryDao. Rather than implement this from scratch, we have chosen to take advantage of the Hibernate support offered in Spring by extending the HibernateDaoSupport class. This class has predefined properties for Hibernate-specific dependencies such as the SessionFactory object, which allows for DI-based configuration of the DAO. All our HibernateEntryDao class needs to worry about is implementing the EntryDao interface. You can see more details on the full Hibernate DAO implementation for SpringBlog in Chapter 9.

Spring provides similar convenience classes for the other ORM frameworks it supports, including iBATIS (covered in Chapter 10), JDO, and Apache's ObJect Relational Bridge (OJB) as well as for plain JDBC.

When using the JDBC support class, JdbcDaoSupport, you may find it necessary to introduce a further layer of abstract classes to factor out database-specific functionality. For instance, when we were building the JDBC DAO for SpringBlog, we found that we could implement nearly all the functionality using standard SQL constructs, but retrieval of newly added primary keys required us to use database-specific functionality. To get around this, we created an abstract implementation of each DAO with the core functionality implemented, and then we created an implementation of each DAO specific to the target database. Figure 11-3 shows a skeleton UML structure for this hierarchy.

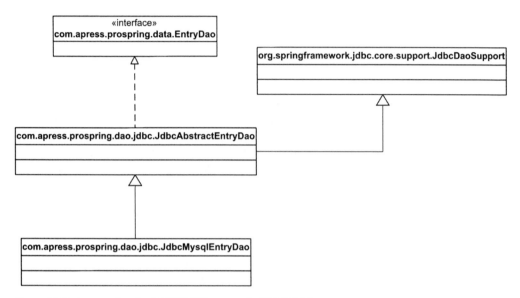

Figure 11-3. *Accounting for DBMS differences in JDBC DAOs*

Here you can see that we have defined a class, JdbcAbstractEntryDao, that implements the EntryDao and extends the JdbcDaoSupport class. This class is abstract and, in addition to providing the base implementation of the EntryDao interface, it defines a single abstract method, getIdentitySql(). Listing 11-12 shows the parts of JdbcAbstractEntryDao in question, with all the implementation code removed for clarity.

Listing 11-12. *Defining an Abstract Hook Method for DB-Specific Functionality*

```
package com.apress.prospring.data.jdbc;

import java.sql.ResultSet;
import java.sql.SQLException;
import java.sql.Types;
import java.util.List;

import javax.sql.DataSource;

import org.springframework.beans.factory.InitializingBean;
import org.springframework.jdbc.core.SqlParameter;
import org.springframework.jdbc.core.support.JdbcDaoSupport;
import org.springframework.jdbc.object.MappingSqlQuery;
import org.springframework.jdbc.object.SqlUpdate;
```

```
import com.apress.prospring.data.EntryDao;
import com.apress.prospring.domain.Entry;

public abstract class JdbcAbstractEntryDao extends JdbcDaoSupport implements
        EntryDao, InitializingBean {

    protected abstract String getIdentitySql();
}
```

Remember, `JdbcAbstractEntryDao` contains the vast majority of the implementation code. Whenever this implementation code needs to find out the last primary key that was auto-generated by the database, it calls the `getIdentitySql()` method and executes the returned command. In this way, we can provide implementations of this method that are specific to a particular database. This is exactly what is done by the `JdbcMysqlEntryDao` class, as shown in Listing 11-13.

Listing 11-13. *Implementing DB-Specific Functionality*

```
package com.apress.prospring.data.jdbc;

public class JdbcMysqlEntryDao extends JdbcAbstractEntryDao {

    protected String getIdentitySql () {
        return "select LAST_INSERT_ID()";
    }
}
```

Note that we have not removed any code here; that is all there is to this class. Now if we want to move the `EntryDao` to another database system, all we need to do is create a new class, derived from `JdbcAbstractEntryDao`, and implement `getIdentitySql()` as appropriate.

DAO Granularity

When deciding how to structure your DAO interfaces, definitely avoid creating one DAO per Domain Object and one DAO per table. Sometimes, these structures appear naturally after thoughtful design, but don't assume that either one of these structures is necessarily the best.

A big problem we often see with projects is the "one DAO per table" problem. When you define a structure like this, you end up with DAOs representing join tables that serve no purpose other than to join two other tables in a many-to-many relationship. Plus, you often find that you have to pass a single Domain Object to lots of different DAOs to have the data persisted.

This is a classic example of letting the database drive the design of your DAO layer. This is something that, in practice, we have found to be a bad idea. The purpose of a DAO is to map Domain Objects to the database and vice versa. Because the bulk of your application is interacting with the Domain Objects, not the database, it makes sense to let the DOM drive database design. Let your DAOs hide the complexity of mapping the data in your Domain Objects to the database; that is their job. You are trying to avoid the situation where persisting a Domain Object requires you to interact with many different DAOs. Situations like this arise naturally, such as when a Domain Object has a reference to another Domain Object of a different type, and both have been modified, and thus need to be persisted. In this case, you can encapsulate that logic in your service layer, but you do not need to create this problem artificially.

So then you might wonder if you should let the DOM drive the design of the DAOs. Well, yes and no. Yes, in that the purpose of the DOM is to get DOM data into and out of the persistent data store so it makes sense to let the DOM act as the driver. No, in that blindly creating one DAO per Domain Object leads to a situation where the persistence of one *logical* unit of data leads to calls to many different DAOs. Consider our earlier example of the Order and OrderLine objects that are created from the Cart and CartItem objects. Because it is unlikely that you are going to want to save or retrieve OrderLine objects without doing the same to an Order object, it makes sense to encapsulate persistence logic for both Domain Objects in a single OrderDao, rather than create OrderDao and OrderLineDao.

Navigating Domain Object Relationships

A problem that we often find when talking to other developers is that they are unsure of when to navigate Domain Object relationships in their DAOs, especially when loading data from the database. Consider the situation in the SpringBlog application of the Entry and Attachment objects. As shown in Figure 11-1, a single Entry can contain many Attachment objects. So the question here is should you load the related Attachment objects when you are loading the Entry objects? Again, the answer is yes and no. We once worked on a project where the developer of the DAO objects had blindly loaded all related data, regardless of whether that data was to be used or not. This led to hundreds of needless database calls being made and hundreds of needless objects being created. There is nothing wrong with loading related data, but only do so when you need to.

In the case of the SpringBlog application, we have the EntryDao.getAll() method that returns a list of all blog entries. We are going to use this method to provide a simple list of entries, with no consideration for the attachments at all. In this case, loading the attachment data from the database and creating corresponding Attachment objects for every Entry is an unnecessary overhead. On the flipside, we also have the EntryDao.getById() method, which loads a single Entry object from the database. SpringBlog uses this method when displaying the full entry along with all comments and attachments. In this case, we *do* want to get the list of attachments for the entry, so we load the list from the database. Listing 11-14 shows a snippet (we have left a *substantial* amount of the code out here!) of code from the JDBC-based implementation of EntryDao, JdbcAbstractEntryDao.

Listing 11-14. *Loading Related Data in a DAO*

```
package com.apress.prospring.data.jdbc;

import java.sql.ResultSet;
import java.sql.SQLException;
import java.sql.Types;
import java.util.List;

import javax.sql.DataSource;
```

```
import org.springframework.beans.factory.InitializingBean;
import org.springframework.jdbc.core.SqlParameter;
import org.springframework.jdbc.core.support.JdbcDaoSupport;
import org.springframework.jdbc.object.MappingSqlQuery;
import org.springframework.jdbc.object.SqlUpdate;

import com.apress.prospring.data.AttachmentDao;
import com.apress.prospring.data.CommentDao;
import com.apress.prospring.data.EntryDao;
import com.apress.prospring.domain.Entry;

    private CommentDao commentDao;

    private AttachmentDao attachmentDao;

    private SelectById selectById;

    private SelectAll selectAll;

    public void setCommentDao(CommentDao commentDao) {
        this.commentDao = commentDao;
    }

    public void setAttachmentDao(AttachmentDao attachmentDao) {
        this.attachmentDao = attachmentDao;
    }

    protected void initDao() throws Exception {
        super.initDao();

        selectById = new SelectById(getDataSource());
    }

    public Entry getById(int entryId) {
        Entry e = (Entry) selectById.findObject(entryId);
        e.setComments(commentDao.getByEntry(e.getEntryId()));
        e.setAttachments(attachmentDao.getByEntry(e.getEntryId()));
        return e;
    }

    public List getAll() {
        return selectAll.execute();
    }
}
```

As you can see, the getAll() method simply loads the List of Entry objects and returns it to the caller. However, in the getById() method, the Entry object is loaded and then populated with the List of Attachment objects using an implementation of AttachmentDao. By being selective about the data we load, and by not loading related data needlessly, we can increase the performance of our application without affecting the functionality.

The code in Listing 11-14 does raise an interesting question though: how should you go about loading related data? Well, essentially, there are two options. The first is to embed the code inside the DAO of the parent Domain Object; the second is to have the DAO of the parent Domain Object use the DAO of the child Domain Object. Both of these approaches are valid, but they are aimed at different scenarios. We tend to use the first approach when the child Domain Object is entirely dependent on the parent Domain Object. The Order and OrderLine structure is an example of this kind of relationship. In most systems we have worked on, it doesn't really make sense to work with OrderLines outside the context of a containing Order. Listing 11-15 shows a snippet of code from the jPetStore sample application supplied with Spring.

Listing 11-15. *Loading Child Data in Parent DAO*

```
package org.springframework.samples.jpetstore.dao.ibatis;

import java.util.List;

import org.springframework.dao.DataAccessException;aff
import org.springframework.orm.ibatis.support.SqlMapDaoSupport;
import org.springframework.samples.jpetstore.dao.OrderDao;
import org.springframework.samples.jpetstore.domain.LineItem;
import org.springframework.samples.jpetstore.domain.Order;

public class SqlMapOrderDao extends SqlMapDaoSupport implements OrderDao {

    public List getOrdersByUsername(String username) throws DataAccessException {
    return getSqlMapTemplate().executeQueryForList(
                                    "getOrdersByUsername", username);
  }

  public Order getOrder(int orderId) throws DataAccessException {
    Object parameterObject = new Integer(orderId);
    Order order = (Order) getSqlMapTemplate().executeQueryForObject(
                        "getOrder", parameterObject);
        if (order != null) {
        order.setLineItems(getSqlMapTemplate().executeQueryForList(
                        "getLineItemsByOrderId", new Integer(order.getOrderId())));
        }
    return order;
  }

 /* omitted for brevity */

}
```

In this code, you can see that the getOrdersByUsername() method loads just the Order objects, whereas the getOrder() method loads the Order object and its associated OrderLines. The logic for loading OrderLine objects is contained in this DAO, not in a DAO specific to the OrderLine object; indeed, no such DAO exists. This implementation approach works well when the child Domain Object is completely dependent on the parent, but when this is not the case, the second approach—having the DAO of the parent Domain Object use the DAO of the child Domain Object—is better.

In the SpringBlog application, we chose to create a specific DAO for the `Attachment` object and then have `EntryDao` and `CommentDao` implementations use this DAO. There are two reasons for this decision. First, an `Attachment` is a child of either an `Entry` or a `Comment`. Using the first approach means that we have to duplicate code for inserting, updating, and deleting `Attachments` across `EntryDao` and `CommentDao` implementations. Refactoring this naturally leads to creating an `AttachmentDao` anyway. Second, we want to be able to manipulate `Attachments` separately from all other objects; a separate DAO is logical anyway.

Nothing is stopping you from being selective about when you load related data and when you do not. For Domain Objects that form a clear parent/child hierarchy with the child completely dependent on the parent, you should choose to encapsulate all DAO logic within the DAO of the parent object. For Domain Objects that do not form this clear relationship or have multiple parents, you should create a separate DAO and use this from within the DAO of the parent object.

Canonicalization and Data Access

Earlier in the chapter we talked about canonicalization and looked at how to implement this in your DOM. Obviously, the lack of a public constructor on a canonicalized Domain Object is going to have an impact on your DAO objects. In this section, we discuss the problems you face when building a DAO for canonicalized Domain Objects.

The first thing to consider when using canonicalization with Domain Objects is identity. If you recall the `ShippingCompany` example presented earlier in Listing 11-9, you will remember that client code can access an instance of `ShippingCompany` using the static `fromInt()` method. Each instance of `ShippingCompany` is given a unique ID that the `fromInt()` method uses to find the appropriate instance. When canonicalizing Domain Objects that are stored in the database, ensure that the appropriate ID is stored in the database to allow you to retrieve the correct `ShippingCompany` instance. In the case of the `ShippingCompany` object, our typical approach is to create a table in the database, `ShippingCompanies`, and then have the primary key field correspond to the ID of the correct `ShippingCompany` object. You don't actually need to create a table in the database when you are using canonicalized objects, but we would recommend it because you can use foreign key constraints to enforce referential integrity in the database. Consider an `Order` object that has a property, `shippedBy`, of type `ShippingCompany`. Without the `ShippingCompanies` table and a foreign key constraint between that table and the `Orders` table, it is possible to store any value in the `shippedBy` column of the `Orders` table.

If you choose to use JDBC to build your DAO objects, using canonicalization should not really have much of an impact. Because you are responsible for creating Domain Objects in the DAO, you can simply switch from using the Domain Object constructor to using the static `fromInt()` method to obtain the appropriate canonicalized object. When using ORM tools such as Hibernate or iBATIS, things become a little less clear-cut.

Hibernate does provide support for canonicalization through the use of the `PersistentEnum` interface, which has your Domain Object implement a structure very similar to that of the `ShippingCompany` object. However, you may be uncomfortable coupling your Domain Objects so closely to a particular persistence technology, especially after you have gone to the trouble of creating a separate DAO that is abstracted by a set of well-defined interfaces. If you are planning on committing to Hibernate long-term, then you may not see this as a big issue, but think carefully about committing to this solution. If you are using iBATIS, then you are completely out of luck; it does not support canonicalization at all. Thankfully, there is an easy solution when your ORM tool either requires too close a coupling for canonicalization or just doesn't support it all—use JDBC.

With Spring support, using JDBC is so simple that you should not discount it because of its complexity. However, if you have chosen to use a particular ORM tool, then you may be reluctant to start replacing entire DAO implementations with JDBC-based ones—so are we. The problem arises when you start to look at having both JDBC and, for instance, Hibernate code in a single class; you lose out on Spring support for one or the other because your DAO can only extend either HibernateDaoSupport or JdbcDaoSupport. Thankfully, there is quite an elegant solution to this problem that allows you to encapsulate both Hibernate and JDBC support in a single DAO without losing out on Spring support for both. The key to this is to factor the JDBC code into an inner class and then delegate calls from the main DAO to this inner class. An example of this is shown in Listing 11-16.

Listing 11-16. *Mixing Hibernate and JDBC in a Single DAO*

```
package com.apress.prospring.ch11.canonicalization;

import org.springframework.jdbc.core.support.JdbcDaoSupport;
import org.springframework.orm.hibernate.support.HibernateDaoSupport;

public class MyDao extends HibernateDaoSupport {

    private MyJdbcDao innerDao;

    public MyDao() {
        innerDao = new MyJdbcDao();
    }

    public void update(MyDomainObject obj) {
        // use Hibernate to persist the data
    }

    public MyDomainObject getById(int someId) {
        return innerDao.getBy(someId);
    }

    private static class MyJdbcDao extends JdbcDaoSupport {

        public MyDomainObject getBy(int someId) {
            // do some real processing
            return null;
        }
    }
}
```

Although this is only a skeleton implementation, you should get the gist. All the JDBC-related code is moved into an inner class that extends `JdbcDaoSupport` whereas all the Hibernate-related functionality is left in the outer class that can still extend `HibernateDaoSupport`. With this class, we can still use Hibernate for persisting Domain Objects, but we can redirect querying calls to the embedded JDBC DAO class.

Utilizing canonicalization effectively in your application can lead to greatly improved memory usage by preventing the creation of vast amounts of needless objects. If you must be able to update data related to canonicalized objects and you are using an ORM framework for your DAO objects, then you can introduce a little JDBC code to add canonicalization support in an ORM framework-independent manner.

Data Access Tier Summary

Creating a Data Access Tier for your application provides the rest of your application components with a standard mechanism for storing and retrieving data. Without a Data Access Tier, you will find that data access code becomes spread out through your application, often resulting in code duplication that is hard to maintain. In the long term, this poorly managed code inevitably leads to bugs and developer headaches.

The DAO pattern provides a good base from which to implement your Data Access Tier. You should always define DAOs as interfaces and then implement these interfaces using your chosen data access technology. When you are using Spring, working with interfaces is trivial and you can easily provide concrete implementations of your DAO interfaces to other components in your application.

In this section, we looked at some of the main design-related issues that are present when you are building a Data Access Tier for your application. In reality, much of the complexity in a Data Access Tier comes from implementation, not design. You can find more details on data access in Chapters 8, 9, and 10 where we discuss JDBC, Hibernate, and iBATIS, respectively.

Designing the Business Tier

At this point in our application design discussion, we have a way of representing the data in our problem domain so that we can manipulate it in code, and we have a way of storing this data in a database and then getting it back out later on. However, currently we are not doing much with this data. Unless your application is especially simplistic, chances are, some kind of logic is going to need implementing. Earlier on, we discussed cases where you should encapsulate logic inside your Domain Objects. In this section, we look at providing a layer of **service objects** to provide a standard interface to the rest of your application logic.

Why Have a Business Tier?

As with the question as to why you should have a Data Access Tier, the answer to this question is plain and simple once you have implemented a few applications without one. If you do not bring together all business logic in a single place, it ends up spread out through your presentation code, typically resulting in lots of code duplication, not to mention creating code that lacks clearly-defined boundaries for responsibilities. Code duplication issues aside, failure to define clear boundaries between code with different responsibilities often results in code that is difficult to debug, because it becomes hard to pinpoint the location of a given function.

A well-defined business layer acts as a sort of gateway into your application, providing your presentation code with a simple, unified way to get at business logic. A good business layer also serves as a definition of what your application can actually perform and what logic is available to be presented to the user.

A significant drawback of not having a Business Tier comes about when you decide to have two kinds of user interface for the same logic. Perhaps you built a web application, but now you want to provide a desktop-based application for users who use the application often. If your business logic code is intertwined with your web presentation code, you are either going to have to refactor the code out of the Presentation Tier, which requires a significant amount of effort in rework and testing, or simply reproduce the business logic code again, this time intertwined with your Swing or SWT code.

We cannot emphasize enough the importance of building a solid Business Tier. Without one, you are setting up your project for failure. Inevitably, the inability to access business logic centrally within an application leads to bugs, maintenance headaches, and unhappy customers.

Designing Business Interfaces

As with most components in your application, you should start by defining a set of interfaces for the service objects in your application. Any code that interacts with your Business Tier should do so through these interfaces. For components that Spring manages, you can supply implementations using DI. If you have to support components Spring does not manage, you may want to supply a simple Factory class to allow for implementation lookup.

Business Tier Dependencies

As with all the interfaces we have talked about, you should avoid defining dependencies in the interfaces of your service objects. The service object should be completely implementation-independent. A well-defined service object interface only has methods that serve business functions. Avoid exposing types from your Data Access Tier through your service objects. Your service objects should insulate the presentation code from the underlying Data Access Tier completely. What is to say that you will be using DAOs anyway? One of your service objects might access all its data using web services or via a JMS queue. A good way to ensure that your service object interface is as accessible as possible is to ensure that return and argument types do not couple the presentation code to anything other than the DOM (and of course Java types!). You are going to be passing Domain Objects through all the tiers of your application, but other components such as DAOs should stay well within their own tiers.

Using Abstract Base Implementations

When building a service object implementation, we always find it useful to create an abstract base class to store all the dependencies. This has two benefits: first, we don't need to define all the dependencies again if all we are doing is changing the implementation; and second, the final implementation class is fully focused on business logic, without the clutter of a bunch of setters for dependency injection. For instance, in the SpringBlog application, we create the AbstractDaoBasedBlogManager class to hold all the DAO dependencies (see Listing 11-17).

Listing 11-17. *The AbstractDaoBasedBlogManager Class*

```
package com.apress.prospring.business;

import com.apress.prospring.data.AttachmentDao;
import com.apress.prospring.data.CommentDao;
import com.apress.prospring.data.EntryDao;
import com.apress.prospring.data.UserDao;

public abstract class AbstractDaoBasedBlogManager implements BlogManager {

    protected UserDao userDao;

    protected EntryDao entryDao;

    protected AttachmentDao attachmentDao;

    protected CommentDao commentDao;

    public void setUserDao(UserDao dao) {
        this.userDao = dao;
    }

    public void setEntryDao(EntryDao dao) {
        this.entryDao = dao;
    }

    public void setAttachmentDao(AttachmentDao dao) {
        this.attachmentDao = dao;
    }

    public void setCommentDao(CommentDao dao) {
        this.commentDao = dao;
    }
}
```

Here you can see that we defined four properties for the DAOs needed by any BlogManager implementation that accesses blog data from the database. If we had a BlogManager that accessed data from XML, we could have defined AbstractXmlBlogManager or AbstractWebServiceBlogManager for a BlogManager that accessed data using web services.

When doing this, only define the dependencies that you know are going to be common to all implementations. It is clear that, if we are creating a base class for all DAO-based BlogManager implementations, then the DAOs are going to be dependencies. When you look at the actual implementation of BlogManager we created, you will see that we actually define another dependency there, one that may not be relevant to all DAO-based implementations.

Service Object Granularity

Something that many developers find quite hard at first, but that is actually quite easy once you are familiar with it, is creating service objects with the correct granularity. The first thing I always tell my developers is that there really is no **correct** level of granularity for service objects. Many different levels of granularity work just as well as each other. However, I also tell my developers that there is a **preferred** level of granularity, and this is the level that makes the service objects simple to use **and** maintain.

For a small application like SpringBlog, a single service object is usually all you need; anything else is overkill and adds unnecessary complexity. In this case, we define application size by the number of business functions an application must perform and the number of logical groups these functions fall into. When you have a larger application with many functions or function groups, this is the time to split these into separate service objects.

Splitting your business functions into different service objects is usually a fairly intuitive process. We start by looking at the collective set of functions and then grouping them into logical sets. For instance, we might have ordering functions, product catalogue functions, and account management functions. From this, we can then create the service object interfaces: OrderManager, ProductManager, and AccountManager in this example. Then we simply define each function in the appropriate service object.

Remember, there is really no right and wrong answer when you are designing service object interfaces. What you are looking for is a set of easy-to-work-with interfaces. If you are going to be writing a lot of code to interact with your business logic layer, you want your service objects to be logically ordered and simple to use.

The DefaultBlogManager Implementation

The SpringBlog doesn't really have too much business logic. Much of the code in the Business Tier is simply acting as a middleman between the presentation code and the Data Access Tier. However, some bits of logic, such as the login code and the auditing code, are of interest.

■**NOTE** Although we have implemented a simple login() method in the DefaultBlogManager class, that is as far as we take any concept of security or user identity in this example application. We did not want to muddy the waters with security issues when we look at the web front end later on. As we write this, an interesting security framework designed specifically for Spring, Acegi, is currently in development. You can check out the website at http://acegisecurity.sourceforge.net/ to see how this project is progressing. Hopefully, this framework will be released by the time the second edition comes around so that we can cover it in some detail.

Listing 11-18 shows the full code for the DefaultBlogManager implementation.

Listing 11-18. *The DefaultBlogManager Class*

```java
package com.apress.prospring.business;

import java.util.Date;
import java.util.List;

import org.springframework.beans.factory.InitializingBean;

import com.apress.prospring.domain.Attachment;
import com.apress.prospring.domain.Comment;
import com.apress.prospring.domain.Entry;
import com.apress.prospring.domain.User;

public class DefaultBlogManager extends AbstractDaoBasedBlogManager implements
        InitializingBean {

    private AuditService auditService;

    public void afterPropertiesSet() throws Exception {
        if (auditService == null) {
            auditService = new DefaultAuditService();
        }
    }

    public void setAuditService(AuditService auditService) {
        this.auditService = auditService;
    }

    public User login(String username, String password)
            throws InvalidCredentialsException {
        User user = userDao.getByUsernameAndPassword(username, password);

        if (user == null) {
            throw new InvalidCredentialsException(
      "The credentials you supplied do not match a known user profile. Try again");
        } else {
            return user;
        }
    }

    public List getMostRecentEntries() {
        return entryDao.getMostRecent(100);
    }

    public List getAllEntries() {
        return entryDao.getAll();
    }
```

```java
public Entry getEntry(int entryId) {
    return entryDao.getById(entryId);
}

public void deleteEntry(int entryId) {
    entryDao.delete(entryId);
    auditService.writeAuditMessage("Entry Id " + entryId + " deleted.",
            User.ROOT);
}

public void saveEntry(Entry entry) {

    if (entry.getEntryId() <= 0) {
        // new entry - make sure
        // post date is set
        entry.setPostDate(new Date());
    }

    entryDao.save(entry);
    auditService.writeAuditMessage("Entry " + entry + " saved", User.ROOT);
}

public void saveComment(Comment comment, User postingUser) {
    comment.setPostedBy(postingUser);

    if (comment.getCommentId() <= 0) {
        // this is a new comment
        comment.setPostDate(new Date());
    }

    commentDao.save(comment);
    auditService.writeAuditMessage("Comment " + comment + " saved.",
            postingUser);
}

public List getEntryAttachments(int entryId) {
    return attachmentDao.getByEntry(entryId);
}

public void attachToEntry(Attachment attachment, int entryId) {
    attachmentDao.insertEntryAttachment(attachment, entryId);
}

public void attachToComment(Attachment attachment, int commentId) {
    attachmentDao.insertCommentAttachment(attachment, commentId);
}
```

```
    public Comment getComment(int commentId) {
        return commentDao.getById(commentId);
    }

    public void deleteComment(int commentId) {
        commentDao.delete(commentId);
        auditService.writeAuditMessage("Comment: " + commentId + " deleted.",
                User.ROOT);
    }

    public List getAllUsers() {
        return userDao.getAll();
    }
}
```

This code shouldn't really need explaining—most of the logic is fairly basic—but there are three things of interest here. First, notice that in some of the methods, such as saveComment() and saveEntry(), we use an AuditService object to create an audit of actions being performed in the database. Originally, we had a private audit() method in the DefaultBlogManager class, but this played havoc with testing, so we refactored it into a new service object. We talk about the reasons behind this decision in greater detail in the next section.

Second, notice that we throw a checked exception for the login() method when a user provides invalid credentials. The reason is simple—this is a recoverable error. In a rich client application, the exception can be caught and the login dialog can be shown again. For a web application, the exception is caught and the user is redirected back to the login page. In this case, using a checked exception is valid and desirable, because it serves as a gentle nudge to code in the Presentation Tier to handle invalid logins correctly.

Finally, you may notice the distinct lack of validation code in this example. We have not forgotten about validation code; it just sits elsewhere in our application. We discuss validation is more detail later in the chapter.

Services Used by Service Objects

It is not uncommon for a service object to require some services itself. The question is whether you should create separate service objects for these services or not. Clearly, if more than one of your service objects needs the same shared service, then you should create another service, but what if only one service object needs the service?

Consider the case of the DefaultBlogManager class in SpringBlog. This class needs to log audit messages whenever an action is taken that modifies the comment or entry data in the database. Originally we had this logic encapsulated in the DefaultBlogManager.audit() method and we used an implementation of AuditDao to store the audit messages in the database. At face value, this approach was fine, but it did cause us some problems in testing. The problem we faced was reliably testing that DefaultBlogManager did in fact invoke audit() when it was supposed to.

The simplest way to do this is to count the number of audit records in the database before invoking a method on DefaultBlogManager and then count them after, checking to see that the number has increased. This is an okay solution, but a better solution would not require database access at all. Adding too many tests that need to query the database really slows down the test run, and this leads to situations where developers stop running tests because they take too long. We overcame this problem by refactoring the audit code into a separate service object behind the AuditService interface shown in Listing 11-19.

Listing 11-19. *The AuditService Interface*

```
package com.apress.prospring.business;

import java.util.Date;

import com.apress.prospring.domain.User;

public interface AuditService {

    public void writeAuditMessage(String data, User user);
    public void purgeAudit(Date oldestDate);
}
```

The default implementation of this interface simply uses AuditDao to store the data in the database. Where this interface becomes useful is in testing. To test that the DefaultBlogManager class is correctly invoking the audit service, we can create a mock implementation of AuditService that counts calls to writeAuditMessage(). In this way, we can accurately determine whether or not the AuditService has been invoked without having to query the database. Because we are not relying on the database at all, we can also pass mock implementations of EntryDao and CommentDao to DefaultBlogManager when testing whether we can reduce the runtime of the tests even more. Listing 11-20 shows the JUnit test that we created to test audit usage.

Listing 11-20. *Testing AuditService Usage*

```
package com.apress.prospring.business;

import java.util.Date;
import java.util.List;

import junit.framework.TestCase;

import com.apress.prospring.data.CommentDao;
import com.apress.prospring.data.EntryDao;
import com.apress.prospring.domain.Comment;
import com.apress.prospring.domain.Entry;
import com.apress.prospring.domain.User;

public class AuditInvokedTest extends TestCase {

    private DefaultBlogManager bm = new DefaultBlogManager();

    private CommentDao commentDao = new MockCommentDao();
```

```java
    private EntryDao entryDao = new MockEntryDao();

    private MockAuditService auditService;

    public AuditInvokedTest() {
        bm.setCommentDao(commentDao);
        bm.setEntryDao(entryDao);
    }

    public void setUp() {
        auditService = new MockAuditService();
        bm.setAuditService(auditService);
    }

    public void testSaveEntry() {
        bm.saveEntry(new Entry());
        performAssert();
    }

    public void testSaveComment() {
        bm.saveComment(new Comment(), new User());
        performAssert();
    }

    private void performAssert() {
        assertEquals("The Audit Service was not invoked",
                                    1, auditService.callCount);
    }

    private class MockAuditService implements AuditService {
        private int callCount = 0;

        public void writeAuditMessage(String data, User user) {
            callCount++;
        }

        public void purgeAudit(Date oldestDate) {

        }

        public int getCallCount() {
            return callCount;
        }
    }

    /* MockCommentDao and MockEntryDao omitted for clarity */

}
```

By using a testing strategy like this, we make it so that we are not dependent on the database to perform a test that has little to do with the database, plus we are keeping test runtimes down, thus reducing the chance that developers will just stop running them. When building any part of your application, be on the lookout for chances to refactor that will improve your ability to test the application. Even if you already have a test for a particular case, you may be able to remove a dependency on the database or on another expensive-to-use component by refactoring parts of your application.

Assembling Domain Object Relationships in the Business Tier

A common practice that we see in many applications is to assemble Domain Object relationships in the Business Tier. This isn't necessarily a bad practice, but you should think about how you are defining the responsibilities of your components. If you find yourself constantly making multiple DAO calls to assemble the same Domain Object relationships in your Business Tier, then this is really a data loading issue and should be moved into the Data Access Tier. However, in some cases, you may need to assemble a large number of Domain Objects into a complex relationship, perhaps to support a reporting or data extraction process, and then this might be more suitably performed in the Business Tier.

When deciding where to assemble Domain Object relationships, I usually ask myself two questions: "Is this relationship typical of how the data is accessed throughout the application?" and "Am I assembling this relationship to support some special business process?" Most relationships, such as the Order and OrderLine relationship, are typical to how those Domain Objects are used in the application; these relationships should be assembled in the Data Access Tier. Other relationships, such as relating Order, OrderLine, User, and Product to support a reporting process, are not typical of the way Order data or Product data is usually loaded from the database, so you would be better off assembling this relationship in the Business Tier.

Business Method Granularity

When designing service interfaces, pay attention to the granularity of your methods. Remember that the responsibility of a service interface is to expose the business functions your application performs to presentation code; the natural level of granularity for methods in a service interface is one per business operation. Sometimes you will have operations that you can invoke individually or as part of a larger operation. In this case, create methods for the smaller and larger operations, and have the larger operation invoke the smaller operation as required.

We often think that many teams spend far too much time worrying about business method granularity. We find that one method per logical business operation provides the simplest and most flexible interface into the business logic of our application.

Transaction Boundaries

One factor that does place additional considerations on the granularity of your business methods is transaction demarcation. If you plan to use the declarative transaction management functions in Spring, then you will be controlling the applicability of transactions at the method level. Although you don't have to apply transactions to your service objects—you can do this at the DAO level—we find it better to mark transactions in the Business Tier; that way, we can integrate as many calls to as many DAOs as we want into a single transaction.

Using the declarative transactions functions in Spring, the methods of your business interfaces serve as boundaries for your transactions. For each method, you can tell Spring that it
must run in a transaction context. If you have methods that can be called individually or as part
of larger transactions, then you can have Spring enlist these methods in existing transactions
or create new ones when a transaction does not exist. Remember, though, for this to work, the
method associated with the smaller operation must be invoked in the control flow of the method
that started the transaction. This means that you cannot invoke methods `foo()` and `bar()` from
your presentation code and expect them to share the same transaction (unless you mark the
transaction in the presentation code, which isn't recommended). Chapter 12 presents a fuller
discussion of the issues surrounding transaction management.

Implementing Validation Logic

A distinct part of the business logic of any application is the logic used to validate the data
provided by the application's users. After all, users are only human, and inevitably, one of them
will make a mistake and enter invalid data. If you fail to validate data as it enters your system,
you are left with bad data floating around, poised to wreak havoc with your finely crafted business logic. The common problem we see with validation logic is that many teams just do not
bother, mainly because writing it is so darn repetitive. However, it is the lesser of two evils
compared to late nights spent debugging your application due to bad data, and thankfully,
many utilities are now available to ease the burden of creating validation logic.

In this section, we explore the validation support in Spring and some of features offered by
the Commons Validator, and we take a quick peek at what features will be available validation-
wise in the next release of Spring.

Where to Call Validation?

Before we start discussing validation support, we should first look at where in your application
you should call your validation code. You may have noticed that we did not call any validation
code in our `DefaultBlogManager`, and you may be wondering why. The reason for this is simple—we
are going to have the Spring MVC framework invoke our validation logic for us. You will almost
always want to perform some kind of validation in the Presentation Tier (remember that one of
the responsibilities of the Presentation Tier is to process user input) so that you can handle bad
data directly and show some kind of error message. If you are only going to have a single front
end for your application then you should invoke your validation logic here; the closer your validation logic is to the presentation code, the easier it is to provide useful feedback to the user.

For applications that have multiple front ends, you will still want to invoke the validation
logic from the presentation code of each front end, but you may also want to call it from your
service objects as well, to serve as a sort of second line of defense against any misbehaved user
interfaces.

Whichever approach you choose, always factor your validation logic into a distinct set of
objects. Avoid being tempted to interweave validation code with your presentation code, because
this makes adding additional user interfaces very difficult and error prone, plus you will lose
out on the reusability that a centralized set of validation rules gives you.

Spring Support for Validation

The current version of Spring provides framework-level support for validation in the form of the Validator interface. When working with Spring, all your validation logic should be encapsulated in objects that implement the Validator interface, which is shown in Listing 11-21.

Listing 11-21. *The Spring Validator Interface*

```
package org.springframework.validation;

public interface Validator {

    boolean supports(Class clazz);

    void validate(Object obj, Errors errors);

}
```

Your Validator implementations indicate which classes they are capable of validating using the supports() method, and then they perform the actual validation in the validate() method. Your code uses the Errors object passed to validate() to define errors that are present in the object in question. The Spring framework then uses this data to render error messages in the Presentation Tier. Currently, only the Spring MVC framework has built-in support for the Validator interface, but in the future, we expect that the same interface will be used for validation in the Spring Rich Client Platform. We are not going to look at how Validators are used in Spring MVC in this section; instead, we focus on creating Validator implementations.

Validation in SpringBlog

Because SpringBlog is such a simple application, not much is required in the way of validation logic. However, we do perform simple validation on Comment and Entry objects that are to be added to the database. In Listing 11-22, you can see the Validator we created for the Entry object, EntryValidator.

Listing 11-22. *The EntryValidator Class*

```
package com.apress.prospring.business.validators;

import org.springframework.validation.Errors;
import org.springframework.validation.ValidationUtils;
import org.springframework.validation.Validator;

import com.apress.prospring.domain.Entry;

public class EntryValidator implements Validator {

    public boolean supports(Class clazz) {
        return clazz.isAssignableFrom(Entry.class);
    }
```

```
public void validate(Object obj, Errors errors) {
    Entry entry = (Entry) obj;

    ValidationUtils.rejectIfEmptyOrWhitespace(errors, "subject",
            "required", null, "required");

    ValidationUtils.rejectIfEmptyOrWhitespace(errors, "body", "required",
            null, "required");
}

}
```

Here you can see that we use the ValidationUtils class to validate that both the subject and body properties of the Entry object are supplied, that they are not empty, and that they do not contain just whitespace. You may be wondering how the ValidationUtils class accesses the value of those properties. They are stored in the Errors object that is passed in and can be accessed using Errors.getFieldValue(). The second argument passed to the rejectIfEmptyOrWhitespace() method is the error code. Spring uses this value to look up the error message to display from a ResourceBundle containing individual properties files for each language you wish to support. Listing 11-23 shows an example of the English property file used in the SpringBlog application.

Listing 11-23. *Internationalized Error Messages*

```
required=This field is required and cannot be empty
```

You will see how to go about configuring the ResourceBundle and your Validators in Chapter 17. The third argument passed to rejectIfEmptyOrWhitespace(), for which we have used null, allows you to pass arguments, as an Object[], to the Spring framework, the elements of which will be replaced for tokens in the error message. For instance, in the message "Hello {0}", the token {0} would be replaced with the 0th element in the Object[]. The final argument passed to rejectIfEmptyOrWhitespace() is the default error message to render if no error message can be found in the ResourceBundle.

This is about as complex as our validation logic gets, and unfortunately, the rejectIfEmptyOrWhitespace() method is about as much help as you are going to get from the current version of Spring. However, don't worry, plenty of tools can help you to implement more complex validation logic, such as Commons Validator, which is covered briefly in the next section.

Using Commons Validator

Commons Validator, available at http://jakarta.apache.org/commons/validator, provides a wide range of validation utilities for many different data types, ranging from different numerics like double and int, to credit card numbers and e-mail addresses. Before starting to create your own routines for validation, first explore what is available in Commons Validator. We have found that for 90 percent of the cases in our applications, Commons Validator has a prebuilt validation routine we can use.

What's in Store for Validation?

There is a lot of work underway to improve validation support in Spring. The first notable addition in the next release will be full integration of Commons Validator, including support for externally defined validation rules that are implemented using Commons Validator and a JSP taglib to add client-side validation in JavaScript using the Commons Validator JavaScript support. The second, although not yet confirmed, addition is rules-based validation. Work is currently underway to add rules support to Spring, and there has been much discussion on providing a `Validator` implementation that uses a rule set as the source for validation rules.

Business Tier Summary

In this section, we looked at the various points you should consider when designing and building a Business Tier for your Spring application. We looked at the SpringBlog Business Tier, and explored how small refactorings in your Business Tier can substantially improve the testability of your application. When looking at method granularity, we discussed the natural granularity level of methods and we considered the impact that transaction demarcation has on your business interfaces. Finally, we finished this section by discussing validation and Spring support for it.

Overall, Spring doesn't provide much in the way of implementing actual business logic, but its support for Dependency Injection, validation, and transaction management make it an ideal platform on which to build your Business Tier.

Summary

In this chapter, we looked at a lot of problems associated with traditional applications and we saw how Spring can help us solve these problems. We discussed a variety of different problems that occur during application development, and we looked at sensible ways in which these problems can be solved effectively. Throughout the chapter, we examined how the practices we discussed were used when we built the SpringBlog application, and we even took a peek at some of the code from the Spring sample applications to see how the principles we discussed were applied there.

This chapter only scratched the surface of application design as a whole, but we have honed in on the issues that are specific to Spring-based applications and problems that you can fix easily when using Spring. For a fuller discussion of application design, refer to the books mentioned throughout the chapter.

In the next chapter we present a detailed look at transaction support, including full examples of both local and distributed transactions and some useful tips for testing transactional methods.

■ ■ ■

CHAPTER 12

Transaction Management

Transactions are pivotal parts of a reliable enterprise application. The common belief is that transactions only relate to database work. The simplistic view of a transaction is begin transaction—SQL updates, deletes, and so on—followed by commit/rollback, but there's much more to transactions than this! In this chapter, we show you how to use declarative transactions rather than manually coded transactions, and how to span transactions across multiple transactional resources. Finally, we give you some hints on how to test transactional code.

Spring offers excellent support for declarative transactions, which means you do not need to clutter your code with transaction management code. All you have to do is declare that a method must participate in a transaction and that Spring will take care of handling the transaction management. To be more specific, in this chapter we look at the following:

Spring transaction abstraction layer: We discuss the base components of Spring transaction abstraction classes and explain how to use these classes to control the properties of the transactions.

Declarative transaction management: We show you how to use Spring to implement declarative transactional management using just plain Java objects. We offer examples for declarative transaction management using the configuration files as well as source level metadata.

Programmatic transaction management: Even though programmatic transactional management is not used very often, we explain how to use the PlatformTransactionManager interface, which gives you ultimate control over the transaction management code.

Transactions over multiple transactional resources: We also cover and give examples of how to use the JTATransactionManager, which allows you to include multiple transactional resources such as a database and message queue in a single transaction.

Exploring the Spring Transaction Abstraction Layer

Whether you use Spring or not, you have to make a fundamental choice when you use transactions—whether to use global or local transactions. Local transactions are specific to a single transactional resource (a JDBC connection, for example), whereas global transactions are managed by the container and can span multiple transactional resources.

Local transactions are easy to manage, and because most operations work with just one transactional resource (such as a JDBC transaction), using local transactions is enough. However, if you are not using Spring, you still have a lot of transaction management code to write, and if in the future the scope of the transaction needs to be extended across multiple transactional resources, you have to drop the local transaction management code and rewrite it to use global transactions.

Global transactions in non-Spring application are, in most cases, coded using JTA, which is a complex API that depends on JNDI. This means that you have to use a J2EE application server. Rather than implementing JTA transactions programmatically, you can use EJB Container Managed Transactions (CMT) functionality, which is provided by a J2EE application server. This allows you to simply declare which operations are to be enlisted in a transaction; once you do, the container takes care of transaction management. This is the preferred way because the code you write does not contain any explicit transactional code and all the hard work is delegated to the container. Another great advantage of EJB CMT is that it removes the need to work with the JTA API directly but, by definition, you still have to use EJBs.

Ideally, you have a container that supports a global and local declarative and programmatic transactions without needing EJBs. Even though declarative transactions are the favored approach, there can be a place for programmatic t ransactions.

Analyzing Transaction Properties

We start with a standard summary of a transaction description. However, keep in mind that all we are going to write about applies to more than just database operations. In most cases, it is true that a database is heavily involved, but nothing stops us from extending the concept of transactions from the database to other transactional resources.

Transactions have the four notoriously known ACID properties—atomicity, consistency, isolation, and durability—and it is up to the transactional resources to maintain these aspects of a transaction. You cannot control the atomicity, consistency, and durability of a transaction, but you can control the **transaction propagation** and **timeout**, which set whether the transaction should be **read-only** and specify the **isolation level**.

Spring encapsulates all these settings in a `TransactionDefinition` interface. This interface is used in the core interface of the transaction support in Spring, the `PlatfromTransactionManager`, whose implementations perform transaction management on a specific platform, such as JDBC or JTA. The core method, `PlatformTransactionManager.getTransaction()`, returns a `TransactionStatus` interface, which is used to control the transaction execution, more specifically to set the transaction result and to check whether the transaction is read-only or whether it is a new transaction.

Exploring the TransactionDefinition Interface

As we mentioned earlier, the `TransactionDefinition` interface controls the properties of a transaction. Let's take a more detailed look at `TransactionDefinition` interface (see Listing 12-1) and describe its methods.

Listing 12-1. *TransactionDefinition Interface*

```
package org.springframework.transaction;
import java.sql.Connection;
public interface TransactionDefinition {
    int getPropagationBehavior();
    int getIsolationLevel();
    int getTimeout();
    boolean isReadOnly();
}
```

The simple and obvious methods of this interface are getTimeout(), which returns the time (in seconds) in which the transaction must complete, and isReadOnly(), which indicates whether the transaction is read-only. The transaction manager implementation can use this value to optimize the execution and to check to make sure that the transaction is performing only reads.

The other two methods, getPropagationBehavior() and getIsolationLevel(), need to be discussed in more detail. We begin with getIsolationLevel(), which controls what changes to the data other transactions see. Table 12-1 lists the transaction isolation levels you can use and explains what changes made in the current transaction other transactions can access.

Table 12-1. *Transaction Isolation Levels*

Isolation Level	Description
TransactionDefinition.ISOLATION_DEFAULT	Default isolation level for individual PlatformTransactionManager.
TransactionDefinition.ISOLATION_READ_UNCOMMITTED	Lowest level of isolation; it is barely a transaction at all because it allows this transaction to see data modified by other uncommitted transactions.
TransactionDefinition.ISOLATION_READ_COMMITTED	Default level in some databases; it ensures that other transactions are not able to read data that has not been committed by other transactions. Unfortunately, you can select data **inserted** or **updated** by other transactions.
TransactionDefinition.ISOLATION_REPEATABLE_READ	More strict than ISOLATION_READ_COMMITED; it ensures that once you select data, you can select at least the same set again. This implies that if another transaction **inserts** new data, you can select the newly inserted data.
TransactionDefinition.ISOLATION_SERIALIZABLE	The most expensive and reliable isolation level; all transactions are treated as if they were executed one after another.

Choosing the appropriate isolation level is very important for the consistency of the data, but making these choices can have a great impact on performance. The highest isolation level, TransactionDefinition.ISOLATION_SERIALIZABLE, is particularly expensive to maintain.

The getPropagationBehavior() method specifies what happens to a transactional call depending on whether there is an active transaction. The values for this method are listed in Table 12-2.

Table 12-2. *Propagation Behavior Values*

Propagation Behavior	Description
TransactionDefinition.PROPAGATION_REQUIRED	Supports a transaction if one already exists. If there is no transaction, it starts a new one.
TransactionDefinition.PROPAGATION_SUPPORTS	Supports a transaction if one already exists. If there is no transaction, it executes non-transactionally.
TransactionDefinition.PROPAGATION_MANDATORY	Supports a transaction if one already exists. Throws an exception if there is no active transaction.
TransactionDefinition.PROPAGATION_REQUIRES_NEW	Always starts a new transaction. If an active transaction already exists, it is suspended.
TransactionDefinition.PROPAGATION_NOT_SUPPORTED	Does not support execution with an active transaction. Always executes non-transactionally and suspends any existing transaction.
TransactionDefinition.PROPAGATION_NEVER	Always executes non-transactionally even if an active transaction exists. Throws an exception if an active transaction exists.
TransactionDefinition.PROPAGATION_NESTED	Runs in a nested transaction if an active transaction exists. If there is no active transaction, the execution is executed as if TransactionDefinition.PROPAGATION_REQUIRED is set.

Using the TransactionStatus Interface

This interface, shown in Listing 12-2, allows a transactional manager to control the transaction execution. The code can check whether the transaction is a new one, or whether it is a read-only transaction and it can initiate a rollback.

Listing 12-2. *TransactionStatus Declaration*

```
public interface TransactionStatus {
    boolean isNewTransaction();
    void setRollbackOnly();
    boolean isRollbackOnly();
}
```

The methods of the TransactionStatus interface are fairly self-explanatory, the most notable one is setRollbackOnly(), which causes a rollback and ends the active transaction.

Implementations of the PlatformTransactionManager

This is an interface that uses the TransactionDefinition and TransactionStatus interfaces to create and manage transactions. The actual implementations of this interface must have detailed knowledge of the transaction manager. The DataSourceTransactionManager controls transactions performed within a DataSource; HibernateTransactionManager controls transactions performed on a Hibernate session, JdoTransactionManager manages JDO transactions, and JtaTransactionManager delegates transaction management to JTA.

Exploring a Transaction Management Sample

The first part of this chapter gave you a quick overview of the transaction infrastructure in Spring, but we are sure you will appreciate an example that demonstrates how to use Spring transaction support.

There are three basic ways to implement an operation that uses transactions: you can use declarative transactions, where you simply declare that a method requires a transaction, you can use source level metadata to indicate that a method requires a transaction, or you can actually write code that handles the transactions. Spring supports all three approaches; we begin with the most flexible and convenient one—declarative transaction management.

First we will show you several implementations of transaction support. Take a look at the UML diagram in Figure 12-1 to get a sense of what is in store in the Hello World application.

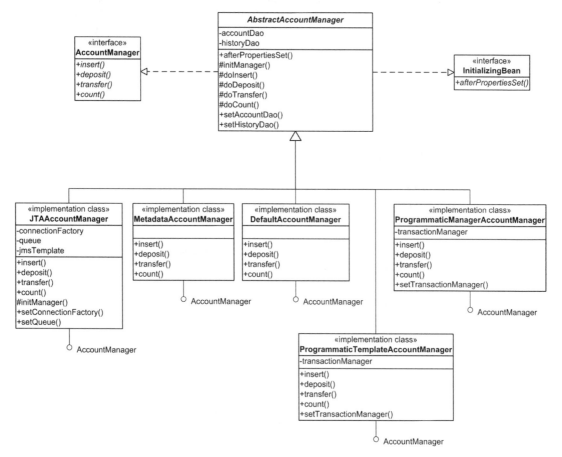

Figure 12-1. *UML diagram for the Hello World application*

AccountManager is the high-level interface we are going to use in our Main class. abstractAccountManager contains code that performs the operations of AccountManager's methods, but in protected methods, the implementation is prefixed with do. AbstractAccountManager has accountDao and historyDao fields and public setters for these DAO interfaces; it also implements InitializingBean.afterPropertiesSet() to check that the DAOs are not null. This method also calls initManager(), which is empty in AbstractAccountManager, but subclasses can override it to perform additional initialization.

As you can guess from the names of the implementation classes, DefaultAccountManager is the default implementation and it relies on declarative transaction specifications, MetadataAccountManager is an implementation that uses source level metadata to declare the transaction requirements, ProgrammaticTemplateAccountManager demonstrates usage of TransactionTemplate, ProgrammaticManagerAccountManager shows how to use PlatformTransactionManager, and finally, JTAAccountManager demonstrates how to use JTA to manage global transactions.

Working with Common Code

Let us begin with code that is common for all the transaction management models we are going to discuss. The example is going to use the well-known concept of bank accounts. In a transaction, each operation on an account is going to write a record to an account history for auditing purposes; a transfer between two accounts is in a transaction as well.

The Account and History tables are defined in the SQL script in Listing 12-3.

Listing 12-3. *Account and History SQL Script*

```
create table Accounts (
    AccountId serial not null,
    AccountNumber varchar(20) not null,
    SortCode varchar(10) not null,
    Balance decimal(10, 2) not null,
    constraint PK_AccountId primary key (AccountId)
);

create unique index IX_Accounts_NumberSortCode on Accounts
    using btree(AccountNumber, SortCode);

create table History (
    HistoryId serial not null,
    Account int not null,
    Operation varchar(50) not null,
    Amount decimal(10, 2) not null,
    TransactionDate timestamp not null,
    TargetAccount int null,
    constraint PK_HistoryId primary key (HistoryId),
    constraint FK_Account foreign key (Account) references Accounts(AccountId)
);
create index IX_History_Account on History using btree(Account);
```

   The data access layer for the tables created in the script above is a simple iBATIS implementation of the AccountDao and HistoryDao interfaces. The SqlMapClientAccountDao is a
standard AccountDao implementation, but HistoryDao has a bit of a twist. It is implemented in
UnreliableSqlMapClientHistoryDao and its insert() method randomly fails. The HistoryDao
and its implementation are shown in Listing 12-4. The reason why the insert() method throws
a RuntimeException randomly is to allow us to prove that only the successful transactions are
committed; the unsuccessful ones are rolled back.

Listing 12-4. *HistoryDao Interface and Implementation*

```
package com.apress.prospring.ch12.data;

// in HistoryDao.java:
import java.util.List;

import com.apress.prospring.ch12.domain.History;

public interface HistoryDao {
    public List getByAccount(int account);
    public History getById(int historyId);
    public void insert(History history);
}

// in UnreliableSqlClientMapHistoryDao
import java.util.List;
import java.util.Random;
import org.springframework.orm.ibatis.support.SqlMapClientDaoSupport;
import com.apress.prospring.ch12.domain.History;

public class UnreliableSqlMapClientHistoryDao
    extends SqlMapClientDaoSupport
    implements HistoryDao {

    private Random r = new Random();

    public List getByAccount(int account) {
        return null;
    }

    public History getById(int historyId) {
        return null;
    }

    public void insert(History history) {
        if (r.nextInt(100) % 3 == 0) {
            throw new RuntimeException("Foobar");
        }
```

```
        getSqlMapClientTemplate().insert("insertHistory", history);
    }

}
```

This HistoryDao implementation fails in about one third of all inserts. To complete the data access layer code, in Listing 12-5, we create an AccountManager interface.

Listing 12-5. *AccountManager Interface*

```
package com.apress.prospring.ch12.business;

import java.math.BigDecimal;

import com.apress.prospring.ch12.domain.Account;

public interface AccountManager {
    public void insert(Account account);
    public void deposit(int accountId, BigDecimal amount);
    public void transfer(int sourceAccount, int targetAccount, BigDecimal amount);
    public int count();
}
```

We use the methods of the interface to manipulate the accounts. The insert() method creates a new account, deposit() deposits a specified sum of money to the account, transfer() moves money between accounts, and finally count() returns the number of accounts in the database.

Finally, we implement AbstractAccountManager, which is going to be a convenient super-class (see Listing 12-6).

Listing 12-6. *AbstractAccountManager Implementation*

```
package com.apress.prospring.ch12.business;

import java.math.BigDecimal;
import java.util.Date;

import org.springframework.beans.factory.BeanCreationException;
import org.springframework.beans.factory.InitializingBean;

import com.apress.prospring.ch12.data.AccountDao;
import com.apress.prospring.ch12.data.HistoryDao;
import com.apress.prospring.ch12.domain.Account;
import com.apress.prospring.ch12.domain.History;

public abstract class AbstractAccountManager
    implements InitializingBean, AccountManager {
```

```java
private AccountDao accountDao;
private HistoryDao historyDao;

protected void doInsert(Account account) {
    getAccountDao().insert(account);
    History history = new History();
    history.setAccount(account.getAccountId());
    history.setAmount(account.getBalance());
    history.setOperation("Initial deposit");
    history.setTargetAccount(null);
    history.setTransactionDate(new Date());
    getHistoryDao().insert(history);
}

protected void doDeposit(int accountId, BigDecimal amount) {
    History history = new History();
    history.setAccount(accountId);
    history.setAmount(amount);
    history.setOperation("Deposit");
    history.setTargetAccount(null);
    history.setTransactionDate(new Date());

    getAccountDao().updateBalance(accountId, amount);
    getHistoryDao().insert(history);
}

protected void doTransfer(int sourceAccount,
    int targetAccount, BigDecimal amount) {
    Account source = getAccountDao().getById(sourceAccount);
    Account target = getAccountDao().getById(targetAccount);

    if (source.getBalance().compareTo(amount) > 0) {
        // transfer allowed
        getAccountDao().updateBalance(sourceAccount, amount.negate());
        getAccountDao().updateBalance(targetAccount, amount);

        History history = new History();
        history.setAccount(sourceAccount);
        history.setAmount(amount);
        history.setOperation("Paid out");
        history.setTargetAccount(target);
        history.setTransactionDate(new Date());
        getHistoryDao().insert(history);

        history = new History();
        history.setAccount(targetAccount);
        history.setAmount(amount);
```

```
                history.setOperation("Paid in");
                history.setTargetAccount(source);
                history.setTransactionDate(new Date());
                getHistoryDao().insert(history);
            } else {
                throw new RuntimeException("Not enough money");
            }
        }

        protected int doCount() {
            return getAccountDao().getCount();
        }


        public final void afterPropertiesSet() throws Exception {
            if (accountDao == null) throw new
                BeanCreationException("Must set accountDao");
            if (historyDao == null) throw new
                BeanCreationException("Must set historyDao");
            initManager();
        }

        protected void initManager() {

        }

        protected AccountDao getAccountDao() {
            return accountDao;
        }

        public void setAccountDao(AccountDao accountDao) {
            this.accountDao = accountDao;
        }

        protected HistoryDao getHistoryDao() {
            return historyDao;
        }

        public void setHistoryDao(HistoryDao historyDao) {
            this.historyDao = historyDao;
        }
    }
```

As you can see, the AbstractAccountManager is totally oblivious to transactions; the code
we wrote simply assumes that everything succeeds and does not deal with any failures.
AbstractAccountManager provides implementation for methods of the AccountManager interface, with a do prefix to allow the implementation classes to simply call the do methods. It also
implements the afterPropertiesSet() method of InitializingBean as final to prevent the

subclasses from overriding it. However, some subclasses may need to perform additional initialization, therefore AbstractAccountManager contains the initManager() method that is called in afterPropertiesSet() and can be overridden in subclasses.

With this infrastructure in place, we can start looking at concrete ways to implement transaction management in Spring.

Supporting Declarative Transactions

In this context, **declarative** means that we tell Spring that a method on a bean has transactional properties and Spring makes sure that the appropriate transaction exists when the method is called. This approach heavily relies on AOP to intercept method calls. For a more detailed description of AOP, refer to Chapter 6.

The major advantage of declarative transaction definition is that we do not have to modify the code we have. When implementing the method, we do not add **any** transaction management at all. Further, it allows us to specify groups of methods that require the same transaction settings. It is not difficult to imagine that we can decide that all methods of a bean require a serializable isolation level, but further down the line, we realize that we can lower the isolation level to READ_COMMITTED. If the configuration file states that, "all methods of the bean require transactions with a serializable isolation level," we can change just one line to downgrade the isolation level.

Another advantage is that the proxy Spring is going to create to process the calls to the target bean allows us to specify additional interceptors. Even though it is not used in this example, we show you how to use this in the SpringBlog sample application.

Let us begin by implementing DefaultAccountManager (see Listing 12-7); remember that all we need to do is call AbstractAccountManager's do*() methods to perform all the work.

Listing 12-7. *DefaultAccountManager Implementation*

```
package com.apress.prospring.ch12.business;

import java.math.BigDecimal;
import java.util.Date;

import com.apress.prospring.ch12.data.AccountDao;
import com.apress.prospring.ch12.data.HistoryDao;
import com.apress.prospring.ch12.domain.Account;
import com.apress.prospring.ch12.domain.History;

public class DefaultAccountManager extends AbstractAccountManager {

    public void insert(Account account) {
        doInsert(account);
    }

    public void deposit(int accountId, BigDecimal amount) {
        doDeposit(accountId, amount);
    }
```

```
    public void transfer(int sourceAccount, int targetAccount, BigDecimal amount) {
        doTransfer(sourceAccount, targetAccount, amount);
    }

}
```

Looking back at the AbstractAccountManager shown in Listing 12-6, you can see that the doInsert(), doDeposit(), and doTransfer() methods require a transaction. This means that you must execute these in an existing transaction or, if no transaction exists, you must start a new one in which to execute them. Because our example bank is very generous, it allows the customers to withdraw (deposit negative amounts) from the account as much as they want, and because creating a new account does not update any data that may be referenced by other transactions, an ISOLATION_READ_COMMITTED isolation level is sufficient. However, the transfer() method inserts new data and updates existing data. It is vital to ensure that no other transactions can select the newly inserted or updated data, thus you must use the highest isolation level, ISOLATION_SERIALIZABLE.

Now that we have the code for the application ready, we need to wire the application up in Spring context file (see Listing 12-8).

Listing 12-8. *applicationContext.xml for the Sample Application*

```xml
<?xml version="1.0" encoding="UTF-8"?>
<!DOCTYPE beans PUBLIC "-//SPRING//DTD BEAN//EN" ➡
"http://www.springframework.org/dtd/spring-beans.dtd">

<beans>

    <!-- Data source bean -->
    <bean id="dataSource" class="org.apache.commons.dbcp.BasicDataSource"
        destroy-method="close">
        <property name="driverClassName">
            <value>org.postgresql.Driver</value></property>
        <property name="url">
            <value>jdbc:postgresql://localhost/prospring</value></property>
        <property name="username"><value>janm</value></property>
        <property name="password"><value>****</value></property>
    </bean>

    <bean id="transactionManager"
        class="org.springframework.jdbc.datasource.DataSourceTransactionManager">
        <property name="dataSource"><ref local="dataSource"/></property>
    </bean>

    <bean id="sqlMapClient"
        class="org.springframework.orm.ibatis.SqlMapClientFactoryBean">
        <property name="configLocation"><value>sqlMapConfig.xml</value></property>
    </bean>
```

```xml
<bean id="accountDao"
    class="com.apress.prospring.ch12.data.SqlMapClientAccountDao">
    <property name="dataSource"><ref local="dataSource"/></property>
    <property name="sqlMapClient"><ref local="sqlMapClient"/></property>
</bean>

<bean id="historyDao"
    class="com.apress.prospring.ch12.data.UnreliableSqlMapClientHistoryDao">
    <property name="dataSource"><ref local="dataSource"/></property>
    <property name="sqlMapClient"><ref local="sqlMapClient"/></property>
</bean>

<bean id="accountManagerTarget"
    class="com.apress.prospring.ch12.business.DefaultAccountManager">
    <property name="accountDao"><ref local="accountDao"/></property>
    <property name="historyDao"><ref local="historyDao"/></property>
</bean>

<bean id="accountManager"
    class="org.springframework.transaction.interceptor➥
            TransactionProxyFactoryBean">
    <property name="transactionManager">
        <ref bean="transactionManager"/></property>
    <property name="target"><ref local="accountManagerTarget"/></property>
    <property name="transactionAttributes">
        <props>
            <prop key="insert*">
                PROPAGATION_REQUIRED, ISOLATION_READ_COMMITTED</prop>
            <prop key="transfer*">
                PROPAGATION_REQUIRED, ISOLATION_SERIALIZABLE</prop>
            <prop key="deposit*">
                PROPAGATION_REQUIRED, ISOLATION_READ_COMMITTED</prop>
        </props>
    </property>
</bean>
</beans>
```

There are a lot of new things in this context file. Let's take a look at the most important bits in more detail.

First of all, we have defined a transactionManager bean, which is implemented in DataSourceTransactionManager. This transaction manager needs to access the dataSource bean to control the JDBC transactions. This is still a fairly standard Spring configuration; the most important and interesting part is that our accountManager bean is actually a proxy to accountManagerTarget. The proxy takes care of the transaction management using the transactionManager bean. When a call to a method defined in transactionAttributes is made on a proxy, the proxy uses the transactionManager to set up the transaction (if needed) and calls the appropriate method on the target. If the target method throws an exception, the proxy instructs the transaction manager to roll back the active transaction. If the target method succeeds, the transaction is committed.

■**NOTE** You can specify exceptions that are allowed to be thrown from the target method and you can define what the proxy is going to do when it catches the exception. By default, the transaction manager rolls back the transaction if a `RuntimeException` is thrown and commits the transaction if a checked exception is thrown. You can fine tune this behavior in the manager bean declaration: If you prefix the exception name with a minus (–), the proxy rolls back the transaction; if you prefix the exception name with a plus (+), the proxy *commits* the transaction. You need to be very careful of the consequences when you specify exceptions that trigger a commit and be absolutely sure you mention this in the documentation!

If we take a more detailed look at the `transactionAttributes` property, we can see that it represents a `Properties` instance, where key is the method name and the value is made up of the transaction propagation, the isolation level, and a list of exceptions. The names are self-explanatory, as you can see here:

```
<prop key="transfer*">PROPAGATION_REQUIRED, ISOLATION_SERIALIZABLE</prop>
```

This code defines that transfer method. Any parameters are included in a transaction if it exists, or a new transaction is started before its execution and the transaction isolation level is set or upgraded to `ISOLATION_SERIALIZABLE`.

The `Main` class of the sample application uses the `accountManager` bean to perform 100 account inserts. Because the `historyDao` is intentionally unreliable, we should get about 66 successful inserts and 34 failures.

Listing 12-9. *Main Class*

```
package com.apress.prospring.ch12;

import java.math.BigDecimal;
import org.springframework.context.ApplicationContext;
import org.springframework.context.support.ClassPathXmlApplicationContext;
import com.apress.prospring.ch12.business.AccountManager;
import com.apress.prospring.ch12.domain.Account;

public class Main {

    private ApplicationContext context;

    private void run() {
        System.out.println("Initializing application");
        context = new ClassPathXmlApplicationContext(new String[] {
            "applicationContext.xml", "applicationContext-local.xml" });
        AccountManager manager = (AccountManager)context.getBean(
            "accountManager");
```

```
        int count = manager.count();
        int failures = 0;
        int attempts = 100;

        for (int i = 0; i < attempts; i++) {
            Account a = new Account();
            a.setBalance(new BigDecimal(10));
            a.setNumber("123 " + i);
            a.setSortCode("xxx " + i);
            try {
                manager.insert(a);
            } catch (RuntimeException ex) {
                System.out.println("Failed to insert account " + ex.getMessage());
                failures++;
            }
        }

        System.out.println("Attempts  : " + attempts);
        System.out.println("Failures  : " + failures);
        System.out.println("Prev count: " + count);
        System.out.println("New count : " + manager.count());

        System.out.println("Done");
    }

    public static void main(String[] args) {
        new Main().run();
    }

}
```

Running this application produces the following output:

```
...
DefaultListableBeanFactory:182 - Invoking BeanPostProcessors after ➥
initialization of bean 'accountManager'
DefaultListableBeanFactory:538 - Calling code asked for FactoryBean ➥
instance for name 'accountManager'
DefaultListableBeanFactory:157 - Returning cached instance of singleton ➥
bean 'accountManager'
DefaultListableBeanFactory:522 - Bean with name 'accountManager' is a factory bean
...
TransactionInterceptor:196 - Getting transaction for method 'insert' in ➥
class [com.apress.prospring.ch12.business.AccountManager]
DataSourceTransactionObject:60 - JDBC 3.0 Savepoint class is available
DataSourceTransactionManager:195 - Using transaction object ➥
[org.springframework.jdbc.datasource.DataSourceTransactionObject@1d381d2]
DataSourceTransactionManager:267 - Creating new transaction
```

```
DataSourceTransactionManager:153 - Opening new connection for JDBC transaction
DataSourceUtils:207 - Changing isolation level of JDBC connection ➥
[org.apache.commons.dbcp.PoolableConnection@afa68a] to 2
DataSourceTransactionManager:170 - Switching JDBC connection ➥
[org.apache.commons.dbcp.PoolableConnection@afa68a] to manual commit
TransactionSynchronizationManager:142 - Bound value ➥
[org.springframework.jdbc.datasource.ConnectionHolder@1dec1dd] for key ➥
[org.apache.commons.dbcp.BasicDataSource@1ee2c2c] to thread [main]
TransactionSynchronizationManager:194 - Initializing transaction synchronization
TransactionSynchronizationManager:117 - Retrieved value ➥
[org.springframework.jdbc.datasource.ConnectionHolder@1dec1dd] for key ➥
[org.apache.commons.dbcp.BasicDataSource@1ee2c2c] bound to thread [main]
Connection:24 - {conn-100003} Connection
PreparedStatement:30 - {pstm-100004} PreparedStatement:➥
    select nextval('Accounts_AccountId_Seq')
PreparedStatement:31 - {pstm-100004} Parameters: []
PreparedStatement:32 - {pstm-100004} Types: []
ResultSet:25 - {rset-100005} ResultSet
ResultSet:45 - {rset-100005} Header: [nextval]
ResultSet:49 - {rset-100005} Result: [6]
PreparedStatement:30 - {pstm-100006} PreparedStatement:➥
    insert into Accounts (AccountId, Number, SortCode, Balance)➥
    values (?, ?, ?, ?)
PreparedStatement:31 - {pstm-100006} Parameters: [6, 123 0, xxx 0, 10]
PreparedStatement:32 - {pstm-100006} Types: [java.lang.Integer, ➥
java.lang.String, java.lang.String, java.math.BigDecimal]
TransactionSynchronizationManager:117 - Retrieved value ➥
[org.springframework.jdbc.datasource.ConnectionHolder@1dec1dd] for key ➥
[org.apache.commons.dbcp.BasicDataSource@1ee2c2c] ➥
bound to thread [main]
Connection:24 - {conn-100007} Connection
PreparedStatement:30 - {pstm-100008} PreparedStatement:➥
    select nextval('History_HistoryId_Seq')
PreparedStatement:31 - {pstm-100008} Parameters: []
PreparedStatement:32 - {pstm-100008} Types: []
ResultSet:25 - {rset-100009} ResultSet
ResultSet:45 - {rset-100009} Header: [nextval]
ResultSet:49 - {rset-100009} Result: [7]
PreparedStatement:30 - {pstm-100010} PreparedStatement:➥
    insert into History (HistoryId, Account, Operation, Amount, ➥
    TransactionDate, TargetAccount) ➥
    values (?, ?, ?, ?, ?, ?)➥
PreparedStatement:31 - {pstm-100010} Parameters: ➥
[7, 6, Initial deposit, 10, 2004-09-16 12:38:12.533, null]
PreparedStatement:32 - {pstm-100010} Types: ➥
```

```
[java.lang.Integer, java.lang.Integer, java.lang.String, ➡
java.math.BigDecimal, java.sql.Timestamp, null]
TransactionInterceptor:239 - Invoking commit for transaction on ➡
method 'insert' in class ➡
[com.apress.prospring.ch12.business.AccountManager]
DataSourceTransactionManager:495 - Triggering beforeCommit synchronization
DataSourceTransactionManager:510 - Triggering beforeCompletion synchronization
DataSourceTransactionManager:372 - Initiating transaction commit
DataSourceTransactionManager:202 - Committing JDBC transaction on ➡
connection [org.apache.commons.dbcp.PoolableConnection@afa68a]
DataSourceTransactionManager:540 - Triggering afterCompletion synchronization
TransactionSynchronizationManager:234 - Clearing transaction synchronization
TransactionSynchronizationManager:165 - Removed value
...
Connection:24 - {conn-100671} Connection
PreparedStatement:30 - {pstm-100672} PreparedStatement:➡
    select count(*) from Accounts
PreparedStatement:31 - {pstm-100672} Parameters: []
PreparedStatement:32 - {pstm-100672} Types: []
ResultSet:25 - {rset-100673} ResultSet
ResultSet:45 - {rset-100673} Header: [count]
ResultSet:49 - {rset-100673} Result: [67]
...
Attempts  : 100
Failures  : 33
Prev count: 0
New count : 67
Done
```

As you can see from the output, when a method in Main asks for an instance of accountManager,
Spring creates the proxy to the accountManagerTarget. When a method is then called on the
accountManager proxy, Spring intercepts the method call and decides whether the method
needs to be enlisted in a transaction. The insert() method required a transaction, and the
proxy creates and manages the transaction; the count() method does not need a transaction,
and the proxy simply delegates the call to the accountManagerTarget method without any
transaction processing. Finally, the results are consistent with our expectations, the (intentionally) unreliable implementation of HistoryDao failed in a third of all calls to its insert() method,
resulting in 67 commits and 33 rollbacks.

Supporting Source Level Metadata Transactions

Source level metadata is a special type of declarative transaction support. Rather than defining
the transaction requirements in the Spring context file, you define the transaction requirements
directly in the source code. By default, Spring includes support for Jakarta Commons Attributes,
more specifically, Commons Attributes 2.1. These attributes look very much like Javadoc
comments, as you can see in Listing 12-10.

Listing 12-10. *Commons Attributes Declaration*

```
/**
 * Tranditional Javadoc comments
 * @author janm
 * @@org.springframework.transaction.interceptor.DefaultTransactionAttribute()
 */
public class Foo {
    /**
     * Javadoc comments
     * @@org.springframework.transaction.interceptor.DefaultTransactionAttribute()
     */
    public void bar() {
    }
}
```

Listing 12-10 shows two attributes: a class-wide attribute and a method attribute. Commons Attributes are not part of standard Java 1.4 SDK, therefore the source code that uses attributes must be compiled. The most convenient way to do this is to create an Ant `taskdef`. You must add the Commons Attributes compiler and the API, the XDoclet, and the commons-collection JAR files to $ANT_HOME/lib; you must also add a `taskdef` element to the Ant build.xml file.

Listing 12-11. *Build.xml taskdef for Commons Attributes Compiler*

```
<taskdef resource="org/apache/commons/attributes/anttasks.properties"/>
```

The next step is to create a target that is going to process the source files, compile the attributes, and place the generated files to the dir.build.commons-attributes directory.

Listing 12-12. *compileAttributes Ant Target*

```
<target name="compile-attributes" >
    <attribute-compiler destdir="${dir.build.commons-attributes}">
        <fileset dir="${dir.main.java.src}" includes="**/*.java"/>
    </attribute-compiler>
</target>
```

The final change to the build.xml script (see Listing 12-13) is to modify the compile target to depend on `compile-attributes` and to compile the generated metadata sources.

Listing 12-13. *Modified Compile Target*

```
<target name="compile" depends="init, compile-attributes">
    <javac destdir="${dir.main.build}" debug="on"
      debuglevel="lines,vars,source">
        <classpath refid="project.classpath"/>
            <src path="${dir.build.commons-attributes}"/>
            <src path="${dir.main.java.src}"/>
    </javac>
</target>
```

Now that we have the Ant build file ready, we can proceed to implement the MetadataAccountManager as a subclass of AbstractAccountManager (see Listing 12-14). This class is going to look very much like DefaultAccountManager, the only difference is the use of Commons Attributes.

Listing 12-14. *MetadataAccountManager Implementation*

```
package com.apress.prospring.ch12.business;

import java.math.BigDecimal;

import com.apress.prospring.ch12.domain.Account;

/**
 * @@org.springframework.transaction.interceptor.DefaultTransactionAttribute()
 */
public class MetadataAccountManager extends AbstractAccountManager {

   public void insert(Account account) {
      doInsert(account);
   }

   public void deposit(int accountId, BigDecimal amount) {
      doDeposit(accountId, amount);
   }

   public void transfer(int sourceAccount, int targetAccount, BigDecimal amount) {
      doTransfer(sourceAccount, targetAccount, amount);
   }

   public int count() {
      return doCount();
   }

}
```

Next, we take the simplistic approach and mark the entire class with DefaultTransactionAttribute. However, something is still missing. How can Spring know how to use the attributes? After all, the attributes are *not* compiled in the MetadataAccountManager.class file. We need to configure Spring AOP autoproxy support. In Listing 12-15, we show you just the basic configuration; we discuss AOP autoproxies in more detail in Chapter 6.

Listing 12-15. *AOP Autoproxies Definition in the Context File*

```xml
<?xml version="1.0" encoding="UTF-8"?>
<!DOCTYPE beans PUBLIC "-//SPRING//DTD BEAN//EN" ➥
"http://www.springframework.org/dtd/spring-beans.dtd">

<beans>

    <bean id="autoproxy"
        class="org.springframework.aop.framework.autoproxy.➥
            DefaultAdvisorAutoProxyCreator"/>
    <bean id="transactionAttributeSource"
        class="org.springframework.transaction.interceptor.➥
            AttributesTransactionAttributeSource"
        autowire="constructor"/>
    <bean id="transactionInterceptor"
        class="org.springframework.transaction.interceptor.TransactionInterceptor"
        autowire="byType"/>
    <bean id="transactionAdvisor"
        class="org.springframework.transaction.interceptor.➥
            TransactionAttributeSourceAdvisor"
        autowire="constructor" />
    <bean id="attributes"
        class="org.springframework.metadata.commons.CommonsAttributes"/>

    <!-- other beans as usual -->

    <bean id="accountManager"
        class="com.apress.prospring.ch12.business.MetadataAccountManager">
        <property name="accountDao"><ref local="accountDao"/></property>
        <property name="historyDao"><ref local="historyDao"/></property>
    </bean>

</beans>
```

The most important new beans from Listing 12-14 are autoproxy and transactionAdvisor. When the application requests an instance of the accountManager bean, Spring automatically creates a proxy to the original bean.

Let's take a closer look at the configuration Spring needs to perform to successfully enable transaction management using source level metadata. The attribute's bean configures support for a generic attributes framework. Spring comes with only Commons Attributes support, but you can easily implement the org.springframework.metadata.Attributes interface to add support for your favorite attributes framework. The transactionAdvisor bean provides advice to the AOP autoproxy to check whether a method call needs to be intercepted by the transactionInterceptor bean. The transactionInterceptor bean is a method call interceptor that checks whether a method or class is marked with a transactional attribute and if so, enlists it in a transaction.

The approach we have implemented in MetadataAccountManager is very simple, but not quite efficient. We have marked the entire class with DefaultTransactionAttribute, which means that all its methods are enlisted in a transaction. Usually there are several methods that do not require transactions; in our example, it is the count() method that does not need to be enlisted in a transaction. To make the example a bit more efficient, in Listing 12-16, we remove the DefaultTransactionAttribute from the class definition and move it to the appropriate methods.

Listing 12-16. *MetadataAccountManager Implementation*

```
package com.apress.prospring.ch12.business;

import java.math.BigDecimal;

import com.apress.prospring.ch12.domain.Account;

/**
 * @@org.springframework.transaction.interceptor.DefaultTransactionAttribute()
 */
public class MetadataAccountManager extends AbstractAccountManager {

    /**
     * @@org.springframework.transaction.interceptor.➥
       DefaultTransactionAttribute()
     */
    public void insert(Account account) {
       doInsert(account);
    }

    /**
     * @@org.springframework.transaction.interceptor.➥
       DefaultTransactionAttribute()
     */
    public void deposit(int accountId, BigDecimal amount) {
       doDeposit(accountId, amount);
    }

    /**
     * @@org.springframework.transaction.interceptor.➥
       DefaultTransactionAttribute()
     */
    public void transfer(int sourceAccount, int targetAccount, BigDecimal amount) {
       doTransfer(sourceAccount, targetAccount, amount);
    }

    public int count() {
       return doCount();
    }

}
```

We have now marked only the insert(), deposit(), and transfer() methods to make sure a transaction and the application correctly wrap calls to these methods in the AOP proxy.

From a programming and configuration point of view, using source level metadata is a very nice way to add transactional support. You have to perform very little configuration in the context files, and the transactional attributes are closely bound with the source code. On the downside, changing the transactional behavior requires you to recompile, retest, and redeploy the application. This gives a declarative transaction in the context files implementation a major advantage over source level metadata implementation.

Using Programmatic Transactions

The last way to implement transactional operations is to write the transaction management code manually. In most cases, this is not an ideal solution because you have to write a fair amount of code that you could avoid writing if you use previously discussed methods. If you choose to implement transactions programmatically, you can either use TransactionTemplate or PlatformTransactionManager; however, always try to use the first option because it is much easier to use. Using PlatformTransactionManager is very much like using JTA UserTransactions—it involves complex and chatty code.

Let's begin by discussing TransactionTemplate. This class is very similar to JdbcTemplate or SqlMapClientTemplate: you call its methods and implement a callback interface where you perform the transactional work. Naturally, TransactionTemplate instances require a PlatformTransactionManager instance; you typically set this in the Spring context file.

In Listing 12-17, we create a ProgrammaticAccountManager class as a subclass of AbstractAccountManager and call its transactional methods in a callback of TransactionTemplate.

Listing 12-17. *ProgrammaticAccountManager Implementation*

```
package com.apress.prospring.ch12.business;

import java.math.BigDecimal;

import org.springframework.transaction.PlatformTransactionManager;
import org.springframework.transaction.TransactionStatus;
import org.springframework.transaction.support.TransactionCallbackWithoutResult;
import org.springframework.transaction.support.TransactionTemplate;

import com.apress.prospring.ch12.domain.Account;

public class ProgrammaticTemplateAccountManager
    extends AbstractAccountManager {

    private PlatformTransactionManager platformTransactionManager;
    private TransactionTemplate transactionTemplate;
```

```
protected void initManager() {
    super.initManager();
    transactionTemplate = new TransactionTemplate(transactionManager);
}

public void insert(final Account account) {
    transactionTemplate.execute(new TransactionCallbackWithoutResult() {

        protected void doInTransactionWithoutResult(TransactionStatus status) {
            doInsert(account);
        }

    });
}

public void deposit(final int accountId, final BigDecimal amount) {
    transactionTemplate.execute(new TransactionCallbackWithoutResult() {

        protected void doInTransactionWithoutResult(TransactionStatus status) {
            doDeposit(accountId, amount);
        }

    });
}

public void transfer(final int sourceAccount, final int targetAccount,
        final BigDecimal amount) {
    transactionTemplate.execute(new TransactionCallbackWithoutResult() {

        protected void doInTransactionWithoutResult(TransactionStatus status) {
            doTransfer(sourceAccount, targetAccount, amount);
        }

    });
}

public int count() {
    return doCount();
}

public void setPlatformTransactionManager(
        PlatformTransactionManager platformTransactionManager) {
    this.platformTransactionManager = platformTransactionManager;
}
}
```

As you can see, the implementation uses TransactionTemplate's execute method and implements TransactionCallbackWithoutResult, which means that we do not have to bother with the return value and the execute method returns null.

If we need to return a value from the transaction, we implement the TransactionCallback interface and its execute() method returns an Object. As you can see in Listing 12-18, the configuration of this bean is simpler than the configuration of the declarative bean shown in Listing 12-8.

Listing 12-18. *accountManager Bean Definition*

```
<?xml version="1.0" encoding="UTF-8"?>
<!DOCTYPE beans PUBLIC "-//SPRING//DTD BEAN//EN" ➥
"http://www.springframework.org/dtd/spring-beans.dtd">

<beans>
    <!-- other beans -->
    <bean id="accountManager"
        class="com.apress.prospring.ch12.business.➥
            ProgrammaticTemplateAccountManager">
        <property name="accountDao"><ref local="accountDao"/></property>
        <property name="historyDao"><ref local="historyDao"/></property>
        <property name="transactionManager">
            <ref bean="transactionManager"/></property>
    </bean>
</beans>
```

Just to illustrate, in Listing 12-19, we show you how to implement the AccountManager using PlatformTransactionManager's methods. However, this is the clumsiest way to do things, and we cannot see a reason why you should choose to make your life so complicated.

Listing 12-19. *ProgrammaticManagerAccountManager Implementation*

```
package com.apress.prospring.ch12.business;

import java.math.BigDecimal;

import org.springframework.transaction.PlatformTransactionManager;
import org.springframework.transaction.TransactionDefinition;
import org.springframework.transaction.TransactionStatus;
import org.springframework.transaction.support.DefaultTransactionDefinition;

import com.apress.prospring.ch12.domain.Account;

public class ProgrammaticManagerAccountManager
    extends AbstractAccountManager {

    private PlatformTransactionManager transactionManager;
```

```
        private TransactionDefinition getDefinition(int isolationLevel) {
            DefaultTransactionDefinition def = new DefaultTransactionDefinition(
                TransactionDefinition.PROPAGATION_REQUIRED);
            def.setIsolationLevel(isolationLevel);

            return def;
        }

        public void insert(final Account account) {
            TransactionStatus status = transactionManager.getTransaction(
                getDefinition(TransactionDefinition.ISOLATION_READ_COMMITTED));
            try {
                doInsert(account);
                transactionManager.commit(status);
            } catch (Throwable t) {
                transactionManager.rollback(status);
            }


        }
        // other methods omitted for clarity
    }
```

In Listing 12-19, we only show the implementation of the insert() method; we hope this is scary enough to convince you not to use this in your code. First of all, there is a lot of repetitive code to write and as a result, the chances of making a coding mistake are much higher. Overall, the concept is quite simple: obtain the TransactionStatus, perform any transactional work, and if it all succeeds, commit the work; otherwise roll it back. As you can see in Listing 12-20, the bean definition remains very similar to the definition from Listing 12-18.

Listing 12-20. *accountManager Bean Definition*

```xml
<?xml version="1.0" encoding="UTF-8"?>
<!DOCTYPE beans PUBLIC "-//SPRING//DTD BEAN//EN" ➥
"http://www.springframework.org/dtd/spring-beans.dtd">

<beans>
    <!-- other beans -->
    <bean id="accountManager"
        class="com.apress.prospring.ch12.business.➥
            ProgrammaticManagerAccountManager">
        <property name="accountDao"><ref local="accountDao"/></property>
        <property name="historyDao"><ref local="historyDao"/></property>
        <property name="transactionManager">
            <ref bean="transactionManager"/></property>
    </bean>
</beans>
```

As you can see, there is far too much code to write, and you are not getting any added benefits from declarative or metadata transaction management.

Working with Transactions Over Multiple Transactional Resources

So far, we have only concerned ourselves with transactions in the Data Access Tier. In a large enterprise application, transactions spread across multiple components, and if the application is to be robust, you cannot simply ignore this and implement local transactional blocks and hope that the overall business process succeeds. If you need to enlist operations that manipulate the database, message queue, and any additional transactional resource in one transaction, you are left with the JTA transaction manager.

JTA is the **only** way to support global transactions. This implies that you need a J2EE application server to run an application with global transactions. Fortunately, this is usually the case because enterprise applications often use JMS, EJBs, and JNDI, which are all implemented by the application server.

The example we show you in this section demonstrates how to use JTA transactions across a database and a message queue. In this example, we create a simple web application, which sends a message to a queue. The message is then picked up by an MDB, which notifies us that it was called. Finally, the `JTAAccountManager.insert()` method throws a `RuntimeException` in about 50 percent of the cases. This exception should then cause the message to be removed from the queue and the database work to be rolled back. If this is the case, the MDB never gets called. We are not going to discuss how to create message-driven beans in Spring in great detail; if you are interested in EJB development using Spring, read Chapter 13.

The sample application we work with in this section requires a JBoss application server and an XA-capable JDBC driver. For this example, we chose the Oracle 10g database and its JDBC driver. Because it is the most complex sample in this chapter, let's begin with a UML diagram (Figure 12-2) that highlights the key components of the sample.

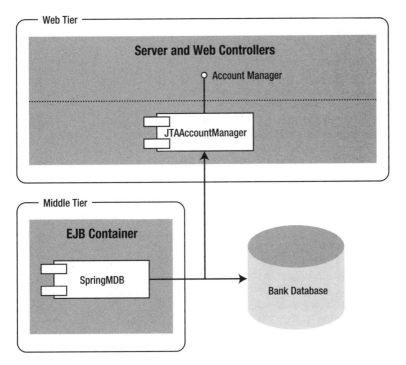

Figure 12-2. *Components of the JTA example*

JTAAccountManager is the actual implementation of the application's business logic; the EJB container is only used to host the message-driven bean. The entire application is packaged in an EAR file with two modules: an EJB JAR file containing the message-driven bean and a web module with the testing web application.

Unfortunately, as you will see in the following more detailed discussion, this design means that we have to split the Spring context files into several files because not all beans are needed and available in the EJB tier. We kept the applicationContext.xml file with the DAO definitions, but we moved the dataSource bean definition using JNDI data sources into the applicationContext-as.xml file. Finally, applicationContext-jms.xml defines the queueConnectionFactory, springQueue, and accountManagerJTATarget beans. Both applicationContext-as.xml and applicationContext-jms.xml can only be used in a J2EE application server. Figure 12-3 shows the source directory structure and sheds some light on how the application is going to be packaged.

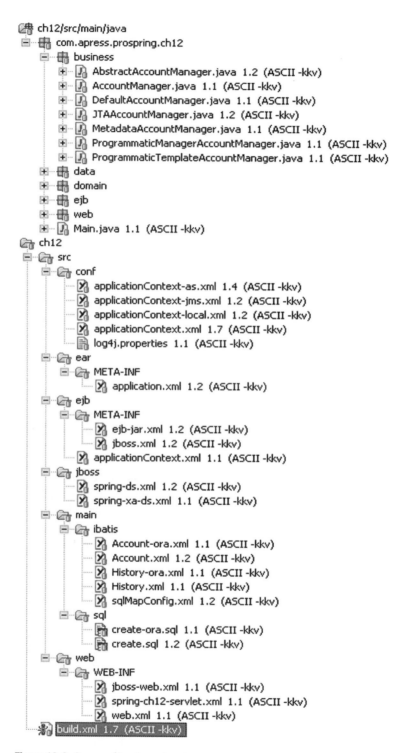

Figure 12-3. *Source directory structure*

Implementing a Message-Driven Bean

Let us begin the source code discussion by looking at the MDB implementation (see Listing 12-21). It contains the "almost empty" applicationContext.xml file in ch12/src/ejb, which is a simple placeholder for the EJB JAR. Spring EJB support needs to build a Spring context to make it available in the EJBs. Because we do not use any Spring beans in the MDB, we can leave the file almost empty, we just need to make sure it is a valid XML according to the DTD. As you just saw, Figure 12-3 shows how the source files are structured and hopefully gives an idea of how the EAR file is going to be built.

Listing 12-21. *SpringMDB Implementation*

```
package com.apress.prospring.ch12.ejb;

import javax.jms.Message;

import org.springframework.ejb.support.AbstractJmsMessageDrivenBean;

public class SpringMDB extends AbstractJmsMessageDrivenBean {

    protected void onEjbCreate() {
        // noop

    }

    public void onMessage(Message message) {
        System.out.println("Message received");
    }

}
```

As you can see from the code, the MDB does not even examine the message, it simply prints "Message received" to standard output. This MDB is packaged in spring-ch12-ejb.jar, along with its null Spring context file and ejb-jar.xml and jboss.xml descriptor files (see Listing 12-22).

Listing 12-22. *EJB JAR Descriptor Files*

```
// applicationContext.xml packaged in the root of the jar
<?xml version="1.0" encoding="UTF-8"?>
<!DOCTYPE beans PUBLIC "-//SPRING//DTD BEAN//EN" ➥
"http://www.springframework.org/dtd/spring-beans.dtd">

<beans>
    <bean id="null"/>
</beans>

// ejb-jar.xml in /META-INF
<?xml version="1.0"?>
```

```
<!DOCTYPE ejb-jar PUBLIC
    "-//Sun Microsystems, Inc.//DTD Enterprise JavaBeans 2.0// EN"
    "http://java.sun.com/dtd/ejb-jar_2_0.dtd" >
<ejb-jar>
    <enterprise-beans>
        <message-driven>
            <ejb-name>SpringMDB</ejb-name>
            <ejb-class>com.apress.prospring.ch12.ejb.SpringMDB</ejb-class>
            <transaction-type>Container</transaction-type>
            <acknowledge-mode>AUTO_ACKNOWLEDGE</acknowledge-mode>
            <message-driven-destination>
                <destination-type>javax.jms.Queue</destination-type>
            </message-driven-destination>
            <env-entry>
                <env-entry-name>ejb/BeanFactoryPath</env-entry-name>
                <env-entry-type>java.lang.String</env-entry-type>
                <env-entry-value>applicationContext.xml</env-entry-value>
            </env-entry>
            <resource-ref>
                <description></description>
                <res-ref-name>jms/SpringMessages</res-ref-name>
                <res-type>javax.jms.XAQueueConnectionFactory</res-type>
                <res-auth>Container</res-auth>
            </resource-ref>
        </message-driven>
    </enterprise-beans>
</ejb-jar>

// jboss.xml in /META-INF
<?xml version="1.0"?>
<jboss>
    <enterprise-beans>
        <message-driven>
            <ejb-name>SpringMDB</ejb-name>
            <destination-jndi-name>queue/springQueue</destination-jndi-name>
            <resource-ref>
                <res-ref-name>jms/SpringMessages</res-ref-name>
                <jndi-name>XAConnectionFactory</jndi-name>
            </resource-ref>
        </message-driven>
    </enterprise-beans>
</jboss>
```

These EJB descriptor files map the MDB implementation in the SpringMDB class to an EJB named SpringMDB, which uses the Container transaction type, references the jms/SpringMessages queue, and has an env-entry of ejb/BeanFactoryPath that references the null Spring context file. Notice that the connection factory for the queue must be XAQueueConnectionFactory because this is the only factory that takes part in JTA transactions. Also, <jndi-name> in the <resource-ref> element in jboss.xml must be XAConnectionFactory because other implementations of the ConnectionFactory cannot participate in JTA transactions.

Using the Web Application

The web application uses the DAO classes you have seen working in the previous paragraphs, so there is no need to revisit them. Because the web application actually performs the database work and because it uses JTA transaction manager, we need to define the data source as a JNDI resource. To do this, we cerate a spring-xa-ds.xml[1] file (Listing 12-23) that references an XA JDBC data source.

Listing 12-23. *spring-xa-ds.xml Data Source Definition*

```
<?xml version="1.0" encoding="UTF-8"?>

<datasources>
    <xa-datasource>
        <jndi-name>XASpringDS</jndi-name>
        <track-connection-by-tx/>
        <isSameRM-override-value>false</isSameRM-override-value>
        <xa-datasource-class>
            oracle.jdbc.xa.client.OracleXADataSource</xa-datasource-class>
        <xa-datasource-property name="URL">
            jdbc:oracle:oci8:@orcl</xa-datasource-property>
        <xa-datasource-property name="User">SCOTT</xa-datasource-property>
        <xa-datasource-property name="Password">****</xa-datasource-property>
        <exception-sorter-class-name>
            org.jboss.resource.adapter.jdbc.vendor.OracleExceptionSorter
        </exception-sorter-class-name>
        <no-tx-separate-pools/>
    </xa-datasource>
    <mbean
        code="org.jboss.resource.adapter.jdbc.xa.oracle.OracleXAExceptionFormatter"
        name="jboss.jca:service=OracleXAExceptionFormatter">
        <depends optional-attribute-name="TransactionManagerService">
            jboss:service=TransactionManager</depends>
    </mbean>
</datasources>
```

---

1. This is application server specific. Thus, spring-ds.xml is going to work only in JBoss.

The spring-xa-ds.xml file defines a JNDI data source and must be deployed in the standard JBoss deploy directory.

■NOTE The driver for your database must support the XA protocol, or the J2EE application server must provide an XA wrapper around the standard JDBC driver. Without XA, the database connection cannot be enlisted in global transactions. Only large and mostly commercial databases support XA natively in their JDBC drivers. We used the Oracle 10g database to run the example in this chapter. You can download Oracle 10g from www.oracle.com/database/index.html.

In Listing 12-24, the web application uses the message queue and the accountManager proxy references accountManagerJTATarget as its target object. The dataSource bean is configured to the JNDI resource. Here, we configure the JNDI references to the message queues in WEB-INF/jboss-web.xml and WEB-INF/web.xml.

Listing 12-24. *WEB-INF Configuration Files*

```
// jboss-web.xml
<?xml version="1.0" encoding="ISO-8859-1"?>
<!DOCTYPE jboss-web
    PUBLIC "-//JBoss//DTD Web Application 2.3V2//EN"
    "http://www.jboss.org/j2ee/dtd/jboss-web_3_2.dtd">

<jboss-web>
    <resource-ref>
        <res-ref-name>queue/springQueue</res-ref-name>
        <jndi-name>queue/springQueue</jndi-name>
    </resource-ref>
</jboss-web>

// web.xml
<?xml version="1.0" encoding="ISO-8859-1"?>
<!DOCTYPE web-app PUBLIC
    "-//Sun Microsystems, Inc.//DTD Web Application 2.3//EN"
    "http://java.sun.com/dtd/web-app_2_3.dtd">
<web-app>
    <display-name>Pro Spring Chapter 12</display-name>
    <context-param>
        <param-name>contextConfigLocation</param-name>
        <param-value>WEB-INF/applicationContext.xml
            WEB-INF/applicationContext-jms.xml
            WEB-INF/applicationContext-as.xml</param-value>
    </context-param>
```

```xml
<servlet>
    <servlet-name>context</servlet-name>
    <servlet-class>
        org.springframework.web.context.ContextLoaderServlet</servlet-class>
    <load-on-startup>1</load-on-startup>
</servlet>

<servlet>
    <servlet-name>spring-ch12</servlet-name>
    <servlet-class>
        org.springframework.web.servlet.DispatcherServlet
    </servlet-class>
    <load-on-startup>2</load-on-startup>
</servlet>

<servlet-mapping>
    <servlet-name>spring-ch12</servlet-name>
    <url-pattern>*.html</url-pattern>
</servlet-mapping>

<resource-ref>
    <res-ref-name>queue/springQueue</res-ref-name>
    <res-type>javax.jms.Queue</res-type>
    <res-auth>Container</res-auth>
</resource-ref>
</web-app>
```

The jboss-web.xml descriptor file defines the JNDI resource mappings and the web.xml defines the Spring ContextLoaderServlet that loads the applicationContext files. The last configuration file, spring-ch12-servlet.xml, is another Spring context file that the DispatcherServlet loads, and it contains the definition for the TestController. We do not discuss web applications in Spring in this chapter; for more details go to Chapter 17. The most important point is that the TestController has an accountManager property that is set to the accountManager proxy defined in applicationContext.xml. The target of the proxy is accountManagerJTATarget. In Listing 12-25, you can see that the implementation of this bean is quite simple; the only thing we have added on top of all the database code is the call to the message queue.

Listing 12-25. *JTAAccountManager Implementation*

```java
package com.apress.prospring.ch12.business;

import java.math.BigDecimal;

import javax.jms.ConnectionFactory;
import javax.jms.JMSException;
import javax.jms.Message;
import javax.jms.Queue;
import javax.jms.Session;
```

```java
import org.springframework.beans.factory.BeanCreationException;
import org.springframework.jms.core.JmsTemplate102;
import org.springframework.jms.core.MessageCreator;

import com.apress.prospring.ch12.domain.Account;

public class JTAAccountManager extends AbstractAccountManager {

    private ConnectionFactory connectionFactory;
    private Queue queue;
    private JmsTemplate102 jmsTemplate;

    protected void initManager() {
        if (connectionFactory == null)
            throw new BeanCreationException("Must set connectionFactory");
        if (queue == null)
            throw new BeanCreationException("Must set queue");
        jmsTemplate = new JmsTemplate102(connectionFactory, false);
    }

    public void insert(Account account) {
        doInsert(account);
        jmsTemplate.send(queue, new MessageCreator() {

            public Message createMessage(Session session) throws JMSException {
                return session.createTextMessage("foobar");
            }

        });

        if (random.nextInt(10) > 5) {
            System.out.println("Fail now");
            throw new IllegalArgumentException("fff");
        }
    }

    public void deposit(int accountId, BigDecimal amount) {
        doDeposit(accountId, amount);
    }

    public void transfer(int sourceAccount, int targetAccount, BigDecimal amount) {
        doTransfer(sourceAccount, targetAccount, amount);
    }

    public int count() {
        return doCount();
    }
```

```
    public void setConnectionFactory(ConnectionFactory connectionFactory) {
        this.connectionFactory = connectionFactory;
    }

    public void setQueue(Queue queue) {
        this.queue = queue;
    }
}
```

As you can see, we override the initManager() method to make sure the queue and connectionFactory properties are set. We also create an instance of JMSTemplate102 in this method. When the insert() method is executed, it calls the inherited doInsert() method and sends a message to the queue. The random generator adds a bit of unreliability to test that the transaction is indeed committed or rolled back.

In Listing 12-26, we define the accountManagerJTATarget bean in the applicationContext-jms.xml file.

Listing 12-26. *applicationContext-jms.xml Descriptor*

```
<?xml version="1.0" encoding="UTF-8"?>
<!DOCTYPE beans PUBLIC "-//SPRING//DTD BEAN//EN" ➥
"http://www.springframework.org/dtd/spring-beans.dtd">

<beans>
    <bean id="queueConnectionFactory"
        class="org.springframework.jndi.JndiObjectFactoryBean">
        <property name="jndiName"><value>UIL2ConnectionFactory</value></property>
    </bean>

    <!-- Test queue -->
    <bean id="springQueue" class="org.springframework.jndi.JndiObjectFactoryBean">
        <property name="jndiName">
            <value>java:comp/env/queue/springQueue</value></property>
    </bean>

    <bean id="accountManagerJTATarget"
        class="com.apress.prospring.ch12.business.JTAAccountManager">
        <property name="accountDao"><ref bean="accountDao"/></property>
        <property name="historyDao"><ref bean="historyDao"/></property>
        <property name="connectionFactory">
            <ref bean="queueConnectionFactory"/></property>
        <property name="queue"><ref bean="springQueue"/></property>
    </bean>

</beans>
```

To make the entire application use JTA transaction manager, we only have to define the correct transaction manager and set a reference to the transaction manager in the accountManager proxy (Listing 12-27).

Listing 12-27. *JNDI dataSource and JTA Transction Manager Definition*

```
<?xml version="1.0" encoding="UTF-8"?>
<!DOCTYPE beans PUBLIC "-//SPRING//DTD BEAN//EN" ➥
"http://www.springframework.org/dtd/spring-beans.dtd">

<beans>

    <!-- Data source bean -->

    <bean id="dataSource"
        class="org.springframework.jndi.JndiObjectFactoryBean">
        <property name="jndiName"><value>java:/XASpringDS</value></property>
    </bean>

    <bean id="transactionManager"
        class="org.springframework.transaction.jta.JtaTransactionManager"/>

    <bean id="sqlMapClient"
        class="org.springframework.orm.ibatis.SqlMapClientFactoryBean">
        <property name="configLocation">
            <value>/WEB-INF/classes/sqlMapConfig.xml</value></property>
    </bean>

</beans>
```

The dataSource is no longer a BasicDataSource; it is up to the J2EE container to manage and pool the connections using its XA data source infrastructure. Now, the transaction manager is a JTATransactionManager and as such, it does not need a reference to the data source because it manages transactions across various transactional resources. The applicationContext.xml file remains unchanged as it only includes references to the transactionManager bean, not the bean itself.

The code in the TestController.handleRequest() method shown in Listing 12-28 is very simple because the controller does not know what implementation of AccountManager it is using; it simply tries to insert 100 accounts—you do not have to worry about the complex JTA transaction management.

Listing 12-28. *TestController Implementation*

```
package com.apress.prospring.ch12.web;

import java.math.BigDecimal;

import javax.servlet.http.HttpServletRequest;
import javax.servlet.http.HttpServletResponse;
```

```java
import org.springframework.beans.factory.BeanCreationException;
import org.springframework.beans.factory.InitializingBean;
import org.springframework.web.servlet.ModelAndView;
import org.springframework.web.servlet.mvc.Controller;

import com.apress.prospring.ch12.business.AccountManager;
import com.apress.prospring.ch12.domain.Account;

public class TestController implements InitializingBean, Controller {

    private AccountManager accountManager;

    public ModelAndView handleRequest(HttpServletRequest request,
        HttpServletResponse response) throws Exception {

        int count = accountManager.count();
        int failures = 0;
        int attempts = 100;
        for (int i = 0; i < attempts; i++) {
            Account account = new Account();
            account.setBalance(new BigDecimal(0));
            account.setNumber("" + System.currentTimeMillis());
            account.setSortCode("dfgdfg");
            try {
                accountManager.insert(account);
            } catch (Exception ex) {
                failures++;
            }
        }

        response.getWriter().println("<br>Attempts:  " + attempts);
        response.getWriter().println("<br>Commits:   " + (attempts - failures));
        response.getWriter().println("<br>Rollbacks: " + failures);
        response.getWriter().println("<hr>");
        response.getWriter().println("<br>Old count: " + count +
            ", new count " + accountManager.count());

        return null;
    }

    public void afterPropertiesSet() throws Exception {
        if (accountManager == null)
            throw new BeanCreationException("Must set accountManager");
    }
```

```
    public void setAccountManager(AccountManager accountManager) {
        this.accountManager = accountManager;
    }
}
```

If we now deploy the application and if JBoss is running on localhost, port 8090, we can go
to `http://localhost:8090/spring-ch12/test.html` and see something like what is shown in
Listing 12-29 in the browser.

Listing 12-29. *Displayed test.html Page*

```
Attempts: 100
Commits: 53
Rollbacks: 47

Old count: 0, new count 53
```

The number of commits you see here depends on the random generator and will probably
be slightly different with every request. You will also see 53 "Message received" messages on
the standard output. This proves that the message queue and database work are enlisted in the
same global transaction.

JTA Transaction Manager Implications

This rather complex example demonstrated how to use global transactions with JTA. Even
though Spring greatly simplifies global transaction management, the example is still quite
complex, especially in terms of deployment and configuration. The performance of the XA
queues and data sources is lower than the performance of their local versions, but the added
benefit of a truly robust application makes this the only viable option in enterprise application
development.

This is all good news; we now have a very robust and scalable application. The downside is
that this application is very difficult to test. To do so, you need a J2EE application server to run
the application, which means you can no longer write any unit tests that run outside of the
container.

Transactions in the Sample Application

In this section, after we discuss the various transaction management approaches in small
sample applications, we show you how we implemented and tested transaction management
in the SpringBlog application.

There are two levels of transaction requirements. First, you need to maintain the integrity
of the data during the kind of insert and update operations that change more than one table.
You also need to be aware of business requirements for transactions. In this example application, the business requirement is that every modification of an Entry must have an audit trail.

This implementation uses declarative transaction definitions in the context file, because
they are easier to manage and because the proxy allows us to specify additional interceptors
for the obscenity filter. In Listing 12-30, we create a blogManager bean that implements the

BlogManager interface and we specify that the saveComment() and saveEntry() methods require a transaction. Further, we specify an obscenityFilterAdvisor post interceptor.

Listing 12-30. *applicationContext.xml Definition*

```
<?xml version="1.0" encoding="UTF-8"?>
<!DOCTYPE beans PUBLIC "-//SPRING//DTD BEAN//EN" ➥
"http://www.springframework.org/dtd/spring-beans.dtd">
<beans>
    <bean id="transactionManager"
        class="org.springframework.jdbc.datasource.DataSourceTransactionManager">
        <property name="dataSource">
            <ref bean="dataSource"/>
        </property>
    </bean>

    <bean id="blogManager"
        class="org.springframework.transaction.interceptor.➥
            TransactionProxyFactoryBean">
        <property name="transactionManager">
            <ref bean="transactionManager"/>
        </property>
        <property name="proxyTargetClass">
            <value>true</value>
        </property>
        <property name="target">
            <ref local="blogManagerTarget"/>
        </property>
        <property name="preInterceptors">
            <list>
                <ref local="obscenityFilterAdvisor"/>
            </list>
        </property>
        <property name="transactionAttributes">
            <props>
                <prop key="saveComment*">PROPAGATION_REQUIRED</prop>
                <prop key="saveEntry*">PROPAGATION_REQUIRED</prop>
            </props>
        </property>
    </bean>
</beans>
```

In Listing 12-30, the bean definition is pretty straightforward with no hidden catches. Now in Listing 12-31, let's take a look at the target bean.

Listing 12-31. *applicationContext.xml Definition*

```xml
<?xml version="1.0" encoding="UTF-8"?>
<!DOCTYPE beans PUBLIC "-//SPRING//DTD BEAN//EN" ➥
"http://www.springframework.org/dtd/spring-beans.dtd">
<beans>
    <bean id="blogManagerTarget"
        class="com.apress.prospring.business.DefaultBlogManager">
        <property name="entryDao"><ref local="entryDao"/></property>
        <property name="userDao"><ref local="userDao"/></property>
        <property name="commentDao"><ref local="commentDao"/></property>
        <property name="auditService"><ref local="auditService"/></property>
    </bean>

    <bean id="auditService"
        class="com.apress.prospring.business.DefaultAuditService">
        <property name="auditDao"><ref local="auditDao"/></property>
    </bean>
</beans>
```

When you look at the `blogManagerTarget` bean, you may be wondering why we did not include the `auditDao` in its dependencies and instead created another bean called `auditService`. There are two fundamental reasons for this. First, the requirement for the audit trail did not specify that the audit needs to be recorded in the database; we did not want to tie the `blogManagerTarget` to using the database for storing the audit information.[2] The second reason is that we need to write deterministic tests that can prove that the transaction proxy is doing its job properly.

Effective Testing of Transactional Methods

We need a way to write tests that **prove** that the transaction management is working. In other words, we needed to prove that if an exception is thrown from within a transaction, the transaction will be rolled back. We also needed to make sure that the `AuditService` implementation gets called exactly once for each Entry operation.

In Listing 12-32, we create two `TestCase`s to demonstrate this: `TransactionTest` proves that the transaction will be committed if and only if the audit is saved successfully; `AuditInvokedTest` proves that the `auditService` bean methods are invoked for operations on entry.

Listing 12-32. *AuditInvokedTest Unit Test Implementation*

```java
package com.apress.prospring.business;

import java.util.Date;
import java.util.List;

import junit.framework.TestCase;
```

---

2. As it is, we **are** using a database table to store the audit information.

```java
import com.apress.prospring.data.CommentDao;
import com.apress.prospring.data.EntryDao;
import com.apress.prospring.domain.Comment;
import com.apress.prospring.domain.Entry;
import com.apress.prospring.domain.User;

public class AuditInvokedTest extends TestCase {

    private DefaultBlogManager bm = new DefaultBlogManager();
    private CommentDao commentDao = new MockCommentDao();
    private EntryDao entryDao = new MockEntryDao();
    private MockAuditService auditService;

    public AuditInvokedTest() {
        bm.setCommentDao(commentDao);
        bm.setEntryDao(entryDao);
    }

    public void setUp() {
        auditService = new MockAuditService();
        bm.setAuditService(auditService);
    }

    public void testSaveEntry() {
        bm.saveEntry(new Entry());
        performAssert();
    }

    public void testSaveComment() {
        bm.saveComment(new Comment(), new User());
        performAssert();
    }

    private void performAssert() {
        assertEquals("The Audit Service was not invoked", 1,
            auditService.callCount);
    }

    private class MockAuditService implements AuditService {
        private int callCount = 0;
        public void writeAuditMessage(String data, User user) {
            callCount++;
        }
        public void purgeAudit(Date oldestDate) {
        }
```

```
        public int getCallCount() {
            return callCount;
        }
    }

    private class MockCommentDao implements CommentDao {
        // all methods implemented as stubs
    }

    private class MockEntryDao implements EntryDao {
        // all methods implemented as stubs
    }

}
```

This test invokes the saveEntry() method on the BlogManager implementation, which, in turn, should call writeAuditMessage() on the AuditService. The key to this test is using mock implementations to make sure that the methods get called appropriately. Once this test succeeds, we know that the BlogManager implementation calls AuditService correctly.

Next, we need to prove that the transaction is rolled back if the audit cannot be written (see Listing 12-33).

Listing 12-33. *TransactionTest Unit Test Implementation*

```
package com.apress.prospring.business;

import java.util.Date;

import org.springframework.context.ApplicationContext;
import org.springframework.context.support.FileSystemXmlApplicationContext;

import com.apress.prospring.domain.Entry;
import com.apress.prospring.domain.User;

import junit.framework.TestCase;

public class TransactionTest extends TestCase {

    private ApplicationContext getApplicationContext() {
        String[] paths = new String[] {
                "./business/src/resources/applicationContext-db.xml",
                "./business/src/resources/applicationContext.xml" };

        return new FileSystemXmlApplicationContext(paths);
    }
```

```java
public void testTransaction() {
    ApplicationContext ctx = getApplicationContext();
    DefaultBlogManager bm = (DefaultBlogManager) ctx.getBean("blogManager");
    bm.setAuditService(new MockAuditService());

    int countBefore = bm.getAllEntries().size();

    Entry e = new Entry();
    e.setSubject("Tester");
    e.setBody("Body");
    e.setPostDate(new Date());

    try {
        bm.saveEntry(e);
        fail("Should have thrown RuntimeException");
    } catch (RuntimeException expected) {
    }

    int countAfter = bm.getAllEntries().size();

    assertEquals("The new Entry should not have been added", countBefore,
            countAfter);

}

private static class MockAuditService implements AuditService {

    public void writeAuditMessage(String data, User user) {
        throw new RuntimeException("Foo!");
    }

    public void purgeAudit(Date oldestDate) {
        // no-op
    }

}
}
```

This test builds the Spring application context from the context files we use in the live application, but it then sets the AuditService implementation to an instance of MockAuditService, which throws a RuntimeException in its writeAuditMessage() method.

In Listing 12-33, we count the number of all entries and attempt to add a new one—this should result in an audit record being created—but because MockAuditService never successfully writes the audit record, we catch a RuntimeException. We go as far as stating that the code fails if no RuntimeException is thrown, because this means that the BlogManager implementation is not using the AuditService implementation correctly. Finally, we count the number of entries in the database and fail the test if the new entry is saved. This proves that an exception thrown from the AuditService causes a transaction rollback in BlogManager.saveEntry() method.

Summary

Transactions are a key part of ensuring data integrity in almost any type of application. In this chapter, you learned how to use Spring to manage transactions with almost no impact on your source code. You now know how to use local and global transactions and are aware of the performance and testing implications of using them.

We provided various examples of transaction implementation—declarative using application context files, declarative using source level metadata, and programmatic—and we discussed the practical uses and implications on coding style and manageability of each.

Local transactions are supported outside of a J2EE application server and almost no additional configuration is made to enable local transaction support in Spring. Unfortunately, the setup for global transactions greatly depends on your J2EE application server. Even though it will most likely be very similar to the JBoss example we showed in this chapter, you will need to refer to the application server documentation for more details.

CHAPTER 13

■■■

Spring and J2EE

$\mathbf{T}$hese days more and more applications are being built on so-called lightweight platforms with technologies like Spring and Tomcat rather than on traditional heavyweight application servers. Despite this move, there is still a place for the application server, and there is certainly a place for many of the J2EE APIs. In this chapter, we cover J2EE support in Spring in detail, focusing in particular on the three following APIs:

JNDI: The Java Naming and Directory Interface (JNDI) provides a standard interface on which Java applications can interact with naming and directory services. In a J2EE setting, we see that JNDI is used to access resources bound to the naming service of the application server. This is the traditional way to look up services in a J2EE context. In this section, we look at the convenience APIs provided by Spring to simplify JNDI coding and how the JndiObjectFactoryBean class provided by Spring acts as an adapter between the world of JNDI lookup and Spring Dependency Injection (DI).

EJB: In traditional J2EE applications, Enterprise Java Beans (EJB) often formed the cornerstone of an application's architecture. Although Spring provides simpler versions of many of the services provided by EJB, such as declarative transaction management and object persistence, many applications will continue to be built using EJBs for some time. Thankfully, you can still utilize Spring in an EJB-based solution, and in this section, we look at how Spring can simplify the creation of EJBs and provide a straightforward, DI–friendly way to access EJB resources.

JMS: The Java Message Service (JMS) provides a standard API from which Java applications can access messaging services. JMS provides the ability for an application to run processes in an asynchronous manner, and it also provides a reliable messaging fabric for distributed applications. Spring comes complete with wrapper APIs around both the 1.0.2 and 1.1 JMS APIs, providing an implementation-agnostic way to access JMS resources of both versions. In addition, Spring provides a greatly simplified API for sending and receiving messages in a JMS environment.

A common misunderstanding we have seen with J2EE is that J2EE is all or nothing—that is to say you either get the full stack or nothing at all. Clearly this is not true; many projects such as Tomcat offer simple servlet containers without providing features for EJB and many of the other J2EE APIs.

The servlet API is a classic example of a J2EE API that has enjoyed considerable success outside of the application server. We often see developers who are keen to use Spring and Tomcat, but because they need a feature such as JMS, they feel that they have to use an application server such as JBoss. This is not the case, however, and part of the beauty of Spring is that it encourages us to piece together our own stack, rather than simply settle for an application server that offers the full stack.

In this chapter, when we look at JNDI and EJB, we are going to go down the traditional route and use the JBoss application server. However, when we look at JMS, we are going to use one of our favorite configurations—Spring, Tomcat, and ActiveMQ. In this way, we get the benefit of the lightweight approach with Spring and Tomcat, and we get a high-quality, open source messaging solution with ActiveMQ.

This chapter is not an introduction to JNDI, EJB, or JMS. We assume that you are already familiar with these APIs, what they are used for, and how they are related. If you are not, then we suggest that you read *Beginning J2EE 1.4: From Novice to Professional* by James L. Weaver, Kevin Mukhar, and Jim Crume (Apress, 2004).

Spring and JNDI

In Chapter 4, we discussed how JNDI represents the Dependency Pull style of IoC. In traditional J2EE applications, JNDI is used to access a variety of different resources, such as EJBs and JMS connection factories. At the basic level, Spring provides a mechanism, using `JndiTemplate`, to simplify the amount of code needed to perform a JNDI lookup. However, this does not overcome the major drawback of using the Dependency Pull style—the component is still responsible for obtaining its own dependencies, and it must maintain some kind of identifying information so it can do so. To overcome this, Spring provides the `JndiObjectFactoryBean`, an implementation of `FactoryBean` that allows resources bound in JNDI to be injected using DI.

In this section, we are going to look at three approaches for accessing resources stored in JNDI. First, we perform a traditional lookup without any Spring classes. Second, we perform a manual lookup again, this time using the `JndiTemplate` class to simplify the amount of code required. Finally, we use the `JndiObjectFactoryBean` to perform DI automatically. However, before we get started with these approaches, we need to examine the common code used by each.

About the JNDI Examples

For each of these JNDI lookup examples, we build a simple servlet that displays a message obtained from JNDI. The message is written out three times, each time using a different approach to retrieve the message. The core of this example is the `MessageResolver` interface, which is implemented by each of the three classes that retrieve the message from JNDI. The `MessageResolver` interface is shown in Listing 13-1.

Listing 13-1. *The MessageResolver Interface*

```
package com.apress.prospring.ch13.jndi;

public interface MessageResolver {

    public String getMessage();
}
```

As you can see, there is nothing special about this interface. The interesting part of this example comes in how the individual examples retrieve the JNDI resource.

The JndiDemoServlet

The MessageResolver interface simply provides a way to implement classes to return a message. The JndiDemoServlet class performs the actual writing of these messages, as shown in Listing 13-2.

Listing 13-2. *The JndiDemoServlet Class*

```
package com.apress.prospring.ch13.jndi;

import java.io.IOException;
import java.io.PrintWriter;

import javax.servlet.ServletException;
import javax.servlet.http.HttpServlet;
import javax.servlet.http.HttpServletRequest;
import javax.servlet.http.HttpServletResponse;

import org.springframework.context.ApplicationContext;
import org.springframework.context.support.ClassPathXmlApplicationContext;

public class JndiDemoServlet extends HttpServlet {

    public static final String JNDI_NAME = "java:comp/env/message";

    private ApplicationContext ctx;

    public void init() throws ServletException {
        ctx = new ClassPathXmlApplicationContext(
                "/WEB-INF/applicationContext.xml");
    }

    protected void doGet(HttpServletRequest request,
            HttpServletResponse response) throws ServletException, IOException {

        PrintWriter writer = response.getWriter();

        writeWithBean("messageWriterTraditional", writer);
        writeWithBean("messageWriterTemplate", writer);
        writeWithBean("messageWriterFactoryBean", writer);
    }
```

```
    private void writeWithBean(String beanName, PrintWriter writer) {
        MessageResolver traditional = (MessageResolver) ctx.getBean(beanName);
        writer.write(traditional.getMessage());
        writer.write("\n");
    }
}
```

JndiDemoServlet is a fairly basic servlet. We start by locating the Spring application context and then, using the writeWithBean() method, we invoke each of the three beans in sequence. Inside the writeWithBean() method, you can see that the message returned by the bean is written to the output stream (using the PrintWriter instance) and is followed by a new line. Notice also that we have defined a public static final field, JNDI_NAME, to hold the JNDI name for the resource that our components are looking for. This resource is defined using the <env-entry> tag in the servlet deployment descriptor, as shown in Listing 13-3.

Listing 13-3. *Binding a JNDI Resource in web.xml*

```xml
<?xml version="1.0" encoding="UTF-8"?>
<!DOCTYPE web-app PUBLIC "-//Sun Microsystems, Inc.//DTD Web Application 2.3//EN"
                        "http://java.sun.com/dtd/web-app_2_3.dtd">
<web-app>
    <servlet>
        <servlet-name>jndi</servlet-name>
        <servlet-class>
          com.apress.prospring.ch13.jndi.JndiDemoServlet</servlet-class>
    </servlet>

    <servlet-mapping>
        <servlet-name>jndi</servlet-name>
        <url-pattern>/jndi</url-pattern>
    </servlet-mapping>

    <env-entry>
        <env-entry-name>message</env-entry-name>
        <env-entry-value>Hello World!</env-entry-value>
        <env-entry-type>java.lang.String</env-entry-type>
    </env-entry>
</web-app>
```

As you can see, we are binding the phrase "Hello World!" to the JNDI resource, so when we access the servlet, we expect to see three lines, each displaying "Hello World!" That covers *how* the messages are displayed; in the next three sections, we look at the different implementations of MessageResolver to see how the message is retrieved.

Traditional JNDI Approach

In this section, we demonstrate the traditional approach to looking up a resource using JNDI. The traditional approach to obtaining a resource from JNDI is to create an instance of

InitialContext and then look up the resource using InitialContext.lookup(). Because we are operating inside a J2EE server, we do not need to set any environmental parameters for the InitialContext, but when we work with JNDI outside of an application server, this is necessary.

Listing 13-4 shows the TraditionalJndiMessageResolver class, an implementation of MessageResolver that does not use any Spring classes.

Listing 13-4. *JNDI Access Using JNDI API*

```
package com.apress.prospring.ch13.jndi;

import javax.naming.Context;
import javax.naming.InitialContext;
import javax.naming.NamingException;

public class TraditionalJndiMessageResolver implements MessageResolver {

    private String message;

    public String getMessage() {
        if (message == null) {
            lookupMessage();
        }
        return message;
    }

    private void lookupMessage() {
        try {
            Context ctx = new InitialContext();
            message = (String) ctx.lookup(JndiDemoServlet.JNDI_NAME);
        } catch (NamingException ex) {
            message = ex.getMessage();
        }
    }
}
```

The bulk of the processing here is in the lookupMessage() method. As you can see, we create an instance of InitialContext and then we perform the lookup using InitialContext.lookup(). Both the InitialContext constructor and the lookupMessage() method are declared as throwing NamingException. In this example, we simply catch any NamingExceptions and set the error message as the message to be displayed.

Using JndiTemplate

In this section, we demonstrate the use of the JndiTemplate class to replace the traditional JNDI lookup code. Using JndiTemplate isn't drastically different from using the InitialContext class to perform the lookup, as shown in Listing 13-5.

Listing 13-5. *Lookup Using JndiTemplate*

```
package com.apress.prospring.ch13.jndi;

import javax.naming.NamingException;

import org.springframework.jndi.JndiTemplate;

public class JndiTemplateMessageResolver implements MessageResolver {

    private String message;

    public String getMessage() {
        if (message == null) {
            lookupMessage();
        }
        return message;
    }

    private void lookupMessage() {
        JndiTemplate template = new JndiTemplate();

        try {
            message = (String) template.lookup(JndiDemoServlet.JNDI_NAME);
        } catch (NamingException ex) {
            message = ex.getMessage();
        }
    }
}
```

As you can see, this implementation does not look much different from the previous one. Although the JndiTemplate constructor does not throw a NamingException, the lookup method does; we handle it in exactly the same way as we did in the previous implementation.

So why use JndiTemplate rather than InitialContext? Both classes can be configured using DI, although only JndiTemplate supports setter injection, so there is nothing to set them apart there. The main reason we would choose to use JndiTemplate over InitialContext is to take advantage of the callback functionality. JndiTemplate defines an execute() method that accepts an instance of JndiCallback. Using this method, you can perform a set of actions in the context of the JNDI Context object, all inside the callback handler. This provides an excellent way to encapsulate JNDI operations; indeed, JndiTemplate implements methods like lookup() using the execute() method. However, this feature is only for very specific cases, and in reality, we would always choose the following implementation over both JndiTemplate and InitialContext when performing a simple lookup.

Using JndiObjectFactoryBean

In this section, we look at the JndiObjectFactoryBean that allows JNDI lookups to be configured declaratively. The implementation of MessageResolver that uses JndiObjectFactoryBean to locate the JNDI message resource is much simpler than the previous implementations. The reason for this is that JndiObjectFactoryBean acts as an adapter between the world of JNDI lookup and the world of Spring DI. For this reason, our JndiObjectFactoryBeanMessageResolver class is, as shown in Listing 13-6, designed to receive the message via DI; in fact, it does not perform any JNDI lookup.

Listing 13-6. *The JndiObjectFactoryBeanMessageResolver Class*

```
package com.apress.prospring.ch13.jndi;

import java.util.Hashtable;

public class JndiObjectFactoryBeanMessageResolver implements MessageResolver {

    private String message;

    public String getMessage() {
        return message;
    }

    public void setMessage(String message) {
        this.message = message;
    }
}
```

As you can see, this class has no dependency on InitialContext or JndiTemplate; the value for the message property can come from anywhere. In this case, however, it comes from JNDI. The bulk of the heavy lifting for JndiObjectFactoryBeanMessageResolver is done in the configuration shown in Listing 13-7.

Listing 13-7. *Using JndiObjectFactoryBean*

```
<bean id="messageResolverFactoryBean"
      class="com.apress.prospring.ch13.jndi.JndiObjectFactoryBeanMessageResolver">
        <property name="message">
            <bean class="org.springframework.jndi.JndiObjectFactoryBean">
                <property name="jndiName">
                    <value>message</value>
                </property>
                <property name="resourceRef">
                    <value>true</value>
                </property>
            </bean>
        </property>
    </bean>
```

Here you can see that we are injecting the value for the message property using the JndiObjectFactoryBean. JndiObjectFactoryBean is configured with the name of the JNDI resource to look up (which should be a type that is compatible with the type of property you are injecting into). In this case, we set the jndiName property to message, but remember that the full JNDI name is java:comp/env/message. By setting the resourceRef property to true, we are informing JndiObjectFactoryBean that this resource is stored in the application environment and as such, it should be prefixed with java:comp/env/ if required.

Running the Example

To run this example, we simply compile all the classes and wrap them up in a WAR file that is deployed into JBoss 3.2.5. Although we do not show this here, you can find the build script for this example in the code download that accompanies this book (you can find it in this chapter's folder of the Downloads section of the Apress website at www.apress.com).

If we point our browser to http://localhost:8080/ch13/jndi, we get the output shown in Figure 13-1.

Figure 13-1. *Running the JNDI example*

As you can see, we get the desired output from each MessageResolver implementation, but we need to use differing levels of effort to create each implementation, and we get differing levels of coupling in the resulting implementations.

Other JNDI Operations

The most common operation using JNDI, especially in a J2EE context, is to look up a resource. However, in some cases, you may need to bind a new resource into the tree, rebind a resource that already exists, or unbind a resource completely. For these operations, you have two options. JndiObjectFactoryBean is not applicable in these circumstances because it performs lookups only. This leaves you with InitialContext and JndiTemplate. Both classes can perform lookup, bind, rebind, and unbind operations on the JNDI tree. As we mentioned earlier, the JndiTemplate class does offer the benefit of being able to execute JNDI operations using the callback mechanism. This allows you to wrap operations involving JNDI in distinct command objects that implement the JndiCallback interface.

Which Approach to Use?

With JndiTemplate and InitialContext offering such similar feature sets, you may find determining which approach to use for a given task confusing. Certainly, when you look up resources in JNDI, you should opt to use JndiObjectFactoryBean. By using JndiObjectFactoryBean, you get all the benefits of DI and you don't have to write any lookup code whatsoever. By choosing one of the other options when you perform a lookup, you are losing the flexibility offered by DI and are needlessly coupling your component to JNDI—not to mention creating extra work for yourself.

For operations such as bind, rebind, and unbind, you can choose between JndiTemplate and InitialContext. We prefer to use JndiTemplate because it offers all the same features as InitialContext but also offers the ability to encapsulate reusable JNDI-related logic in command objects that implement JndiCallback. Listing 13-8 shows a simple example of this that performs a bulk lookup of messages from JNDI.

Listing 13-8. *Using JndiCallback*

```
package com.apress.prospring.ch13.jndi;

import javax.naming.Context;
import javax.naming.NamingException;

import org.springframework.jndi.JndiCallback;
import org.springframework.jndi.JndiTemplate;

public class BulkLookupBean {

    private static final String MESSAGE1 = "java:/comp/env/message1";

    private static final String MESSAGE2 = "java:/comp/env/message2";

    private static final String MESSAGE3 = "java:/comp/env/message3";

    private static final String MESSAGE4 = "java:/comp/env/message4";

    public void doLookup() {
        String[] names = new String[] { MESSAGE1, MESSAGE2, MESSAGE3, MESSAGE4 };

        JndiTemplate template = new JndiTemplate();
```

```
        try {
            String[] messages = (String[]) template
                    .execute(new BulkLookupCallback(names));
        } catch (NamingException ex) {
            ex.printStackTrace();
        }
    }

    private class BulkLookupCallback implements JndiCallback {

        private String[] names;

        public BulkLookupCallback(String[] names) {
            this.names = names;
        }

        public Object doInContext(Context ctx) throws NamingException {
            String[] messages = new String[names.length];

            for (int x = 0; x < names.length; x++) {
                messages[x] = (String) ctx.lookup(names[x]);
            }

            return messages;
        }
    }
}
```

Here you can see that we have created an implementation of JndiCallback that looks up a given set of JNDI names and returns a String[] that corresponds to the values stored under these names. InitialContext provides no functionality similar to this, so for complex JNDI operations, JndiTemplate provides a useful way to compartmentalize your code.

Spring and EJB

With the advent of Spring, developers now have, for the first time, a truly lightweight alternative to EJB. Using Spring, you can take advantage of many of the features offered by EJB, such as declarative transaction management, object pooling, and simple ORM functionality. That said, we anticipate that EJB will continue to be used for application development for the foreseeable future. Although we do not look at reasons for or against using EJB in this book, our experience with Spring has been excellent, and we recommend that you use it instead of EJB whenever you can. For a more complete discussion of the pros and cons of both Spring and EJB, read *Expert One-on-One J2EE without EJB* by Rod Johnson and Juergen Hoeller (Wrox, 2004). What we *are* going to focus on in this section is how you can continue to use Spring even though you are building your application using EJB.

EJB Support in Spring

EJB support in Spring can be loosely grouped into two categories: access and implementation. The access support classes in Spring make it easier for you to access EJB resources. You have already seen an example of some of the base access support classes in the section on JNDI. In this section, we look at how Spring extends the basic JNDI support framework to ease EJB access and utilizes AOP support to provide proxy-based access to EJB resources.

The EJB implementation support in Spring provides abstract base classes that make it simpler for you to create three types of EJB: stateless session beans, stateful session beans, and message-driven beans. The basic premise behind these base classes is not so much to ease the burden of creating an EJB, but to enable you to access Spring-managed resources easily from within your beans and, more importantly, to aid you in factoring your business logic out of the EJB implementation and into a POJO used by the EJB. Don't worry if this sounds a little unclear at this point; we discuss this in detail in the next section alongside two examples that should make this crystal clear.

In this section, we build a simple web application that uses two EJB services. The first, a stateless session bean, implements the EchoService business interface and provides simple echoing capabilities. The second, a stateful session bean, implements the CounterService business interface and provides stateful services for counting.

These are trivial examples, but they help to demonstrate the recommended approach to building EJBs with Spring as well as different components involved in Spring's EJB support. As with the JNDI section, we do not go into great detail about the EJB spec itself, other than to discuss the various deployment descriptors that make up our sample. We do, however, peek inside the implementation of Spring's EJB support at the various components and how they affect your application. In particular, we look at how Spring locates the ApplicationContext for your EJBs and how JNDI resources are located using the JNDI infrastructure discussed earlier.

You may have noticed that we mentioned that Spring supports three kinds of EJB, but we are only going to be implementing two types in this chapter. The message-driven bean support classes follow a similar pattern to those for stateless and stateful session beans, and you will find an example of how to build a message-driven bean with Spring in Chapter 12.

Building EJBs with Spring

Spring provides three abstract classes to serve as base classes for your EJB bean classes: AbstractStatelessSessionBean, AbstractStatefulSessionBean, and AbstractMessageDrivenBean. When building an EJB using Spring, you still have to provide all the different interfaces and the home class, but when implementing your bean class, you derive from the appropriate Spring base class. The base classes provided by Spring allow your EJBs to access a Spring ApplicationContext, and thus allow them to access resources that are managed by Spring.

Before we jump into the details of building our EchoService and CounterService beans using Spring, we are going to look at **how** Spring goes about locating an ApplicationContext for your EJBs and the recommended approach for building an EJB when you are using Spring.

The Spring EJB Class Hierarchy

Spring provides a well-defined class hierarchy for the EJB support classes, as shown in Figure 13-2.

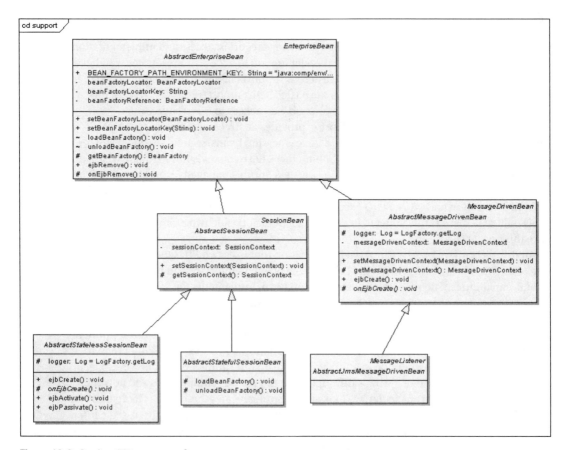

Figure 13-2. *Spring EJB support classes*

As you can see, the central base class, `AbstractEnterpriseBean`, exposes the `beanFactoryLocator` property to allow subclasses access to the `BeanFactoryLocator` instance being used. The `BeanFactoryLocator` interface is discussed in more detail in the next section, along with the `loadBeanFactory()` and `unloadBeanFactory()` methods. Notice that the `AbstractStatelessSessionBean` class has already implemented the `ejbCreate()`, `ejbActivate()`, and `ejbPassivate()` methods, whereas `AbstractStatefulSessionBean` has not. Spring has special requirements regarding bean passivation that we discuss in more detail later, in the section entitled "Building a Stateful Session Bean."

The BeanFactoryLocator Interface

One of the key features offered by the base EJB classes in Spring is the ability to access an `ApplicationContext` from which you can load Spring-managed resources. This functionality is not provided by the base classes themselves; rather, it is delegated to an implementation of the `BeanFactoryLocator` interface, like the one shown in Listing 13-9.

Listing 13-9. *The BeanFactoryLocator Interface*

```
public interface BeanFactoryLocator {

  BeanFactoryReference useBeanFactory(String factoryKey) throws BeansException;

}
```

A `BeanFactoryLocator` is used in circumstances when Spring has no control over the creation of a resource and thus cannot automatically configure it. In these circumstances, a `BeanFactoryLocator` allows a resource to locate the `BeanFactory` itself in an externally configurable way. Of course, in such cases, the resource can simply mandate where the `BeanFactory` configuration must be, but that means that you, as the application developer, have no control over the application. By using `BeanFactoryLocator`, you can fully control how your EJBs locate the `BeanFactory` or `ApplicationContext` they use for configuration.

Notice that the `BeanFactoryLocator` doesn't return a `BeanFactory` instance directly; instead it returns a `BeanFactoryReference`. A `BeanFactoryReference` is a lightweight wrapper around a `BeanFactory` or `ApplicationContext` that allows the resource using the `BeanFactory` to release its reference to the `BeanFactory` gracefully. The actual implementation of this interface is specific to both the `BeanFactoryLocator` implementation and the `BeanFactory` or `ApplicationContext` interface. We investigate this functionality a little more in Listing 13-21 when we look at stateful session beans that use their ability to release a `BeanFactoryReference` to enable bean passivation.

By default, all of the base EJB classes use the `ContextJndiBeanFactoryLocator` implementation of `BeanFactoryLocator`. Essentially, this class looks in a given JNDI location for a comma-separated list of configuration file names and creates an instance of `ClassPathXmlApplicationContext` using these configuration files. You can provide your own implementation of `BeanFactoryLocator` by setting the `beanFactoryLocator` property that is exposed by all three base EJB classes via the `AbstractEnterpriseBean` class. However, if you do so, be aware that each instance of your bean has its own instance of `ContextJndiBeanFactoryLocator`, and likewise, each instance of `ContextJndiBeanFactoryLocator` has its own instance of `ClassPathXmlApplicationContext`.

Although all the `ApplicationContext` instances created for your EJB instances are identically configured, the beans are not identical. Consider a Spring configuration that defines the `echoService` bean the `EchoServiceEJB` will use. If your application server creates 100 instances of your EJB, then 100 instances of `ContextJndiBeanFactoryLocator` are created, along with 100 instances of `ClassPathXmlApplicationContext` and 100 instances of the `echoService` bean. If this behavior is undesirable for your application, then Spring provides the `SingletonBeanFactoryLocator` and `ContextSingletonBeanFactoryLocator` classes that load singleton instances of `BeanFactory` and `ApplicationContext`, respectively. See the JavaDoc for these classes for more information.

The Spring Approach to EJBs

One of the biggest drawbacks of EJB is that it is very difficult to test EJB components separately from the EJB container, which makes unit testing EJB-implemented business logic a feat only attempted by the particularly masochistic. However, a workaround to this problem has been around in the Java world for a long while; it involves implementing your business logic in a POJO that implements the same business interface as your EJB bean class; you can then have the bean class delegate to the POJO. Using Spring makes this implementation much simpler and much more flexible, because you don't have to embed any logic inside the EJB as to how the POJO implementation is located and created. Figure 13-3 shows how we employ this approach when building the EchoService EJB.

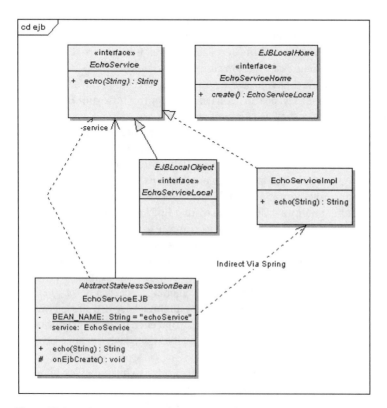

Figure 13-3. *Using a POJO implementation for an EJB*

Here you can see that, as expected, the bean class, EchoServiceEJB, implements the EchoService interface, but also notice that EchoServiceEJB has a dependency on the EchoService interface and a private field of type EchoService.

Building a Stateless Session Bean

A stateless session bean is the easiest EJB to build with Spring; this is because it requires no special handling whatsoever and all the ejbXXX() methods are implemented by the AbstractStatelessSessionBean class.

We start by creating the service interface, as shown in Listing 13-10.

Listing 13-10. *The EchoService Interface*

```
package com.apress.prospring.ch13.ejb;

public interface EchoService {

    public String echo(String message);
}
```

Notice that the service interface is not EJB-specific, and indeed, it is not required when implementing the EJB. The traditional approach to EJB development is to define business methods in the EJB-specific local and remote interfaces. In this approach, the business methods are defined in a standard Java interface and the local and remote bean interfaces extend this standard interface. This service interface not only provides a standard interface for the local and remote interfaces to extend, but it also provides a common interface that both the EJB bean class and the POJO implementation class can implement. Although we recommend that your EJB bean class *does not* implement either the local or remote interface, there is no problem with the EJB bean implementing the service interface. By having all the components that make up the EJB share a common interface, it is easier to ensure that your local interface defines the methods you intend it to, that your bean class implements the methods expected by the local interface, and that the POJO implementation implements the methods required by the EJB bean class.

The next step is to create the bean interface. In this example, we do not use the EJB in a remote container, so we stick to a local interface, as shown in Listing 13-11.

Listing 13-11. *The Local Interface for the EchoService EJB*

```
package com.apress.prospring.ch13.ejb;

import javax.ejb.EJBLocalObject;

public interface EchoServiceLocal extends EchoService, EJBLocalObject {

}
```

Notice that, as we discussed earlier, no business methods are defined in this interface. Instead, the EchoServiceLocal interface extends the service interface, EchoService.

Next, we need to create the EJB home interface. For this example, we are not going to be invoking the EJB remotely, so we stick to a simple local home interface, as shown in Listing 13-12.

Listing 13-12. *Local Home Interface for EchoService EJB*

```
package com.apress.prospring.ch13.ejb;

import javax.ejb.CreateException;
import javax.ejb.EJBLocalHome;

public interface EchoServiceHome extends EJBLocalHome {

    public EchoServiceLocal create() throws CreateException;
}
```

That takes care of most of the boilerplate code required by the EJB specification.

When you are building an EJB using traditional architecture, the next step is to create the bean class. However, we are going to factor the implementation of the EchoService into a POJO and have the EJB bean class delegate to this POJO implementation. Listing 13-13 shows the POJO implementation of the EchoService interface.

Listing 13-13. *POJO Implementation of EchoService*

```
package com.apress.prospring.ch13.ejb;

public class EchoServiceImpl implements EchoService {

    public String echo(String message) {
        return message;
    }
}
```

Here the implementation of EchoService is contained in a POJO that you can easily test outside of the EJB container (not that this implementation needs much testing!).

The final step in the implementation of the EchoService EJB is to create the bean class itself. This is where Spring comes into the equation. With the actual implementation of the EchoService interface contained in EchoServiceImpl, we can simply choose to create an instance of this implementation in EchoServiceEJB and be done with it.

However, what happens if we want to change the implementation? We need to recompile and redeploy the EJB. By using Spring, we can load the implementation class, and any dependencies, from the ApplicationContext. This means that you can take full advantage of all of Spring's features for the actual implementation class, including DI, AOP, and external configuration support. Listing 13-14 shows the implementation of the EchoService bean class.

Listing 13-14. *The EchoServiceEJB Class*

```
package com.apress.prospring.ch13.ejb;

import javax.ejb.CreateException;

import org.springframework.ejb.support.AbstractStatelessSessionBean;

public class EchoServiceEJB extends AbstractStatelessSessionBean implements
        EchoService {

    private static final String BEAN_NAME = "echoService";

    private EchoService service;

    public String echo(String message) {
        return service.echo(message);
    }

    protected void onEjbCreate() throws CreateException {
        service = (EchoService) getBeanFactory().getBean(BEAN_NAME);
    }
}
```

There are a few interesting points to note in this code. First, you should notice that EchoServiceEJB extends the Spring base class AbstractStatelessSessionBean and implements the EchoService interface. Second, all the methods on the EchoService interface are delegated to the wrapped implementation of EchoService. Third, this bean has no ejbXXX() methods— these are all implemented in AbstractStatelessSessionBean. And finally, notice the onEjbCreate() method. This is a hook method provided by AbstractStatelessSessionBean, and it is called during ejbCreate(). This method is perfect for obtaining any Spring-managed resources the EJB needs, in particular, the actual implementation of the service interface. As you can see, we retrieved the echoService bean from Spring and stored it in the service field. This bean is the implementation of EchoService to which the EchoServiceEJB delegates.

Remember from Figure 13-2 that the getBeanFactory() method is declared on the AbstractEnterpriseBean class that forms the base of all Spring EJB implementation support classes. By default, the AbstractEnterpriseBean class uses an instance of ContextJndiBeanFactoryLocator to locate and load an ApplicationContext to return from getBeanFactory(). ContextJndiBeanFactoryLocator works by looking in a particular JNDI location for a list of file names from which to load the ApplicationContext configuration. We can specify this list in the deployment descriptor for the EJB, as shown in Listing 13-15.

Listing 13-15. *Configuring ContextJndiBeanFactoryLocator in Deployment Descriptor*

```
<session>
    <description>Echo Service Bean</description>
    <ejb-name>EchoServiceEJB</ejb-name>
    <local-home>com.apress.prospring.ch13.ejb.EchoServiceHome</local-home>
    <local>com.apress.prospring.ch13.ejb.EchoServiceLocal</local>
    <ejb-class>com.apress.prospring.ch13.ejb.EchoServiceEJB</ejb-class>
    <session-type>Stateless</session-type>
    <transaction-type>Container</transaction-type>
    <env-entry>
        <env-entry-name>ejb/BeanFactoryPath</env-entry-name>
        <env-entry-type>java.lang.String</env-entry-type>
        <env-entry-value>applicationContext.xml</env-entry-value>
    </env-entry>
</session>
```

The important part in this deployment descriptor is the `<env-entry>` tag that sets the value of the `ejb/BeanFactoryPath` JNDI location to `applicationContext.xml`. The JNDI path `ejb/BeanFactoryPath` is the default location where `ContextJndiBeanFactoryLocator` looks for the configuration file path. The configuration in Listing 13-15 is essentially telling the instance of `ContextJndiBeanFactoryLocator` associated with the `EchoServiceEJB` to create an `ApplicationContext` configured using the details in the applicationContext.xml file.

An important point to note is that this configuration file is specific to the EJB and is separate from any applicationContext.xml file you may have for the main application. When we package up the application, we place the applicationContext.xml file specific to the EJBs in the EJB JAR, and then we have the applicationContext.xml file for the web application in the WAR file.

To finish up with the deployment of the `EchoServiceEJB`, we also need the JBoss-specific deployment descriptor for the bean. This is shown in Listing 13-16.

Listing 13-16. *JBoss Deployment Descriptor*

```
<jboss>
    <enterprise-beans>
        <session>
            <ejb-name>EchoServiceEJB</ejb-name>
            <local-jndi-name>ejb/echoService</local-jndi-name>
        </session>
    </enterprise-beans>
</jboss>
```

The important part in this deployment descriptor is the `<local-jndi-name>` tag, which tells JBoss the JNDI name to which to bind the EJB home. In this case, we are able to locate an instance of `EchoServiceHome` under `ejb/echoService`.

That's all for the stateless session bean. As you can see, the implementation steps aren't vastly different from the traditional approach to EJB implementation. However, with the approach taken here, you gain the ability to test your business logic easily and without any dependency on the EJB container. By using Spring, we have made the POJO-based implementation approach much more flexible, and we are easily able to avoid coupling the EJB bean to a particular POJO implementation.

Building a Stateful Session Bean

Building a stateful session bean is slightly more complex than building a stateless session bean because you now have to consider what happens to the ApplicationContext when the bean is passivated. Recall from Figure 13-2 that AbstractStatefulSessionBean does not implement ejbCreate(), ejbActivate(), and ejbPassivate(). The reason for this is that none of the default BeanFactory and ApplicationContext implementations Spring provides is serializable, and as a result, none can be passivated along with your stateful session bean.

To get around this, you have two options. The simplest option is to implement the ejbActivate() and ejbPassivate() to load and unload the ApplicationContext as appropriate, which allows the bean to be passivated without storing the ApplicationContext and reconstructing the ApplicationContext when the bean is activated again. The second option is to provide your own implementation of BeanFactoryLocator that creates a BeanFactory or an ApplicationContext that *is* serializable. When you use the first approach, be aware that when you use the ContextJndiBeanFactoryLocator, bean activation results in the ApplicationContext being loaded from scratch. If this is unacceptable overhead for your application, you can swap ContextJndiBeanFactoryLocator for ContextSingletonBeanFactoryLocator, as discussed earlier.

As before, to start building the bean, we start with the service interface, shown here in Listing 13-17.

Listing 13-17. *The CounterService Interface*

```
package com.apress.prospring.ch13.ejb;

public interface CounterService {

    public int increment();

    public int decrement();
}
```

Again, we created a basic service interface that will be implemented by the local interface, the bean class, and the implementation class.

The next step is to create the local interface, shown in Listing 13-18.

Listing 13-18. *Local Interface for CounterService*

```
package com.apress.prospring.ch13.ejb;

import javax.ejb.EJBLocalObject;

public interface CounterServiceLocal extends CounterService, EJBLocalObject {

}
```

Again, the local interface itself contains no method definitions, and all the business methods are inherited from the CounterService interface.

Next up, we need to create the home interface, as shown in Listing 13-19.

Listing 13-19. *The Local Home Interface for CounterService*

```
package com.apress.prospring.ch13.ejb;

import javax.ejb.CreateException;
import javax.ejb.EJBLocalHome;

public interface CounterServiceHome extends EJBLocalHome {

    public CounterServiceLocal create() throws CreateException;
}
```

Again, there is nothing special about this implementation; it is just the standard EJB approach.

The fourth component required for the CounterService EJB is the POJO implementation. This implementation is stateful and is marked as Serializable, so it can be passivated along with the CounterServiceEJB. Listing 13-20 shows the CounterServiceImpl class.

Listing 13-20. *Basic CounterService Implementation*

```
package com.apress.prospring.ch13.ejb;

import java.io.Serializable;

public class CounterServiceImpl implements CounterService, Serializable {

    private int count = 0;

    public int increment() {
        return ++count;
    }

    public int decrement() {
        return --count;
    }
}
```

Thus far, the implementation of the stateful session bean has been similar to the implementation of the stateless session bean. However, there are notable differences when implementing the bean class. Listing 13-21 shows the bean class for the CounterServiceEJB.

Listing 13-21. *The CounterServiceEJB Class*

```java
package com.apress.prospring.ch13.ejb;

import java.rmi.RemoteException;

import javax.ejb.CreateException;
import javax.ejb.EJBException;

import org.springframework.ejb.support.AbstractStatefulSessionBean;

public class CounterServiceEJB extends AbstractStatefulSessionBean implements
        CounterService {

    private CounterService service;

    public int increment() {
        return service.increment();
    }

    public int decrement() {
        return service.decrement();
    }

    public void ejbCreate() throws CreateException {
        load();
        service = (CounterService) getBeanFactory().getBean("counterService");
    }

    public void ejbActivate() throws EJBException, RemoteException {
        load();
        service = (CounterService) getBeanFactory().getBean("counterService");
    }

    public void ejbPassivate() throws EJBException, RemoteException {
        unload();
    }

    private void load() {
        loadBeanFactory();
    }

    private void unload() {
        unloadBeanFactory();
        setBeanFactoryLocator(null);
    }
}
```

The first part of the bean class implementation is similar to that of the `EchoServiceEJB` that we created earlier. However, the noticeable differences here are in the `ejbCreate()`, `ejbActivate()`, and `ejbPassivate()` methods. In `ejbCreate()`, we invoke the `load()` method, which in turn invokes `loadBeanFactory()` on `AbstractEnterpriseBean`. This causes the `BeanFactoryLocator` implementation to load the `BeanFactory` and makes it available via a call to `getBeanFactory()`. Finally the `ejbCreate()` method uses the `BeanFactory` to access the `counterService` bean and stores it in the `service` field.

The bean is now configured for use and will continue to function happily until the container chooses to passivate it. When this happens, the `ejbPassivate()` method is invoked and, in turn, the `unload()` method. The first step `unload()` takes is to invoke `unloadBeanFactory()`, which clears out the `ApplicationContext` loaded by the `ContextJndiBeanFactoryLocator` and sets the reference to `null`. As we mentioned earlier, the reason for this is that `ClassPathXmlApplicationContext` (the `ApplicationContext` implementation used by `ContextJndiBeanFactoryLocator`) is not serializable and as a result, it cannot be passivated along with the bean. Finally, `unload()` removes all references to the `BeanFactoryLocator` implementation because, like `ClassPathXmlApplicationContext`, `ContextJndiBeanFactoryLocator` is not serializable.

When the container is ready to reactivate a bean after passivation, it invokes `ejbActivate()` on the bean to let the bean know it can reestablish any state that could not be passivated. In this case, we simply invoke `load()` again to reload the `ApplicationContext`. Note that if you are using a custom `BeanFactoryLocator` implementation, then you need to reinstantiate it in `ejbActivate()` as well. Once the `ApplicationContext` is reloaded, we reload the `counterService` bean from the `ApplicationContext`.

You may well be wondering why we bother to reload the `ApplicationContext` in `ejbCreate()`. Given that the `CounterServiceImpl` class is serializable, it will be passivated along with the bean, so all we really need to do is close the `BeanFactory` once we obtain the `counterService` bean. However, remember that you can configure *any* `CounterService` implementation in the `ApplicationContext`, including one that is not serializable. If you can guarantee that all implementations are serializable then you can opt for this approach, perhaps supplementing it with a check in `ejbCreate()` to ensure that the implementation is actually serializable. Where you cannot guarantee that the implementation is serializable, you have to assume that it is not; therefore, you have to unload the `BeanFactory` at passivation and reload it on activation.

As with the stateless session bean, we need to define the location of the configuration for the `ApplicationContext` in the EJB deployment descriptor; this is shown in Listing 13-22.

Listing 13-22. *Deployment Descriptor for Stateful Session Bean*

```
<session>
    <description>Counter Service Bena</description>
    <ejb-name>CounterServiceEJB</ejb-name>
    <local-home>
        com.apress.prospring.ch13.ejb.CounterServiceHome</local-home>
    <local>com.apress.prospring.ch13.ejb.CounterServiceLocal</local>
    <ejb-class>com.apress.prospring.ch13.ejb.CounterServiceEJB</ejb-class>
    <session-type>Stateful</session-type>
    <transaction-type>Container</transaction-type>
    <env-entry>
```

```
    <env-entry-name>ejb/BeanFactoryPath</env-entry-name>
    <env-entry-type>java.lang.String</env-entry-type>
    <env-entry-value>applicationContext.xml</env-entry-value>
    </env-entry>
</session>
```

Accompanying this is the corresponding entry in the JBoss-specific deployment descriptor, shown in Listing 13-23.

Listing 13-23. *JBoss Deployment Descriptor for CounterServiceEJB*

```
<session>
    <ejb-name>CounterServiceEJB</ejb-name>
    <local-jndi-name>ejb/counterService</local-jndi-name>
</session>
```

EJB Implementation Summary

Implementing EJBs with Spring is not drastically different from implementing EJBs using traditional approaches. However, Spring support makes it simple to factor out the implementation of your EJBs into a POJO class, thus reducing the barriers to testing and helping you deliver quality software.

As you saw, implementing a stateless session bean is pretty painless—you have no special requirements to bear in mind. When implementing stateful session beans, be aware of how the particular implementation of BeanFactoryLocator your bean is using affects the bean's ability to passivate successfully. If the BeanFactory returned by the BeanFactoryLocator is not serializable, then you need to remember to call loadBeanFactory() from ejbActivate() and unloadBeanFactory() from ejbPassivate(). Likewise, if the implementation of BeanFactoryLocator being used is not serializable, you need to set it to null in ejbPassivate() and, if you are not using the default implementation, re-create it in ejbActivate().

In some applications you can get around this requirement if you can ensure that any resources you obtain from the BeanFactory are serializable. If this is the case, you can simply store the resources in ejbCreate() and then unload the BeanFactory immediately, with no need to reload and unload because the bean is activated and passivated. If you need to access resources that aren't serializable, then consider using the ContextSingletonBeanFactoryLocator class to reduce the overhead of the ApplicationContext constantly being reloaded.

That concludes the implementation of the EJBs using Spring. Next, you see how to access these resources easily using Spring's EJB access support classes.

Accessing EJBs with Spring

Now that we have created our EJBs, we want, of course, to access them. Earlier in the chapter, you saw how to use Spring's JNDI support to simplify the lookup of JNDI resources. This comes in handy when we are trying to access the stateful CounterServiceEJB, because we can expose the home interface as a Spring-managed resource using JndiObjectFactoryBean. However, for the stateless EchoServiceEJB, we can go a step further. We use the LocalStatelessSessionProxyFactoryBean to create a proxy to the EchoServiceEJB and access it directly using the EchoService interface.

In this section, we are going to demonstrate how you can access both stateless and stateful session beans in a simpler manner using Spring's built-in features. We are going to jump ahead of ourselves slightly and show just the relevant methods from the example servlet. We show the full servlet code later in the section entitled "Testing EchoService and CounterService."

The JndiObjectLocator Infrastructure Component

Before we jump into the juicy details of EJB access, we want to talk about the JndiObjectLocator class in Spring. Earlier in the chapter, we showed you how you can use JndiObjectFactoryBean to look up a resource in JNDI automatically and make it available via DI. In this section, we show you how to use LocalStatelessSessionProxyFactoryBean to look up an EJB home interface in JNDI and automatically build a proxy to the EJB resource associated with that home interface. Both JndiObjectFactoryBean and LocalStatelessSessionProxyFactoryBean share a common ancestor in JndiObjectLocator. This class, along with its parent, JndiLocatorSupport, provides the common logic for obtaining JNDI objects. What does this mean for you? Simply that configuring a LocalStatelessSessionProxyFactoryBean is just like configuring a JndiObjectFactoryBean because most of the properties are exposed on the common base classes. You will see this in practice in the next two sections.

Accessing a Stateless Session Bean via a Proxy

The easiest way to access a stateless session bean in a Spring application is to use a proxy. Spring provides two proxy FactoryBean classes for stateless session beans: LocalStatelessSessionProxyFactoryBean for local beans and SimpleRemoteStatelessSessionProxyFactoryBean for remote beans.

Because the EchoServiceEJB is only exposed through a local interface, we use LocalStatelessSessionProxyFactoryBean in this example, but the configuration is identical for both classes. All you need to do to create the proxy is configure the appropriate FactoryBean in your application configuration file.

Listing 13-24 shows the configuration for the echoService bean, which is a proxy to the EchoServiceEJB.

Listing 13-24. *Configuring a Stateless Session Bean Proxy*

```
<bean id="echoService"
    class="org.springframework.ejb.access.LocalStatelessSessionProxyFactoryBean">
        <property name="jndiName">
            <value>ejb/echoService</value>
        </property>
        <property name="resourceRef">
            <value>true</value>
        </property>
        <property name="businessInterface">
            <value>com.apress.prospring.ch13.ejb.EchoService</value>
        </property>
</bean>
```

The first thing you should notice here is that two of the properties, jndiName and resourceRef, are identical to those used in JndiObjectFactoryBean. This is because, as we described, LocalStatelessSessionProxyFactoryBean and JndiObjectFactoryBean share the same JNDI infrastructure base classes. The third property specified in the configuration, businessInterface, tells the LocalStatelessSessionProxyFactoryBean which interface the proxy should implement. In general, this is the business interface used for the EJB. You can use another interface, perhaps to limit the methods exposed, but be sure that the methods in your interface match methods in the local interface of the EJB. Remember that because LocalStatelessSessionProxyFactoryBean is a FactoryBean, Spring does not return the bean instance itself; instead, it returns the result of FactoryBean.getObject(), which in this case is the proxy to the EJB.

In the simple example servlet that we built, we placed all code related to the stateless EchoServiceEJB in the doStatelessExample() method (see Listing 13-25).

Listing 13-25. *Working with the EJB Proxy*

```
private void doStatelessExample(ApplicationContext ctx, PrintWriter writer) {
        // access the EJB proxy
        EchoService service = (EchoService) ctx.getBean("echoService");
        writer.write(service.echo("Foo"));
}
```

Here you can see that the EchoServiceEJB is accessed via the proxy, as though it were just a standard Spring bean. Using this approach makes it simple to swap out EJBs for standard POJOs and vice versa without affecting any dependency components.

Simplifying Stateful Session Bean Access

When accessing stateful session beans, be aware that currently, no proxy classes are available for you to use. However, you can still simplify your code somewhat by using the JNDI support in Spring.

The first step is to configure a bean in your ApplicationContext to access the EJB home interface, as shown in Listing 13-26.

Listing 13-26. *Accessing EJB Home Using Spring*

```
<bean id="counterServiceHome"
            class="org.springframework.jndi.JndiObjectFactoryBean">
        <property name="jndiName">
            <value>ejb/counterService</value>
        </property>
        <property name="resourceRef">
            <value>true</value>
        </property>
</bean>
```

Here we simply use the JndiObjectFactoryBean to perform the lookup of the home interface automatically. In the code, we can avoid performing this lookup manually and instead access the home interface using Spring. Listing 13-27 shows the example code for the stateful session bean.

Listing 13-27. *Using the CounterServiceEJB*

```
private void doStatefulExample(ApplicationContext ctx, PrintWriter writer,
        HttpSession session) {
    CounterService service = (CounterService) session
            .getAttribute("counterService");

    if (service == null) {

        try {
            CounterServiceHome home = (CounterServiceHome) ctx
                    .getBean("counterServiceHome");

            service = (CounterService) home.create();

            session.setAttribute("counterService", service);
        } catch (CreateException ex) {
            ex.printStackTrace(writer);
            return;
        }
    }

    writer.write("Counter: " + service.increment());
}
```

Notice that we are able to avoid performing the JNDI lookup. Instead, we rely on Spring to do that for us. Because we are storing the handle to the stateful session bean in the HttpSession, subsequent requests to this servlet use the same instance and thus, we see the counter on the page increase.

EJB Access Summary

When using EJBs in your Spring-based applications, you have a lot of options for simplifying how you access them. When using stateful session beans, you can use Spring's JNDI support to simplify the EJB home interface lookup. For stateless session beans, you can go a few steps further and create a proxy to the EJB; this allows you to treat it as a POJO bean and frees you and your application from EJB-specific details.

Testing EchoService and CounterService

All that remains for this example is to finish off the example servlet and package up the application.

Finishing the EjbTestServlet

You have already seen the bulk of the code for the EjbTestServlet class in the doStatelessExample() and doStatefulExample() methods shown earlier. All that is left is the doGet() method, which loads the ApplicationContext and invokes both doStatelessExample() and doStatefulExample(). The code for doGet() is shown in Listing 13-28.

Listing 13-28. *The doGet() Method*

```
protected void doGet(HttpServletRequest request,
            HttpServletResponse response) throws ServletException, IOException {

    PrintWriter writer = response.getWriter();

    response.setContentType("text/html");

    writer.write("<html><head><title>EJB Samples</title></head>");

    writer.write("<body>");

    writer.write("<h1>Echo Service (Stateless Session Bean)</h1>");

    doStatelessExample(ctx, writer);

    writer.write("<h1>Counter Service (Stateful Session Bean)</h1>");

    doStatefulExample(ctx, writer, request.getSession());

    writer.write("</body></html>");

}
```

This code is fairly basic, so we do not need to go into great detail explaining it; the
only point of note is that the ApplicationContext is loaded in the init() method as it was in
Listing 13-2.

Packaging the Sample Application

We are not going to go into great detail regarding the packaging of the sample application, but
we do want to point out that it actually has *two* applicationContext.xml files to configure
Spring. The first, shown in Listing 13-29, goes inside the EJB JAR and is used by the EJBs for
configuration.

Listing 13-29. *ApplicationContext Configuration for EJBs*

```
<?xml version="1.0" encoding="UTF-8"?>
<!DOCTYPE beans PUBLIC "-//SPRING//DTD BEAN//EN"
"http://www.springframework.org/dtd/spring-beans.dtd">

<beans>
    <bean id="echoService"
        class="com.apress.prospring.ch13.ejb.EchoServiceImpl"/>

    <bean id="counterService"
        class="com.apress.prospring.ch13.ejb.CounterServiceImpl"/>
</beans>
```

Here you can see that the POJO implementations of the EchoService and CounterService interfaces are configured and made available for access by the EchoServiceEJB and CounterServiceEJB classes. The second applicationContext.xml file sits in the WEB-INF directory of the web applications WAR file. This file, shown in Listing 13-30, contains the configuration for the EchoServiceEJB proxy and the CounterServiceEJB home interface lookup.

Listing 13-30. *Configuring the Sample Application*

```
<beans>
      <bean id="echoService"
           class="org.springframework.ejb.access.➥
                              LocalStatelessSessionProxyFactoryBean">
      <property name="jndiName">
         <value>ejb/echoService</value>
      </property>
      <property name="resourceRef">
         <value>true</value>
      </property>
      <property name="businessInterface">
         <value>com.apress.prospring.ch13.ejb.EchoService</value>
      </property>
   </bean>
   <bean id="counterServiceHome"
        class="org.springframework.jndi.JndiObjectFactoryBean">
      <property name="jndiName">
         <value>ejb/counterService</value>
      </property>
      <property name="resourceRef">
         <value>true</value>
      </property>
   </bean>
</beans>
```

If you have problems packaging your application, check out the build script included with the code download; it shows how we go about assembling the sample application.

Running the Sample Application

Running the sample application is easy—just drop the EAR file created by the build script into the deploy directory in JBoss and you are on your way. The first time the screen is displayed, it looks something like Figure 13-4.

Here you can see that the foo message is echoed back to the screen by the EchoServiceEJB and that the CounterServiceEJB is currently displaying the count as one. Refreshing this screen results in the same message from EchoServiceEJB, but the counter displayed by CounterServiceEJB steadily increases.

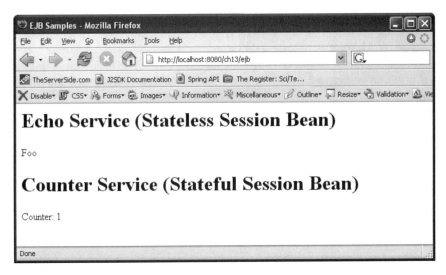

Figure 13-4. *First run of the sample application*

EJB Summary

In this section, we looked at Spring's support for EJB, specifically focusing on support for stateless and stateful session beans. Using Spring's base classes, you can easily create EJBs that are simply wrappers around dynamically loaded business logic. Using this approach makes for easier testing and looser coupling in your application. When accessing stateless session beans, Spring provides proxy support, freeing you of the coding burden of accessing EJB resources and decreasing the coupling in your application.

Spring and JMS

One of the most popular and widely used J2EE APIs, certainly in applications that we have worked on, is JMS. JMS provides a standardized API for accessing messaging services from a Java application. A wide range of JMS-compliant messaging services is available. Every J2EE-compliant application server provides a JMS messaging system and a large number of stand-alone messaging systems support JMS, both open source and commercial. With such a large set of choices available, when choosing a messaging provider, you can easily pick one that is ideal for your solution.

We do not go into great detail on choosing a JMS provider; so many are available and there are so many considerations that the discussion would require a chapter unto itself. What we do point out is that you should not assume that the need for JMS mandates the use of a full J2EE server; plenty of stand-alone JMS providers are available. We have enjoyed considerable success on projects using a simple combination of Spring, Tomcat, and ActiveMQ. Of course, if another requirement of your application leads you to choose an application server—for instance, you may want to use message-driven beans to receive JMS messages—then do not avoid the application server. On the other hand, do not let your need for JMS mean that you have to use an application server.

Spring's support for JMS was introduced in version 1.1 and a whole set of additional functionality is scheduled for 1.2. In this section, we look at how you can send and receive messages easily, to both queues and topics, using Spring JMS support classes. We also look at how you can use Spring's `PlatformTransactionManager` architecture to manage JMS local transactions transparently. In addition to this, we take a peek at the additional functionality scheduled for version 1.2 of Spring.

As with previous sections, we assume that you have a working knowledge of JMS; we won't be discussing JMS basics in any detail.

Introducing ActiveMQ

For the examples in this section, we are going to be using ActiveMQ, which is available from Codehaus at `http://activemq.codehaus.org`. ActiveMQ is an open source, stand-alone JMS messaging service written in 100-percent Java. Because this is a book on Spring, we do not spend a vast amount of time on ActiveMQ, and thankfully you do not need to perform any configuration to get ActiveMQ up and running—other than creating a simple startup script, that is. At the time of writing, version 1.1 of ActiveMQ is currently in development, but we chose to use the stable version 1.0 to ensure that you are able to run the examples.

The feature set of ActiveMQ is huge, but importantly, ActiveMQ supports version 1.1 of JMS, which you must have for some of the examples in this section. Of particular interest to Spring developers is the configuration mechanism of ActiveMQ, which is Spring-based and provides the ability to host an ActiveMQ message broker in your Spring application. We do not cover these features here, but you can find out more about them from the ActiveMQ website.

To get started, download the 1.0 release of ActiveMQand extract the files to a directory on your machine. A notable omission from version 1.0, which is fixed in version 1.1, is a startup script. Thankfully it is fairly easy to create one yourself; Listing 13-31 shows the startup script we created for Windows.

Listing 13-31. *Startup Script for ActiveMQ*

```
java -cp "activemq-1.0.jar;lib\commons-logging-1.0.3.jar;➡
lib\concurrent-1.3.4.jar;lib\geronimo-spec-j2ee-1.0-M1.jar" ➡
org.codehaus.activemq.broker.impl.Main tcp://localhost:61626
```

Save this file into the root directory of your ActiveMQ installation with the .bat extension. Unix users need to swap the backslashes (\) for forward slashes (/) and the semicolons (;) for colons (:). Notice in the last line of the startup script that we pass in a single argument to the `Main` class; this is the URL on which the ActiveMQ message broker should listen for client connections. ActiveMQ supports a number of different communication protocols including TCP, UDP, and SSL. We chose to stick with plain old TCP and instructed the broker to listen on port 61626.

This startup script runs the basic ActiveMQ broker that uses in-memory persistence for messages. This means that if you shut down the ActiveMQ broker, any messages that are not picked up are lost. In the lib directory of the ActiveMQ directory, you will find JAR files for Berkeley DB and JDBM. If you include these JARs (either Berkeley DB or JDBM) in the classpath in your startup script, then ActiveMQ uses a corresponding persistence system for message persistence. See the ActiveMQ website for more details on the different persistence options.

Once you run the startup script, you should receive a message telling you that the ActiveMQ message broker has started and the TCP transport is listening on the configured port.

ActiveMQ, JNDI, JMS, and Spring

One of the nicest features of ActiveMQ is that it is easy to configure. As you saw in the previous section, ActiveMQ runs right out of the box with very little configuration. With a traditional JMS server, such as the one included in a J2EE application server, you configure the JMS ConnectionFactory along with the various Destinations using a vendor-specific mechanism; these are then made available via JNDI. With ActiveMQ, you can configure the ConnectionFactory directly in your Spring ApplicationContext configuration file and inject it into your components just as you would with any standard bean. In addition, you can also configure the different Destinations your application uses in the configuration file; ActiveMQ will create them on the fly as your application attempts to connect. Using these features means that you no longer need to have JNDI service available, nor does your code need to interact with it; in addition, now you can keep the configuration for your messaging resources alongside the resources for the rest of your application.

Throughout this section, we use the ActiveMQ approach to JMS component configuration. If you deploy a Spring-based JMS application into a JMS provider that exposes JMS resources via JNDI, you can make these resources available for DI using the JndiObjectFactoryBean discussed earlier in the chapter.

JMS Domain Model Unification

As you may be aware, JMS defines two distinct messaging domains: point-to-point and publish/subscribe. In version 1.0.2 of JMS, the API was structured in a way that required your application to have prior knowledge of the messaging domain it was using. That is to say, you could not start your application off with a point-to-point model and then switch it to publish/subscribe without making changes to your code. As of version 1.1, the two domains have been unified, and for the most part, your application can remain blissfully unaware.

The JMS helper classes in Spring follow a similar model, allowing your application to code in a domain-independent manner. What makes this interesting is that Spring supports this for both JMS 1.1 and JMS 1.0.2. It should be noted that some of the features we look at, specifically those scheduled for the 1.2 release, are currently 1.1-specific.

The JmsTemplate and JmsTemplate102 Classes

For the most part, applications using Spring JMS interact with the JMS provider via the JmsTemplate class or the JmsTemplate102 class. The JmsTemplate102 class is actually a subclass of the JmsTemplate, which is intended for use with JMS 1.1 providers, and it simply overrides certain methods to work with JMS 1.0.2 providers. Because we are running against a JMS 1.1 provider, we use the JmsTemplate class instead of JmsTemplate102. Unless otherwise specified, you can simply switch to the JmsTemplate102 class if you are using a 1.0.2 provider.

Sending and Receiving Messages Synchronously

The most basic of operations you can perform using JmsTemplate are send and synchronous receive. In general, JMS is more suited to an asynchronous receive style, but as of version 1.1,

Spring JMS does provide a solution for this. We discuss alternatives in more detail later, in the section entitled "Receiving Messages Asynchronously."

In this example, we are going to create two simple console-based applications: one that sends a single message to a queue, and one that listens for a message and displays it once it is received.

To start with, we need to configure the basic JMS ConnectionFactory and JmsTemplate. Because we use the same ConnectionFactory and JmsTemplate settings for all examples in this section, we factor these settings into a common configuration file. Remember that ActiveMQ allows you to configure the ConnectionFactory in your Spring configuration file. You can create JmsTemplate instances directly in your code, but it is better to configure them in your Spring configuration file. That way, you can change settings without having to edit the code, plus you can easily switch between JmsTemplate102 and JmsTemplate if you decide to swap JMS providers.

Listing 13-32 shows the configuration that is shared by all the examples in this section.

Listing 13-32. *Configuring a ConnectionFactory and a JmsTemplate*

```
<!DOCTYPE beans PUBLIC "-//SPRING//DTD BEAN//EN"
"http://www.springframework.org/dtd/spring-beans.dtd">
<beans>

    <!-- configure connection factory -->
    <bean id="connectionFactory"
            class="org.codehaus.activemq.ActiveMQConnectionFactory">
        <property name="brokerURL">
            <value>tcp://localhost:61626</value>
        </property>
    </bean>

    <bean id="jmsTemplate" class="org.springframework.jms.core.JmsTemplate">
        <property name="connectionFactory">
            <ref local="connectionFactory"/>
        </property>
    </bean>

</beans>
```

If you are using a JMS provider that uses JNDI to expose the ConnectionFactory, you can replace the connectionFactory with a JndiObjectFactoryBean to load the ConnectionFactory from JNDI. The only dependency the JmsTemplate class requires is the ConnectionFactory; we set it here using DI. JmsTemplate has a selection of configuration parameters that are mainly related to underlying JMS configuration parameters. You can read more about these in the API docs.

However, there are three properties used by JmsTemplate that you should be aware of. The first property is defaultDestination. It allows you to define a default JMS Destination to send messages to when an explicit Destination is not defined. The second, destinationResolver, allows you to specify the implementation of DestinationResolver that is used to locate Destinations based on a String name. We cover DestinationResolver in more detail later in the chapter.

The final property, pubSubDomain, is only relevant to the JmsTemplate102 class, and it allows you to inform Spring whether or not it should use classes that correspond to the publish/subscribe messaging model in a JMS 1.0.2 environment.

The next step is to configure a Destination to which to send the messages. Because we are just going from one client to another, we can use point-to-point messaging, so we need to configure a JMS Queue. As we mentioned, ActiveMQ allows you to configure Destinations directly in your Spring configuration file, and it creates them on the fly. If you are using a different JMS provider, then you may need to create the Queue explicitly, and you can use JndiObjectFactoryBean to retrieve the Queue from JNDI. Listing 13-33 shows the Queue configuration.

Listing 13-33. *Configuring the Hello World Queue*

```
<!DOCTYPE beans PUBLIC "-//SPRING//DTD BEAN//EN"
"http://www.springframework.org/dtd/spring-beans.dtd">
<beans>

    <bean id="destination" class="org.codehaus.activemq.message.ActiveMQQueue">
        <!-- Set the Queue Name -->
        <constructor-arg index="0">
            <value>HelloWorldQueue</value>
        </constructor-arg>
    </bean>
</beans>
```

Here you can see that we use constructor injection to set the name of the Queue. That is all the configuration needs for this example. To recap, we configured a ConnectionFactory and a JmsTemplate in the common configuration file. The ConnectionFactory is provided to the JmsTemplate as a dependency. In the example-specific configuration file, we configured a single Destination, a Queue. This is where our example application sends to and receives from.

For the code, we start by looking at the HelloWorldSender class which, unsurprisingly, sends the message "Hello World" to the Queue defined in the configuration file. Listing 13-34 shows the code for HelloWorldSender.

Listing 13-34. *Sending a Message Using JmsTemplate*

```
package com.apress.prospring.ch13.jms.helloworld;

import javax.jms.Destination;
import javax.jms.JMSException;
import javax.jms.Message;
import javax.jms.Session;

import org.springframework.context.ApplicationContext;
import org.springframework.context.support.FileSystemXmlApplicationContext;
import org.springframework.jms.core.JmsTemplate;
import org.springframework.jms.core.MessageCreator;
```

```
public class HelloWorldSender {

    public static void main(String[] args) {
        ApplicationContext ctx = new FileSystemXmlApplicationContext(
                new String[] { "./ch13/src/conf/applicationContext-common.xml",
                        "./ch13/src/conf/applicationContext-helloWorld.xml"

        });

        JmsTemplate template = (JmsTemplate) ctx.getBean("jmsTemplate");
        Destination destination = (Destination) ctx.getBean("destination");

        template.send(destination, new MessageCreator() {
            public Message createMessage(Session session) throws JMSException {
                return session.createTextMessage("Hello World");
            }
        });

        System.out.println("Message Sent");
    }
}
```

Most of this code should look familiar, but notice that when we create the
FileSystemXmlApplicationContext, we are passing in a String[] so that both the common
and example-specific configuration files get picked up. The interesting part of this application
is the call to JmsTemplate.send(). JmsTemplate allows you to send using either send() or
convertAndSend(). You see convertAndSend() in action in one of the later examples; for now, we
will stick with send(). The send() method has three overloads: one that accepts a Destination
and a MessageCreator, as shown in the example; one that accepts a String and a MessageCreator;
and one that accepts just MessageCreator. If you use the first of these overloads, Spring sends
the Message created by the MessageCreator to the Destination supplied. Using the second overload, Spring attempts to locate the Destination using the supplied destination name and the
configured DestinationResolver implementation. We use this overload in one of the later
examples. The final overload simply sends the created Message to the configured default
Destination, which by default is null. In Listing 13-34, we use an anonymous implementation
of MessageCreator that simply creates a TextMessage that contains the text "Hello World".

That is really all there is to sending a message using JmsTemplate. Notice that, in Listing 13-34,
we never use any messaging domain-specific classes or interfaces such as Queue. Everything is
expressed in generic terms; only the configuration file points to exactly which messaging model
is being used, and you can change that without affecting the code.

The final part of this example is the HelloWorldReceiver, which receives a single message
from a given Destination, writes it to stdout, and then exits. We configure this class with the
same Destination as the HelloWorldSender class, and it is able to pick up messages sent by the
HelloWorldSender class. Listing 13-35 shows the code for the HelloWorldReceiver class.

Listing 13-35. *Receiving Messages Synchronously with JmsTemplate*

```
package com.apress.prospring.ch13.jms.helloworld;

import javax.jms.Destination;
import javax.jms.Message;

import org.springframework.context.ApplicationContext;
import org.springframework.context.support.FileSystemXmlApplicationContext;
import org.springframework.jms.core.JmsTemplate;

public class HelloWorldReceiver {

    public static void main(String[] args) {
        ApplicationContext ctx = new FileSystemXmlApplicationContext(
                new String[] { "./ch13/src/conf/applicationContext-common.xml",
                        "./ch13/src/conf/applicationContext-helloWorld.xml"

                });

        JmsTemplate template = (JmsTemplate) ctx.getBean("jmsTemplate");
        Destination destination = (Destination) ctx.getBean("destination");

        System.out.println("Will wait " + template.getReceiveTimeout()
                + " seconds for message");

        Message msg = template.receive(destination);
        System.out.println("Received Message: " + msg);
    }
}
```

Notice that much of the code here is very similar to the code in the HelloWorldSender class. The interesting part here is the call to JmsTemplate.receive() in order to retrieve the message from the specified Destination. The receive() method has two other overloads besides the one that accepts Destination. The first of these accepts a String that is used to look up the Destination using the currently configured DestinationResolver. The second of these overloads accepts no arguments and uses the default Destination that is configured in the JmsTemplate instance.

The call to receive() blocks for the number of milliseconds shown by the getReceiveTimeout() method. By default, the timeout is set to –1, which indicates that there is no timeout and that receive() should wait indefinitely for a message. Because this class shares the same configuration as the HelloWorldSender class, no other configuration is required.

Now let's try this example out. First, make sure that ActiveMQ is running on your machine and then start up the HelloWorldReceiver class. This gives you the following message:

```
Will wait -1 seconds for message
```

As we mentioned, the default timeout is set as –1 second, hence the message that is displayed. The `HelloWorldReceiver` class now sits patiently and waits for a message to go into the queue. All that remains is for you to start the `HelloWorldSender` and send the message into the queue. As soon as `HelloWorldSender` exits, notice that `HelloWorldReceiver` also exits, after writing a message similar to the following to `stdout`:

```
Received Message: ACTIVEMQ_TEXT_MESSAGE: dest = HelloWorldQueue, ➥
id = ID:meerkat-1747-1096023135651-10:0, text = Hello World
```

As you can see, you do not need very much code to get send and receive functionality up and running in your application. Using `JmsTemplate`, you can work in a JMS domain-agnostic manner, regardless of whether you are using JMS 1.0.2 or JMS 1.1. The send functionality described here is pretty typical of a standard JMS-based application, but in general, you will want to receive messages in an asynchronous manner; we cover this in more detail later. Before we do, however, we should look at how you can use publish/subscribe `Destinations` in your Spring JMS code.

Using Publish/Subscribe Messaging

You will not be surprised to learn that there really is not a vast amount of difference in your application code when you are using publish/subscribe `Destinations` rather than point-to-point `Destinations`. The main difference is in the application configuration because we need to configure a `Topic` rather than a `Queue` as the `Destination` for our messages. Listing 13-36 shows the configuration for this example.

Listing 13-36. *Configuring a Topic*

```xml
<!DOCTYPE beans PUBLIC "-//SPRING//DTD BEAN//EN"
"http://www.springframework.org/dtd/spring-beans.dtd">
<beans>

    <bean id="destination" class="org.codehaus.activemq.message.ActiveMQTopic">
        <!-- Set the Destination Name -->
        <constructor-arg index="0">
            <value>FantasyFootballTopic</value>
        </constructor-arg>
    </bean>
</beans>
```

Again we configure the ActiveMQ class appropriate to the `Destination` type directly in the configuration file rather than obtaining the object from a JNDI registry. The send part of this example (see Listing 13-37) is very similar to the previous example shown in Listing 13-34, except this time, we send multiple messages and use the `convertAndSend()` method to do so.

Listing 13-37. *Sending Messages to a Topic*

```
package com.apress.prospring.ch13.jms.pubsub;

import javax.jms.Destination;

import org.springframework.context.ApplicationContext;
import org.springframework.context.support.FileSystemXmlApplicationContext;
import org.springframework.jms.core.JmsTemplate;

public class Producer {

    public static void main(String[] args) throws Exception{
        ApplicationContext ctx = new FileSystemXmlApplicationContext(
                new String[] { "./ch13/src/conf/applicationContext-common.xml",
                        "./ch13/src/conf/applicationContext-pubsub.xml"

        });

        JmsTemplate template = (JmsTemplate) ctx.getBean("jmsTemplate");
        final Destination destination = (Destination) ctx.getBean("destination");

        for(int x = 0; x < 2; x++) {
            System.out.println("Sending Message: " + x);
            template.convertAndSend(destination, "Foo: " + x);
            Thread.sleep(400);
        }
    }
}
```

You will recognize much of this code from the previous example (see Listing 13-34), but the interesting part here is inside the for loop. The convertAndSend() method is capable of converting Java objects into Message instances and sending them directly. To perform the conversion, convertAndSend() uses the instance of MessageConverter that is currently configured with the JmsTemplate. We discuss MessageConverters in more detail in the next section; for now, it is enough to know that the String we supply gets converted to a TextMessage instance. The call to Thread.sleep() simply slows the producer down, because we noticed that with these basic settings, the messages are being sent so fast that the consumers lose some arbitrarily.

The receive portion of this example, the Consumer class, is also very similar to the last example; the main difference here is that we put Consumer in an infinite loop, constantly waiting for new messages. Listing 13-38 shows the code for the Consumer class.

Listing 13-38. *The Consumer Class*

```
package com.apress.prospring.ch13.jms.pubsub;

import javax.jms.Destination;
import javax.jms.Message;

import org.springframework.context.ApplicationContext;
import org.springframework.context.support.FileSystemXmlApplicationContext;
import org.springframework.jms.core.JmsTemplate;

public class Consumer {

    public static void main(String[] args) throws Exception {
        ApplicationContext ctx = new FileSystemXmlApplicationContext(
                new String[] { "./ch13/src/conf/applicationContext-common.xml",
                        "./ch13/src/conf/applicationContext-pubsub.xml"

                });

        System.out.println("Starting Consumer");

        JmsTemplate template = (JmsTemplate) ctx.getBean("jmsTemplate");
        final Destination destination = (Destination) ctx
                .getBean("destination");

        while (true) {
            System.out.println("Waiting...");
            Message msg = template.receive(destination);
            System.out.println("Received: " + msg);
        }
    }
}
```

At this point, nothing in this code should look unfamiliar. To test out this application, first start up three instances of the Consumer class; each instance should display the following message on screen:

```
Starting Consumer
Waiting...
```

Next, run a single instance of the Producer class to send two messages to the publish/subscribe Destination. Once the Producer class exits, notice that all three of the running Consumer instances display something similar to this:

```
Received: ACTIVEMQ_TEXT_MESSAGE: dest = FantasyFootballTopic, ➥
id = ID:meerkat-1879-1096026129573-10:0, text = Foo: 0
Waiting...
Received: ACTIVEMQ_TEXT_MESSAGE: dest = FantasyFootballTopic, ➥
id = ID:meerkat-1879-1096026129573-20:0, text = Foo: 1
Waiting...
```

As with the point-to-point example, there is not really much to say about this example. The code is extremely clear and simple to understand. However, notice that nothing in the code is specific to working with a publish/subscribe Destination. As we already stated, Spring provides this domain model-independent API regardless of whether you use JMS 1.1 or not.

A Note on MessageConverters

In the previous example, shown in Listing 13-37, we used the JmsTemplate.convertAndSend() method to convert a String to an instance of TextMessage and send it to a given Destination—all automatically. Behind the scenes, Spring uses an implementation of the MessageConverter interface to convert the Java object to an instance of Message that can be sent to the JMS provider. When receiving a message with the receiveAndConvert() method, which has overloads similar to receive(), Spring uses the MessageConverter to perform the reverse operation, transforming an instance of Message into an instance of an arbitrary object.

The default implementation of MessageConverter, SimpleMessageConverter, performs a variety of simple conversions both to and from Messages, including String to TextMessage and Map to MapMessage. You can find the full details of all the conversions performed by this class in the JavaDoc.

If you have a special requirement for your application, then you can create your own MessageConverter and configure it for a given JmsTemplate using the messageConverter property. As usual, it is best to configure this externally in the Spring configuration file.

Using JMS Local Transactions

In Chapter 12, we discussed Spring's support for transaction management and demonstrated how to use distributed transactions across multiple resource providers including a JMS provider. In this section, we expand on this discussion and look at how you can use Spring's PlatformTransactionManager to manage JMS local transactions declaratively in your applications. If you have not yet read the previous chapter, you might want to look at it now because we do not discuss the transaction architecture in any detail here.

To take advantage of Spring's transaction management functionality, first we need to wrap the JMS operations we want to perform inside a single method in a business object. We can then get Spring to create the transaction proxy of this business interface and send messages to a Destination as part of a transaction. Listing 13-39 shows the code for the Sender class that we use to highlight this functionality.

Listing 13-39. *The Sender Class*

```
package com.apress.prospring.ch13.jms.trans;

import org.springframework.jms.core.JmsTemplate;

public class Sender {

    public static final String DESTINATION_NAME = "transDemo";

    private JmsTemplate template;

    public void setJmsTemplate(JmsTemplate template) {
        this.template = template;
    }

    public void sendMessages() {
        for(int x = 0; x < 10; x++) {
            template.convertAndSend(DESTINATION_NAME, "bar");

            if(x == 8) {
                throw new RuntimeException("Ha Ha!");
            }
        }
    }
}
```

Most of this code should look familiar to you by now; however, there are two points of interest. First, notice that after nine messages are sent, a RuntimeException is thrown, which prevents the final message from being sent. When this code is running as part of a transaction, none of these messages should be in the queue once the transaction rolls back, but when this is executing outside of a transaction, the nine messages sent before the RuntimeException is thrown continue to exist in the queue.

Second, notice that we have used the overload of convertAndSend() that accepts a String instead of a Destination. When using this overload, Spring uses the instance of DestinationResolver that is configured for the JmsTemplate to locate the Destination object using the String value you supplied as the key. The exact meaning of the key differs between the different implementations of DestinationResolver; for instance, in the default implementation, DynamicDestinationResolver, the key is simply used as the Destination name. This is very useful when coupled with ActiveMQ, which creates the Destinations on the fly. The other implementation included with Spring is JndiDestinationResolver, which looks for Destination in JNDI—the key is the JNDI name that Spring should look under for the Destination.

The next step in this example is to create the configuration file. We want to demonstrate how to use the Sender class both inside and outside a transaction. To do this, we create a bean of instance Sender and then we create a transactional proxy to this bean. The code for this configuration is shown in Listing 13-40.

Listing 13-40. *Configuring the Sender Class*

```
<!DOCTYPE beans PUBLIC "-//SPRING//DTD BEAN//EN"
"http://www.springframework.org/dtd/spring-beans.dtd">
<beans>

    <bean id="senderTarget" class="com.apress.prospring.ch13.jms.trans.Sender">
        <property name="jmsTemplate">
                <ref bean="jmsTemplate"/>
        </property>
    </bean>

    <bean id="transactionManager"
class="org.springframework.jms.connection.JmsTransactionManager">
        <property name="connectionFactory">
            <ref bean="connectionFactory"/>
        </property>
    </bean>

    <bean id="sender"
class="org.springframework.transaction.interceptor.TransactionProxyFactoryBean">
        <property name="transactionManager">
            <ref local="transactionManager"/>
        </property>
        <property name="target">
            <ref local="senderTarget"/>
        </property>
        <property name="transactionAttributes">
            <props>
                <prop key="send*">PROPAGATION_REQUIRED</prop>
            </props>
        </property>
    </bean>
</beans>
```

Much of the detail in this configuration file has already been discussed in this chapter or the last. The interesting point is that, because we are looking to manage JMS transactions, we use the JmsTransactionManager implementation of PlatformTransactionManager. As you saw previously, using JMS along with another resource provider in a distributed transaction requires JtaTransactionManager. Notice that when configuring the JmsTransactionManager, we pass it a reference of the ConnectionFactory so that it can manage transactions appropriately.

With the configuration in place, all that remains is to test both the transaction and nontransaction Sender beans. Listing 13-41 shows the code for this.

Listing 13-41. *JMS Transactions in Action*

```
package com.apress.prospring.ch13.jms.trans;

import javax.jms.Message;

import org.springframework.aop.support.AopUtils;
import org.springframework.context.ApplicationContext;
import org.springframework.context.support.FileSystemXmlApplicationContext;
import org.springframework.jms.core.JmsTemplate;

public class TransactionDemo {

    public static void main(String[] args) {
        ApplicationContext ctx = new FileSystemXmlApplicationContext(
                new String[] { "./ch13/src/conf/applicationContext-common.xml",
                        "./ch13/src/conf/applicationContext-trans.xml"

                });

        Sender transactional = (Sender) ctx.getBean("sender");
        Sender nonTransactional = (Sender) ctx.getBean("senderTarget");

        System.out.println("Trying Transactional...");
        runTest(transactional, ctx);
        System.out.println("Trying Non Transactional...");
        runTest(nonTransactional, ctx);
    }

    private static void runTest(Sender sender, ApplicationContext ctx) {
        System.out.println("Got Transactional Proxy?: "
                + AopUtils.isAopProxy(sender));

        try {
            sender.sendMessages();
        } catch (Exception ex) {
            System.out.println("Sender Threw Exception");
        }

        // now try to receive messages
        JmsTemplate template = (JmsTemplate) ctx.getBean("jmsTemplate");

        // set timeout so that eventually
        // we stop trying to receive
        template.setReceiveTimeout(2000);
```

```
        Message msg = null;
        int count = 0;

        do {
            msg = template.receive(Sender.DESTINATION_NAME);

            if (msg != null)
                count++;

        } while (msg != null);

        System.out.println("Received " + count + " messages.");
    }
}
```

Much of this code you have already seen in this chapter; the interesting part is inside the runTest() method. Once we have invoked Sender.sendMessages(), we attempt to retrieve any messages that are in the queue and count them to see if the transaction was applied correctly. By setting the timeout to 2 seconds, we ensure that the JmsTemplate.receive() method does not block forever and eventually, when there are no messages left, we get a count of the messages received. When running this code, we should see that for the first execution of runTest(), which uses the transactional Sender bean, the message count should be 0, because the whole sending process happened inside a transaction that was rolled back due to the RuntimeException thrown by the Sender class. When the runTest() method executes for the second time, this time with the nontransactional Sender bean, we should see a message count of nine, since nine messages are sent before the RuntimeException is raised.

Running the example proves this to be the case, as shown here:

```
Trying Transactional...
Got Transactional Proxy?: true
Sender Threw Exception
Received 0 messages.
Trying Non Transactional...
Got Transactional Proxy?: false
Sender Threw Exception
Received 9 messages.
```

As you can see, the transaction kicked in as appropriate and caused a rollback when the RuntimeException was thrown, preventing the first nine messages sent from being committed to the queue. As this example shows, using JMS transactions with Spring is just as simple as using any other transactional resource supported by Spring. By using the declarative transaction features, you remove your need to manage transactions, and you can easily define transactional boundaries in terms of the methods on your business objects.

Receiving Messages Asynchronously

Earlier in this section, we looked at how you can send messages to a Destination and then receive them in a synchronous manner using JmsTemplate. The main drawback with this approach is that it doesn't accurately reflect the way JMS is used in most nontrivial applications—

with asynchronous receive. As of version 1.1, the only support class for receiving messages asynchronously is the AbstractMessageDrivenBean class (covered in Chapter 12) that helps you build a message-driven EJB. When using a J2EE application server, message-driven beans are an excellent way to receive messages in an asynchronous manner, but when using a simple servlet container such as Tomcat, they obviously do not work.

Thankfully, the lack of support for asynchronous receive in Spring 1.1 is currently being addressed and the solution, from our tests, seems functionally complete. Currently available in the sandbox area of the Spring CVS repository is a selection of FactoryBean implementations. These are designed for use with JMS and make creating a JMS application with asynchronous receive simple. In this section, we preview these classes to see how they are used. Be aware that the classes discussed here are not yet finalized and may change before release. That said, they are already functionally complete, and we anticipate that the changes, if any, will be minimal.

To run the examples in this section, you need to check out the Spring source code from CVS. You can find instructions on doing so at http://sourceforge.net/cvs/?group_id=73357. Once you have the source code, you need to build both the main code branch and the sandbox code branch. You can do this by running the fulljar and sandboxjar targets in the Ant build script supplied with the code. Once you have the two JAR files, be sure to include them in your classpath so you can run the examples in this section.

Previewing Spring 1.2 JMS Support

The biggest addition to JMS support that Spring 1.2 will bring is a set of FactoryBeans that allow you to configure many more aspects of your JMS application in your configuration. One of the main features offered by this approach is that you can hook up a MessageListener implementation to a JMS Destination completely within your application configuration.

Before we look into the configuration of the different JMS components, we need a MessageListener implementation. Listing 13-42 shows this (very basic) implementation.

Listing 13-42. *A Simple MessageListener Implementation*

```
package com.apress.prospring.ch13.jms.asynch;

import javax.jms.Message;
import javax.jms.MessageListener;

public class Listener implements MessageListener {
    public void onMessage(Message msg) {
        System.out.println("Received Message: " + msg);
    }
}
```

Here you can see that when a message is received, we simply write it to stdout. In a real application, you would, no doubt, perform much more processing than this, but for example purposes, this implementation is fine.

With the MessageListener implementation completed, we can now move on to configure the various JMS components. What we are looking for is a way to configure a MessageProducer that we can use to create messages and a MessageConsumer to link up our MessageListener. Before we can create either of these, we need a Session, and before we can create the Session, we need a Connection. Thankfully, FactoryBeans for all of these components are provided. Listing 13-43 shows the configuration for these different components.

Listing 13-43. *Wiring JMS Components with Spring*

```
<!DOCTYPE beans PUBLIC "-//SPRING//DTD BEAN//EN"
"http://www.springframework.org/dtd/spring-beans.dtd">
<beans>
    <bean id="destination" class="org.codehaus.activemq.message.ActiveMQQueue">
        <!-- Set the Destination Name -->
        <constructor-arg index="0">
            <value>BarQueue</value>
        </constructor-arg>
    </bean>

    <bean id="connection" class="org.springframework.jms.JmsConnectionFactoryBean">
        <property name="connectionFactory">
            <ref bean="connectionFactory"/>
        </property>
    </bean>

    <bean id="session" class="org.springframework.jms.JmsSessionFactoryBean">
        <property name="connection">
            <ref local="connection"/>
        </property>
    </bean>

    <bean id="producer" class="org.springframework.jms.JmsProducerFactoryBean">
        <property name="destination">
            <ref local="destination"/>
        </property>
        <property name="session">
            <ref local="session"/>
        </property>
    </bean>

    <bean id="consumer" class="org.springframework.jms.JmsConsumerFactoryBean">
        <property name="destination">
            <ref local="destination"/>
        </property>
        <property name="session">
            <ref local="session"/>
        </property>
        <property name="messageListener">
            <ref local="messageListener"/>
        </property>
    </bean>
```

```
    <bean id="messageProducer"
              class="com.apress.prospring.ch13.jms.asynch.Producer">
        <property name="messageProducer">
            <ref local="producer"/>
        </property>
        <property name="session">
            <ref local="session"/>
        </property>
    </bean>

    <bean id="messageListener"
              class="com.apress.prospring.ch13.jms.asynch.Listener"/>
</beans>
```

There are a number of beans in this configuration file, but the overall effect should be simple to understand. Using the connectionFactory bean from the common configuration file, we create a JMS Connection using the JmsConnectionFactoryBean. With this Connection, we create a Session using JmsSessionFactoryBean. From here, we create both a MessageProducer and a MessageConsumer using the appropriate FactoryBean, wiring in our MessageListener implementation to the MessageConsumer. Notice as well that we have configured an instance of the Producer class, the code for which is shown in Listing 13-44.

Listing 13-44. *Sending Messages with MessageProducer*

```
package com.apress.prospring.ch13.jms.asynch;

import javax.jms.Message;
import javax.jms.MessageProducer;
import javax.jms.Session;

import org.springframework.context.ApplicationContext;
import org.springframework.context.support.FileSystemXmlApplicationContext;

public class Producer {

    private MessageProducer producer;
    private Session session;

    public static void main(String[] args) throws Exception{
        ApplicationContext ctx = new FileSystemXmlApplicationContext(
                new String[] { "./ch13/src/conf/applicationContext-common.xml",
                    "./ch13/src/conf/applicationContext-asynch.xml"

                });
```

```
            Producer p = (Producer)ctx.getBean("messageProducer");
            p.createMessages();
            System.out.println("Done");
        }

        public void setMessageProducer(MessageProducer producer) {
            this.producer = producer;
        }

        public void setSession(Session session) {
            this.session = session;
        }

        public void createMessages() throws Exception{
            for(int x = 0; x < 10; x++) {
                Message m = session.createTextMessage("Foo " + x);
                producer.send(m);
                System.out.println("Sent Message: " + x);
            }
        }
    }
}
```

In this class, we use the MessageProducer and Session beans configured in Spring to send ten messages to a given Destination; the particular Destination is defined in the configuration for the MessageProducer bean. This covers the send part of the example. All that is required at the receive end is a simple application that starts the JMS Connection, and then the MessageListener starts receiving messages sent to the queue. Listing 13-45 shows the code for the Consumer class that does just this.

Listing 13-45. *The Consumer Class*

```
package com.apress.prospring.ch13.jms.asynch;

import javax.jms.Connection;

import org.springframework.context.ApplicationContext;
import org.springframework.context.support.FileSystemXmlApplicationContext;

public class Consumer{

    public static void main(String[] args) throws Exception{
        ApplicationContext ctx = new FileSystemXmlApplicationContext(
                new String[] { "./ch13/src/conf/applicationContext-common.xml",
                    "./ch13/src/conf/applicationContext-asynch.xml"

        });
```

```
            Connection connection = (Connection)ctx.getBean("connection");
            connection.start();

            System.out.println("Started");
            System.in.read();
        }
    }
```

There really isn't much to say about this class, other than if you do not start the Connection, the MessageListener will not receive any messages. To test this, first start up an instance of the Consumer class which, once started, displays the Started message and sits happily waiting for new messages. Once the Consumer class starts, run the Producer class a few times; each time you run it, your Consumer class receives a new set of messages.

JMS Summary

Current Spring support for JMS allows you to send messages quickly and easily in a manner that is independent of the underlying JMS domain model, be it point-to-point or publish/subscribe. This is a feature that is already enjoyed by users of JMS 1.1–compliant providers, but Spring brings this functionality to JMS 1.0.2 users as well.

Using MessageConverters, you can support a complex conversion between JMS Messages and arbitrary Java types. Using the JmsTransactionManager, you can manage local JMS transactions using Spring's PlatformTransactionManager architecture. With features coming in Spring 1.2, you will be able to support full asynchronous messaging easily and without EJB.

Summary

In this chapter, we took a detailed look at Spring's support for building applications using traditional J2EE technologies. We looked at how Spring can simplify the use of JNDI in your application, and in particular, how Spring acts as an adapter layer between resources held in JNDI and beans managed by Spring.

In the EJB section, we examined Spring's EJB support class for building both stateless and stateful session beans. In addition, we analyzed how Spring's EJB classes sit on top of the JNDI support classes and the AOP framework to provide proxy-based access to stateless session beans.

In the final part of this chapter, we explored how to use Spring to simplify JMS-based applications and how Spring's JMS support is integrated into the PlatformTransactionManager architecture. As part of the coverage of JMS, we peeked inside the Spring sandbox to see what JMS-related features are coming up in Spring 1.2; in particular, we discussed support for the asynchronous send.

In the next chapter, we talk about how Spring integrates with the popular Quartz scheduling engine to provide job scheduling capabilities to your application.

■ ■ ■

CHAPTER 14

Job Scheduling with Spring

Most application logic happens in response to some form of user action, such as a button click or a form submission. However, in many applications certain processes must be invoked *without* user interaction, usually at a given interval. For example, you might have a process that cleans out temporary files once an hour or a process that creates a data export from a database and sends it to an external system once a day at midnight. Most nontrivial applications require some kind of scheduling support, if not directly related to business logic of the application, then to support system housekeeping.

When you are building scheduled tasks for your application, it is fairly simple to create a task that runs once an hour or once a day. But what about a task that runs at 15:00 every Monday, Wednesday, and Friday? This is a little more difficult to code, and it makes sense to use prebuilt scheduling solutions rather than attempt to create your own scheduling framework.

When talking about scheduling from a programming perspective, we tend to talk about three distinct concepts. A **job** is a unit of work that needs to be scheduled to run at a specific interval. A **trigger** is a condition that causes a job to run, perhaps a fixed interval or a given piece of data. A **schedule** is a collection of triggers that govern the complete schedule of a job. Typically, you encapsulate a job by implementing some interface or extending some given base class. You define your triggers in whatever terms your scheduling framework supports. Some frameworks may support only basic interval-based triggers, whereas others, such as Quartz, provide much more flexible trigger schemes. In general, a job only has a single trigger in its schedule, and the terms schedule and trigger are often used interchangeably.

Scheduling support in Spring comes in two distinct forms: JDK Timer-based and Quartz-based. The JDK Timer-based approach provides scheduling capabilities on any 1.3 or later JVM, and it does not need external dependencies beyond Spring. Timer-based scheduling is quite primitive and provides limited flexibility when defining job schedules. However, Timer support is included with Java and requires no external libraries, which might be beneficial if you are restricted by application size or corporate policy. Quartz-based scheduling is much more flexible and allows triggers to be defined in a much more real-world way, such as the earlier example of 15:00 every Monday, Wednesday, and Friday.

In this chapter, we explore both of the scheduling solutions included with Spring. In particular, this chapter discusses three core topics:

- **Scheduling with the JDK Timer:** In this section, we explore Spring's support for JDK Timer-based scheduling. This section introduces the different trigger types available with Timer-based scheduling and looks at how you can schedule any arbitrary logic without needing to create additional Java code.

- **Quartz-based scheduling:** In this section, we look at the comprehensive Quartz scheduling engine and how it is integrated into Spring. In particular, we examine Quartz support for cron expressions allowing for highly complex schedules to be configured using a concise format. As with the JDK Timer section, in this section, you see how to schedule any logic without needing to encapsulate it for Quartz.

- **Job scheduling considerations:** In this section, we discuss the various points to consider when choosing a scheduling implementation and patterns to use when creating logic for scheduled execution.

Scheduling Jobs Using JDK Timer

The most basic scheduling support with Spring is based on the JDK java.util.Timer class. When scheduling using Timer, you are limited to simple interval-based trigger definitions, which makes Timer-based scheduling only suitable for jobs that you need to execute just once at some given future time, or that you need to execute at some fixed frequency.

Trigger Types with Timer

Timer-based scheduling offers you the three types of triggers described in Table 14-1.

Table 14-1. *Trigger Types for Timer-Based Scheduling*

Trigger Type	Description
One-Off	When you use a one-off trigger, job execution is scheduled for some given point in the future, defined as the number of milliseconds from a given date. After the job executes, it is not rescheduled for further execution. We have found that one-off triggers are great for scheduling jobs that need to be done once, because you might forget to do them yourself. For instance, if a web application has scheduled maintenance coming up in a week, then we can schedule a task to switch on the "In Maintenance" page when the maintenance is due to begin.
Repeating, Fixed-Delay	When you use a fixed-delay trigger, you schedule the first execution of the job just like you did for a one-off trigger, but after that, it is rescheduled to execute after a given interval. When you are using fixed-delay, the interval is relative to the actual execution time of the previous job. This means that the interval between successive executions is always approximately the same, even if this means that executions occur "late" when compared to the original schedule. With this type of trigger, the interval you specify is the actual interval between subsequent executions. Use this approach when the interval between executions must be kept as constant as possible.
Repeating, Fixed-Rate	Fixed-rate triggers function in a similar way to fixed-delay triggers, but the next execution time is always calculated based on the initial scheduled execution time. This means that if a single execution is delayed, subsequent executions are not delayed as a result. With this type of trigger, the interval you specify is not necessarily the actual interval between subsequent executions. Use this approach when the interval between executions is not important, but the actual execution time is.

You may find it quite difficult to visualize the differences between fixed-delay and fixed-rate triggers and, unfortunately, it is very difficult for us to create an example that causes enough of a delay in execution to highlight the differences reliably. That said, here is a simple example that should highlight the differences.

Consider a task that starts executing at 13:00 and has a specified interval for 30 minutes. The task runs fine until 16:30 when the system experiences a heavy load and a particularly nasty garbage collection; these cause the actual execution time to be a minute late—16:31. Now, with fixed-delay scheduling it is the *actual* interval that is important, that is to say, we want 30 minutes between each actual execution, so the next execution is scheduled for 17:01 rather than 17:00. With fixed-rate scheduling, the interval defines the *intended* interval—that is to say, we intend the job to execute every 30 minutes based on start time, not on the time of the last job—so the job is scheduled for execution at 17:00.

Both of these trigger types have their uses. In general, you use fixed-rate triggers for real-time–sensitive operations such as those that must execute every hour on the hour. You use fixed-delay triggers for situations where you want the time between each execution to be as regular as possible or when you want to avoid the possibility of two executions happening too close together, as can happen with fixed-rate execution if a particular execution is delayed long enough.

Creating a Simple Job

To create a job to use with the Timer class, you simply extend the TimerTask class and implement the run() method to execute your job's logic. Listing 14-1 shows a simple TimerTask implementation that writes "Hello World" to stdout.

Listing 14-1. *Creating a Basic TimerTask*

```
package com.apress.prospring.ch14.timer;

import java.util.TimerTask;

public class HelloWorldTask extends TimerTask {

    public void run() {
        System.out.println("Hello World!");
    }
}
```

Here you can see that in the run() method, we simply write the "Hello World" message to stdout. Each time a job is executed, Timer invokes the TimerTask's run() method. The simplest possible trigger we can create for this job is a one-off trigger to start the job in 1 second; Listing 14-2 shows this.

Listing 14-2. *Using a One-Off Trigger with the HelloWorldTask*

```
package com.apress.prospring.ch14.timer;

import java.util.Timer;

public class OneOffScheduling {

    public static void main(String[] args) {
        Timer t = new Timer();
        t.schedule(new HelloWorldTask(), 1000);
    }
}
```

In order to schedule a job using a given trigger when you are using the JDK Timer class, you must first create an instance of the Timer class and then create the trigger using one of the schedule() or scheduleAtFixedRate() methods. In Listing 14-2, we used the schedule() method to schedule an instance of HelloWorldTask to run after a delay of 1,000 milliseconds. If you run this example, after the initial delay of 1 second, you get the following message:

```
Hello World!
```

This kind of one-off trigger is fairly useless—how often are you going to need to schedule a one-off task to run an arbitrary period of time after application startup? For this reason, you can also specify an absolute date when you create a one-off trigger. So if we want to create a job to remind us 7 days before an important birthday, we can replace our call to Timer.schedule() with something like this:

```
Calendar cal = Calendar.getInstance();
cal.set(2005, Calendar.NOVEMBER, 30);
t.schedule(new HelloWorldTask(), cal.getTime());
```

In this example, you can see that we created an instance of Calendar for the date November 30, 2005. Then, using the Calendar instance, we scheduled the HelloWorldTask to run. This is clearly more useful than the first example, because no matter what time the application starts, the job is always scheduled to run at the same time. The only drawback with this approach is that we will not be reminded about the birthday in 2006 or 2007 unless we explicitly add more triggers. By using a repeating trigger, we can get around this.

Both types of repeating trigger, fixed-delay and fixed-rate, are configured in the same way—you specify a starting point, using either a number of milliseconds relative to the call to schedule() or an absolute date, and then you specify an interval in milliseconds to control when subsequent executions occur. Remember that "interval" is interpreted differently depending on whether you are using a fixed-delay or fixed-rate trigger.

We can schedule the HelloWorldTask job to run every 3 seconds with a 1-second delay using the code shown in Listing 14-3.

Listing 14-3. *Scheduling a Repeating Task*

```
package com.apress.prospring.ch14.timer;

import java.util.Timer;

public class FixedDelayScheduling {

    public static void main(String[] args) throws Exception{
        Timer t = new Timer();
        t.schedule(new HelloWorldTask(), 1000, 3000);
    }
}
```

If you run this application you will see the first "Hello World" message displayed after about 1 second, followed by further "Hello World" messages every 3 seconds. To schedule this job using a fixed-rate trigger, simply replace the call to Timer.schedule() with a call to Timer.scheduleAtFixedRate(), as shown in Listing 14-4.

Listing 14-4. *Scheduling a Job Using a Fixed-Rate Trigger*

```
package com.apress.prospring.ch14.timer;

import java.util.Timer;

public class FixedRateScheduling {

    public static void main(String[] args) throws Exception {
        Timer t = new Timer();
        t.scheduleAtFixedRate(new HelloWorldTask(), 1000, 1000);
    }
}
```

As with the one-off trigger, you can start both fixed-delay and fixed-rate triggers using an absolute date. Using this approach, we can create a trigger for our birthday reminder example that runs on a given date and then repeats each year. This is shown in Listing 14-5.

Listing 14-5. *Scheduling Birthday Reminders*

```
package com.apress.prospring.ch14.timer;

import java.util.Calendar;
import java.util.Timer;

public class SimpleBirthdayReminderScheduling {

    private static final long MILLIS_IN_YEAR = 1000 * 60 * 60 * 24 * 365;
```

```
    public static void main(String[] args) {
        Timer t = new Timer();

        Calendar cal = Calendar.getInstance();
        cal.set(2005, Calendar.NOVEMBER, 30);
        t.schedule(new HelloWorldTask(), cal.getTime());

        t.scheduleAtFixedRate(new HelloWorldTask(), cal.getTime(),
                MILLIS_IN_YEAR);
    }
}
```

In this example, you can see that we calculate the number of milliseconds in a year, and then using a `Calendar` instance, we define a starting point of November 30th and then define the interval to be one year. Now every year on November 30th, provided that this application is running, the "Hello World" message is written to `stdout`. Clearly this is not a fully functional example, because there is no real notification mechanism, and each time we want to add a new birthday reminder, we need to change the code. In the next section, we create a more robust birthday reminder application using Spring's JDK `Timer` support classes.

Spring Support for JDK Timer Scheduling

As you saw in the previous section, it is easy to create and schedule jobs using the JDK `Timer` and `TimerTask` classes. That said, there are some problems with the approach we took in the previous examples. First, we created the `TimerTask` instances within the application rather than using Spring. For the `HelloWorldTask`, this is acceptable because we did not need to configure the job at all, but many jobs require some configuration data, and as a result, we should manage these using Spring to allow for easy configuration. Second, the trigger information is hard-coded into the application, meaning that any changes to the time a job is triggered require a change to the application code along with a recompilation. Finally, scheduling new jobs or removing a job requires changes to the application code when ideally, we should be able to configure this externally. By using Spring's `Timer` support classes, we can externalize all job and trigger configuration as well as hand over control of `Timer` creation to Spring, thus allowing jobs and their triggers to be defined externally.

The core of Spring's `Timer` support comes in the form of the `ScheduledTimerTask` and `TimerFactoryBean` classes. The `ScheduledTimerTask` class acts as a wrapper around your `TimerTask` implementations and allows you to define trigger information for the job. Using the `TimerFactoryBean`, you can have Spring automatically create `Timer` instances for a given list of `ScheduledTimerTask` beans using the trigger configuration data when creating the trigger.

Using ScheduledTimerTask and TimerFactoryBean

Before we dive in and look at our new and improved birthday reminder application, we should first look at the basics of how `ScheduledTimerTask` and `TimerFactoryBean` work. For each scheduled job you want to create, you need to configure an instance of the job class and an instance of `ScheduledTimerTask` containing the trigger details. You can share the same `TimerTask` instance across many `ScheduledTimerTask` instances if you want to create many triggers for the same job. Once you have these components configured, simply configure a `TimerFactoryBean` and specify the list of ScheduledTimerTask beans. Spring then creates an instance of Timer and schedules all the jobs defined by the ScheduledTimerTask beans using that Timer class.

This might sound complex at first, but in reality it is not. Listing 14-6 shows a simple configuration for scheduling the HelloWorldTask to run every 3 seconds with a delay of 1 second before the first execution.

Listing 14-6. *Configuring Job Scheduling Using TimerFactoryBean*

```
<!DOCTYPE beans PUBLIC "-//SPRING//DTD BEAN//EN"
"http://www.springframework.org/dtd/spring-beans.dtd">
<beans>
    <bean id="job" class="com.apress.prospring.ch14.timer.HelloWorldTask"/>

    <bean id="timerTask"
        class="org.springframework.scheduling.timer.ScheduledTimerTask">
        <property name="delay">
            <value>1000</value>
        </property>
        <property name="period">
            <value>3000</value>
        </property>
        <property name="timerTask">
            <ref local="job"/>
        </property>
    </bean>

    <bean id="timerFactory"
        class="org.springframework.scheduling.timer.TimerFactoryBean">
        <property name="scheduledTimerTasks">
            <list>
                <ref local="timerTask"/>
            </list>
        </property>
    </bean>
</beans>
```

Here you can see that we have configured a bean, job, of type HelloWorldTask and then using this bean, we have configured a bean of type ScheduledTimerTask, setting the delay to 1,000 milliseconds and the period to 3,000 milliseconds. The final part of the configuration is the timerFactory bean, which is passed a list of beans of type ScheduledTimerTask. In this case, we only have one task to schedule, represented by the timerTask bean. Be aware that when specifying trigger information using ScheduledTimerTask, you can only supply a delay in milliseconds, not an initial date for startup. We show you a way around this when we build the birthday reminder application in the next section.

With all of the scheduling and job definition information contained in the configuration, there is very little for our sample application to do. In fact, all we need to do is load the ApplicationContext, and Spring goes away and creates the Timer class and schedules the HelloWorldTask as per the configuration file. This code is shown in Listing 14-7.

Listing 14-7. *The TimerFactoryBeanExample Class*

```
package com.apress.prospring.ch14.timer;

import org.springframework.context.ApplicationContext;
import org.springframework.context.support.FileSystemXmlApplicationContext;

public class TimerFactoryBeanExample {

    public static void main(String[] args) throws Exception {
        ApplicationContext ctx = new FileSystemXmlApplicationContext(
                "./ch14/src/conf/timer.xml");
        System.in.read();
    }
}
```

If you run this application, you will see that the message "Hello World" is written to stdout every 3 seconds after an initial delay of 1 second. As you can see from this example, it is very simple to configure job scheduling external to your application's code. Using this approach, it is much simpler to make changes to a job's schedules or to add new scheduled jobs and remove existing ones.

A More Comprehensive Birthday Reminder Application

In this section, we create a more complex birthday reminder application using Spring's Timer support. With this example, we want to be able to schedule multiple reminder jobs, each with a specific configuration, to identify whose birthday the reminder is for. We also want to be able to add and remove reminders without having to modify the application code.

To get started, we need to create a job to perform the actual reminder. Because we are going to create these jobs using Spring, we can allow all configuration data to be provided using dependency injection. Listing 14-8 shows the BirthdayReminderTask.

Listing 14-8. *The BirthdayReminderTask*

```
package com.apress.prospring.ch14.timer.bday;

import java.util.TimerTask;

public class BirthdayReminder extends TimerTask {

    private String who;

    public void setWho(String who) {
        this.who = who;
    }
```

```
    public void run() {
        System.out.println("Don't forget it is " + who
                + "'s birthday is 7 days");
    }
}
```

Notice here that we defined a property on the task, who, that allows us to specify who the birthday reminder is for. In a real birthday reminder application, the reminder would no doubt be sent to e-mail or some similar medium. In the next chapter, where we cover Spring e-mail support, we flesh out this example even more so it sends reminders to e-mail. For now, however, you'll have to be content with reminder messages written to stdout!

With this task complete, we are almost ready to move on to the configuration stage. However, as we pointed out earlier, you cannot specify the start time of a scheduled job using a date when you are using ScheduledTimerTask. This is problematic for our sample application because we do not want to have to specify reminder dates as a relative offset to the startup time of the application! Thankfully, we can overcome this problem quite easily by extending the ScheduledTimerTask class and overriding the getDelay() method used by TimerFactoryBean to determine what delay it should assign to a trigger. At the same time, we can also override the getPeriod() method to return the number of milliseconds in a year so that you do not have to add that literal into configuration files! Listing 14-9 shows the code for our custom ScheduledTimerTask, BirthdayScheduledTask.

Listing 14-9. *Customizing ScheduledTimerTask*

```
package com.apress.prospring.ch14.timer.bday;

import java.text.DateFormat;
import java.text.ParseException;
import java.text.SimpleDateFormat;
import java.util.Calendar;
import java.util.Date;

import org.springframework.scheduling.timer.ScheduledTimerTask;

public class BirthdayScheduledTask extends ScheduledTimerTask {

    private static final long MILLIS_IN_YEAR = 1000 * 60 * 60 * 24 * 365;

    private DateFormat dateFormat = new SimpleDateFormat("yyyy-MM-dd");

    private Date startDate;

    public void setDate(String date) throws ParseException {
        startDate = dateFormat.parse(date);
    }
```

```
    public long getDelay() {
        Calendar now = Calendar.getInstance();
        Calendar then = Calendar.getInstance();
        then.setTime(startDate);

        return (then.getTimeInMillis() - now.getTimeInMillis());
    }

    public long getPeriod() {
        return MILLIS_IN_YEAR;
    }
}
```

Here you can see that we define a new property for the BirthdayScheduledTask class, date, which allows us to specify the start date as a date rather than a delay period. This property is of type String, because we use an instance of SimpleDateFormat configured with the pattern yyyy-MM-dd to parse dates such as 2005-11-30. You can see that we override the getPeriod() method, which TimerFactoryBean uses when it configures the interval for the trigger, to return the number of milliseconds in a year. Also notice that we override getDelay(), and using the Calendar class, we calculate the number of milliseconds between the current time and the specified start date. This value is then returned as the delay. With this complete, we can now complete the configuration for our sample application, as shown in Listing 14-10.

Listing 14-10. *Configuring the Birthday Reminder Application*

```
<!DOCTYPE beans PUBLIC "-//SPRING//DTD BEAN//EN"
"http://www.springframework.org/dtd/spring-beans.dtd">
<beans>
    <bean id="mum"
          class="com.apress.prospring.ch14.timer.bday.BirthdayScheduledTask">
        <property name="date">
            <value>2005-11-30</value>
        </property>
        <property name="fixedRate">
            <value>true</value>
        </property>
        <property name="timerTask">
            <bean class="com.apress.prospring.ch14.timer.bday.BirthdayReminder">
                <property name="who">
                    <value>Mum</value>
                </property>
            </bean>
        </property>
    </bean>
```

```
<bean id="timerFactory"
    class="org.springframework.scheduling.timer.TimerFactoryBean">
    <property name="scheduledTimerTasks">
        <list>
            <ref local="mum"/>
        </list>
    </property>
</bean>
</beans>
```

This code should look familiar to you by now. Notice that we used our BirthdayScheduledTask class in place of the ScheduledTimerTask class and instead of specifying a delay and a period, we have simply specified the date. Also, we rely on the overridden getDelay() and getPeriod() methods to provide the TimerFactoryBean with the delay and period values. In addition, notice that we set the fixedRate property of the BirthdayScheduledTask bean to true. This property is inherited from ScheduledTimerTask; TimerFactoryBean uses it to decide whether or not it should create a fixed-rate or fixed-delay trigger.

Scheduling Arbitrary Jobs

When you are scheduling jobs, you often need to schedule the execution of logic that already exists. If this is the case, you might not want to go to the trouble of creating a TimerTask class just to wrap your logic. Thankfully, you don't have to. Using the MethodInvokingTimerTaskFactoryBean, you can schedule the execution of any method on any given bean or a static method on a specific class; you can even provide method arguments if your logic method requires them.

As an example of this, consider the FooBean shown in Listing 14-11.

Listing 14-11. *The FooBean Class*

```
package com.apress.prospring.ch14.timer;

public class FooBean {

    public void someJob(String message) {
        System.out.println(message);
    }
}
```

If we want to schedule the someJob() method to run every 3 seconds with a given argument rather than create a TimerTask just to do that, we can simply use the MethodInvokingTimerTaskFactoryBean to create a TimerTask for us. The configuration for this is shown in Listing 14-12.

Listing 14-12. *Using MethodInvokingTimerTaskFactoryBean*

```
<!DOCTYPE beans PUBLIC "-//SPRING//DTD BEAN//EN"
"http://www.springframework.org/dtd/spring-beans.dtd">
<beans>
    <bean id="target" class="com.apress.prospring.ch14.timer.FooBean"/>

    <bean id="task"
                class="org.springframework.scheduling.timer.➥
                                    MethodInvokingTimerTaskFactoryBean">
        <property name="targetObject">
            <ref local="target"/>
        </property>
        <property name="targetMethod">
            <value>someJob</value>
        </property>
        <property name="arguments">
            <value>Hello World!</value>
        </property>
    </bean>

    <bean id="timerTask"
class="org.springframework.scheduling.timer.ScheduledTimerTask">
        <property name="delay">
            <value>1000</value>
        </property>
        <property name="period">
            <value>3000</value>
        </property>
        <property name="timerTask">
            <ref local="task"/>
        </property>
    </bean>

    <bean id="timerFactory"
                class="org.springframework.scheduling.timer.TimerFactoryBean">
        <property name="scheduledTimerTasks">
            <list>
                <ref local="timerTask"/>
            </list>
        </property>
    </bean>

</beans>
```

Here you can see that we can replace the definition of our own custom TimerTask bean with a definition using the MethodInvokingTimerTaskFactoryBean. In order to configure MethodInvokingTimerTaskFactoryBean, we specify the target of the invocation as a reference

to another bean, the method to execute, and the argument to use when executing. The
TimerTask supplied by MethodInvokingTimerTaskFactoryBean is used in the normal way,
wrapped in a ScheduledTimerTask, and passed to the TimerFactoryBean.

Listing 14-13 shows a simple driver program to test this out.

Listing 14-13. *Testing the MethodInvokingTimerTaskFactoryBean*

```
package com.apress.prospring.ch14.timer;

import org.springframework.context.ApplicationContext;
import org.springframework.context.support.FileSystemXmlApplicationContext;

public class MethodInvokerScheduling {

    public static void main(String[] args) throws Exception {
        ApplicationContext ctx = new FileSystemXmlApplicationContext(
                "./ch14/src/conf/timerMethodInvoker.xml");
        System.in.read();
    }
}
```

Running this example gives you the now familiar timed appearance of "Hello World!"
messages on your console. Clearly, using MethodInvokingTimerTaskFactoryBean removes the
need to create custom TimerTask implementations that simply wrap the execution of a business method.

Timer Scheduling Summary

JDK Timer-based scheduling provides support for an application's basic scheduling needs
using a simple and easy-to-understand architecture. Although the trigger system for JDK Timer
is not extremely flexible, it does provide basic schemes that allow you to control simple scheduling. Using Spring's support classes for Timer, you externalize a task scheduling configuration
and make it easier to add and remove tasks from the scheduler without having to chance any
application code. Using MethodInvokingTimerTaskFactoryBean, you avoid having to create
TimerTask implementations that do nothing more than invoke a business method, thus reducing
the amount of code you need to write and maintain.

The main drawback of JDK Timer scheduling comes when you need to support complex
triggers such as a trigger to execute a job every Monday, Wednesday, and Friday at 15:00. In the
next part of this chapter, we look at the Quartz scheduling engine, which provides much more
comprehensive support for scheduling and, just like Timer, is fully integrated into Spring.

Scheduling Jobs Using Quartz

The open source Quartz project is a dedicated job scheduling engine designed to be used in
both J2EE and J2SE settings. Quartz provides a huge range of features such as persistent jobs,
clustering, and distributed transactions. We do not look at the clustering or distributed transaction features here—you can find out more about these online at www.opensymphony.com/quartz.

Spring's Quartz integration is very similar to Spring's Timer integration in that it provides for declarative configuration of jobs, triggers, and schedules. In addition to this, Spring provides additional job persistence features that allow the scheduling of a Quartz job to take part in a Spring-managed transaction.

Introducing Quartz

Quartz is an extremely powerful job scheduling engine, and we cannot hope to cover everything about it in the remainder of this chapter. However, we do cover the main aspects of Quartz that are related to Spring, and we discuss how you can use Quartz from a Spring application. As with our Timer discussion, we start by looking at Quartz separately from Spring, and then we look at Quartz/Spring integration.

The core of Quartz is made up of two interfaces, Job and Scheduler, and two classes, JobDetail and Trigger. From their names, it should be apparent what most of these do, but the role of the JobDetail class is not clear. Unlike Timer-based scheduling, tasks are not executed using a single instance of your job class; instead, Quartz creates instances as it needs them. You can use the JobDetail class to encapsulate the job state and to pass information to a job and between subsequent executions of a job. With Timer-based scheduling, there was no notion of a Trigger with Trigger logic encapsulated by the Timer class itself. Quartz supports a pluggable architecture for Triggers, which allows you to create your own implementations as you see fit. That said, you rarely create your own Trigger implementations because Quartz provides the super-powerful CronTrigger out of the box, which allows you to use cron expressions (more on that shortly) to have fine-grained control over job execution.

Simple Job Scheduling

To create a job for use in Quartz, simply create a class that implements the Job interface. The Job interface defines a single method, execute(), which is where you call your business logic from. Quartz passes an instance of JobExecutionContext context to the execute() method, allowing you to access context data about the current execution. We look at this in more detail in the next section.

Listing 14-14 show a simple Job implementation that writes "Hello World" to stdout.

Listing 14-14. *Creating a Simple Job*

```
package com.apress.prospring.ch14.quartz;

import org.quartz.Job;
import org.quartz.JobExecutionContext;
import org.quartz.JobExecutionException;

public class HelloWorldJob implements Job {

    public void execute(JobExecutionContext context)
            throws JobExecutionException {
        System.out.println("Hello World!");
    }

}
```

To schedule this job to run, we first need to obtain a Scheduler instance, then create a JobDetail bean that contains information about the job, and then create a Trigger to govern job execution. The code for this is shown in Listing 14-15.

Listing 14-15. *Scheduling Jobs in Quartz*

```
package com.apress.prospring.ch14.quartz;

import java.util.Date;

import org.quartz.JobDetail;
import org.quartz.Scheduler;
import org.quartz.SimpleTrigger;
import org.quartz.Trigger;
import org.quartz.impl.StdSchedulerFactory;

public class HelloWorldScheduling {

    public static void main(String[] args) throws Exception {

        Scheduler scheduler = new StdSchedulerFactory().getScheduler();
        scheduler.start();

        JobDetail jobDetail = new JobDetail("helloWorldJob",
                Scheduler.DEFAULT_GROUP, HelloWorldJob.class);

        Trigger trigger = new SimpleTrigger("simpleTrigger",
                Scheduler.DEFAULT_GROUP, new Date(), null,
                SimpleTrigger.REPEAT_INDEFINITELY, 3000);

        scheduler.scheduleJob(jobDetail, trigger);
    }
}
```

This code starts by obtaining an instance of Scheduler using the StdSchedulerFactory class. We are not going to look at this class in any detail here, but you can find out more information in the Quartz tutorial, which is available on the website. For now, it is enough to know that the StdSchedulerFactory.getScheduler() class returns a Scheduler instance that is ready to run. In Quartz, a Scheduler can be started, stopped, and paused. If a Scheduler has not been started or is paused, then no Triggers fire, so we start the Scheduler using the start() method.

Next, we create the JobDetail instance of the job we are scheduling, passing in three arguments to the constructor. The first argument is the job name and is used to refer to this job when using one of the Scheduler interface's administration methods, such as pauseJob(), which allows a particular job to be paused. The second argument is the group name for which we are using the default group name. Group names can be used to refer to a group of jobs together, perhaps to pause them all using Scheduler.pauseJobGroup(). You should note that job names are unique within a group. The third and final argument is the Class, which implements this particular job.

With the JobDetail instance created, we now move on to create a Trigger. In this example, we use the SimpleTrigger class, which provides JDK Timer-style trigger behavior. The first and second arguments passed to the SimpleTrigger constructor are trigger name and group name, respectively. Both of these arguments perform similar functions for a Trigger as they do for a JobDetail. Trigger names are also unique within a group. The third and fourth arguments, both of type Date, are the start and end date for this Trigger. By specifying null for the end date, we are saying there is no end date. The ability to specify an end date for a trigger is not available when you are using Timer. The next argument is the repeat count, which allows you to specify the maximum number of times the Trigger can fire. We use the constant REPEAT_INDEFINITELY to allow the Trigger to fire without a limit. The final argument is the interval between Trigger firings and is defined in milliseconds. We have defined an interval of 3 seconds.

The final step in this example is to schedule the job with a call to Scheduler.schedule() that passes in the JobDetail instance and the Trigger. If you run this application, you see the familiar stream of "Hello World!" messages appearing gradually in your console.

Using JobDetail Beans

In the previous example, all information for the job execution was contained in the job itself. However, you can pass state into the job using the JobDetail class. Each instance of JobDetail has an associated JobDataMap instance, which implements Map, and allows you to pass in job data in key/value pairs. Your jobs can modify data in the JobDataMap to allow for the passing of data between subsequent executions of the job. However, there are some considerations related to job persistence when using this approach. We discuss these later in the section entitled "About Job Persistence."

In Listing 14-16, you can see an example of a Job that uses data contained in the JobDataMap to perform its processing.

Listing 14-16. *Using the JobDataMap*

```
package com.apress.prospring.ch14.quartz;

import java.util.Map;

import org.quartz.Job;
import org.quartz.JobExecutionContext;
import org.quartz.JobExecutionException;

public class MessageJob implements Job {

    public void execute(JobExecutionContext context)
            throws JobExecutionException {
        Map properties = context.getJobDetail().getJobDataMap();

        System.out.println("Previous Fire Time: "
                + context.getPreviousFireTime());
        System.out.println("Current Fire Time: " + context.getFireTime());
        System.out.println("Next Fire Time: " + context.getNextFireTime());
```

```
        System.out.println(properties.get("message"));

        System.out.println("");
    }
}
```

Here you can see that we access the JobDetail using the JobExecutionContext instance
that is passed to the execute() method. Using this JobDetail instance, we can then obtain the
JobDataMap and from there, we are able to extract the Object that is keyed as message and write
it to stdout. Also notice that we are able to get information about the previous, current, and
next execution of this job from the JobExecutionContext.

In Listing 14-17, you can see an example of how you populate the JobDataMap with data
when scheduling the Job.

Listing 14-17. *Adding Data to the JobDataMap*

```
package com.apress.prospring.ch14.quartz;

import java.util.Date;
import java.util.Map;

import org.quartz.JobDetail;
import org.quartz.Scheduler;
import org.quartz.SimpleTrigger;
import org.quartz.Trigger;
import org.quartz.impl.StdSchedulerFactory;

public class MessageScheduling {

    public static void main(String[] args) throws Exception{
        Scheduler scheduler = new StdSchedulerFactory().getScheduler();
        scheduler.start();

        JobDetail jobDetail = new JobDetail("messageJob",
                Scheduler.DEFAULT_GROUP, MessageJob.class);

        Map map = jobDetail.getJobDataMap();
        map.put("message", "This is a message from Quartz");

        Trigger trigger = new SimpleTrigger("simpleTrigger",
                Scheduler.DEFAULT_GROUP, new Date(), null,
                SimpleTrigger.REPEAT_INDEFINITELY, 3000);

        scheduler.scheduleJob(jobDetail, trigger);
    }
}
```

You will recognize much of this code from the previous example shown in Listing 14-15, but notice that once the JobDetail instance has been created, we access the JobDataMap and add it to a message, keyed as message. If you run this example and leave it running for a few iterations, you end up with output similar to this:

```
Previous Fire Time: null
Current Fire Time: Tue Sep 28 17:16:48 BST 2005
Next Fire Time: Tue Sep 28 17:16:51 BST 2005
This is a message from Quartz

Previous Fire Time: Tue Sep 28 17:16:48 BST 2005
Current Fire Time: Tue Sep 28 17:16:51 BST 2005
Next Fire Time: Tue Sep 28 17:16:54 BST 2005
This is a message from Quartz

Previous Fire Time: Tue Sep 28 17:16:51 BST 2005
Current Fire Time: Tue Sep 28 17:16:54 BST 2005
Next Fire Time: Tue Sep 28 17:16:57 BST 2005
This is a message from Quartz
```

Here you can see that the message contained in the JobDataMap is written to stdout after the information about the execution times of the previous, current, and next execution is displayed. As you will see shortly, when using Spring to configure Quartz scheduling, you can create the JobDataMap in your Spring configuration file, allowing you to externalize all Job configuration completely.

Using the CronTrigger

In the previous examples, we used the SimpleTrigger class, which provides trigger functionality very similar to that of the JDK Timer class. However, where Quartz excels is in its support for complex trigger expressions using the CronTrigger. CronTrigger is based on the Unix cron daemon, a scheduling application that supports a simple, yet extremely powerful, trigger syntax. Using CronTrigger, you can quickly and accurately define trigger expressions that would be extremely difficult or impossible to do with the SimpleTrigger class. For instance, you can create a trigger that says, "fire every 5 seconds of every minute, starting at the third second of the minute, but only between the hours of 14:00 and 17:00" or "fire on the last Friday of every month."

A CronTrigger syntax expression, referred to as a cron expression, contains six required components and one optional component. A cron expression is written on a single line and each component is separated from the next by space. Only the last, or rightmost, component is optional. Table 14-2 describes the cron components in detail.

Each component accepts the typical range of values that you would expect, such as 0–59 for seconds and minutes and 1–31 for day of the month. For the month and day of the week components, you can use numbers, such as 1–7 for day of the week, or text such as SUN–SAT.

Table 14-2. *Components of a Cron Expression*

Position	Meaning	Allowed Special Characters
1	Seconds (0–59)	, , -, *, /
2	Minutes (0–59)	, , -, *, /
3	Hours (0–23)	, , -, *, /
4	Day of month (1–31)	, , -, *, /, ?, L, C
5	Month	(either JAN–DEC or 1–12), , -, *, /
6	Day of week (either SUN–SAT or 1–7)	, , -, *, /, ?, L, C, #
7	Year (optional, 1970–2099), when empty, full range is assumed	, , -, *, /

Each field also accepts a given set of special symbols, so placing a * in the hours component means every hour, and using an expression such as 6L in the day-of-the-week component means last Friday of the month. Table 14-3 describes cron wildcards and special symbols in detail.

Table 14-3. *Cron Expression Wildcards and Special Symbols*

Special Character	Description
*	Any value. This special character can be used in any field to indicate that the value should not be checked. Therefore, our example cron expression will be fired on any day of the month, any month, and any day of the week between 1970 and 2099.
?	No specific value. This special character is usually used with other specific values to indicate that a value must be present but will not be checked.
-	Range. For example 10-12 in the Hours field means hours 10, 11, and 12.
,	List separator. Allows you to specify a list of values, such as MON, TUE, WED in the Day of week field.
/	Increments. This character specifies increments of a value. For example 0/1 in the Minute field in our example means every 1-minute increment of the minute field, starting from 0.
L	L is an abbreviation for Last. The meaning is a bit different in Day of month and Day of week. When used in the Day of month field, it means the last day of the month (31st of March, 28th or 29th of February, and so on). When used in Day of week, it has the same value as 7—Saturday. The L special character is most useful when you use it with a specific Day of week value. For example, 6L in the Day of week field means the last Friday of each month.
#	This value is allowed only for the Day of week field and it specifies the *n*th day in a month. For example 1#2 means the first Monday of each month.
C*	The Calendar value is allowed for the Day of month and Day of week fields. The values of days are calculated against a specified calendar. Specifying 20C in the Day of month field fires the trigger on the first day included in the calendar on or after the 20th. Specifying 6C in the Day of week field is interpreted as the first day included in the calendar on or after Friday.

* At the time of writing, support for the C special character and specifying both Day of week and Day of month values has not been not completed.

The last thing to bear in mind when writing cron expressions is daylight saving time changes. This may cause a trigger to fire twice in the spring or not to fire at all in the fall (sorry, southern hemisphere).

There are many more permutations for cron expressions than we can discuss here and you can find a detailed description of cron syntax in the JavaDoc for the CronTrigger class.

Listing 14-18 shows an example of the CronTrigger class in action.

Listing 14-18. *Using the CronTrigger Class*

```
package com.apress.prospring.ch14.quartz;

import java.util.Map;

import org.quartz.CronTrigger;
import org.quartz.JobDetail;
import org.quartz.Scheduler;
import org.quartz.Trigger;
import org.quartz.impl.StdSchedulerFactory;

public class CronTriggerExample {

    public static void main(String[] args) throws Exception {
        Scheduler scheduler = new StdSchedulerFactory().getScheduler();
        scheduler.start();

        JobDetail jobDetail = new JobDetail("messageJob",
                Scheduler.DEFAULT_GROUP, MessageJob.class);

        Map map = jobDetail.getJobDataMap();
        map.put("message", "This is a message from Quartz");

        String cronExpression = "3/5 * 14,15,16,17 * * ?";

        Trigger trigger = new CronTrigger("cronTrigger",
                Scheduler.DEFAULT_GROUP, cronExpression);

        scheduler.scheduleJob(jobDetail, trigger);
    }
}
```

Much of this code should look familiar to you; the only major difference here is that we use the cron expression. The actual creation of the CronTrigger class is very similar to the creation of the SimpleTrigger class in that you have a name and a group name. To help you understand the cron expression in the example, we break it down into components. The first component, 3/5, means every 5 seconds starting at the third second of the minute. The second component, *, simply says every minute. The third component, 14, 15, 16, 17, restricts this trigger to running between 14:00 and 17:59—that is, when the time begins with 14, 15, 16, or 17. The next two components are both wildcards saying that this trigger can run in any month or any year.

The final component uses the wildcard, ?, to indicate that this trigger can run on any day of the week. This expression has the net effect of firing every 5 seconds, starting on the third second of the minute, but only between 14:00 and 17:59.

If you run this example, depending on the time of day, you either see a blank screen or the ever increasing list of "Hello World"s. Try modifying the first component in the expression to change the frequency or at which second in the minute the trigger starts. You should also try modifying other components to see what effects you get.

The CronTrigger is great for almost all trigger requirements; however, expressions can quickly get convoluted when you need to consider exceptions to the rule. For instance, consider a process that checks a task list for a user every Monday, Wednesday, and Friday at 11:00 and 15:00. Now consider what happens when you want to prevent this trigger from firing when the user is on vacation. Thankfully, Quartz provides support for this via the Calendar interface. Using the Calendar interface, you can accurately define a period that should either be explicitly included or explicitly excluded from a trigger's normal schedule. Quartz comes with six implementations of Calendar, one of which is the HolidayCalendar that stores a list of days to be excluded from a trigger's schedule. Listing 14-19 shows a modification of the previous example that uses a HolidayCalendar to exclude December 25, 2005.

Listing 14-19. *Explicitly Excluding Dates with HolidayCalendar*

```
package com.apress.prospring.ch14.quartz;

import java.util.Calendar;
import java.util.Map;

import org.quartz.CronTrigger;
import org.quartz.JobDetail;
import org.quartz.Scheduler;
import org.quartz.Trigger;
import org.quartz.impl.StdSchedulerFactory;
import org.quartz.impl.calendar.HolidayCalendar;

public class CronWithCalendarExample {

    public static void main(String[] args) throws Exception {
        Scheduler scheduler = new StdSchedulerFactory().getScheduler();
        scheduler.start();

        // create a calendar to exclude a particular date
        Calendar cal = Calendar.getInstance();
        cal.set(2005, Calendar.DECEMBER, 25);

        HolidayCalendar calendar = new HolidayCalendar();
        calendar.addExcludedDate(cal.getTime());
```

```
            // add to scheduler
            scheduler.addCalendar("xmasCalendar", calendar, true, false);

            JobDetail jobDetail = new JobDetail("messageJob",
                    Scheduler.DEFAULT_GROUP, MessageJob.class);

            Map map = jobDetail.getJobDataMap();
            map.put("message", "This is a message from Quartz");

            String cronExpression = "3/5 * 14,15,16,17 * * ?";

            Trigger trigger = new CronTrigger("cronTrigger",
                    Scheduler.DEFAULT_GROUP, cronExpression);

            trigger.setCalendarName("xmasCalendar");

            scheduler.scheduleJob(jobDetail, trigger);
    }
}
```

Here you can see that we create an instance of HolidayCalendar and then, using the
addExcludedDate() method, we exclude the 25th of December. With the Calendar instance
created, we add the Calendar to the Scheduler using the addCalendar() method, giving it a
name of xmasCalendar. Then later, before adding the CronTrigger, we associate it with the
xmasCalendar. Using this approach saves you from having to create complex cron expressions
just to exclude a few arbitrary dates.

About Job Persistence

Quartz provides support for Job persistence, allowing you to add jobs at runtime or make
changes to existing jobs and have these changes and additions persist for subsequent executions of the Job. Central to this concept is the JobStore interface, implementations of which are
used by Quartz when it is performing persistence. By default, Quartz uses the RAMJobStore
implementation, which simply stores Jobs in memory. Other available implementations are
JobStoreCMT and JobStoreTX. Both of these classes persist job details using a configured
DataSource and support the creation and modification of Jobs as part of a transaction. The
JobStoreCMT implementation is intended to be used in an application server environment and
takes part in container-managed transactions. For stand-alone applications you should use
the JobStoreTX implementation. Spring provides its own LocalDataSourceJobStore implementation of JobStore, which can take part in Spring-managed transactions. We take a look at this
implementation when we discuss Spring support for Quartz.

Earlier on, you saw how you can modify the contents of the JobDataMap to pass information
between different executions of the same Job. However, if you try to run that example using a
JobStore implementation other the RAMJobStore, you will be surprised to see that it doesn't
work. The reason for this is that Quartz supports the notion of stateless and stateful jobs. When
using the RAMJobStore and modifying the JobDataMap, you are actually modifying the store
directly, so the type of Job is unimportant, but this is not the case when you are using implementations other than RAMJobStore. A stateless Job only has the data in the JobDataMap persisted

when it is added to the Scheduler, whereas stateful Jobs have their JobDataMap persisted after every execution. To mark a Job as stateful, implement the StatefulJob interface instead of the Job interface. StatefulJob is a subinterface of Job, so you do not need to implement Job as well. You should also be aware that any data you place in the JobDataMap when using Job persistence must be serializable, because Quartz writes the JobDataMap as a serialized blob to the database.

Quartz Support in Spring

Spring's Quartz integration follows a similar pattern to the integration with Timer in that it allows you to configure your job scheduling fully within the Spring configuration file. In addition to this, Spring provides further classes to integrate with the Quartz JobStore, thus allowing you to configure Job persistence in your configuration and for Job modification to take part in Spring-managed transactions.

Scheduling a Job with Spring

As you would expect, much of the code you need to schedule a Quartz Job using Spring goes into the Spring configuration file. Indeed, you only need to load the ApplicationContext in your application for the configuration to take effect and for Spring to start the Scheduler automatically.

In Listing 14-20, you can see the configuration code required to configure the MessageJob class you saw in Listing 14-16 to run once every 3 seconds.

Listing 14-20. *Configuring Scheduling Declaratively*

```
<!DOCTYPE beans PUBLIC "-//SPRING//DTD BEAN//EN"
"http://www.springframework.org/dtd/spring-beans.dtd">
<beans>
    <bean id="job" class="org.springframework.scheduling.quartz.JobDetailBean">
        <property name="jobClass">
            <value>com.apress.prospring.ch14.quartz.MessageJob</value>
        </property>
        <property name="jobDataAsMap">
            <map>
                <entry key="message">
                    <value>This is a message from the Spring configuration file!
                    </value>
                </entry>
            </map>
        </property>
    </bean>

    <bean id="trigger"
            class="org.springframework.scheduling.quartz.SimpleTriggerBean">
        <property name="jobDetail">
            <ref local="job"/>
        </property>
```

```
            <property name="startDelay">
                <value>1000</value>
            </property>
            <property name="repeatInterval">
                <value>3000</value>
            </property>
        </bean>

        <bean id="schedulerFactory"
                class="org.springframework.scheduling.quartz.SchedulerFactoryBean">
            <property name="triggers">
                <list>
                    <ref local="trigger"/>
                </list>
            </property>
        </bean>
</beans>
```

Here you can see that we use the JobDetailBean class, which extends the JobDetail class, to configure the job data in a declarative manner. The JobDetailBean provides more JavaBeans-style properties that are accessible by Spring, and it also provides sensible defaults for properties that you usually have to specify yourself. For instance, notice that we did not specify a job name or a group name. By default, the JobDetailBean uses the ID of the <bean> tag as the job name and the default group of the Scheduler as the group name. Notice that we are able to add data to the JobDataMap property using the jobDataAsMap property. The name of this property is not a typo—you can't add directly to the jobDataMap property because it is of type JobDataMap and this type is not supported in Spring configuration files.

With the JobDetailBean configured, the next step is to create a trigger. Spring offers two classes, SimpleTriggerBean and CronTriggerBean, that wrap the SimpleTrigger and CronTrigger classes, allowing you to configure them declaratively and to associate them with a JobDetail-Bean—all within your configuration file. Notice that in the example above, shown in Listing 14-20, we defined a starting delay of 1 second and then a repeat interval of 3 seconds. By default, the SimpleTriggerBean sets the repeat count to infinite.

The final piece of configuration you need is for the SchedulerFactoryBean. By default, SchedulerFactoryBean creates an instance of StdSchedulerFactory from which to create the Scheduler implementation. You can override this behavior by setting the schedulerFactoryClass property to the name of a Class that implements SchedulerFactory, which you wish to use in place of StdSchedulerFactory. The only property that you need to configure scheduling is the triggers property, which accepts a List of TriggerBeans.

Because all of the job scheduling configuration is contained in the configuration, you need very little code to actually start the Scheduler and have the Jobs execute. In fact, all you need to do is create the ApplicationContext, as shown in Listing 14-21.

Listing 14-21. *Testing Declarative Quartz Configuration*

```
package com.apress.prospring.ch14.quartz.spring;

import org.springframework.context.ApplicationContext;
import org.springframework.context.support.FileSystemXmlApplicationContext;

public class SimpleSpringQuartzIntegrationExample {

    public static void main(String[] args) {
        ApplicationContext ctx = new FileSystemXmlApplicationContext(
        "./ch14/src/conf/quartzSimple.xml");
    }
}
```

As you can see, this class does nothing more than create an instance of `ApplicationContext` using the configuration shown in Listing 14-20. If you run this application and leave it running for a few iterations, you end up with something like this:

```
Previous Fire Time: null
Current Fire Time: Wed Sep 29 14:59:08 BST 2005
Next Fire Time: Wed Sep 29 14:59:11 BST 2005
This is a message from the Spring configuration file!

Previous Fire Time: Wed Sep 29 14:59:08 BST 2005
Current Fire Time: Wed Sep 29 14:59:11 BST 2005
Next Fire Time: Wed Sep 29 14:59:14 BST 2005
This is a message from the Spring configuration file!

Previous Fire Time: Wed Sep 29 14:59:11 BST 2005
Current Fire Time: Wed Sep 29 14:59:14 BST 2005
Next Fire Time: Wed Sep 29 14:59:17 BST 2005
This is a message from the Spring configuration file!
```

Notice that it is running just like it was for the previous `MessageJob` example, but the message displayed is the message configured in the Spring configuration file.

Using Persistent Jobs

One of the great features of Quartz is its ability to create stateful, persistent `Job`s. This opens up some great functionality that is not available when you are using `Timer`-based scheduling. With persistent `Job`s, you can add `Job`s to Quartz at runtime and they will still be in your application after a restart. Plus, you can modify the `JobDataMap` passed between executions of a `Job` and changes will still be in effect after a restart.

In this example, we are going to schedule two jobs, one using Spring configuration mechanisms, and one at runtime. We then see how the Quartz persistence mechanism copes with changes to the JobDataMap for these Jobs and what happens in subsequent executions of the application.

To start with, you need to create a database in which Quartz can store the Job information. In the Quartz distribution—we used version 1.4.2—you will find a selection of database scripts for a variety of different RDMBS flavors. For the example here, we use MySQL, but you should not encounter problems using a different database as long as Quartz has a database script for it. Once you have located the script for your database, execute it against your database and verify that 12 tables, each with the prefix qrtz, have been created.

Next, create your test Job. Because we want to make changes to JobDataMap during Job execution, we need to flag to Quartz that it should treat this as a stateful Job. We do this by implementing the StatefulJob interface rather than the Job interface. This is shown in Listing 14-22.

Listing 14-22. *Creating a Stateful Job*

```
package com.apress.prospring.ch14.quartz.spring;

import java.util.Map;

import org.quartz.JobExecutionContext;
import org.quartz.JobExecutionException;
import org.quartz.StatefulJob;

public class PersistentJob implements StatefulJob {

    public void execute(JobExecutionContext context)
            throws JobExecutionException {
        Map map = context.getJobDetail().getJobDataMap();
        System.out.println("[" + context.getJobDetail().getName() + "]"
                + map.get("message"));
        map.put("message", "Updated Message");
    }

}
```

The StatefulJob interface does not add additional methods for your class to implement; it is simply a marker telling Quartz that it should persist the JobDetail after every execution. Here you can see that we display the message that is stored in the JobDataMap along with the name of the Job.

The next step is to configure the Job in Spring and configure the Scheduler with a DataSource it can use for persistence. This is shown in Listing 14-23.

Listing 14-23. *Configuring Quartz Persistence in Spring*

```
<!DOCTYPE beans PUBLIC "-//SPRING//DTD BEAN//EN"
"http://www.springframework.org/dtd/spring-beans.dtd">
<beans>
    <bean id="job" class="org.springframework.scheduling.quartz.JobDetailBean">
        <property name="jobClass">
            <value>com.apress.prospring.ch14.quartz.spring.PersistentJob</value>
        </property>
        <property name="jobDataAsMap">
            <map>
                <entry key="message">
                    <value>Original Message</value>
                </entry>
            </map>
        </property>
    </bean>
    <bean id="dataSource"
            class="org.springframework.jdbc.datasource.SingleConnectionDataSource">
        <property name="driverClassName">
            <value>com.mysql.jdbc.Driver</value>
        </property>
        <property name="url">
            <value>jdbc:mysql://localhost:3306/quartz</value>
        </property>
        <property name="username"><value>root</value></property>
        <property name="password"><value></value></property>
    </bean>
    <bean id="trigger"
                class="org.springframework.scheduling.quartz.SimpleTriggerBean">
        <property name="jobDetail">
            <ref local="job"/>
        </property>
        <property name="startDelay">
            <value>1000</value>
        </property>
        <property name="repeatInterval">
            <value>3000</value>
        </property>
    </bean>
    <bean id="schedulerFactory"
                class="org.springframework.scheduling.quartz.SchedulerFactoryBean">
        <property name="triggers">
            <list>
                <ref local="trigger"/>
            </list>
        </property>
```

```
        <property name="dataSource">
            <ref local="dataSource"/>
        </property>
    </bean>
</beans>
```

You will recognize much of this configuration code from Listing 14-20; the important part here is the dataSource bean. In this code, we use the Spring class SingleConnectionDataSource; this is a useful DataSource implementation for testing but never use it in production. And remember, you need to modify the connection details in the configuration as is appropriate for your environment. For more details on configuring other DataSources with Spring, see Chapter 8. Using the configured dataSource bean, we set the dataSource property of the SchedulerFactoryBean. By doing this, we instruct Spring to create a Scheduler that is configured to persist Job data using the given DataSource. Internally, this is achieved using Spring's own JobStore implementation, LocalDataSourceJobStore.

With the configuration complete, all that remains is to load it in an application and add another Job to the Scheduler at runtime. Listing 14-24 shows the code for this.

Listing 14-24. *Testing Job Persistence*

```
package com.apress.prospring.ch14.quartz.spring;

import java.util.Date;

import org.quartz.JobDetail;
import org.quartz.Scheduler;
import org.quartz.SimpleTrigger;
import org.quartz.Trigger;
import org.springframework.context.ApplicationContext;
import org.springframework.context.support.FileSystemXmlApplicationContext;

public class SpringWithJobPersistence {

    public static void main(String[] args) throws Exception {
        ApplicationContext ctx = new FileSystemXmlApplicationContext(
                "./ch14/src/conf/quartzPersistent.xml");

        // get the scheduler
        Scheduler scheduler = (Scheduler) ctx.getBean("schedulerFactory");

        JobDetail job = scheduler.getJobDetail("otherJob",
                Scheduler.DEFAULT_GROUP);

        if (job == null) {
            // the job has not yet been created
            job = (JobDetail) ctx.getBean("job");
            job.setName("otherJob");
            job.getJobDataMap().put("message", "This is another message");
```

```
        Trigger trigger = new SimpleTrigger("simpleTrigger",
                Scheduler.DEFAULT_GROUP, new Date(), null,
                SimpleTrigger.REPEAT_INDEFINITELY, 3000);

        scheduler.scheduleJob(job, trigger);
    }
  }
}
```

This code requires little explanation; however, note that before we schedule the second job, we check to see if it already exists using the `Scheduler.getJobDetail()` method. This is so we do not overwrite the `Job` on subsequent runs of the application.

The first time you run this example, you get output something like this:

```
[otherJob]This is another message
[job]Original Message
[otherJob]Updated Message
[job]Updated Message
[otherJob]Updated Message
[job]Updated Message
```

As you can see, the first time each `Job` executes, the message displayed is the original message that was configured in the `JobDataMap` when the `Job` was scheduled. On subsequent executions, each `Job` displays the updated message that was set during the previous execution. If you stop the application and then restart it, you see something slightly different:

```
[otherJob]Updated Message
[job]Updated Message
[otherJob]Updated Message
[job]Updated Message
[otherJob]Updated Message
[job]Updated Message
```

This time you can see that because the `Job` data was persisted, you do not need to re-create the second `Job` and the `JobDataMap` accurately reflects changes that were made during the last run of the application.

Scheduling Arbitrary Jobs with Quartz

Like the `Timer`-based scheduling classes, Spring provides the ability to schedule the execution of arbitrary methods using Quartz. We are not going to go into any detail on this because it works in an almost identical manner to the `Timer` approach. Instead of using `MethodInvokingTimerTaskFactoryBean`, you use `MethodInvokingJobDetailFactoryBean`, and instead of creating `TimerTasks` automatically, you create `JobDetails` automatically.

Job Scheduling Considerations

If you are going to be adding job scheduling to your application, then there are a few considerations that you should bear in mind when you choose which scheduler and which approach to take.

Choosing a Scheduler

The first decision you have to make when adding scheduling to your application is which scheduler to use. This is actually quite an easy choice. If you only have very simple scheduling requirements or you are restricted in the external libraries that you can package with your application, then you should use `Timer`-based scheduling; otherwise use Quartz.

Even if you find that your requirements are simple, you might want to go with Quartz anyway, especially if you have to create an explicit `Job` implementation. This way, if your requirements become more advanced, you can easily add persistence, transactions, or more complex triggers without having to change a `TimerTask` to a `Job`. In general, we have found that using Quartz for all of our scheduling allows us to become familiar with a single scheduling approach and prevents our developers from having to worry about two different approaches, when one provides everything they need.

Package Job Logic Separate from Job Class

A common approach that we see many developers take when they are adding scheduling to an application is to place business logic inside a `Job` or a `TimerTask`. Generally, this is a bad idea. In many cases, you also need to have scheduled tasks available for execution on demand, which requires the logic to be separate from the scheduling framework.

Also, you do not need to couple your business logic unduly to a particular scheduler. We have found that a better approach is to keep business logic in separate classes and then either create a simple wrapper around this that is specific to your scheduler or, more preferably, use the appropriate `MethodInvoker*FactoryBean` to create the wrapper for you.

Summary

In this chapter, we showed you various different mechanisms for scheduling jobs with Spring. We looked at the basic support offered when you use JDK `Timer` and the more sophisticated support offered through Quartz. We looked at how the different trigger types are used, and in particular, we explored the `CronTrigger` in Quartz as a means of creating complex schedules that match real-world scenarios.

Job scheduling is an important part of enterprise applications and Spring provides excellent support for adding scheduling to your own applications. In the next chapter, we examine Spring's support for sending e-mail messages using both JavaMail and COS Mail.

CHAPTER 15

Mail Support in Spring

For many applications, e-mail is a perfect medium for a wide variety of tasks such as user notification, marketing, and, in some cases, application integration. In the Java world, there is a large selection of e-mail solutions, the most well known of which is JavaMail from Sun. Although JavaMail is exceptionally powerful, it is quite a complex API; as a result, sending a simple e-mail with JavaMail is not a trivial task. Thankfully, Spring provides full support for e-mail through a much-simplified API. The Spring Mail API is fully pluggable, and out of the box, you get two implementations: one that uses JavaMail, and another that uses the `MailMessage` class written by Jason Hunter as part of the `com.oreilly.servlet` (COS) package available at `www.servlets.com`. In this chapter, we are going to examine the Spring e-mail abstraction layer, including both the `JavaMail` and COS `MailMessage` implementations.

Spring's e-mail abstraction layer is split into two parts: one for basic mail support and one for more complex mail support. The JavaMail implementation supports both parts, whereas the COS implementation only supports the sending of simple messages. For this reason, much of the discussion in this chapter is focused on the JavaMail implementation. To follow the examples in this chapter, you should familiarize yourself with the JavaMail and `MailMessage` APIs, because we will not go into great detail about either of these APIs.

In particular, this chapter focuses on the following topics:

The Spring Mail API structure: In this section, we introduce the various interfaces and classes that make up the Spring Mail API along with the two implementations that are provided out of the box. We look at how the mail API is structured for use in a DI-based environment and how this benefits your application.

Sending simple e-mails: In this section, we start off with basic examples for sending plain text e-mail using a completely programmatic approach with both JavaMail and COS. The final example in this section revisits the birthday reminder application from the previous chapter and demonstrates how to use the Spring Mail API in a more declarative fashion.

Sending MIME messages: This section is wholly focused on the JavaMail implementation of the Spring Mail API and shows you how to assemble nontrivial mail messages. In particular, we look at how to construct complex multipart messages with embedded image content, alternative formats, and attachments.

Using Mail with Velocity: In this section, we look at a practical extension to the mail support using the Jakarta Velocity templating engine to simplify message creation. We also demonstrate how you can build a simple framework for creating and sending messages containing alternative formats using Spring Mail and Velocity.

In order to run the examples in this section, you need to download both JavaMail and COS MailMessage. If you downloaded the full Spring distribution with all the dependencies included, you will find all the JAR files there. Otherwise, you can obtain JavaMail along with the JavaBeans Activation Framework, which is required by JavaMail, from http://java.sun.com. You can obtain COS MailMessage from http://servlets.com/cos.

The Spring Mail API Structure

Central to the Spring Mail abstraction layer are the MailSender and JavaMailSender interfaces shown in Figure 15-1.

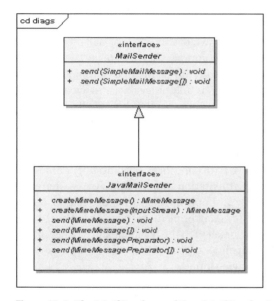

Figure 15-1. *The MailSender and JavaMailSender interfaces*

The MailSender interface is intended for implementations that only support simple, plain text e-mails. As you can see, JavaMailSender extends the MailSender interface with methods for constructing and sending MIME messages.

COS MailMessage does not support complex MIME messages, and as a result, the implementation based on MailMessage only includes an implementation of MailSender and can only be used for sending plain text e-mails. When you require something more complex than this, you can use the JavaMail-based implementation, which provides an implementation of the JavaMailSender interface, allowing you to send complex MIME messages.

In general, if you are just sending plain text e-mails, it is better to have your application code to the MailSender interface, which provides an extremely simple API for sending messages. If you need to send more complex e-mails, perhaps with attachments or inline images, then you need to code to the JavaMailSender interface and use the JavaMail implementation of the mail abstraction layer.

Configuring Mail Settings Using Spring

Both the JavaMail and COS `MailMessage` mail layer implementations provide JavaBean-style properties to allow you to configure mail settings in your Spring configuration file. For the COS implementation, the only parameter you can set is the host name of the SMTP server to use for sending mail, but the JavaMail implementation provides a much wider set of parameters to control the protocol, mail host, host port, and server authentication details. In addition to the JavaBean properties for basic configuration, the JavaMail implementation allows you to provide any of the recognized JavaMail configuration parameters using an instance of `Properties` and the `<properties>` tag in your configuration file.

The SimpleMailMessage Class

One of the core classes used by both the COS and JavaMail implementations is `SimpleMailMessage`. This class encapsulates the details of a basic mail message in a simple JavaBean. Using this class, you can create templates for your messages in your configuration file, specifying details such as the sender address and the subject, and then just modify the appropriate details in your application code. To avoid threading issues, `SimpleMailMessage` has a copy constructor that accepts another instance of `SimpleMailMessage`, allowing you to create a sandbox instance of your message that can be modified separately on your thread without affecting the shared instance.

Sending Simple E-Mails

The most basic task when sending e-mail is to send a simple, plain text e-mail. Both the COS and JavaMail implementations support this functionality, and both allow this to be achieved using both programmatic and declarative mechanisms. In the first part of this section, you learn how to create and send messages programmatically, and in the second part, we look at an alternative implementation that uses the declarative approach to configure both the `MailSender` implementations and the `SimpleMailMessage`.

Constructing and Sending E-Mail Programmatically

To send mail programmatically, the first task is to create an instance of `SimpleMailMessage` and then configure it with the appropriate details, such as subject, body text, and recipient address. The next step is to create an instance of `MailSender` and then set the appropriate configuration details; in particular, you need to set the host address of the mail server.

In Listing 15-1, you can see the `SimpleMailSender` class, which acts as a base class for the examples in this section.

Listing 15-1. *The SimpleMailSender Class*

```
package com.apress.prospring.ch15.simple;

import org.springframework.mail.MailSender;
import org.springframework.mail.SimpleMailMessage;

public abstract class SimpleMailSender {

    protected abstract MailSender getMailSender();

    public final void sendMessage(String to, String text) {
        SimpleMailMessage msg = new SimpleMailMessage();
        msg.setTo(to);
        msg.setSubject("Test Message");
        msg.setFrom("test@apress.com");
        msg.setText(text);

        MailSender sender = getMailSender();
        sender.send(msg);
    }
}
```

The first thing to notice here is that this class is declared abstract and has an abstract method, getMailSender(). We will create two different base classes: one that returns an instance of CosMailSenderImpl and one that returns JavaMailSenderImpl. In this way, we can reuse the logic in sendMessage(). In the sendMessage() method, we assemble an instance of SimpleMailMessage with content for the subject and body and addresses for the sender and recipient. Once this instance is assembled, we use the instance of MailSender returned by the getMailSender() method to send the message. The MailSender interface includes two send() methods, one that accepts a single instance of SimpleMailMessage and another that accepts an array of SimpleMailMessage objects for sending messages in bulk.

In Listing 15-2, you can see the JavaMailSimpleMailSender class that extends SimpleMailSender to return an instance of JavaMailSenderImpl from the getMailSender() method.

Listing 15-2. *The JavaMailSimpleMailSender Class*

```
package com.apress.prospring.ch15.simple;

import org.springframework.mail.MailSender;
import org.springframework.mail.javamail.JavaMailSenderImpl;

public class JavaMailSimpleMailSender extends SimpleMailSender {
```

```
    protected MailSender getMailSender() {
        JavaMailSenderImpl sender = new JavaMailSenderImpl();
        sender.setHost("localhost");
        return sender;
    }
}
```

Notice that in the getMailSender() method, we create an instance of JavaMailSenderImpl and configure the mail host using the setHost() method. Most likely, you will need to change the mail host address for your environment. Be aware that the setHost() method is not defined on either the MailSender or JavaMailSender interfaces, so you cannot configure the mail host in a implementation-agnostic manner when using this approach. In Listing 15-3, you can see the CosSimpleMailSender class, which shows a simple implementation like that shown in Listing 15-2 but for the CosMailSenderImpl class.

Listing 15-3. *The CosSimpleMailSender Class*

```
package com.apress.prospring.ch15.simple;

import org.springframework.mail.MailSender;
import org.springframework.mail.cos.CosMailSenderImpl;

public class CosSimpleMailSender extends SimpleMailSender {

    protected MailSender getMailSender() {
        CosMailSenderImpl sender = new CosMailSenderImpl();
        sender.setHost("localhost");
        return sender;
    }
}
```

Here you can see that aside from the class instance that is created, this implementation is identical to that of the JavaMailSimpleMailSender class. At this point, we have two classes that, using different MailSender implementations, can send a message containing some arbitrary text to a single recipient. Listing 15-4 shows the SimpleMailTest class that tests out the CosSimpleMailSender and JavaMailSimpleMailSender classes.

Listing 15-4. *Sending the E-Mails*

```
package com.apress.prospring.ch15.simple;

public class SimpleMailTest {

    private static final String TO = "robh@cakesolutions.net";

    private static final String TEXT = "Hello World!";
```

```
    public static void main(String[] args) {

        SimpleMailSender sender1 = new JavaMailSimpleMailSender();
        SimpleMailSender sender2 = new CosSimpleMailSender();

        sender1.sendMessage(TO, TEXT);
        sender2.sendMessage(TO, TEXT);
    }
}
```

Here we are using an instance of JavaMailSimpleMailSender and an instance of CosSimpleMailSender to send two copies of the same message to the same recipient. When you run this example, it takes a few seconds to execute depending on your mail server and the connection speed and it then terminates. In Figure 15-2, you can see the results of this code rendered in our mail client.

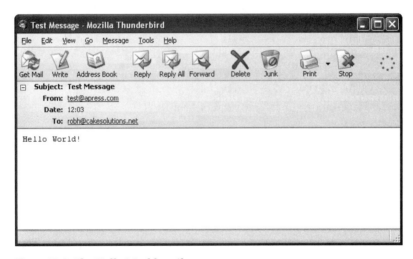

Figure 15-2. *The Hello World mail message*

As you can see from this example, sending simple, plain text e-mails is extremely straightforward. However, this approach has a big drawback: all configuration data for the MailSender implementations and the SimpleMailMessage objects is contained in the code. In the next example, you will see how to configure the MailSender and SimpleMailMessage in the Spring configuration file.

Constructing E-Mail Declaratively

In the previous section, we alluded to the fact that it is possible to configure a MailSender in your Spring configuration file and to create a template SimpleMailMessage containing the basic details of your mail. In this section, we revisit the birthday reminder example from the previous chapter to add e-mail-based reminders.

The first step in this example is to create a TimerTask implementation that sends reminders to e-mail. This is shown in Listing 15-5.

Listing 15-5. *The ReminderTask Class*

```
package com.apress.prospring.ch15.birthday;

import java.util.TimerTask;

import org.springframework.mail.MailSender;
import org.springframework.mail.SimpleMailMessage;

public class ReminderTask extends TimerTask {

    private SimpleMailMessage defaultMessage;
    private MailSender sender;
    private String who;

    public void setMailMessage(SimpleMailMessage defaultMessage) {
        this.defaultMessage = defaultMessage;
    }

    public void setMailSender(MailSender sender) {
        this.sender = sender;
    }

    public void setWho(String who) {
        this.who = who;
    }

    public void run() {
        SimpleMailMessage msg = new SimpleMailMessage(defaultMessage);
        msg.setText("Remember! It is " + who + "'s birthday in 7 days.");
        sender.send(msg);
        System.out.println("Sent reminder for: " + who);
    }
}
```

The first thing you should notice in this code is that we defined two JavaBean properties, `mailSender` and `mailMessage`. These allow for instances of `MailSender` and `SimpleMailMessage` to be set using DI. In the `run()` method, we create an instance of `SimpleMailMessage` using the externally provided instance as a template. Then we set the message text to be the reminder, and we send it using the externally provided `MailSender` instance. Notice that we haven't specified any configuration properties for the `MailSender` nor do we specify a subject, sender address, or recipient address for the `SimpleMailMessage`. These parameters are all set in the configuration file shown in Listing 15-6.

Listing 15-6. *Configuring Mail Settings Externally*

```
<!DOCTYPE beans PUBLIC "-//SPRING//DTD BEAN//EN"
"http://www.springframework.org/dtd/spring-beans.dtd">
<beans>
    <bean id="mum"
          class="com.apress.prospring.ch14.timer.bday.BirthdayScheduledTask">
        <property name="date">
            <value>2004-11-29</value>
        </property>
        <property name="fixedRate">
            <value>true</value>
        </property>
        <property name="timerTask">
            <bean class="com.apress.prospring.ch15.birthday.ReminderTask">
                <property name="who">
                    <value>Mum</value>
                </property>
                <property name="mailSender">
                    <ref local="sender"/>
                </property>
                <property name="mailMessage">
                    <ref local="mailMessage"/>
                </property>
            </bean>
        </property>
    </bean>

    <bean id="sender" class="org.springframework.mail.javamail.JavaMailSenderImpl">
        <property name="host">
            <value>localhost</value>
        </property>
    </bean>

    <bean id="mailMessage" class="org.springframework.mail.SimpleMailMessage">
        <property name="from">
            <value>reminders@apress.com</value>
        </property>
        <property name="to">
            <value>robh@cakesolutions.net</value>
        </property>
        <property name="subject">
            <value>Birthday Reminder!!</value>
        </property>
    </bean>
```

```
    <bean id="timerFactory"
        class="org.springframework.scheduling.timer.TimerFactoryBean">
        <property name="scheduledTimerTasks">
            <list>
                <ref local="mum"/>
            </list>
        </property>
    </bean>
</beans>
```

You should recognize much of this configuration code from the previous chapter; the important parts are the mailMessage and sender bean declarations. For the sender bean, we use the JavaMailSenderImpl class and we configure the host property to be localhost, as we did when using the programmatic approach. For the mailMessage bean we have set the to, from, and subject properties. Each of these properties is inherited by the instance of SimpleMailMessage created in the run() method, because we use this instance of SimpleMailMessage as a template.

Listing 15-7 shows a simple driver class that loads the configuration shown in Listing 15-6 and then simply waits.

Listing 15-7. *Loading the Mail Configuration*

```
package com.apress.prospring.ch15.birthday;

import org.springframework.context.ApplicationContext;
import org.springframework.context.support.FileSystemXmlApplicationContext;

public class Runner {

    public static void main(String[] args) throws Exception {

        ApplicationContext ctx = new FileSystemXmlApplicationContext(
                "./ch15/src/conf/birthdayReminder.xml");
        System.in.read();
    }
}
```

Until the date in the configuration file is reached, no e-mail is sent, so you might want to change the date to one that is more relevant or change the configuration for the scheduled task to use a different schedule altogether. Figure 15-3 shows a sample message generated by this example.

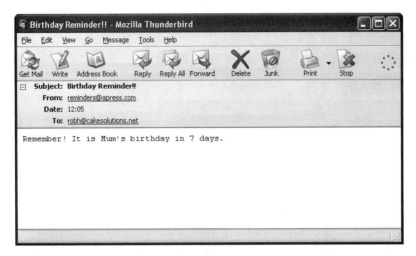

Figure 15-3. *The birthday reminder e-mail*

The declarative approach for configuration is generally preferred to the wholly programmatic approach, because it allows you to externalize fully all configuration, including basic message configuration, and you can take advantage of Dependency Injection (DI) when providing your application components with instances of MailSender and SimpleMailMessage. This is particularly useful because it allows you to swap out one implementation of MailSender for another.

Constructing and Sending MIME Messages

In the previous section, all the e-mails we created were simple, plain text e-mails with no fancy extras like HTML formatting, embedded images, or attachments. This might be okay for some applications where the e-mail is simply for information purposes or is used entirely within an organization, but often applications require the ability to send much more complex e-mail messages. The JavaMail implementation of MailSender, or more accurately of JavaMailSender, provides the ability to send MIME (Multipart Internet Message Encoding) messages, allowing for messages in HTML format, messages with embedded images, and messages with attachments.

In this section, we consider five separate scenarios for sending complex MIME messages:

- Sending a message with HTML content

- Sending an HTML message with embedded images

- Sending a message with attachments

- Sending an HTML message with a plain text alternative

- Sending a MIME message with a complex structure

All of these examples rely on features in the JavaMailSenderImpl class and as a result, they do not work with CosMailSenderImpl. A major drawback of sending MIME messages is that you cannot use the SimpleMailMessage class for external configuration because the MIME-aware methods on JavaMailSenderImpl do not work with this class. For this reason, it is often better to create a class to encapsulate your MIME message that Spring can configure externally. For the examples in this section, we define a common base class that allows for external configuration of the messages, as shown in Listing 15-8.

Listing 15-8. *The AbstractMessageSender Class*

```
package com.apress.prospring.ch15.mime;

import org.springframework.mail.javamail.JavaMailSender;

public abstract class AbstractMessageSender {

    protected String to;
    protected String from;
    protected String subject;
    protected JavaMailSender sender;


    public void setTo(String to) {
        this.to = to;
    }

    public void setFrom(String from) {
        this.from = from;
    }

    public void setSubject(String subject) {
        this.subject = subject;
    }

    public void setJavaMailSender(JavaMailSender sender) {
        this.sender = sender;
    }
}
```

The idea behind this class is that each of our examples inherits from it and can then be configured in the Spring configuration file. Also, all examples in this section require an instance of JavaMailSender, which is set via the javaMailSender property exposed by the AbstractMessageSender. To configure this JavaMailSender instance, we use a shared configuration file (shown in Listing 15-9) across all of the examples.

Listing 15-9. *The Shared Configuration File*

```
<!DOCTYPE beans PUBLIC "-//SPRING//DTD BEAN//EN"
"http://www.springframework.org/dtd/spring-beans.dtd">
<beans>
    <bean id="sender" class="org.springframework.mail.javamail.JavaMailSenderImpl">
        <property name="host">
            <value>localhost</value>
        </property>
    </bean>
</beans>
```

Here you can see that we configured a sender bean, of type JavaMailSenderImpl, and we configured the host property for our environment. You may need to modify the host for these examples to work in your environment.

In addition to the shared configuration file, each example uses a custom configuration such as that shown in Listing 15-10.

Listing 15-10. *The Example-Specific Configuration File*

```
<!DOCTYPE beans PUBLIC "-//SPRING//DTD BEAN//EN"
"http://www.springframework.org/dtd/spring-beans.dtd">
<beans>
    <bean id="messageSender"
            class="com.apress.prospring.ch15.mime.AlternativeFormatMessageSender">
        <property name="javaMailSender">
            <ref bean="sender"/>
        </property>
        <property name="to">
            <value>robh@cakesolutions.net</value>
        </property>
        <property name="from">
            <value>mail@apress.com</value>
        </property>
        <property name="subject">
            <value>Alternative Formats</value>
        </property>
    </bean>
</beans>
```

The only thing that changes in each of these configuration files is the class attribute of the messageSender bean. For this reason, we do not show each of these configurations in the text, but you can still find them in the code download.

Sending a Basic HTML E-Mail

An HTML message is created in a similar manner to plain text e-mail, but you must be sure to specify the MIME type of the message that you are creating—in this case, text/html. Although you can't use the SimpleMailMessage class when working with MIME messages, Spring provides the MimeMessageHelper class that allows you to work with MIME messages in a similar manner to the SimpleMailMessage class and to avoid some of the complexities of working with the JavaMail API directly.

In Listing 15-11, you can see the SimpleHtmlMessageSender class that builds and sends a simple HTML mail.

Listing 15-11. *The SimpleHtmlMessageSender Class*

```
package com.apress.prospring.ch15.mime;

import javax.mail.MessagingException;
import javax.mail.internet.MimeMessage;

import org.springframework.context.ApplicationContext;
import org.springframework.context.support.FileSystemXmlApplicationContext;
import org.springframework.mail.javamail.MimeMessageHelper;

public class SimpleHtmlMessageSender extends AbstractMessageSender {

    public void sendMessage() throws MessagingException {
        MimeMessage msg = sender.createMimeMessage();
        MimeMessageHelper helper = new MimeMessageHelper(msg);

        helper.setTo(to);
        helper.setFrom(from);
        helper.setSubject(subject);
        helper.setText("<html><head></head><body><h1>Hello World!"
                + "</h1></body></html>", true);

        sender.send(msg);
    }

    public static void main(String[] args) throws Exception {
        ApplicationContext ctx = new FileSystemXmlApplicationContext(
                new String[] { "./ch15/src/conf/simpleHtmlMessageSender.xml",
                        "./ch15/src/conf/javaMailSender.xml" });

        SimpleHtmlMessageSender sender = (SimpleHtmlMessageSender) ctx
                .getBean("messageSender");
        sender.sendMessage();
    }
}
```

Much of this code is fairly self-explanatory, but there are a few points of note. First, notice that an instance of MimeMessage is retrieved by calling the createMimeMessage() method of the JavaMailSender interface. Second, this instance is wrapped in an instance of MimeMessageHelper and we use this to set the various parameters. The final point of note in this example is that in the call to MimeMessageHelper.setText(), we pass in true as the second argument to flag that this message is an HTML format message. Once the message is assembled, it is sent with a call to `JavaMailSender.send()`.

Figure 15-4 shows the results of this code rendered in our e-mail client.

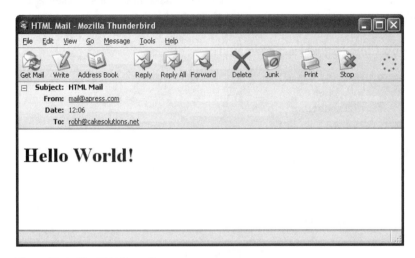

Figure 15-4. *The HTML mail message*

Sending an HTML Mail with Embedded Images

In the previous example, you saw how to assemble and send an HTML format e-mail. In this section, you see how to add embedded images to your mail and display these in the HTML body content.

NOTE In general, we have found that it is better to avoid embedded images and to use images that are accessed via a standard URL in your e-mails. Many e-mail clients have trouble dealing with embedded images especially when they form part of more complex MIME structures like the one shown later in the section entitled "Sending Complex MIME Messages."

In order to send an HTML e-mail that uses embedded images, you have to assemble the HTML message first and then add the images as additional parts to the MIME message. When adding a MIME part, you can associate a **Content-ID** with it; a Content-ID is used if you are referring to the image from the HTML. When using `MimeMessageHelper`, Spring takes care of much of the logic behind this process for you.

Listing 15-12 shows the `InlineImageMessageSender` class that demonstrates how to build a message with inline images.

Listing 15-12. *The InlineImageMessageSender Class*

```java
package com.apress.prospring.ch15.mime;

import java.io.File;

import javax.mail.MessagingException;
import javax.mail.internet.MimeMessage;

import org.springframework.context.ApplicationContext;
import org.springframework.context.support.FileSystemXmlApplicationContext;
import org.springframework.core.io.FileSystemResource;
import org.springframework.mail.javamail.MimeMessageHelper;

public class InlineImageMessageSender extends AbstractMessageSender {

    public void sendMessage() throws MessagingException {
        MimeMessage msg = sender.createMimeMessage();
        MimeMessageHelper helper = new MimeMessageHelper(msg, true);

        helper.setTo(to);
        helper.setFrom(from);
        helper.setSubject(subject);

        helper.setText("<html><head></head><body><h1>Hello World!</h1>"
                + "<img src=\"cid:abc\"></body></html>", true);

        // add the image
        FileSystemResource img = new FileSystemResource(new File(
                "./ch15/src/images/apress.gif"));
        helper.addInline("abc", img);

        sender.send(msg);
    }

    public static void main(String[] args) throws Exception {
        ApplicationContext ctx = new FileSystemXmlApplicationContext(
                new String[] { "./ch15/src/conf/inlineImageMessageSender.xml",
                        "./ch15/src/conf/javaMailSender.xml" });

        InlineImageMessageSender sender = (InlineImageMessageSender) ctx
                .getBean("messageSender");
        sender.sendMessage();
    }
}
```

This example is very similar to the previous example, but there are three noticeable differences in the sendMessage() method.

First, in the HTML that is added to the message body, there is an <img> tag whose src attribute is set to cid:abc. This tells the mail client to use the embedded resource with Content-ID abc when rendering this image.

Second, you can see that the image resource itself is embedded in the message using the MimeMessageHelper.addInline() method. When you are adding inline resources, it is important that you add the message body first and the resources second; otherwise, the message does not render correctly in the mail client. As of version 1.1, the Spring manual reports, incorrectly, that you must add inline resources first, followed by the message body. This is corrected in subsequent releases, but be aware that older releases still have this error in the documentation.

Finally, you will notice that when constructing the instance of MimeMessageHelper, we passed in a second, boolean, argument. This argument specifies whether or not the MimeMessageHelper should work in multipart mode, which is required to add attachments to a message.

Figure 15-5 shows the result of running this example rendered in a mail client.

Figure 15-5. *Displaying a message with embedded images*

As you can see from the figure, the embedded image is rendered as part of the message body. Using this approach for including images in your messages means that you avoid needing to store images on a server that is accessible by the recipients; however, many mail clients do not handle embedded images well when they are combined with other MIME features such as alternative message formats.

Sending a Message with Attachments

Sending attachments with a message is very much like including embedded resources; in fact, behind the scenes, both features create additional MIME parts in your message. The main difference is that embedded resources have their **content disposition** set to inline, indicating that they should not be considered as attachments.

Listing 15-13 shows a slight modification to the previous example—instead of embedding, the image attaches to the message.

Listing 15-13. *Sending Attachments*

```java
package com.apress.prospring.ch15.mime;

import java.io.File;

import javax.mail.MessagingException;
import javax.mail.internet.MimeMessage;

import org.springframework.context.ApplicationContext;
import org.springframework.context.support.FileSystemXmlApplicationContext;
import org.springframework.core.io.FileSystemResource;
import org.springframework.mail.javamail.MimeMessageHelper;

public class AttachmentMessageSender extends AbstractMessageSender {

    public void sendMessage() throws MessagingException {
        MimeMessage msg = sender.createMimeMessage();
        MimeMessageHelper helper = new MimeMessageHelper(msg, true);

        helper.setTo(to);
        helper.setFrom(from);
        helper.setSubject(subject);

        helper.setText(
                "<html><head></head><body><h1>Hello World!</h1></body></html>",
                true);

        // add the image
        FileSystemResource img = new FileSystemResource(new File(
                "./ch15/src/images/apress.gif"));
        helper.addAttachment("apress.gif", img);

        sender.send(msg);
    }

    public static void main(String[] args) throws Exception {
        ApplicationContext ctx = new FileSystemXmlApplicationContext(
                new String[] { "./ch15/src/conf/attachmentMessageSender.xml",
                        "./ch15/src/conf/javaMailSender.xml" });

        AttachmentMessageSender sender = (AttachmentMessageSender) ctx
                .getBean("messageSender");
        sender.sendMessage();
    }
}
```

As we mentioned, this example is very similar to the last. The only important difference here is that we have swapped the call to addInline() with a call to addAttachment(). Because attachments are included in the mail in the same way as embedded resources, they are also given a Content-ID, which most mail clients recognize as the file name. Figure 15-6 shows this message in the mail client; notice the file name that is displayed for the attachment.

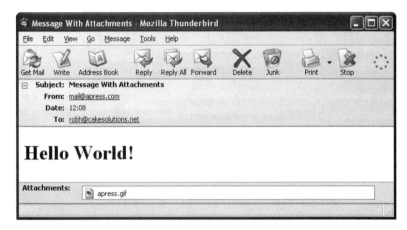

Figure 15-6. *Message with an attachment*

Sending an HTML Mail Message with Plain Text Alternative

In the examples so far, there has been very little direct interaction with the JavaMail APIs, and we have been able to rely on Spring helper classes when assembling the MIME messages. However, in some cases, the complexity of the MIME message structure requires you to interact directly with the JavaMail API. This example and the one that follows are examples of this.

When you need more control over how a MIME message is assembled, you can create an implementation of the MimeMessagePreparator callback interface and pass this to the JavaMailSender.send() method in place of the MimeMessage. The main reason for doing this rather than attempting to assemble the MimeMessage directly is that JavaMail throws a lot of checked exceptions from which it is impossible to recover. Spring takes care of wrapping these checked exceptions in runtime exceptions, thus reducing the complexity of your code. You should note that you can still use the MimeMessageHelper class when assembling your own MimeMessages, but we choose not do so here to illustrate how to interact directly with JavaMail.

In this example you see how to assemble an HTML message with a plain text alternative. When rendered in a mail client that either doesn't support HTML or has had HTML disabled, the plain text alternative contained in the message is used in place of the HTML. This is like sending two copies of the same letter, each in a different language, in the same envelope. In general, both the HTML and plain text message parts contain the same message, albeit in different formats. In this example, we are going to make the plain text message different from the HTML one to illustrate how this works.

The code for this example is quite complex, so we explain it in pieces. Listing 15-14 shows the basic class that obtains the required beans from Spring and then sends the message with a call to JavaMailSender.send().

Listing 15-14. *The AlternativeFormatMessageSender Class*

```
package com.apress.prospring.ch15.mime;

import javax.mail.BodyPart;
import javax.mail.Message;
import javax.mail.internet.InternetAddress;
import javax.mail.internet.MimeBodyPart;
import javax.mail.internet.MimeMessage;
import javax.mail.internet.MimeMultipart;

import org.springframework.context.ApplicationContext;
import org.springframework.context.support.FileSystemXmlApplicationContext;
import org.springframework.mail.javamail.MimeMessagePreparator;

public class AlternativeFormatMessageSender extends AbstractMessageSender {

    public void sendMessage() {
        sender.send(new MessagePreparator());
    }

    public static void main(String[] args) throws Exception {
        ApplicationContext ctx = new FileSystemXmlApplicationContext(
                new String[] {
                        "./ch15/src/conf/alternativeFormatMessageSender.xml",
                        "./ch15/src/conf/javaMailSender.xml" });

        AlternativeFormatMessageSender sender =
                (AlternativeFormatMessageSender) ctx.getBean("messageSender");
        sender.sendMessage();
    }
}
```

Much of this code will be familiar to you by now, but notice that the call to send passes in an instance of the MessagePreparator class instead of an instance of MimeMessage. The MessagePreparator class is an inner class that implements the MimeMessagePreparator interface and it is responsible for actually constructing the MimeMessage object. Note that Spring creates the MimeMessage instance and passes it to the MimeMessagePreparator.prepare() method. The MessagePreparator is only responsible for configuring this object; it does not need to create the MimeMessage itself.

Listing 15-15 shows the MimeMessagePreparator class.

Listing 15-15. *The MimeMessagePreparator Class*

```
private class MessagePreparator implements MimeMessagePreparator {

    public void prepare(MimeMessage msg) throws Exception {

        // set header details
        msg.addFrom(InternetAddress.parse(from));
        msg.addRecipients(Message.RecipientType.TO, InternetAddress
                .parse(to));
        msg.setSubject(subject);

        // create wrapper multipart/alternative part
        MimeMultipart ma = new MimeMultipart("alternative");
        msg.setContent(ma);

        // create the plain text
        BodyPart plainText = new MimeBodyPart();
        plainText.setText("This is the plain text version of the mail.");
        ma.addBodyPart(plainText);

        //  create the html part
        BodyPart html = new MimeBodyPart();
        html.setContent(
            "<html><head></head><body><h1>This is the HTML version of the mail."
                    + "</h1></body></html>", "text/html");
        ma.addBodyPart(html);
    }
  }
}
```

Here the prepare() method starts by setting the sender and recipient addresses along with the subject. Notice that when setting the addresses of the sender and recipient, we have to use the InternetAddress.parse() method to create an instance of InternetAddress from a String. This is one of the details that are hidden by the MimeMessageHelper class, and it is often preferable to use MimeMessageHelper for configuring message properties, even when assembling the message directly.

Next, we create an instance of MimeMultipart, a wrapper class to hold multiple message parts, and we specify the MIME type as multipart/alternative, signifying that the parts contained in this multipart are alternative formats of the same data. This MimeMultipart instance is specified as the content of the MimeMessage instance using the MimeMessage.setContent() method.

Next, we create two instances of MimeBodyPart: one for the plain text body and one for the HTML body. When assembling the plain text BodyPart, it is enough simply to call the setText() method passing in the part content. This sets the MIME type of the BodyPart to text/plain. For the HTML BodyPart, we use the setContent() method in place of setText() and we explicitly pass in the MIME type of text/html as the second argument. Both of these BodyParts are then added to the MimeMultipart instance and as a result, they are added to the MimeMessage. The order in which you add BodyParts to the MimeMultipart is important, and you should add the BodyPart with the most preferable message format last.

The result of this code is to populate a MimeMessage instance so that the top-level MIME type is multipart/alternative and within the message there are two parts: one with the MIME type text/plain and the other with the MIME type text/html.

Figure 15-7 shows this message rendered as HTML in the mail client and Figure 15-8 shows it rendered as plain text.

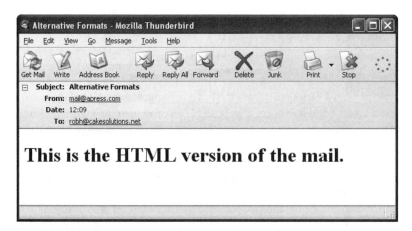

Figure 15-7. *The HTML message*

Figure 15-8. *The plain text message*

Most mail clients allow you to select which format you want to view messages in. We have found that Mozilla Thunderbird is very useful during testing because it allows you to quickly swap between the different message formats. Another useful tool for testing is the Pegasus mail client for Microsoft Windows that allows you to view the individual parts of the message as a graphical tree representation. You can download Pegasus from www.pmail.com. Figure 15-9 shows the tree representation of this message rendered in Pegasus.

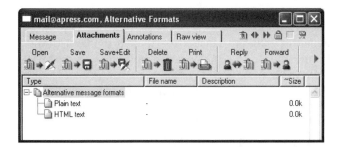

Figure 15-9. *Checking the message structure with Pegasus*

Sending Complex MIME Messages

So far you have seen how to send a variety of different MIME messages, including HTML messages with embedded images and messages with both HTML and plain text content, but how can you send a message that has HTML content with embedded images and a plain text alternative? In this section, we show you how.

The code required to send an HTML message with both embedded images and a plain text alternative is not that different from the code required to send the HTML message with the plain text alternative. The main change is that we need to wrap the HTML content along with the embedded images inside an additional multipart wrapper. This wrapper groups the HTML together with the embedded images and instructs the mail client that HTML together with the images forms the second message format, not just the HTML on its own. Listing 15-16 shows the code you need to do this.

Listing 15-16. *Assembling Complex MIME Messages*

```
package com.apress.prospring.ch15.mime;

import javax.activation.DataHandler;
import javax.activation.FileDataSource;
import javax.mail.BodyPart;
import javax.mail.Message;
import javax.mail.MessagingException;
import javax.mail.internet.InternetAddress;
import javax.mail.internet.MimeBodyPart;
import javax.mail.internet.MimeMessage;
import javax.mail.internet.MimeMultipart;

import org.springframework.context.ApplicationContext;
import org.springframework.context.support.FileSystemXmlApplicationContext;
import org.springframework.mail.javamail.MimeMessagePreparator;

public class ComplexMessageSender extends AbstractMessageSender {
```

```java
public void sendMessage() throws MessagingException {
    sender.send(new MessagePreparator());
}

public static void main(String[] args) throws Exception {
    ApplicationContext ctx = new FileSystemXmlApplicationContext(
            new String[] {
                    "./ch15/src/conf/complexMessageSender.xml",
                    "./ch15/src/conf/javaMailSender.xml" });

    ComplexMessageSender sender = (ComplexMessageSender) ctx
            .getBean("messageSender");
    sender.sendMessage();
}

private class MessagePreparator implements MimeMessagePreparator {

    public void prepare(MimeMessage msg) throws Exception {

        // set header details
        msg.addFrom(InternetAddress.parse(from));
        msg.addRecipients(Message.RecipientType.TO, InternetAddress
                .parse(to));
        msg.setSubject(subject);

        // create wrapper multipart/alternative part
        MimeMultipart ma = new MimeMultipart("alternative");
        msg.setContent(ma);

        // create the plain text
        BodyPart plainText = new MimeBodyPart();
        plainText.setText("This is the plain text version of the mail.");
        ma.addBodyPart(plainText);

        //  create the html and image multipart wrapper
        BodyPart related = new MimeBodyPart();
        MimeMultipart mr = new MimeMultipart("related");
        related.setContent(mr);
        ma.addBodyPart(related);

        BodyPart html = new MimeBodyPart();
        html.setContent(
            "<html><head></head><body><h1>This is the HTML version of the mail."
                    + "</h1><img src=\"cid:0001\"></body></html>", "text/html");
        mr.addBodyPart(html);
```

```
        BodyPart img = new MimeBodyPart();
        img.setHeader("Content-ID", "0001");
        img.setDisposition("inline");
        img.setDataHandler(new DataHandler(
                    new FileDataSource("./ch15/src/images/apress.gif")));
        mr.addBodyPart(img);
    }
  }
}
```

The important piece of this code is the prepare() method of the MessagePreparator class. Up to and including the code that adds the plain text BodyPart, the prepare() method is identical to the one in the last example. When it comes to the HTML format message, we start by creating a BodyPart and a second MimeMultipart instance. This MimeMultipart instance is given the MIME type multipart/related, indicating that the BodyParts it contains are related and, for the purposes of the enclosing MimeMultipart, should be treated as one. The MimeMultipart of type multipart/related is then set as the content for a BodyPart and this BodyPart is added to the top-level multipart/alternative MimeMultipart instance. The reason we create a BodyPart in this case is that you cannot add one MimeMultipart to another without first wrapping it in a BodyPart—essentially you are saying that a part of the top-level multipart is made up of another multipart.

Next we add the HTML BodyPart to the multipart/related MimeMultipart followed by the embedded image. In general, it is much easier to use the MimeMessageHelper class to add embedded resources to a MimeMultipart, but we wanted to show how to do it manually. The first two steps required when adding an embedded, inline resource are to set the Content-ID header of the multipart and to set the content disposition to inline. Once this is done, you can supply the content of the actual BodyPart using the setDataHandler() method. The setDataHandler() method requires an instance of javax.activation.DataHandler, which in turn requires an instance of a class that implements javax.activation.DataSource—we use the javax.activation.FileDataSource class. JavaMail and the JavaBeans Activation Framework take care of encoding the resource data for inclusion in the message as well as identifying the correct MIME type for the data and including this in the BodyPart.

In Figure 15-10, you can see the plain text version of this message and Figure 15-11 shows the HTML version with the embedded image.

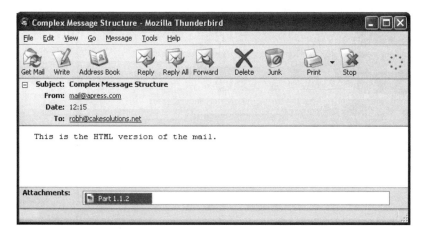

Figure 15-10. *The plain text message*

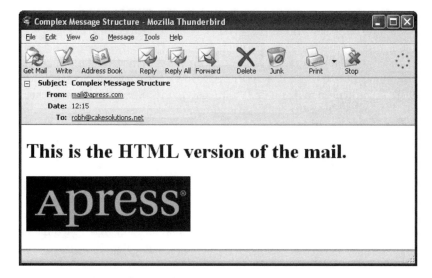

Figure 15-11. *The HTML message*

Notice that in the plain text view, the inline image is treated as an attachment even though we set the content disposition to `inline`. This is just one example of how different mail clients treat the mail structure differently. Again, you can use Pegasus to view the structure of the message in graphical form as shown in Figure 15-12.

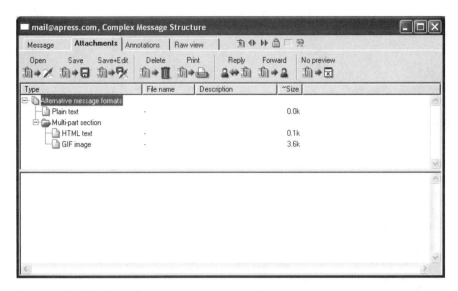

Figure 15-12. *Checking the message structure in Pegasus*

Here you can see that the plain text mail sits in the second level of the tree along with a multipart section containing both the HTML and GIF image in the third level of the tree. Interestingly, when Pegasus is configured to ignore the HTML part of the message, it displays the plain text part without showing the GIF image as an attachment.

Using Spring Mail with Velocity

Mail is a common feature in many applications and even with the support provided by Spring, you may find yourself creating the same code in every application just to build the correct structure for a message. You will also find that using a wholly programmatic approach to message construction places too much of the message content inside your application, making it difficult to modify this content. We have found that a flexible solution to this problem is to create a reusable implementation of the MimeMessagePreparator interface that creates a message in a common structure and obtains message content from Velocity templates.

Velocity is a templating engine that allows you to create any kind of textual output by merging text-based templates with Java Objects. Velocity is most widely used as a replacement or complement to JSP in the Web Tier, as discussed in Chapter 18, but it has many uses beyond that. If you are unfamiliar with Velocity, you can visit the website at http://jakarta.apache.org/velocity, or you can read *Pro Jakarta Velocity: From Professional to Expert* by Rob Harrop (Apress, 2004).

We have found that a message structure that works well in most mail clients is simply to provide both plain text and HTML content in a single multipart. We have found that it is better to avoid embedded images and host them on a web server instead. You can link to them in the standard way from within the HTML content.

For the solution shown in this section, we created a class, VelocityMimeMessagePreparator, that is designed to be configured using DI. This means you can define an instance of VelocityMimeMessagePreparator in your Spring configuration, setting important properties such as the sender and recipients addresses as well the Velocity templates to use for the plain text and HTML message parts. At runtime, you simply obtain the VelocityMimeMessagePreparator bean from Spring and pass it a Map containing the data you wish to merge with the templates. Spring also provides excellent support for Velocity, meaning that you can configure the VelocityEngine instance used by the VelocityMimeMessagePreparator in your configuration file. Listing 15-17 shows the code for the VelocityMimeMessagePreparator class.

Listing 15-17. *The VelocityMimeMessagePreparator Class*

```
package com.apress.prospring.ch15.velocity;

import java.util.Map;

import javax.mail.BodyPart;
import javax.mail.Message;
import javax.mail.internet.InternetAddress;
import javax.mail.internet.MimeBodyPart;
import javax.mail.internet.MimeMessage;
import javax.mail.internet.MimeMultipart;

import org.apache.velocity.app.VelocityEngine;
import org.springframework.beans.factory.InitializingBean;
import org.springframework.mail.javamail.MimeMessagePreparator;
import org.springframework.ui.velocity.VelocityEngineUtils;

public class VelocityMimeMessagePreparator implements MimeMessagePreparator,
        InitializingBean {

    private VelocityEngine velocityEngine;

    private String plainTextTemplate = "plainText.vm";

    private String htmlTemplate = "html.vm";

    private String from;

    private String to;

    private String subject;

    private Map data;

    public void prepare(MimeMessage msg) throws Exception {
        // set header details
        msg.addFrom(InternetAddress.parse(from));
        msg.addRecipients(Message.RecipientType.TO, InternetAddress.parse(to));
        msg.setSubject(subject);
```

```java
        // create wrapper multipart/alternative part
        MimeMultipart ma = new MimeMultipart("alternative");
        msg.setContent(ma);

        // create the plain text
        BodyPart plainText = new MimeBodyPart();
        plainText.setText(VelocityEngineUtils.mergeTemplateIntoString(
                velocityEngine, plainTextTemplate, data));
        ma.addBodyPart(plainText);

        //  create the html part
        BodyPart html = new MimeBodyPart();
        html.setContent(VelocityEngineUtils.mergeTemplateIntoString(
                velocityEngine, htmlTemplate, data), "text/html");
        ma.addBodyPart(html);
    }

    public void afterPropertiesSet() throws Exception {
        if (velocityEngine == null) {
            throw new IllegalArgumentException(
                    "Must set the velocityEngine property of "
                            + getClass().getName());
        }
    }

    public void setPlainTextTemplatePath(String plainTextTemplate) {
        this.plainTextTemplate = plainTextTemplate;
    }

    public void setHtmlTemplatePath(String htmlTemplate) {
        this.htmlTemplate = htmlTemplate;
    }

    public void setVelocityEngine(VelocityEngine velocityEngine) {
        this.velocityEngine = velocityEngine;
    }

    public void setTo(String to) {
        this.to = to;
    }

    public void setFrom(String from) {
        this.from = from;
    }
```

```
    public void setSubject(String subject) {
        this.subject = subject;
    }

    public void setData(Map data) {
        this.data = data;
    }

}
```

As you can see, there is nothing particularly clever about this code. We create a MimeMessage using the structure shown earlier in the section entitled "Sending an HTML Mail Message with Plain Text Alternative." Notice, however, that we do not directly create an instance of VelocityEngine—this is provided using DI, because we use the VelocityEngineUtils class provided by Spring to interact with Velocity. A more complex implementation of this class would provide support for adding CC and BCC recipients, but note that this implementation does support multiple TO recipients, because the call to InternetAddress.parse() returns InternetAddress[] and successfully parses comma-separated lists of addresses.

Listing 15-18 shows a simple plain text template you can use with this class.

Listing 15-18. *A Simple Plain Text Template*

```
This is the plain text mail.

The message of the day is: $msg.
```

Here you can see we have a Velocity template that contains a single variable field, $msg. At runtime, we can specify a value for that field. Listing 15-19 shows the corresponding HTML template, which also contains a $msg variable.

Listing 15-19. *The HTML Message Template*

```
<html>
    <head></head>
    <body>
    <h1>This is the HTML mail</h1>
    <h2>Today's message is: <em>$msg</em></h2>
    <img src="http://www.apress.com/img/v2/hdr_logo.gif">
    </body>
</html>
```

Notice that instead of using a Content-ID for the image source, we used a standard URL pointing to an image stored on the Apress web server.

In Listing 15-20, you can see a sample configuration file that configures a VelocityMimeMessagePreparator bean.

Listing 15-20. *Configuring the VelocityMimeMessagePreparator*

```
<!DOCTYPE beans PUBLIC "-//SPRING//DTD BEAN//EN"
"http://www.springframework.org/dtd/spring-beans.dtd">
<beans>
    <bean id="preparator"
          class="com.apress.prospring.ch15.velocity.VelocityMimeMessagePreparator">
        <property name="to">
            <value>robh@cakesolutions.net</value>
        </property>
        <property name="from">
            <value>mail@apress.com</value>
        </property>
        <property name="subject">
            <value>Mail Using Velocity</value>
        </property>
        <property name="plainTextTemplatePath">
            <value>./ch15/src/vm/plainText.vm</value>
        </property>
        <property name="htmlTemplatePath">
            <value>./ch15/src/vm/html.vm</value>
        </property>
        <property name="velocityEngine">
          <bean class="org.springframework.ui.velocity.VelocityEngineFactoryBean"/>
        </property>
    </bean>
</beans>
```

This configuration is fairly basic but you can see that it allows for easy modification not only of basic message parameters, such as the sender address, but also of the templates that make up the plain text and HTML parts of the message. To supply the VelocityMimeMessagePreparator class with an instance of VelocityEngine, we use the VelocityEngineFactoryBean supplied by Spring. We use the default VelocityEngine configuration, but had we wanted to, we could have modified this configuration using the VelocityEngineFactoryBean.

To use this class in an application, all you need to do is obtain the bean from Spring along with an instance of JavaMailSender, configure the VelocityMimeMessagePreparator with some data to merge into the template, and then invoke the JavaMailSender.send() method, as shown in Listing 15-21.

Listing 15-21. *Using the VelocityMimeMessagePreparator Class*

```
package com.apress.prospring.ch15.velocity;

import java.util.HashMap;
import java.util.Map;
```

```
import org.springframework.context.ApplicationContext;
import org.springframework.context.support.FileSystemXmlApplicationContext;
import org.springframework.mail.javamail.JavaMailSender;

public class VelocityRunner {

    public static void main(String[] args) {
        ApplicationContext ctx = new FileSystemXmlApplicationContext(
                new String[] { "./ch15/src/conf/velocity.xml",
                        "./ch15/src/conf/javaMailSender.xml" });

        JavaMailSender sender = (JavaMailSender) ctx.getBean("sender");
        VelocityMimeMessagePreparator preparator =
                        (VelocityMimeMessagePreparator) ctx.getBean("preparator");

        Map data = new HashMap();
        data.put("msg", "Hello World!");

        preparator.setData(data);

        sender.send(preparator);
    }
}
```

Figure 15-13 shows the resulting plain text message and Figure 15-14 shows the resulting HTML message.

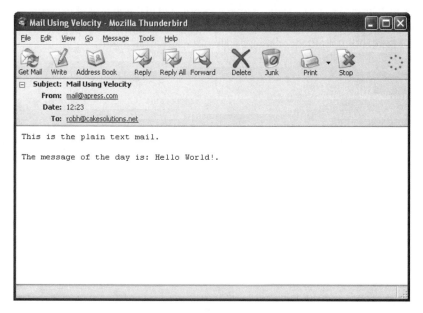

Figure 15-13. *Plain text message generated by Velocity*

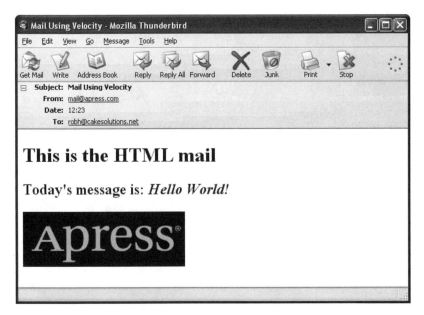

Figure 15-14. *HTML message generated by Velocity*

Summary

In this chapter, you learned how to use Spring to simplify the creation of e-mail messaging functionality for your applications. You saw how to use both JavaMail and COS `MailMessage` to create and send simple, plain text messages, and we demonstrated how you can configure these messages externally using Spring DI features. In the second half of the chapter, we discussed how you can use JavaMail to construct complex MIME messages to support advanced features such as HTML message content, embedded images, and message attachment.

CHAPTER 16

Using Spring Remoting

So far, all of the examples we have looked at have assumed that all the components in your application are running on the same machine, and indeed, in the same JVM. In many cases, this architecture is preferable to one where components are distributed across many different machines. In some cases, however, running an application on a single machine does not sufficiently meet the requirements of the application, and you need component distribution to meet these requirements.

In this chapter, we discuss four of the five remote component architectures Spring provides, looking at how you can use Spring's support classes to create, expose, and access remote services using each different architecture. Although Spring provides five different remoting architectures, shown later in Table 16-1, the Hessian and Burlap classes are identical, so we just focus on Hessian rather than repeat the same content for Burlap.

In particular, this chapter focuses on the following:

Remoting with RMI: In this section, you see how to develop remote services using RMI and Spring. You learn how to expose any POJO service object over RMI using Spring's RMI service exporter. This section also demonstrates the creation and usage of CORBA services using Spring and JNDI.

Spring and XML web services: No remoting architecture is complete without support for XML web services and in this section, you learn to build JAXRPC web services using Spring and Apache Axis.

The Spring HTTP Invoker architecture: Spring comes complete with its own built-in remoting architecture that uses standard Java serialization over HTTP. This section shows you how to expose your POJO services using HTTP Invoker and also how to secure your services using HTTP Basic authentication.

Caucho Hessian integration: In addition to support for the standard RMI and JAXRPC remoting architectures plus its own native architecture, Spring also integrates with the Caucho projects, Hessian and Burlap. In this section, you see how to use the HTTP-based Hessian alongside Spring as the remoting architecture for your applications. This section also shows you how to use HTTP Basic authentication with Hessian to provide a level of security for your applications.

For this chapter, we assume that you have a basic understanding of both RMI and JAXRPC. If you are not familiar with the basics of either of these, we suggest that you read the RMI tutorial at http://java.sun.com/docs/books/tutorial/rmi/ and the Java web services tutorial at http://java.sun.com/webservices/docs/1.3/tutorial/doc/index.html.

Remoting, Spring, and EJB

For EJB applications, you can best achieve component distribution by using built-in features of the EJB specification. Recently, EJB has come under a lot of industry scrutiny, but the fact remains that EJB does simplify the creation of distributed applications, which makes it a useful tool when you are developing distributed J2EE applications.

For non-EJB, the common choice for building distributed applications is Java's Remote Method Invocation (RMI), which allows Java objects running in one JVM to be accessed from another. RMI is quite complex to work with, and part of the allure of EJB is that it hides the underlying details of RMI from the developer.

For both EJB and non-EJB applications, the most common kind of distribution is to have one Java component talk to another Java component, but in many cases, the components that make up a distributed system are not written in the same language. Using RMI, you can have Java components interoperate with components written in other languages using Common Object Request Broker Architecture (CORBA). More recently, Java has gained support for web services, allowing you to build applications in Java that interoperate with arbitrary services using XML as a means of communication.

The two main problems you face when you go to create distributed applications in Java are complexity and the sheer amount of code you need to create distributed components. EJB goes some way toward solving this by hiding some of the details of RMI and, as of J2EE 1.4, web services from your applications. However, for non-EJB applications, this does not help because EJB is not available. In EJB applications, we are seeing a shift away from heavyweight EJB concepts toward lightweight frameworks such as Spring.

Thankfully, Spring provides a comprehensive set of features, known as Spring remoting, that ease the creation of distributed applications. For non-EJB applications, you can use Spring remoting to radically simplify the creation of remote services and to reduce the amount of code you need to access these services. For EJB applications, Spring remoting provides a viable alternative to EJB for building many distributed applications that, when coupled with other features in Spring, may remove the need for EJB altogether, allowing for much more flexibility in how you choose to deploy your EJB application.

■NOTE Although Spring's RMI support provides a viable alternative to EJB in many cases, out of the box, there is no support for standard role-based authentication nor is there support for propagating remote transactions. It is possible to add this support, although this is outside the scope of this chapter. If you require either of these two features, we recommend that you use EJB to create your remote components.

Spring provides support for five distinct types of remoting architecture that cover both homogenous (Java-to-Java) and heterogeneous (Java-to-Other) communication. These architectures are detailed in Table 16-1.

Table 16-1. *Remoting Support in Spring*

Architecture	Description
RMI	RMI is a standard part of J2SE, which allows for the creation of distributed applications. Using Spring's RMI support, you can reduce the amount of code you need to expose and access RMI services and have Spring handle most of the plumbing associated with RMI, such as the handling of `RemoteExceptions`. Spring also provides integration support for RMI and JNDI, which is most useful when you are exposing and accessing CORBA services.
JAXRPC	The Java API for XML-based Remote Procedure Calls, JAXRPC, provides a standard Java API for accessing and exposing RPC-style SOAP web services. Spring provides support classes to ease the creation of JAXRPC client applications and servlet-based service endpoints. Like many of the Java XML APIs, JAXRPC comes in many different flavors, the most popular of which is Apache Axis, a fully JAXRPC-compliant SOAP stack that is available from `http://ws.apache.org/axis`. We use Axis for the JAXRPC examples in this chapter.
HTTP Invoker	The HTTP Invoker architecture is a Spring-native remoting architecture that uses standard Java serialization and HTTP to provide a simple solution for building remote components. The HTTP Invoker relies on a servlet container at the server side to host remote services. A benefit of this is that you can secure your remote services using HTTP authentication methods.
Hessian	Hessian is a binary protocol created by Caucho (`www.caucho.com`) to simplify the creation of web services. Hessian is not linked to any particular transport, although in general, it is used with HTTP. Spring provides support classes to make it easier to create Hessian services. These classes use HTTP as the transport and also provide proxy support, allowing Hessian services to be accessed transparently.
Burlap	Burlap is an XML-based protocol also created by Caucho. Burlap is a complement to the Hessian protocol. Aside from the details of the protocol, Burlap is used in an identical manner to Hessian. Burlap support in Spring is a mirror of the support offered for Hessian; indeed, the Burlap classes are designed to be drop-in replacements for the Hessian classes, should you need to swap protocols.

Spring Remoting Architecture

Central to the Spring remoting architecture are the concepts of a **service exporter** and a **proxy generator**. One of the first tasks that you need to perform when you build a distributed application is to expose your remote services so that clients can access them. Spring simplifies this by providing a set of service exporters that allow you to configure and expose services declaratively, thus dramatically reducing the amount of code you need to write to expose remote services.

Once you have exposed a remote service, you need to create a client that accesses the service. This is often one of the most complex areas of building a distributed application because you often need to be intimately aware of the plumbing of your remote architecture of choice. With Spring, you can use a proxy generator to create a proxy to the remote resource; this allows you to access the remote service via a simple Java interface. By using this approach, you not only reduce the complexity of client code, because Spring is dealing with the plumbing, but you also decouple your application from your chosen remote architecture, because Spring hides all the implementation-level details.

Both of these components are available for four of the five remoting architectures supported by Spring. In the case of JAXRPC, there is no service exporter because the method for service exposure is dependent on the JAXRPC implementation you are using. However, Spring does provide the `ServletEndpointSupport` class to simplify the creation of JAXRPC service endpoints that are exposed via a servlet.

Remote Method Invocation

RMI has been part of Java since version 1.1 and is central to how many of the platform's remoting solutions are created. CORBA support in Java is provided using RMI, and EJB uses RMI as the underlying mechanism for bean communication. Also, in the "Web Services with JAXRPC" section later in this chapter, you will see that JAXRPC builds on RMI concepts to expose Java objects as web services.

In this section, we look at four distinct examples. First, you see how to expose an arbitrary Java object as an RMI service. Second, you learn how to access this service via a proxy. The third topic we cover is how to expose an RMI service to CORBA using Spring, and finally, you see how to access this service using a Spring-created proxy.

Exposing Arbitrary Services

The traditional approach to building an RMI service involves first defining an interface for your service that extends the `java.rmi.Remote` interface. Your RMI service then implements this interface and most likely extends the `java.rmi.server.UnicastRemoteObject` class. The main drawback to this approach is that your remote service is then coupled to the RMI framework, thus reducing the chances for component reuse and making it difficult to change the remoting architecture used by your application.

Spring remoting allows you to overcome this problem using the `RmiServiceExporter` class. By using `RmiServiceExporter`, you can expose any arbitrary Java object as an RMI service using any Java interface. Your interface is not required to extend `Remote`, nor is your service class required to extend `UnicastRemoteObject`. In addition, `RmiServiceExporter` allows your remote service to be configured and exposed declaratively, which reduces your need to create executable code just to expose remote services. Another benefit of using Spring to expose RMI services is that you can avoid having to create stubs for your service because this is handled automatically by Spring.

The main benefit of Spring's approach to RMI service exposure is that it allows you to expose existing service objects in your application as remote services with no modifications. Provided that your service classes implement an interface, which is good design anyway, you can easily expose your application services remotely with minimal effort.

In Listing 16-1, you can see the `HelloWorld` interface that acts as the interface for our remote service.

Listing 16-1. *The HelloWorld Interface*

```
package com.apress.prospring.ch16.remoting;

public interface HelloWorld {

    public String getMessage();
}
```

Notice that this interface does not extend the Remote interface, and the getMessage() method is not declared to throw RemoteException as required by the RMI specification. In fact, this interface provides no indication that it will be exposed remotely at all. Likewise, the implementation of the HelloWorld interface shown in Listing 16-2 is equally RMI-independent.

Listing 16-2. *The SimpleHelloWorld Class*

```
package com.apress.prospring.ch16.remoting;
ss
public class SimpleHelloWorld implements HelloWorld {

    public String getMessage() {
        return "Hello World";
    }
}
```

As with the HelloWorld interface, the SimpleHelloWorld class is free from any RMI-specific details—indeed, it could well have been created before exposing it as an RMI service was even considered. To expose the SimpleHelloWorld class as an RMI service via the HelloWorld interface, simply configure an instance of RmiServiceExporter in your ApplicationContext with the appropriate details, as shown in Listing 16-3.

Listing 16-3. *Exposing RMI Services with RmiServiceExporter*

```
<!DOCTYPE beans PUBLIC "-//SPRING//DTD BEAN//EN"

"http://www.springframework.org/dtd/spring-beans.dtd">
<beans>
    <bean id="helloWorldService"
        class="com.apress.prospring.ch16.remoting.SimpleHelloWorld"/>

    <bean id="serviceExporter"
        class="org.springframework.remoting.rmi.RmiServiceExporter">
        <property name="serviceName">
            <value>HelloWorld</value>
        </property>
        <property name="service">
            <ref local="helloWorldService"/>
        </property>
        <property name="serviceInterface">
            <value>com.apress.prospring.ch16.remoting.HelloWorld</value>
        </property>
        <property name="registryPort">
            <value>9000</value>
        </property>
```

```
        <property name="servicePort">
            <value>9001</value>
        </property>
    </bean>

</beans>
```

Here we declared two beans: the helloWorldService bean, which is the bean we want to expose, and the serviceExporter bean, which exposes the helloWorldService bean as an RMI service. In the serviceExporter bean, we set the serviceName property to HelloWorld. The RmiServiceExporter class requires this property and uses it as the service name when registering the service with the RMI registry. The service property is used to pass the RmiServiceExporter the bean instance that should be exported, and the serviceInterface property defines the interface that should be used as the remote interface. You can remotely invoke only methods on the service interface—if you have a method on your service object but not on the service interface, it cannot be invoked remotely. The registryPort property allows you to specify the port of the RMI registry, and the servicePort property allows you to specify which port the service uses for communication. By default, servicePort is set to 0, meaning a random port number is used.

With the configuration of the RmiServiceExporter complete, all you need to do in your server application is load the ApplicationContext. When you do, Spring invokes the RmiServiceExporter automatically and exposes the service. Internally, the RmiServiceExporter class implements the InitializingBean interface to perform the actual service exposure process. This means that if you want service exposure to happen automatically, you must use an ApplicationContext, not a BeanFactory, because a BeanFactory does not auto-instantiate singletons.

Listing 16-4 shows a simple class that loads the configuration from Listing 16-3; it then simply waits for connections to the service.

Listing 16-4. *Hosting the HelloWorld Service*

```
package com.apress.prospring.ch16.remoting.rmi;

import org.springframework.context.ApplicationContext;
import org.springframework.context.support.FileSystemXmlApplicationContext;

public class HelloWorldHost {

    public static void main(String[] args) throws Exception {
        ApplicationContext ctx = new FileSystemXmlApplicationContext(
        "./ch16/src/conf/rmi/helloWorld.xml");
        System.out.println("Host Started...");
    }
}
```

If you run this example, you will notice that it does not exit immediately because the remote service is running in the background, waiting for connections from clients. As you can see from the examples in this section, you can expose any of your service objects as a remote service quickly and easily using the `RmiServiceExporter` class, all without modifications to the service object or to the service interface. In the next section, you will see how to access this remote service transparently using a Spring-generated proxy.

Accessing an RMI Service Using Proxies

One of the most complex parts of building RMI-based applications is creating the client application. If it uses the traditional approach to creating RMI clients, your client application becomes coupled to RMI, making it difficult to change to a new remoting architecture. If this is the case, you are forced to deal with all the messy internals of RMI, such as `RemoteExceptions` and service lookup.

Thankfully, Spring provides a much simpler mechanism for interacting with an RMI service—a proxy generator, which removes the need for you to create plumbing code and eliminates the coupling of your application to Spring. Using the proxy generator, you can have Spring generate a proxy to the remote service that implements the service interface, thus allowing you to interact with the remote service via the service interface as though it were a local component. Spring hides all the RMI details, such as service lookup and exception handling; this allows you to code to the business interface rather than to a particular implementation.

The RMI proxy generator, `RmiProxyFactoryBean`, as with all proxy generators, implements the `FactoryBean` interface, which allows the proxy to be created and configured declaratively and then injected into a component as a dependency. Listing 16-5 shows a class that defines such a dependency.

Listing 16-5. *The HelloWorldClient Class*

```
package com.apress.prospring.ch16.remoting.rmi;

import org.springframework.context.ApplicationContext;
import org.springframework.context.support.FileSystemXmlApplicationContext;

import com.apress.prospring.ch16.remoting.HelloWorld;

public class HelloWorldClient {

    private HelloWorld helloWorldService;

    public static void main(String[] args) throws Exception {
        ApplicationContext ctx = new FileSystemXmlApplicationContext(
                "./ch16/src/conf/rmi/helloWorldClient.xml");

        HelloWorldClient helloWorldClient = (HelloWorldClient) ctx
                .getBean("helloWorldClient");
        helloWorldClient.run();

    }
```

```
    public void run() {
        System.out.println(helloWorldService.getMessage());
    }

    public void setHelloWorldService(HelloWorld helloWorldService) {
        this.helloWorldService = helloWorldService;
    }
}
```

Here you can see that the HelloWorldClient class defines the helloWorldService class that expects an instance of HelloWorld to be provided. By using the RMI proxy generator, we can create a proxy to the SimpleHelloWorld service exposed in Listing 16-5. This proxy implements the HelloWorld interface and is injected into an instance of the HelloWorldClient class. Listing 16-6 shows the appropriate configuration for this.

Listing 16-6. *Configuring an RMI Proxy*

```
<!DOCTYPE beans PUBLIC "-//SPRING//DTD BEAN//EN"
"http://www.springframework.org/dtd/spring-beans.dtd">
<beans>
    <bean id="helloWorldService"
          class="org.springframework.remoting.rmi.RmiProxyFactoryBean">
        <property name="serviceUrl">
            <value>rmi://localhost:9000/HelloWorld</value>
        </property>
        <property name="serviceInterface">
            <value>com.apress.prospring.ch16.remoting.HelloWorld</value>
        </property>
    </bean>

    <bean id="helloWorldClient"
          class="com.apress.prospring.ch16.remoting.rmi.HelloWorldClient">
        <property name="helloWorldService">
            <ref local="helloWorldService"/>
        </property>
    </bean>
</beans>
```

The important piece of code here is the helloWorldService declaration. Notice that two properties are required: serviceInterface and serviceUrl. The serviceInterface property tells the proxy generator which interface the generated proxy should implement. The serviceUrl points the proxy at the correct RMI service—in this case, this is the HelloWorld service running in the registry at port 9000 on the localhost.

Because the RmiProxyFactoryBean class implements the FactoryBean interface, you can treat it as though it is an instance of the service interface because this is the type that the FactoryBean is defined to return. Because of this, you can use the helloWorldService bean to satisfy the helloWorldService dependency of the helloWorldClient bean.

To test this example, first make sure the host class from Listing 16-4 is running, then run the `HelloWorldClient` class. After a short delay, you will see "Hello World" displayed in the `HelloWorldClient` window. Note that you can run the `HelloWorldClient` class as many times as you wish, provided the `HelloWorldHost` class is still running.

As is evident from this example, using proxies is a simple yet powerful way to access remote services. By using a proxy, you remove the burden on you to handle all the plumbing code involved with your remoting architecture of choice. As a result, you decrease the chance that bugs will creep into your application and increase the speed at which you can create applications. Another key benefit of using proxies is that doing so reduces the coupling between your application and your remoting architecture, making it easier for you to swap out remote components for local ones or to change the remoting architecture for another one.

Exposing CORBA Services

One excellent feature offered by RMI is that it allows you to expose access services using the Internet Inter-Orb Protocol (IIOP). This means that components written in other languages can access these services using CORBA. CORBA is a popular solution for interoperating between components written in different languages; as such, it enjoys extensive support in many of the most popular programming languages available today.

Exposing a Java service via RMI using IIOP rather than the default Java Remote Method Protocol (JRMP) is simply a matter of generating the correct stubs and then exposing the service via a CORBA Object Request Broker (ORB). As you saw in the earlier examples, when you are exposing a service using JRMP, Spring not only removes the need for your components to be coupled to the RMI infrastructure, but it also removes the need to create stubs. When you are exposing CORBA services, Spring is not quite as helpful, although it does take care of registering your service with the ORB.

In fact, Spring does not really supply classes to simplify CORBA service exposure and utilization; instead, it provides features to expose and look up remote services using JNDI. However, this feature is most useful when you are dealing with CORBA components because your application can interact with the ORB via JNDI.

In this section, you learn how to build an RMI service, generate the appropriate IIOP stubs, and then expose the IIOP service to the ORB using Spring. In order to run the example in this section, you need to obtain a JNDI provider for the CORBA Common Object Services (COS) name server. You can obtain the Sun implementation from the JNDI home page at `http://java.sun.com/products/jndi/`. This provider allows you to access the COS naming service using the JNDI API, thus allowing Spring to interact with it as well.

The first step you need to take when building an RMI service is to create the remote service interface. Your remote service interface must extend the `java.rmi.Remote` interface, and all methods in the interface must throw `RemoteException`. Listing 16-7 shows the remote service interface for this example.

Listing 16-7. *The RemoteHelloWorld Interface*

```
package com.apress.prospring.ch16.remoting.rmi;

import java.rmi.Remote;
import java.rmi.RemoteException;

public interface RemoteHelloWorld extends Remote {

    String getMessage() throws RemoteException;
}
```

This interface is very similar to the HelloWorld interface shown in Listing 16-1 except that it now meets the contract required by the RMI specification.

Next, you need to create an implementation of your remote interface. Listing 16-8 shows a trivial implementation of the RemoteHelloWorld interface.

Listing 16-8. *The SimpleRemoteHelloWorld Class*

```
package com.apress.prospring.ch16.remoting.rmi;

import java.rmi.RemoteException;

public class SimpleRemoteHelloWorld implements RemoteHelloWorld {

    public String getMessage() throws RemoteException {
        return "Hello World";
    }
}
```

As with the RemoteHelloWorld interface, this class is not much different from its corresponding nonremote implementation shown in Listing 16-2. At this point, you should compile both the RemoteHelloWorld interface and the SimpleRemoteHelloWorld class so that they are available to create the IIOP stub.

■**NOTE** If you are unfamiliar with the concepts of stubs or ties, we recommend that you read *Java RMI* by William Grosso (O'Reilly, 2001) for a comprehensive discussion of all things RMI.

Generating IIOP Stubs and Tags

To generate a remote stub for an RMI service, use the rmic tool that is included with your JDK. The rmic tool takes the remote service class and from this, generates the appropriate stubs. By default, rmic generates stubs for JRMP, but if you specify the -iiop switch, it generates IIOP stubs and ties instead. To generate stubs for the SimpleRemoteHelloWorld class, you must run the following command:

```
rmic -classpath bin -d bin -iiop ➥
com.apress.prospring.ch16.remoting.rmi.SimpleRemoteHelloWorld
```

The -classpath switch specifies the location of any classes needed by rmic. The rmic tool needs to be able to access both the class and the interface for your remote service, so make sure that they are both on the classpath specified by the -classpath switch. The -d switch specifies the root folder to which the generated classes should be written. The final argument is the fully qualified class name of the service class for which you are generating stubs. Running this command generates the _SimpleRemoteHelloWorld_Tie and _RemoteHelloWorld_stub class files in the same directory as the SimpleRemoteHelloWorld class.

Exposing the Service to CORBA Using Spring and JNDI

After you generate the stubs, the next step is to configure an instance of JndiRmiServiceExporter in your ApplicationContext to export the remote service to a JNDI location. In this case, we use the COS provider for JNDI to register the service with the CORBA ORB. Listing 16-9 shows this configuration file.

Listing 16-9. *Exposing an RMI Service to CORBA Using JNDI*

```
<!DOCTYPE beans PUBLIC "-//SPRING//DTD BEAN//EN"
"http://www.springframework.org/dtd/spring-beans.dtd">
<beans>
    <bean id="helloWorldService"
          class="com.apress.prospring.ch16.remoting.rmi.SimpleRemoteHelloWorld"/>

    <bean id="serviceExporter"
          class="org.springframework.remoting.rmi.JndiRmiServiceExporter">
        <property name="jndiName">
            <value>HelloWorld</value>
        </property>
        <property name="service">
            <ref local="helloWorldService"/>
        </property>
        <property name="jndiEnvironment">
            <props>
                <prop key="java.naming.factory.initial">
                            com.sun.jndi.cosnaming.CNCtxFactory</prop>
                <prop key="java.naming.provider.url">iiop://localhost:1050</prop>
            </props>
        </property>
    </bean>
</beans>
```

In this configuration, we declare two beans, helloWorldService and serviceExporter. The helloWorldService bean is simply an instance of the SimpleRemoteHelloWorld class to be managed by Spring. The important part of this code is the serviceExporter bean. For the serviceExporter bean, we specified three properties: jndiName, which is the name used to register the remote service with the ORB; service, which is the actual service object and must be of type Remote; and jndiEnvironment.

The jndiEnvironment property allows you to configure the InitialContext that Spring uses internally to perform JNDI operations. Here we specify that the CNCtxFactory class should be used to create the actual InitialContext implementation. CNCtxFactory is part of the COS JNDI provider and performs lookup and registration operations against the CORBA ORB specified using the java.naming.provider.url property. Basically this means that you should execute operations against the ORB running on port 1050 of the local machine. Do not worry too much about this yet; we discuss the ORB later in this section.

Creating a Host Application

With the configuration of the service exporter complete, all that remains from a code perspective is to create the host application that loads the ApplicationContext. Listing 16-10 shows the HelloWorldJndiHost class that loads the ApplicationContext and waits for user connections to the service.

Listing 16-10. *The HelloWorldJndiHost Class*

```
package com.apress.prospring.ch16.remoting.rmi;

import org.springframework.context.ApplicationContext;
import org.springframework.context.support.FileSystemXmlApplicationContext;

public class HelloWorldJndiHost {

    public static void main(String[] args) throws Exception {
        ApplicationContext ctx = new FileSystemXmlApplicationContext(
        "./ch16/src/conf/rmi/helloWorldJndi.xml");
        System.out.println("Host Started...");
    }
}
```

Here, the main() method simply loads the ApplicationContext using the configuration shown in Listing 16-9; it then prints a message to the console to notify the user that the host has started. As with the host class shown in Listing 16-4, this class does not exit automatically when it is run; this is because it is kept alive by the RMI framework that is exposing the remote service to CORBA.

Starting the Object Request Broker

If you try to run the host application at this point, it returns an error, informing you that it is unable to connect to the ORB. The JDK comes complete with an ORB that you can use when you develop CORBA applications using Java. You can start the ORB using the orbd application, which you can find in the bin directory of your JDK. To start the ORB using port 1050, as the host application requires in Listing 16-10, run the following command:

```
orbd -port 1050
```

Once the ORB is started, you can start up the host and host your CORBA component.

Accessing a CORBA Service

Just as Spring provides proxy support for JRMP RMI services, it can also generate a proxy for any remote service that can be accessed via JNDI. Using this feature, you can create a proxy to a remote IIOP service hosted in an ORB. In this section, you see how to use the JndiRmiProxyFactoryBean to generate a proxy to an RMI/IIOP service exposed via an ORB.

In order to create a proxy from a JNDI-accessible RMI resource, you must configure an instance of JndiRmiProxyFactoryBean with the appropriate JNDI access information and the name of the interface you want the proxy to implement. Listing 16-11 shows a configuration that generates a proxy for the SimpleRemoteHelloWorld service we created in Listing 16-8.

Listing 16-11. *Configuring a JNDI RMI Proxy*

```
<!DOCTYPE beans PUBLIC "-//SPRING//DTD BEAN//EN"
"http://www.springframework.org/dtd/spring-beans.dtd">
<beans>
    <bean id="helloWorldService"
        class="org.springframework.remoting.rmi.JndiRmiProxyFactoryBean">
        <property name="jndiName">
            <value>HelloWorld</value>
        </property>
        <property name="serviceInterface">
            <value>com.apress.prospring.ch16.remoting.HelloWorld</value>
        </property>
        <property name="jndiEnvironment">
            <props>
                <prop key="java.naming.factory.initial">
                        com.sun.jndi.cosnaming.CNCtxFactory</prop>
                <prop key="java.naming.provider.url">iiop://localhost:1050</prop>
            </props>
        </property>
    </bean>
</beans>
```

Here you can see that we configured the JndiRmiProxyFactoryBean class with the same JNDI information we used to configure JndiRmiServiceExporter in Listing 16-9; this is because it is the service we want to access. An interesting point to note here is that we used the HelloWorld interface from Listing 16-1 as the service interface, not the RemoteHelloWorld interface from Listing 16-7. One of the major benefits of the Spring-generated proxies is that you can use any interface you want for the proxy, as long as the names, return types, and parameter lists of the methods match those exposed by the remote service. In this case, we use the HelloWorld interface that exposes a getMessage() method; this method is identical to the RemoteHelloWorld .getMessage() method but does not throw RemoteException. The Spring-generated proxy takes care of handling any RemoteException on your behalf, leaving your client code free to code to the business interface rather than the remote interface.

Using the proxy is as simple as loading ApplicationContext and obtaining the corresponding bean in your application, as shown in Listing 16-12.

Listing 16-12. *The HelloWorldJndiClient Class*

```
package com.apress.prospring.ch16.remoting.rmi;

import org.springframework.context.ApplicationContext;
import org.springframework.context.support.FileSystemXmlApplicationContext;

import com.apress.prospring.ch16.remoting.HelloWorld;

public class HelloWorldJndiClient {

    public static void main(String[] args) throws Exception {
        ApplicationContext ctx = new FileSystemXmlApplicationContext(
                "./ch16/src/conf/rmi/helloWorldJndiClient.xml");

        HelloWorld helloWorld = (HelloWorld) ctx.getBean("helloWorldService");
        System.out.println(helloWorld.getMessage());

    }
}
```

Running this example with the `HelloWorldJndiHost` class also running results in the following output:

```
Hello World
```

From this example and the earlier example that shows the creation of a proxy to an RMI/JMRP service, you can see that Spring proxies greatly reduce the amount of code you need to write to access remote RMI services. One of the biggest benefits of Spring RMI proxies is that you can actually hide the fact that the service is remote; this allows your application to work directly with a business interface, relying on Spring to take care of all the RMI plumbing.

Web Services with JAXRPC

Just as RMI provides a standard API for creating remote services that are exposed using binary protocols, JAXRPC provides a standard API for creating remote services that are exposed using RPC-style SOAP messages. JAXRPC is used to create SOAP-based services, called **endpoints** in web service lingo, and clients in an implementation-agnostic way. On the server side, JAXRPC is a fairly simple API that borrows much from RMI. The complexity lies in the definition of service endpoints, which is often an implementation-specific issue, and the code on the client side, which is convoluted and problematic.

Unfortunately, Spring cannot help much with service endpoint issues, because the way in which this functions is dependent on the JAXRPC implementation you are using. However, Spring does provide the `ServletEndpointSupport` class, which makes it simple for endpoints that sit behind a servlet to access a Spring `ApplicationContext`. On the client side, Spring provides the `JaxRpcPortProxyFactoryBean` class, which allows you to create a proxy to a SOAP web service, reducing the complexity inherent in creating a JAXRPC client and shielding your client application from any JAXRPC-specific details.

In this section, you create a simple web service that uses the ServletEndpointSupport class to load dependencies from a Spring ApplicationContext and you learn a useful pattern for building service endpoints when you are using Spring. In addition, you use the JaxRpcPortProxyFactoryBean to create a proxy for accessing your service and you look at Axis-specific details for handling complex Java objects in your services.

Introducing Apache Axis

For the examples in this section, we are going to use the Apache Axis SOAP stack, which provides a fully compliant JAXRPC implementation. Axis provides support for SOAP over a variety of different transports such as HTTP, JMS, and SMTP. For the examples in this section, we use the HTTP transport, which is implemented as a servlet that dispatches requests to your service automatically. HTTP is the traditional transport for SOAP and Spring provides additional support for service endpoints that sit behind a servlet.

In this section, we assume a basic knowledge of the Axis framework and JAXRPC. If you are unfamiliar with JAXRPC, refer to the tutorial mentioned at the beginning of this chapter. For a quick introduction to Axis, check out the user guide at http://ws.apache.org/axis/java/user-guide.html, which provides a rundown of Axis features and how they work.

If you downloaded the full distribution of Spring including all the dependencies, you already have Axis and its dependencies. Otherwise, you can download Axis from http://ws.apache.org/axis. For the examples in this section, we use version 1.1 of Axis.

Creating a Web Service with ServletEndpointSupport

In this section, you build a basic web service that is analogous to the "Hello World" RMI services you saw earlier. Creating JAXRPC services is where most of the implementation-specific details come into play. From a Java code perspective, everything is pretty much standard, but on a deployment front, everything is implementation-specific. If you want to build a web service using a JAXRPC implementation other than Axis, you need to modify the deployment details as appropriate for your implementation of choice.

A basic Axis web service is constructed of four parts: the Axis servlet, the Axis deployment descriptor, the remote interface, and the service implementation. The Axis servlet sits between your services and SOAP clients and is responsible for creating the Web Services Description Language (WSDL) description of your service so that a SOAP client can access your service, for translating SOAP requests into Java method calls, and for translating method return values into SOAP responses. The Axis servlet hides most of the plumbing code related to building a web service from you; indeed, you rarely, if ever, have to create code to handle SOAP messages manually because the Axis servlet takes care of all of this.

The Axis deployment descriptor is an XML document that provides information to the Axis servlet about the services you wish to expose and how they should be exposed. Axis uses the information contained in the deployment descriptor to determine which classes in your web application should be exposed via SOAP and also to obtain additional information about the service that cannot be obtained from the remote interface or the service implementation.

The remote interface is identical to the remote interface used for an RMI service. It must extend the java.rmi.Remote interface and all methods must be declared to throw RemoteException. This similarity with RMI makes it simple to reuse remote interfaces across both RMI services and web services; indeed, in this example, we reuse the RemoteHelloWorld interface from Listing 16-7 for our web service.

The service implementation is simply an implementation of the remote interface similar to the SimpleRemoteHelloWorld implementation you saw in Listing 16-8. Indeed, we could have reused this implementation to create our services; however, unlike the RMI service, our application is not responsible for creating instances of the service class—that is the job of Axis—thus making it impossible for us to use Spring DI. As a workaround to this, Spring provides the ServletEndpointSupport base class, which you can use to obtain a Spring ApplicationContext automatically that is configured as part of your web application. This functionality sits on top of the special support for ApplicationContext loading in web applications that Spring provides. We cover this in more detail in Chapter 17, but for now, it is enough to know that Spring provides a mechanism for loading an ApplicationContext once in a web application and makes it available through the ServletContext class.

Creating the Remote Interface

When building a JAXRPC web service, the first step is to create the remote interface. As we mentioned in the previous section, JAXRPC remote interfaces are exactly the same as RMI remote interfaces. For this example, we reuse the RemoteHelloWorld interface shown in Listing 16-7.

Implementing the Web Service

After you create the remote interface for your web service, the next step is to create your service implementation class. As we mentioned previously, creating a basic service class is just like creating a service class for an RMI service—you simply implement the remote interface. Indeed, we could choose to reuse the SimpleRemoteHelloWorld class from Listing 16-8. However, this approach has a drawback—you cannot use DI. A much better solution is to make your service class a simple wrapper around a POJO service object, which is loaded from a Spring ApplicationContext and thus can be configured using DI. Spring makes this simple by providing the ServletEndpointSupport class, which allows you to access the ApplicationContext that is loaded for a web application. In Listing 16-13, you can see the JaxRpcHelloWorld class, which shows an example of this approach.

Listing 16-13. *Creating a JAXRPC Service Wrapper*

```
package com.apress.prospring.ch16.remoting.jaxrpc;

import java.rmi.RemoteException;

import javax.xml.rpc.ServiceException;

import org.springframework.remoting.jaxrpc.ServletEndpointSupport;

import com.apress.prospring.ch16.remoting.HelloWorld;
import com.apress.prospring.ch16.remoting.rmi.RemoteHelloWorld;

public class JaxRpcHelloWorld extends ServletEndpointSupport implements
        RemoteHelloWorld {
```

```
    private HelloWorld helloWorld;

    protected void onInit() throws ServiceException {
        helloWorld = (HelloWorld) getApplicationContext().getBean(
                "helloWorldService");
    }

    public String getMessage() throws RemoteException {
        return helloWorld.getMessage();
    }
}
```

There are two important parts to this class: the implementation of the getMessage() method and the onInit() method. In getMessage(), you can see that the actual processing is delegated to an instance of the HelloWorld interface shown in Listing 16-1. The HelloWorld interface and the RemoteHelloWorld interface share methods with the same signature, but HelloWorld does not extend Remote and its methods do not throw RemoteException. Implementations of the HelloWorld interface can easily be tested away from the servlet container and reused in many environments because they are not coupled to the Java remote interfaces. We could have just made the JaxRpcHelloWorld class delegate to another RemoteHelloWorld, but the reusability of implementations of RemoteHelloWorld is impaired by the fact that all methods throw the checked RemoteException. By using the HelloWorld interface, we can use implementations that can be used easily in other environments.

In the onInit() method, you can see that an actual implementation of HelloWorld is loaded from a Spring ApplicationContext. The ServletEndpointSupport class provides the getApplicationContext() method, which allows you to access the ApplicationContext that is configured for the web application containing the service class. The actual mechanism for configuring this ApplicationContext is discussed later in the "Creating the Web Application Deployment Descriptor" section, but in Listing 16-14, you can see the contents of the ApplicationContext configuration file.

Listing 16-14. *ApplicationContext Configuration for JaxRpcHelloWorld*

```
<!DOCTYPE beans PUBLIC "-//SPRING//DTD BEAN//EN"
"http://www.springframework.org/dtd/spring-beans.dtd">
<beans>
    <bean id="helloWorldService"
          class="com.apress.prospring.ch16.remoting.SimpleHelloWorld"/>
```

As you can see, the helloWorldService bean is defined as an instance of the SimpleHelloWorld class shown in Listing 16-2. This class implements the HelloWorld interface but has nothing to do with the RemoteHelloWorld interface implemented by the JaxRpcHelloWorld service class.

Behind the scenes, the ServletEndpointSupport class implements the javax.xml.rpc.server.ServiceLifecycle interface, which allows it to receive notifications from Axis at certain points throughout its lifecycle. Through this interface, the ServletEndpoint class is able to access the ServletContext of the currently running web application, and from there, it can access the ApplicationContext that is configured for the web application.

Creating the Axis Deployment Descriptor

Once you have created the service implementation class, you are ready to create the Axis deployment descriptor for your web service. The Axis deployment descriptor is an XML file that you should name server-config.wsdd and place in the WEB-INF directory of your web application. Listing 16-15 shows the server-config.wsdd file for the JaxRpcHelloWorld service.

Listing 16-15. *Axis Deployment Descriptor for JaxRpcHelloWorld*

```
<deployment xmlns="http://xml.apache.org/axis/wsdd/"
xmlns:java="http://xml.apache.org/axis/wsdd/providers/java">
    <handler name="URLMapper" type="java:org.apache.axis.handlers.http.URLMapper"/>

    <service name="HelloWorld" provider="java:RPC">
        <parameter name="className"
                value="com.apress.prospring.ch16.remoting.jaxrpc.JaxRpcHelloWorld"/>
        <parameter name="allowedMethods" value="*"/>
    </service>

    <transport name="http">
        <requestFlow>
            <handler type="URLMapper"/>
        </requestFlow>
    </transport>
</deployment>
```

There are three important parts to this deployment descriptor: the <handler> tag, the <transport> tag, and the <service> tag. The <handler> tag allows you to configure a Handler that you can integrate into the control flow for a SOAP request/response sequence. The URLMapper Handler is required as part of the request flow of the HTTP transport that you configure using the <transport> tag. The URLMapper is used by Axis to map the URIs of incoming requests to service names; this is the desirable approach when you are using HTTP as the transport. For instance, if the Axis servlet is mapped to handle requests on http://localhost:8080/app/services and you have a service called FooService, then the URL for your service is http://localhost:8080/app/services/FooService. Without this Handler, your service is not accessible and Axis is not able to generate the WSDL for it because it cannot locate the service for the given URI. You can find more details about the <handler> and <transport> tags on the Axis website.

The most important tag is the <service> tag, which is used to configure the actual service. The <service> tag itself has two attributes: name and provider. The name attribute can be any value, but each service must have a valid name. Bear in mind that this name forms part of the URL for your web service, so it should be concise and you should avoid special characters that overcomplicate the URL. The provider attribute specifies what kind of web service you are creating. In this case, we specify java:RPC, indicating that this is an RPC-style service. Inside the <service> tag are two <parameter> tags—one that specifies the fully qualified name of the service implementation class and one that defines a filter for which methods of the service are exposed in the service.

Axis supports many more configuration parameters than those shown in this example, but they are outside the scope of this chapter. For more details, read the Axis reference guide at `http://ws.apache.org/axis/java/reference.html`.

Creating the Web Application Deployment Descriptor

Once you have created the Axis deployment descriptor, all that remains is to create the web application deployment descriptor, package the web application for deployment, and then deploy it in your servlet container of choice.

In the deployment descriptor for a web service built using `ServletEndpointSupport`, you need to configure not only the Axis servlet, but also the Spring `ContextLoaderServlet` (or `ContextLoaderListener` for 2.4 servlet containers) to load the `ApplicationContext` for your web service. Listing 16-16 shows an example of this configuration for the `JaxRpcHelloWorld` service.

Listing 16-16. *Configuring the Axis Servlet and Spring ContextLoaderServlet*

```
<?xml version="1.0" encoding="UTF-8"?>
<!DOCTYPE web-app PUBLIC "-//Sun Microsystems, Inc.//DTD Web Application 2.3//EN"
                    "http://java.sun.com/dtd/web-app_2_3.dtd">
<web-app>
    <context-param>
        <param-name>contextConfigLocation</param-name>
        <param-value>/WEB-INF/applicationContext.xml</param-value>
    </context-param>

    <servlet>
        <servlet-name>context</servlet-name>
        <servlet-class>
            org.springframework.web.context.ContextLoaderServlet
        </servlet-class>
        <load-on-startup>1</load-on-startup>
    </servlet>

    <servlet>
        <servlet-name>axis</servlet-name>
        <servlet-class>org.apache.axis.transport.http.AxisServlet</servlet-class>
        <load-on-startup>2</load-on-startup>
    </servlet>

    <servlet-mapping>
        <servlet-name>axis</servlet-name>
        <url-pattern>/services/*</url-pattern>
    </servlet-mapping>
</web-app>
```

Here you can see a deployment descriptor that configures two servlets: the Spring `ContextLoaderServlet` and the Axis `AxisServlet` class. The `ContextLoaderServlet` loads an `ApplicationContext` using the path provided in the `contextConfigLocation` context parameter and then stores it in the `ServletContext`. Without this servlet declaration, the `ServletEndpointSupport` class is not able to locate the `ApplicationContext`, and thus `JaxRpcHelloWorld` cannot load the `helloWorldService` bean it requires. You should always ensure that the `ContextLoaderServlet` is loaded before all other servlets by explicitly setting the `<load-on-startup>` parameter for each servlet. This avoids problems arising when a servlet attempts to access an `ApplicationContext` that is not yet loaded.

The configuration of the Axis service is fairly basic and you should be more than familiar with the code you see. Note that the choice of URL mapping was not arbitrary—Axis generates a web page for your services that expects them to be mapped under /services/*. Figure 16-1 shows an example of the page generated by Axis for the HelloWorld service configured in Listing 16-16.

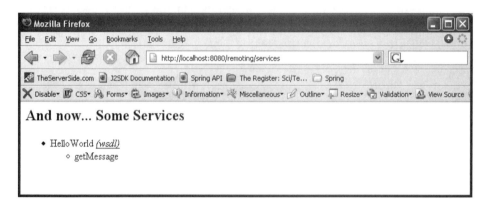

Figure 16-1. *Viewing web services in your web browser*

Clicking the `wsdl` link next to the listing for the HelloWorld service brings up the WSDL definition for your service. It is evident from looking at the WSDL that Axis is saving you an awful lot of work by generating the WSDL automatically. We certainly would not want to have to generate a WSDL document manually for every service we create.

Accessing RPC-Style Web Services Using Proxies

Traditionally, accessing a web service using JAXRPC has been quite a complex process that bears little resemblance to working with the service interface of the web service. Although some web service toolkits, Axis included, provide the ability to generate proxies to a web service, these are generally implementation-dependent and might not function exactly as you would expect.

Thankfully, Spring provides a JAXRPC proxy generator that allows you to access any RPC-style SOAP service using a simple Java interface. In this example, you learn how to configure an instance of `JaxRpcPortProxyFactoryBean` to create a proxy to the HelloWorld service that you built and deployed in the previous section.

One of the biggest benefits of using a Spring proxy for accessing JAXRPC services is that you can have the proxy implement a business interface rather than the remote interface of the JAXRPC service. The remote interface is still required so that Spring can use it internally, but externally, you can interact with a proxy through the business interface. In this example, you see how to construct a proxy to the HelloWorld service that uses the `HelloWorld` interface shown in Listing 16-1 rather than the RemoteHelloWorld interface that is implemented by the JaxRpcHelloWorld service class.

Configuring the JaxRpcPortProxyFactoryBean

Creating a JAXRPC proxy is very similar to creating an RMI proxy—all you need to do is configure an instance of the JaxRpcPortProxyFactoryBean in your ApplicationContext. This instance can then be accessed in your application using your chosen business interface. Listing 16-17 shows an example configuration that uses JaxRpcPortProxyFactoryBean to create a proxy to the HelloWorld service.

Listing 16-17. *Configuring a JAXRPC Proxy*

```
<!DOCTYPE beans PUBLIC "-//SPRING//DTD BEAN//EN"
"http://www.springframework.org/dtd/spring-beans.dtd">
<beans>
    <bean id="helloWorldService"
            class="org.springframework.remoting.jaxrpc.JaxRpcPortProxyFactoryBean">
        <property name="serviceFactoryClass">
            <value>org.apache.axis.client.ServiceFactory</value>
        </property>
        <property name="wsdlDocumentUrl">
            <value>http://localhost:8080/remoting/services/HelloWorld?wsdl</value>
        </property>
        <property name="namespaceUri">
            <value>http://localhost:8080/remoting/services/HelloWorld</value>
        </property>
        <property name="serviceName">
            <value>JaxRpcHelloWorldService</value>
        </property>
        <property name="portName">
            <value>HelloWorld</value>
        </property>
        <property name="portInterface">
            <value>com.apress.prospring.ch16.remoting.rmi.RemoteHelloWorld</value>
        </property>
        <property name="serviceInterface">
            <value>com.apress.prospring.ch16.remoting.HelloWorld</value>
        </property>
    </bean>
</beans>
```

Here you can see that we configured an instance of JaxRpcPortProxyFactoryBean with values for seven properties. The values for four of these properties—serviceFactoryClass, wsdlDocumentUrl, portInterface, and serviceInterface—are simple to obtain. Obtaining values for the rest requires peeking inside the WSDL that is generated for your service.

The serviceFactoryClass is used to point Spring at the implementation of the javax.xml.rpc.ServiceFactory interface provided by your SOAP stack. In the case of Axis, this class is org.apache.axis.client.ServiceFactory.

The wsdlDocumentUrl, obviously, specifies the URL of the WSDL document for your service; you can obtain it by browsing to your service in a web browser and clicking the wsdl link.

The serviceInterface property allows you to specify which interface you want the generated proxy to implement. If this is the remote interface of the JAXRPC service, you do not need to provide a value for the portInterface property; otherwise, you must set portInterface to the fully qualified name of the remote interface. As you can see, we specify that the proxy should implement the HelloWorld interface, which is not a remote interface, so we also specify that the portInterface is RemoteHelloWorld. In general, it is better to use a separate service interface for your proxies rather than the remote interface because it removes the need for your application code to deal with RemoteExceptions explicitly.

To obtain values for the namespaceUri, portName, and serviceName properties, you need to look at the WSDL generated for your service. The root node of the WSDL document is <wsdl:definitions>, which has an attribute, targetNamespace, the value of which corresponds to the value of the namespaceUri property.

Toward the end of your WSDL document, you will see a snippet of code similar to that shown in Listing 16-18.

Listing 16-18. *Service Definition in WSDL*

```
<wsdl:service name="JaxRpcHelloWorldService">
    <wsdl:port binding="impl:HelloWorldSoapBinding" name="HelloWorld">
      <wsdlsoap:address
              location="http://localhost:8080/remoting/services/HelloWorld"/>
    </wsdl:port>
  </wsdl:service>
```

Here the value of the name attribute of the <wsdl:service> tag corresponds to the value of the serviceName property, and the value of the name attribute of the <wsdl:port> tag corresponds to the value of the portName property.

These seven properties provide the JaxRpcPortProxyFactoryBean class with all the information it needs to generate a proxy that implements the HelloWorld interface but internally uses the RemoteHelloWorld interface. The proxy is generated using the WSDL document at http://localhost:8080/remoting/services/HelloWorld?wsdl and it expects the target namespace of this WSDL document to be http://localhost:8080/remoting/services/HelloWorld.

Using JAXRPC Proxies

As with RmiProxyFactoryBean, the JaxRpcPortProxyFactoryBean class implements the FactoryBean interface so that when it is accessed using ApplicationContext.getBean() it returns the proxy instead of a reference to itself. Listing 16-19 shows the HelloWorldClient class, which loads an ApplicationContext using the configuration shown in Listing 16-17, grabs the proxy, and uses it to execute the getMessage() method of the web service.

Listing 16-19. *Using a JAXRPC Proxy*

```
package com.apress.prospring.ch16.remoting.jaxrpc;

import org.springframework.context.ApplicationContext;
import org.springframework.context.support.FileSystemXmlApplicationContext;

import com.apress.prospring.ch16.remoting.HelloWorld;

public class HelloWorldClient {

    public static void main(String[] args) {
        ApplicationContext ctx = new FileSystemXmlApplicationContext(
        "./ch16/src/conf/jaxrpc/client.xml");

        HelloWorld helloWorld = (HelloWorld)ctx.getBean("helloWorldService");
        System.out.println(helloWorld.getMessage());
    }
}
```

As you can see from this example, the client is free to interact with the web service using the HelloWorld interface, which is much simpler than the RemoteHelloWorld interface because it does not require code to deal with the checked RemoteExceptions.

Make sure that your web service is deployed in your servlet container and that the servlet container is running, then run this application. After a short delay, you should see the message "Hello World" written to the console. As this example shows, building a web service client is extremely simple when you are using Spring, thanks to the support for proxies. By allowing proxies to implement a business interface that is separate from the remote interface of a service, Spring also makes the code required to interact with the proxy much simpler as well.

Working with JavaBeans in Axis Services

In the previous example, the value returned by the getMessage() method of the HelloWorld service was a simple String, which is mapped directly to the xsd:string type in SOAP. This mapping is handled automatically by Axis, but when you use complex return types such as JavaBeans, Axis cannot map the type automatically, and using such a type requires additional configuration at both the server and client side.

As an example of this, consider the remote interface shown in Listing 16-20.

Listing 16-20. *The MessageService Interface*

```
package com.apress.prospring.ch16.remoting.jaxrpc;

import java.rmi.Remote;
import java.rmi.RemoteException;

import com.apress.prospring.ch16.remoting.MessageBean;
```

```java
public interface MessageService extends Remote {

    MessageBean getMessage() throws RemoteException;
}
```

Here you can see that the getMessage() method of the MessageService interface does not return a String like RemoteHelloWorld.getMessage(); instead, it returns an instance of the MessageBean, the code for which is shown in Listing 16-21.

Listing 16-21. *The MessageBean Class*

```java
package com.apress.prospring.ch16.remoting;

import java.io.Serializable;

public class MessageBean implements Serializable {

    private String message;
    private String senderName;

    public String getMessage() {
        return message;
    }

    public void setMessage(String message) {
        this.message = message;
    }

    public String getSenderName() {
        return senderName;
    }

    public void setSenderName(String senderName) {
        this.senderName = senderName;
    }

    public String toString() {
            return "Message: " + message + "\nSender: " + senderName;
    }
}
```

As you can see, MessageBean is just a simple JavaBean class with two properties, both of type String. You will need additional configuration when you use this class as part of an Axis service, as the return type of a method or as a method parameter.

■**NOTE** Although the MessageBean class implements Serializable, this is **not** a requirement of JAXRPC. MessageBean is used in a later example that does require it to implement Serializable.

Deploying a Service with Complex Types

On the server side, when configuring your service in server-config.wsdd, you need to specify additional configuration details that tell Axis how it should serialize and deserialize your complex types to and from SOAP messages. Axis provides built-in support for serializing and deserializing JavaBean-style classes; this means that other than a small amount of additional configuration information, you do not need to expend any effort to use JavaBeans in your web services.

For non-JavaBean-style classes, you must provide custom implementations of the SerializerFactory and DeserializerFactory interfaces. Indeed, behind the scenes, Axis' Java-Beans support is implemented using prebuilt implementations of these interfaces. The topic of custom serialization is outside the scope of this chapter, but you can find more details online in the Axis User Guide.

To configure a JavaBean for use with an Axis web service, you need to add a <beanMapping> definition to the <service> definition for your service. In Listing 16-22, you can see the <service> definition for the MessageService complete with <beanMapping>.

Listing 16-22. *Configuring a <beanMapping>*

```
<service name="MessageService" provider="java:RPC">
        <parameter name="className"
            value="com.apress.prospring.ch16.remoting.jaxrpc.JaxRpcMessageService"/>
        <parameter name="allowedMethods" value="*"/>
        <beanMapping qname="apress:MessageBean"
                xmlns:apress="http://www.apress.com"
                    languageSpecificType="➥
                    java:com.apress.prospring.ch16.remoting.jaxrpc.MessageBean"/>
    </service>
```

Here you can see that we have defined a <beanMapping> tag for the MessageBean class, specifying that the XML-qualified name of the MessageBean class in SOAP form should be apress:MessageBean, where apress is the namespace and MessageBean is the local name. In addition, we map the apress namespace to the URI http://www.apress.com.

From the service configuration in Listing 16-22, note also that the implementation class is set to JaxRpcMessageService; the code for this is shown in Listing 16-23.

Listing 16-23. *The JaxRpcMessageService Class*

```
package com.apress.prospring.ch16.remoting.jaxrpc;

import java.rmi.RemoteException;

import com.apress.prospring.ch16.remoting.MessageBean;

public class JaxRpcMessageService implements MessageService {

    public MessageBean getMessage() throws RemoteException {
        MessageBean bean = new MessageBean();
        bean.setMessage("Hello World!");
        bean.setSenderName("Rob Harrop");
        return bean;
    }

}
```

This implementation is trivial and requires no explanation. At this point, you are ready to deploy your web service. Once the web service is deployed in your servlet container, you should navigate to the WSDL for it to ensure that the <beanMapping> has been correctly applied. In Listing 16-24, you can see a snippet of the WSDL from the MessageService that is created by the <beanMapping>.

Listing 16-24. *Complex Types in WSDL*

```
<wsdl:types>
    <schema targetNamespace="http://www.apress.com"
                            xmlns="http://www.w3.org/2001/XMLSchema">
        <import namespace="http://schemas.xmlsoap.org/soap/encoding/" />
        <complexType name="MessageBean">
            <sequence>
                <element name="message" nillable="true" type="xsd:string" />
                <element name="senderName" nillable="true" type="xsd:string" />
            </sequence>
        </complexType>
    </schema>
</wsdl:types>
```

In the definition of the MessageBean <complexType>, the name for which is derived from the qname attribute of your <beanMapping>, you can see that Axis has successfully defined two attributes, message and senderName, based on the JavaBean properties of the MessageBean class.

Accessing a Service with Complex Types

Once you have successfully deployed a service using complex types, all that remains is to create a client application to access the service. Unfortunately, in Spring, there is no declarative way to define complex type mappings for use with JAXRPC clients. Instead, you must subclass the

JaxRpcPortProxyFactoryBean class to post-process the JAXRPC service created by the proxy creator and add your custom type mappings.

When registering custom type mappings, you are essentially informing your JAXRPC framework which implementations of the SerializerFactory and DeserializerFactory classes to use for a given type. Although the code to register a custom type mapping is largely provider-independent, the implementations of SerializerFactory and DeserializerFactory are either supplied by your SOAP stack or by your application. In this case, we use the BeanSerializerFactory and BeanDeserializerFactory classes provided by Axis when we register our custom type mapping. This is shown in Listing 16-25.

Listing 16-25. *Registering a Custom Type Mapping*

```
package com.apress.prospring.ch16.remoting.jaxrpc;

import javax.xml.namespace.QName;
import javax.xml.rpc.Service;
import javax.xml.rpc.encoding.TypeMapping;
import javax.xml.rpc.encoding.TypeMappingRegistry;

import org.apache.axis.encoding.ser.BeanDeserializerFactory;
import org.apache.axis.encoding.ser.BeanSerializerFactory;
import org.springframework.remoting.jaxrpc.JaxRpcPortProxyFactoryBean;

import com.apress.prospring.ch16.remoting.MessageBean;

public class MessageServiceJaxRpcProxyFactoryBean extends
        JaxRpcPortProxyFactoryBean {

    protected void postProcessJaxRpcService(Service service) {
        TypeMappingRegistry tmr = service.getTypeMappingRegistry();
        TypeMapping tm = tmr.createTypeMapping();

        QName qname = new QName("http://www.apress.com", "MessageBean");

        tm.register(MessageBean.class, qname,
                new BeanSerializerFactory(MessageBean.class, qname),
                new BeanDeserializerFactory(MessageBean.class, qname));

        tmr.register("http://schemas.xmlsoap.org/soap/encoding/", tm);
    }
}
```

To register a custom type mapping in your custom JaxRpcPortProxyFactoryBean implementation, you must override the postProcessJaxRpcService() method, which allows you to access the Service instance once it is configured by the base class. The code in Listing 16-25 is fairly self-explanatory—if you cannot follow the code, you should refer to the JAXRPC JavaDocs, which are available from http://java.sun.com/xml/jaxrpc/.

To access a service that uses complex types using a proxy, replace
`JaxRpcPortProxyFactoryBean` with your custom implementation in the
`ApplicationContext` configuration. In this case, we replace `JaxRpcPortProxyFactoryBean`
with `MessageServiceJaxRpcProxyFactoryBean`, as shown in Listing 16-26.

Listing 16-26. *Proxy Configuration Using Custom Proxy Factory*

```
<!DOCTYPE beans PUBLIC "-//SPRING//DTD BEAN//EN"
"http://www.springframework.org/dtd/spring-beans.dtd">
<beans>
    <bean id="messageService"
             class="➥
   com.apress.prospring.ch16.remoting.jaxrpc.MessageServiceJaxRpcProxyFactoryBean">
        <property name="serviceFactoryClass">
            <value>org.apache.axis.client.ServiceFactory</value>
        </property>
        <property name="wsdlDocumentUrl">
            <value>
                http://localhost:8080/remoting/services/MessageService?wsdl
            </value>
        </property>
        <property name="namespaceUri">
            <value>http://localhost:8080/remoting/services/MessageService</value>
        </property>
        <property name="serviceName">
            <value>JaxRpcMessageServiceService</value>
        </property>
        <property name="portName">
            <value>MessageService</value>
        </property>
        <property name="serviceInterface">
            <value>com.apress.prospring.ch16.remoting.jaxrpc.MessageService</value>
        </property>
    </bean>
</beans>
```

As you can see, the proxy is configured in the same way as it would be if you used the standard `JaxRpcPortProxyFactoryBean` class; the only thing that changes is the class used in the
`<bean>` declaration. Notice that in this example, we use the remote interface as the value for the
`serviceInterface` property; this means that the proxy itself actually implements the remote
interface of the service. We do this only for illustration purposes—it is certainly preferable to
use a nonremote business interface as the interface for your proxy.

Using the proxy from your application code is no different than working with any other
object that implements the `MessageService` interface, as shown by the code in Listing 16-27.

Listing 16-27. *The MessageServiceClient Class*

```
package com.apress.prospring.ch16.remoting.jaxrpc;

import org.springframework.context.ApplicationContext;
import org.springframework.context.support.FileSystemXmlApplicationContext;

import com.apress.prospring.ch16.remoting.MessageBean;

public class MessageServiceClient {

    public static void main(String[] args) throws Exception {
        ApplicationContext ctx = new FileSystemXmlApplicationContext(
        "./ch16/src/conf/jaxrpc/messageServiceClient.xml");
        MessageService service = (MessageService)ctx.getBean("messageService");
        MessageBean bean = service.getMessage();
        System.out.println(bean);
    }
}
```

Provided that the MessageService is deployed in your servlet container, running this example results in the following output to the console after a short delay:

```
Message: Hello World!
Sender: Rob Harrop
```

Spring HTTP Invoker

As you saw from the previous section, JAXRPC is quite a complex way to expose services over HTTP. Not only that, the use of XML adds a certain amount of overhead, because incoming requests and outgoing responses have to be converted to and from SOAP. In many cases, all you need is a simple mechanism for two Java applications to communicate with each other using HTTP as the transport.

In this case, JAXRPC may be overkill, because both sides are using Java and using XML as a communication fabric adds unnecessary complexity. Likewise, RMI is unsuitable for this scenario, because it cannot be used over HTTP. Thankfully, quite a few solutions provide simple mechanisms for exposing services over HTTP. Spring provides support for three such services on top of the support offered by JAXRPC: Hessian, Burlap, and Spring HTTP Invokers. Hessian and Burlap are covered in more detail later in the chapter; in this section, you learn how to use Spring's native HTTP Invoker remoting architecture to build distributed components in a 100-percent Spring environment.

From a user perspective, Spring HTTP Invokers are deceptively simple and provide a powerful mechanism for remote component communication. On the server side, services are exposed on top of Spring's comprehensive web framework, using a 100-percent Spring-native configuration mechanism. Unlike JAXRPC, you are in full control of the creation semantics for your service objects and thus you can configure them using Spring DI.

On the client side, Spring provides proxy capabilities that allow you to access HTTP Invoker–exposed services via a business interface. Internally, Spring uses the built-in capabilities of the JDK for HTTP communication, although you can configure it to use Jakarta Commons HttpClient (http://jakarta.apache.org/commons/httpclient), which provides a more complete HTTP implementation. By using HttpClient on the client and standard servlet security on the server, you can secure your HTTP Invoker services using HTTP Basic authentication.

In this section, we show you how to build services using the HTTP Invoker architecture and how to access these services using Spring-generated proxies. You also see how Spring handles the transmission of complex types and how you can provide basic security using HTTP Basic authentication.

Exposing Simple Services

To build and deploy a service using the HTTP Invoker architecture, you need to follow four distinct steps. First you must create the service interface. Spring does not place any special constraints on the service interface, so feel free to use one of your normal business interfaces. However, you may wish to restrict the operations that are exported in your service, in which case you can create a specific interface for your service. For the example in this section, we use the standard HelloWorld interface from Listing 16-1.

The second step you need to take is to build the actual service implementation. Again, Spring places no special constraints on the implementation class such as those specified by RMI. Indeed, with Spring HTTP Invokers, it is generally easier to use one of your standard service classes. If you need to restrict the exposure of operations on your service class, do this in the service interface. For the example in this section, we use the SimpleHelloWorld implementation of HelloWorld shown in Listing 16-2.

The third step is to configure an instance of HttpInvokerServiceExporter in your ApplicationContext. Behind the scenes, HttpInvokerServiceExporter is implemented as a Spring Controller that is capable of receiving an HTTP request and returning an arbitrary response. Also, when configuring your HttpInvokerServiceExporter, you must specify a mapping for the service to a URL. We discuss a lot of different mechanisms for mapping beans to a URL in Chapter 17, but for the examples in this section, we use BeanNameUrlHandlerMapping, which uses the name of the bean as the URL mapping.

The fourth step you need to follow is to configure an instance of Spring's DispatcherServlet in your web application deployment descriptor. DispatcherServlet is responsible for routing incoming HTTP requests to the appropriate Controllers based on their URL mappings. If you are unclear about the basic concept behind the MVC pattern in a web application, you might want to skip ahead to Chapter 17 for a rundown of MVC and the roles played by Spring's DispatcherServlet class and Controller interface.

Creating the Service Interface and Service Implementation

As we mentioned, Spring places no special constraints on your service interface or service implementation when you are using the HTTP Invoker stack. In most cases, you simply use standard business interfaces along with some arbitrary implementation, although in some cases, you may choose to restrict the operations that are exposed remotely using a specific service interface.

For the example in this section, we are going to use the HelloWorld interface and SimpleHelloWorld class from Listings 16-1 and 16-2, respectively. Because we have already shown and discussed these, we will not cover them again here.

Exporting an HTTP Invoker Service

Configuring the HttpInvokerServiceExporter is much like configuring the RmiServiceExporter, although HttpInvokerServiceExporter only requires two properties: the service bean and the service interface. Listing 16-28 shows a sample configuration that configures an HttpInvokerServiceExporter for the helloWorldService bean that we configured in Listing 16-14.

Listing 16-28. *Exporting an HTTP Invoker Service*

```
<!DOCTYPE beans PUBLIC "-//SPRING//DTD BEAN//EN"
"http://www.springframework.org/dtd/spring-beans.dtd">
<beans>
    <bean id="defaultHandlerMapping"
class="org.springframework.web.servlet.handler.BeanNameUrlHandlerMapping"/>

    <bean name="/helloWorld"
        class="org.springframework.remoting.httpinvoker.HttpInvokerServiceExporter">
        <property name="service">
            <ref bean="helloWorldService"/>
        </property>
        <property name="serviceInterface">
            <value>com.apress.prospring.ch16.remoting.HelloWorld</value>
        </property>
    </bean>
</beans>
```

This configuration is fairly straightforward, but it has two points of note. First, notice that the bean name for the HttpInvokerServiceExporter is specified as /helloWorld. When processing incoming requests, Spring's DispatcherServlet uses any defined HandlerMapping beans to find a Controller to which the request should be routed. In this case, we define a BeanNameUrlHandlerMapping bean as our only HandlerMapping implementation. As its name implies, BeanNameUrlHandlerMapping attempts to map the URL of the incoming request to a bean based on the bean's name. So in this case, if a request comes in whose URL (after taking out the host name, context path, and servlet mapping) is /helloWorld, BeanNameUrlHandlerMapping routes it to the /helloWorld bean.

The second point of note here is that when we set the service property of the HttpInvokerServiceExporter, we point to a bean that is contained in a separate configuration file. When you create a web application using Spring, it is traditional to separate your bean definitions into at least two ApplicationContexts. You place all non-web-specific bean definitions, such as service objects and data access objects, in one ApplicationContext and all web-specific beans, such as Controllers and HandlerMappings, in another. The ApplicationContext that contains your business interfaces is loaded by the ContextLoaderServlet, whereas the ApplicationContext containing the web components is loaded by the DispatcherServlet. Spring ensures that beans in the web-specific ApplicationContext can access beans in the business ApplicationContext but not vice versa. The reason for this separation is simple—it increases reusability. Because the business ApplicationContext does not contain any web-specific bean declarations, you can reuse it in other applications.

In our example, we reuse the helloWorldBean definition that is shown in Listing 16-14. This single bean definition constitutes the business ApplicationContext and it is loaded by the ContextLoaderServlet. The defaultHandlerMapping and /helloWorld beans shown in Listing 16-28 make up our web ApplicationContext, which is loaded by the DispatcherServlet. The name and location of the web ApplicationContext file is very important. You must place the file in the WEB-INF directory of your web application and you must name it *<servlet_name>*-servlet.xml where *<servlet_name>* is the name given to the DispatcherServlet in your web application deployment descriptor.

Configuring Spring's DispatcherServlet

Configuring the DispatcherServlet is really simple; it is just a standard servlet configuration. The only point to note is that you must remember to configure the ContextLoaderServlet, or ContextLoaderListener if it is compatible with your container, if you split your bean definitions across multiple files as we did. Listing 16-29 shows the DispatcherServlet configuration for this example.

Listing 16-29. *Configuring DispatcherServlet*

```xml
<?xml version="1.0" encoding="UTF-8"?>
<!DOCTYPE web-app PUBLIC "-//Sun Microsystems, Inc.//DTD Web Application 2.3//EN"
                    "http://java.sun.com/dtd/web-app_2_3.dtd">
<web-app>
    <context-param>
        <param-name>contextConfigLocation</param-name>
        <param-value>/WEB-INF/applicationContext.xml</param-value>
    </context-param>

    <servlet>
        <servlet-name>context</servlet-name>
        <servlet-class>
            org.springframework.web.context.ContextLoaderServlet
        </servlet-class>
        <load-on-startup>1</load-on-startup>
    </servlet>

    <servlet>
        <servlet-name>httpinvoker</servlet-name>
        <servlet-class>
            org.springframework.web.servlet.DispatcherServlet
        </servlet-class>
        <load-on-startup>3</load-on-startup>
    </servlet>
```

```
<servlet-mapping>
    <servlet-name>httpinvoker</servlet-name>
    <url-pattern>/http/*</url-pattern>
</servlet-mapping>
```

`</web-app>`

This configuration should be self-explanatory, so we do not go into any detail here. The only thing to be aware of is that because we named the `DispatcherServlet` httpinvoker, the `ApplicatonContext` configuration file associated with this servlet must be named httpinvoker-servlet.xml.

Unfortunately, unlike Axis, the `HttpInvokerServiceExporter` does not provide a nice interface to test whether or not the service is deployed correctly. However, you can test to see whether the servlet is configured correctly by pointing your browser at the service URL, in this case `http://localhost:8080/remoting/http/helloWorld`. If you get an error screen that indicates that a `java.io.EOFException` has been thrown, then the service is being invoked as you wanted it to be but no data is available. If you get another error, then it is likely that Spring cannot find your `ApplicationContext` configuration files, that they contain errors, or that the URL mapping is incorrectly defined. Check all the configuration files for mistakes and make sure that they are all correctly named and sit in the correct places in your web application, then redeploy.

Accessing an HTTP Invoker Service Using Proxies

As with both RMI and JAXRPC, accessing an HTTP Invoker service is done using proxies that hide all the messy details from your application, which allows you to code purely to business interfaces. Just like the `FactoryBeans` provided for RMI and JAXRPC proxies, Spring provides the `HttpInvokerProxyFactoryBean` that creates a proxy for your HTTP Invoker service. Listing 16-30 shows a sample configuration that uses `HttpInvokerProxyFactoryBean` to create a proxy to the service created in the last section.

Listing 16-30. *Creating an HTTP Invoker Proxy*

```
<!DOCTYPE beans PUBLIC "-//SPRING//DTD BEAN//EN"
"http://www.springframework.org/dtd/spring-beans.dtd">
<beans>
    <bean id="helloWorldService"
      class="org.springframework.remoting.httpinvoker.HttpInvokerProxyFactoryBean">
        <property name="serviceUrl">
            <value>http://localhost:8080/remoting/http/helloWorld</value>
        </property>
        <property name="serviceInterface">
            <value>com.apress.prospring.ch16.remoting.HelloWorld</value>
        </property>
    </bean>
</beans>
```

This configuration is fairly self-explanatory and demonstrates the ease with which you can configure a proxy for HTTP Invoker services. You can use this proxy in your application just like you would use any instance of HelloWorld, as shown in Listing 16-31.

Listing 16-31. *Using an HTTP Invoker Proxy*

```
package com.apress.prospring.ch16.remoting.http;

import org.springframework.context.ApplicationContext;
import org.springframework.context.support.FileSystemXmlApplicationContext;

import com.apress.prospring.ch16.remoting.HelloWorld;

public class HelloWorldClient {

    public static void main(String[] args) {
        ApplicationContext ctx = new FileSystemXmlApplicationContext(
                                    "./ch16/src/conf/http/helloWorld.xml");

        HelloWorld helloWorld = (HelloWorld)ctx.getBean("helloWorldService");
        System.out.println(helloWorld.getMessage());
    }
}
```

As with earlier examples of the HelloWorld service, running this class results in a short delay before the message "Hello World" is printed to the console.

Using Arbitrary Objects in HTTP Invoker Services

In the previous example, the return type of the getMessage() method was a Java String that implements the Serializable interface and thus is transmittable by HTTP Invoker, which builds on top of Java serialization as a mechanism for transmitting objects across the wire. Recall from the discussion of JAXRPC that you need substantial effort to use a complex Java type as a return type or an argument of a remote method. With HTTP Invokers, you need very little effort to make your own types transmittable—all you need to do is implement Serializable for any classes you wish to use in your service.

As an example of this, consider the MessageService interface we showed you earlier in Listing 16-20. This interface defines a single method, getMessage(), that returns an instance of MessageBean. Recall from Listing 16-21 that the MessageBean class implements the Serializable interface and as such, it is perfectly acceptable to use in an HTTP Invoker service. Listing 16-32 shows an HttpInvokerServiceExporter that configures a new HTTP Invoker service at the URL /messageService.

Listing 16-32. *Configuring the /messageService HTTP Invoker Service*

```
<bean name="/messageService"
      class="org.springframework.remoting.httpinvoker.HttpInvokerServiceExporter">
      <property name="service">
```

```
            <ref bean="messageService"/>
        </property>
        <property name="serviceInterface">
            <value>com.apress.prospring.ch16.remoting.MessageService</value>
        </property>
</bean>
```

Notice that in this example we point the `HttpInvokerServiceExporter` to the `messageService` that needs to be added to the business `ApplicationContext`, as shown in Listing 16-33.

Listing 16-33. *Adding the messageService Bean to the ApplicationContext*

```
<!DOCTYPE beans PUBLIC "-//SPRING//DTD BEAN//EN"
"http://www.springframework.org/dtd/spring-beans.dtd">
<beans>
    <bean id="helloWorldService"
            class="com.apress.prospring.ch16.remoting.SimpleHelloWorld"/>
    <bean id="messageService"
            class="com.apress.prospring.ch16.remoting.http.SimpleMessageService"/>
</beans>
```

Mapping this service to a URL requires that you configure a `BeanNameUrlHandlerMapping` definition in the web `ApplicationContext`, as shown earlier in Listing 16-28.

Because a `DispatcherServlet` is already configured for the `ApplicationContext` containing the HTTP Invoker services, you do not need to make any additional modifications to the deployment descriptor for the web application.

As with the previous HTTP Invoker service, you can test that this service has been deployed correctly by pointing your browser at the correct location, but to test it fully, you need to build a client. As you saw in the previous section, this is much simplified by the use of proxies. Listing 16-34 shows a proxy configuration for accessing the `MessageService`.

Listing 16-34. *HTTP Invoker Proxy for MessageService*

```
<!DOCTYPE beans PUBLIC "-//SPRING//DTD BEAN//EN"
"http://www.springframework.org/dtd/spring-beans.dtd">
<beans>
    <bean id="messageService"
 class="org.springframework.remoting.httpinvoker.HttpInvokerProxyFactoryBean">
        <property name="serviceUrl">
            <value>http://localhost:8080/remoting/http/messageService</value>
        </property>
        <property name="serviceInterface">
            <value>com.apress.prospring.ch16.remoting.MessageService</value>
        </property>
    </bean>
</beans>
```

You should be more than familiar with code needed to use this proxy, but we included it in Listing 16-35 for the sake of completeness.

Listing 16-35. *Accessing the MessageService*

```
package com.apress.prospring.ch16.remoting.http;

import org.springframework.context.ApplicationContext;
import org.springframework.context.support.FileSystemXmlApplicationContext;

import com.apress.prospring.ch16.remoting.MessageService;

public class MessageServiceClient {

    public static void main(String[] args) {
        ApplicationContext ctx = new FileSystemXmlApplicationContext(
                "./ch16/src/conf/http/messageService.xml");

        MessageService messageService = (MessageService) ctx
                .getBean("messageService");
        System.out.println(messageService.getMessage());
    }
}
```

Running this class results in the following output:

```
Message: Hello World!
Sender: Rob Harrop
```

Using HTTP Basic Authentication

One of the best features of the HTTP Invoker architecture is that it can use built-in servlet container security services to provide secure services. In this example, you learn how to create a secure version of the MessageService we created in the previous section that requires users to authenticate using HTTP Basic authentication.

For the purposes of this example, we reuse most of the server-side configuration from the previous example. The only modifications are to the web ApplicationContext file to add a new URL mapping and to the web application deployment descriptor to configure the security. The bulk of the work in this example is on the client side, where we create an authentication-aware proxy.

Configuring a URL Mapping for the Secure Service

The new secure service requires a new URL mapping that can be mapped as a secured resource in the web application deployment descriptor. Because we use BeanNameUrlHandlerMapping, this involves creating a new bean definition with the new URL, as shown in Listing 16-36.

Listing 16-36. *URL Mapping for Secure Service*

```
<bean name="/messageServiceSecure"
      class="org.springframework.remoting.httpinvoker.HttpInvokerServiceExporter">
      <property name="service">
          <ref bean="messageService"/>
      </property>
      <property name="serviceInterface">
          <value>com.apress.prospring.ch16.remoting.MessageService</value>
      </property>
</bean>
```

Remember to add this declaration to the web `ApplicationContext`, not the business `ApplicationContext`.

Configuring Container Security

Most of you are already familiar with the details of container security—it is a fairly well-known part of the servlet specification—so we do not go into a great amount of detail on this topic. To secure a service, you need to configure the web application to use HTTP Basic authentication, map a security role into your application, and then mark the service URL as secure. Listing 16-37 shows a configuration that achieves these three points.

Listing 16-37. *Configuring Container Security*

```
<security-constraint>
    <web-resource-collection>
        <web-resource-name>Secure HTTP Services</web-resource-name>
        <url-pattern>/http/messageServiceSecure</url-pattern>
    </web-resource-collection>
    <auth-constraint>
        <role-name>manager</role-name>
    </auth-constraint>
</security-constraint>

<login-config>
    <auth-method>BASIC</auth-method>
    <realm-name>remoting</realm-name>
</login-config>

<security-role>
    <role-name>manager</role-name>
</security-role>
```

In this configuration, we define a security role named manager. How these roles are obtained is container specific. For testing, we used Tomcat, which allows you to specify users and roles in a simple XML file called tomcat-users.xml.

The <login-config> element configures the servlet container to use HTTP Basic authentication, and the <security-constraint> element restricts access to the /http/messageServiceSecure URL members of the manager role only. If you deploy this example to your servlet container, you can check that the security is active by pointing your browser at http://localhost:8080/ remoting/http/messageServiceSecure, which should prompt you for a user name and password.

Adding Authentication Capabilities to a Proxy

Deploying a secure HTTP service is the easy part; accessing it is not quite so simple. From our initial discussion of the HttpInvokerProxyFactoryBean, recall that we mentioned that internally, this bean can use either built-in JDK HTTP support or the Jakarta Commons HttpClient project. The built-in support for HTTP in the JDK does not include support for HTTP Basic authentication, meaning that you need to use HttpClient if you want to use HTTP Basic authentication to access a secure service.

Configuring HttpInvokerProxyFactoryBean to use HttpClient is simply a matter of setting the httpInvokerRequestExecutor property to an instance of CommonsHttpInvokerRequestExecutor. This is where it gets complex. CommonsHttpInvokerRequestExecutor does not allow you to set user names and passwords as properties, but it does allow you to pass in an instance of the HttpClient class, which is core to the HttpClient project. However, it is not possible to configure HttpClient with credentials for HTTP Basic authentication using Spring DI. The workaround for this is to create a FactoryBean implementation that can return an appropriately configured implementation of HttpClient, as shown in Listing 16-38.

Listing 16-38. *The HttpClientFactoryBean Class*

```
package com.apress.prospring.ch16.remoting.http;

import org.apache.commons.httpclient.Credentials;
import org.apache.commons.httpclient.HttpClient;
import org.apache.commons.httpclient.UsernamePasswordCredentials;
import org.springframework.beans.factory.FactoryBean;
import org.springframework.beans.factory.InitializingBean;

public class HttpClientFactoryBean implements FactoryBean, InitializingBean {

    private HttpClient httpClient;
    private String username;
    private String password;
    private String authenticationHost;
    private String authenticationRealm;

    public Object getObject() throws Exception {
        return httpClient;
    }
}
```

```
    public Class getObjectType() {
        return HttpClient.class;
    }

    public boolean isSingleton() {
        return true;
    }

    public void setPassword(String password) {
        this.password = password;
    }

    public void setUsername(String username) {
        this.username = username;
    }

    public void setAuthenticationHost(String authenticationHost) {
        this.authenticationHost = authenticationHost;
    }

    public void setAuthenticationRealm(String authenticationRealm) {
        this.authenticationRealm = authenticationRealm;
    }

    public void afterPropertiesSet() throws Exception {
        if ((username == null) || (password == null)) {
            throw new IllegalArgumentException(
                    "You must set the username, password");
        }

        httpClient = new HttpClient();
        httpClient.getState().setAuthenticationPreemptive(true);

        Credentials credentials = new UsernamePasswordCredentials(username,
                password);
        httpClient.getState().setCredentials(authenticationRealm,
                authenticationHost, credentials);
    }
}
```

Most of the code in the HttpClientFactoryBean class is self-explanatory; the important part is
the afterProperties() method. The afterProperties() method ensures that values for the
username and password properties have been supplied before it moves on to create an instance of
HttpClient, which is stored in the httpClient field. The call to setAuthenticationPreemptive()
instructs the HttpClient that it should send credentials to the server in advance of any requests
from the server in an attempt to authenticate preemptively.

In the final part of afterProperties(), an instance of UsernamePasswordCredentials is created and assigned to the HttpClient, along with the values of the authenticationRealm and authenticationHost properties. Both of these properties can be left null, but specifying them allows you to restrict the supplied credentials to a set host or authentication realm.

By using the HttpClientFactoryBean, it is now possible to configure an instance of CommonsHttpInvokerRequestExecutor with a correctly configured instance of HttpClient. In turn, you can use this CommonsHttpInvokerRequestExecutor bean to configure an instance of HttpInvokerProxyFactoryBean so that it can take advantage of HTTP Basic authentication. This is shown in Listing 16-39.

Listing 16-39. *Configuring HttpInvokerProxyFactoryBean for HTTP Basic Authentication*

```
<!DOCTYPE beans PUBLIC "-//SPRING//DTD BEAN//EN"
"http://www.springframework.org/dtd/spring-beans.dtd">
<beans>
    <bean id="messageService"
      class="org.springframework.remoting.httpinvoker.HttpInvokerProxyFactoryBean">
        <property name="serviceUrl">
            <value>http://localhost:8080/remoting/http/messageServiceSecure</value>
        </property>
        <property name="serviceInterface">
            <value>com.apress.prospring.ch16.remoting.MessageService</value>
        </property>
        <property  name="httpInvokerRequestExecutor">
            <ref local="requestExecutor"/>
        </property>
    </bean>

    <bean id="requestExecutor"
class="org.springframework.remoting.httpinvoker.CommonsHttpInvokerRequestExecutor">
        <property name="httpClient">
            <bean
              class="com.apress.prospring.ch16.remoting.http.HttpClientFactoryBean">
                <property name="username">
                    <value>tomcat</value>
                </property>
                <property name="password">
                    <value>tomcat</value>
                </property>
            </bean>
        </property>
    </bean>
</beans>
```

You can use the resulting proxy created by this configuration just like any proxy, as shown in Listing 16-40.

Listing 16-40. *The MessageServiceSecureClient Class*

```
package com.apress.prospring.ch16.remoting.http;

import org.springframework.context.ApplicationContext;
import org.springframework.context.support.FileSystemXmlApplicationContext;

import com.apress.prospring.ch16.remoting.MessageService;

public class MessageServiceSecureClient {

    public static void main(String[] args) {
        ApplicationContext ctx = new FileSystemXmlApplicationContext(
                "./ch16/src/conf/http/messageServiceSecure.xml");

        MessageService messageService = (MessageService) ctx
                .getBean("messageService");
        System.out.println(messageService.getMessage());
    }
}
```

If you run this example, as long as you configured validation credentials in the ApplicationContext, then you will see output similar to that from the example in Listing 16-35. You should experiment with different sets of credentials to see the security in action.

Hessian and Burlap

Using the HTTP Invoker remoting architecture is a really simple way to create distributed applications when all components use both Java and Spring. This setup is sufficient in many cases, but it is unrealistic to think that Spring, and indeed Java, will always be used in all components in a remote application.

In these cases, Hessian and Burlap provide a suitable alternative to HTTP Invoker. Hessian is a lightweight framework for the creation of web services using a binary protocol. Burlap is a similar framework, although the underlying protocol uses XML rather than a binary representation. The only implementation of Burlap available at the time of writing is for Java, although implementing Burlap in other languages should not be restrictively difficult. Hessian has, at the time of writing, three different implementations, which cover Java, Python, and C++; this makes it suitable for communicating between components written in different languages. In this section, we focus on Hessian rather than Burlap; but remember, in the context of Spring, usage of both is identical. To make the examples in this section run with Burlap instead of Hessian, replace all instances of Hessian in class names with Burlap.

The way you use Hessian and Burlap in Spring is similar to the way you use HTTP Invoker. At the server side, the Spring DispatcherServlet is responsible for dispatching incoming requests to the HessianServiceExporter that, like HttpInvokerServiceExporter, implements the Controller interface and is thus capable of handling requests passed from the DispatcherServlet.

At the client side, you access Hessian services using a proxy you create using the HessianProxyFactoryBean. Like HTTP Invoker, Hessian services support HTTP Basic authentication and whereas configuration at the server side is identical, the client side configuration for Hessian is much simpler.

In this section, you see how to expose services using Hessian and Spring, as well as how to access these services using the Spring Hessian proxy generator. You also learn how to secure your Hessian services using HTTP Basic authentication and how to configure a Hessian proxy to access a secure service.

Exposing Services Using Hessian

Like HTTP Invoker, Hessian places no constraints on the service interface or the service implementation class. This allows you to use your standard business objects and removes the need to create any special interfaces or implementations. As with HTTP Invoker, you can choose to create a specific service interface if you wish to restrict the methods that are exposed. For the example in this section, we reuse the HelloWorld interface and SimpleHelloWorld class shown in Listings 16-1 and 16-2, respectively.

Because the HessianServiceExporter uses the same basic architecture as the HttpInvokerServiceExporter, configuring a HessianServiceExporter requires very similar XML. Listing 16-41 shows the definition of a HessianServiceExporter and a BeanNameUrlHandlerMapping.

Listing 16-41. *Configuring a Hessian Service*

```
<!DOCTYPE beans PUBLIC "-//SPRING//DTD BEAN//EN"
"http://www.springframework.org/dtd/spring-beans.dtd">
<beans>
    <bean id="defaultHandlerMapping"
      class="org.springframework.web.servlet.handler.BeanNameUrlHandlerMapping"/>

    <bean name="/helloWorld"
      class="org.springframework.remoting.caucho.HessianServiceExporter">
        <property name="service">
            <ref bean="helloWorldService"/>
        </property>
        <property name="serviceInterface">
            <value>com.apress.prospring.ch16.remoting.HelloWorld</value>
        </property>
    </bean>
</beans>
```

As you can see, the only difference between this configuration and the configuration for the corresponding HTTP Invoker service shown in Listing 16-28 is that the class attribute for the /helloWorld bean is set to the HessianServiceExporter.

As with HTTP Invoker services, Hessian services are fronted by an instance of
DispatcherServlet, which you need to configure in the web application deployment
descriptor along with a URL mapping for the servlet. This is shown in Listing 16-42.

Listing 16-42. *Configuring DispatcherServlet*

```
<servlet>
    <servlet-name>caucho</servlet-name>
    <servlet-class>
            org.springframework.web.servlet.DispatcherServlet</servlet-class>
    <load-on-startup>4</load-on-startup>
</servlet>

<servlet-mapping>
    <servlet-name>caucho</servlet-name>
    <url-pattern>/caucho/*</url-pattern>
</servlet-mapping>
```

Remember that the servlet name is important and indicates the name that we should give
to the configuration file shown in Listing 16-43.

Accessing Hessian Services

Configuring a Hessian proxy is just like configuring an HTTP Invoker proxy; the only difference
is that you replace HttpInvokerProxyFactoryBean with HessianProxyFactoryBean, as shown in
Listing 16-43.

Listing 16-43. *Configuring a Hessian Proxy*

```
<!DOCTYPE beans PUBLIC "-//SPRING//DTD BEAN//EN"
"http://www.springframework.org/dtd/spring-beans.dtd">
<beans>
    <bean id="helloWorldService"
      class="org.springframework.remoting.caucho.HessianProxyFactoryBean">
        <property name="serviceUrl">
            <value>http://localhost:8080/remoting/caucho/helloWorld</value>
        </property>
        <property name="serviceInterface">
            <value>com.apress.prospring.ch16.remoting.HelloWorld</value>
        </property>
    </bean>
</beans>
```

By now, you should be more than familiar with the details of this configuration, so we do
not go into any details on it. As you can probably guess, using this proxy in a client application
does not require any special handling, as you can see in Listing 16-44.

Listing 16-44. *Using a Hessian Proxy*

```
package com.apress.prospring.ch16.remoting.caucho;

import org.springframework.context.ApplicationContext;
import org.springframework.context.support.FileSystemXmlApplicationContext;

import com.apress.prospring.ch16.remoting.HelloWorld;

public class HelloWorldClient {

    public static void main(String[] args) {
        ApplicationContext ctx = new FileSystemXmlApplicationContext(
        "./ch16/src/conf/caucho/helloWorld.xml");

        HelloWorld helloWorld = (HelloWorld)ctx.getBean("helloWorldService");
        System.out.println(helloWorld.getMessage());
    }
}
```

Running this example displays the message "Hello World!" in the console after a short delay.

Using HTTP Basic Authentication

As with HTTP Invoker, you can secure Hessian services using HTTP Basic authentication. As we mentioned earlier, configuration at the server side is the same as it was for HTTP Invoker, but at the client side, the Hessian configuration for HTTP Basic authentication is much simpler.

Listing 16-45 shows the configuration of a new Hessian service using the MessageService interface and SimpleMessageClass that appeared in Listings 16-20 and 16-21, respectively.

Listing 16-45. *Configuring the Secure Message Service*

```
<bean name="/messageServiceSecure"
      class="org.springframework.remoting.caucho.HessianServiceExporter">
    <property name="service">
        <ref bean="messageService"/>
    </property>
    <property name="serviceInterface">
        <value>com.apress.prospring.ch16.remoting.MessageService</value>
    </property>
</bean>
```

Although you should be more familiar with this configuration, note that you do not need to take any special steps to handle the use of complex types in a Hessian service. The MessageService.getMessage() method returns an instance of MessageBean, which was marked as Serializable for use in HTTP Invoker services. For Hessian services, this is not necessary because Hessian has its own serialization mechanism.

Because you have already configured container security for the sample services in Listing 16-29, all you need to do to make this service secure is add a new `<url-pattern>` tag to the `<web-resource-collection>` tag, as shown in Listing 16-46.

Listing 16-46. *Adding an Additional Secure URL*

```
<web-resource-collection>
    <web-resource-name>Secure HTTP Services</web-resource-name>
    <url-pattern>/http/messageServiceSecure</url-pattern>
    <url-pattern>/caucho/messageServiceSecure</url-pattern>
</web-resource-collection>
```

Configuring a Hessian proxy to access this secure service is much simpler than configuring an HTTP Invoker proxy to access a secure service, because the HessianProxyFactoryBean allows you to specify the user name and password you need to use for authentication using Spring DI, as shown in Listing 16-47.

Listing 16-47. *Configuring a Hessian Proxy for HTTP Basic Authentication*

```
<!DOCTYPE beans PUBLIC "-//SPRING//DTD BEAN//EN"
"http://www.springframework.org/dtd/spring-beans.dtd">
<beans>
    <bean id="messageService"
        class="org.springframework.remoting.caucho.HessianProxyFactoryBean">
        <property name="serviceUrl">
            <value>
                http://localhost:8080/remoting/caucho/messageServiceSecure
            </value>
        </property>
        <property name="serviceInterface">
            <value>com.apress.prospring.ch16.remoting.MessageService</value>
        </property>
        <property name="username">
            <value>tomcat</value>
        </property>
        <property name="password">
            <value>tomcat</value>
        </property>
    </bean>
</beans>
```

You can use this proxy just like any other, as shown in Listing 16-48.

Listing 16-48. *The MessageServiceSecureClient Class*

```java
package com.apress.prospring.ch16.remoting.caucho;

import org.springframework.context.ApplicationContext;
import org.springframework.context.support.FileSystemXmlApplicationContext;

import com.apress.prospring.ch16.remoting.MessageService;

public class MessageServiceSecureClient {

    public static void main(String[] args) {
        ApplicationContext ctx = new FileSystemXmlApplicationContext(
                "./ch16/src/conf/caucho/messageServiceSecure.xml");

        MessageService messageService = (MessageService) ctx
                .getBean("messageService");
        System.out.println(messageService.getMessage());
    }
}
```

Try running this example with both valid and invalid credentials to test the security of the service.

Choosing a Remoting Architecture

With so many options available for remoting, you may wonder which solution to use. Thankfully, the decision is often quite clear for a given set of requirements. The Spring documentation provides quite a comprehensive discussion on how to choose a remoting implementation. We expanded on this here and you should certainly read it in conjunction with this discussion.

As the documentation states, RMI is a good solution for Java-to-Java solutions that require transmission of complex object models. Because RMI uses built-in Java serialization capabilities, creating a distributed application that transmits complex models across the network requires very little effort on your part. Using RMI in conjunction with Spring allows you to hide RMI-specific implementation details from your application, making it easier to plug in a new remoting architecture, should your requirements change.

RMI is also a good solution for you to use in heterogeneous environments because it allows you to communicate using CORBA IIOP, which is widely supported in a variety of other languages. Indeed, you may find that if you are deploying a new component into an existing environment, the architecture in place is CORBA. In this case, RMI is the best solution for your needs.

The biggest drawback of RMI is that it is not easily usable across HTTP, so if you need to communicate across the Internet or you need to punch through corporate firewalls easily, one of the other available architectures will better meet your needs.

The use of JAXRPC is usually mandated if you need to communicate across HTTP with systems written in other languages; this is because SOAP is widely supported. Remember, think twice before you adopt JAXRPC for Java-to-Java communication, because many more efficient solutions exist. Even if you feel that you may need SOAP support in the future, you can easily create a SOAP service for non-Java clients and use some other framework for your Java clients with both services backed by the same implementation class.

The Spring-native HTTP Invoker architecture is a good candidate for having Java-to-Java communication with Spring available at both ends, and because it builds on Java serialization, it is more than capable of transmitting complex object models between components.

Hessian and, to a certain degree, Burlap are excellent candidates for use in both homogenous and heterogeneous environments. You should prefer Hessian over Burlap unless XML is explicitly required, because Hessian performs much better than Burlap and is more widely supported outside of Java. In Java-to-Java environments, Hessian is a valid alternative to HTTP Invokers and may be the only solution if both ends are not using Spring. The only problem is that Hessian's serialization support is not quite as comprehensive as that provided by Java serialization, so for complex object models, you may be restricted to HTTP Invoker in order to have your application function correctly.

Summary

In this chapter, you learned how to create and access remote services using Spring and a wide variety of different remoting architectures. In the first part of the chapter, you saw how to use Spring remoting to simplify the creation of RMI-based services and how you can use Spring to create and access CORBA services via JNDI. In the second part of the chapter, you explored how to create and access SOAP web services using Spring's support for JAXRPC. We then introduced you to Spring's native remoting solution—HTTP Invoker. Using the HTTP Invoker architecture, you can easily expose and access remote services over HTTP, using Java serialization to format complex object graphs to be transmitted across the wire. We then covered how to expose services over HTTP using the Hessian binary protocol. You saw how Hessian provides a viable solution for many use cases even in heterogeneous environments, although we did highlight that Hessian has some problems with complex object graphs that you do not encounter when you are using the HTTP Invoker architecture.

In the next chapter, you will see how to use the Spring MVC framework to build complex web applications in a simple and organized manner. You will explore how to take advantage of the Spring Controller architecture to solve common problems such as adding CRUD behavior to an application and building wizard-style forms that span multiple pages.

PART 6

Web Applications with Spring

CHAPTER 17

Web Applications
with Spring MVC

Web applications have become a very important part of any enterprise system. The key requirement for a web framework is to simplify development of the Web Tier as much as possible. The Spring web framework naturally uses Inversion of Control (IoC) to set the dependencies in the controllers. Before we dive into discussing Spring MVC, we need to take a look at what MVC stands for and how it can help develop more flexible web applications.

More specifically, we cover the following key components of a web application:

MVC architecture: We need to start by explaining the MVC architecture, including both the Model 1 and Model 2 architectures. In this section, we provide a generic explanation of the MVC architecture, but we do not focus on J2EE in great detail.

Spring MVC: In this section, we explain in more detail how the components of the MVC architecture are implemented in Spring web applications.

Controllers: Controllers are one of the most important parts in Spring web applications. We explain how the controllers are implemented in Spring and how Spring identifies the controller to handle specific requests.

Themes and locales: Finally, we discuss how Spring allows the web applications to be internationalized and themed according to users' preferences.

What Is MVC?

MVC is an acronym for the Model View Controller architecture. The purpose of this pattern is to simplify the implementation of applications that need to act upon user requests and manipulate and display data. There are three distinct components of this pattern:

- **Model** represents data that the user is expecting to see. In most cases, the model consists of Java beans.

- **View** is responsible for rendering the model. A view in a text editor probably displays the text in appropriate formatting; in most cases, a view in a web application generates an HTML output that the client's browser can interpret.

- **Controller** is a piece of logic that is responsible for processing and acting upon the user requests, building an appropriate model, and passing it to the view for rendering. In case of Java web applications, the controller is in most cases a servlet. Of course, the controller can be implemented in any language a web container can execute.

Currently, there are two models of MVC. In the domain of web applications, Model 1 architecture can be illustrated using the diagram in Figure 17-1.

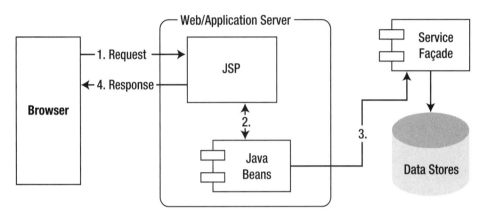

Figure 17-1. *MVC type 1 architecture*

As you can see, the JSP pages are in the center of the application. They contain *both* the control logic and presentation logic. The client makes a request to a JSP page; the logic in the page then builds (typically plain old Java objects) and renders the model. The separation of the presentation layer and control layer is not very clear. In fact, with the exception of "Hello world" applications, Model 1 quickly grows out of control, simply because of the amount of logic that different JSP pages need to perform.

Model 2 is far more manageable in a larger application. Whereas in Model 1, a JSP page was both the view and controller, in Model 2, there is a separate JSP page for the controller.

It is now the controller that intercepts the user requests, prepares the model, and passes it to the view for rendering. The JSP pages no longer contain logic for processing the requests; they simply display the model prepared by the controller.

We used JSP in place of the view and controller in Model 1 and the view in Model 2. This is obviously incorrect because the view is not limited to just JSP pages. Spring MVC architecture is an implementation of Model 2 MVC, hence the view can be anything that can render the model and return it to the client.

Now that we have covered the basics of the MVC pattern, we can explore how this pattern is implemented in Spring and how you can use it in your web applications.

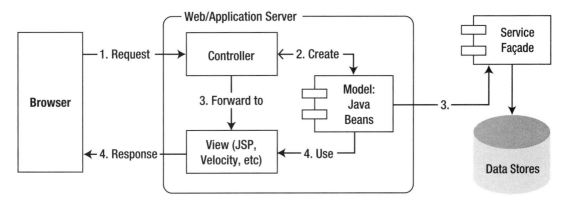

Figure 17-2. *MVC type 2 architecture*

Introducing Spring MVC

Spring MVC support allows us to build flexible applications using an MVC Model 2 pattern. The implementation is truly generic, the model is a simple Map that holds the data, View is an interface whose implementations render the data, and the controller is an implementation of the Controller interface.

Introduction and Overview

Spring's implementation of the MVC architecture for web applications is based around DispatcherServlet. This servlet processes the requests and invokes appropriate controllers to handle the request.

The DispatcherServlet intercepts the incoming requests and determines which Controller will handle the request. The Spring controllers return a ModelAndView class from their handling methods. The ModelAndView instance holds a reference to a view and a model. The model is a simple Map instance that holds Java beans that the view is going to render. The View is an interface that, when implemented, defines the render method. It makes sense that the View implementation can be virtually anything the client can interpret.

Implementation

If we want to create a web application with Spring, we need to start with the basic web.xml, where we need to specify the DispatcherServlet and set the mapping for the specified url-pattern, as shown in Listing 17-1.

Listing 17-1. *web.xml Descriptor*

```
<?xml version="1.0" encoding="ISO-8859-1"?>
<!DOCTYPE web-app PUBLIC
"-//Sun Microsystems, Inc.//DTD Web Application 2.3//EN"
    "http://java.sun.com/dtd/web-app_2_3.dtd">
<web-app>
    <display-name>Pro Spring Chapter 17 Sample application</display-name>
    <description>dtto</description>

    <servlet>
        <servlet-name>ch171819</servlet-name>
        <servlet-class>
            org.springframework.web.servlet.DispatcherServlet
        </servlet-class>
        <load-on-startup>1</load-on-startup>
    </servlet>
    <servlet-mapping>
        <servlet-name>ch17</servlet-name>
        <url-pattern>*.html</url-pattern>
    </servlet-mapping>
    <servlet-mapping>
        <servlet-name> ch171819</servlet-name>
        <url-pattern>*.tile</url-pattern>
    </servlet-mapping>
</web-app>
```

This web.xml file defines the ch171819 servlet of the DispatcherServlet class that maps to all requests to *.html[1] or *.tile.

Using Handler Mappings

Before we can talk about all the exciting components of the Spring MVC framework, we must take the time to explain how URL mapping works in Spring. You need the URL mapping to tell Spring which controller to invoke for the specific request. Even though it sounds complicated, it is not too difficult and can be done easily in the Spring application context file.

Spring uses HandlerMapping implementations to identify the controller to invoke and comes with the implementations of HandlerMapping shown in Table 17-1.

We are not going to use the BeanNameUrlHandlerMapping in our application; instead, we start using the SimpleUrlHandlerMapping. An example of BeanNameUrlHandlerMapping is shown in Chapter 16.

---

1. I usually create mapping to *.html because it is a recognized extension and it easily fools the search engines into thinking that it is not a dynamically generated page.

Table 17-1. *HandlerMapping Implementations*

HandlerMapping	Description
BeanNameUrlHandlerMapping	The bean name is identified by the URL. If the URL is /product/index.html, the controller id that handles this mapping would have to be set to /product/index.html. This mapping is useful for smaller applications because it does not support wildcards in the requests.
SimpleUrlHandlerMapping	This handler mapping allows you to specify the requests (using full names and wildcards) that specify which controller is going to handle the request.

Using Handler Interceptors

Interceptors are closely related to mappings because you can specify a list of interceptors that are called for each mapping. HandlerInterceptor implementations can process each request before or after the appropriate controller has processed it. You can choose to implement the HandlerInterceptor interface or extend HandlerInterceptorAdapter, which provides a default implementation for all HandlerInterceptor methods. As an example, we are going to implement a BigBrotherHandlerInterceptor that is going process each request.

Listing 17-2. *BigBrotherHandlerInterceptor Implementation*

```
package com.apress.prospring.ch17.web;

import javax.servlet.http.HttpServletRequest;
import javax.servlet.http.HttpServletResponse;

import org.springframework.web.servlet.ModelAndView;
import org.springframework.web.servlet.handler.HandlerInterceptorAdapter;

public class BigBrotherHandlerInterceptor extends HandlerInterceptorAdapter {

    public void postHandle(HttpServletRequest request,
        HttpServletResponse response, Object handler,
        ModelAndView modelAndView) throws Exception {
        // process the request
    }
}
```

The actual implementation of such an interceptor probably processes the request parameters and stores them in an audit log. To use the interceptor, we create URL mapping and interceptor bean definitions in the Spring application context file, as shown in Listing 17-3.

Listing 17-3. *HandlerMapping and HandlerInterceptor Definitions*

```xml
<?xml version="1.0" encoding="UTF-8" ?>
<!DOCTYPE beans PUBLIC "-//SPRING//DTD BEAN//EN" ➥
"http://www.springframework.org/dtd/spring-beans.dtd">

<beans>
    <bean id="bigBrotherHandlerInterceptor"
        class="com.apress.prospring.ch17.web.BigBrotherHandlerInterceptor"/>

    <bean id="publicUrlMapping"
        class="org.springframework.web.servlet.handler.SimpleUrlHandlerMapping">
        <property name="interceptors">
            <list>
                <ref local="bigBrotherHandlerInterceptor"/>
            </list>
        </property>
        <property name="mappings">
            <props>
                <prop key="/index.html">indexController</prop>
                <prop key="/product/index.html">productController</prop>
                <prop key="/product/view.html">productController</prop>
                <prop key="/product/edit.html">productFormController</prop>
            </props>
        </property>
    </bean>
</beans>
```

You can specify as many HandlerMapping and HandlerInterceptor beans as you like, provided that the actual mappings do not collide with each other.

Now that you know how Spring maps the URLs to controllers, let's take a look at the pivotal component of the Spring MVC architecture—the controllers.

Working with Controllers

Controllers do all the work to process the request, build the model based on the request, and pass the model to the view for rendering. Spring's DispatcherServlet intercepts the requests from the client and uses a HandlerAdapter implementation that is responsible for delegating the request for further processing. You can implement the HandlerAdapter yourself, which allows you to modify the chain of command the request must pass through.

The DispatcherServlet has a List handlerAdapters property that allows you to specify the HandlerAdapters you wish to use. To make sure the HandlerAdapter implementations are called in the right order, you can choose to implement the Ordered interface in your HandlerAdapter to indicate its position of among other HandlerAdapters.

If the handlerAdapters property of DispatcherServlet is null, the DispatcherServlet uses SimpleControllerHandlerAdapter. Because we are not going to provide any additional HandlerAdapter implementations, our application is going to use the SimpleControllerHandlerAdapter.

Because the SimpleControllerHandlerAdapter's handle() method calls ((Controller) handler).handleRequest(request, response), the Spring handler beans that are to act as controllers must implement the Controller interface. This approach makes it very easy to write your own implementation from scratch or to use one of the convenience superclasses. The Controller interface depends on HttpServletRequest and HttpServletResponse, which means that you can use it only in web applications.

Let's take a look at the most basic implementation of the Controller interface. In Listing 17-4, we create an IndexController that simply writes "Hello, World" to the response stream.

Listing 17-4. *IndexController Implementation*

```
package com.apress.prospring.ch17.web;

import javax.servlet.http.HttpServletRequest;
import javax.servlet.http.HttpServletResponse;

import org.springframework.web.servlet.ModelAndView;
import org.springframework.web.servlet.mvc.Controller;

public class IndexController implements Controller {

    public ModelAndView handleRequest(HttpServletRequest request,
        HttpServletResponse response) throws Exception {

        response.getWriter().println("Hello, world");

        return null;
    }

}
```

The only method we need to implement is ModelAndView handleRequest(HttpServletRequest, HttpServletResponse). We return null as ModelAndView, which means that no view is rendered and the output written to the output of the response is committed and returned to the client.

Implementing the Controller interface is not, in most cases, too much work because Spring provides a number of useful superclasses.

AbstractController

At the first glance, it might seem that AbstractController is simply a wrapper around the interface that forces you to implement the handleRequestInternal method to process the request. This is only partially true because AbstractController extends a WebContentGenerator class that allows you to set additional properties to control the request and response. Additionally, the WebContentGenerator extends WebApplicationObjectSupport, which, in turn, extends an ApplicationObjectSupport class that implements ApplicationContextAware. In other words, extending your controller from AbstractController rather than implementing the Controller interface directly gives you access to the ServletContext, WebApplicationContext, ApplicationContext, Log, and MessageSourceAccessor.

In Table 17-2, we examine the properties you can set that are related to the web application environment.

Table 17-2. *WebContentGenerator/AbstractController Properties*

Property	Description	Default Value
supportedMethods	Supported and allowed HTTP methods.	GET, POST
requiresSession	Specifies whether an HttpSession instance is required to process the request.	false
useExpiresHeader	Specifies whether to use the HTTP 1.0 expires header.	true
useCacheControlHeader	Specifies whether to use the HTTP 1.1 cache-control header.	true
cacheSeconds	Instructs the client to cache the generated content for the specified number of seconds.	−1
synchronizeOnSession	Specifies whether the controller should synchronize instances of HttpSession before invoking handleRequestInternal. This is useful for serializing reentrant request handling from the same client.	false

As an example, in Listing 17-5, we set the cacheSeconds property to 10 and then refresh the page in the client (making sure we are not instructing the client to bypass the cache). As a result, we should only see new content from the server every 10 seconds.

Listing 17-5. *IndexController Implementation Using AbstractController*

```
package com.apress.prospring.ch17.web;

import javax.servlet.http.HttpServletRequest;
import javax.servlet.http.HttpServletResponse;

import org.springframework.web.servlet.ModelAndView;
import org.springframework.web.servlet.mvc.AbstractController;
```

```
public class IndexController extends AbstractController {

    protected ModelAndView handleRequestInternal(HttpServletRequest request,
        HttpServletResponse response) throws Exception {
        setCacheSeconds(10);
        response.getWriter().println("Hello, world at " +
            System.currentTimeMillis());
        return null;
    }

}
```

If you compare the implementations of IndexController in Listing 17-4 and Listing 17-5, you will see that there is very little difference between them, except for the fact that the code in Listing 17-5 now has full access to the context (both servlet and application) and can manipulate the HTTP headers more easily. In Listing 17-14 later in this chapter, we show you how to access the application context.

ParameterizableViewController

This is a ridiculously simple subclass of AbstractController; it implements the handleRequestInternal method to return a new model with a name set in its viewName property. No data is inserted into the model, and the only reason you would chose to use this controller is to simply display a view using its name.

Listing 17-6 shows the ParameterizableIndexController we created to demonstrate the functionality of ParameterizableViewController.

Listing 17-6. *ParameterizableIndexController Implementation*

```
package com.apress.prospring.ch17.web;

import org.springframework.web.servlet.mvc.ParameterizableViewController;

public class ParameterizableIndexController extends ParameterizableViewController {

}
```

In Listing 17-7, we add a parameterizableIndexController bean to the application context file and set its viewName property to product-index as well as add a reference to it to the publicUrlMapping bean.

Listing 17-7. *parameterizableIndexController Bean Declarations*

```xml
<?xml version="1.0" encoding="UTF-8" ?>
<!DOCTYPE beans PUBLIC "-//SPRING//DTD BEAN//EN" ➥
"http://www.springframework.org/dtd/spring-beans.dtd">

<beans>
    <bean id="publicUrlMapping"
        class="org.springframework.web.servlet.handler.SimpleUrlHandlerMapping">
        <property name="interceptors">
            <list>
                <ref local="bigBrotherHandlerInterceptor"/>
            </list>
        </property>
        <property name="mappings">
            <props>
                <prop key="/index.html">indexController</prop>
                <prop key="/pindex.html">parameterizableIndexController</prop>
                <prop key="/product/index.html">productController</prop>
                <prop key="/product/view.html">productController</prop>
                <prop key="/product/edit.html">productFormController</prop>
                <prop key="/product/image.html">productImageFormController</prop>
            </props>
        </property>
    </bean>

    <bean id="parameterizableIndexController"
        class="com.apress.prospring.ch17.web.ParameterizableIndexController">
        <property name="viewName"><value>products-index</value></property>
    </bean>
</beans>
```

MultiActionController

This Controller implementation is far more interesting than ParameterizableViewController. It is also a subclass of AbstractController, which means it has access to all its properties and methods. Most importantly, it lets you provide as many implementations of public ModelAndView(HttpServletRequest, HttpServletResponse) throws Exception as you need. You can choose to implement the methods in your subclass of MultiActionController, or you can specify a delegate object that implements these methods. In the latter case, the MultiActionController invokes the methods on the delegate object.

The two additional properties to AbstractController, delegate and methodNameResolver, are used to tell MultiActionController which method on which object to invoke for each request. If the delegate property is left to its default value of null, the method is looked up and invoked on MultiActionController subclass; if delegate is not null, the method is invoked on delegate.

The methodNameResolver must be set to an implementation of MethodNameResolver. There are three implementations of MethodNameResolver, which are described in Table 17-3.

Table 17-3. *MethodNameResolver Implementations*

Implementation	Description
InternalPathMethodNameResolver	The method name is taken from the last ("file") part of the path, excluding the extension. When using this resolver path, /servlet/foo.html maps to a method declared as public ModelAndView foo(HttpServletRequest, HttpServletResponse). This is also the default implementation used in MultiActionController.
ParameterMethodNameResolver	The method name is taken from the specified request parameter. The default parameter name is action; you can change the parameter name in the context file.
PropertiesMethodNameResolver	The method name is resolved from an external properties file. You can specify exact mapping, such as /test.html=handleTest or you can use wildcards, such as /*=handleAllTs.

If none of the resolvers shown in Table 17-3 are suitable for your application, you can implement your own MethodNameResolver, but the resolvers already provided out of the box by Spring are usually sufficient. In Listing 17-8, we take a look at the simplest implementation of the MultiActionController subclass.

Listing 17-8. *MultiActionController Subclass*

```
package com.apress.prospring.ch17.web.product;

import javax.servlet.http.HttpServletRequest;
import javax.servlet.http.HttpServletResponse;

import org.springframework.web.servlet.ModelAndView;
import org.springframework.web.servlet.mvc.multiaction.MultiActionController;


public class ProductController extends MultiActionController {

    public ModelAndView view(HttpServletRequest request,
        HttpServletResponse response) throws Exception{

        response.getOutputStream().print("Viewing product " +
            request.getParameter("productId"));

        return null;
    }

}
```

The ProductController from Listing 17-8 adds only one method, view(). If the path /product/* is mapped to this controller, and if the request is /product/view.html?productId=10, the output displayed in the browser is going to be Viewing product 10.

This proves that, by default, MultiActionController uses InternalPathMethodNameResolver as a methodNameResolver and that the delegate property is null, because the view() method is called on ProductController. Let's take a look at how we can configure other methodNameResolvers, starting with ParameterMethodNameResolver.

By default, ParameterMethodNameResolver uses action as the parameter name from which to get the method name; we can change (as we do in Listing 17-9) that by setting the paramName property. We can also specify the method name that is invoked when the paramName parameter is not present in the request by setting the defaultMethodName property to the name of the method to be invoked.

Listing 17-9. *ch17-servlet.xml Definition with ParameterMethodNameResolver*

```xml
<?xml version="1.0" encoding="UTF-8" ?>
<!DOCTYPE beans PUBLIC "-//SPRING//DTD BEAN//EN"
    "http://www.springframework.org/dtd/spring-beans.dtd">

<beans>
    <!-- other beans -->
    <bean id="productController"
        class="com.apress.prospring.ch17.web.product.ProductController">
        <property name="methodNameResolver">
            <ref local="productMethodNameResolver"/></property>
    </bean>

    <bean id="productMethodNameResolver"
        class="org.springframework.web.servlet.mvc.multiaction.➥
            ParameterMethodNameResolver">
            <property name="paramName"><value>method</value></property>
            <property name="defaultMethodName"><value>view</value></property>
        </property>
    </bean>
</beans>
```

If we now make a request to /product/a.html and do not specify the method parameter, ProductController.view is invoked; we get the same behavior if we make a request to /product/a.html?method=view. However, if we make a request to /product/a.html?method=foo, we get an error message because method public ModelAndView foo(HttpServletRequest, HttpServletResponse) is not implemented in ProductController.

The last method name resolver we discuss is PropertiesMethodNameResolver (see Listing 17-10). This method resolver relies on the request URI, but unlike InternalPathMethodNameResolver, we can specify the method names in the Spring context file.

Listing 17-10. *ch17-servlet.xml Definition with PropertiesMethodNameResolver*

```
<?xml version="1.0" encoding="UTF-8" ?>
<!DOCTYPE beans PUBLIC "-//SPRING//DTD BEAN//EN"
"http://www.springframework.org/dtd/spring-beans.dtd">

<beans>
    <!-- other beans -->
    <bean id="productController"
        class="com.apress.prospring.ch17.web.product.ProductController">
        <property name="methodNameResolver">
            <ref local="productMethodNameResolver"/></property>
    </bean>

    <bean id="productMethodNameResolver"
        class="org.springframework.web.servlet.mvc.multiaction.➥
            PropertiesMethodNameResolver">
        <property name="mappings">
            <props>
                <prop key="/product/view.html">view</prop>
                <prop key="/product/v*.html">view</prop>
            </props>
        </property>
    </bean>
</beans>
```

This code demonstrates how to use `PropertiesMethodNameResolver`—we need to configure its `mappings` property and add a list of mappings and their handler methods. The example from Listing 17-10 declares that /product/view.html as well as /product/v*.html map to the `public ModelAndView view(HttpServletRequest, HttpServletResponse)` method in `ProductController`. The benefit of this `MethodNameResolver` is that we can use wildcards in the mapping strings.

All these controllers are very useful, but if we have to process input submitted by a user, we have to write a lot of code to get the submitted values and process error messages. Spring simplifies this process by providing several command controllers. Before we can move ahead to the command controllers, however, we must discuss Spring views. This enables us to create pages that the command controllers will use to process the data the users enter.

Views, Locales, and Themes

We already touched on the `View` interface, but we simply stated its uses. It is now time to examine it in more detail. Let's start with a custom implementation of the `View` interface. This demonstrates how simple it is to create a custom view and what Spring does to look up (and instantiate) an appropriate instance of a view when we refer to the view by its name.

Using Views Programmatically

In this example, we manually implement a View and return this implementation in the
ModelAndView class, which is a result of the AbstractController.handleRequestInternal() method.

Our view must implement only a single method from the View interface: render(Map,
HttpServletRequest, HttpServletResponse). The View implementation we create in Listing 17-11
outputs all data from the model to a text file and sets the response headers to indicate to the
client that the returned content is a text file and that it should be treated as an attachment.

Listing 17-11. *PlainTextView Implementation*

```java
package com.apress.prospring.ch17.web.views;

import java.io.PrintWriter;
import java.util.Iterator;
import java.util.Map;

import javax.servlet.http.HttpServletRequest;
import javax.servlet.http.HttpServletResponse;

import org.springframework.web.servlet.View;


public class PlainTextView implements View {

    public void render(Map model, HttpServletRequest request,
        HttpServletResponse response) throws Exception {

        response.setContentType("text/plain");
        response.addHeader("Content-disposition",
            "attachment; filename=output.txt");

        PrintWriter writer = response.getWriter();
        for (Iterator k = model.keySet().iterator(); k.hasNext();) {
            Object key = k.next();
            writer.print(key);
            writer.println(" contains:");
            writer.println(model.get(key));
        }
    }

}
```

In Listing 17-12, we modify the IndexController class from Listing 17-5 to return our custom view.

Listing 17-12. *Modified IndexController Class*

```
public class IndexController extends AbstractController {

    protected ModelAndView handleRequestInternal(
        HttpServletRequest request, HttpServletResponse response)
        throws Exception {

        setCacheSeconds(10);
        Map model = new HashMap();
        model.put("Greeting", "Hello World");
        model.put("Server time", new Date());

        return new ModelAndView(new PlainTextView(), model);
    }

}
```

Let's now make a request to the /index.html path. The IndexController.handleRequestInternal method is called and it returns an instance of ModelAndView with View set to the instance of PlainTextView and a model Map containing the keys Greeting and Server time. The render() method of PlainTextView sets the header information that prompts the client to display a Save As window like the one shown in Figure 17-3.

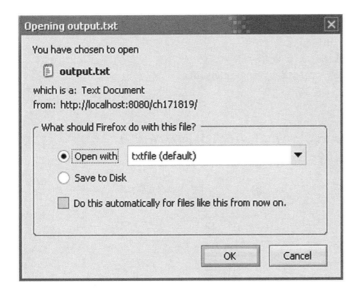

Figure 17-3. *PlainTextView implementation*

The content of the output.txt file, shown in Figure 17-4, is simply the model displayed as plain text.

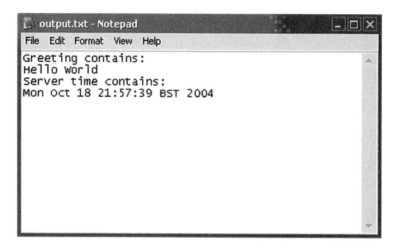

Figure 17-4. *Downloaded output.txt file*

The result is exactly what we expected: there were two entries in the model Map—Greeting and Server time—with Hello World and a current Date value.

This example has one disadvantage: the code in IndexController creates an instance of PlainTextView for each request. This is not necessary, because the view is a stateless object. In Listing 17-13, we improve the application and make PlainTextView a Spring bean.

Listing 17-13. *PlainTextView as Spring Bean*

```xml
<?xml version="1.0" encoding="UTF-8" ?>
<!DOCTYPE beans PUBLIC "-//SPRING//DTD BEAN//EN"
    "http://www.springframework.org/dtd/spring-beans.dtd">

<beans>
    <bean id="plainTextView"
        class="com.apress.prospring.ch17.web.views.PlainTextView"/>
    <!-- other beans as usual -->
</beans>
```

We need to modify the IndexController's handleRequestInternal() method to use the plainTextView bean instead of the instantiating the instance of PlainTextView for each request. We do this in Listing 17-14.

Listing 17-14. *Modified IndexController Class*

```
public class IndexController extends AbstractController {

    protected ModelAndView handleRequestInternal(
        HttpServletRequest request, HttpServletResponse response)
        throws Exception {

        setCacheSeconds(10);
        Map model = new HashMap();
        model.put("Greeting", "Hello World");
        model.put("Server time", new Date());
        View view = (View)getApplicationContext().getBean("plainTextView");

        return new ModelAndView(view, model);
    }

}
```

This is better—each request gets the same instance of the PlainTextView bean. However, it is still far from ideal. A typical web application consists of a rather large number of views, and it is inconvenient to configure all views this way. Moreover, certain views require further configuration. Take a JSP view, for example; it needs a path to the JSP page. If we configure all views as Spring beans manually, we have to configure each JSP page as a separate bean. It would be nice if we had an easier way to define the views and delegate all the work to Spring. This is where view resolvers come into play.

Using ViewResolver Implementations

A ViewResolver is a strategy interface Spring uses to look up and instantiate an appropriate view based on its name and locale. Various view resolvers all implement the ViewResolver interface's single method—View resolveViewName(String viewName, Locale locale) throws Exception—which allows your applications to be much easier to maintain. The locale parameter suggests that the ViewResolver can return views for different client locales.

Table 17-4 explores the various implementations of the ViewResolver interface.

Table 17-4. *ViewResolver Implementations*

Implementation	Description
BeanNameViewResolver	This is a simple ViewResolver implementation that tries to get the view as a bean configured in the application context. You may find this resolver useful for smaller applications where you do not want to create another file that holds the view definitions. However, this resolver has several limitations; the most annoying one is that you have to configure the views as Spring beans in the application context. Also, it does not support internalization.
ResourceBundleViewResolver	This is a far more complex resolver. In this case, the view definitions are kept in a separate configuration file; you do not have to configure the view beans in the application context file. This resolver supports internalization.
UrlBasedViewResolver	This resolver instantiates the appropriate view based on the URL. You can configure the URL to have prefixes and suffixes. This resolver gives you more control over the views than BeanNameViewResolver, but it can become difficult to manage in a larger application and does not support internalization.
XmlViewResolver	This view resolver is similar to ResourceBundleViewResolver because the view definitions are kept in a separate file. Unfortunately, this resolver does not support internalization.

Now that we know what ViewResolvers are available in Spring and their advantages and disadvantages, we can improve the sample application. We are going to discuss the ResourceBundleViewResolver because it offers the most complex functionality.

In Listing 17-15, we start by updating the application context file to include the viewResolver bean definition.

Listing 17-15. *ResourceBundleViewResolver Definition*

```
<?xml version="1.0" encoding="UTF-8" ?>
<!DOCTYPE beans PUBLIC "-//SPRING//DTD BEAN//EN" ➥
"http://www.springframework.org/dtd/spring-beans.dtd">

<beans>
    <bean id="viewResolver"
        class="org.springframework.web.servlet.view.ResourceBundleViewResolver">
        <property name="basename"><value>views</value></property>
    </bean>
    <!-- etc -->
</beans>
```

This introduces the viewResolver bean that Spring uses to resolve all view names. The class is ResourceBundleViewResolver, and its basename property is views. This means that the ViewResolver is going to look for the views_<LID>.properties file on the classpath, where LID is the locale identifier (EN, CS, and so on). If the resolver cannot locate the views_<LID>.properties file, it tries to open the views.properties file. To demonstrate the internalization support in this resolver, we create views.properties and views_CS.properties. We use the first file for any language other than Czech. The syntax of the properties file is viewname.class=class-name and viewname.url=view-url, as shown in Listing 17-16.

Listing 17-16. *Views.properties File Syntax*

```
#index
products-index.class=org.springframework.web.servlet.view.JstlView
products-index.url=/WEB-INF/views/product/index.jsp
```

We found that the best way to keep this file reasonably easy to maintain is to follow the logical structure of the application, using a dash as the directory separator. If you create a User ➤ Edit view definition, we recommend using code similar to that presented in Listing 17-17.

Listing 17-17. *Additions to the views.properties File*

```
#index
user-edit.class=org.springframework.web.servlet.view.JstlView
user-edit.url=/WEB-INF/views/user /edit.jsp
```

Similarly, we create index.jsp and index_CS.jsp in /web-src/as-web/WEB-INF/views/product. Finally, in Listing 17-18, we modify ProductController to return a dummy list of Product objects and display this list in the view.

Listing 17-18. *Modified ProductController*

```
package com.apress.prospring.ch17.web.product;

public class ProductController extends MultiActionController {

    private List products;

    private Product createProduct(int productId, String name,
        Date expirationDate) {
        Product product = new Product();
        product.setProductId(productId);
        product.setName(name);
        product.setExpirationDate(expirationDate);

        return product;
    }
```

```
    public ProductController() {
        products = new ArrayList();
        Date today = new Date();
        products.add(createProduct(1, "test", today));
        products.add(createProduct(2, "Pro Spring Appes", today));
        products.add(createProduct(3, "Pro Velocity", today));
        products.add(createProduct(4, "Pro VS.NET", today));
    }

    public ModelAndView index(HttpServletRequest request,
        HttpServletResponse response) {

        return new ModelAndView("products-index", "products", products);
    }
    // other methods omitted for clarity
}
```

As you can see, we did not modify `ProductController` in any unexpected way; the only change is that the `ModelAndView` constructor we call in the `index()` method is `ModelAndView(String, String, Object)` instead of `ModelAndView(View, …)`.

To test the application, make sure to set the preferred language in your browser to anything other than Czech. Spring creates `product-index` View of type `JstlView` with the URL set to `/WEB-INF/product/index.jsp` and renders the output, which appears in Figure 17-5.

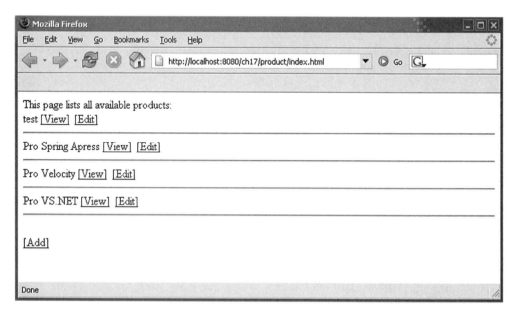

Figure 17-5. *English version of the site*

If we now change the preferred language to Czech, the view resolver creates an instance of index_CS, which is a JstlView, and its URL property points to /WEB-INF/products/index_CS.jsp. Figure 17-6 shows the resulting site.

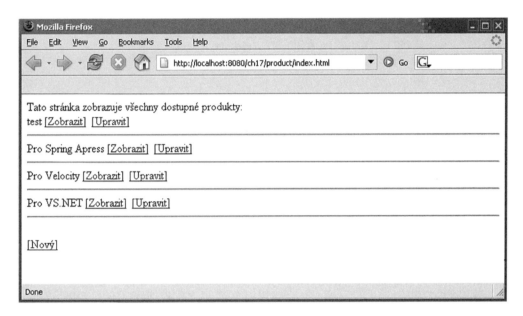

Figure 17-6. *Czech version of the site*

Using view resolvers rather than manually instantiating the views has the obvious benefit of simpler configuration files, but it also reduces the application's memory footprint. If we define each view as a Spring bean, it is instantiated on application start; if we use view resolvers, the view is instantiated and cached on first request.

Using Localized Messages

Before we can discuss using Locales in Spring web applications, we must look at how Spring resolves the actual text for messages to be displayed either in the spring:message tag (covered in Chapter 18) or as part of the validation process. The code interface, MessageSource, uses the MessageSourceResolvable interface to find the message key to be displayed. Spring comes with two implementations of the MessageSource interface: the ResourceBundleMessageSource and the ReloadableResourceBundleMessageSource. Both implementations use a standard properties file to load the messages, but the ReloadableResourceBundleMessageSource can reload the contents of the properties file if it detects a change, thus eliminating the need to restart the application when the content of the properties file is updated.

The default bean name Spring looks up is messageSource; our definition of this bean is shown in Listing 17-19.

Listing 17-19. *messageSource Bean Definition*

```xml
<?xml version="1.0" encoding="UTF-8" ?>
<!DOCTYPE beans PUBLIC "-//SPRING//DTD BEAN//EN" ➥
"http://www.springframework.org/dtd/spring-beans.dtd">

<beans>
    <bean id="messageSource"
        class="org.springframework.context.support.ResourceBundleMessageSource">
        <property name="basename"><value>messages</value></property>
    </bean>
</beans>
```

A more detailed discussion of MessageSource is offered in Chapter 18.

Using Locales

We have already discussed the internalization support in ResourceBundleViewResolver; let's now take a look at how things work under the hood.

Spring uses the LocaleResolver interface to intercept the request and calls its methods to get or set the locale. There are several implementations of LocaleResolver, each with its particular uses and properties, shown in Table 17-5.

Table 17-5. *LocaleResolver Implementations*

Implementation	Description
AcceptHeaderLocaleResolver	This locale resolver returns the locale based on an accept-language header sent by the user agent to the application. If this resolver is used, the application automatically appears in the user's preferred language (if you take the time to implement it). If the user wishes to switch to another language, he has to change his browser settings.
CookieLocaleResolver	This locale resolver uses cookie on the client's machine to identify the locale. This allows the user to specify the language she wants the application to appear in without changing her browser settings. It is not hard to imagine that a user in Prague has an English web browser, yet she expects to see the application in Czech. Using this locale resolver, we can store the locale settings using the user's browser cookie store.
FixedLocaleResolver	This is a very simple implementation of LocaleResolver that always returns one configured locale.
SessionLocaleResolver	This resolver works very much like CookieLocaleResolver, but the locale settings are not persisted in a cookie and are lost when the session expires.

Using Themes

In addition to providing the application's views in the users' language, you can use themes to further improve the users' experience. Theme is usually a collection of stylesheets and images embedded into the rendered output. Spring also provides a tag library that you can use to enable theme support in your JSP pages. Let's start with a directory structure we are going to use to demonstrate the usage of themes, as shown in Figure 17-7.

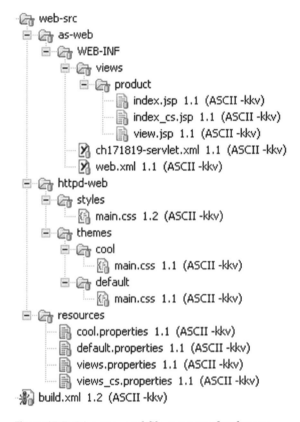

Figure 17-7. *Directory and file structure for themes*

As you can see from Figure 17-7, we added a themes directory and created two new properties files: cool.properties and default.properties. The content of the properties file specifies the location of static theme resources, as shown in Listing 17-20.

Listing 17-20. *cool.properties File*

```
css=/themes/cool/main.css
```

The key in the properties file specifies the key that is exposed by the theme resolver, and the value of the property specifies the location of the themed resource. We can use this definition in a JSP page using the Spring tag library, as shown in Listing 17-21.

Listing 17-21. *Contents of the index.jsp File*

```
<%@taglib prefix="c" uri="http://java.sun.com/jstl/core"%>
<%@taglib prefix="spring" uri="http://www.springframework.org/tags"%>

<html>
    <head>
        <c:set var="css"><spring:theme code="css"/></c:set>
        <c:if test="${not empty css}">
            <link rel="stylesheet"
                    href="<c:url value="${css}"/>" type="text/css" />
        </c:if>
    </head>
<body>
This page lists all available products:<br>
<c:forEach items="${products}" var="product">
    <c:out value="${product.name}"/>
    <a href="view.html?productId=
        <c:out value="${product.productId}"/>">[View]</a> 
    <a href="edit.html?productId=
        <c:out value="${product.productId}"/>">[Edit]</a> <br>
    <hr>
</c:forEach><br>
<a href="edit.html">[Add]</a>
</body>
</html>
```

Finally, we need to modify the Spring application context and add a themeResolver bean,
as shown in Listing 17-22.

Listing 17-22. *themeResolver Bean Definition*

```
<?xml version="1.0" encoding="UTF-8" ?>
<!DOCTYPE beans PUBLIC "-//SPRING//DTD BEAN//EN" ➥
"http://www.springframework.org/dtd/spring-beans.dtd">

<beans>
    <bean id="themeResolver"
          class="org.springframework.web.servlet.theme.FixedThemeResolver">
        <property name="defaultThemeName"><value>cool</value></property>
    </bean>
    <!-- other beans as usual -->
</beans>
```

This application context file specifies that the application uses FixedThemeResolver with
defaultThemeName set to cool. The theme is therefore loaded from the cool.properties file in the
root of the classpath.

Themes can contain references to any kind of static content, such as images and movies,
not just stylesheets. This also means that themes must support internalization because the

images may contain text that needs to be translated into other languages. The internalization support in theme resolvers works exactly the same as internalization support in ResourceBundleViewResolver. The theme resolver tries to load theme_<LID>.properties, where LID is the locale identifier (EN, CS, and so on). If the properties file with the LID does not exist, the resolver tries to load the properties file without the LID.

Just like the ViewResolvers and the LocaleResolvers, there are several implementations of ThemeResolvers, as shown in Table 17-6.

Table 17-6. *ThemeResolver Implementations*

Theme Resolver	Description
CookieThemeResolver	This allows the theme to be set per user and stores the theme preferences by storing a cookie on the client's computer.
FixedThemeResolver	This theme resolver returns one fixed theme, which is set in the bean's defaultThemeName property.
SessionThemeResolver	This allows the theme to be set per a user's session. The theme is not persisted between sessions.

Adding support for themes is not very difficult and it can give your application an extra visual kick with very little programming effort.

Using Command Controllers

Up until now, we have talked about the ways to get the data to the user based on the request parameters and how to render the data passed from the controllers. A typical application also gathers and processes data from the user. Spring supports this scenario by providing command controllers that process the data posted to the controllers. Before we can start discussing the various command controllers, we must examine the concept of command controllers.

The command controller allows a command object's properties to be populated from the form submission. The command controllers closely work with the Spring tag library to simplify data validation. The command controller is an ideal place to perform all business validation. As the validation occurs on the server, it is impossible for the users to bypass the validation, but you should not rely on the Web Tier to perform all validation, and you should revalidate in the Business Tier.

On the technical side, the command controller implementations expose a so-called command object, which is (in general) a domain object. Let's take a look at the command controllers we can use in our application.

AbstractCommandController: The first member of the command controller inheritance hierarchy we discuss is AbstractCommandController. Just like AbstractController, it implements the Controller interface. This class is not designed to actually handle HTML form submissions, but it provides basic support for validation and data binding. You can use this class to implement your own command controller in case the Spring controllers are insufficient for your needs.

AbstractFormController: The AbstractFormController class extends AbstractCommandController and can actually handle HTML form submission. In other words, this command controller processes the values in HttpServletRequest and populates the controller's command object. The AbstractFormController also has the ability to detect duplicate form submission, and it allows you to specify the views that are to be displayed in the code rather than in the Spring context file.

SimpleFormController: This is the most commonly used command controller to process HTML forms. It is also designed to be very easy to use—you can specify the views to display for the initial view and a success view, and you can set the command object you need to populate with the submitted data.

AbstractWizardFormController: As the name suggests, this command controller is useful for implementing a wizard style set of pages. This also implies that you must keep the command object in the current HttpSession and you need to implement the validatePage() method to check whether the data on the current page is valid and whether the wizard can continue to the next page. In the end, AbstractWizardFormController executes the processFinish() method to indicate that it has processed the last page of the wizard process and that the data is valid and can be passed to the Business Tier.

Using Form Controllers

Now that you know which form controller to choose, let's create an example that demonstrates how a form controller is used. We start with the simplest form controller implementation and then move on and add validation and custom formatters.

The most basic controller implementation extends SimpleFormController, overrides its onSubmit() method, and provides a default constructor, as shown in Listing 17-23.

Listing 17-23. *ProductFormController Implementation*

```
package com.apress.prospring.ch17.web.product;

public class ProductFormController extends SimpleFormController {

    public ProductFormController() {
        super();
        setCommandClass(Product.class);
        setFormView("products-edit");
    }

    protected ModelAndView onSubmit(HttpServletRequest request,
        HttpServletResponse response, Object command,
        BindException errors) throws Exception {
        System.out.println(command);

        return new ModelAndView("products-index-r");
    }

}
```

The ProductFromController's constructor defines that the command class is Product.class; this means that the object this controller creates is an instance of Product.

Next, we override the onSubmit() method, which gets called when the user submits the form. The command object has already passed the validation and it is safe to pass it to the Business Tier of the application, if appropriate. The onSubmit() method returns a products-index-r view, which is a RedirectView that redirects to the products/index.html page. We need this because we want the ProductController.handleIndex() method to take care of the request.

Finally, the call to setFormView() specifies the view that is used to display the form. In our case, it is a JSP page, as shown in Listing 17-24.

Listing 17-24. *edit.jsp Page*

```jsp
<%@taglib prefix="c" uri="http://java.sun.com/jstl/core"%>
<%@taglib prefix="spring" uri="http://www.springframework.org/tags"%>

<html>
<head>
    <c:set var="css"><spring:theme code="css"/></c:set>
        <c:if test="${not empty css}">
            <link rel="stylesheet"
                href="<c:url value="${css}"/>" type="text/css" />
        </c:if>
</head>
<body>
<form action="edit.html" method="post">
<input type="hidden" name="productId"
    value="<c:out value="${command.productId}"/>">
<table>
    <tr>
        <td>Name</td>
        <td><spring:bind path="command.name">
                <input name="name" value="<c:out value="${status.value}"/>">
                <span class="error"><c:out value="${status.errorMessage}"/></span>
            </spring:bind>
        </td>
    </tr>
    <tr>
        <td>Expiration Date</td>
        <td><spring:bind path="command.expirationDate">
                <input name="expirationDate"
                    value="<c:out value="${status.value}"/>">
                <span class="error"><c:out value="${status.errorMessage}"/></span>
            </spring:bind>
        </td>
    </tr>
```

```
    <tr>
        <td></td>
        <td><input type="submit"></td>
    </tr>
</table>
</form>
</body>
</html>
```

The `spring:bind` tag Spring provides allows us to pass the values from the form in a very simple way and also provides simple validation. First, we bind a value to a path, which is the command object name (as set in the form controller; the default value is `command`) and the property we set in the field. Inside the `spring:bind` tag, Spring defines the object status, whose value field represents the value of the property defined in the `spring:bind` tag. The `status.errorMessage` defines any validation error message.

The last thing we need to do is modify the application context file, the `productFormController` bean, and a mapping from /product/edit.html to the form controller. This is shown in Listing 17-25.

Listing 17-25. *ProductFormController Definition and URL Mapping*

```
<?xml version="1.0" encoding="UTF-8" ?>
<!DOCTYPE beans PUBLIC "-//SPRING//DTD BEAN//EN" ➥
"http://www.springframework.org/dtd/spring-beans.dtd">

<beans>
    <bean id="publicUrlMapping"
        class="org.springframework.web.servlet.handler.SimpleUrlHandlerMapping">
        <property name="mappings">
            <props>
                <prop key="/index.html">indexController</prop>
                <prop key="/product/index.html">productController</prop>
                <prop key="/product/view.html">productController</prop>
                <prop key="/product/edit.html">productFormController</prop>
            </props>
        </property>
    </bean>

    <!-- Product -->
    <bean id="productFormController"
        class="com.apress.prospring.ch17.web.product.ProductFormController">
    </bean>
    <!-- other beans as usual -->
</beans>
```

As you can see, there is nothing unusual about the new definitions in the Spring application context file. If we now navigate to `http://localhost:8080/ch17/product/edit.html`, we see a typical web page with a form to enter the data (see Figure 17-8).

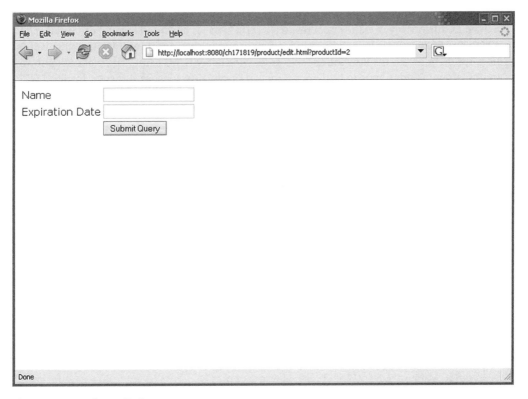

Figure 17-8. *Product edit form*

Unfortunately, the expirationDate property is of type Date, and Java date formats are a bit difficult to use. You cannot expect users to type **Sun Oct 24 19:20:00 BST 2004** for Date values. To make things a bit easier for the users, in Listing 17-26, we register a custom editor with the current binder. To do this, we are going to override the initBinder() method.

Listing 17-26. *CustomEditor Registration in ProductFormController*

```
package com.apress.prospring.ch17.web.product;

public class ProductFormController extends SimpleFormController {

    // other methods omitted for clarity

    protected void initBinder(HttpServletRequest request,
        ServletRequestDataBinder binder) throws Exception {
        SimpleDateFormat dateFormat = new SimpleDateFormat("dd/MM/yyyy");
        dateFormat.setLenient(false);
        binder.registerCustomEditor(Date.class, null,
            new CustomDateEditor(dateFormat, false));
    }
}
```

The newly registered custom editor is applied to all Date.class values and the values are parsed as dd/MM/yyyy values, as a result, "24/10/2004" is accepted instead of "Sun Oct 24 19:20:00 BST 2004" as a valid Date value. There is one other important thing missing: validation. We do not want to allow the users to add a product with no name. The most elegant way to implement validation is to implement the Validator interface, as shown in Listing 17-27, register the ProductValidator bean as a Spring-managed bean, and set the ProductFormController's validator property to the productValidator bean.

Listing 17-27. *ProductValidator Bean Implementation*

```
package com.apress.prospring.ch17.business.validators;

import org.springframework.validation.Errors;
import org.springframework.validation.Validator;

import com.apress.prospring.ch17.domain.Product;

public class ProductValidator implements Validator {

    public boolean supports(Class clazz) {
        return clazz.isAssignableFrom(Product.class);
    }

    public void validate(Object obj, Errors errors) {
        Product product = (Product)obj;
        if (product.getName() == null || product.getName().length() == 0) {
            errors.rejectValue("name", "required", "");
        }
    }

}
```

This Validator implementation adds a validation error with errorCode set to required. This code identifies a message resource, which needs to be resolved using a messageSource bean. The messageSource bean allows the message strings to be externalized and supports internalization as well. The rules for creating internalized messages are exactly the same as the rules for creating internationalized views and themes. We only show the final application context file in Listing 17-28; we do not show the contents of the messages.properties and messages_CS.properties files.

Listing 17-28. *ProductFormController Definition and URL Mapping*

```
<?xml version="1.0" encoding="UTF-8" ?>
<!DOCTYPE beans PUBLIC "-//SPRING//DTD BEAN//EN" ➥
"http://www.springframework.org/dtd/spring-beans.dtd">
```

```
<beans>
    <bean id="messageSource"
        class="org.springframework.context.support.ResourceBundleMessageSource">
        <property name="basename"><value>messages</value></property>
    </bean>

    <bean id="productValidator"
        class="com.apress.prospring.ch17.business.validators.ProductValidator"/>

    <!-- Product -->
    <bean id="productFormController"
        class="com.apress.prospring.ch17.web.product.ProductFormController">
        <property name="validator"><ref bean="productValidator"/></property>
    </bean>
    <!-- other beans as usual -->
</beans>
```

When we rebuild and redeploy the application, go to the product/edit.html page, and try
to submit the form without filling in the name but provide a valid expiration date, we see an
error message in the appropriate language, as shown in Figure 17-9.

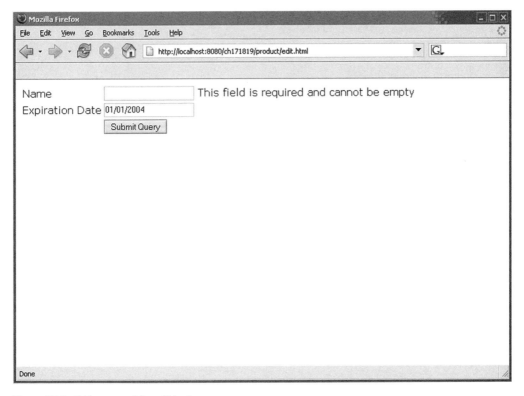

Figure 17-9. *Edit page with validation errors*

You now know how to get **new** data from the users, but in a typical application, you have to deal with edits as well. There must be a way to prepare the command object so it contains data retrieved from the Business Tier. Typically, this means that the request to the edit page contains a request parameter that specifies the object's identity. The object is then loaded in a call to the Business Tier and presented to the user. To do this, override the formBackingObject() method, as shown in Listing 17-29.

Listing 17-29. *Overriding the formBackingObject() Method*

```
package com.apress.prospring.ch17.web.product;

public class ProductFormController extends SimpleFormController {

    // other methods omitted for clarity

    protected Object formBackingObject(HttpServletRequest request)
        throws Exception {
        Product command = new Product();
        int productId = RequestUtils.getIntParameter(request, "productId", 0);
        if (productId != 0) {
            // load the product
            command.setProductId(productId);
            command.setName("loaded");
        }

        return command;
    }
}
```

And behold: when we make a request to edit.html with request parameter productId set to 2, the command object's name property is set to loaded. Of course, instead of creating an instance of the Product object in the controller, we use a Business Tier to pass the object identified by productId.

The other controllers follow the same rules for processing form submission and validation, so you do not need to describe them any further. The Spring sample applications explain the uses of other controllers.

Exploring the AbstractWizardFormController

A very useful subclass of AbstractFormController is AbstractWizardFormController, which allows you to implement a wizard-like series of pages. To demonstrate how to use this Controller implementation, we begin with a simple set of JSP pages: step1.jsp, step2.jsp, and finish.jsp (see Listing 17-30). The code of these JSP pages is not too different from the code used in the edit.jsp page used in Listing 17-24.

Listing 17-30. *Code for the step1.jsp, step2.jsp, and finish.jsp Pages*

```jsp
// step1.jsp
<%@taglib prefix="c" uri="http://java.sun.com/jstl/core"%>
<%@taglib prefix="spring" uri="http://www.springframework.org/tags"%>


<html>
<head>
    <c:set var="css"><spring:theme code="css"/></c:set>
        <c:if test="${not empty css}"><link rel="stylesheet"
            href="<c:url value="${css}"/>" type="text/css" /></c:if>
</head>
<body>
<form action="wizard.html?_target1" method="post">
<input type="hidden" name="_page" value="0">
<table>
    <tr>
        <td>Name</td>
        <td><spring:bind path="command.name">
                <input name="name" value="<c:out value="${status.value}"/>">
                <span class="error"><c:out value="${status.errorMessage}"/></span>
            </spring:bind>
        </td>
    </tr>
    <tr>
        <td></td>
        <td><input type="submit" value="Next"></td>
    </tr>
</table>
</form>
</body>
</html>


// step2.jsp
<%@taglib prefix="c" uri="http://java.sun.com/jstl/core"%>
<%@taglib prefix="spring" uri="http://www.springframework.org/tags"%>


<html>
<head>
    <c:set var="css"><spring:theme code="css"/></c:set>
        <c:if test="${not empty css}"><link rel="stylesheet"
            href="<c:url value="${css}"/>" type="text/css" /></c:if>
</head>
<body>
<form action="wizard.html?_target2" method="post">
<input type="hidden" name="_page" value="1">
```

```
<table>
    <tr>
        <td>Expiration Date</td>
        <td><spring:bind path="command.expirationDate">
                <input name="expirationDate"
                    value="<c:out value="${status.value}"/>">
                <span class="error"><c:out value="${status.errorMessage}"/></span>
            </spring:bind>
        </td>
    </tr>
    <tr>
        <td></td>
        <td><input type="submit" value="Next"></td>
    </tr>
</table>
</form>
</body>
</html>


// finish.jsp
<%@taglib prefix="c" uri="http://java.sun.com/jstl/core"%>
<%@taglib prefix="spring" uri="http://www.springframework.org/tags"%>


<html>
<head>
    <c:set var="css"><spring:theme code="css"/></c:set>
        <c:if test="${not empty css}"><link rel="stylesheet"
            href="<c:url value="${css}"/>" type="text/css" /></c:if>
</head>
<body>
<form action="wizard.html?_finish" method="post">
<input type="hidden" name="_page" value="2">
<table>
    <tr>
        <td>Register now?</td>
        <td><c:out value="${command}"/></td>
    </tr>
    <tr>
        <td></td>
        <td><input type="submit" value="Next"></td>
    </tr>
</table>
</form>
</body>
</html>
```

As you can see, the step1.jsp and step2.jsp pages simply populate the name and expirationDate properties of the command object, which is an instance of the Product domain object.

Now that we have set up the JSP pages, we must take a look at how the AbstractWizardFormController uses request parameters to control the page flow of the wizard. These parameters are summarized in Table 17-7.

Table 17-7. *Page Flow Request Parameters*

Parameter	Description
_target<value>	The value is a number that specifies the index in the pages[] property that the controller should go to when the current page is submitted and is valid or when the allowDirtyForward or allowDirtyBack properties are set to true.
_finish	If this parameter is specified, the AbstractWizardFormController invokes the processFinish() method and removes the command object from the session.
_cancel	If this parameter is specified, the AbstractWizardFormController invokes the processCancel() method, which, if not overridden, just removes the command object from the session. If you choose to override this method, do not forget to call the super() method or remove the command object from the session manually.
_page	This parameter (usually specified as <input type="hidden" name="_page" value="">) specifies the index of the page in the pages[] property.

Now that we have the JSP pages that form the wizard steps, we need to implement the RegistrationController as a subclass of the AbstractWizardFormController, as shown in Listing 17-31.

Listing 17-31. *RegistrationController Implementation*

```
package com.apress.prospring.ch17.web.registration;

public class RegistrationController extends AbstractWizardFormController {

    public RegistrationController() {
        setPages(new String[] {"registration-step1", "registration-step2",
            "registration-finish"});
        setSessionForm(true);
        setCommandClass(Product.class);
    }

    protected ModelAndView processFinish(HttpServletRequest request,
        HttpServletResponse response, Object command,
        BindException errors) throws Exception {
        Product product = (Product)command;

        System.out.println("Register " + product);
        return null;
    }
```

```
    protected void initBinder(HttpServletRequest request,
        ServletRequestDataBinder binder) throws Exception {
        SimpleDateFormat dateFormat = new SimpleDateFormat("dd/MM/yyyy");
        dateFormat.setLenient(false);
        binder.registerCustomEditor(Date.class, null,
            new CustomDateEditor(dateFormat, false));
    }

    protected void validatePage(Object command, Errors errors, int page,
        boolean finish) {
        getValidator().validate(command, errors);
    }
}
```

The code shown in Listing 17-31 represents almost the simplest implementation of the
AbstractWizardFormController subclass. Technically, all we have to implement is the
processFinish() method; but in our case, we also need to register a custom editor for the Date
class. Finally, we want to set the commandClass property to Product.class. We can set the pages
and sessionForm properties in the bean definition, which is shown in Listing 17-32, but we
decided to set the properties in the constructor instead.

Listing 17-32. *RegistrationController Bean and URL Mappings*

```xml
<?xml version="1.0" encoding="UTF-8" ?>
<!DOCTYPE beans PUBLIC "-//SPRING//DTD BEAN//EN"
    "http://www.springframework.org/dtd/spring-beans.dtd">

<beans>
    <bean id="publicUrlMapping"
        class="org.springframework.web.servlet.handler.SimpleUrlHandlerMapping">
        <property name="interceptors">
            <list>
                <ref local="bigBrotherHandlerInterceptor"/>
            </list>
        </property>
        <property name="mappings">
            <props>
                <!-- other props omitted -->
                <prop key="/registration/wizard.html">registrationController</prop>
            </props>
        </property>
    </bean>
    <bean id="registrationController"
        class="com.apress.prospring.ch17.web.registration.RegistrationController">
        <property name="validator"><ref bean="productValidator"/></property>
    </bean>
</beans>
```

Notice that we have not created mappings for the step1.jsp, step2.jsp, and finish.jsp pages; instead we have only created a single mapping for /registration/wizard.html, which is handled by the registrationController bean. We also set the validator property of the registrationController to the productValidator bean. We use the validator property in the validatePage() method to show that we can validate each page. The implementation we choose is exactly the same as the default implementation in AbstractWizardFormController, but if we want to, we can allow the user to move to the next page. The AbstractWizardFormController performs the validation before calling the processFinish() method, so there is no way to avoid validation and it is safe to skip validation on certain pages—the command object in the processFinish() method is guaranteed to be valid.[2]

The explanation of the AbstractWizardFormController we offer here is quite simple, but even so, it should give you a good starting point if you decide to use AbstractWizardFormController subclasses in your application.

File Upload

Spring handles file upload through implementations of the MultipartResolver interface. Out of the box, Spring comes with support for COS FileUpload and Commons FileUpload. By default, no default multipartResolver bean is declared, so if you want to use either the Commons or COS implementations or provide your own implementation, you have to declare the multipartResolver bean in the Spring application context, as shown in Listing 17-33.

Listing 17-33. *multipartResolver Declaration for Commons and COS FileUpload*

```
<?xml version="1.0" encoding="UTF-8" ?>
<!DOCTYPE beans PUBLIC "-//SPRING//DTD BEAN//EN" ➥
"http://www.springframework.org/dtd/spring-beans.dtd">

<beans>
    <bean id="multipartResolver"
        class="org.springframework.web.multipart.➥
            commons.CommonsMultipartResolver">
        <property name="maxUploadSize"> <value>100000</value> </property>
    </bean>

    <bean id="multipartResolver"
        class="org.springframework.web.multipart.cos.CosMultipartResolver">
        <property name="maxUploadSize"><value>100000</value></property>
    </bean>
    <!-- other beans as usual -->
</beans>
```

Do not forget that you can only have one multipartResolver bean; this means you have to choose which one to use when you declare the beans. Once the multipartResolver bean is configured, Spring knows how to handle multipart/form-data encoded requests to transform the form data into a byte[] array. To demonstrate that our newly configured multipartResolver

---

2. The command object is valid only if we supply an appropriate Validator implementation.

works, we are going to create ProductImageForm (see Listing 17-34) and
ProductImageFormController (see Listing 17-35) classes. The first one extends
SimpleFormController and handles the image upload, while the second one contains
properties for the image name and contents.

Listing 17-34. *ProductImageForm Implementation*

```
package com.apress.prospring.ch17.web.product;

public class ProductImageForm {

    private String name;
    private byte[] contents;

    public byte[] getContents() {
        return contents;
    }

    public void setContents(byte[] contents) {
        this.contents = contents;
    }

    public String getName() {
        return name;
    }

    public void setName(String name) {
        this.name = name;
    }
}
```

There is nothing spectacular about this class; it is a simple Java bean that exposes the
name and contents properties.

The ProductImageFormController's initBinder() method is much more interesting
(see Listing 17-35).

Listing 17-35. *ProductImageFormController Implementation*

```
package com.apress.prospring.ch17.web.product;

import javax.servlet.http.HttpServletRequest;
import javax.servlet.http.HttpServletResponse;

import org.springframework.validation.BindException;
import org.springframework.web.bind.ServletRequestDataBinder;
import org.springframework.web.multipart.support.ByteArrayMultipartFileEditor;
import org.springframework.web.servlet.ModelAndView;
import org.springframework.web.servlet.mvc.SimpleFormController;
```

```java
public class ProductImageFormController extends SimpleFormController {

    public ProductImageFormController() {
        super();
        setCommandClass(ProductImageForm.class);
        setFormView("products-image");
    }

    protected ModelAndView onSubmit(HttpServletRequest request,
        HttpServletResponse response, Object command,
        BindException errors) throws Exception {
        ProductImageForm form = (ProductImageForm)command;

        System.out.println(form.getName());
        byte[] contents = form.getContents();
        for (int i = 0; i < contents.length; i++) {
            System.out.print(contents[i]);
        }

        return new ModelAndView("products-index-r");
    }

    protected void initBinder(HttpServletRequest request,
        ServletRequestDataBinder binder) throws Exception {
        binder.registerCustomEditor(byte[].class,
            new ByteArrayMultipartFileEditor());
    }

}
```

The ByteArrayMultipartResolver class uses the multipartResolver bean from the application context to parse the contents of the multipart stream and return it as a byte[] array, which is then processed in the onSubmit() method.

Be careful when coding the JSP page for the file upload. Our favorite error is to forget the enctype attribute (highlighted in Listing 17-36) of the form element.

Listing 17-36. *Image.jsp Form*

```jsp
<%@taglib prefix="c" uri="http://java.sun.com/jstl/core"%>
<%@taglib prefix="spring" uri="http://www.springframework.org/tags"%>

<html>
<head>
    <c:set var="css"><spring:theme code="css"/></c:set>
        <c:if test="${not empty css}"><link rel="stylesheet"
            href="<c:url value="${css}"/>" type="text/css" /></c:if>
</head>
```

```
<body>
<form action="image.html" method="post" enctype="multipart/form-data">
<table>
    <tr>
        <td>Name</td>
        <td><spring:bind path="command.name">
                <input name="name" value="<c:out value="${status.value}"/>">
                <span class="error"><c:out value="${status.errorMessage}"/></span>
            </spring:bind>
        </td>
    </tr>
    <tr>
        <td>Image</td>
        <td><spring:bind path="command.contents">
                <input name="contents" type="file">
                <span class="error"><c:out value="${status.errorMessage}"/></span>
            </spring:bind>
        </td>
    </tr>
    <tr>
        <td></td>
        <td><input type="submit"></td>
    </tr>
</table>
</form>
</body>
</html>
```

As you can see, the JSP page is a standard HTML page, except for the enctype attribute. We must not forget to define this JSP page as a view in the views.properties file. Once we have done all that and recompiled and redeployed the application, we should be able to use the file upload page at products/image.html (see Figure 17-10).

File upload—or multipart handling in general—concludes the discussion of Spring MVC.

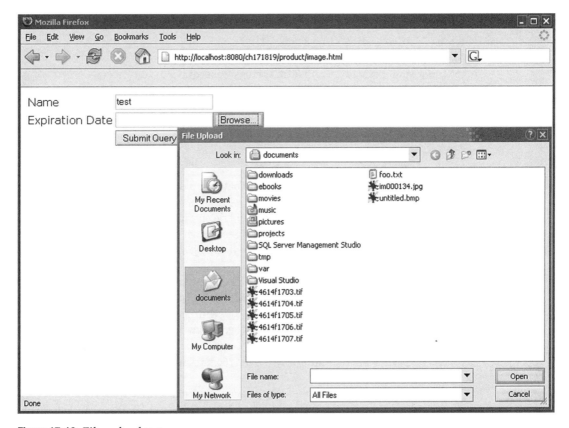

Figure 17-10. *File upload test*

Using Spring MVC in the Sample Application

We tried to use all technologies described in this chapter in the SpringBlog application, and in this section, we show the most interesting implementation details.

We start the implementation discussion with the URL mappings. To map the request URLs to the controllers in our application, we use a single `SimpleUrlHandlerMapping` bean. This bean maps all *.html and *.tile requests to the appropriate controller. The bean definition is shown in Listing 17-37, and as you can see, it is not too much different from the code presented in the "Using Handler Mappings" section earlier in this chapter.

Listing 17-37. *urlMapping Bean Definition*

```xml
<?xml version="1.0" encoding="UTF-8" ?>
<!DOCTYPE beans PUBLIC "-//SPRING//DTD BEAN//EN"
    "http://www.springframework.org/dtd/spring-beans.dtd">
<beans>
    <bean id="urlMapping"
        class="org.springframework.web.servlet.handler.SimpleUrlHandlerMapping">
        <property name="mappings">
            <props>
                <!-- Index -->
                <prop key="/index.html">indexController</prop>
                <!-- Entry -->
                <prop key="/entry/view.html">entryController</prop>
                <prop key="/entry/delete.html">entryController</prop>
                <prop key="/entry/edit.html">editEntryFormController</prop>
                <!-- Comment -->
                <prop key="/comment/index.html">commentController</prop>
                <prop key="/comment/delete.html">commentController</prop>
                <prop key="/comment/view.html">commentController</prop>
                <prop key="/comment/edit.html">editCommentFormController</prop>
                <!-- Audit -->
                <prop key="/admin/audit/*">auditController</prop>
                <!-- Tiles -->
                <prop key="/tiles/menu.html">menuTileController</prop>
                <!-- Users -->
                <prop key="/admin/users/index.html">usersController</prop>
                <!-- Login -->
                <prop key="/security/login.html">loginController</prop>
                <!-- Attachments -->
                <prop key="/attachment/*">attachmentController</prop>
            </props>
        </property>
    </bean>
</beans>
```

To support localized validation messages and messages in general, we configure a
ResourceBundleMessageSource bean. We chose this implementation over
ReloadableResourceBundleMessageSource because we did not need to reload the messages
in the lifecycle of the application. The definition of the messageSource bean is shown in
Listing 17-38.

Listing 17-38. *messageSource Bean Definition*

```xml
<?xml version="1.0" encoding="UTF-8" ?>
<!DOCTYPE beans PUBLIC "-//SPRING//DTD BEAN//EN"
    "http://www.springframework.org/dtd/spring-beans.dtd">
<beans>
    <bean id="messageSource"
        class="org.springframework.context.support.ResourceBundleMessageSource">
        <property name="basename">
            <value>messages</value>
        </property>
    </bean>
</beans>
```

Here, we created two messages properties files: one for the Czech language stored in the messages_cs.properties and one in messages.properties, which contains the text in English and also represents the fallback properties file.

To use `messageSource` and to make sure the blog entries are valid before we pass them to the Business Tier, we implement `CommentValidator` and `EntryValidator`. These validators are a standard implementation; the only interesting point to consider is the implementation of the `supports()` method, which we show in Listing 17-39.

Listing 17-39. *CommentValidator Implementation*

```java
package com.apress.prospring.business.validators;

import org.springframework.validation.Errors;
import org.springframework.validation.Validator;

import com.apress.prospring.domain.Comment;

public class CommentValidator implements Validator {

    public boolean supports(Class clazz) {
        return Comment.class.isAssignableFrom(clazz);
        // return clazz.isAssignableFrom(Comment.class);
    }

    public void validate(Object obj, Errors errors) {
        Comment comment = (Comment)obj;
        if (comment.getSubject() == null || comment.getSubject().length() == 0) {
            errors.rejectValue("subject", "required", null, "required");
        }
        if (comment.getBody() == null || comment.getBody().length() == 0) {
            errors.rejectValue("body", "required", null, "required");
        }
    }

}
```

We implemented the `supports()` method using `Comment.class.isAssignableFrom(clazz)` because we had to create a subclass of the `Comment` domain class to support the uploading of the attachments. We defined the validators as regular Spring beans, and the controllers that require validation simply reference the validator beans, as shown in Listing 17-40.

Listing 17-40. *Validator Beans and Their Usage*

```xml
<?xml version="1.0" encoding="UTF-8" ?>
<!DOCTYPE beans PUBLIC "-//SPRING//DTD BEAN//EN"
    "http://www.springframework.org/dtd/spring-beans.dtd">
<beans>
    <bean id="commentValidator"
        class="com.apress.prospring.business.validators.CommentValidator"/>
    <bean id="editCommentFormController"
        class="com.apress.prospring.web.comment.EditCommentFormController">
        <property name="blogManager"><ref bean="blogManager"/></property>
        <property name="validator"><ref local="commentValidator"/></property>
    </bean>

    <bean id="entryValidator"
        class="com.apress.prospring.business.validators.EntryValidator"/>
    <bean id="editEntryFormController"
        class="com.apress.prospring.web.entry.EditEntryFormController">
        <property name="blogManager"><ref bean="blogManager"/></property>
        <property name="validator"><ref local="entryValidator"/></property>
    </bean>
</beans>
```

The implementation of the controllers in the application is not different from the sample code offered in the "Working with Controllers" section earlier in this chapter. However, here we create a set of convenience classes that give their subclasses access to the `blogManager` property. The convenience classes we implement are the `AbstractBlogManagerController`, `AbstractBlogManagerFormController`, and `AbstractBlogManagerMultiactionController`. All these abstract classes implement the `InitializingBean` interface to make sure that the `blogManager` property is set to an instance of the `BlogManager` implementation; moreover, the `AbstractBlogManagerController` is not a subclass of `AbstractController`, it just implements the `Controller` interface, making the class much more lightweight.

Typical usage of the `AbstractBlogManagerMultiactionController` is shown in Listing 17-41.

Listing 17-41. *Typical Usage of AbstractBlogManagerMultiactionController*

```
package com.apress.prospring.web.entry;

import java.util.HashMap;
import java.util.Map;

import javax.servlet.http.HttpServletRequest;
import javax.servlet.http.HttpServletResponse;

import org.springframework.web.bind.RequestUtils;
import org.springframework.web.servlet.ModelAndView;

import com.apress.prospring.domain.Entry;
import com.apress.prospring.web.AbstractBlogManagerMultiactionController;
import com.apress.prospring.web.security.SessionSecurityManager;

public class EntryController extends AbstractBlogManagerMultiactionController {

    public ModelAndView handleView(HttpServletRequest request,
        HttpServletResponse response) throws Exception {
        int entryId = RequestUtils.getRequiredIntParameter(request, "entryId");
        Entry e = getBlogManager().getEntry(entryId);
        Map model = new HashMap();
        model.put("entry", e);
        return new ModelAndView("entry-view", model);
    }

    public ModelAndView handleDelete(HttpServletRequest request,
        HttpServletResponse response) throws Exception {
        boolean confirm = RequestUtils.getIntParameter(request, "confirm", 0) == 1;
        int entryId = RequestUtils.getRequiredIntParameter(request, "entryId");
        if (confirm) {
            getBlogManager().deleteEntry(entryId,
                SessionSecurityManager.getUser(request));
            return new ModelAndView("entry-deleted");
        } else {
            Map model = new HashMap();
            model.put("entry", getBlogManager().getEntry(entryId));
            return new ModelAndView("entry-delete", model);
        }
    }
}
```

Notice that you do not need to implement the `InitializingBean` interface to make sure that the required properties are set. In fact, the `afterPropertiesSet()` is implemented as `final`, which actually prevents the subclasses from providing their own implementation.

We do not implement any security the way you would expect in standard web applications. Instead, we create the `SessionSecurityManager` class that contains static methods that perform just a very basic support for retrieving user identities. To extend the security code a bit further to make sure it actually restricts the actions that require a user to be logged in, you can implement a `HandlerInterceptor`, that makes sure the `User` domain object is set in the session and redirect it to a login page if this is not the case. To allow some of the URLs to be accessible without the user being logged in, you split the `urlMapping` bean into two beans. One contains the mappings with no restrictions, and the other contains the `HandlerInterceptor` implementation and the mappings that require a user to be logged in.

For view technologies, we use JSP pages to render the output returned to the client and we use Tiles to aggregate the output of the JSP pages into the final page layout. A more detailed discussion of the Tiles framework and other view technologies follows in Chapter 18.

Summary

In this chapter, you learned how to use the Spring MVC architecture to build flexible and powerful web applications. You know how to use Spring to configure your controllers, and you know which controller to use for different usage scenarios. You also know how to validate the data the users enter on the forms, how to build applications that display the output in the user's language, and how to make the user's experience even better by providing themes. File upload is also quite easy to implement.

But there is more! We have barely covered the various view implementations Spring offers. Read on and you will find out how to use Tiles to make your web applications extremely flexible, elegant, and easy to maintain. You will also find out about other view technologies, such as PDF and Excel as well as a very fast Velocity template engine.

■ ■ ■

CHAPTER 18

Beyond JSP

In the previous chapter, we used JSP pages to generate the output that was then sent to the client's browser for rendering. Naturally, we can build the entire application using just JSP pages, but if we did, the application and JSP pages would probably become too complex to manage.

Even though JSP pages are very powerful, they can present a considerable processing overhead. Because Spring MVC fully decouples the view from the logic, the JSP pages should not contain any Java scriptlets. Even if the JSP pages contain no scriptlets, they still need to be compiled—a lengthy operation—and the runtime performance is sometimes not as good as we would like to see. Velocity is a viable alternative; it offers much faster rendering times while not restricting the developer too much.

In this chapter, we are going to explore the Tiles framework, which allows you to organize the output generated by the controllers into separate components that you can assemble together using a master template. This greatly simplifies the visual design of the application, and you can make any changes to the overall layout of the output very quickly and you will need very little space for coding mistakes.

However, there are some cases where HTML output is simply not suitable and we have to use PDF or Excel output to present the data to the user.

To summarize, we are going to cover the following view technologies:

JSP pages: We begin with the most widely used view technology in J2EE applications. Specifically we cover the Spring tag library and show you how to use it in your JSP pages.

Velocity: In this section, you learn how to create and use Velocity to render the model prepared by the controllers. We are also going to cover Spring Velocity macros that work almost exactly like the Spring JSP tags.

XSLT: If you have an existing XML document that represents the data you want to render, you should consider using XSLT views. We explain how to use the XSLT view to render the data easily and efficiently.

PDF and Excel: Expanding on the XSLT views, we show you how to use PDF and Excel views. We explain how to create an Excel and a PDF view using the model data.

Tiles: Finally, this chapter explores how to create a final output that consists of small components that are combined into a final page output. This allows you to create more flexible page layouts.

Using JSP Pages

JSP pages are a tested technology with which many developers are familiar. Because JSP pages are compiled into Java classes, and because they can contain Java code, developers may be too tempted to move parts of the business logic into the JSP pages. Needless to say, that is a very bad thing: not only does it violate the MVC type 2 architecture, it also makes the application very difficult to maintain.

There is no way to stop the developers from using Java scriptlets in the JSP pages, but you should not need to use them. If you ever find yourself needing a scriptlet, or if you find yourself performing much logic using the standard JSTL tags, consider writing a custom tag.

Spring offers a list of custom tags that simplify access to Spring features in your JSP pages, as shown in Table 18-1.

Table 18-1. *Spring Custom Tags*

Custom Tag	Description
htmlEscape	Sets a value indicating whether the output of other Spring tags should be escaped. If true, the HTML formatting strings (such as <, />, &, etc.) are replaced by their HTML visual codes.
message	Displays a message retrieved from the Spring messageSource beans; the message is identified by its code.
theme	Retrieves a value for an element defined in the current theme.
hasBindErrors	Evaluates a nested body if the page has validation errors.
nestedPath	Sets a nested path that is then used by the bind tag.
bind	Binds to an object and provides an object that allows you to access the bound value and any error messages.
transform	Transforms a variable to a string using the currently registered PropertyEditor. You can only use this with the bind tag.

Let's take a closer look at using the Spring custom tags. We begin with the message tag.

Using the message Tag

Let's create a messageSource bean definition in the application context file and an appropriate message.properties file. Listing 18-1 shows the definition of the messageSource bean.

Listing 18-1. *messageSource Bean Definition*

```
<?xml version="1.0" encoding="UTF-8" ?>
<!DOCTYPE beans PUBLIC "-//SPRING//DTD BEAN//EN" ➥
"http://www.springframework.org/dtd/spring-beans.dtd">

<beans>
    <bean id="messageSource"
        class="org.springframework.context.support.ResourceBundleMessageSource">
        <property name="basename"><value>messages</value></property>
    </bean>
    <!-- other beans omitted -->
</beans>
```

If you want to learn more about messageSource beans in web applications, go back to
Chapter 17. Let's create a trivial message.properties file. If you want to, you can create
message.properties files for multiple languages. Listing 18-2 shows the message.properties file
in English.

Listing 18-2. *message.properties File*

```
greeting=Hello <b>Spring</b> Framework
required=This field is required and cannot be empty
```

Now, we create a default.jsp page that uses the Spring JSTL library to display the greeting
message inside an H1 element. Listing 18-3 shows the code for this page.

Listing 18-3. *Code for default.jsp Page*

```
<%@taglib prefix="spring" uri="http://www.springframework.org/tags"%>
<%@taglib prefix="c" uri="http://java.sun.com/jstl/core"%>

<html>
<head>
<title>Pro Spring</title>
</head>
<body>
<h1><spring:message code="greeting"/></h1>
</body>
</html>
```

The usage of the message tag in this code is quite simple: we simply use it to output text that is looked up in the messageSource bean. This is obviously the simplest use of this tag, which you can modify by setting its attributes as shown in Table 18-2.

Table 18-2. *message Tag Attributes*

Attribute	Description
code	The code you use to look up the message text in the messageSource bean.
arguments	A comma-separated list of arguments passed to the getMessage() method of the messageSource bean.
text	Text that is displayed if the entry code is not found in the messageSource. Internally, this is used as an argument in the MessageSource.getMessage() call.
var	Specifies an object that is set to the value of the message.
scope	Specifies a scope to which the object specified in the var attribute is going to be inserted.
htmlEscape	Indicates whether the message tag should escape the HTML text. If not specified, the global value defined by the htmlEscape tag is used.

Using the theme Tag

The theme tag allows you to create themed pages. It uses the themeResolver bean to load all theme element definitions. For a more detailed explanation of the themeResolver bean, refer to Chapter 17. To see the tag work, you need to make sure that there is a themeResolver bean definition in the application context file, as shown in Listing 18-4.

Listing 18-4. *themeResolver Bean Definition*

```
<?xml version="1.0" encoding="UTF-8" ?>
<!DOCTYPE beans PUBLIC "-//SPRING//DTD BEAN//EN" ➥
"http://www.springframework.org/dtd/spring-beans.dtd">

<beans>
    <bean id="themeResolver"
        class="org.springframework.web.servlet.theme.FixedThemeResolver">
        <property name="defaultThemeName"><value>cool</value></property>
    </bean>
    <!-- other beans omitted -->
</beans>
```

The code fragment of the default.jsp page in Listing 18-5 displays the typical usage of the theme bean.

Listing 18-5. *theme Tag Usage*

```
<link rel="stylesheet" href="<spring:theme code="css"/>">
```

The theme tag has similar attributes to the message tag, which allows you to further control the values it generates. In fact, the theme tag is a subclass of the message tag, the only difference is that the codes are looked up in a themeResolver rather than messageSource bean. The attributes you can use are summarized in Table 18-3.

Table 18-3. *theme Tag Attributes*

Attribute	Description
code	The code used to look up the theme element text in the themeResolver bean.
arguments	A comma-separated list of arguments that is passed to the getMessage() method of the messageSource bean.
text	Text that is displayed if the entry code is not found in the messageSource. Internally, this is used as an argument in the MessageSource.getMessage() call.
var	Specifies an object that is set to the value of the theme resource.
scope	Specifies a scope to which the object specified in the var attribute is going to be inserted.
htmlEscape	Indicates whether the message tag should escape the HTML text. If not specified, the global value defined by the htmlEscape tag is used.

Using the hasBindErrors Tag

This tag evaluates its body if the bean specified in its name attribute has validation errors. If there are no errors, the body of the tag is skipped. Listing 18-7 demonstrates how to use this tag in a JSP page.

Listing 18-6. *hasBindErrors Tag*

```
<spring:hasBindErrors name="command">
    There were validation errors: <c:out value="${errors}"/>
</spring:hasBindErrors>
```

As with other beans, Table 18-4 lists attributes you can use to fine-tune the behavior of this tag.

Table 18-4. *hasBindErrors Attributes*

Attribute	Description
name	Name of the bean for which errors will be looked up.
htmlEscape	Indicates whether the message tag should escape the HTML text. If not specified, the global value defined by the htmlEscape tag is used.

Using the nestedPath Tag

This tag is used to include another object in the path resolution operation performed by the bind tag. The nestedPath tag also copies objects in an existing nestedPath to the nestedPath it creates.

The only attribute of this tag is path, which specifies a path to the object that is to be included in the nestedPath. The code in Listing 18-7 shows how to use the nestedPath tag to add a user attribute to the nestedPath, thus giving the bind tag access to properties exposed by the user bean.

Listing 18-7. *nestedPath Tag Usage*

```
<spring:nestedPath name="user"/>
```

Using the bind Tag

The bind tag is the most important tag exposed by the Spring tag library. It greatly simplifies data entry and validation. In its simplest form, it looks up an object's property, identified by the path attribute, and exposes a new variable named status that holds the object's value and validation errors. This is the most common usage scenario and it is shown in code fragment in Listing 18-8.

Listing 18-8. *The bind Tag*

```
<spring:bind path="command.name">
    <input name="name" value="<c:out value="${status.value}"/>">
    <span class="error"><c:out value="${status.errorMessage}"/></span>
</spring:bind>
```

This code assumes a command object is in the current scope, and that it exposes the name property. The bind tag then creates a status object and sets its status property to an instance of the BindStatus object for the property identified by the path attribute. If there are any validation errors, the errors property contains an instance of Errors; the PropertyEditor used to parse the value is in the propertyEditor property.

You can further control this tag with the attributes listed in Table 18-5.

Table 18-5. *bind Tag Attributes*

Attribute	Description
path	Identifies the object and its property that are used to create the status, errors, and propertyEditor properties.
ignoreNestedPath	If set to true, the bind tag ignores any available nested paths as set by the nestedPath tag.
htmlEscape	Indicates whether the message tag should escape the HTML text. If not specified, the global value defined by the htmlEscape tag is used.

Using the transform Tag

The `transform` tag looks up the appropriate `PropertyEditor` for the object specified in the `value` attribute and uses it to output the `String` representation. You can use this attribute instead of the Format JSTL tags to keep the formatting rules in Spring. The tag's usage is shown in Listing 18-9.

Listing 18-9. *transform Tag Usage*

```
<spring:transform value="command.expirationDate"/>
```

If the `expirationDate` property of the `command` object is of the `Date` class, and if there is a `PropertyEditor` registered for `Date.class` with specified formatting rules, the `transform` tag outputs the appropriately formatted date string. All attributes of the `transform` tag are listed in Table 18-6.

Table 18-6. *transform Tag Attributes*

Attribute	Description
value	Identifies the value to be formatted.
var	If specified, this attribute sets the output to the object specified in the value attribute.
scope	Specifies the scope to which the object specified in the var attribute is going to be inserted.
htmlEscape	Indicates whether the message tag should escape the HTML text. If this is not specified, the global value defined by the htmlEscape tag is used.

JSP Best Practices

As we have stated before, JSP pages offer the largest set of features you can use to generate HTML output. Because the JSP pages are *compiled* into Java classes, the applications using JSPs can suffer from low performance, especially when the pages are still being compiled. Another consideration is that if the content of the page is too big, the JSP will not compile into a Java class because Java methods cannot be more than 64KB long.

From an architectural point of view, there is a danger that developers will use Java code in the pages to perform business operations. This is clearly a violation of the MVC architecture and it *will* cause problems in the future development of the application.

If you keep all these potential limitations in mind, you will no doubt find that JSP pages are an excellent technology to use, especially when combined with tag libraries. However, there are other view technologies that may not be as feature-rich as JSP, but offer other benefits; the first in line is Velocity.

Using Velocity

Velocity is another view technology that you can use in the Spring views. Unlike JSP pages, Velocity templates are not compiled into Java classes. They are interpreted by the Velocity engine.

Even though the pages are interpreted, the time needed to generate the output is very short; in fact, in most cases, Velocity templates outperform the JSP pages. However, there are a couple of drawbacks: the JSP custom tags cannot be used in Velocity and the developers have to familiarize themselves with the syntax of the Velocity Template Language.

Velocity is a stand-alone project that is used in many applications that produce text output. You can download the latest version of the Velocity libraries from `http://jakarta.apache.org/velocity/`. We are going to use version 1.4 in this chapter. In addition to Velocity, you need the VelocityTools you can download from `http://jakarta.apache.org/velocity/tools/`.

Integrating Velocity and Spring

A Velocity engine must be initialized before you can use it. The `VelocityConfigurer` class performs this initialization. We need the `velocityConfigurer` bean to set up resource paths to the Velocity template files.

Once an instance of the `VelocityConfigurer` class is created in the application context, we can use Velocity just like any other view in our application. Listing 18-10 shows how to declare a `velocityConfigurer` bean.

Listing 18-10. *velocityConfigurer Bean Declaration*

```
<?xml version="1.0" encoding="UTF-8" ?>
<!DOCTYPE beans PUBLIC "-//SPRING//DTD BEAN//EN" ➥
"http://www.springframework.org/dtd/spring-beans.dtd">

<beans>
    <bean id="velocityConfigurer"
        class="org.springframework.web.servlet.view.velocity.VelocityConfigurer">
        <property name="resourceLoaderPath">
            <value>WEB-INF/views/</value></property>
    </bean>
</beans>
```

Next, we add a view definition in the views.properties file, as shown in Listing 18-11.

Listing 18-11. *Velocity View Definition*

```
#product/index
product-index.class=org.springframework.web.servlet.view.velocity.VelocityView
product-index.url=product/index.vm
```

The `product-index` view is going to be created as an instance of `VelocityView` and the template file is going to be loaded from WEB-INF/views/product/index.vm. The first part of the path to the template file is defined in the `velocityConfigurer` bean and the second part is declared in the views.properties file. All that is left to do is create a simple Velocity template (see Listing 18-12).

Listing 18-12. *The product/index.vm Velocity Template*

```
<html>
<head>
</head>
<body>

All products:<br>
#foreach($product in $products)
    ${product.name}<br>
#end

</body>
</html>
```

Finally, in Listing 18-13, we are going to modify the `ProductController` from Chapter 17 to make sure it returns an instance of `ModelAndView("product-index", …)`.

Listing 18-13. *Modified ProductController*

```
public class ProductController extends MultiActionController {
    private List<Product> products;

    public ModelAndView index(HttpServletRequest request,
        HttpServletResponse response) {
        return new ModelAndView("product-index", "products", products);
    }

}
```

When the application is rebuilt and deployed, we should see a list of products at /ch18/ product/index.html, as shown in Figure 18-1.

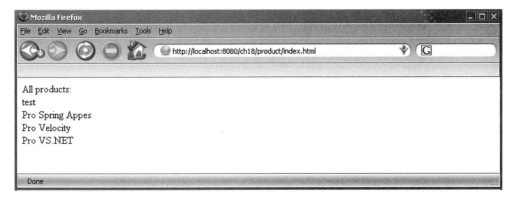

Figure 18-1. *Output of the ProductController.index() method in the browser*

Advanced Velocity Concepts

Just a simple `View` implementation would be a very limited Velocity support. Spring goes much further by allowing you to customize the properties of the Velocity engine by setting its properties through the `velocityConfigurer` bean, and by providing you with macros that have functionality similar to the Spring JSTL tags introduced in the "Using JSP Pages" section.

You can set the properties of the Velocity Engine in one of two ways: either by providing a standard properties file or by setting the properties directly in the `velocityConfigurer` bean definition, as shown in Listing 18-14.

Listing 18-14. *Setting Velocity Engine Properties*

```xml
<?xml version="1.0" encoding="UTF-8" ?>
<!DOCTYPE beans PUBLIC "-//SPRING//DTD BEAN//EN" ➡
"http://www.springframework.org/dtd/spring-beans.dtd">

<beans>
    <bean id="velocityConfigurer"
        class="org.springframework.web.servlet.view.velocity.VelocityConfigurer">
        <property name="resourceLoaderPath">
            <value>WEB-INF/views/</value></property>
        <property name="velocityProperties">
            <props>
                <prop key="file.resource.loader.cache">false</prop>
            </props>
        </property>
        <property name="configLocation">
            <value>/WEB-INF/classes/velocity.properties</value>
        </property>
    </bean>
</beans>
```

Naturally, you have to decide whether you want to set the Velocity engine properties in a properties file or whether you want to keep them in the bean definition.

Perhaps the most important Velocity support comes from the Velocity macros Spring exposes in the Velocity templates; these macros work just like the Spring JSTL tags. The most important macro is the `#springBind` macro. It gives you access to the Spring Validator framework from your Velocity templates. If you need to use the Spring macros in a particular view, you must set Spring's `exposeSpringMacroHelpers` property to `true`.

To demonstrate the usage of the Velocity macros, we will now create a Velocity template that allows the users to enter product details. In this template, we provide full validation and error control. We use the `ProductFormController` from Chapter 17 but modify the views.properties file and, obviously, create the edit.vm template. Let's get started with Listing 18-15, which shows the modified views.properties file.

Listing 18-15. *views.properties File*

```
#products
product-index.class=org.springframework.web.servlet.view.velocity.VelocityView
product-index.url=product/index.vm
product-index-r.class=org.springframework.web.servlet.view.RedirectView
product-index-r.url=/ch17/product/index.html
product-edit.class=org.springframework.web.servlet.view.velocity.VelocityView
product-edit.url=product/edit.vm
product-edit.exposeSpringMacroHelpers=true

#other views omitted
```

In Listing 18-15, the code in bold shows the lines we added to support the `product-edit` view as a Velocity template. Notice that we set the `exposeSpringMacroHelpers` property to `true`; this allows us to create the edit.vm template, as shown in Listing 18-16.

Listing 18-16. *edit.vm template Contents*

```
<form action="edit.html" method="post">
<input type="hidden" name="productId" value="${command.productId}">
<table>
    <tr>
        <td>Name</td>
        <td>#springBind("command.name")
                <input name="name" value="$!status.value">
                <span class="error">$status.errorMessage</span>
        </td>
    </tr>
    <tr>
        <td>Expiration Date</td>
        <td>#springBind("command.expirationDate")
                <input name="expirationDate" value="$!status.value">
                <span class="error">$status.errorMessage</span>
        </td>
    </tr>
    <tr>
        <td></td>
        <td><input type="submit"></td>
    </tr>
</table>
</form>
```

Notice that we can use the `#springBind` macro in the template. This macro does precisely the same work its JSTL counterpart does: it allows us to access the Spring Validator framework from the template. The result is exactly what you would expect—the /product/edit.html file shows a standard HTML form with a working validator (see Figure 18-2).

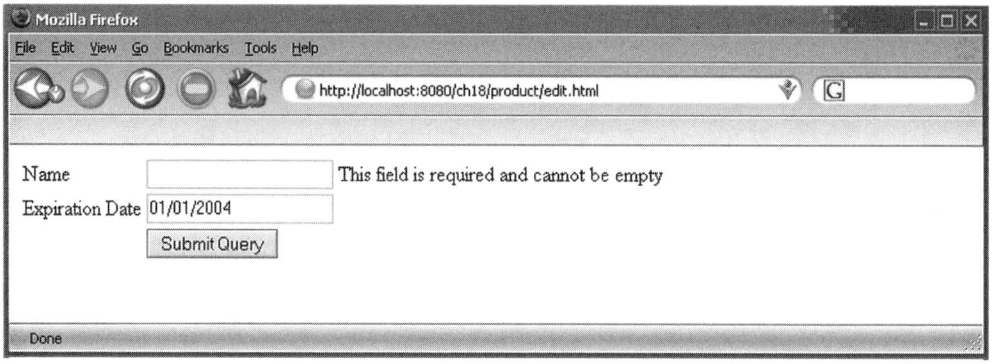

Figure 18-2. *Edit form with validator message*

There is no difference between the ProductFormController code when you are using Velocity views and the code you use in the JSP views; the only differences are the view definition in the views.properties file and the presence of the velocityConfigurer bean in the application context.

The code we used in the edit.vm file in Listing 18-16 still doesn't take full advantage of the available Spring macros. We could further simplify the code by using the #springFormInput, #springFormTextarea, #springFormSingleSelect, #springFormMultiSelect, #springFormRadioButtons, #springCheckboxes, and #showErrors macros, but there is little advantage in doing so. A better solution is to spend a little more time writing the code, and making sure that it does exactly what we need it to, instead of relying on too many tools to do **all** the work for us.

The final set of properties of the VelocityView that is worth your attention is composed of velocityFormatterAttribute, dateToolAttribute, and numberToolAttribute. If you specify these values in the views.properties file, the instances of the VelocityFormatter, the DateTool, and the NumberTool are inserted into the VelocityContext using the names set in the views.properties file.

Velocity provides a good alternative to JSP pages; the lack of features is well justified by its speed. Unfortunately, you cannot yet use Velocity in Tiles, which is a great disadvantage.

Using XSLT Views

XSLT offers an elegant way to transform XML data into any other plain text format. If you already have an XML document, it may be worth using an XSLT view to transform it to HTML output.

Let's create a ProductsXsltView that takes the List of Product objects, builds an XML document, and then uses XSLT to transform it to HTML. Listing 18-17 shows the implementation of the ProductsXsltView class.

Listing 18-17. *ProductsXsltView Implementation*

```java
package com.apress.prospring.ch18.web.views;

import java.util.Iterator;
import java.util.List;
import java.util.Map;

import javax.servlet.http.HttpServletRequest;
import javax.servlet.http.HttpServletResponse;

import org.jdom.Document;
import org.jdom.Element;
import org.jdom.output.DOMOutputter;
import org.springframework.web.servlet.view.xslt.AbstractXsltView;
import org.w3c.dom.Node;

import com.apress.prospring.ch18.domain.Product;

public class ProductsXsltView extends AbstractXsltView {

    protected Node createDomNode(Map model, String root,
        HttpServletRequest request, HttpServletResponse response)
        throws Exception {

        List products = (List)model.get("products");
        if (products == null)
            throw new NullPointerException("Products not in model");
        Document document = new Document();
        Element rootElement = new Element(root);
        document.setRootElement(rootElement);

        for (Iterator i = products.iterator(); i.hasNext();) {
            Product product = (Product)i.next();
            Element pe = new Element("product");
            pe.setAttribute("productId", Integer.toString(product.getProductId()));
            pe.setAttribute("expirationDate",
                product.getExpirationDate().toString());
            pe.setText(product.getName());

            rootElement.addContent(pe);
        }

        return new DOMOutputter().output(document);
    }

}
```

Remember, it is not important how you create the Node object that the createDomNode() method returns. In this case, we used JDOM, because it is a bit easier to use than the W3C XML API.

The AbstractXsltView class allows you to add additional name/value pairs that you can pass as the stylesheet parameters. For each <xsl:param name="param-name">param-value</xsl:param>, you must add an entry to a Map returned from the getParameters() method.

To test our view, we are going to create an XSLT template that transforms the XML document to a very simple HTML page, as shown in Listing 18-18.

Listing 18-18. *XSLT Template*

```xml
<?xml version="1.0"?>
<xsl:stylesheet version="1.0" xmlns:xsl="http://www.w3.org/1999/XSL/Transform">
    <xsl:template match="/">
        <html>
            <head>
                <title>Pro Spring</title>
            </head>
            <body>
                <h1>Available Products</h1>
                <xsl:for-each select="products/product">
                    <xsl:value-of select="."/>
                    <br />
                </xsl:for-each>
            </body>
        </html>
    </xsl:template>
</xsl:stylesheet>
```

Just like with any other view, we now need to declare ProductsXsltView in the views.properties file, as shown in Listing 18-19.

Listing 18-19. *views.properties Declaration of the ProductsXsltView*

```
product-index.class=com.apress.prospring.ch18.web.views.ProductsXsltView
product-index.root=root
product-index.stylesheetLocation=/WEB-INF/views/product/index.xslt
```

When we deploy the application, we can see the product listing as a regular HTML page.

Be careful when you use XSLT views because the processing involved is very complex, and in most cases, an XSLT view is the slowest view available. In Listings 18-17 to 18-19, we have actually built the XML document and then used XSLT to transform it to HTML, this is, without a doubt, the worst way to use XSLT views. However, if you already have an XML document and all you need to do is transform it to HTML, you can certainly benefit from implementing an XSLT view.

Using PDF Views

Even though the previously discussed view technologies are powerful, they still depend on the browser to interpret the generated HTML code. Even though basic HTML renders without any problems on all browsers, you cannot guarantee that a page with complex formatting is going to look the same on all browsers. What's more, sometimes HTML is not suitable if you need to print the output, or use a particularly complex formatting. If this is the case, your best solution is to use a document format that renders consistently on all clients. For this, you need to include the iText (www.lowagie.com/iText/) JAR file, which is already included in the Spring distribution.

Unfortunately, there is no PDF template language, so we have to implement the views ourselves. As you saw in Chapter 17, implementing a custom view is not a difficult task, and Spring provides a convenience superclass, `AbstractPdfView`, which you can use in your PDF view implementation.

Implementing a PDF View

The PDF view we implement in this section displays product details. We do not change the `ProductController` whose `view()` method processes the requests to view a product, but we do need to change to the views.properties file and implement the `ProductPdfView` class to create the PDF output.

Let us begin by looking at Listing 18-20, which shows the implementation of the `ProductPdfView` class using the iText library.

Listing 18-20. *ProductPdfView Implementation*

```
package com.apress.prospring.ch18.web.views;

import java.util.Map;

import javax.servlet.http.HttpServletRequest;
import javax.servlet.http.HttpServletResponse;

import org.springframework.web.servlet.view.document.AbstractPdfView;

import com.apress.prospring.ch18.domain.Product;
import com.lowagie.text.Document;
import com.lowagie.text.Paragraph;
import com.lowagie.text.pdf.PdfWriter;

public class ProductPdfView extends AbstractPdfView {

    protected void buildPdfDocument(Map model, Document document,
        PdfWriter writer, HttpServletRequest request,
        HttpServletResponse response) throws Exception {
        Product product = (Product) model.get("product");
        if (product == null) throw new
            NullPointerException("Product not present in the model");
```

```
        Paragraph header = new Paragraph("Product details");
        header.font().setSize(20);
        document.add(header);

        Paragraph content = new Paragraph(product.getName());
        document.add(content);

        Paragraph footer = new Paragraph("Pro Spring Chapter 18");
        footer.setAlignment(Paragraph.ALIGN_BOTTOM);
        document.add(footer);
    }

}
```

This view simply extracts the Product domain object from the model and uses its data to add Paragraphs to the document instance. Because the ProductPdfView is a subclass of AbstractPdfView, we do not have to take care of setting the appropriate HTTP headers or performing any I/O—the superclass takes care of all that.

Before we can verify that the newly created ProductPdfView class works, we need to modify the views.properties file, make sure that the product-view's class is set to ProductPdfView, and make sure that the ProductController.view() adds a Product instance to the model. Listing 18-21 shows the changes we need to make to the views.properties file.

Listing 18-21. *views.properties File for product-view*

```
product-view.class=com.apress.prospring.ch18.web.views.ProductPdfView
```

You may notice that we do not need to set any additional properties on product-view.

Next, in Listing 18-22, we make sure that the ProductController.view() method returns the correct instance of ModelAndView.

Listing 18-22. *ProductController.view Implementation*

```
public class ProductController extends MultiActionController {
    private Product createProduct(int productId, String name,
        Date expirationDate) {
        Product product = new Product();
        product.setProductId(productId);
        product.setName(name);
        product.setExpirationDate(expirationDate);

        return product;
    }
```

```
    public ModelAndView view(HttpServletRequest request,
        HttpServletResponse response) throws Exception {
        Product product = createProduct(1, "Pro Spring", new Date());
        return new ModelAndView("product-view", "product", product);
    }
}
```

When the application is rebuilt and deployed, we should see the PDF document in Figure 18-3 returned for /product/view.html.

Figure 18-3. *ProductPdfView output*

Generating a PDF from your Spring web application is not too difficult, even though a lot of coding is involved.

Using Excel Views

If your application requires Excel output, you can use Spring to create an Excel view rather than directly writing the contents of an Excel file to the output stream. Just like AbstractPdfView, Spring provides AbstractExcelView, which you can subclass to further simplify development of new Excel views. You are going to need the Jakarta POI (http://jakarta.apache.org/poi/) library to perform the actual Excel I/O; the POI JAR file comes with the Spring distribution.

Now we are going to show you a simple ProductsExcelView that renders a list of products into an Excel spreadsheet. We implement ProductsExcelView and modify the views.properties file. The implementation of ProductsExcelView extends AbstractExcelView, as shown in Listing 18-23.

Listing 18-23. *ProductsExcelView Implementation*

```
package com.apress.prospring.ch18.web.views;

import java.util.List;
import java.util.Map;

import javax.servlet.http.HttpServletRequest;
import javax.servlet.http.HttpServletResponse;

import org.apache.poi.hssf.usermodel.HSSFSheet;
import org.apache.poi.hssf.usermodel.HSSFWorkbook;
import org.springframework.web.servlet.view.document.AbstractExcelView;

import com.apress.prospring.ch18.domain.Product;

public class ProductsExcelView extends AbstractExcelView {

    private static final int COL_PRODUCT_ID = 0;
    private static final int COL_NAME = 1;
    private static final int COL_EXPIRATION_DATE = 2;

    protected void buildExcelDocument(Map model, HSSFWorkbook wb,
        HttpServletRequest request, HttpServletResponse response)
        throws Exception {
        List<Product> products = (List<Product>)model.get("products");
        HSSFSheet sheet = wb.createSheet("Products");
        int row = 0;
        getCell(sheet, row, COL_PRODUCT_ID).setCellValue("ProductId");
        getCell(sheet, row, COL_NAME).setCellValue("Name");
        getCell(sheet, row, COL_EXPIRATION_DATE).setCellValue("ExpirationDate");
        row++;
        for (Product product : products) {
            getCell(sheet, row, COL_PRODUCT_ID).setCellValue(
                product.getProductId());
            getCell(sheet, row, COL_NAME).setCellValue(
                product.getName());
            getCell(sheet, row, COL_EXPIRATION_DATE).setCellValue(
                product.getExpirationDate());
            row++;
        }
    }

}
```

The code for the `ProductsExcelView` class is quite simple: we get a `List` of `Product` objects and iterate over the list, adding a row to the Excel workbook in each iteration.

Next, we make sure that the `product-index` view declared in views.properties is referencing the newly created `ProductsExcelView` class, as shown in Listing 18-24.

Listing 18-24. *views.properties with ProductsExcelView Definition*

```
product-index.class=com.apress.prospring.ch18.web.views.ProductsExcelView
```

Again, we do not need to set any additional properties for this view. The `ProductController.index()` method does not need to be modified because it already returns `ModelAndView("product-index", …)`. When we make a request to /product/index.html, we get an Excel spreadsheet, as shown on Figure 18-4.

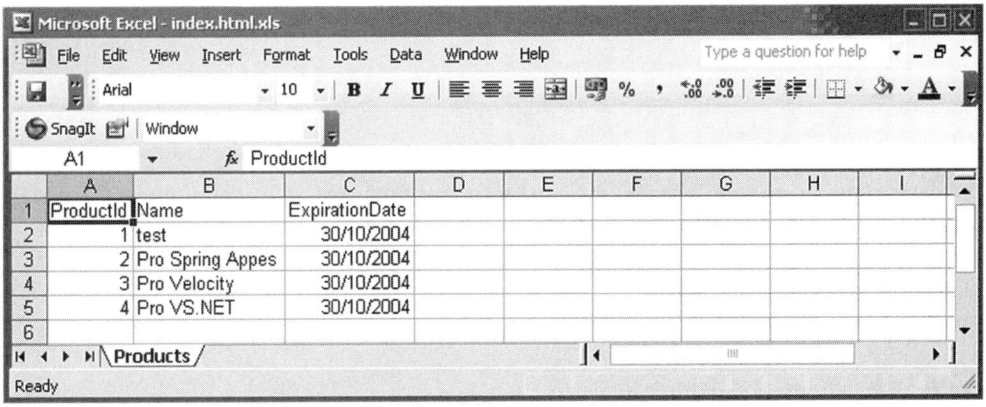

Figure 18-4. *Output of the ProductsExcelView*

Using `AbstractExcelView` is very similar to using `AbstractPdfView`: in both cases, we have to implement code that creates the **content** of the document; we do not need to handle the I/O.

Using Tiles

Unlike all the previous view technologies, Tiles is not actually used to generate the output. Instead, it can combine the output from various views into a master view. Each individual tile can consist of a collection of tiles, a JSP page, or output directly written to the `HttpResponse` object in the `handleRequest()` method of a Spring controller.

Tiles is a part of the Jakarta Struts project (`http://struts.apache.org/`). At the time of writing, the latest version of Struts was 1.2.4. Do not forget to include the Struts library (struts.jar) in your Spring project.

Integrating Tiles and Spring

Tiles requires some initialization to be performed. In a Struts application, the initialization is performed when Tiles is loaded as a plugin; in Spring, we need to create a `TilesConfigurer` bean that loads the tile definitions XML file and configures the Tiles framework, as shown in Listing 18-25.

Listing 18-25. *TilesConfigurer Definition in Application Context*

```
<?xml version="1.0" encoding="UTF-8" ?>
<!DOCTYPE beans PUBLIC "-//SPRING//DTD BEAN//EN" ➥
"http://www.springframework.org/dtd/spring-beans.dtd">

<beans>
    <bean id="tilesConfigurer"
        class="org.springframework.web.servlet.view.tiles.TilesConfigurer">
        <property name="definitions">
            <list>
                <value>/WEB-INF/tiles-layout.xml</value>
            </list>
        </property>
    </bean>
</beans>
```

This bean creates the Tiles DefinitionsFactory instance using the definition files listed in the definitions property of the TilesConfigurer bean.

Before we can use Tiles in our application, we must create the tiles-layout.xml file. We start with a very simple file (see Listing 18-26) that simply verifies that the Tiles support is properly configured in our Spring application.

Listing 18-26. *Simple Tiles Definition File*

```
<?xml version="1.0" encoding="ISO-8859-1" ?>
<!DOCTYPE tiles-definitions PUBLIC
    "-//Apache Software Foundation//DTD Tiles Configuration 1.1//EN"
    "http://jakarta.apache.org/struts/dtds/tiles-config_1_1.dtd">

<tiles-definitions>
    <definition name=".dummy"/>
</tiles-definitions>
```

When we build and deploy the application, the application server's console prints log messages like the following from the TilesConfigurer class to indicate that the Tiles support has been correctly configured.

```
21:07:58,001 INFO  [TilesConfigurer] TilesConfigurer: initializion started
21:07:58,011 INFO  [TilesConfigurer] TilesConfigurer: adding definitions ➥
[/WEB-INF/tiles-layout.xml]
21:07:58,211 INFO  [TilesConfigurer] TilesConfigurer: initialization completed
```

Now that we have verified that the Tiles support is working, we need to think about the tiles we want to use in our application. A typical layout of a web page might look like the one shown in Figure 18-5. We are going to call this page a root page. It is a JSP page that uses the Tiles tag library to insert the appropriate tiles according to their definitions in the tiles configuration files.

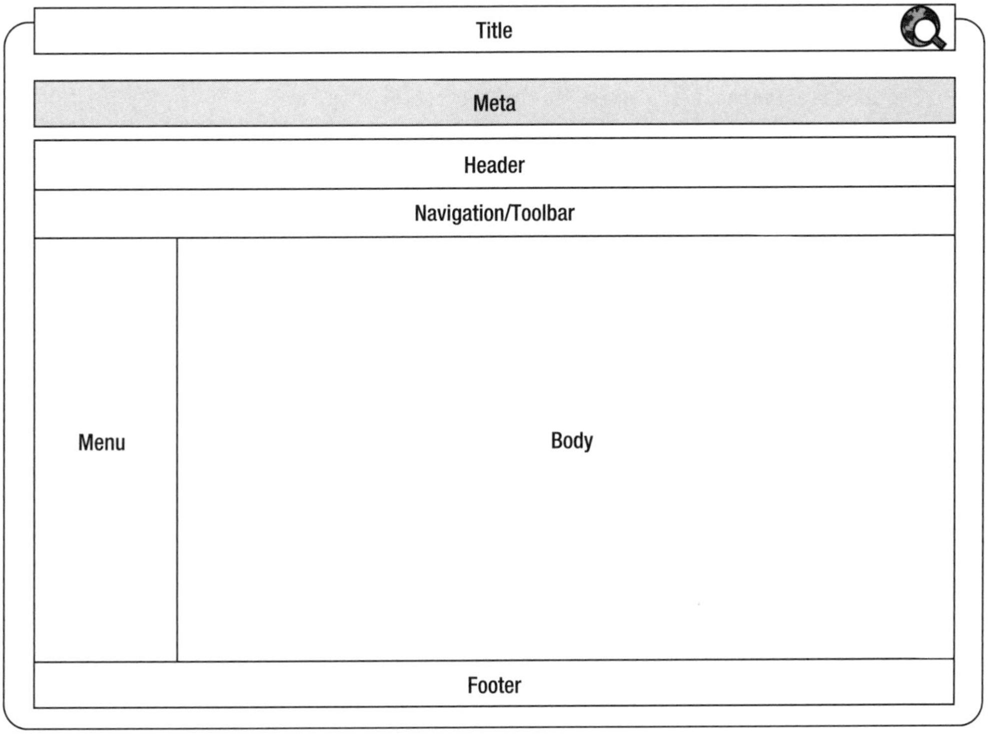

Figure 18-5. *Tiles layout*

Looking at this layout, you might think that we are going to create five tiles—one for each section of the final page layout. In fact, we are going to add another tile, which is going to output the content of the <meta> tag in the root layout.

Let's begin by creating the root.jsp page that places all the tiles into an HTML table, as shown in Listing 18-27.

Listing 18-27. *The root.jsp Page*

```
<%@taglib prefix="spring" uri="http://www.springframework.org/tags"%>
<%@taglib prefix="tiles" uri="http://jakarta.apache.org/struts/tags-tiles"%>
<%@taglib prefix="c" uri="http://java.sun.com/jstl/core"%>

<html>
<head>
    <c:set var="css"><spring:theme code="css"/></c:set>
        <c:if test="${not empty css}">
            <link rel="stylesheet" href="<c:url value="${css}"/>"
                type="text/css" />
        </c:if>
    <tiles:insert attribute="meta"/>
    <title><tiles:getAsString name="title"/></title>
</head>

<table cellspacing="0" cellpadding="0" width="700px" align="center"
    bgcolor="#ffffff">
    <tr>
        <td colspan="2"><tiles:insert attribute="header"/></td>
    </tr>
    <tr>
        <td colspan="2"><tiles:insert attribute="toolbar"/></td>
    </tr>
    <tr height="400px">
        <td width="150px" valign="top"><tiles:insert attribute="menu"/></td>
        <td width="550px" valign="top"><tiles:insert attribute="body"/></td>
    </tr>
    <tr>
        <td colspan="2"><tiles:insert attribute="footer"/></td>
    </tr>
</table>

</body>
</html>
```

The root layout page is quite straightforward: we define the layout of the page, and we use Tiles tags to specify where Tiles should insert the appropriate pages. However, the Tiles framework still does not know what content to insert for all <tiles:insert> and <tiles:getAsString> tags. To solve this problem, we need to create the Tiles definition file, as shown in Listing 18-28.

Listing 18-28. *Tiles Definition File*

```
<?xml version="1.0" encoding="ISO-8859-1" ?>
<!DOCTYPE tiles-definitions PUBLIC
    "-//Apache Software Foundation//DTD Tiles Configuration 1.1//EN"
    "http://jakarta.apache.org/struts/dtds/tiles-config_1_1.dtd">

<tiles-definitions>
    <!-- Abstract root definition -->
    <definition name=".root" path="/WEB-INF/views/tiles/root.jsp">
        <put name="title" value="CHANGE-ME"/>
        <put name="meta" value="/WEB-INF/views/tiles/meta.jsp"/>
        <put name="header" value="/WEB-INF/views/tiles/header.jsp"/>
        <put name="menu" value="/WEB-INF/views/tiles/menu.jsp"/>
        <put name="toolbar" value="/WEB-INF/views/tiles/toolbar.jsp"/>
        <put name="footer" value="/WEB-INF/views/tiles/footer.jsp"/>
    </definition>

    <!-- Index -->
    <definition name=".index" extends=".root">
        <put name="title" value="Main Page"/>
        <put name="body" value="/WEB-INF/views/index.jsp"/>
    </definition>
</tiles-definitions>
```

This definition file introduces a number of Tiles concepts. Let's go through the features used here, line by line. The first definition element's attribute name is set to .root, and the element also includes the path attribute. This instructs Tiles to use the JSP page specified in the path attribute and to use the values specified in the put elements to display their content. However, the .root definition is missing the body attribute we are using in the root.jsp page. The definition we created is an abstract definition because it does not define all the attributes used. We must extend this abstract definition to ensure that all the necessary attributes are defined, as shown in the second definition element. Its name attribute is set to .index and its extends attribute specifies that it should inherit all the values in the put elements from the definition element whose name is .root. It **overrides** the title value and **adds** the body value—just as you would expect in Java code.

Before we can move ahead and configure the Spring views to use Tiles, we need to stress that the individual pages that are used as tiles **must not** include the standard HTML headers. However, if you are using JSP pages, they **must** include all taglib references. The requirement for no document HTML tags is obvious because the document tags are already included in the root page. The taglibs must be included in the JSP pages because Tiles requests each tile individually—the tiles are not actually aware that the output they are rendering is being collected by another layer and formatted using the root layout.

Now that we know how what the requirements are for individual tiles, we must configure the Spring views to use the Tiles framework. To do this, we are going to modify the views.properties file, as shown in Listing 18-29.

Listing 18-29. *views.properties Definition*

```
#index
index.class=org.springframework.web.servlet.view.tiles.TilesJstlView
index.url=.index
```

This file defines that the view name index is going to be created as an instance of TilesJstlView and its url is going to be .index.

■**NOTE** You may be wondering why we are using dots (.) in the Tiles definition names and no dots in the view names. This is simply a practice we find useful when managing applications with a large number of views and Tiles definitions. By looking at the names, you can immediately identify which one is a tile and which one is a Spring view.

The last step we need to do before we can test our application (shown in Listing 18-30) is to make sure that the IndexController's handleRequestInternal() method is returning the correct view.

Listing 18-30. *IndexController Class*

```java
package com.apress.prospring.ch18.web;

public class IndexController extends AbstractController {

    protected ModelAndView handleRequestInternal(HttpServletRequest request,
        HttpServletResponse response) throws Exception {

        setCacheSeconds(10);
        Map<String, Object> model = new HashMap<String, Object>();
        model.put("Greeting", "Hello World");
        model.put("Server time", new Date());

        return new ModelAndView("index", model);
    }

}
```

When we now deploy the application and make a request to the /index.html page, the TilesConfigurer bean parses the Tiles configuration, loads the .root and .index definitions, calls each JSP page, renders their output, and then finally takes the JSP output and outputs it into the appropriate places in the root.jsp page, whose output is returned to the client, as shown in Figure 18-6.

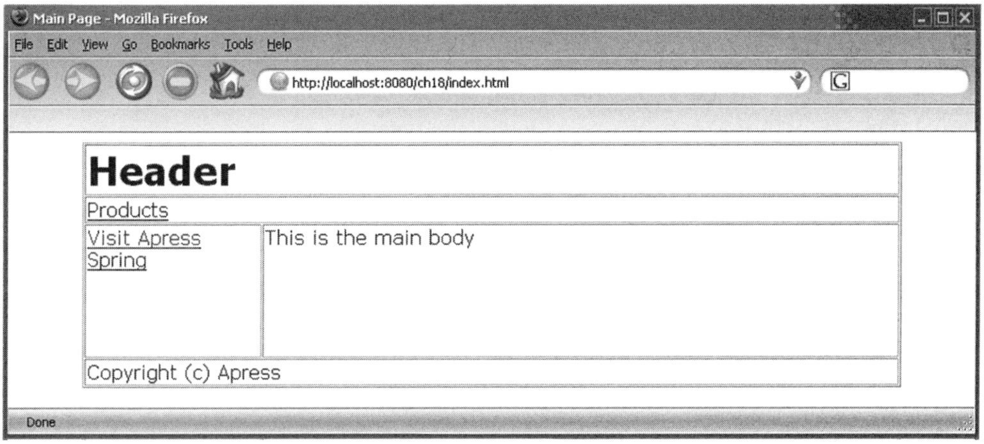

Figure 18-6. *The .root Tiles view*

Advanced Tiles Concepts

In the previous section, we showed you how to use Tiles in your Spring application in a way that is not too different from the @include JSP directive. The true power of Tiles comes from the fact that Tiles can take any output and paste it into the appropriate place. A tile can consist of other tiles, JSP pages, or even simple output from a controller. We start with a tile whose content is the output written to the response stream by a simple controller.

First, we create a tile that prints out the memory usage information directly to the HttpServletResponse's Writer object. We create another servlet mapping in web.xml to map all *.tile requests to the ch18 servlet. The only reason for this is to keep the request namespace clean of any ambiguous request URLs. The modified web.xml file is shown in Listing 18-31.

Listing 18-31. *web.xml Descriptor*

```
<?xml version="1.0" encoding="ISO-8859-1"?>
<!DOCTYPE web-app PUBLIC
    "-//Sun Microsystems, Inc.//DTD Web Application 2.3//EN"
    "http://java.sun.com/dtd/web-app_2_3.dtd">
<web-app>
    <!-- omitted for clarity -->
    <servlet-mapping>
        <servlet-name>ch18</servlet-name>
        <url-pattern>*.tile</url-pattern>
    </servlet-mapping>
</web-app>
```

Next, we create a TileController that is a subclass of MultiActionController. We implement only one method in the TileController, the handleStatus(), which prints out the memory information. Listing 18-32 shows that this implementation is quite trivial.

Listing 18-32. *TileController.handleStatus Implementation*

```java
package com.apress.prospring.ch18.web.tiles;

import java.io.PrintWriter;
import java.lang.management.ManagementFactory;
import java.lang.management.MemoryPoolMXBean;
import java.util.List;

import javax.servlet.http.HttpServletRequest;
import javax.servlet.http.HttpServletResponse;

import org.springframework.web.servlet.ModelAndView;
import org.springframework.web.servlet.mvc.multiaction.MultiActionController;

public class TileController extends MultiActionController {

    private void writeMemoryPoolMXBean(MemoryPoolMXBean bean,
        PrintWriter writer) {
        writer.append("<pre><tt>");

        writer.append("Name: "); writer.append(bean.getName());
        writer.append("\n");
        writer.append("Type: "); writer.append(bean.getType().name());
        writer.append("\n");
        writer.append("Usage: "); writer.append(bean.getUsage().toString());
        writer.append("\n");

        writer.append("</pre></tt>");
    }


    public ModelAndView handleStatus(HttpServletRequest request,
        HttpServletResponse response) throws Exception {
        List<MemoryPoolMXBean> beans =
                ManagementFactory.getMemoryPoolMXBeans();
        PrintWriter writer = response.getWriter();
        for (MemoryPoolMXBean bean : beans) {
            writeMemoryPoolMXBean(bean, writer);
        }
        return null;
    }

}
```

Notice that the handleStatus() method returns null, which means that Spring does not attempt to perform any view processing.

Next, we declare the `tileController` bean in the application context file together with a `tileMethodNameResolver` bean and an entry in the `publicUrlMapping` bean, as shown in Listing 18-33.

Listing 18-33. *The tileController and tileMethodNameResolver Beans*

```xml
<?xml version="1.0" encoding="UTF-8" ?>
<!DOCTYPE beans PUBLIC "-//SPRING//DTD BEAN//EN" ➥
"http://www.springframework.org/dtd/spring-beans.dtd">

<beans>
    <bean id="publicUrlMapping"
        class="org.springframework.web.servlet.handler.SimpleUrlHandlerMapping">
        <property name="mappings">
            <props>
                <prop key="/index.html">indexController</prop>
                <prop key="/product/index.html">productController</prop>
                <prop key="/product/view.html">productController</prop>
                <prop key="/product/edit.html">productFormController</prop>
                <prop key="/product/image.html">productImageFormController</prop>

                <prop key="/tile/*.tile">tileController</prop>
            </props>
        </property>
    </bean>

    <!-- Tile -->
    <bean id="tileController"
        class="com.apress.prospring.ch18.web.tiles.TileController">
        <property name="methodNameResolver">
            <ref local="tileMethodNameResolver"/>
        </property>
    </bean>
    <bean id="tileMethodNameResolver"
        class="org.springframework.web.servlet.mvc.multiaction.➥
PropertiesMethodNameResolver">
        <property name="mappings">
            <props>
                <prop key="/tile/status.tile">handleStatus</prop>
            </props>
        </property>
    </bean>
</beans>
```

We test that our `tileController` works by making a request to /ch18/tile/status.tile. This prints the JVM memory status information.

Finally, we create a StatusController as a subclass of AbstractController, add it to the application context file, and add an entry to the publicUrlMapping bean to map /status.html to the StatusController, as shown in Listing 18-34.

Listing 18-34. *The statusController Bean Definition and a New Entry in the publicUrlMapping Bean*

```xml
<?xml version="1.0" encoding="UTF-8" ?>
<!DOCTYPE beans PUBLIC "-//SPRING//DTD BEAN//EN" ➥
"http://www.springframework.org/dtd/spring-beans.dtd">

<beans>
    <bean id="publicUrlMapping"
        class="org.springframework.web.servlet.handler.SimpleUrlHandlerMapping">
        <property name="mappings">
            <props>
                <prop key="/index.html">indexController</prop>
                <prop key="/status.html">statusController</prop>
                <prop key="/product/index.html">productController</prop>
                <prop key="/product/view.html">productController</prop>
                <prop key="/product/edit.html">productFormController</prop>
                <prop key="/product/image.html">productImageFormController</prop>

                <prop key="/tile/*.tile">tileController</prop>
            </props>
        </property>
    </bean>
    <bean id="statusController"
        class="com.apress.prospring.ch18.web.StatusController"/>
</beans>
```

The code in the StatusController.handleRequestInternal() method simply returns an instance of ModelAndView("status"). This means that we need to add an entry to the tiles-layout.xml file and views.properties, as shown in Listing 18-35.

Listing 18-35. *Additions to tiles-layout.xml and views.properties*

tiles-layout.xml:
```xml
<?xml version="1.0" encoding="ISO-8859-1" ?>
<!DOCTYPE tiles-definitions PUBLIC
    "-//Apache Software Foundation//DTD Tiles Configuration 1.1//EN"
    "http://jakarta.apache.org/struts/dtds/tiles-config_1_1.dtd">
```

```
<tiles-definitions>
    <!-- other definitions omitted -->

    <definition name=".status" extends=".root">
        <put name="title" value="Status"/>
        <put name="body" value="/tile/status.tile"/>
    </definition>
</tiles-definitions>
```

views.properties:
```
status.class=org.springframework.web.servlet.view.tiles.TilesJstlView
status.url=.status
```

When we make a request to /ch18/status.html, Spring instantiates the status view defined in views.properties. This view points to the .status tile definition, which specifies that the value for the body element should be taken from the output generated by /ch18/tile/status.tile. The final result may look like what appears in Figure 18-7.

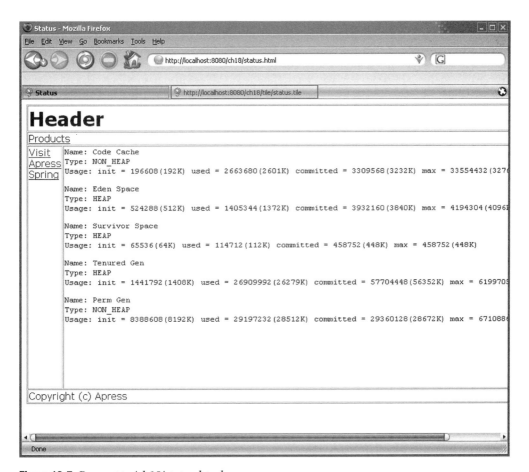

Figure 18-7. *Request to /ch18/status.html*

You would rarely use a controller that prints out the output directly to the output stream; in most cases, a controller returns a ModelAndView that identifies a view and data to be rendered by the view. You can use this approach in a Tiles application. To demonstrate this, we add the handleMenu() method to the TileController, which is going to read the links from the configuration file and render them using a JSP page.

First, we modify the TileController, as shown in Listing 18-36.

Listing 18-36. *Modified TileController*

```
public class TileController extends MultiActionController {

    public ModelAndView handleMenu(HttpServletRequest request,
        HttpServletResponse response) throws Exception {
        return new ModelAndView("tile-menu", "menu", menu);
    }

    public void setMenu(Map menu) {
        this.menu = menu;
    }
}
```

The handleMenu() method takes the menu property set in the application context file and forwards it to the tile-menu view, which is defined as JstlView in views.properties, as shown in Listing 18-37.

Listing 18-37. *views.properties Contents*

```
#index
index.class=org.springframework.web.servlet.view.tiles.TilesJstlView
index.url=.index

#status
status.class=org.springframework.web.servlet.view.tiles.TilesJstlView
status.url=.status

#menu tile
tile-menu.class=org.springframework.web.servlet.view.JstlView
tile-menu.url=/WEB-INF/views/tiles/menu2.jsp
```

Listing 18-38 shows that the JSP page that displays the menu is quite trivial; it uses the core JSTL tags to iterate over all items in a map.

Listing 18-38. *The tile/menu2.jsp Page*

```
<%@taglib prefix="c" uri="http://java.sun.com/jstl/core"%>

<c:forEach items="${menu}" var="item">
    <a href="<c:out value="${item.value}"/>"><c:out value="${item.key}"/></a><br>
</c:forEach>
```

Finally, in Listing 18-39, we modify the tiles-layout.xml and the ch18-servlet.xml files to use the newly created menu.

Listing 18-39. *The tiles-layout.xml and ch18-servlet.xml Files*

tiles-layout.xml:
```
<tiles-definitions>
    <!-- Abstract root definition -->
    <definition name=".root" path="/WEB-INF/views/tiles/root.jsp">
        <put name="title" value="CHANGE-ME"/>
        <put name="meta" value="/WEB-INF/views/tiles/meta.jsp"/>
        <put name="header" value="/WEB-INF/views/tiles/header.jsp"/>
        <put name="menu" value="/tile/menu.tile"/>
        <put name="toolbar" value="/WEB-INF/views/tiles/toolbar.jsp"/>
        <put name="footer" value="/WEB-INF/views/tiles/footer.jsp"/>
    </definition>
    <!-- other definitions omitted -->
</tiles-definitions>
```

ch18-servlet.xml:
```
<beans>
    <bean id="tileController"
        class="com.apress.prospring.ch18.web.tiles.TileController">
        <property name="methodNameResolver">
            <ref local="tileMethodNameResolver"/></property>
        <property name="menu">
            <map>
                <entry key="Apress">
                    <value>http://www.apress.com</value></entry>
                <entry key="Spring">
                    <value>http://www.springframework.org</value></entry>
                <entry key="Cake Solutions">
                    <value>http://www.cakesolutions.net</value></entry>
            </map>
        </property>
    </bean>
    <bean id="tileMethodNameResolver"
        class="org.springframework.web.servlet.mvc.multiaction.➥
PropertiesMethodNameResolver">
        <property name="mappings">
            <props>
                <prop key="/tile/status.tile">handleStatus</prop>
                <prop key="/tile/menu.tile">handleMenu</prop>
            </props>
        </property>
    </bean>
</beans>
```

Because we modified the `.root` tile definition, we can use our new menu in all the definitions that extend the `.root` definition. You can see the newly displayed menu in Figure 18-8.

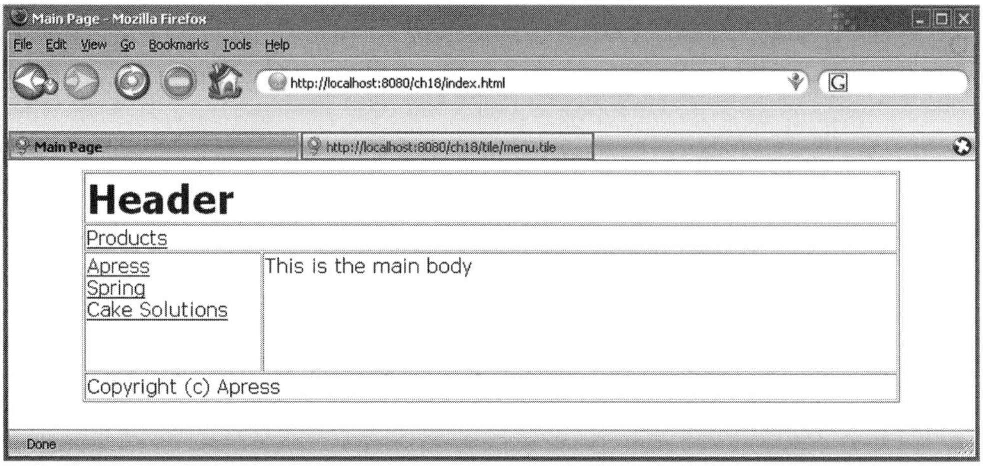

Figure 18-8. *New menu tile*

Tiles Best Practices

Tiles is a very powerful framework that can greatly simplify the development of web applications. With its power comes the complexity of configuration files and different request paths. Because of this power, it is important to make sure you use and enforce a logical naming convention in the entire project.

We feel that the best way to organize the requests URLs is to use *.html for the final pages returned to the client and *.tile for requests whose output is to be rendered as a tile. The view naming conventions follow the directory structure of the source files, so a Spring `JstlView` definition for a JSP page located in tile/menu.jsp is named `tile-menu`. And finally, a tile definition that you might use to render the output of the /product/index.html page is best named `.product.index`.

At the time of writing, there was only experimental support for Tiles Velocity views, so for the time being your only option is to use JSP pages as the source for individual tiles.

Using Views in the Sample Application

The SpringBlog sample application uses the Tiles framework extensively. We also implement an Excel view in SpringBlog to allow the users to download the Excel spreadsheet version of all blog entries. The sources for the tiles are JSP pages and there is also static content that does not need to be served by the web container.

The directory structure shown in Figure 18-9 explains the situation better: the /web/src/as-web/WEB-INF directory contains files that are served and processed by the web container, whereas the /web/src/httpd-web contains files that can be served by the web server. Finally, the /web/src/resources folder contains the various properties and additional configuration files.

Figure 18-9. *Directory structure of the web component of the sample application*

We believe that this directory structure is the best way to organize files you need for the Web Tier of an application. The Ant build script packages the files into a WAR file, keeping the directory structure shown in Figure 18-9. The only exception is the resources directory. All files from this directory are packaged to WEB-INF/classes directory.

Let's take a closer look at the files we needed to create to successfully implement the various views used in the Web Tier of the application.

resources/messages.properties: This is the default message source file. If no localized messages_<LID>.properties is found, the messageSource bean falls back to using this file.

resources/messages_cs.properties: This is the Czech translation of the messages used in the messageSource bean.

resources/tiles-config.xml: This is the Tiles layout file. The contents of this file follow the rules outlined in the "Using Tiles" section.

resources/views.properties: This is the configuration file the ResourceBundleViewResolver uses to allow Spring to create instances of the View implementations using only the view name in the ModelAndView constructor.

views/.jsp:** These are standard JSP tile pages. This means that the JSPs contain the standard HTML tags. The only file that starts with the <HTML> tag is the views/tiles/root-layout.jsp, which represents the root tile layout.

To demonstrate other view technologies, in the SpringBlog application, we included the Excel view that allows the users to download all entries in an Excel spreadsheet. The implementation of this view is simply an extension of the view we introduced in the "Using Excel Views" section.

We encourage you to go through the source tree yourselves, focusing on the naming conventions used for the view names, JSP pages, and Tile names. We believe that it is very important to have a clearly defined naming strategy, even for such small projects as SpringBlog.

Summary

In this chapter, you learned about the view technologies available in a Spring application. Now you know that there's a lot more to generating web output than using JSP pages. You can use Velocity if you need top performance, and you can control PDF or Excel file output if you need to ensure that the formatting is the same on all browsers or if you need to generate output that the users will print out. You also saw how to set up Tiles to integrate all the different views together.

If you are interested in mastering Velocity, look for *Pro Jakarta Velocity: From Professional to Expert* by Rob Harrop (Apress, 2004), which covers the Velocity Template Language and its uses as well as all the internals of Velocity.

The next chapter concludes the web applications development section of the book by focusing on using the Struts framework in Spring web applications.

CHAPTER 19

Spring and Struts

This chapter concludes the section on web application development. We focus on the integration of Struts in Spring web applications. To follow the examples in this chapter, you need the Struts libraries, which you can obtain from `http://struts.apache.org/`.

Whether you decide to use Struts or Spring MVC in the web layer of your application greatly depends on the amount of code you have already implemented. If you are starting the implementation from scratch, we recommend that you use Spring MVC because it represents cleaner implementations of the MVC architecture.

In this chapter, we specifically focus on the following aspects of using Struts in a Spring web application:

Introducing Struts: Even though we do not mean for this text to be a complete description of Struts, we do explore the Struts architecture and explain how it integrates with the MVC architecture; we also provide a simple Struts application.

Accessing Spring beans: If you find that you need to use Spring in your Struts application, refer to this section. Here we show you how to gain access to the Spring application context and how to retrieve beans from the context programmatically in Struts actions.

Using other views: If you are writing a hybrid application, you may be surprised to find out that the views you configured in your Spring application context are not available to the Struts framework. In this section, we show you how to configure Struts to use other view technologies and we discuss the implications of doing so.

Struts actions as Spring beans: This section explains how to configure Struts actions as regular Spring beans; doing so allows you to take advantage of the full feature set of the Spring framework.

Combining Struts and Spring MVC: The last section explores how to integrate and connect the Struts actions and Spring MVC controllers so that you can take advantage of Spring views and other features accessible only to Spring MVC controllers.

Exploring the Struts Architecture

Struts represents an implementation of MVC type 2 architecture. The most important components of Struts are the `ActionServlet`, `Action`, and `ActionForm` subclasses. `ActionServlet` represents the controller that intercepts the requests and forwards them for further processing based on the configuration file for the `ActionForm` and `Action` subclasses. `ActionForm` transfers data users entered to `Action`, which performs necessary operations using the Business Tier components of the application and finally forwards to a view. An overview of the Struts MVC architecture appears in Figure 19-1.

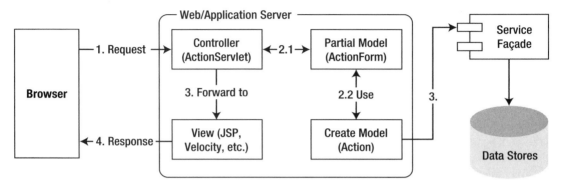

Figure 19-1. *Struts MVC architecture*

The controller (`ActionServlet`) uses a configuration file (typically struts-config.xml) to load definitions of the `Action` subclasses that will be used to handle the requests. Based on the request URL, the controller finds an action definition that is going to handle the request. The Struts framework processes the request, checks the configuration files, and performs the following actions:

- If the action requires a form bean, the controller creates an appropriate instance of it. The form bean is used to collect data from the user; it usually exposes properties for the data to be collected. It can also validate the data by overriding the `validate()` method.

- The action instance is created and its `execute()` method is called. The primary purpose of the action bean is to perform any logic necessary to process the request. Once the action bean finishes processing the request, it returns an `ActionForward` instance to indicate to the controller the action that needs to be performed next. The `ActionForward` instance can represent a forward to another action or a view that displays the model represented by the form bean and any attributes set in the request and session scopes.

The architecture of Struts offers much more than we covered in this short introduction. In this chapter, we continue to use Struts plugins to demonstrate details of Spring integration and the use of other view technologies.

First Struts Application

With the Struts architecture in mind, in this section, we create a simple Struts application with just one Struts action that forwards to a JSP page. It does not perform any special processing; it simply proves that the Struts framework is loaded and that the Spring application is using it to process the requests.

Now we create a web.xml descriptor, a struts-config.xml Struts descriptor file, and Spring applicationContext.xml files. The web.xml file includes the Spring servlets as well as the Struts servlet, both of which appear in Listing 19-1.

Listing 19-1. *The web.xml Descriptor*

```xml
<?xml version="1.0" encoding="ISO-8859-1"?>
<!DOCTYPE web-app PUBLIC
    "-//Sun Microsystems, Inc.//DTD Web Application 2.3//EN"
    "http://java.sun.com/dtd/web-app_2_3.dtd">
<web-app>
    <display-name>Pro Spring Chapter 19 Sample application</display-name>
    <description>dtto</description>
    <context-param>
        <param-name>contextConfigLocation</param-name>
        <param-value>WEB-INF/applicationContext.xml</param-value>
    </context-param>
    <servlet>
        <servlet-name>context</servlet-name>
        <servlet-class>org.springframework.web.context.ContextLoaderServlet
        </servlet-class>
        <load-on-startup>1</load-on-startup>
    </servlet>
    <servlet>
        <servlet-name>ch19</servlet-name>
        <servlet-class>
            org.springframework.web.servlet.DispatcherServlet
        </servlet-class>
        <load-on-startup>2</load-on-startup>
    </servlet>
    <servlet>
        <servlet-name>action</servlet-name>
        <servlet-class>org.apache.struts.action.ActionServlet</servlet-class>
        <load-on-startup>3</load-on-startup>
    </servlet>
    <servlet-mapping>
        <servlet-name>ch19</servlet-name>
        <url-pattern>*.html</url-pattern>
    </servlet-mapping>
    <servlet-mapping>
        <servlet-name>ch19</servlet-name>
        <url-pattern>*.tile</url-pattern>
    </servlet-mapping>
    <servlet-mapping>
        <servlet-name>action</servlet-name>
        <url-pattern>*.do</url-pattern>
    </servlet-mapping>
</web-app>
```

The web.xml file still holds references to the ch19, which is a Spring DispatcherServlet, but it adds a definition of the action servlet, which is a Struts ActionServlet that is mapped to Struts-recommended *.do requests.

Next, we create the struts-config.xml file, which is a standard Struts configuration file. We start off with just a single action with one action forward definition, as shown in Listing 19-2.

Listing 19-2. *The struts-config.xml File*

```
<?xml version="1.0" encoding="ISO-8859-1"?>
<!DOCTYPE struts-config PUBLIC
    "-//Apache Software Foundation//DTD Struts Configuration 1.1//EN"
    "http://jakarta.apache.org/struts/dtds/struts-config_1_1.dtd">

<struts-config>

    <action-mappings>
        <action path="/index"
            type="com.apress.prospring.ch19.web.actions.IndexAction"
            validate="false">
            <forward name="success" path="/WEB-INF/views/default.jsp"/>
        </action>
    </action-mappings>

</struts-config>
```

Here, the /index action is implemented in the IndexAction, which is a subclass of the Action class. It does not require any form beans, and it has one forward declaration to the index.jsp page, which is stored in /WEB-INF/views/default.jsp. The implementation of the IndexAction is shown in Listing 19-3.

Listing 19-3. *IndexAction Implementation*

```
package com.apress.prospring.ch19.web.actions;

import javax.servlet.http.HttpServletRequest;
import javax.servlet.http.HttpServletResponse;

import org.apache.struts.action.Action;
import org.apache.struts.action.ActionForm;
import org.apache.struts.action.ActionForward;
import org.apache.struts.action.ActionMapping;

public class IndexAction extends Action {

    public ActionForward execute(ActionMapping mapping, ActionForm form,
        HttpServletRequest request, HttpServletResponse response)
        throws Exception {
        return mapping.findForward("success");
    }
}
```

The class overrides the execute() method to process the request and return an ActionForward object, which Struts looks up based on its name passed to the findForward() method. The JSP page is just a simple "Hello, World" style page because there is no model to be displayed.

When we build and deploy the application and make a request to /index.do URL, we see the output generated by the index.jsp page.

Accessing Spring Beans

The application we built in the last section works fine, but the IndexAction has no access to any Spring beans. Let's create a ProductManager interface and the StaticListProductManager implementation class and define a productManager bean. The ProductManager interface contains only one method: List<Product> findAll(). This method returns all available products and StaticListProductManager implements this method by returning a hard-coded list of products. The productManager bean is defined in the applicationContext.xml file, as shown in Listing 19-4.

Listing 19-4. *productManager Definition in the applicationContext.xml*

```xml
<?xml version="1.0" encoding="UTF-8" ?>
<!DOCTYPE beans PUBLIC "-//SPRING//DTD BEAN//EN"
    "http://www.springframework.org/dtd/spring-beans.dtd">

<beans>
    <bean id="productManager"
        class="com.apress.prospring.ch19.business.StaticListProductManager" />
</beans>
```

The ProductManager interface implemented by StaticListProductManager is quite simple: it has only one method that returns all the products. Listing 19-5 shows the ProductManager interface.

Listing 19-5. *ProductManager Interface*

```java
package com.apress.prospring.ch19.business;

import java.util.List;

import com.apress.prospring.ch19.domain.Product;

public interface ProductManager {
    public List<Product> findAll();
}
```

This interface is implemented by StaticListProductManager, which returns only a hard-coded list of products, as shown in Listing 19-6.

Listing 19-6. *StaticListProductManager Implementation*

```
package com.apress.prospring.ch19.business;

import java.util.ArrayList;
import java.util.List;

import com.apress.prospring.ch19.domain.Product;

public class StaticListProductManager implements ProductManager {

    private List<Product> products;

    private Product createProduct(int productId, String name, String description) {
        Product product = new Product();
        product.setProductId(productId);
        product.setName(name);
        product.setDescription(description);

        return product;
    }

    public StaticListProductManager() {
        products = new ArrayList<Product>();
        products.add(createProduct(1, "Pro Spring",
            "The best book ever"));
        products.add(createProduct(2, "Pro Jakarta Struts",
            "That's a good one, too"));
    }

    public List<Product> findAll() {
        return products;
    }

}
```

This is a pretty standard way of implementing the Business Tier of a Spring application. Unfortunately, we do not define the Struts Action subclasses as Spring beans, which means we cannot use the Spring DI.

We need to take another approach. Because our application is running in a container that provides the ServletContext implementation and because it is a Spring application, the context's attribute WebApplicationContext.ROOT_WEB_APPLICATION_CONTEXT_ATTRIBUTE is set to an instance of Spring WebApplicationContext. We can use WebApplicationContextUtils. getRequiredWebApplicationContext(servletContext) to get WebApplicatonContext and then call its getBean() method to get an instance of a Spring bean.

Listing 19-7 shows how to use the technique described in the preceding paragraph to get an instance of the productManager bean.

Listing 19-7. *Getting a Spring Bean in a Struts Action Subclass*

```
public class IndexAction extends Action {

    private ProductManager productManager;

    public void setServlet(ActionServlet actionServlet) {
        super.setServlet(actionServlet);
        ServletContext servletContext = actionServlet.getServletContext();
        WebApplicationContext wac =
            WebApplicationContextUtils.
                getRequiredWebApplicationContext(servletContext);
        productManager = (ProductManager)wac.getBean("productManager");
    }

    public ActionForward execute(ActionMapping mapping, ActionForm form,
        HttpServletRequest request, HttpServletResponse response)
        throws Exception {
        request.setAttribute("products", productManager.findAll());

        return mapping.findForward("success");
    }
}
```

In Listing 19-7, you can see that the declaration of the ProductManager property looks just like the same declaration in a Spring controller. To get an instance of the ProductManager implementation declared in the productManager bean, we need to get the ServletContext from the ActionServlet instance by calling the getServletContext() method. Next, we use the WebApplicatonContextUtils utility class to get a WebApplicationContext instance associated with the ServletContext. Finally, we manually get the instance of the productManager bean by calling the getBean() method and passing in the bean name. Because getBean() returns Object, we must cast the returned instance to ProductManager. The execute() method can use the ProductManager instance in the usual way.

This is a very clumsy way to access the Spring beans. To simplify the access to the Spring-managed beans, Spring offers the ActionSupport class. It is a convenience superclass that extends Action and offers a number of methods that allow the subclasses to access the Spring API. Let's take a closer look at the methods offered by the ActionSupport class in Table 19-1.

We can now refactor our IndexAction class to extend the ActionSupport class. To do so, we remove the setServlet() method and replace it by overriding the onInit() method. All these changes are shown in Listing 19-8.

Table 19-1. *Methods Offered by ActionSupport*

Method	Description
setServlet()	Gets the WebApplicationContext and MessageSourceAccessor instances from the Spring context. Calls onInit() when the servlet is being initialized and onDestroy() when it is being destroyed.
initWebApplicationContext()	Called from setServlet(), performs the WebApplicationServlet instance lookup. The default implementation is to find the root WebApplicationContext.
final getWebApplicationConext()	Returns an instance of WebApplicationContext.
final getMessageSourceAccessor()	Returns an instance of MessageSourceAccessor.
final getServletContext()	Returns an instance of ServletContext.
final getTempDir()	Returns the temporary directory for the web application.
onInit()	Subclasses can override this method to perform their own initialization. It is the last method called in the setServlet() method when the servlet is being loaded.
onDestroy()	Subclasses can override this method to perform their own deinitialization. It is the first method called in the setServlet() method when the servlet is being unloaded.

Listing 19-8. *Refactored IndexAction*

```
package com.apress.prospring.ch19.web.actions;

import javax.servlet.http.HttpServletRequest;
import javax.servlet.http.HttpServletResponse;

import org.apache.struts.action.ActionForm;
import org.apache.struts.action.ActionForward;
import org.apache.struts.action.ActionMapping;
import org.springframework.web.struts.ActionSupport;

import com.apress.prospring.ch19.business.ProductManager;

public class IndexAction extends ActionSupport {

    private ProductManager productManager;

    protected void onInit() {
        productManager = (ProductManager)getWebApplicationContext().
            getBean("productManager");
    }
```

```
    public ActionForward execute(ActionMapping mapping, ActionForm form,
        HttpServletRequest request, HttpServletResponse response)
        throws Exception {
        request.setAttribute("products", productManager.findAll());

        return mapping.findForward("success");
    }
}
```

As you can see, the code is much cleaner and still allows you to access the Spring beans.

Using Other Views

Unfortunately, you cannot use Spring views in your Struts actions simply because the Struts Action subclasses are not Spring-managed beans and because the execute() methods must return an instance of ActionForward rather than ModelAndView. If you want to take advantage of Tiles, for example, you must configure the Tiles support in the Struts configuration files. Declaring the tilesConfigurer bean in Spring application context has no effect on the Struts actions. And if you attempt to set the forward to a tile definition, most likely you end up in an IllegalArgumentException with a message saying that Path .index does not start with a slash (/) character being thrown.

If you wish to use Tiles, remove the tilesConfigurer bean from the Spring application context file and replace it with a Struts plugin definition, as shown in Listing 19-9.

Listing 19-9. *Struts Plugin Definition*

```xml
<?xml version="1.0" encoding="ISO-8859-1"?>
<!DOCTYPE struts-config PUBLIC
    "-//Apache Software Foundation//DTD Struts Configuration 1.1//EN"
    "http://jakarta.apache.org/struts/dtds/struts-config_1_1.dtd">

<struts-config>
    <action-mappings>
        <action path="/index"
            type="com.apress.prospring.ch19.web.actions.IndexAction"
            validate="false">
            <forward name="success" path=".index"/>
        </action>
    </action-mappings>

    <plug-in className="org.apache.struts.tiles.TilesPlugin" >
        <set-property property="definitions-config"
            value="/WEB-INF/tiles-layout.xml" />
        <set-property property="moduleAware" value="true" />
        <set-property property="definitions-parser-validate" value="true" />
        <set-property property="definitions-debug" value="2" />
    </plug-in>
</struts-config>
```

The tiles-layout.xml and the JSP pages for the individual tiles are a copy of the files discussed in Chapter 18. Provided that all these files are in place, we can see that `IndexAction` is successfully forwarding to the `.index` view defined in the Tiles definition file. The final result is shown in Figure 19-2.

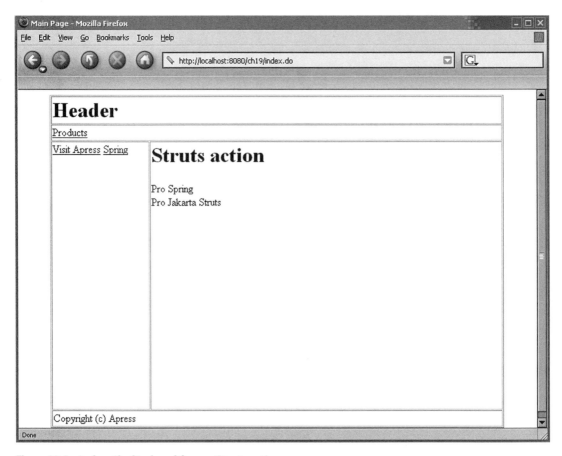

Figure 19-2. *.index tile displayed from a Struts action*

Note that you need to keep the `tilesConfigurer` bean definition in place if you are slowly migrating the Struts actions to Spring controllers. In this case, you need to fully configure the Spring web framework as well as the Struts framework. You should only use this approach in situations in which you need to support the legacy Struts code. Do not mix Struts and Spring MVC in a new application. The reasons are obvious: first, if you use both the Spring MVC and Struts, you are wasting the server resources, and then by having to maintain two sets of configuration files, you are unnecessarily increasing the complexity of your application.

The same rules we discussed here apply to any other view technologies that are used in a Struts application.

Using Struts Actions as Spring Beans

The approach we described in the previous section represents a working solution, but it is still a bit too clumsy to use in a real application. The ideal solution is to declare the Struts actions as Spring beans and let Spring set all the required dependencies. You can achieve this using ContextLoaderPlugin. This Struts plugin loads Spring application context for a Struts ActionServlet. The loader automatically refers to the root WebApplicationContext; the namespace for the context loaded by the plugin is the name of the Struts ActionServlet with –servlet appended to it. By default, the XmlWebApplicationContext is used to load the context file.

This still does not solve the problem of having to create the actions as subclasses of ActionSupport, as shown in Listing 19-8. It would be better if we could define that the beans in the Spring application context are proxies to the Struts Actions. Let's create a SpringIndexAction class that is a direct subclass of the Action class, as shown in Listing 19-10.

Listing 19-10. *SpringIndexAction Implementation*

```
package com.apress.prospring.ch19.web.actions;

import javax.servlet.http.HttpServletRequest;
import javax.servlet.http.HttpServletResponse;

import org.apache.struts.action.Action;
import org.apache.struts.action.ActionForm;
import org.apache.struts.action.ActionForward;
import org.apache.struts.action.ActionMapping;

import com.apress.prospring.ch19.business.ProductManager;

public class SpringIndexAction extends Action {

    private ProductManager productManager;

    public final ActionForward execute(ActionMapping mapping, ActionForm form,
        HttpServletRequest request, HttpServletResponse response)
        throws Exception {
        request.setAttribute("products", productManager.findAll());

        return mapping.findForward("success");
    }

    public final void setProductManager(ProductManager productManager) {
        this.productManager = productManager;
    }
}
```

Furthermore, the SpringIndexAction declares a setter for the productManager property. We need to add an action declaration to the Struts configuration file (see Listing 19-11).

Listing 19-11. *SpringIndexAction Declaration*

```
<?xml version="1.0" encoding="ISO-8859-1"?>
<!DOCTYPE struts-config PUBLIC
    "-//Apache Software Foundation//DTD Struts Configuration 1.1//EN"
    "http://jakarta.apache.org/struts/dtds/struts-config_1_1.dtd">

<struts-config>
    <action-mappings>
        <action path="/index"
            type="com.apress.prospring.ch19.web.actions.IndexAction"
            validate="false">
            <forward name="success" path=".index"/>
        </action>
        <action path="/sindex"
            type=" org.springframework.web.struts.DelegatingActionProxy "
            validate="false">
            <forward name="success" path=".index"/>
        </action>
    </action-mappings>
    <!-- the rest of the file as usual -->
</struts-config>
```

Notice that the action type is set to DelegatingActionProxy, which is a Spring class that delegates all calls to the real bean of the SpringIndexAction class.

Before we can use DelegatingActionProxy, we first need to add the ContextLoaderPlugin bean to the Struts configuration file, as shown in Listing 19-12.

Listing 19-12. *ContextLoaderPlugin Definition*

```
<?xml version="1.0" encoding="ISO-8859-1"?>
<!DOCTYPE struts-config PUBLIC
    "-//Apache Software Foundation//DTD Struts Configuration 1.1//EN"
    "http://jakarta.apache.org/struts/dtds/struts-config_1_1.dtd">

<struts-config>
    <!-- other definitions omitted -->
    <plug-in className="org.springframework.web.struts.ContextLoaderPlugIn">
        <set-property property="contextConfigLocation"
            value="/WEB-INF/ch19-context.xml"/>
    </plug-in>
</struts-config>
```

We set the default location of contextConfigFile to /WEB-INF/ch19-context.xml because we declare the SpringIndexAction there. The context file is empty; to be more precise, it contains a single bean defined as <bean id="null"/>, that only passes the DTD validation. The last pieces of the puzzle that connect the SpringIndexAction to the Spring DI mechanism are the DelegatingActionProxy beans in the Spring application context file. You must set the bean name to the action path from the Struts configuration file. We can then set all the properties in the usual Spring way. Listing 19-13 shows the Spring application context file that introduces the true DI to Struts.

Listing 19-13. *Spring Application Context File*

```xml
<?xml version="1.0" encoding="UTF-8" ?>
<!DOCTYPE beans PUBLIC "-//SPRING//DTD BEAN//EN"
    "http://www.springframework.org/dtd/spring-beans.dtd">

<beans>
    <bean name="/sindex"
        class="com.apress.prospring.ch19.web.actions.SpringIndexAction">
        <property name="productManager"><ref bean="productManager"/></property>
    </bean>

</beans>
```

When we now make a request to the /sindex.do URL, `DelegatingActionProxy` looks up the bean with its name set to `/sindex`. It uses the beans defined in the `WebApplicationContext` that is loaded by the `ContextLoaderPlugin` declared in the file specified in its `contextConfigLocation` property. The `/sindex` bean is the actual `SpringIndexAction`, it is instantiated, and its `productManager` property is set.

The final result is no different from the output you saw in Listing 19-10 except that the `SpringIndexAction` is a fully Spring-managed bean and we have no manual dependency lookup code in the `Action`.

Combining Struts and Spring MVC

If you are migrating an existing Struts application to Spring MVC, you may find yourself in a situation in which you have a Struts action that you need to forward to a Spring MVC controller implementation. This is quite easy to implement: all you need to do is create a Spring MVC controller and a Struts action that forwards to that controller's URL. If you create these, you will be able to pass data from your Struts actions to Spring controllers, which means that you will be able to use Spring views to display the output of Struts actions.

■**NOTE** This is a very clumsy way to use Spring views from Struts actions. Use this approach only if your Struts actions perform large amount of processing that are too difficult or too time-consuming to implement in Spring MVC. This is just a **temporary** solution.

To demonstrate how to pass data from Struts actions to the Spring MVC infrastructure, let's create the `IndexController` class as a subclass of the `MultiActionController` and define the mapping for its `handleIndex()` method in the Spring application context file. The `handleIndex()` method returns a `ModelAndView` instance with the view name set to `.index`, and the model contains a list of all `Products`. Listing 19-14 shows the Spring bean configuration for the `IndexController`.

Listing 19-14. *IndexController Beans*

```xml
<?xml version="1.0" encoding="UTF-8" ?>
<!DOCTYPE beans PUBLIC "-//SPRING//DTD BEAN//EN" ➥
"http://www.springframework.org/dtd/spring-beans.dtd">

<beans>
    <bean id="tilesConfigurer"
        class="org.springframework.web.servlet.view.tiles.TilesConfigurer">
        <property name="definitions">
            <list>
                <value>/WEB-INF/tiles-layout.xml</value>
            </list>
        </property>
    </bean>

    <bean id="viewResolver"
        class="org.springframework.web.servlet.view.ResourceBundleViewResolver">
        <property name="basename"><value>views</value></property>
    </bean>

    <bean id="publicUrlMapping"
        class="org.springframework.web.servlet.handler.SimpleUrlHandlerMapping">
        <property name="mappings">
            <props>
                <prop key="/index.html">indexController</prop>
            </props>
        </property>
    </bean>

    <!-- Index -->
    <bean id="indexController"
        class="com.apress.prospring.ch19.web.IndexController">
        <property name="productManager"><ref bean="productManager"/></property>
        <property name="methodNameResolver">
            <ref local="indexMethodNameResolver"/></property>
    </bean>

    <bean id="indexMethodNameResolver"
        class="org.springframework.web.servlet.mvc.multiaction.➥
            PropertiesMethodNameResolver">
        <property name="mappings">
            <props>
                <prop key="/index.html">handleIndex</prop>
            </props>
        </property>
    </bean>

</beans>
```

The definitions in Listing 19-14 are nothing out of the ordinary; however, it is important to notice that we had to define the tilesConfigurer in Spring, even though we already configured it in Struts. Next, we declare the usual viewResolver, publicUrlMapping, indexController, and indexMethodNameResolver beans. To test that the IndexController is working, you need to make a request to /index.html; you should see a page that looks exactly like the page generated by the /sindex.do action, which is shown in Listing 19-3.

Next, we create a Struts ForwardAction that simply forwards to the success forward, which passes the control to the IndexController, which, in turn, displays the .index tile. Listing 19-15 shows the implementation of the ForwardAction.

Listing 19-15. *ForwardAction Implementation*

```
package com.apress.prospring.ch19.web.actions;
// imports omitted
public class ForwardAction extends Action {

    public final ActionForward execute(ActionMapping mapping, ActionForm form,
        HttpServletRequest request, HttpServletResponse response)
        throws Exception {
        request.setAttribute("fromStruts", "Hello");
        return mapping.findForward("success");
    }

}
```

We now need to add the action definition to the Struts configuration file, as shown in Listing 19-16.

Listing 19-16. *Struts Configuration File*

```
<?xml version="1.0" encoding="ISO-8859-1"?>
<!DOCTYPE struts-config PUBLIC
    "-//Apache Software Foundation//DTD Struts Configuration 1.1//EN"
    "http://jakarta.apache.org/struts/dtds/struts-config_1_1.dtd">

<struts-config>
    <action-mappings>
        <!-- other actions as usual -->
        <action path="/fwd"
            type="com.apress.prospring.ch19.web.actions.ForwardAction"
            validate="false">
            <forward name="success" path="/index.html"/>
        </action>
    </action-mappings>
    <!-- the rest of the file omitted -->
</struts-config>
```

When we make a request to /fwd.do, the `ForwardAction.execute()` method runs and forwards to the /index.html, which is handled by the `IndexController`. As a result, you see the same output as is generated by the `IndexController.handleIndex()` method, whose implementation is shown in Listing 19-17.

Listing 19-17. *IndexController.handleIndex Implementation*

```
package com.apress.prospring.ch19.web;

public class IndexController extends MultiActionController {

    private ProductManager productManager;

    public ModelAndView handleIndex(HttpServletRequest request,
        HttpServletResponse response) throws Exception {
        Map<String, Object> model = new HashMap<String, Object>();
        model.put("products", productManager.findAll());
        model.put("fromStruts", request.getAttribute("fromStruts"));

        return new ModelAndView("index", model);
    }

    public final void setProductManager(ProductManager productManager) {
        this.productManager = productManager;
    }
}
```

As you can see, in the `handleIndex()` method, we added the `fromStruts` request parameter to the `model` Map, thus enabling any Spring view to access it. This is a quick and dirty solution if you need to display the data generated by a Struts action in a Spring view.

Summary

In this chapter, you learned how to use Struts in your Spring application. You now know how to get the beans in the Struts actions programmatically and, more importantly, you know how to configure your Struts actions as regular Spring beans, which allows you to take advantage of the full feature set of the Spring framework. You also learned how to combine Struts actions and Spring controllers, which means you can create a quick interim solution while migrating an existing Struts application to Spring.

Unfortunately, we did not offer a full description of the Struts framework in this chapter; if you want to find out more, take a look at the excellent second edition of *Pro Jakarta Struts* by John Carnell and Rob Harrop (Apress, 2004).

PART 7

■■■

Appendixes

■■■
Testing with Spring

Testing is a crucial part of software development; we believe you should not even think about releasing a piece of software that has not been tested in some way. The easiest testing technique is unit testing. It allows you to test each component of the application separately, in a controlled environment. Once you know that all components work on their own, it may be appropriate to run integration tests; however, these tests are difficult to implement, especially when you are dealing with large applications that use EJBs and JTA transactions. In these cases, integration tests may be impossible to write. Once you have tested your application and have found it to be fully functional, it is time to do some performance testing. This type of testing may bring up threading and JVM heap usage issues that you would not notice otherwise.

Some of the testing methods are far too complex for the scope of this appendix, leaving us with just the following issues to discuss:

Introducing unit testing: In this section, we look at how unit tests work, focusing in particular on JUnit framework. We discuss the importance of mock objects in this section.

Unit tests: It is important to write the tests so that you can repeat them any time and always get the same results. We show you methods that allow you to test local transactions and business logic components.

Integration tests: Even though integration testing is difficult in terms of environment setup, we show you some techniques you can use to test the component integration as thoroughly as possible.

Test coverage: Even though this topic is not directly linked to the actual testing procedures, we mention a few test coverage frameworks that help you identify areas of your code that do not have appropriate unit tests.

Performance testing: Finally, we show you the tools to use for performance testing and discuss the issues you might encounter.

Introducing Unit Testing

As the name suggests, **unit testing** tests the components of your applications on their own. It allows you to prove that a single class works in terms of contract checking and functionality.

Contract checking means that the class should check that it is called within specifications. Let's assume a class with a method returns a square root of a real (`double`) number. If the argument passed to the function is negative or NaN, the method throws an `IllegalArgumentException`.

The unit test for such a class should test the contract by calling the method with a negative argument and then with a NaN. In both cases, an IllegalArgumentException must be thrown. Once we have tested the contract, we must also test the functionality. Using our square root method, we call it with 9 and then check that the returned value is 3.[1]

Unfortunately, we rarely test such simple methods; in most cases, the tests are far more complex, making it very easy to miss a situation that might cause the tested class to fail. This is not a problem of unit testing as such; it is a problem for the programmer who writes incomplete unit tests. Later in the chapter, we discuss the ways to make sure that the unit tests cover all the code.

To simplify the task of writing the unit tests, we use existing unit test frameworks, such as JUnit. You can download the latest version of JUnit from www.junit.org/index.htm; if you are using a Java IDE such as Eclipse, JBuilder, or others, chances are that JUnit is already bundled with the IDE. Here, we cover JUnit usage in Eclipse.

Let's write our first JUnit test in Eclipse; Listing A-1 shows that the code of the unit test always succeeds because it is not actually testing anything.

Listing A-1. *JUnit Test*

```
package com.apress.propspring.apa;

import junit.framework.TestCase;

public class TestAll extends TestCase {
    public void testFoo() {


    }
}
```

The individual JUnit tests are subclasses of TestCase, which offers basic assertion and failure methods. The failure methods are often used in contract testing, whereas the assertion methods are used in functionality testing. The individual tests are simple public void methods whose names begin with test. Each test method is allowed to throw Exception.

To see our test for our imaginary square root method, see Listing A-2.

Listing A-2. *Test for the Square Root Method*

```
public void testSqrt() {
    try {
        sqrt(-1);
        fail("This function returns only real results");
    } catch (IllegalArgumentException expected) {
        // OK
    }
```

---

1. Note that doubles cannot represent certain numbers precisely, hence the test should allow for some tolerance. This tolerance is determined by the expected usage of the method we are testing.

```
    try {
        sqrt(Double.NaN);
        fail("This function cannot take +/-NaN as argument");
    } catch (IllegalArgumentException expected) {
        // OK
    }

    assertEquals(3.0, sqrt(9), 0);
}
```

As you can see, the test for the simple `sqrt()` method is much longer than the actual implementation, but once it is tested, we can be sure that the `sqrt()` method functions correctly and that any errors are handled correctly. Listing A-2 also demonstrates how to use the `fail()` and `assert*()` methods to perform the testing.

In most cases, the classes being tested (targets) require other objects to function. Imagine a unit test for a piece of business logic—it probably requires data access classes to retrieve and store the data it processes. Let's imagine you are testing a discount calculation that applies a discount to an order based on the value of the order and the value of the previous orders. You *can* use the data access layer that takes the data from the database, but this is rarely a good solution. The unit test does not test the business component in isolation; instead it tests the data access components as well as the database. Furthermore, the tables in the database must contain suitable data to test all nuances of the discount calculation algorithm. This makes the test very fragile: a change in the data may influence the result of the test.

It is better to create mock classes for the target's dependencies. In the case of the discount calculation business component, you probably have to create a mock order data access component. Let's assume that `OrderDao` is an interface for the data access component that is used throughout the application. It is easy to provide an implementation of `OrderDao` so that it *always* returns the correct data for the test without accessing the database. This way the unit test is completely isolated and allows you to run repeated tests without influencing any other components of your application.

Unit Tests

Now that you know what unit tests are and you know the basics of the JUnit framework, we can show you how to implement tests so that you can be sure they accurately test all aspects of your code in an unobtrusive way.

It is important to realize that even though we are developing the application using Spring and we are taking advantage of all its DI and Proxy features, we still need to make sure that the classes that implement our application's interfaces work correctly on their own. This is why we do not create the Spring application context, but instead manually create instances of the tested classes and set their dependencies. The dependencies are mock implementations of the dependency interfaces. Let's take a look at Listing A-3, which shows how we implement the tests for the `DefaultBlogManager` implementation of the `BlogManager` interface.

Listing A-3. *AuditTest Unit Test*

```java
package com.apress.prospring.business;

import java.util.Date;
import java.util.List;

import junit.framework.TestCase;

import com.apress.prospring.data.CommentDao;
import com.apress.prospring.data.EntryDao;
import com.apress.prospring.domain.Comment;
import com.apress.prospring.domain.Entry;
import com.apress.prospring.domain.User;

public class AuditInvokedTest extends TestCase {
    private DefaultBlogManager bm = new DefaultBlogManager();
    private CommentDao commentDao = new MockCommentDao();
    private EntryDao entryDao = new MockEntryDao();
    private MockAuditService auditService;

    public AuditInvokedTest() {
        bm.setCommentDao(commentDao);
        bm.setEntryDao(entryDao);
    }

    public void setUp() {
        auditService = new MockAuditService();
        bm.setAuditService(auditService);
    }

    public void testSaveEntry() {
        bm.saveEntry(new Entry());
        performAssert();
    }

    public void testSaveComment() {
        bm.saveComment(new Comment(), new User());
        performAssert();
    }

    private void performAssert() {
        assertEquals("The Audit Service was not invoked", 1,
            auditService.callCount);
    }
```

```java
private class MockAuditService implements AuditService {
    private int callCount = 0;

    public void writeAuditMessage(String data, User user) {
        callCount++;
    }

    public void purgeAudit(Date oldestDate) {

    }

    public int getCallCount() {
        return callCount;
    }
}

private class MockCommentDao implements CommentDao {
    public List getByEntry(int entry) {
        return null;
    }
    public Comment getById(int commentId) {
        return null;
    }
    public void save(Comment comment) {
    }
    public void delete(int commentId) {
    }
}

private class MockEntryDao implements EntryDao {
    public List getAll() {
        return null;
    }
    public void save(Entry entry) {
    }
    public void delete(int entryId) {
    }
    public Entry getById(int entryId) {
        return null;
    }
    public List getMostRecent(int count) {
        return null;
    }
}

}
```

If this test case succeeds, we have proof that the DefaultBlogManager calls the writeAudit() method of the AuditService for each operation that modifies an entry. The DefaultBlogManager requires three dependencies—EntryDao, CommentDao, and AuditService—and we provided mock implementations for each of these interfaces. We do not need to worry about the EntryDao and CommentDao mock implementations, but we do check that the AuditService.writeAudit() implementation gets called when DefaultBlogManager.saveEntry() or DefaultBlogManager.saveComment() is called. This test successfully proves that the DefaultBlogManager performs the necessary auditing functions and yet the test does not require any other external resources. We can run it as many times as we want and still the test succeeds or fails consistently. The result of running this unit test from Eclipse is shown in Figure A-1.

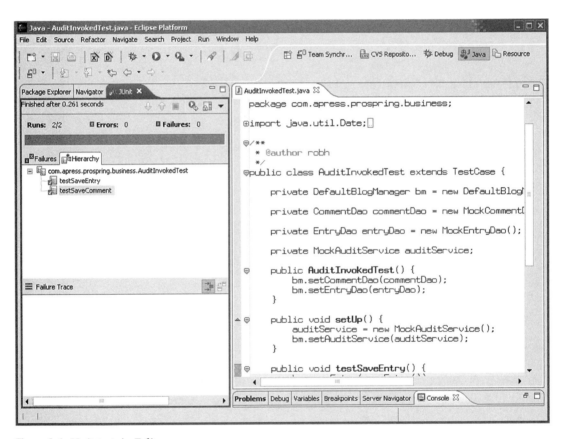

Figure A-1. *Unit tests in Eclipse*

Writing all the mock classes manually can mean a lot of repetitive work. This is where EasyMock (www.easymock.org/) comes it. It is a framework that allows you to create mock classes automatically. You can even add behavior to the generated mock classes. Let's take a look at Listing A-4, which shows the refactored AuditInvokedTest class that uses the EasyMock library to generate the mock classes.

Listing A-4. *AuditInvokedTest Using EasyMock*

```
package com.apress.prospring.business;

import org.easymock.MockControl;

import junit.framework.TestCase;

import com.apress.prospring.data.CommentDao;
import com.apress.prospring.data.EntryDao;
import com.apress.prospring.domain.Comment;
import com.apress.prospring.domain.Entry;

public class AuditInvokedTest2 extends TestCase {

    private DefaultBlogManager bm = new DefaultBlogManager();

    private MockControl auditServiceControl;
    private AuditService auditService;

    public void setUp() {
        CommentDao commentDao;
        EntryDao entryDao;

        entryDao = (EntryDao)
            MockControl.createControl(EntryDao.class).getMock();
        commentDao = (CommentDao)
            MockControl.createControl(CommentDao.class).getMock();

        auditServiceControl = MockControl.createControl(AuditService.class);
        auditService = (AuditService) auditServiceControl.getMock();

        bm.setAuditService(auditService);
        bm.setCommentDao(commentDao);
        bm.setEntryDao(entryDao);
    }

    public void testSaveEntry() {
        Entry entry = new Entry();
         auditService.writeAuditMessage("Entry " + entry + " saved", null);
        auditServiceControl.replay();
        bm.saveEntry(entry, null);
    }
```

```
    public void testSaveComment() {
        Comment comment = new Comment();
        auditService.writeAuditMessage("Comment " + comment + " saved.", null);
        auditServiceControl.replay();
        bm.saveComment(comment, null);
    }

}
```

The code in the setUp() method creates mock implementations for the EntryDao and CommentDao interfaces. Because we do not need to include any behavior in the mock classes, we do not have to store the MockControl object returned by the MockControl.createControl() method.

However, we actually need to test that the writeAuditMessage() method gets called on the AuditService, but at the same time, we do not want to manually create a mock implementation for it. In the testSaveEntry() and testSaveComment() method, we call the writeAuditMessage() method on the generated mock class with the expected arguments and then we call auditServiceControl.replay(). Doing this actually makes EasyMock check to make sure that the writeAuditMessage() method gets called and that the parameters passed to it are set to the expected values.

As you can see, using EasyMock is a very convenient way to generate mock implementations of your interfaces, and doing so allows for a certain level of control over the behavior of the generated mock classes.

Sometimes we need to test the components' links to the external components, which means that we need to write integration tests.

Writing Integration Tests

Integration tests may sound too complex, but a simple integration test is a data access layer implementation test that actually connects to the database and accesses the data in the appropriate tables. Such a test requires interaction of the database, the Spring framework, and the code being tested. If any part of this chain fails, the entire test fails.

Manually creating beans for an integration test may be too difficult and unnecessary to code manually. Instead, we create the Spring application context and let the framework instantiate the beans for us. In most cases, you will be using XmlApplicationContext, thus you need to instantiate one of the XmlApplicationContext implementations. Let's take a look at the code in Listing A-5 to see how we can go about this.

Listing A-5. *Creating the Application Context*

```
public class TransactionTest extends TestCase {

    private ApplicationContext getApplicationContext() {
        String[] paths = new String[] {
                "./business/src/resources/applicationContext-db.xml",
                "./business/src/resources/applicationContext.xml" };
```

```
        return new FileSystemXmlApplicationContext(paths);
    }

}
```

The paths[] array specifies the file that is read to build the application context; the actual implementation we use is FileSystemXmlApplicationContext. We can then use the application context to programmatically get instances of the beans we need to test. Let's take a look at how we implemented the database transaction test in the sample application in Listing A-6.

Listing A-6. *TransactionTest Test Case*

```
package com.apress.prospring.business;

import java.util.Date;

import org.springframework.context.ApplicationContext;
import org.springframework.context.support.FileSystemXmlApplicationContext;

import com.apress.prospring.domain.Entry;
import com.apress.prospring.domain.User;

import junit.framework.TestCase;

public class TransactionTest extends TestCase {

    private ApplicationContext getApplicationContext() {
        String[] paths = new String[] {
                "./business/src/resources/applicationContext-db.xml",
                "./business/src/resources/applicationContext.xml" };

        return new FileSystemXmlApplicationContext(paths);
    }

    public void testTransaction() {
        ApplicationContext ctx = getApplicationContext();
        DefaultBlogManager bm =
            (DefaultBlogManager) ctx.getBean("blogManager");
        bm.setAuditService(new MockAuditService());

        int countBefore = bm.getAllEntries().size();
        Entry e = new Entry();
        e.setSubject("Tester");
        e.setBody("Body");
        e.setPostDate(new Date());
```

```
        try {
            bm.saveEntry(e);
            fail("Should have thrown RuntimeException");
        } catch (RuntimeException ex) {

        }
        int countAfter = bm.getAllEntries().size();
        assertEquals("The new Entry should not have been added", countBefore,
                countAfter);

    }

    private static class MockAuditService implements AuditService {
        public void writeAuditMessage(String data, User user) {
            throw new RuntimeException("Foo!");
        }
        public void purgeAudit(Date oldestDate) {
        }
    }
}
```

In this test, we used Spring to get an instance of BlogManager, but we have set its auditService property to a mock implementation of the AuditService. The mock implementation always throws an exception in its writeAuditMessage() method, which must cause the BlogManager.saveEntry() work to be rolled back. We test this by getting the total number of entries, and then calling the saveEntry() method, failing the test if the saveEntry() method succeeds, and finally checking the new number of entries, which must be the same as the number of entries before we called the saveEntry() method.

Unfortunately, this type of testing is only going to work when you are testing local transactions. If your application must be run in an application server because it uses JTA transactions or any other services provided by the application server, your only option is to use some kind of EJB unit testing framework, such as Cactus (http://jakarta.apache.org/cactus). This type of testing is well beyond the scope of this appendix.

Since version 1.1.1, Spring has come up with a collection of convenience superclasses that simplify the creation of integration tests. All these classes are packaged in the spring-mock.jar file and extend the TestCase class; they are summarized in Table A-1.

Now that you know the classes available in a Spring mock package, take a look at Listing A-7, which shows how we can refactor the TransactionTest class.

Table A-1. *TestCase Subclasses in a Spring Mock Package*

Class	Description
AbstractSpringContextTests	Maintains a map of Spring contexts so that they are not re-created for each JUnit test. The getContext() method returns and caches either context loaded in the loadContextLocations() method if the argument is instanceof String[] or context loaded in the loadContext() method if the argument is not instanceof String[].
AbstractDependencyInjectionSpringContextTests	Subclass of AbstractSpringContextTests. When used as a superclass of your test, it allows the Spring beans to be set using either setters (default strategy) or protected fields. You no longer have to manually create the application context and get the bean you wish to test from it.
AbstractTransactionalSpringContextTests	A subclass of AbstractDependencyInjectionSpringContext-Tests that makes sure the work performed as part of each test is automatically rolled back when the test finishes. This is useful if you want to maintain a consistent state of the database between tests.
AbstractTransactionalDataSourceSpringContextTests	Convenience subclass of AbstractTransactionalSpringContextTests that allows the tables that are affected in the test to be cleared by executing a delete from SQL command.

Listing A-7. *Refactored TransactionTest*

```
package com.apress.prospring.business;

import java.util.Date;
import java.util.List;

import org.springframework.context.ConfigurableApplicationContext;
import org.springframework.context.support.FileSystemXmlApplicationContext;
import org.springframework.test.AbstractDependencyInjectionSpringContextTests;
```

```
import com.apress.prospring.domain.Entry;
import com.apress.prospring.domain.User;

public class TransactionTest2
    extends AbstractDependencyInjectionSpringContextTests {

    private DefaultBlogManager blogManager;

    protected ConfigurableApplicationContext loadContextLocations(
        String[] paths) {
        return new FileSystemXmlApplicationContext(paths);
    }

    public void setBlogManager(DefaultBlogManager blogManager) {
        this.blogManager = blogManager;
    }

    protected String[] getConfigLocations() {
        return new String[] { "./business/src/resources/applicationContext-db.xml",
            "./business/src/resources/applicationContext.xml",
            "./business/src/resources/applicationContext-jdbc.xml"};
    }

    public void testTransaction2() {
        // use the blogManager as usual
    }

    private static class MockAuditService implements AuditService { }

}
```

As you can see from Listing A-7, we removed the code that creates the application context and looks up the blogManager bean. Instead, we use the AbstractDependencyInjectionSpringContextTests as a superclass of our test case, create a setter for the blogManager property, override the loadContextLocations() method, and implement the abstract getConfigLocations() method to make sure the context files are loaded properly. The rest of the code in this test performs the same actions as the test shown in Listing A-6.

Another aspect of integration testing is represented by the Web Tier tests. Generally, you could use HttpUnit (http://httpunit.sourceforge.net/) to write the tests, but Spring allows you to get instances of the controller beans and then use classes from the org.springframework.mock.web package to write tests for the Web Tier without having to use a web server.

Test Coverage

It is important that your tests are as thorough as possible. An elegant way to make sure you are testing enough is to use a test coverage tool. There are several test coverage tools available, starting with the commercial Clover (`www.cenqua.com/clover/`), which offers truly amazing analysis of your code and tests. If you want to use open source alternatives, you can use jcoverage (`www.jcoverage.com/downloads.html`) or EMMA (`http://emma.sourceforge.net/`).

In general, test coverage tools work by adding another layer of code to your application and generally require you to modify the build procedure to include the test coverage tool instrumentation layer in the final binary. The test coverage tools are well outside the scope of this chapter, but we do encourage you to try at least one of them. You will be amazed (shocked) to see how much code goes untested.

Performance Testing

The last thing we feel we should mention in this appendix is performance testing. We waited to cover it until the last section intentionally. Performance is an important aspect of the application, but it is far more important to have a stable and robust application. Users will be much happier to get a slower but working application rather than a fast application that is unreliable and buggy.

However, if at all possible, it is useful to run a performance test before you release the application using a multi-processor machine. This may reveal concurrent programming problems (deadlocks and race conditions), which would otherwise go unnoticed.

We use JMeter for our web performance testing. You can download the latest version of JMeter from `http://jakarta.apache.org/jmeter/`. JMeter allows you to test the raw throughput of your application as well as its robustness and memory usage under extreme stress. You can start hundreds of user sessions and make as many requests per second as your machine can handle. The result of JMeter testing is shown in Figure A-2.

As you can see, we managed to squeeze out about 37 requests per second on a single Pentium IV 2GHz machine with 1GB of RAM and a JBoss 3.2.6 application server.

It is very useful to combine performance testing with memory profiling. One of our favorite memory profiling applications is JProbe, which is now available for free download at `www.quest.com/`. Even though memory profiling is not directly related to testing, it helps you identify situations where objects are not garbage collected because you have forgotten to free a reference to them. This is usually the case with forgotten attributes in the `HttpSession`; these can slowly kill a web application with an `OutOfMemoryError`.

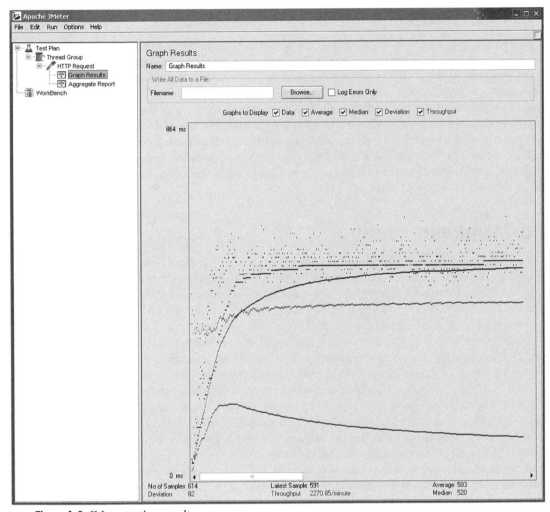

Figure A-2. *JMeter testing results*

Summary

This appendix showed you how to test the components of your application either on their own using unit tests or in cooperation with other components in integration tests. You can also be confident that most of your code is tested by using test coverage tools. In addition, you can prove that the code you have implemented runs fast enough and does not crash under extreme stress if it passes the performance tests.

You also know which tools to choose for your tests, whether it is JUnit for unit and integration testing, Cactus EJB for web testing, JMeter for web and performance testing, or Clover, jcoverage, or EMMA for test coverage.

■■■

The Spring Rich Project

The Spring Rich (Spring Rich Client) framework allows you to develop Swing-based applications using all the concepts you have learned in this book. More specifically, Spring Rich offers you all the following features:

- A declarative configuration, a bean lifecycle, and transaction management.

- An abstraction layer for building MDI-style rich client applications.

- A comprehensive GUI framework that links specific actions to the user interface (UI) elements. You can further group the actions using standard UI elements such as menus, toolbars, and pop-up menus.

- A data binding framework you can use to transfer the values from the UI elements to the underlying model. This model can be represented by simple JavaBeans, Maps, rowsets, or any custom data access strategy implementation.

- Forms and a form builder API that simplifies development of declarative forms with UI elements you can create using the provided metadata. In other words, the UI elements are created based on the type of the underlying property.

- Helper classes for producing GUI standards following dialogs, wizards, tables, and lists.

- Helper services for i18n and centralized component construction.

- Integration with JGoodies Forms, JGoodies Looks, Glazed Lists, Acegi, Spin, and Foxtrot.

- Integration in progress with FlexDock, InfoNode, JIDE, and JDNC component libraries.

We do not build a new sample application because it is far too complex to fit into this appendix. Instead, we explore the sample Petclinic application and explain the core concepts of Spring Rich and its influence on this application's code. Here, we focus only on the standalone version of the sample application and leave the client/server version for you to explore.

It is important to realize that even though we have tried to make descriptions as general as possible in this appendix, some details are specific to the version we checked out from CVS. It is likely that by the time this book is published, a lot of these details will have changed and many new features will have been added. Specifically, we are going to cover the following concepts:

Getting Spring Rich: First, we show you how to get the latest version of Spring Rich from CVS.

Compiling Spring Rich: Next, we explain how to compile the source code obtained from CVS and how to build the Petclinic sample application.

Exploring the Spring Rich architecture: We examine the core components of the Spring Rich framework and explain their usage in the Petclinic sample application.

Getting Spring Rich

Spring Rich is a separate project on SourceForge.net; you can check out the latest version from CVS using the commands shown in Listing B-1.

Listing B-1. *CVS Commands to Check Out Spring Rich*

```
cvs -d:pserver:anonymous@cvs.sourceforge.net:/cvsroot/spring-rich-c login

cvs -z3 -d:pserver:anonymous@cvs.sourceforge.net:/cvsroot/spring-rich-c ➡
co modulename
```

Spring Rich contains the .project file Eclipse uses to identify a Java project, which means you can just as easily use Eclipse's CVS client to check out the framework. Figure B-1 shows Eclipse with the Spring Rich repository.

At the time of this writing, the only way to get Spring Rich is to check out the latest source from CVS. In the future, you will always be able to get the current version from the same repository location, even when official binary and source distributions become available. The Spring Rich team expects to have two binary releases (lite and with dependencies) ready by February 2005.

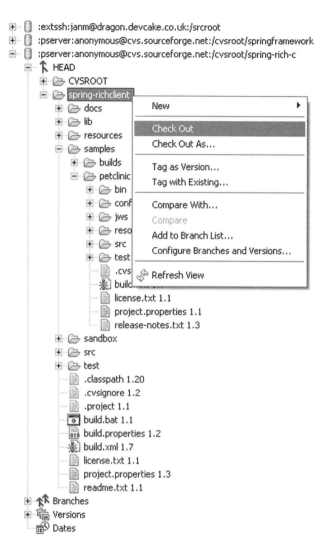

Figure B-1. *Eclipse with the Spring Rich CVS repository explorer*

Compiling Spring Rich and the Petclinic Sample Application

Now that you have the latest source code for Spring Rich, you can build the framework by building the `alljars` and the `sandboxjar` targets (see Listing B-2).

Listing B-2. *Building Spring Rich*

```
[ in spring-rcp-c directory ]
ant alljars
   [output from ant]
ant sandboxjar
   [output from ant]
```

Building these targets produces the spring-richclient.jar, the spring-richclient-resources.jar, the spring-richclient-sandbox.jar, and the spring-richclient-src.zip files in the dist directory.

If you want to build the Petclinic sample application, you need to make a few changes to the samples/petclinic/build.xml [1.7] file, as shown in Listing B-3.

Listing B-3. *Petclinic build.xml File*

```xml
<?xml version="1.0"?>
<project name="petclinic-rich" basedir="." default="usage">
    <property file="build.properties" />
    <property file="project.properties" />
    <target name="build-standalone">
        <jar jarfile="${dist.dir}/petclinic-standalone.jar">
            <manifest>
                <attribute name="Main-Class"
                    value=➥
                       "org.springframework.richclient.samples.petclinic.➥
                        PetClinicStandalone" />
                <attribute name="Class-Path"
                            value="lib/acegi-security.jar
    lib/aopalliance.jar lib/burlap.jar
    lib/commons-codec.jar lib/commons-logging.jar lib/concurrent.jar
    lib/forms.jar lib/hessian.jar lib/hsqldb.jar
    lib/looks.jar lib/spring.jar lib/spring-sandbox.jar lib/spring-petclinic.jar
    lib/spring-richclient.jar lib/spring-richclient-sandbox.jar
    lib/spring-richclient-resources.jar" />
            </manifest>
        </jar>
    </target>
</project>
```

Once the application is built, you should have the petclinic-standalone.jar and the petclinic-clientserver.jar files in the dist directory. Now run the standalone version by executing java -jar petclinic-standalone.jar in the dist directory, which starts the Petclinic sample using the HSQL database implementation. Use user name **scott** and password **wombat** to log in. Figure B-2 shows the main window of the Petclinic sample.

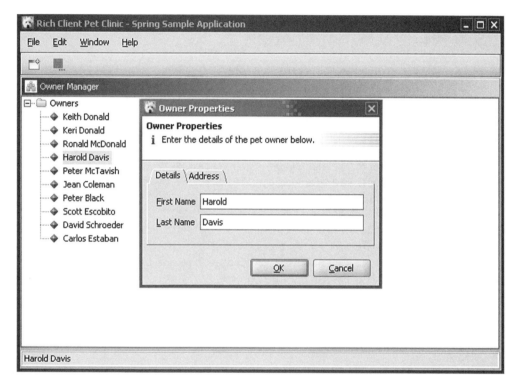

Figure B-2. *Running the Petclinic application*

Examining the Petclinic Startup Sequence

In the remainder of this appendix, we cover the noteworthy code and configuration files you need to run the Petclinic application.

Because the Petclinic sample is a regular Java application, it must have a main() method that configures the application environment. Listing B-4 shows that the main() method is implemented in the PetClinicStandalone class.

Listing B-4. *PetClinicStandalone Main Class*

```java
package org.springframework.richclient.samples.petclinic;

import org.springframework.richclient.application.ApplicationLauncher;

public class PetClinicStandalone {

    public static void main(String[] args) {
        try {
            String rootContextDirectoryClassPath =
                "/org/springframework/richclient/samples/petclinic/ctx";
            String startupContextPath = rootContextDirectoryClassPath +
                "/common/richclient-startup-context.xml";
            String richclientApplicationContextPath =
                rootContextDirectoryClassPath +
                "/common/richclient-application-context.xml";
            String richclientPreferenceContextPath =
                rootContextDirectoryClassPath +
                "/common/richclient-preference-context.xml";
            String businessLayerContextPath = rootContextDirectoryClassPath +
                "/common/business-layer-context.xml";
            String securityContextPath = rootContextDirectoryClassPath +
                "/standalone/security-context.xml";

            new ApplicationLauncher(startupContextPath,
                new String[] { richclientApplicationContextPath,
                    richclientPreferenceContextPath, businessLayerContextPath,
                    securityContextPath });
        } catch (Exception e) {
            System.exit(1);
        }
    }
}
```

The main() method simply sets up variables representing paths to the Spring application context files and creates an instance of the ApplicationLauncher. The first parameter is the path to the startup context file, which is loaded before the root application context is constructed. Typically, you need to include the beans that are essential to the application startup stage and keep the remaining beans in the files in the root context.

The code in Listing B-5 shows the ctx/common/richclient-startup-context.xml file, which defines the splashScreen bean. The ApplicationLauncher looks up the bean with this ID and if it exists, it is displayed while the full application context is being built.

Listing B-5. *richclient-startup-context.xml File*

```xml
<?xml version="1.0" encoding="UTF-8"?>
<!DOCTYPE beans PUBLIC "-//SPRING//DTD BEAN//EN"
    "http://www.springframework.org/dtd/spring-beans.dtd">
<beans>
    <bean id="splashScreen"
        class="org.springframework.richclient.application.SplashScreen"
        singleton="false">
        <property name="imageResourcePath">
            <value>/images/splash-screen.jpg</value>
        </property>
    </bean>
</beans>
```

The usage and purpose of the startup context file is to quickly build a minimal platform and to display basic user interface elements to let the user know that the application is starting up.

Using the Base Components of Spring Rich

The Spring Rich application consists of several key components that cooperate to create and manage the application's views and process commands the views generate in response to the user actions. In this section, we examine the key beans used in the Petclinic application.

Application and ApplicationLifecycleAdvisor

The most important beans that govern the lifecycle of a Spring Rich application are `Application` and `ApplicationLifecycleAdvisor`. The `Application` bean uses the `ApplicationLifecycleAdvisor` subclasses to manage the lifecycle of the application. The `DefaultApplicationLifecycleAdvisor` overrides the `createWindowCommandManager()` method to look up an instance of the `ApplicationWindowCommandManager` bean. This bean intercepts commands from the UI and performs the associated actions. The Petclinic application extends `ApplicationLifecycleAdvisor` in `PetClinicLifecycleAdvisor` and overrides the `onPreWindowOpen()` and `onCommandsCreated()` methods to perform extra initialization.

The declaration of `ApplicationWindowCommandManager`, stored in commands-context.xml, is shown in Listing B-6.

Listing B-6. *ApplicationWindowCommandManager Bean Declaration*

```xml
<?xml version="1.0" encoding="UTF-8"?>
<!DOCTYPE beans PUBLIC "-//SPRING//DTD BEAN//EN"
    "http://www.springframework.org/dtd/spring-beans.dtd">
<beans>
    <bean id="windowCommandManager"
        class="org.springframework.richclient.application.support.➥
            ApplicationWindowCommandManager">
        <property name="sharedCommandIds">
            <list>
             <!-- commands -->
            </list>
        </property>
    </bean>

    <bean id="aboutCommand"
        class="org.springframework.richclient.command.support.AboutCommand">
        <property name="aboutTextPath">
            <value>
                org/springframework/richclient/samples/petclinic/about.txt
            </value>
        </property>
    </bean>
</beans>
```

The commands themselves are other Spring-managed beans, some of which are also declared in this file. The commands usually extend the ApplicationWindowAwareCommand class, which attaches the command to the appropriate user interface element and handles the events the user interface element generates.

Using Commands

Now take a look at aboutCommand. This command's definition is shown in Listing B-6 and it is implemented in the AboutCommand class. It extends the ApplicationWindowAwareCommand and most importantly, it overrides the doExecuteCommand() method to perform the required action (see Listing B-7).

Listing B-7. *AboutCommand Implementation*

```java
package org.springframework.richclient.command.support;

import org.springframework.core.io.Resource;
import org.springframework.richclient.application.support.AboutBox;

public class AboutCommand extends ApplicationWindowAwareCommand {
    private static final String ID = "aboutCommand";
```

```
private AboutBox aboutBox = new AboutBox();

public AboutCommand() {
    super(ID);
}

public void setAboutTextPath(Resource path) {
    this.aboutBox.setAboutTextPath(path);
}

protected void doExecuteCommand() {
    aboutBox.display(getApplicationWindow().getControl());
}

}
```

This particular implementation shows a dialog window displaying the contents of the file specified in the path Resource; the user interface item and the result of the doExecuteCommand() method are shown in Figure B-3.

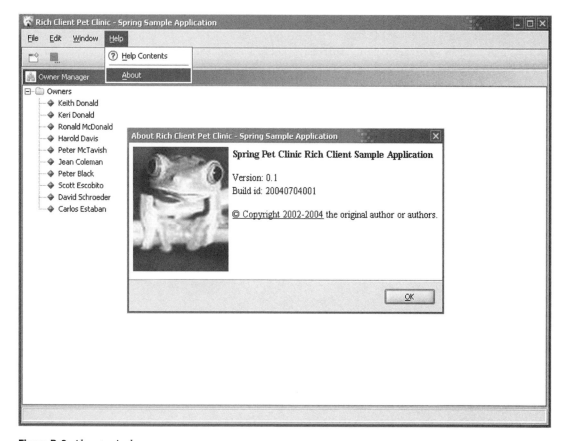

Figure B-3. *About window*

You can execute a command in another way, which is perhaps more suitable when you are implementing commands in your own application. You can use the `TargetableActionCommand` as a bean class and set its `commandExecutor` property to an instance of the bean that implements the `ActionCommandExecutor` interface. The `ActionCommandExecutor` interface contains a single method, `execute()`, that your class must implement to perform the actions of the command. This is clearly demonstrated in the `NewOwnerWizard` class shown in Listing B-8.

Listing B-8. *NewOwnerWizard Implementation*

```
package org.springframework.richclient.samples.petclinic.ui;

import org.springframework.richclient.application.event.LifecycleApplicationEvent;
import org.springframework.richclient.command.ActionCommandExecutor;
import org.springframework.richclient.forms.CompoundForm;
import org.springframework.richclient.wizard.AbstractWizard;
import org.springframework.richclient.wizard.FormBackedWizardPage;
import org.springframework.richclient.wizard.WizardDialog;
import org.springframework.samples.petclinic.Clinic;
import org.springframework.samples.petclinic.Owner;
import org.springframework.util.Assert;

public class NewOwnerWizard
    extends AbstractWizard implements ActionCommandExecutor {

    public void execute() {
        if (wizardDialog == null) {
            wizardDialog = new WizardDialog(this);
            wizardForm = new CompoundForm();
        }
        wizardForm.setFormObject(new Owner());
        wizardDialog.showDialog();
    }
    // other methods omitted
}
```

The application context contains a `newOwnerCommand` bean definition that references the `NewOwnerWizard` (see Listing B-9).

Listing B-9. *newOwnerCommand Bean Definition*

```xml
<?xml version="1.0" encoding="UTF-8"?>
<!DOCTYPE beans PUBLIC "-//SPRING//DTD BEAN//EN"
    "http://www.springframework.org/dtd/spring-beans.dtd">
<beans>
    <bean id="newOwnerCommand"
        class="org.springframework.richclient.command.TargetableActionCommand">
        <property name="commandExecutor">
            <ref bean="newOwnerWizard"/>
        </property>
    </bean>
</beans>
```

We now know how to implement a command to perform the operations we need, however, we still do not know how to create a menu item or a toolbar button and associate it with the command.

Several beans of type CommandGroupFactoryBean with quite intuitive names take care of this. Now we go back to the file shown in Listing B-9 and add those beans into the context file. By default, DefaultApplicationLifecycleAdvisor looks up beans using the names shown in Listing B-10.

Listing B-10. *Menu Bar and Toolbar Beans*

```xml
<?xml version="1.0" encoding="UTF-8"?>
<!DOCTYPE beans PUBLIC "-//SPRING//DTD BEAN//EN"
    "http://www.springframework.org/dtd/spring-beans.dtd">
<beans>

    <bean id="menuBar"
        class="org.springframework.richclient.command.CommandGroupFactoryBean">
        <property name="members">
            <list>
                <ref bean="fileMenu"/>
                <ref bean="editMenu"/>
                <ref bean="windowMenu"/>
                <ref bean="helpMenu"/>
            </list>
        </property>
    </bean>
```

```xml
<bean id="toolBar"
    class="org.springframework.richclient.command.CommandGroupFactoryBean">
    <property name="members">
        <list>
            <ref bean="newMenu"/>
            <value>saveAsCommand</value>
        </list>
    </property>
</bean>

<bean id="fileMenu"
    class="org.springframework.richclient.command.CommandGroupFactoryBean">
    <property name="members">
        <list>
            <ref bean="newMenu"/>
            <value>separator</value>
            <ref bean="loginCommand"/>
            <ref bean="logoutCommand"/>
            <value>separator</value>
            <value>saveAsCommand</value>
            <value>separator</value>
            <value>propertiesCommand</value>
            <value>separator</value>
            <bean
                class="org.springframework.richclient.command.support.➥
                    ExitCommand"/>
        </list>
    </property>
</bean>

<bean id="newMenu"
    class="org.springframework.richclient.command.CommandGroupFactoryBean">
    <property name="members">
        <list>
            <ref bean="newOwnerCommand"/>
        </list>
    </property>
</bean>

<bean id="editMenu"
    class="org.springframework.richclient.command.CommandGroupFactoryBean">
    <property name="members">
        <list>
            <value>undoCommand</value>
            <value>redoCommand</value>
            <value>separator</value>
            <value>cutCommand</value>
```

```
                    <value>copyCommand</value>
                    <value>pasteCommand</value>
                    <value>separator</value>
                    <value>selectAllCommand</value>
                    <value>deleteCommand</value>
                </list>
            </property>
        </bean>

        <bean id="windowMenu"
            class="org.springframework.richclient.command.CommandGroupFactoryBean">
            <property name="members">
                <list>
                    <bean
                        class="org.springframework.richclient.command.support.➥
                            NewWindowCommand"/>
                    <value>separator</value>
                    <bean
                        class="org.springframework.richclient.command.support.➥
                            ShowViewMenu"/>
                    <value>separator</value>
                    <ref bean="preferenceCommand"/>
                </list>
            </property>
        </bean>

        <bean id="helpMenu"
            class="org.springframework.richclient.command.CommandGroupFactoryBean">
            <property name="members">
                <list>
                    <ref bean="helpContentsCommand"/>
                    <value>separator</value>
                    <ref bean="aboutCommand"/>
                </list>
            </property>
        </bean>
</beans>
```

We can now create menu bars and toolbars and we can specify which commands to execute when the user selects an item from the menu or clicks a toolbar button. In most cases, executing a command results in another user interface element being displayed. Each Command can be bound to multiple user interface elements and any CommandGroup can group any number of pop-up menus, menus, menu bars, and toolbars. The newOwnerCommand, for example, is referenced from the fileMenu as well as the newMenu. In the next section, we are going to take a look at the views used in the Petclinic application.

Using Views

There are two major groups of user interface elements: views and forms. A view is an atomic part of the user interface (such as a tree view with a search box) that you can insert into another view or a form. A form represents a window displayed by the operating system.

An example of a view is the list of owners shown in the main window, while an example of a form is the New Owner dialog. Now we show you how the OwnerManager view is implemented and how it uses the OwnerGeneralForm and OwnerAddressForm to edit the selected owner. The definition of the ownerManagerView bean is shown in Listing B-11.

Listing B-11. *OwnerManagerView Bean*

```
<?xml version="1.0" encoding="UTF-8"?>
<!DOCTYPE beans PUBLIC "-//SPRING//DTD BEAN//EN"
    "http://www.springframework.org/dtd/spring-beans.dtd">
<beans>
    <bean id="ownerManagerView"
        class="org.springframework.richclient.application.support.➥
            DefaultViewDescriptor">
        <property name="viewClass">
            <value>
                org.springframework.richclient.samples.petclinic.ui.➥
            OwnerManagerView
            </value>
        </property>
        <property name="viewProperties">
            <map>
                <entry key="clinic">
                    <ref bean="clinic"/>
                </entry>
            </map>
        </property>
    </bean>
</beans>
```

The OwnerManagerView implementation is a subclass of the AbstractView, which allows our subclass to be used as a viewClass of DefaultViewDescriptor. This property is used in the DefaultViewDescriptor's createView() method, which instantiates the specified class. Alternatively, you can override DefaultViewDescriptor.createView() either by subclassing DefaultViewDescriptor or by using method injection.

Next, we want to find out how OwnerManagerView controls the context menu displayed when you right-click an owner, and how it displays the Edit Owner dialog. This is best demonstrated in the code in Listing B-12.

Listing B-12. *OwnerManagerView Implementation*

```
package org.springframework.richclient.samples.petclinic.ui;

// imports omitted

public class OwnerManagerView
    extends AbstractView implements ApplicationListener {

    private Clinic clinic;
    private String ownerLastName = "";
    private JTree ownersTree;
    private DefaultTreeModel ownersTreeModel;
    private RenameCommand renameCommand = new RenameCommand();
    private DeleteCommandExecutor deleteExecutor = new DeleteCommandExecutor();
    private PropertiesCommandExecutor propertiesExecutor =
        new PropertiesCommandExecutor();

    protected void registerLocalCommandExecutors(
        PageComponentContext context) {
        context.register(GlobalCommandIds.DELETE, deleteExecutor);
        context.register(GlobalCommandIds.PROPERTIES, propertiesExecutor);
    }

    protected JComponent createControl() {
        JPanel view = new JPanel(new BorderLayout());
        createOwnerManagerTree();
        JScrollPane sp = new JScrollPane(ownersTree);
        view.add(sp, BorderLayout.CENTER);
        return view;
    }

    private class PropertiesCommandExecutor
        extends AbstractActionCommandExecutor {
        private NestingFormModel ownerFormModel;
        private CompositeDialogPage compositePage;

        public void execute() {
            final Owner owner = getSelectedOwner();
            ownerFormModel = SwingFormModel.createCompoundFormModel(owner);
            compositePage = new TabbedDialogPage("ownerProperties");
            compositePage.addForm(new OwnerGeneralForm(ownerFormModel));
            compositePage.addForm(new OwnerAddressForm(ownerFormModel));
```

```
        TitledPageApplicationDialog dialog =
            new TitledPageApplicationDialog(compositePage,
                getWindowControl()) {
            protected boolean onFinish() {
                ownerFormModel.commit();
                clinic.storeOwner(owner);
                ownersTreeModel.nodeChanged(getSelectedOwnerNode());
                return true;
            }
        };
        dialog.showDialog();
    }
}


}
```

The most important bits of the code are shown in Listing B-12. The first method called is the createControl(), which sets up the visual representation of the view. In Petclinic, the OwnerManagerView instance is realized by instances of JTree in JScrollPane. Next, the registerLocalCommandExecutors() method is called. This method registers commands local to the view. These commands are activated when the view receives focus. This is precisely what the implementation in Listing B-12 does: it registers deleteExecutor and propertiesExecutor, two logical actions that are shared between views.

Now we need to focus on propertiesExecutor, which is set to an instance of the inner class PropertiesCommandExecutor. This class is a subclass of AbstractActionCommandExecutor and overrides the well-known execute() method to perform the operations the command requires. When execute() is called, perhaps as the result of a menu-item click, a TitledApplicationDialog containing a tabbed dialog page appears. On the dialog's first tab, the OwnerGeneral form is displayed, allowing editing of general identification properties like firstName and lastName. On the dialog's second tab, the Address form is displayed, allowing you to edit the Owner's location.

When you click the dialog OK button, onFinish() is automatically called. Next, any buffered edits are committed to the backing Owner domain model object in ownerFormModel.commit(). Because the forms are backed by the Owner JavaBean, updates to it are easily persistable using an ORM tool such as Hibernate. The clinic business façade is responsible for updating the owner in the database in its onFinish() method.

Note also, because of Spring Rich's declarative validation system, the finish command is only enabled when all validation rules are satisfied. If a validation rule is violated, the dialog displays a descriptive error message and automatically disables the finish command. The framework manages all of this for you. Figure B-4 shows the Owner Properties form with the Last Name field failing validation; this causes the OK button to be disabled.

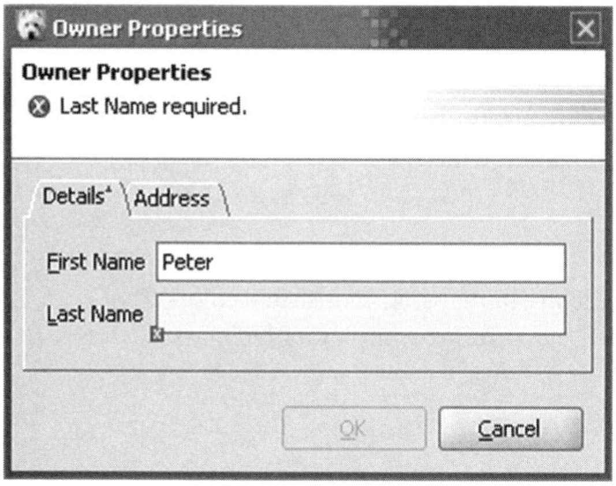

Figure B-4. *Owner Properties window*

Typically, you want to configure an initial view to display when the application starts. The default view is configured in the `ApplicationLifecycleAdvisor` bean; in our case, this is the `petclinicLifecycleAdvisor` bean shown in Listing B-13.

Listing B-13. *petclinicLifecycleAdvisor Bean Definition*

```
<?xml version="1.0" encoding="UTF-8"?>
<!DOCTYPE beans PUBLIC "-//SPRING//DTD BEAN//EN"
    "http://www.springframework.org/dtd/spring-beans.dtd">
<beans>

    <bean id="application"
        class="org.springframework.richclient.application.Application">
        <constructor-arg index="0">
            <ref bean="petclinicLifecycleAdvisor"/>
        </constructor-arg>
    </bean>

    <bean id="petclinicLifecycleAdvisor"
        class="org.springframework.richclient.samples.petclinic.➥
            PetClinicLifecycleAdvisor">
        <property name="windowCommandBarDefinitions">
            <value>
             org/springframework/richclient/samples/petclinic/ui/➥
             commands-context.xml</value>
        </property>
        <property name="startingPageId">
            <value>ownerManagerView</value>
        </property>
    </bean>
</beans>
```

These two beans, application and petcliniclifecycleAdvisor, are the final two beans that bind all the application's other beans together into one rich client application. The petcliniclifecycleAdvisor's startingPageId property specifies the bean that implements the PageDescriptor that is displayed when the application starts. By default, the instance of SingleViewPageDescriptor is created for the main application window.

Prettying Up the Application

The users of desktop applications are used to seeing nice icons, bitmaps, and consistent colors. The Spring Rich framework supports these elements of the user interface–implemented classes shown in Table B-1.

Table B-1. *User Interface Configuration Classes*

Class	Description
UIManagerConfigurer	Displays user interface elements in a way that is consistent with the host OS.
JGoodiesLooksConfigurer	Sets the UIManagerConfigurer instance to use JGoodies.
DefaultImageSource	This bean uses the ResourceMapFactoryBean to load the image definitions.
DefaultIconSource	This bean loads the icons from the ImageSource bean.

In general, all Spring Rich GUI elements created using implementations of ButtonFactory, ComponentFactory, ControlFactory, LabelInfoFactory, and MenuFactory have their visual properties configured using DI. The result of this is that you do not need to hard-code the visual settings in Java. A good example of this declarative configuration is the imageResourcesFactory bean in the richclient-application-context.xml file.

The other user interface beans (such as MessageSource) you already know from Chapters 17 and 18.

Summary

Spring Rich represents a solid platform for building rich client applications using Spring, while allowing you to use the features of the Spring framework, which allows you to enforce the key concepts of Spring application design. Even though Spring Rich is still a young project, we believe it is a framework that deserves your attention.

Because Spring Rich is still in the alpha stages, it is undergoing rapid development, and chances are, by the time you read this book, some of its features will have changed. However, we are sure that none of the existing features will be removed and therefore, this appendix will be a valuable starting point for your own experiments with Spring Rich.

■ ■ ■

Spring IDE

As you have seen throughout this book, Spring simplifies many facets of application development including configuration, component interaction, and data access. However, Spring is not without its own complexities. In particular, many users find managing the large amount of information present in the Spring configuration files quite difficult, especially in large applications where the number of bean definitions can easily reach into the hundreds.

Thankfully, you can alleviate much of this burden using the Spring IDE, a plugin for the Eclipse platform that provides a custom Spring configuration file editor that makes it simple to manage a large number of beans. In this appendix, we demonstrate how the features in the Spring IDE can make your life easier when you are developing Spring applications. Specifically, we look at the following features:

Installing Spring IDE: In this section, we show you how to install the Eclipse platform on your machine, how to configure the Graphical Editor Framework (GEF)—a required component of Spring IDE—and finally, how to install Spring IDE into the Eclipse platform.

Configuring a Spring IDE project: The Spring IDE provides a **nature** for the Eclipse environment, allowing you to add Spring IDE features to any project type. Using this nature, you can create a standard Java project in the Eclipse IDE and then add and remove the Spring IDE features as you see fit.

Managing Spring configuration files: Most of the features in the Spring IDE are provided through extensions to the Eclipse text editor architecture. The Spring IDE provides a set of features, which you can use with any Eclipse text editor, that identifies invalid class names, invalid bean names, and nonexistent parent bean references. In addition to these features, the Spring IDE provides support for configurations spread across multiple files and can highlight inadvertent usage of bean overriding.

Visualizing Spring configuration files: The Spring IDE provides two graphical views, one tree-based and one graph-based, that offer you an easy way to visualize the beans in your application and to view the relationships between them.

This appendix is not intended as an introduction to the Eclipse platform. If you are interested in using Eclipse to develop applications using Java and Spring, you should read *Eclipse* by Steve Holzner (O'Reilly, 2004).

Installing Spring IDE

Spring IDE is a plugin for the Eclipse platform. Before you can use Spring IDE, you must install both the Eclipse platform and the GEF, a standard Eclipse extension that provides platform-level support for graphical editors. Spring IDE uses the GEF to render the bean graph.

Installing Eclipse

Installing Eclipse could not be simpler. Start by obtaining the appropriate distribution for your platform from the Eclipse download site (`www.eclipse.org/downloads`). Eclipse is packaged in a variety of different ways for each platform depending on the features you require. We recommend that you download the Eclipse SDK package, which includes the Eclipse platform, the Java development tools, and the plugin development. This is the base package if you want to use Eclipse for Java development, and it is the package we used for developing the examples in this book.

At the time of writing, Eclipse is at version 3.0.1, with the milestone three (M3) release of version 3.1 also available. For the examples in this book, we use a mixture of both 3.0.1 and 3.1M3 on both Windows and Mac OS X.

Once you have downloaded the Eclipse distribution for your platform, simply extract the files to your chosen location. In the root directory of the Eclipse distribution, you will find the Eclipse executable for your platform. Running this starts Eclipse immediately, and you are prompted for a location for your workspace files. You can choose to have Eclipse prompt you for a workspace location every time it starts up or remember a given location and use that every time.

Installing the Graphical Editor Framework

As the name implies, the GEF is a standard framework for building applications with graphical editors for the Eclipse platform. Spring IDE uses the GEF to create the graphical bean map, which is discussed later in the section entitled "Viewing the Bean Graph."

The easiest way to install the GEF is to use the Update Manager, which downloads the latest version of the GEF and installs it automatically. You can access the Update Manager using Help ➤ Software Updates ➤ Find and Install. When the Update Manager appears, you are offered the options of searching for updates to currently installed features or searching for new features. When you choose to search for new features, the Update Sites to Visit screen shown in Figure C-1 appears.

The Update Sites to Visit screen allows you to configure which update sites Eclipse should search for new features. The Eclipse.org update site is already configured, and collapsing the corresponding node in the site tree displays the list of features available at Eclipse.org. In this list, you see one or more nodes for the GEF SDK. Check the one with the most recent version number and then click Next.

The next screen displays the list of feature packages available for the version of the GEF SDK you chose, as shown in Figure C-2.

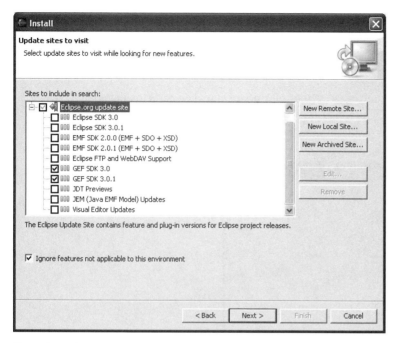

Figure C-1. *The Update Sites to Visit screen*

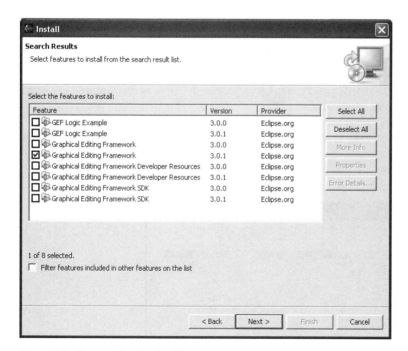

Figure C-2. *FeatureList for the GEF*

Unless you plan to develop your own GEF-based plugins, the only feature you need to install is the GEF itself and not the GEF SDK or its associated packages. To install the GEF, check the GEF node in the feature list and then click Next to proceed to the licensing screen. Before you can download the GEF, you are prompted to read the license and must indicate that you accept the license terms.

After you agree to the license terms, the Update Manager starts to download the GEF components from the Eclipse.org site. You can monitor the progress of the download in the Update Manager progress window, as shown in Figure C-3.

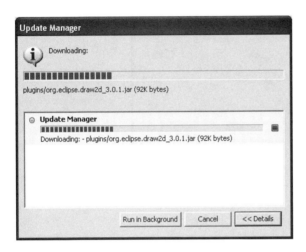

Figure C-3. *Monitoring download progress*

Once the Update Manager finishes downloading the GEF components, you are asked to confirm that you want to install the GEF features; after you do so, you are prompted to restart Eclipse to complete the installation.

Once Eclipse restarts, you can verify that the GEF has been installed correctly using Help ➤ About Eclipse Platform ➤ Plug-in Details. This displays a list of all the plugins present in your Eclipse platform installation, as shown in Figure C-4. The GEF should be listed along with the other plugins.

Provider	Plug-in Name	Version	Plug-in Id
Eclipse.org	File Buffers	3.1.0	org.eclipse.core.filebuffers
Eclipse.org	Graphical Editing Framework	3.0.1	org.eclipse.gef
Eclipse.org	Help Application Server	3.0.0	org.eclipse.help.appserver
Eclipse.org	Help System Base	3.0.0	org.eclipse.help.base
Eclipse.org	Help System Core	3.0.0	org.eclipse.help
Eclipse.org	Help System IDE	3.0.0	org.eclipse.help.ide
Eclipse.org	Help System UI	3.0.0	org.eclipse.help.ui
Eclipse.org	Help System Webapp	3.0.0	org.eclipse.help.webapp
Eclipse.org	Install/Update Configurator	3.0.0	org.eclipse.update.configura..
Eclipse.org	Install/Update Core	3.0.0	org.eclipse.update.core

Figure C-4. *Verifying the GEF installation*

Installing Spring IDE

As with the GEF, the easiest way to install Spring IDE is to use the Update Manager. However, unlike the GEF, Spring IDE does not have a preconfigured update site so you need to create one yourself.

When you get to the Update Site screen, click the New Remote Site button to bring up the New Update Site window, as shown in Figure C-5.

Figure C-5. *Adding a new update site*

Give the new update site a meaningful name, such as Spring IDE, and set the URL to `http://springframework.sourceforge.net/spring-ide/eclipse/updatesite/`. Click OK to add the new update site to your Eclipse configuration. Now you will see the Spring IDE site listed in the Update Site screen. Expand the Spring IDE node to display the list of features available. You need to install both Spring IDE and the Spring Framework into your Eclipse IDE, so check both of these features and click Next to proceed to the feature list.

In the feature list screen, you will see that a number of different versions are available for both the Spring Framework and the Bean Configuration Support features, as shown in Figure C-6.

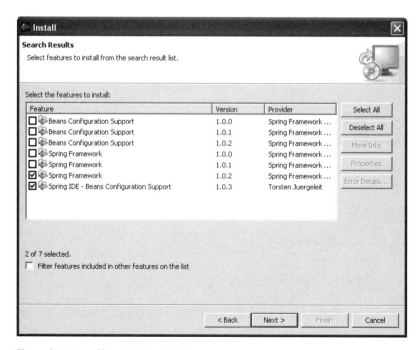

Figure C-6. *Installing Spring IDE features*

At the time of writing, Bean Configuration Support was at version 1.0.3 whereas the Spring Framework was at version 1.0.2. You must install a version of both components in order to use Spring IDE. Because the maximum version of the Spring Framework supported by Spring IDE is 1.0.2, it does not provide support for any of the Spring 1.1–specific features such as method injection; however, Spring IDE is still perfectly usable for your Spring 1.1 projects.

Adding the Spring IDE Nature

Many Eclipse plugins provide their own project type to replace the Java Project type. This is often quite restrictive if you need to start using a plugin's feature mid-project, because you need to re-create the Eclipse project from scratch—something that requires considerable effort. To avoid this problem, Spring IDE is packaged as a **nature**, which acts as a sort of decorator for project types, extending the feature set provided by the project type in question. This means that you can use Spring IDE with a wide variety of different project types, including the built-in Java Project.

To add the Spring IDE nature to an existing Java project, simply right-click the project icon in Navigator and choose Add Spring Beans Project Nature from the drop-down menu, as shown in Figure C-7.

Figure C-7. *Adding Spring Beans Nature to a project*

If you decide later that you do not want to use Spring IDE for your project, you can remove the Spring Beans Project Nature by right-clicking the Project icon and choosing Remove Spring Beans Project Nature.

Editing and Validating Configuration Files

You access most of the features of Spring IDE when editing the configuration files for your application. Spring IDE itself does not provide any XML editing capabilities; instead, it uses standard extension mechanisms to add features to any Eclipse text editor. This means that you can use Spring IDE with the plain text editor included with Eclipse or with any one of the many XML plugins available for the Eclipse platform.

We have found that Spring IDE works best in conjunction with a full XML editor such as the freely available XMLBuddy (`http://xmlbuddy.com/`) from Bocaloco Software or the fantastic <oXygen/> XML Editor (`www.oxygenxml.com`) from SyncRO Soft. We have used both of these XML editors to great effect with Spring IDE, and we recommend that you give them both a try. For the examples in this appendix, we used the <oXygen/> XML Editor version 5.0.

Configuring the Spring Beans Nature

Before you can take advantage of Spring IDE's features for editing your configuration files, you must tell Spring IDE which files in your application you want it to work on. To do this, right-click the project icon in Navigator and choose Properties from the menu to bring up the project's Properties dialog. In the panel list on the left side of the Properties dialog, you will see a list of property panels for the project, one of which is the Spring Beans Project; click this to bring up the Spring Beans Project properties sheet.

The Spring Beans Project properties sheet contains two tabs: Config Files and Config Sets. The Config Files tab allows you to configure which files Spring IDE should treat as Spring configuration files. The Config Sets tab is covered later in the section entitled "Using Multiple Configuration Files." To add files to the Config Files set of your Spring project, use the Add button to select all the XML files present in your application.

Figure C-8 shows the property sheet for a Spring Beans–enabled project containing four separate Spring configuration files.

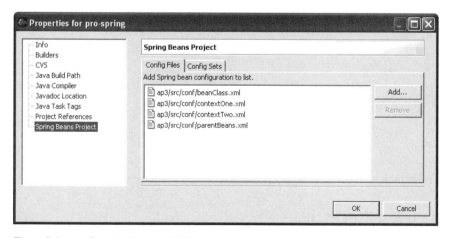

Figure C-8. *Configuring Spring IDE*

If a configuration file is not configured in the Spring Beans Project tab, then you cannot use Spring IDE's features when editing that file.

Validating Bean Classes

One of most frustrating aspects of developing a Spring application is the number of runtime errors that arise during development from misspelled class names in the configuration file. Before we started using Spring IDE, we were used to the configure/run/reconfigure cycle of creating Spring applications that resulted from misspelled class names. Using Spring IDE, we can validate class names contained in our configuration files at design time, thus reducing the number of runtime errors we experience during development.

To experience an example of this, try constructing a <bean> definition using an invalid class name, such as that shown in Figure C-9.

Figure C-9. *Detecting invalid class names*

Here you can see that we used a nonexistent class name for the testBean definition, and this is highlighted by Spring IDE using the error icon next to the offending line of XML. In addition to the error icon shown in the code editor, Spring IDE adds a comprehensive description of the error to the Eclipse Problems window, as shown in Figure C-10.

Description	Resource	In Folder
⊗ Class 'com.apress.prospring.ap3.NonExistentClass' not found	beanClass.xml	pro-spring/ap3/src/conf

Figure C-10. *Viewing configuration problems*

This is one of our favorite Spring IDE features, simply because it saves so much time by reducing the number of runtime errors we experience during development.

Validating Bean Properties

Another big annoyance when developing Spring applications is the number of runtime errors caused by misspelled property names in configuration files. Just like misspelled class names, this is a problem that can easily present itself and is a frequent cause of frustration for developers. Using Spring IDE, you can validate that the bean properties you configure in your configuration files correspond to actual setXXX() methods in the bean class.

Figure C-11 shows what happens when you try to configure an invalid property when you are using Spring IDE.

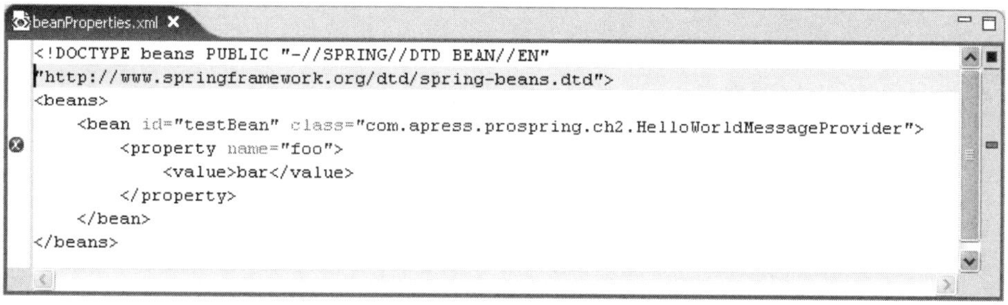

Figure C-11. *Configuring invalid properties*

As you can see, Spring IDE highlights the invalid property name right in the code window using the error marker. As with invalid class names, errors regarding invalid property names are shown in the Eclipse Problems window (see Figure C-12).

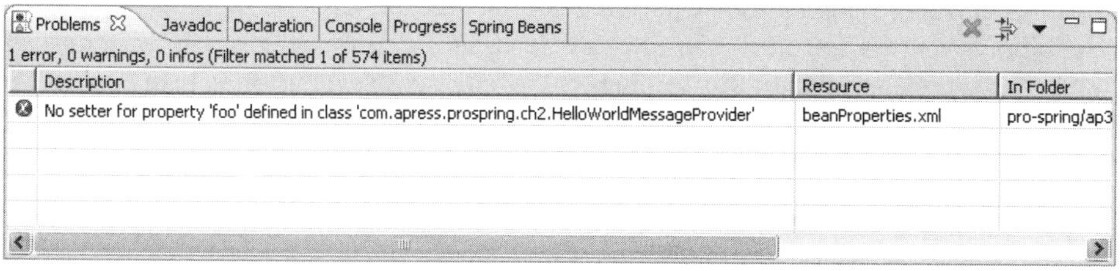

Figure C-12. *Identifying invalid property names*

Validating Parent Beans

You can validate many bean references using a standard XML editor or parser; however, a reference to a parent element cannot be validated in this way, because it is possible that the parent bean may exist in a completely different configuration file and this functionality is not supported by standard XML parsers.

With Spring IDE, it is possible to validate that the bean specified as the parent of another bean does exist, as shown in Figure C-13.

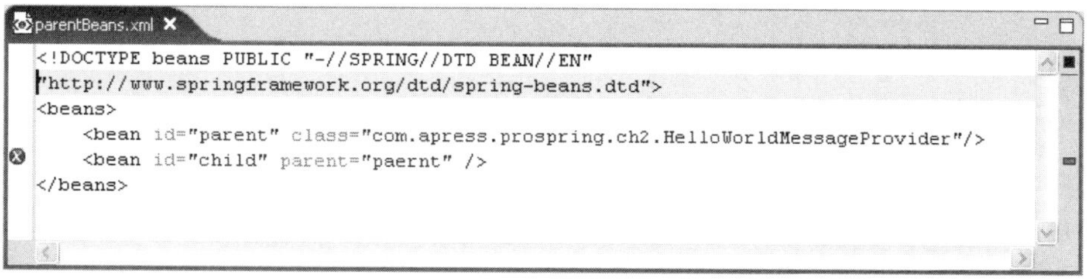

Figure C-13. *Validating parent bean existence*

As you can see from Figure C-13, Spring IDE highlights references to nonexistent parent beans directly in the code editor using the error marker. As you would expect, and as Figure C-14 shows, this is backed up by an entry in the Problems window.

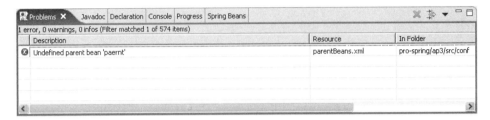

Figure C-14. *Identifying nonexistent parent beans*

Using Multiple Configuration Files

In most nontrivial Spring applications, it is common to see the configuration spread across multiple physical configuration files. In this case, Spring IDE allows you to group configuration files into named Config Sets. When working on a file in a Config Set, Spring IDE checks all files in the Config Set when trying to resolve parent bean references.

To configure a Config Set, open up the Spring Beans Project property sheet for your project and choose the Config Sets tab. In the Config Sets tab, click the New button to bring up the Create New Spring Beans Config Set dialog, as shown in Figure C-15.

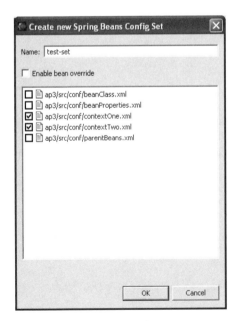

Figure C-15. *Adding a Config Set*

To create the Config Set, give it a meaningful name and choose the files you want to be part of it. By default, Spring IDE checks to see if a bean definition in one file of the Config Set overrides a definition in another file in the set. Figure C-16 gives an example of this.

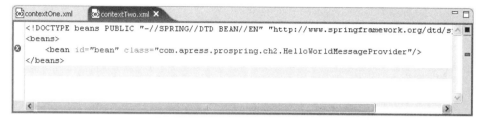

Figure C-16. *Identifying bean overriding*

Here, the contextTwo.xml file is part of a Config Set with the contextOne.xml file. Both files contain a definition of the bean bean, and Spring IDE flags the definition in contextTwo.xml as an invalid override using error marking. In many cases, bean overriding is done by mistake and indicates an error in the configuration, but in some cases, such as when you are using nested ApplicationContexts, bean overriding is a desirable feature. In this case, Spring IDE allows you to disable overriding warnings for a Config Set by checking the Enable bean override box when you are creating the Config Set.

Visualizing a Spring Application

A big complaint we hear from many developers is that it is often hard to get a high-level view of the beans declared in your application and how they are interrelated. Spring IDE solves this by offering two different views of your configuration: a tree-based view that shows beans along with the properties configured for them, and a graph-based view that shows your beans and their relationships to each other.

Viewing Project Configurations

The first view Spring IDE provides for your application is the tree-based Spring Beans view, which you access by right-clicking the code window for any Spring IDE–managed configuration file and choosing Show In Spring Beans View.

The Spring Beans view, as shown in Figure C-17, provides a tree-based view of all beans across the configuration files and Config Sets for your application.

This view provides you with a mechanism you can use to assess quickly all the beans configured for your application and the values assigned to them. You can collapse each bean node in the tree to show the properties configured for that bean, along with the values provided.

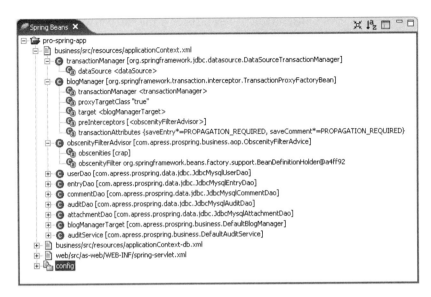

Figure C-17. *Using the Spring Beans view*

Viewing the Bean Graph

The Spring Beans view is great for seeing what beans you have configured and what values have been configured for your bean properties, but it is not so good at showing how the beans are interrelated. For this, you need the Bean Graph view. You can activate the Bean Graph view by right-clicking a file or Config Set in the Spring Beans view and choosing Show Graph from the context menu. Figure C-18 shows the Bean Graph for the SpringBlog application.

As you can see, the Bean Graph shows each bean as a rectangular block with the names of configured properties listed in the lower region. Dependencies between beans are represented by arrows, with the arrow pointing from the dependent bean to the dependency. This view provides you with a good overview of your application, and it is often useful for providing developers who are new to the project with an overview of how all the beans in your application interact.

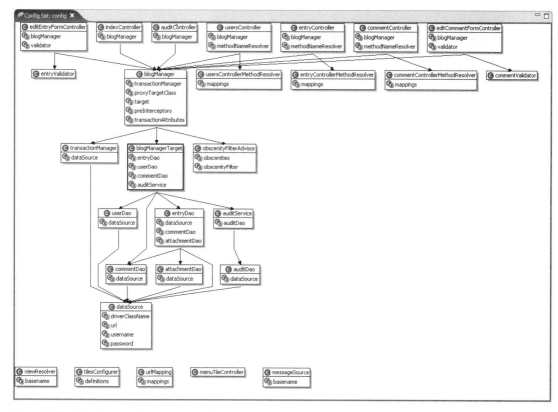

Figure C-18. *The SpringBlog Bean Graph*

Summary

Spring IDE is a valuable part of any Spring developer's toolbox. Using the additional editing capabilities provided by Spring IDE, you can reduce the number of runtime errors you experience during development due to incorrect configuration. This, in turn, increases your productivity and leaves you with more time to focus on the goal at hand—delivering quality software. Using the Spring Beans and Bean Graph views, you can get a quick overview of all the beans in your application, including both configured property values and bean relationships.

The Future of Spring

One of the most attractive features of Spring is that both the Spring development team and the community at large are constantly developing it. This has led to a framework that already encompasses a great deal of the tools and techniques a programmer must use when building an application. The number of tools and techniques Spring supports is growing all the time, and Spring is constantly improving its existing feature set. In this appendix, we discuss a selection of the new features and improvements that are currently in development or are scheduled to begin development at any time. In particular, we look at the following:

`BeanFactory` **script support:** Using script support, you can define bean dependencies using a script language, currently BeanShell or Groovy. Spring then dynamically creates instances of your script classes as required. In this section, we take a quick peek at how this works using the Groovy scripting language.

J2SE 5.0 annotations metadata support: As you saw in Chapter 12, Spring provides an implementation-independent mechanism for using source level metadata in your applications via the `Attributes` interface. As of version 1.1 of Spring, the only implementation of the `Attributes` interface was `CommonsAttributes`, which used the Jakarta Commons Attributes framework. Currently under development, the `AnnotationsAttributes` class allows J2SE 5.0 annotations to be used in place of Commons Attributes for applications running on a 5.0-compliant JVM.

Spring JMX: Using Java Management eXtensions (JMX), you can expose and manage application components in a standard way. JMX has been around for quite a while and, as of version 5.0 of J2SE, is now a standard part of the Java platform. Spring JMX simplifies the use of JMX in your application by removing the need to create much of the JMX plumbing code by hand. In this section, you see how to expose your Spring beans via JMX, how to access JMX-managed resources using proxies, and how to use JSR-160 support for remote JMX management.

Spring JMS: As you saw in Chapter 13, Spring already provides substantial support for using JMS in your applications. However, the current support classes do not really compete with those offered in EJB containers via message-driven beans. The JMS code in the Spring sandbox hopes to fix this. In this section, we take a quick peek at this code.

JasperReports support: The Spring MVC framework is a major part of the overall framework and already provides comprehensive support for a wide range of view technologies. Soon to be added to this range is support for JasperReports, which allows you to add reporting capabilities to your Spring-based applications quickly and easily.

Note that many of the features we discuss in this appendix are still in development and may change before they are released. For that reason, we do not go into great detail on every single feature; instead, we simply discuss what the features will do for you and present some simple examples.

To run the JSR-175 annotation example, you need to install the J2SE 5.0 JDK on your machine, and you need to check out the samples module, which contains the `AnnotationsAttributes` class, from the Spring CVS server.

Using Scripting Languages with BeanFactory

As of version 1.1 of Spring, the `BeanFactory` implementations could only create beans from already compiled Java classes. For the most part, this is what you want, but in some cases, you might find it useful to define a bean as a script and have this script compiled automatically. With the new scripting support features that are in development, this will soon be possible.

The main goal for this functionality is that you are able to define Web Tier controllers using a scripting language and enable quick and easy modification of these controller scripts. This makes sense for most, if not all, web applications where controllers are essentially wrappers that invoke logic in the Business Tier. Using a scripting language makes developing and modifying Web Tier controllers much easier.

The typical usage pattern for the scripting functionality is to define an interface or base class in Java or to use preexisting interfaces or classes such as `Controller` or `AbstractController`, then implement this interface in a scripting language, and then have Spring compile the script on the fly for you. For example, consider the interface shown in Listing D-1.

Listing D-1. *The PersonBean Interface*

```
package com.apress.prospring.apd.groovy;

public interface PersonBean {

    String getName();
    int getAge();
}
```

Here you can see a simple interface that defines two methods: `getName()` and `getAge()`.

Now consider the code shown in Listing D-2 that loads two instances of `PersonBean` from the `BeanFactory` and displays the value returned by `getName()`.

Listing D-2. *Using the PersonBean Interface*

```
package com.apress.prospring.apd.groovy;

import org.springframework.context.ApplicationContext;
import org.springframework.context.support.FileSystemXmlApplicationContext;

public class Example {

    public static void main(String[] args) {
        ApplicationContext ctx = new FileSystemXmlApplicationContext(
                "./ap4/src/conf/groovy/groovy.xml");

        PersonBean robh = (PersonBean) ctx.getBean("robh");
        System.out.println("Name: " + robh.getName());

        PersonBean janm = (PersonBean) ctx.getBean("janm");
        System.out.println("Name: " + janm.getName());
    }
}
```

Here you can see that we are loading two beans of type PersonBean from the
ApplicationContext. As of yet, we have not created an implementation of PersonBean in Java
and we are not going to. Instead, we create two implementations in Groovy and have Spring
compile them on the fly. If you are unfamiliar with Groovy, visit http://groovy.codehaus.org.
Listing D-3 shows the Groovy class for the robh bean and Listing D-4 shows the class for the
janm bean.

Listing D-3. *Groovy Class for robh Bean*

```
package com.apress.prospring.apd.groovy;

class RobHarrop implements PersonBean {

    String getName() {
        return "Rob Harrop";
    }

    int getAge() {
        return 100;
    }
}
```

Listing D-4. *Groovy Class for janm Bean*

```
package com.apress.prospring.apd.groovy;

class JanMachacek implements PersonBean {

    String getName() {
        return "Jan Machacek";
    }

    int getAge() {
        return 100;
    }
}
```

To have Spring compile these scripts into beans automatically, we use the factory-bean and factory-method attributes of the bean tag in conjunction with the GroovyScriptFactory class, as shown in Listing D-5.

Listing D-5. *Compiling Groovy Scripts into Beans*

```
<?xml version="1.0" encoding="UTF-8"?>
<!DOCTYPE beans PUBLIC "-//SPRING//DTD BEAN//EN"
"http://www.springframework.org/dtd/spring-beans.dtd">
<beans>
    <bean id="groovyScriptFactory"
      class="org.springframework.beans.factory.script.groovy.GroovyScriptFactory"/>
    <bean id="robh" factory-bean="groovyScriptFactory" factory-method="create">
        <constructor-arg index="0">
            <value>./ap4/src/conf/groovy/robh.groovy</value>
        </constructor-arg>
    </bean>
    <bean id="janm" factory-bean="groovyScriptFactory" factory-method="create">
        <constructor-arg index="0">
            <value>./ap4/src/conf/groovy/janm.groovy</value>
        </constructor-arg>
    </bean>
</beans>
```

Here we use the factory-bean attribute of the bean tag to inform Spring that the groovyScriptFactory bean, which is of type GroovyScriptFactory, should be used to create the robh and janm beans. In addition, we use the factory-method attribute to instruct Spring to use the create() method of the groovyScriptFactory bean when it creates the beans and the <constructor-arg> tag to pass arguments to this method.

If you run this example, after a short delay, you see the following output:

```
Name: Rob Harrop
Name: Jan Machacek
```

As you can see, Spring compiled the scripts shown in Listings D-3 and D-4 and used the resulting classes to create the beans. As mentioned, you do experience a short delay when you start this application—a result of the script compilation process.

In its current incarnation, `BeanFactory` script integration has support for both Groovy and BeanShell scripts. Currently, script support is scheduled for version 1.2 of Spring; however, the development team is discussing bringing the 1.2 release forward so that features such as JMX and JSR-175 support can be released earlier. As a result, script support might not appear until Spring 1.3.

Using J2SE 5.0 Annotations

As you saw in Chapter 12 when looking at transactions, Spring provides the ability to define configuration options using source level metadata. As of Spring 1.1, this functionality was provided solely through the Commons Attributes metadata library, because at the time, there was no native Java support for source level metadata. With the advent of J2SE 5.0, Java now has native support for source level metadata using **annotations**.

Using Spring's annotation support, which will most likely be released in Spring 1.2, you can now access Java annotations using the Spring `Attributes` interface. In addition to this, many of the Spring features that use Commons Attributes for configuration will also begin to support Java annotations; indeed, the appropriate annotations for the transaction classes are almost complete.

NOTE We have assumed a certain familiarity with the new language features of Java 5.0 in this section. If you are unfamiliar with the new language features, read *Java 5.0 Tiger: A Developer's Notebook* by David Flanagan and Brett McLaughlin (O'Reilly, 2004).

Java annotations introduce a whole new set of syntax features into the language. To create an annotation, you use the `@interface` keyword; you can assign default values for annotation properties using the `default` keyword. Listing D-6 shows a simple example of this.

Listing D-6. *The Name Annotation*

```
package com.apress.prospring.apd.jsr175;

import java.lang.annotation.ElementType;
import java.lang.annotation.Retention;
import java.lang.annotation.RetentionPolicy;
import java.lang.annotation.Target;

@Retention(RetentionPolicy.RUNTIME)
@Target(ElementType.TYPE)
public @interface Name {

    String first() default "John";
    String last() default "Smith";
}
```

Here you can see that we create an annotation called Name with two attributes, first and last. We give each of the annotation attributes a default value using the default keyword. Also notice that this annotation definition is itself annotated with two of the standard annotations. We use the Retention annotation to define how the annotation metadata should be retained during the compile/run process. We use RetentionPolicy.RUNTIME to indicate that this annotation should be accessible at runtime using reflection. In addition, the Target annotation defines those parts of your code, such as methods and classes, to which the annotation can be applied. The use of ElementType.TYPE means that you can apply this annotation to classes only.

Using this annotation to annotate another class is simple, as shown in Listing D-7.

Listing D-7. *Using the Name Annotation*

```
package com.apress.prospring.apd.jsr175;

@Name(first="Rob", last="Harrop")
public class AttributeDemo {


}
```

Here you can see that we annotate the AttributeDemo class with the Name annotation, providing values for both the first and last attributes. Accessing the annotation information at runtime is easy using Spring's AnnotationsAttributes class, as shown in Listing D-8.

Listing D-8. *Accessing Annotations at Runtime*

```
package com.apress.prospring.apd.jsr175;

import java.util.Collection;
import java.util.Iterator;

import org.springframework.metadata.Attributes;
import org.springframework.metadata.annotations.AnnotationsAttributes;

public class Example {

    public static void main(String[] args) {
        Attributes attributes = new AnnotationsAttributes();

        Collection attrs = attributes.getAttributes(AttributeDemo.class,
                Name.class);

        for (Iterator i = attrs.iterator(); i.hasNext();) {
            Name nameAttr = (Name) i.next();
            System.out.println("Found name attribute: " + nameAttr.first()
                    + " " + nameAttr.last());
        }
    }
}
```

Using Spring JMX

JMX is quite a popular part of Java; this popularity has caused it to become part of the standard Java distribution as of Java 5.0. If you are unfamiliar with JMX, we recommend that you read the documentation available at `http://java.sun.com/products/JavaManagement/`.

Using Spring JMX you can expose your Spring beans as JMX resources without having to couple your beans to the JMX API. In addition to this, you can access JMX-managed resources through proxies, thus removing the need for your application to interact with the complex and loosely typed JMX client API.

Until recently, there was no standard mechanism for exposing JMX resources to remote clients; as a result, a variety of different adaptors emerged from a variety of vendors. With the advent of JSR-160, there is now a standard way for JMX resources to be exposed and accessed remotely. Spring JMX provides full support for exposing JSR-160 services and for accessing remote services using proxy classes.

In this section, we take a quick look at some of the basic functionality provided by Spring JMX.

Exposing Beans to JMX

The central class in Spring JMX is `JmxMBeanAdapter`, which orchestrates the entire process of creating JMX management interfaces for your beans, obtaining `ObjectNames` for your beans, and registering your beans with `MBeanServer`. The `JmxMBeanAdapter` class supports full declarative configuration, allowing you to expose your beans via JMX without writing a single line of Java code.

As an example of this, consider the `JmxBean` class shown in Listing D-9.

Listing D-9. *The JmxBean Class*

```
package com.apress.prospring.apd.jmx;

public class JmxBean {

    private String name;

    private int age;

    private String favoriteColor;

    public int getAge() {
        return age;
    }

    public void setAge(int age) {
        this.age = age;
    }

    public String getFavoriteColor() {
        return favoriteColor;
    }
```

```
    public void setFavoriteColor(String favoriteColor) {
        this.favoriteColor = favoriteColor;
    }

    public String getName() {
        return name;
    }

    public void setName(String name) {
        this.name = name;
    }
}
```

As you can see, this is just a plain JavaBean containing no JMX-specific code at all. To register this bean with MbeanServer, simply pass it into an instance of JmxMBeanAdapter using the beans property, as shown in Listing D-10.

Listing D-10. *Exposing a Bean via JMX*

```xml
<?xml version="1.0" encoding="UTF-8"?>
<!DOCTYPE beans PUBLIC "-//SPRING//DTD BEAN//EN"
"http://www.springframework.org/dtd/spring-beans.dtd">
<beans>
    <bean id="adaptor" class="org.springframework.jmx.JmxMBeanAdapter">
        <property name="beans">
            <map>
                <entry key="spring:name=someBean">
                    <ref local="someBean"/>
                </entry>
            </map>
        </property>
        <property name="server">
            <ref local="mbeanServer"/>
        </property>
    </bean>

    <bean id="mbeanServer"
          class="org.springframework.jmx.factory.MBeanServerFactoryBean"/>

    <bean id="someBean" class="com.apress.prospring.apd.jmx.JmxBean">
        <property name="name"><value>Rob Harrop</value></property>
        <property name="age"><value>100</value></property>
        <property name="favoriteColor"><value>Blue</value></property>
    </bean>
</beans>
```

There are two interesting parts to this configuration. First, notice that we define a bean, mbeanServer, of type MBeanServerFactoryBean and use this to set the value of the JmxMBeanAdapter.server property. Internally, JmxMBeanAdapter attempts to locate a running instance of MBeanServer, which is useful when your application is running in an application server such as JBoss, which provides a default MBeanServer. However, when MBeanServer is not available, you should use MBeanServerFactoryBean to create one and pass it to JmxMBeanAdapter.

Second, notice that when passing in someBean to JmxMBeanAdapter via the beans property, the key of the Map entry is a JMX ObjectName. By default, JmxMBeanAdapter uses the key of the beans Map as the ObjectName when registering the bean with MBeanServer. As you will see in subsequent sections, this behavior can be modified.

In Listing D-11, you can see a simple example that loads the configuration shown in Listing D-10 and accesses someBean via JMX.

Listing D-11. *Accessing someBean via JMX*

```
package com.apress.prospring.apd.jmx;

import javax.management.Attribute;
import javax.management.MBeanServer;
import javax.management.ObjectName;

import org.springframework.context.ApplicationContext;
import org.springframework.context.support.FileSystemXmlApplicationContext;

public class SimpleExample {

    public static void main(String[] args) throws Exception {

        ApplicationContext ctx = new FileSystemXmlApplicationContext(
                "./ap4/src/conf/jmx/simple.xml");

        MBeanServer server = (MBeanServer) ctx.getBean("mbeanServer");
        JmxBean bean = (JmxBean) ctx.getBean("someBean");

        System.out.println(bean.getName());

        // invoke JMX operation
        server.setAttribute(ObjectName.getInstance("spring:name=someBean"),
                new Attribute("name", "Jan Machacek"));

        System.out.println(bean.getName());
    }
}
```

Here you can see that after loading `ApplicationContext`, we retrieve both the `someBean` and `mbeanServer` beans. Then we write out the value of the `name` property of `someBean` twice, in between which we change the value of this property using JMX. Running this code results in the following output:

```
Rob Harrop
Jan Machacek
```

As you can see, the call to `MBeanServer.setAttribute()` changed the value of `someBean`, indicating that `someBean` was registered as a JMX resource under the `spring:name=someBean` `ObjectName`.

Accessing a Managed Resource Using a Proxy

As you saw from the example in Listing D-11, accessing JMX-managed resources can be messy and may cause you to lose all the compile-time benefits of the strongly typed nature of Java. Using Spring JMX, you can overcome this by creating a proxy to a JMX-managed resource using the `JmxProxyFactoryBean` class. Listing D-12 shows a bean declaration that you can add to the configuration shown in Listing D-10 to create a proxy to the `spring:name=someBean` MBean.

Listing D-12. *Configuring a JMX Proxy*

```
<bean id="proxy" class="org.springframework.jmx.proxy.JmxProxyFactoryBean">
    <property name="server">
        <ref local="mbeanServer"/>
    </property>
    <property name="objectName">
        <value>spring:name=someBean</value>
    </property>
</bean>
```

Here you can see that we pass in both the `MBeanServer` and the `ObjectName` of the resource we wish to proxy to `JmxProxyFactoryBean`. By default, `JmxProxyFactoryBean` attempts to determine the class of the managed resource and then creates a dynamic subclass of this. If you are using `JmxProxyFactoryBean` to access a remote resource and the managed resource class is not accessible locally, then you can create an interface for the proxy and pass this to the `JmxProxyFactoryBean` class using the `proxyInterfaces` property.

In Listing D-13, you can see a simplified version of the code in Listing D-11 that uses the proxy defined in Listing D-12 to access the `spring:name=someBean` MBean.

Listing D-13. *Using a JMX Proxy*

```
package com.apress.prospring.apd.jmx;

import org.springframework.context.ApplicationContext;
import org.springframework.context.support.FileSystemXmlApplicationContext;

public class WithProxyExample {
```

```
    public static void main(String[] args) throws Exception {

        ApplicationContext ctx = new FileSystemXmlApplicationContext(
                "./ap4/src/conf/jmx/simple.xml");


        JmxBean bean = (JmxBean) ctx.getBean("someBean");
        JmxBean proxy = (JmxBean) ctx.getBean("proxy");

        System.out.println(bean.getName());

        // invoke JMX operation
        proxy.setName("Jan Machacek");

        System.out.println(bean.getName());
    }
}
```

The output of this example is the same as the output of the example shown in Listing D-11.

Defining the Management Interface Using Metadata

Up to now, all the JMX examples shown have exposed all methods and properties on JmxBean via JMX; this is the default behavior of JmxMBeanAdapter. Thankfully, you can customize this behavior using an implementation of the ModelMBeanInfoAssembler interface to which the JmxMBeanAdapter delegates. By default, JmxMBeanAdapter uses the ReflectiveModelMBeanInfoAssembler interface, which uses reflection to access all public methods and properties of a class and exposes them via JMX. Spring JMX comes complete with a second implementation of the ModelMBeanInfoAssembler interface, MetadataModelMBeanInfoAssembler, which uses source level metadata to determine which methods and properties should be exposed via JMX. At the time of writing, only Commons Attributes metadata is supported by Spring JMX, although JSR-175 metadata will be included with the final release.

Listing D-14 shows a modification of the JmxBean class complete with source level metadata defining which properties should be exposed via JMX.

Listing D-14. *Using Source Level Metadata to Define a JMX-Managed Interface*

```
package com.apress.prospring.apd.jmx;

/**
 * @@org.springframework.jmx.metadata.support.ManagedResource
 *    (description="My Managed Resource", objectName="spring:name=jmxBean")
 */
public class JmxBean {

    private String name;
```

```java
    private int age;

    private String favoriteColor;

    /**
     * @@org.springframework.jmx.metadata.support.ManagedAttribute
     * (description="The Age Attribute")
     */
    public int getAge() {
        return age;
    }

    /**
     * @@org.springframework.jmx.metadata.support.ManagedAttribute
     * (description="The Age Attribute")
     */
    public void setAge(int age) {
        this.age = age;
    }

    /**
     * @@org.springframework.jmx.metadata.support.ManagedAttribute
     * (description="The Favourite Color Attribute")
     */
    public String getFavoriteColor() {
        return favoriteColor;
    }

    public void setFavoriteColor(String favoriteColor) {
        this.favoriteColor = favoriteColor;
    }

    /**
     * @@org.springframework.jmx.metadata.support.ManagedAttribute
     * (description="The Name Attribute")
     */
    public String getName() {
        return name;
    }

    public void setName(String name) {
        this.name = name;
    }
}
```

Here you can see that the JmxBean class and various methods of the class are marked with metadata that defines them as part of the JMX management interface. The ManagedResource attribute used on the class itself defines the description of the managed resource that graphical JMX clients will display in addition to the ObjectName. The ManagedAttribute attribute used on some of the getXXX()/setXXX() methods is used to mark a method as part of the interface to a JMX attribute. Notice that you can also provide a description for the attributes as well. You can see that in some cases, we have not placed a ManagedAttribute on the setXXX() method of a property, making that property read-only when accessed via JMX. The ManagedAttribute attribute can only be used on getXXX()/setXXX() methods; to mark a normal method for exposure as a JMX operation, use the ManagedOperation attribute.

Using Commons Attributes requires an initial phase in the build process prior to compilation to generate additional Java source for the attributes. Listing D-15 shows a sample Ant build script that does just this.

Listing D-15. *Compiling Commons Attributes*

```
<project name="ap4" default="compile" basedir="../../../../../../../../">

    <property name="spring.dir" value="${basedir}/../spring" />
    <property name="src.dir" value="${basedir}/ap4/src/java" />
    <property name="dest.dir" value="${basedir}/bin" />

    <path id="project.classpath">
        <fileset dir="${spring.dir}/lib">
            <include name="**/*.jar" />
        </fileset>
        <path location="${spring.dir}/target/sandbox/classes" />
    </path>

    <taskdef classpathref="project.classpath"
             resource="org/apache/commons/attributes/anttasks.properties" />

    <target name="compile">
        <attribute-compiler destdir="${src.dir}">
            <fileset dir="${src.dir}" includes="**/*.java" />
        </attribute-compiler>
        <javac source="1.4" srcdir="${src.dir}" destdir="${dest.dir}"
               classpathref="project.classpath" />
    </target>
</project>
```

In the sample code, this build file sits in the same directory as the JmxBean source file. Listing D-16 shows how to configure JmxMBeanAdapter to use the MetadataModelMBeanInfoAssembler class to assemble the management interface for your beans.

Listing D-16. *Configuring MetadataModelMBeanInfoAssembler*

```xml
<?xml version="1.0" encoding="UTF-8"?>
<!DOCTYPE beans PUBLIC "-//SPRING//DTD BEAN//EN"
"http://www.springframework.org/dtd/spring-beans.dtd">
<beans>
    <bean id="adaptor" class="org.springframework.jmx.JmxMBeanAdapter">
        <property name="namingStrategy">
            <ref local="metadataNamingStrategy"/>
        </property>
        <property name="assembler">
            <ref local="metadataAssembler"/>
        </property>
        <property name="server">
            <ref local="mbeanServer"/>
        </property>
    </bean>

    <bean id="mbeanServer"
          class="org.springframework.jmx.factory.MBeanServerFactoryBean"/>

    <bean id="metadataNamingStrategy"
          class="org.springframework.jmx.naming.MetadataNamingStrategy"/>

    <bean id="metadataAssembler"
class="org.springframework.jmx.assemblers.metadata.MetadataModelMBeanInfoAssembler
"/>

    <bean id="someBean" class="com.apress.prospring.apd.jmx.JmxBean">
        <property name="name"><value>Rob Harrop</value></property>
        <property name="age"><value>100</value></property>
        <property name="favoriteColor"><value>Blue</value></property>
     </bean>

    <bean id="proxy" class="org.springframework.jmx.proxy.JmxProxyFactoryBean">
        <property name="server">
            <ref local="mbeanServer"/>
        </property>
        <property name="objectName">
            <value>spring:name=jmxBean</value>
        </property>
    </bean>
</beans>
```

Here you can see that we set the assembler property of the `JmxMBeanAdapter` class to an instance of `MetadataModelMBeanInfoAssembler`, which means that the metadata of each bean is read by Spring when it creates the management interface.

The second thing to notice about this example is that we set the
JmxMBeanAdapter.namingStrategy property to an instance of MetadataNamingStrategy. When
determining what ObjectName to use when registering a bean, JmxMBeanAdapter consults its
configured implementation of the NamingStrategy interface. The NamingStrategy interface has
a single method, getObjectName(), to which Spring passes the Map key associated with the bean
and the bean instance itself. MetadataNamingStrategy uses the ObjectName configured via the
ManagedResource attribute that you saw in Listing D-14.

The third and final point of interest in this example is that no beans are passed to
JmxMBeanAdapter via the beans property. The reason for this is that the
MetadataModelMBeanInfoAssembler class implements the
AutodetectCapableModelMBeanInfoAssembler interface and JmxMBeanAdapter gives it a chance
to identify beans that should be exposed to JMX. The MetadataModelMBeanInfoAssembler class
adds any bean whose class is marked with the ManagedResource attribute to the set of beans to
be exposed. When using this approach, the bean name is used in place of the Map key when
obtaining the ObjectName from the configured NamingStrategy implementation.

Listing D-17 demonstrates the role of metadata in the construction of the management
interface by attempting to write to the name attribute that is marked as read-only in the code
(i.e., setName() has no ManagedAttribute).

Listing D-17. *Testing MetadataModelMBeanInfoAssembler*

```
package com.apress.prospring.apd.jmx;

import javax.management.MBeanServer;

import org.springframework.context.ApplicationContext;
import org.springframework.context.support.FileSystemXmlApplicationContext;

public class MetadataExample {

    public static void main(String[] args) throws Exception {

        ApplicationContext ctx = new FileSystemXmlApplicationContext(
                "./ap4/src/conf/jmx/attributes.xml");

        MBeanServer server = (MBeanServer) ctx.getBean("mbeanServer");
        JmxBean proxy = (JmxBean) ctx.getBean("proxy");

        System.out.println(proxy.getName());
        try {
            proxy.setName("Jan Machacek");
        } catch(Exception ex) {
            System.out.println(ex.getMessage());
        }
    }
}
```

Running this example results in the following output:

```
Rob Harrop
Operation/Attribute setName is not exposed on the management interface
```

As you can see, invoking the getName() method is acceptable because it is marked with a ManagedAttribute attribute, but invoking setName() causes an exception because it does not have a ManagedAttribute.

Using JSR-160 Support

With the advent of JSR-160, you can now expose an MBeanServer to remote clients in a standard way; clients can also access remote MBeanServers in a standard way. Spring JMX provides JSR-160 support classes to allow MBeanServer instances to be exposed to remote clients in an entirely declarative manner and to allow remote JMX resources to be accessed via proxy.

In Listing D-18 you can see an example configuration that exposes an MBeanServer, and thus all its managed resources, to remote clients using ConnectorServiceBean.

Listing D-18. *Exposing an MBeanServer Using JSR-160*

```
<?xml version="1.0" encoding="UTF-8"?>
<!DOCTYPE beans PUBLIC "-//SPRING//DTD BEAN//EN"
"http://www.springframework.org/dtd/spring-beans.dtd">
<beans>
    <bean id="adaptor" class="org.springframework.jmx.JmxMBeanAdapter">
        <property name="beans">
            <map>
                <entry key="spring:name=someBean">
                    <ref local="someBean"/>
                </entry>
            </map>
        </property>
        <property name="server">
            <ref local="mbeanServer"/>
        </property>
    </bean>

    <bean id="mbeanServer"
class="org.springframework.jmx.factory.MBeanServerFactoryBean"/>

    <bean id="someBean" class="com.apress.prospring.apd.jmx.JmxBean">
        <property name="name">
            <value>Rob Harrop</value>
        </property>
        <property name="age">
            <value>100</value>
        </property>
```

```
    <property name="favoriteColor">
        <value>Blue</value>
    </property>
</bean>

<bean id="connectorService"
class="org.springframework.jmx.remote.ConnectorServiceBean">
    <property name="server">
        <ref local="mbeanServer"/>
    </property>
</bean>
</beans>
```

You will recognize much of this code from Listing D-10, although the connectorService bean is new. Using the ConnectorServiceBean class, you can expose MBeanServer via JSR-160 to remote clients. By default, ConnectorServiceBean uses the service URL service:jmx:jmxmp:// localhost:9876, although you can change this by setting the serviceUrl property of ConnectorServiceBean.

ConnectorServiceBean automatically starts listening for remote connections as soon as your ApplicationContext initializes it, so hosting a remote MBeanServer requires little Java code, as shown in Listing D-19.

Listing D-19. *Hosting MBeanServer*

```
package com.apress.prospring.apd.jmx;

import org.springframework.context.ApplicationContext;
import org.springframework.context.support.FileSystemXmlApplicationContext;

public class Jsr160Server {

    public static void main(String[] args) throws Exception {
        ApplicationContext ctx = new FileSystemXmlApplicationContext(
        "./ap4/src/conf/jmx/jsr160.xml");
        System.out.println("Waiting...");
        System.in.read();
    }
}
```

To access a managed resource in a remote MbeanServer, you can use the JmxProxyFactoryBean as you would with a local resource, but instead of passing in an MBeanServer instance, you pass in an MBeanServerConnection instance, which you can configure using MBeanServerConnectionFactoryBean, as shown in Listing D-20.

Listing D-20. *Configuring a Remote JMX Proxy*

```xml
<?xml version="1.0" encoding="UTF-8"?>
<!DOCTYPE beans PUBLIC "-//SPRING//DTD BEAN//EN"
"http://www.springframework.org/dtd/spring-beans.dtd">
<beans>
    <bean id="mbeanServerConnection"
class="org.springframework.jmx.remote.MBeanServerConnectionFactoryBean">
        <property name="serviceUrl">
            <value>service:jmx:jmxmp://localhost:9876</value>
        </property>
    </bean>
    <bean id="proxy" class="org.springframework.jmx.proxy.JmxProxyFactoryBean">
        <property name="server">
            <ref local="mbeanServerConnection"/>
        </property>
        <property name="objectName">
            <value>spring:name=someBean</value>
        </property>
    </bean>
</beans>
```

Here you can see that we configure JmxProxyFactoryBean with an instance of
MBeanServerConnection using MBeanServerConnectionFactoryBean, which itself is configured
with the service URL of the remote MBeanServer. The resulting proxy can be used just like any
other, as shown in Listing D-21.

Listing D-21. *Using a Remote JMX Proxy*

```java
package com.apress.prospring.apd.jmx;

import org.springframework.context.ApplicationContext;
import org.springframework.context.support.FileSystemXmlApplicationContext;

public class Jsr160Client {

    public static void main(String[] args) {
        ApplicationContext ctx = new FileSystemXmlApplicationContext(
        "./ap4/src/conf/jmx/jsr160-client.xml");

        JmxBean bean = (JmxBean)ctx.getBean("proxy");
        System.out.println(bean.getName());

    }
}
```

Spring JMS

As you saw in Chapter 13, Spring already has substantial support for JMS. However, this support still does not match the feature set offered by message-driven EJBs; work is underway to fix this. We do not discuss this new feature set here, because we already previewed it in Chapter 13.

Building JasperReports Views

JasperReports is an open source reporting engine written in 100-percent Java. JasperReports has been in development for quite some time and provides a comprehensive feature set for building reporting applications using Java. The current version of JasperReports, 0.6.1, provides support for four output formats: CSV, Microsoft Excel, HTML, and PDF. Using Spring's Jasper-Reports view support, you can easily integrate JasperReports into your web applications.

　　To run the example in this section, you need to download JasperReports from `http://jasperreports.sourceforge.net`.

Designing Reports

Unlike many commercial reporting tools, JasperReports uses an open, XML-based file format for the report designs. For those of you who have wrestled with graphical report designers in the past and have tried to get the report layout just right, the ability to edit a report design at such a low level will no doubt be more than welcome. Thankfully, however, you do not need to hand-code all your report files because there is a wide range of graphical tools for working with JasperReports design files. You can find complete details of these tools on the JasperReports website.

　　For the example in this section, we use one of the sample report designs that comes with JasperReports. We are not going to show the code for the report design here, because there is quite a lot of it and this is not a chapter about JasperReports. It is enough to know that the report design displays a list of people's names along with the street and city in which they live. The full code for the report file is available in the code download (visit this chapter's folder in the Downloads section of the Apress website at `www.apress.com`).

Compiling Reports

Before you can use reports, you must compile the design file, which has a .jrxml extension, into a report file, which has a .jasper extension. When using JasperReports with Spring, you have two options for report compilation: you can use the Ant task that comes with JasperReports or you can let Spring compile your report on the fly. When associating a Spring `Controller` with a JasperReports view, you can provide either the .jasper or the .jrxml file. When you supply a .jrxml file, Spring compiles the report for you and caches the compiled form to serve future requests.

Using JasperReports View Classes

Using the JasperReports view classes is just like using any other view class in Spring. You have to link a `Controller` to the URLs behind which you want the reports to sit, populate a `ModelAndView` object with the report data and the name of the view, and link the view name to the report file. If you are unfamiliar with these concepts, refer to Chapters 17 and 18 before continuing with this section.

Building a Controller to handle requests for reports is easy, as shown in Listing D-22.

Listing D-22. *Creating a Controller to Handle Report Requests*

```java
package com.apress.prospring.apd.jasperreports;

import java.util.ArrayList;
import java.util.HashMap;
import java.util.List;
import java.util.Map;

import javax.servlet.http.HttpServletRequest;
import javax.servlet.http.HttpServletResponse;

import net.sf.jasperreports.engine.data.JRBeanCollectionDataSource;

import org.springframework.web.servlet.ModelAndView;
import org.springframework.web.servlet.mvc.multiaction.MultiActionController;

public class ReportController extends MultiActionController {

    public ModelAndView handleSimpleReportPdf(HttpServletRequest request,
            HttpServletResponse response) throws Exception {
        return new ModelAndView("simpleReportPdf", getModel());
    }

    public ModelAndView handleSimpleReportHtml(HttpServletRequest request,
            HttpServletResponse response) throws Exception {

        return new ModelAndView("simpleReportHtml", getModel());
    }

    public ModelAndView handleSimpleReportCsv(HttpServletRequest request,
            HttpServletResponse response) throws Exception {

        return new ModelAndView("simpleReportCsv", getModel());
    }

    public ModelAndView handleSimpleReportExcel(HttpServletRequest request,
            HttpServletResponse response) throws Exception {

        return new ModelAndView("simpleReportExcel", getModel());
    }
```

```
    private Map getModel() {
        Map model = new HashMap();
        model.put("ReportTitle", "My Demo Report!");
        model.put("dataSource", new JRBeanCollectionDataSource(getData()));

        return model;
    }

    private List getData() {
        List list = new ArrayList();

        for (int x = 0; x < 10; x++) {
            ReportBean bean = new ReportBean();
            bean.setId(x);
            bean.setName("Rob Harrop");
            bean.setStreet("1 Some Street");
            bean.setCity("Manchester");

            list.add(bean);
        }

        return list;
    }
}
```

Here you can see that we create four handleXXX() methods that correspond to requests for reports in the four different output formats supported by JasperReports. The interesting part of this code is how we construct the model data. JasperReports allows you to pass in two kinds of data to the report: parameter data and report data.

Parameter data is just general data and is used to customize the overall output of the report, but it has nothing to do with the actual data itself. In Listing D-22, you can see that we add an entry to the model Map called ReportTitle. Behind the scenes, Spring passes this parameter to JasperReports when filling the report with data.

Report data is the actual data the report is created to display. Report data in JasperReports is represented by an instance of a class that implements the JRDataSource interface. In this case, we use the JRBeanCollectionDataSource, which is used to wrap a Collection of JavaBeans where each bean in the Collection corresponds to a single row of output in the report and the properties of each bean correspond to the fields defined in the report. This JRDataSource is added to the model data along with the parameter data. Behind the scenes, Spring picks up this JRDataSource instance and passes it to JasperReports when filling the data.

Listing D-23 shows the ApplicationContext configuration for the ReportController class.

Listing D-23. *Configuring the ReportController Class*

```xml
<?xml version="1.0" encoding="UTF-8" ?>
<!DOCTYPE beans PUBLIC "-//SPRING//DTD BEAN//EN"
"http://www.springframework.org/dtd/spring-beans.dtd">
<beans>
    <bean id="viewResolver"
          class="org.springframework.web.servlet.view.ResourceBundleViewResolver">
        <property name="basename">
            <value>views</value>
        </property>
    </bean>

    <bean id="urlMapping"
          class="org.springframework.web.servlet.handler.SimpleUrlHandlerMapping">
        <property name="mappings">
            <props>
                <prop key="/simpleReportPdf.pdf">controller</prop>
                <prop key="/simpleReportHtml.html">controller</prop>
                <prop key="/simpleReportCsv.csv">controller</prop>
                <prop key="/simpleReportExcel.xls">controller</prop>
            </props>
        </property>
    </bean>

    <bean id="controller"
            class="com.apress.prospring.apd.jasperreports.ReportController">
        <property name="methodNameResolver">
            <ref local="resolver"/>
        </property>
    </bean>

    <bean id="resolver"
            class="org.springframework.web.servlet.mvc.multiaction.➥
                        PropertiesMethodNameResolver">
        <property name="mappings">
            <props>
                <prop key="/simpleReportPdf.pdf">handleSimpleReportPdf</prop>
                <prop key="/simpleReportHtml.html">handleSimpleReportHtml</prop>
                <prop key="/simpleReportCsv.csv">handleSimpleReportCsv</prop>
                <prop key="/simpleReportExcel.xls">handleSimpleReportExcel</prop>
            </props>
        </property>
    </bean>
</beans>
```

You should be more than familiar with this configuration by now. Notice, however, that we use `ResourceBundleViewResolver` to map the request URLs to actual view classes using the data contained in the views.properties file, shown in Listing D-24.

Listing D-24. *Mapping Requests to View Classes*

```
simpleReportPdf.class=➡
org.springframework.web.servlet.view.jasperreports.JasperReportsPdfView
simpleReportPdf.url=/WEB-INF/reports/DataSourceReport.jasper

simpleReportHtml.class=➡
org.springframework.web.servlet.view.jasperreports.JasperReportsHtmlView
simpleReportHtml.url=/WEB-INF/reports/DataSourceReport.jasper

simpleReportCsv.class=➡
org.springframework.web.servlet.view.jasperreports.JasperReportsCsvView
simpleReportCsv.url=/WEB-INF/reports/DataSourceReport.jasper

simpleReportExcel.class=➡
org.springframework.web.servlet.view.jasperreports.JasperReportsExcelView
simpleReportExcel.url=/WEB-INF/reports/DataSourceReport.jasper
```

Notice that each report format has a corresponding view class, which encapsulates rendering behavior for that format. To test this example out, deploy it into your servlet container—we used Tomcat—and point your browser at `http://localhost:8080/jasper/simpleReportPdf.pdf` to bring up the filled report in PDF format.

Using JasperReports Outside the Web Tier

Spring support for JasperReports is not just constrained to the Web Tier. Using the `JasperReportsUtils` class, you can simplify the use of JasperReports in non-web applications with a variety of convenience methods for compiling, filling, and rendering reports in all four report formats. The `JasperReportsUtils` class provides methods for all of the operations performed by the view classes—indeed, the view classes are implemented using `JasperReportsUtils`.

Summary

In this appendix, we presented a quick peek at some of the new features that will be included in future releases. You saw how to integrate scripting languages into your application using Spring's dynamic compilation capabilities, which allow you to use arbitrary scripts as beans within your application. We demonstrated how to use the `AnnotationsAttributes` class as a mechanism for reading J2SE 5.0 annotations at runtime. In the Spring JMX section, you saw how to expose your beans as JMX-manageable resources and how to access JMX resources, both local and remote, using Spring's proxy support. In the final part of this appendix, you learned how to add reporting capabilities to a web application using Spring's JasperReports support.

Index

forums.apress.com

FOR PROFESSIONALS BY PROFESSIONALS™

JOIN THE APRESS FORUMS AND BE PART OF OUR COMMUNITY. You'll find discussions that cover topics of interest to IT professionals, programmers, and enthusiasts just like you. If you post a query to one of our forums, you can expect that some of the best minds in the business—especially Apress authors, who all write with *The Expert's Voice*™—will chime in to help you. Why not aim to become one of our most valuable participants (MVPs) and win cool stuff? Here's a sampling of what you'll find:

DATABASES

Data drives everything.

Share information, exchange ideas, and discuss any database programming or administration issues.

INTERNET TECHNOLOGIES AND NETWORKING

Try living without plumbing (and eventually IPv6).

Talk about networking topics including protocols, design, administration, wireless, wired, storage, backup, certifications, trends, and new technologies.

JAVA

We've come a long way from the old Oak tree.

Hang out and discuss Java in whatever flavor you choose: J2SE, J2EE, J2ME, Jakarta, and so on.

MAC OS X

All about the Zen of OS X.

OS X is both the present and the future for Mac apps. Make suggestions, offer up ideas, or boast about your new hardware.

OPEN SOURCE

Source code is good; understanding (open) source is better.

Discuss open source technologies and related topics such as PHP, MySQL, Linux, Perl, Apache, Python, and more.

PROGRAMMING/BUSINESS

Unfortunately, it is.

Talk about the Apress line of books that cover software methodology, best practices, and how programmers interact with the "suits."

WEB DEVELOPMENT/DESIGN

Ugly doesn't cut it anymore, and CGI is absurd.

Help is in sight for your site. Find design solutions for your projects and get ideas for building an interactive Web site.

SECURITY

Lots of bad guys out there—the good guys need help.

Discuss computer and network security issues here. Just don't let anyone else know the answers!

TECHNOLOGY IN ACTION

Cool things. Fun things.

It's after hours. It's time to play. Whether you're into LEGO® MINDSTORMS™ or turning an old PC into a DVR, this is where technology turns into fun.

WINDOWS

No defenestration here.

Ask questions about all aspects of Windows programming, get help on Microsoft technologies covered in Apress books, or provide feedback on any Apress Windows book.

HOW TO PARTICIPATE:

Go to the Apress Forums site at **http://forums.apress.com/**.
Click the New User link.